D1326395

Vauxhall/Opel Vectra
Owners Workshop Manual

John S. Mead

Models covered

(4618 - 400)

Hatchback, Saloon & Estate, including special/limited editions
Petrol: 1.8 litre (1796cc) & 2.2 litre (2198cc)
Turbo-Diesel: 1.9 litre (1910cc), 2.0 litre (1994cc) & 2.2 litre (2171cc)

Does NOT cover 1.6 litre or 2.0 litre turbo 4-cyl petrol, 3.2 litre V6 petrol, or 3.0 litre V6 diesel engines.
Does NOT cover CVTronic transmission, dual fuel models or 'facelifted' range introduced October 2005

© Haynes Publishing 2008

A book in the **Haynes Owners Workshop Manual Series**

ABCDE
FGHIJ
KLMNO
PQRST

ISBN **978 1 84425 618 1**

British Library Cataloguing in Publication Data
A catalogue record for this book is available from the British Library.

Printed in the USA

Haynes Publishing
Sparkford, Yeovil, Somerset BA22 7JJ, England

Haynes North America, Inc
861 Lawrence Drive, Newbury Park, California 91320, USA

Haynes Publishing Nordiska AB
Box 1504, 751 45 UPPSALA, Sverige

Contents

Contents

REPAIRS AND OVERHAUL

Engine and Associated Systems

Transmission

Brakes and suspension

Body equipment

REFERENCE

Index

Advanced driving

Many people see the words 'advanced driving' and believe that it won't interest them or that it is a style of driving beyond their own abilities. Nothing could be further from the truth. Advanced driving is straightforward safe, sensible driving - the sort of driving we should all do every time we get behind the wheel.

An average of 10 people are killed every day on UK roads and 870 more are injured, some seriously. Lives are ruined daily, usually because somebody did something stupid. Something like 95% of all accidents are due to human error, mostly driver failure. Sometimes we make genuine mistakes - everyone does. Sometimes we have lapses of concentration. Sometimes we deliberately take risks.

For many people, the process of 'learning to drive' doesn't go much further than learning how to pass the driving test because of a common belief that good drivers are made by 'experience'.

Learning to drive by 'experience' teaches three driving skills:

- [ ] Quick reactions. (Whoops, that was close!)
- [ ] Good handling skills. (Horn, swerve, brake, horn).
- [ ] Reliance on vehicle technology. (Great stuff this ABS, stop in no distance even in the wet...)

Drivers whose skills are 'experience based' generally have a lot of near misses and the odd accident. The results can be seen every day in our courts and our hospital casualty departments.

Advanced drivers have learnt to control the risks by controlling the position and speed of their vehicle. They avoid accidents and near misses, even if the drivers around them make mistakes.

The key skills of advanced driving are **concentration,** effective all-round **observation, anticipation** and **planning.** When **good vehicle handling** is added to these skills, all driving situations can be approached and negotiated in a safe, methodical way, leaving nothing to chance.

Concentration means applying your mind to safe driving, completely excluding anything that's not relevant. Driving is usually the most dangerous activity that most of us undertake in our daily routines. It deserves our full attention.

Observation means not just looking, but seeing and seeking out the information found in the driving environment.

Anticipation means asking yourself what is happening, what you can reasonably expect to happen and what could happen unexpectedly. (One of the commonest words used in compiling accident reports is 'suddenly'.)

Planning is the link between seeing something and taking the appropriate action. For many drivers, planning is the missing link.

If you want to become a safer and more skilful driver and you want to enjoy your driving more, contact the Institute of Advanced Motorists at www.iam.org.uk, phone 0208 996 9600, or write to IAM House, 510 Chiswick High Road, London W4 5RG for an information pack.

Working on your car can be dangerous. This page shows just some of the potential risks and hazards, with the aim of creating a safety-conscious attitude.

General hazards

Scalding

• Don't remove the radiator or expansion tank cap while the engine is hot.
• Engine oil, automatic transmission fluid or power steering fluid may also be dangerously hot if the engine has recently been running.

Burning

• Beware of burns from the exhaust system and from any part of the engine. Brake discs and drums can also be extremely hot immediately after use.

Crushing

• When working under or near a raised vehicle, always supplement the jack with axle stands, or use drive-on ramps. *Never venture under a car which is only supported by a jack.*
• Take care if loosening or tightening high-torque nuts when the vehicle is on stands. Initial loosening and final tightening should be done with the wheels on the ground.

Fire

• Fuel is highly flammable; fuel vapour is explosive.
• Don't let fuel spill onto a hot engine.
• Do not smoke or allow naked lights (including pilot lights) anywhere near a vehicle being worked on. Also beware of creating sparks (electrically or by use of tools).
• Fuel vapour is heavier than air, so don't work on the fuel system with the vehicle over an inspection pit.
• Another cause of fire is an electrical overload or short-circuit. Take care when repairing or modifying the vehicle wiring.
• Keep a fire extinguisher handy, of a type suitable for use on fuel and electrical fires.

Electric shock

• Ignition HT voltage can be dangerous, especially to people with heart problems or a pacemaker. Don't work on or near the ignition system with the engine running or the ignition switched on.

• Mains voltage is also dangerous. Make sure that any mains-operated equipment is correctly earthed. Mains power points should be protected by a residual current device (RCD) circuit breaker.

Fume or gas intoxication

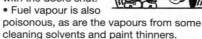

• Exhaust fumes are poisonous; they often contain carbon monoxide, which is rapidly fatal if inhaled. Never run the engine in a confined space such as a garage with the doors shut.
• Fuel vapour is also poisonous, as are the vapours from some cleaning solvents and paint thinners.

Poisonous or irritant substances

• Avoid skin contact with battery acid and with any fuel, fluid or lubricant, especially antifreeze, brake hydraulic fluid and Diesel fuel. Don't syphon them by mouth. If such a substance is swallowed or gets into the eyes, seek medical advice.
• Prolonged contact with used engine oil can cause skin cancer. Wear gloves or use a barrier cream if necessary. Change out of oil-soaked clothes and do not keep oily rags in your pocket.
• Air conditioning refrigerant forms a poisonous gas if exposed to a naked flame (including a cigarette). It can also cause skin burns on contact.

Asbestos

• Asbestos dust can cause cancer if inhaled or swallowed. Asbestos may be found in gaskets and in brake and clutch linings. When dealing with such components it is safest to assume that they contain asbestos.

Special hazards

Hydrofluoric acid

• This extremely corrosive acid is formed when certain types of synthetic rubber, found in some O-rings, oil seals, fuel hoses etc, are exposed to temperatures above 400°C. The rubber changes into a charred or sticky substance containing the acid. *Once formed, the acid remains dangerous for years. If it gets onto the skin, it may be necessary to amputate the limb concerned.*
• When dealing with a vehicle which has suffered a fire, or with components salvaged from such a vehicle, wear protective gloves and discard them after use.

The battery

• Batteries contain sulphuric acid, which attacks clothing, eyes and skin. Take care when topping-up or carrying the battery.
• The hydrogen gas given off by the battery is highly explosive. Never cause a spark or allow a naked light nearby. Be careful when connecting and disconnecting battery chargers or jump leads.

Air bags

• Air bags can cause injury if they go off accidentally. Take care when removing the steering wheel and/or facia. Special storage instructions may apply.

Diesel injection equipment

• Diesel injection pumps supply fuel at very high pressure. Take care when working on the fuel injectors and fuel pipes.

⚠ *Warning: Never expose the hands, face or any other part of the body to injector spray; the fuel can penetrate the skin with potentially fatal results.*

Remember...

DO

• Do use eye protection when using power tools, and when working under the vehicle.

• Do wear gloves or use barrier cream to protect your hands when necessary.

• Do get someone to check periodically that all is well when working alone on the vehicle.

• Do keep loose clothing and long hair well out of the way of moving mechanical parts.

• Do remove rings, wristwatch etc, before working on the vehicle – especially the electrical system.

• Do ensure that any lifting or jacking equipment has a safe working load rating adequate for the job.

DON'T

• Don't attempt to lift a heavy component which may be beyond your capability – get assistance.

• Don't rush to finish a job, or take unverified short cuts.

• Don't use ill-fitting tools which may slip and cause injury.

• Don't leave tools or parts lying around where someone can trip over them. Mop up oil and fuel spills at once.

• Don't allow children or pets to play in or near a vehicle being worked on.

The Vauxhall/Opel Vectra was introduced in the UK in October 1995 as a replacement for the Cavalier. It was originally available in Saloon and Hatchback versions with 1.6, 1.8, 2.0 and 2.5 litre petrol engines and 1.7 litre normally aspirated diesel engines. The Estate range was launched in October 1996. Since its introduction, the Vectra has had various mechanical revisions and facelifts during the course of the production run. This manual covers versions from mid-2002, which were the subject of the second facelift, together with further mechanical revisions. Earlier models are covered in previous editions of the Haynes Vauxhall/Opel Vectra Service and Repair Manual.

A variety of engines are available in the Vectra range: 1.8 and 2.2 litre petrol engines and 1.9, 2.0 and 2.2 litre diesel engines. All engines are of the four-cylinder, in-line type, featuring single or double overhead camshafts. The engines all have fuel injection, and are fitted with a range of emission control systems. 1.6, 2.0 and 3.2 litre petrol, and 3.0 litre diesel engines are also available, but are not covered in this manual.

The Vectra is available in Saloon, Hatchback and Estate body styles, with a wide range of fittings and interior trim depending on the model specification.

Fully-independent front and rear suspension is fitted; the front being of the MacPherson-strut type and the rear being of multi-link design.

According to engine type, the manual gearbox is of the five- or six-speed all synchromesh type, with five- and six-speed electronically-controlled automatic transmissions optionally available on certain models.

A wide range of standard and optional equipment is available within the Vectra range to suit most tastes, including power steering, air conditioning, remote central locking, electric windows, electric sunroof, anti-lock braking system, electronic alarm system and supplemental restraint systems.

For the home mechanic, the Vectra is a relatively straightforward vehicle to maintain, and most of the items requiring frequent attention are easily accessible.

Your Vauxhall/Opel Vectra manual

The aim of this manual is to help you get the best value from your vehicle. It can do so in several ways. It can help you decide what work must be done (even should you choose to get it done by a garage), provide information on routine maintenance and servicing, and give a logical course of action and diagnosis when random faults occur. However, it is hoped that you will use the manual by tackling the work yourself. On simpler jobs, it may even be quicker than booking the car into a garage and going there twice, to leave and collect it. Perhaps most important, a lot of money can be saved by avoiding the costs a garage must charge to cover its labour and overheads.

The manual has drawings and descriptions to show the function of the various components, so that their layout can be understood. Then the tasks are described and photo-graphed in a clear step-by-step sequence.

References to the 'left' or 'right' are in the sense of a person in the driver's seat, facing forward.

Project vehicles

The main vehicle used in the preparation of this manual, and which appears in many of the photographic sequences, was a Vauxhall Vectra Hatchback with a 1.9 litre DOHC diesel engine. Other vehicles included a Vectra Estate with a 1.9 litre SOHC diesel engine, a Vectra Hatchback with a 2.0 litre diesel engine and a Vectra Hatchback with a 2.2 litre petrol engine.

Acknowledgements

Certain illustrations are the copyright of Vauxhall Motors Limited, and are used with their permission. Thanks are also due to Draper Tools Limited, who provided some of the workshop tools, and to all those people at Sparkford who helped in the production of this manual.

We take great pride in the accuracy of information given in this manual, but vehicle manufacturers make alterations and design changes during the production run of a particular vehicle of which they do not inform us. No liability can be accepted by the authors or publishers for loss, damage or injury caused by any errors in, or omissions from, the information given.

Vauxhall Vectra 1.9 SRi Hatchback

The following pages are intended to help in dealing with common roadside emergencies and breakdowns. You will find more detailed fault finding information at the back of the manual, and repair information in the main chapters.

If your car won't start and the starter motor doesn't turn

☐ If it's a model with automatic transmission, make sure the selector is in P or N.
☐ Open the bonnet and make sure that the battery terminals are clean and tight.
☐ Switch on the headlights and try to start the engine. If the headlights go very dim when you're trying to start, the battery is probably flat. Get out of trouble by jump starting (see next page) using a friend's car.

If your car won't start even though the starter motor turns as normal

☐ Is there fuel in the tank?
☐ Is there moisture on electrical components under the bonnet? Switch off the ignition, then wipe off any obvious dampness with a dry cloth. Spray a water-repellent aerosol product (WD-40 or equivalent) on ignition and fuel system electrical connectors like those shown in the photos. (Note that diesel engines don't usually suffer from damp).

1 On petrol engines, remove the engine cover and check that the wiring to the ignition module is connected firmly.

2 Check that the air mass meter wiring is connected securely.

3 Check the security and condition of the battery connections.

4 Check all multiplugs and wiring connectors for security.

Check that electrical connections are secure (with the ignition switched off) and spray them with a water-dispersant spray like WD-40 if you suspect a problem due to damp

5 Check that all fuses are still in good condition and none have blown.

Jump starting

When jump-starting a car using a booster battery, observe the following precautions:

✔ Before connecting the booster battery, make sure that the ignition is switched off.

✔ Ensure that all electrical equipment (lights, heater, wipers, etc) is switched off.

✔ Take note of any special precautions printed on the battery case.

✔ Make sure that the booster battery is the same voltage as the discharged one in the vehicle.

✔ If the battery is being jump-started from the battery in another vehicle, the two vehicles MUST NOT TOUCH each other.

✔ Make sure that the transmission is in neutral (or PARK, in the case of automatic transmission).

 HAYNES HINT *Jump starting will get you out of trouble, but you must correct whatever made the battery go flat in the first place. There are three possibilities:*

1 *The battery has been drained by repeated attempts to start, or by leaving the lights on.*

2 *The charging system is not working properly (alternator drivebelt slack or broken, alternator wiring fault or alternator itself faulty).*

3 *The battery itself is at fault (electrolyte low, or battery worn out).*

1 Connect one end of the red jump lead to the positive (+) terminal of the flat battery

2 Connect the other end of the red lead to the positive (+) terminal of the booster battery.

3 Connect one end of the black jump lead to the negative (-) terminal of the booster battery

4 Connect the other end of the black jump lead to a bolt or bracket on the engine block, well away from the battery, on the vehicle to be started.

5 Make sure that the jump leads will not come into contact with the fan, drive-belts or other moving parts of the engine.

6 Start the engine using the booster battery and run it at idle speed. Switch on the lights, rear window demister and heater blower motor, then disconnect the jump leads in the reverse order of connection. Turn off the lights etc.

Wheel changing

 Warning: Do not change a wheel in a situation where you risk being hit by other traffic. On busy roads, try to stop in a lay-by or a gateway. Be wary of passing traffic while changing the wheel – it is easy to become distracted by the job in hand.

Preparation

☐ When a puncture occurs, stop as soon as it is safe to do so.
☐ Park on firm level ground, if possible, and well out of the way of other traffic.
☐ Use hazard warning lights if necessary.

☐ If you have one, use a warning triangle to alert other drivers of your presence.
☐ Apply the handbrake and engage first or reverse gear (or Park on models with automatic transmission).

☐ Chock the wheel diagonally opposite the one being removed – a couple of large stones will do for this.
☐ If the ground is soft, use a flat piece of wood to spread the load under the jack.

Changing the wheel

1 Lift the floor covering and unscrew the spare wheel clamp nut. Lift out the spare wheel.

2 Remove the tools from the carrier stored beneath the spare wheel.

3 On models with steel wheels, use the special tool to pull the wheel trim from the wheel. On models with alloy wheels, use the screwdriver provided inserted at the wheel bolt holes to prise off the trim.

4 Slacken each wheel bolt by half a turn.

5 Locate the jack head below the jacking point nearest the wheel to be changed; the jacking point is indicated by an arrow in the sill. Turn the handle until the base of the jack touches the ground ensuring that the jack is vertical. Raise the vehicle until the wheel is clear of the ground. If the tyre is flat make sure that the vehicle is raised sufficiently to allow the spare wheel to be fitted.

6 Remove the bolts and lift the wheel from the vehicle. Place it beneath the sill in place of the spare as a precaution against the jack failing. Fit the spare wheel and tighten the bolts moderately with the wheelbrace.

Finally . . .

☐ Remove the wheel chocks.
☐ Stow the jack and tools in the correct locations in the car.
☐ Check the tyre pressure on the wheel just fitted. If it is low, or if you don't have a pressure gauge with you, drive slowly to the nearest garage and inflate the tyre to the correct pressure.
☐ Have the damaged tyre or wheel repaired as soon as possible, or another puncture will leave you stranded.

7 Lower the vehicle to the ground, then finally tighten the wheel bolts in a diagonal sequence. Refit the wheel trim. Note that the wheel bolts should be tightened to the specified torque at the earliest opportunity.

Identifying leaks

Puddles on the garage floor or drive, or obvious wetness under the bonnet or underneath the car, suggest a leak that needs investigating. It can sometimes be difficult to decide where the leak is coming from, especially if the engine bay is very dirty already. Leaking oil or fluid can also be blown rearwards by the passage of air under the car, giving a false impression of where the problem lies.

Warning: Most automotive oils and fluids are poisonous. Wash them off skin, and change out of contaminated clothing, without delay.

 The smell of a fluid leaking from the car may provide a clue to what's leaking. Some fluids are distinctively coloured.
It may help to clean the car carefully and to park it over some clean paper overnight as an aid to locating the source of the leak.
Remember that some leaks may only occur while the engine is running.

Sump oil

Engine oil may leak from the drain plug...

Oil from filter

...or from the base of the oil filter.

Gearbox oil

Gearbox oil can leak from the seals at the inboard ends of the driveshafts.

Antifreeze

Leaking antifreeze often leaves a crystalline deposit like this.

Brake fluid

A leak occurring at a wheel is almost certainly brake fluid.

Power steering fluid

Power steering fluid may leak from the pipe connectors on the steering rack.

Towing

When all else fails, you may find yourself having to get a tow home – or of course you may be helping somebody else. Long-distance recovery should only be done by a garage or breakdown service. For shorter distances, DIY towing using another car is easy enough, but observe the following points:

☐ Use a proper tow-rope – they are not expensive. The vehicle being towed must display an ON TOW sign in its rear window.

☐ Always turn the ignition key to the 'On' position when the vehicle is being towed, so that the steering lock is released, and the direction indicator and brake lights work.

☐ Only attach the tow-rope to the towing eyes provided. A towing eye is provided with the tool kit in the luggage compartment.

☐ To fit the towing eye, remove the circular cover from the front or rear bumper, as required, then screw in the towing eye anti-clockwise as far as it will go using the handle of the wheelbrace to turn the eye. **Note that the towing eye has a left-hand thread**.

☐ Before being towed, release the handbrake and select neutral on the transmission. On models with automatic transmission, special precautions apply. If in doubt, do not tow, or transmission damage may result.

☐ Note that greater-than-usual pedal pressure will be required to operate the brakes, since the vacuum servo unit is only operational with the engine running.

☐ Because the power steering will not be operational, greater-than-usual steering effort will be required.

☐ The driver of the car being towed must keep the tow-rope taut at all times to avoid snatching.

☐ Make sure that both drivers know the route before setting off.

☐ Only drive at moderate speeds and keep the distance towed to a minimum. Drive smoothly and allow plenty of time for slowing down at junctions.

Introduction

There are some very simple checks which need only take a few minutes to carry out, but which could save you a lot of inconvenience and expense.

These *Weekly checks* require no great skill or special tools, and the small amount of time they take to perform could prove to be very well spent, for example:

☐ Keeping an eye on tyre condition and pressures, will not only help to stop them wearing out prematurely, but could also save your life.

☐ Many breakdowns are caused by electrical problems. Battery-related faults are particularly common, and a quick check on a regular basis will often prevent the majority of these.

☐ If your car develops a brake fluid leak, the first time you might know about it is when your brakes don't work properly. Checking the level regularly will give advance warning of this kind of problem.

☐ If the oil or coolant levels run low, the cost of repairing any engine damage will be far greater than fixing the leak, for example.

Underbonnet check points

◄ 1.8 litre petrol

1 *Engine oil level dipstick*

2 *Engine oil filler cap*

3 *Coolant reservoir (expansion tank)*

4 *Hydraulic fluid reservoir*

5 *Washer fluid reservoir*

6 *Battery*

◄ 2.2 litre petrol

1 *Engine oil level dipstick*

2 *Engine oil filler cap*

3 *Coolant reservoir (expansion tank)*

4 *Hydraulic fluid reservoir*

5 *Washer fluid reservoir*

6 *Battery*

◄ **1.9 litre DOHC diesel**

1 *Engine oil level dipstick*
2 *Engine oil filler cap*
3 *Coolant reservoir (expansion tank)*
4 *Hydraulic fluid reservoir*
5 *Washer fluid reservoir*
6 *Battery*

◄ **2.0 litre diesel**

1 *Engine oil level dipstick*
2 *Engine oil filler cap*
3 *Coolant reservoir (expansion tank)*
4 *Hydraulic fluid reservoir*
5 *Washer fluid reservoir*
6 *Battery*

Engine oil level

Before you start

✔ Make sure that the car is on level ground.
✔ The oil level must be checked with the engine at normal operating temperature, however, wait at least 5 minutes after the engine has been switched off.

HAYNES HiNT *If the oil is checked immediately after driving the vehicle, some of the oil will remain in the upper engine components, resulting in an inaccurate reading on the dipstick.*

The correct oil

Modern engines place great demands on their oil. It is very important that the correct oil for your car is used (see *Lubricants and fluids*).

Car care

● If you have to add oil frequently, you should check whether you have any oil leaks. Place some clean paper under the car overnight, and check for stains in the morning. If there are no leaks, then the engine may be burning oil.
● Always maintain the level between the upper and lower dipstick marks (see photo 3). If the level is too low, severe engine damage may occur. Oil seal failure may result if the engine is overfilled by adding too much oil.

1 The dipstick is brightly-coloured for easy identification (see *Underbonnet check points* for exact location). Withdraw the dipstick.

3 Note the level on the end of the dipstick, which should be between the upper (MAX) mark and lower (MIN) mark. Approximately 1.0 litre of oil will raise the level from the lower mark to the upper mark.

2 Using a clean rag or paper towel remove all oil from the dipstick. Insert the clean dipstick into the tube as far as it will go, then withdraw it again.

4 Oil is added through the filler cap. Unscrew the cap and top-up the level. A funnel may help to reduce spillage. Add the oil slowly, checking the level on the dipstick frequently. Avoid overfilling (see *Car care*).

Coolant level

 Warning: Do not attempt to remove the expansion tank pressure cap when the engine is hot, as there is a very great risk of scalding. Do not leave open containers of coolant about, as it is poisonous.

Car Care

● With a sealed-type cooling system, adding coolant should not be necessary on a regular basis. If frequent topping-up is required, it is likely there is a leak. Check the radiator, all hoses and joint faces for signs of staining or wetness, and rectify as necessary.

● It is important that antifreeze is used in the cooling system all year round, not just during the winter months. Don't top up with water alone, as the antifreeze will become diluted.

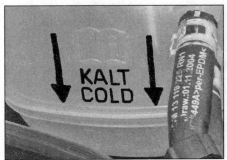

1 The coolant level varies with the temperature of the engine. When the engine is cold, the coolant level should be slightly above the KALT/COLD mark on the side of the tank. When the engine is hot, the level will rise.

2 If topping-up is necessary, wait until the engine is cold. Slowly unscrew the expansion tank cap, to release any pressure present in the cooling system, and remove it.

3 Add a mixture of water and antifreeze to the expansion tank until the coolant is up to the KALT/COLD level mark. Refit the cap and tighten it securely.

Tyre condition and pressure

It is very important that tyres are in good condition, and at the correct pressure - having a tyre failure at any speed is highly dangerous. Tyre wear is influenced by driving style - harsh braking and acceleration, or fast cornering, will all produce more rapid tyre wear. As a general rule, the front tyres wear out faster than the rears. Interchanging the tyres from front to rear ("rotating" the tyres) may result in more even wear. However, if this is completely effective, you may have the expense of replacing all four tyres at once! Remove any nails or stones embedded in the tread before they penetrate the tyre to cause deflation. If removal of a nail does reveal that the tyre has been punctured, refit the nail so that its point of penetration is marked. Then immediately change the wheel, and have the tyre repaired by a tyre dealer.

Regularly check the tyres for damage in the form of cuts or bulges, especially in the sidewalls. Periodically remove the wheels, and clean any dirt or mud from the inside and outside surfaces. Examine the wheel rims for signs of rusting, corrosion or other damage. Light alloy wheels are easily damaged by "kerbing" whilst parking; steel wheels may also become dented or buckled. A new wheel is very often the only way to overcome severe damage.

New tyres should be balanced when they are fitted, but it may become necessary to re-balance them as they wear, or if the balance weights fitted to the wheel rim should fall off. Unbalanced tyres will wear more quickly, as will the steering and suspension components. Wheel imbalance is normally signified by vibration, particularly at a certain speed (typically around 50 mph). If this vibration is felt only through the steering, then it is likely that just the front wheels need balancing. If, however, the vibration is felt through the whole car, the rear wheels could be out of balance. Wheel balancing should be carried out by a tyre dealer or garage.

1 *Tread Depth - visual check*
The original tyres have tread wear safety bands (B), which will appear when the tread depth reaches approximately 1.6 mm. The band positions are indicated by a triangular mark on the tyre sidewall (A).

2 *Tread Depth - manual check*
Alternatively, tread wear can be monitored with a simple, inexpensive device known as a tread depth indicator gauge.

3 *Tyre Pressure Check*
Check the tyre pressures regularly with the tyres cold. Do not adjust the tyre pressures immediately after the vehicle has been used, or an inaccurate setting will result.

Tyre tread wear patterns

Shoulder Wear

Underinflation (wear on both sides)
Under-inflation will cause overheating of the tyre, because the tyre will flex too much, and the tread will not sit correctly on the road surface. This will cause a loss of grip and excessive wear, not to mention the danger of sudden tyre failure due to heat build-up.
Check and adjust pressures
Incorrect wheel camber (wear on one side)
Repair or renew suspension parts
Hard cornering
Reduce speed!

Centre Wear

Overinflation
Over-inflation will cause rapid wear of the centre part of the tyre tread, coupled with reduced grip, harsher ride, and the danger of shock damage occurring in the tyre casing.
Check and adjust pressures

If you sometimes have to inflate your car's tyres to the higher pressures specified for maximum load or sustained high speed, don't forget to reduce the pressures to normal afterwards.

Uneven Wear

Front tyres may wear unevenly as a result of wheel misalignment. Most tyre dealers and garages can check and adjust the wheel alignment (or "tracking") for a modest charge.
Incorrect camber or castor
Repair or renew suspension parts
Malfunctioning suspension
Repair or renew suspension parts
Unbalanced wheel
Balance tyres
Incorrect toe setting
Adjust front wheel alignment
Note: *The feathered edge of the tread which typifies toe wear is best checked by feel.*

Brake (and clutch) fluid level

Before you start

✔ Make sure that the car is on level ground.
✔ Cleanliness is of great importance when dealing with the braking system, so take care to clean around the reservoir cap before topping-up. Use only clean brake fluid.

Safety first!

● If the reservoir requires repeated topping-up, this is an indication of a fluid leak somewhere in the system, which should be investigated immediately.

● If a leak is suspected, the car should not be driven until the braking system has been checked. Never take any risks where brakes are concerned.

 HAYNES HINT *The fluid level in the reservoir will drop slightly as the brake pads and shoes wear down, but the fluid level must never be allowed to drop below the MIN mark.*

⚠ *Warning: Hydraulic fluid can harm your eyes and damage painted surfaces, so use extreme caution when handling and pouring it. Do not use fluid which has been standing open for some time, as it absorbs moisture from the air, which can cause a dangerous loss of braking effectiveness.*

1 The MAX and MIN marks are indicated on the front of the reservoir. The fluid level must be kept between the marks at all times.

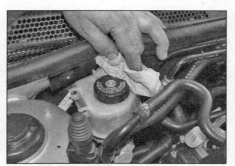

2 If topping-up is necessary, first wipe clean the area around the filler cap to prevent dirt entering the hydraulic system. Unscrew the reservoir cap.

3 Carefully add fluid, taking care not to spill it onto the surrounding components. Use only the specified fluid; mixing different types can cause damage to the system. After topping-up to the correct level, securely refit the cap and wipe off any spilt fluid.

Washer fluid level

● Screenwash additives not only keep the windscreen clean during bad weather, they also prevent the washer system freezing in cold weather – which is when you are likely to need it most. Don't top-up using plain water, as the screenwash will become diluted, and will freeze in cold weather.

⚠ *Warning: On no account use engine coolant antifreeze in the screen washer system – this may damage the paintwork.*

1 The reservoir for the windscreen, rear window and headlight (where applicable) washer systems is located on the front left-hand side of the engine compartment. If topping-up is necessary, prise open the cap and lift out the dipstick attached to it.

2 When topping-up the reservoir a screenwash additive should be added in the quantities recommended on the bottle.

Wiper blades

1 Check the condition of the wiper blades; if they are cracked or show any signs of deterioration, or if the glass swept area is smeared, renew them. Wiper blades should be renewed annually.

2 To remove a windscreen wiper blade, pull the arm fully away from the screen until it locks. Swivel the blade through 90°, press the locking tab with your fingers and slide the blade out of the arm's hooked end.

3 Don't forget to check the tailgate wiper blade as well. To remove the blade, depress the retaining tab and slide the blade out of the hooked end of the arm.

Battery

Caution: Before carrying out any work on the vehicle battery, read the precautions given in 'Safety first!' at the start of this manual. If the battery is to be disconnected, refer to 'Disconnecting the battery' in the Reference Chapter, before proceeding.

✔ Make sure that the battery tray is in good condition, and that the clamp is tight. Corrosion on the tray, retaining clamp and the battery itself can be removed with a solution of water and baking soda. Thoroughly rinse all cleaned areas with water. Any metal parts damaged by corrosion should be covered with a zinc-based primer, then painted.

✔ Periodically (approximately every three months), check the charge condition of the battery as described in Chapter 5A.

✔ If the battery is flat, and you need to jump start your vehicle, see *Roadside Repairs*.

1 The battery is located at the front, left-hand side of the engine compartment, housed in a protective plastic box. Open the battery box, for access to the terminals, by releasing the lid at the front and pivoting it upwards. Where fitted, unclip the insulation jacket and lift open the jacket cover.

2 Check the tightness of battery clamps to ensure good electrical connections. You should not be able to move them. Also check each cable for cracks and frayed conductors.

HAYNES HINT

Battery corrosion can be kept to a minimum by applying a layer of petroleum jelly to the clamps and terminals after they are reconnected.

3 If corrosion (white, fluffy deposits) is evident, remove the cables from the battery terminals, clean them with a small wire brush, then refit them. Automotive stores sell a tool for cleaning the battery post . . .

4 . . . as well as the battery cable clamps

Electrical systems

✔ Check all external lights and the horn. Refer to the appropriate Sections of Chapter 12 for details if any of the circuits are found to be inoperative.

✔ Visually check all accessible wiring connectors, harnesses and retaining clips for security, and for signs of chafing or damage.

HAYNES HiNT *If you need to check your brake lights and indicators unaided, back up to a wall or garage door and operate the lights. The reflected light should show if they are working properly.*

1 If a single indicator light, stop-light or headlight has failed, it is likely that a bulb has blown and will need to be renewed. Refer to Chapter 12 for details. If both stop-lights have failed, it is possible that the switch has failed (see Chapter 9).

2 If more than one indicator light or headlight has failed, it is likely that either a fuse has blown or that there is a fault in the circuit (see Chapter 12). The main fuses are located behind a cover on the left-hand edge of the facia. Pull open and remove the cover for access to the fuses.

3 Additional fuses and relays are located in the fuse/relay box on the left-hand side of the engine compartment . . .

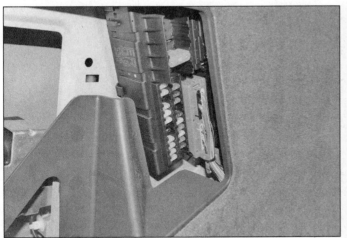

4 . . . and in the left-hand side of the luggage compartment. Refer to the wiring diagrams at the end of Chapter 12 for details of the fuse locations and circuits protected.

5 To renew a blown fuse, remove it, where applicable, using the plastic tool provided. Fit a new fuse of the same rating, available from car accessory shops. It is important that you find the reason that the fuse blew (see *Electrical fault finding* in Chapter 12).

Lubricants and fluids

Engine*

Petrol . . . . Multigrade engine oil, viscosity SAE 0W/30, 0W/40, 5W/30 or 5W/40 to specification ACEA A3, ACEA A3/B3, ACEA A3/B3/B4 or higher

Diesel . . . . Multigrade engine oil, viscosity SAE 0W/30, 0W/40, 5W/30 or 5W/40 to specification ACEA B3, ACEA A3/B3, ACEA A3/B3/B4 or higher

Manual transmission . . . . Vauxhall/Opel gear oil (09 120 541)

Automatic transmission:

AF23/AF33 . . . . Vauxhall/Opel automatic transmission fluid (93 160 393)

AF40 . . . . Vauxhall/Opel automatic transmission fluid (93 165 147)

Power steering reservoir . . . . Vauxhall/Opel steering fluid (93 160 548)

Cooling system. . . . . Vauxhall/Opel silicate-free coolant (09 194 431/19 40 650)

Brake/clutch fluid reservoir. . . . . Hydraulic fluid to DOT 4

* The engine oil specification shown is for vehicles operating under the normal maintenance intervals given at the start of Chapters 1A and 1B. If the vehicle is operating under the extended ECOService-Flex maintenance intervals, long-life oil (Vauxhall specification GM-LL-A-025 for petrol engines, or GM-LL-B-025 for diesel engines) **must** *be used at all times. Refer to Chapter 1A or 1B for further information.*

Tyre pressures (cold)

Note: *Pressures apply to original-equipment tyres, and may vary if any other make or type of tyre is fitted; check with the tyre manufacturer or supplier for correct pressures if necessary.*

Normal load (up to 3 passengers)	Front	Rear
1.8 litre petrol models		
All except 235/35 R 19.	2.0 bar (29 psi)	2.2 bar (32 psi)
235/35 R 19	2.6 bar (38 psi)	2.3 bar (33 psi)
2.2 litre petrol models		
195/65 R 15 and 205/55 R 16	2.3 bar (33 psi)	2.3 bar (33 psi)
215/55 R 16, 215/50 R 17, 225/45 R 17 and 225/45 R 18.	2.2 bar (32 psi)	2.2 bar (32 psi)
235/35 R 19	2.6 bar (38 psi)	2.3 bar (33 psi)
1.9 litre Z19DTH diesel models		
195/65 R 15 and 205/55 R 16	2.4 bar (35 psi)	2.4 bar (35 psi)
215/55 R 16, 215/50 R 17, 225/45 R 17 and 225/45 R 18.	2.3 bar (33 psi)	2.3 bar (33 psi)
235/35 R 19	3.0 bar (44 psi)	2.7 bar (39 psi)
1.9 litre Z19DT, 2.0 and 2.2 litre diesel models		
195/65 R 15 and 205/55 R 16	2.3 bar (33 psi)	2.3 bar (33 psi)
215/55 R 16, 215/50 R 17, 225/45 R 17 and 225/45 R 18.	2.2 bar (32 psi)	2.2 bar (32 psi)
235/35 R 19	2.6 bar (38 psi)	2.3 bar (33 psi)
Fully laden		
1.8 litre petrol models		
All except 235/35 R 19.	2.2 bar (32 psi)	2.7 bar (39 psi)
235/35 R 19	2.8 bar (41 psi)	3.3 bar (48 psi)
2.2 litre petrol models		
195/65 R 15 and 205/55 R 16	2.5 bar (36 psi)	3.0 bar (44 psi)
215/55 R 16, 215/50 R 17, 225/45 R 17 and 225/45 R 18.	2.3 bar (33 psi)	2.8 bar (41 psi)
235/35 R 19	2.8 bar (41 psi)	3.3 bar (48 psi)
1.9 litre Z19DTH diesel models		
195/65 R 15 and 205/55 R 16	2.5 bar (36 psi)	3.0 bar (44 psi)
215/55 R 16, 215/50 R 17, 225/45 R 17 and 225/45 R 18.	2.4 bar (35 psi)	2.9 bar (42 psi)
235/35 R 19	3.2 bar (46 psi)	3.5 bar (51 psi)
1.9 litre Z19DT, 2.0 and 2.2 litre diesel models		
195/65 R 15 and 205/55 R 16	2.5 bar (36 psi)	3.0 bar (44 psi)
215/55 R 16, 215/50 R 17, 225/45 R 17 and 225/45 R 18.	2.3 bar (33 psi)	2.8 bar (41 psi)
235/35 R 19	2.8 bar (41 psi)	3.3 bar (48 psi)
Space-saver temporary spare tyre		
All models.	4.2 bar (61 psi)	4.2 bar (61 psi)

Chapter 1 Part A:
Routine maintenance and servicing – petrol models

Contents

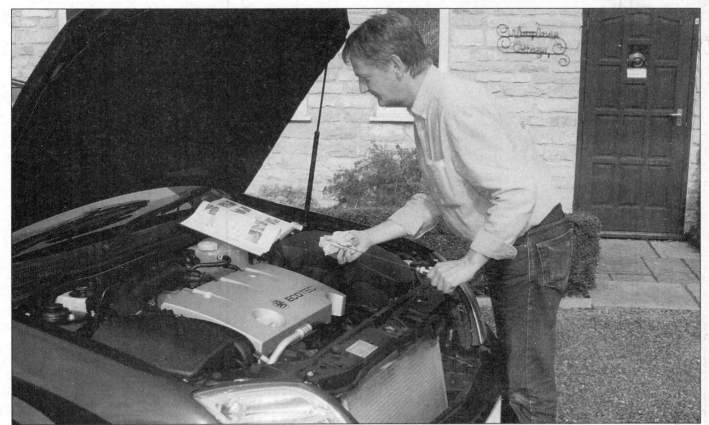

Degrees of difficulty

Easy, suitable for novice with little experience	**Fairly easy,** suitable for beginner with some experience	**Fairly difficult,** suitable for competent DIY mechanic	**Difficult,** suitable for experienced DIY mechanic	**Very difficult,** suitable for expert DIY or professional

Lubricants and fluids............................... Refer to *Weekly checks*

Capacities

Engine oil (including oil filter)

1.8 litre engines	4.25 litres
2.2 litre engines	5.0 litres

Difference between MIN and MAX dipstick marks:

All except 2.2 litre Z22SE engines	1.0 litre
2.2 litre Z22SE engines	0.75 litre

Cooling system

1.8 litre engines	5.5 litres

2.2 litre Z22SE engines:

Manual transmission without air conditioning	7.1 litres
Manual transmission with air conditioning	7.4 litres
Automatic transmission with or without air conditioning	7.6 litres

2.2 litre Z22YH engines:

Manual transmission without air conditioning	6.9 litres
Manual transmission with air conditioning	7.2 litres
Automatic transmission with or without air conditioning	7.4 litres

Transmission

Manual transmission:

F17+ transmission	1.6 litres
F23 transmission	1.55 litres
Automatic transmission (at fluid change)	3.0 to 3.5 litres (approximately)

Washer fluid reservoir

Without headlight washers	2.9 litres
With headlight washers	5.6 litres

Fuel tank

Saloon and Hatchback models	60 litres
Estate models	61 litres

Cooling system

Antifreeze mixture:

40% antifreeze	Protection down to -28°C
50% antifreeze	Protection down to -40°C

Ignition system

Spark plugs:

	Type	Gap
1.8 litre engines	Bosch FQR 8 LEU2	1.35 mm
2.2 litre engines:		
Z22SE engines	Bosch HLR 8 STEX	1.1 mm
Z22YH engines	Beru 14 FGR-8DQU7	0.8 mm

Brakes

Friction material minimum thickness (including backing plate):

Front brake pads	9.0 mm
Rear brake pads	8.0 mm

Torque wrench settings

	Nm	lbf ft
Engine oil filter:		
1.8 litre engines	15	11
2.2 litre engines	25	18
Engine oil filter housing retaining bolt (1.8 litre engines)	45	33
Roadwheel bolts	110	81
Spark plugs:		
1.8 litre engines	25	18
2.2 litre engines:		
Z22SE engines	20	15
Z22YH engines	25	18
Sump drain plug:		
1.8 litre engines	14	10
2.2 litre engines	25	18

The maintenance intervals in this manual are provided with the assumption that you, not the dealer, will be carrying out the work. These are the minimum maintenance intervals based on the standard service schedule recommended by the manufacturer for vehicles driven daily. If you wish to keep your vehicle in peak condition at all times, you may wish to perform some of these procedures more often. We encourage frequent maintenance, because it enhances the efficiency, performance and resale value of your vehicle.

If the vehicle is driven in dusty areas, used to tow a trailer, or driven frequently at slow speeds (idling in traffic) or on short journeys, more frequent maintenance intervals are recommended.

When the vehicle is new, it should be serviced by a dealer service department (or other workshop recognised by the vehicle manufacturer as providing the same standard of service) in order to preserve the warranty. The vehicle manufacturer may reject warranty claims if you are unable to prove that servicing has been carried out as and when specified, using only original equipment parts or parts certified to be of equivalent quality.

Flexible maintenance intervals

All Vectra models covered by this manual are also capable of operating under the flexible maintenance interval plan known as Vauxhall/Opel ECOService-Flex. Under this flexible maintenance plan, a maximum service interval of 2 years or 25 000 miles can be achieved under ideal conditions. Information on a number of variables such as distance driven, driving cycles, engine operating conditions, coolant temperature and oil temperature are obtained and stored in the engine management ECU. Based on this information, the ECU calculates the remaining distance until the next service is due and displays this distance on the service interval indicator.

The ECOService-Flex plan is entirely dependent on the exclusive use of specially developed 'long-life' engine oils meeting Vauxhall/Opel specification GM-LL-A-025. If any other type of oil is used (such as engine oils meeting the conventional ACEA specifications) then the shorter maintenance intervals shown in the following schedule must be adhered to.

As stated earlier, it is our philosophy that frequent maintenance is always the preferred option, however it is up to the individual owner as to the course of action to be adopted.

Every 250 miles or weekly

☐ Refer to *Weekly checks*

Every 9000 miles or 6 months – whichever comes first

☐ Renew the engine oil and filter (Section 3)*

* Note: Vauxhall/Opel recommend that the engine oil and filter are changed every 18 000 miles or 12 months if the vehicle is being operated under the standard service schedule. However, oil and filter changes are good for the engine and we recommend that the oil and filter are renewed more frequently, especially if the vehicle is used on a lot of short journeys.

Every 18 000 miles or 12 months – whichever comes first

☐ Check all underbonnet and underbody components, pipes and hoses for leaks (Section 4)
☐ Check the condition of the brake pads (renew if necessary), the calipers and discs (Section 5)
☐ Check the condition of all brake fluid pipes and hoses (Section 6)
☐ Check the condition of the front suspension and steering components, particularly the rubber gaiters and seals (Section 7)
☐ Check the condition of the driveshaft joint gaiters, and the driveshaft joints (Section 8)
☐ Check the condition of the exhaust system components (Section 9)
☐ Check the condition of the rear suspension components (Section 10)
☐ Check the bodywork and underbody for damage and corrosion, and check the condition of the underbody corrosion protection (Section 11)
☐ Check the tightness of the roadwheel bolts (Section 12)
☐ Lubricate all door, bonnet and tailgate hinges and locks (Section 13)
☐ Check the operation of the horn, all lights, and the wipers and washers (Section 14)

Every 18 000 miles or 12 months – whichever comes first (continued)

☐ Check the headlight beam alignment (Section 15)
☐ Carry out a road test (Section 16)
☐ Reset the service interval indicator (Section 17)

Every 18 000 miles or 2 years – whichever comes first

☐ Renew the pollen filter (Section 18)

Every 36 000 miles or 2 years – whichever comes first

☐ Check the auxiliary drivebelt and tensioner (Section 19)

Every 2 years, regardless of mileage

☐ Renew the battery for the remote control handset (Section 20)
☐ Renew the brake and clutch fluid (Section 21)
☐ Renew the coolant (Section 22)*
☐ Exhaust emission test (Section 23)

* Note: Vauxhall/Opel do not specify renewal intervals for the antifreeze mixture, as the mixture used to fill the system when the vehicle is new is designed to last the lifetime of the vehicle. See Section 22.

Every 36 000 miles or 4 years – whichever comes first

☐ Renew the air cleaner filter element (Section 24)
☐ Renew the spark plugs (Section 25)
☐ Renew the timing belt, tensioner and idler pulleys – 1.8 litre engines (Section 26)*
☐ Renew the fuel filter (Section 27)
☐ Renew the automatic transmission fluid (Section 28)

* Note: The normal interval for timing belt renewal is 54 000 miles or 6 years, however, it is strongly recommended that the interval used is 36 000 miles on vehicles which are subjected to intensive use, ie, mainly short journeys or a lot of stop-start driving. The actual belt renewal interval is therefore very much up to the individual owner, but bear in mind that severe engine damage will result if the belt breaks.

Underbonnet view of a 1.8 litre engine model

1 Engine oil level dipstick
2 Engine oil filler cap
3 Air cleaner assembly
4 Front suspension strut
   upper mounting
5 Screen washer fluid
   reservoir
6 Airflow meter
7 Brake (and clutch) fluid
   reservoir
8 Throttle body/housing
9 Ignition module
10 Coolant expansion tank
11 Battery
12 Fuse/relay box
13 ABS hydraulic modulator

Underbonnet view of a 2.2 litre engine model

1 Engine oil level dipstick
2 Engine oil filler cap
3 Air cleaner assembly
4 Front suspension strut
   upper mounting
5 Screen washer fluid
   reservoir
6 Airflow meter
7 Brake (and clutch) fluid
   reservoir
8 Throttle body/housing
9 Ignition module
10 Coolant expansion tank
11 Battery
12 Fuse/relay box
13 ABS hydraulic modulator
14 Oil filter
15 Engine management ECU

Front underbody view of a 1.8 litre model

1 Exhaust front pipe
2 Steering track rods
3 Front suspension lower arms
4 Front brake calipers
5 Engine mounting front torque link
6 Engine mounting rear torque link
7 Right-hand driveshaft
8 Final drive cover plate
9 Manual transmission
10 Engine oil drain plug
11 Engine oil filter
12 Air conditioning compressor
13 Electric cooling fan
14 Front subframe

Rear underbody view of a 1.8 litre model

1 Handbrake cable
2 Exhaust intermediate pipe
3 Exhaust heat shield
4 Rear axle body
5 Rear hub carrier
6 Lower control arm
7 Upper control arm
8 Auxiliary control arm
9 Shock absorber
10 Rear anti-roll bar
11 Rear suspension trailing arm
12 Fuel filter
13 Fuel tank
14 Charcoal canister

1 General information

1 This Chapter is designed to help the home mechanic maintain his/her vehicle for safety, economy, long life and peak performance.

2 The Chapter contains a master maintenance schedule, followed by Sections dealing specifically with each task in the schedule. Visual checks, adjustments, component renewal and other helpful items are included. Refer to the accompanying illustrations of the engine compartment and the underside of the vehicle for the locations of the various components.

3 Servicing your vehicle in accordance with the mileage/time maintenance schedule and the following Sections will provide a planned maintenance programme, which should result in a long and reliable service life. This is a comprehensive plan, so maintaining some items but not others at the specified service intervals will not produce the same results.

4 As you service your vehicle, you will discover that many of the procedures can – and should – be grouped together, because of the particular procedure being performed, or because of the proximity of two otherwise-unrelated components to one another. For example, if the vehicle is raised for any reason, the exhaust can be inspected at the same time as the suspension and steering components.

5 The first step in this maintenance programme is to prepare yourself before the actual work begins. Read through all the Sections relevant to the work to be carried out, then make a list and gather all the parts and tools required. If a problem is encountered, seek advice from a parts specialist, or a dealer service department.

2 Regular maintenance

1 If, from the time the vehicle is new, the routine maintenance schedule is followed closely, and frequent checks are made of fluid levels and high-wear items, as suggested throughout this manual, the engine will be kept in relatively good running condition, and the need for additional work will be minimised.

2 It is possible that there will be times when the engine is running poorly due to the lack of regular maintenance. This is even more likely if a used vehicle, which has not received regular and frequent maintenance checks, is purchased. In such cases, additional work may need to be carried out, outside of the regular maintenance intervals.

3 If engine wear is suspected, a compression test (refer to the appropriate part of Chapter 2) will provide valuable information regarding the overall performance of the main internal components. Such a test can be used as a basis to decide on the extent of the work to be carried out. If, for example, a compression test indicates serious internal engine wear, conventional maintenance as described in this Chapter will not greatly improve the performance of the engine, and may prove a waste of time and money, unless extensive overhaul work is carried out first.

4 The following series of operations are those most often required to improve the performance of a generally poor-running engine:

Primary operations

a) *Clean, inspect and test the battery (refer to Weekly checks).*
b) *Check all the engine-related fluids (refer to Weekly checks).*
c) *Check the condition and tension of the auxiliary drivebelt (Section 19).*
d) *Renew the spark plugs (Section 25).*
e) *Check the condition of the air filter, and renew if necessary (Section 24).*
f) *Renew the fuel filter (Section 27).*
g) *Check the condition of all hoses, and check for fluid leaks (Section 4).*

5 If the above operations do not prove fully effective, carry out the following secondary operations:

Secondary operations

All items listed under *Primary operations*, plus the following:

a) *Check the charging system (refer to Chapter 5A).*
b) *Check the ignition system (refer to Chapter 5B).*
c) *Check the fuel, exhaust and emission control systems (refer to the appropriate Parts of Chapter 4).*

Every 9000 miles or 6 months

3 Engine oil and filter renewal

> **HAYNES HiNT** *Frequent oil and filter changes are the most important preventative maintenance procedures which can be undertaken by the DIY owner. As engine oil ages, it becomes diluted and contaminated, which leads to premature engine wear.*

1 Before starting this procedure, gather together all the necessary tools and materials. Also make sure that you have plenty of clean rags and newspapers handy, to mop-up any spills. Ideally, the engine oil should be warm, as it will drain more easily, and more built-up sludge will be removed with it. Take care not to touch the exhaust or any other hot parts of the engine when working under the vehicle. To avoid any possibility of scalding, and to protect yourself from possible skin irritants and other harmful contaminants in used engine oils, it is advisable to wear gloves when carrying out this work.

2 Access to the underside of the vehicle will be greatly improved if it can be raised on a lift, driven onto ramps, or jacked up and supported on axle stands (see *Jacking and vehicle support*). Whichever method is chosen, make sure that the vehicle remains level, or if it is at an angle, that the drain plug is at the lowest point. The drain plug is located at the rear of the sump.

3 Remove the oil filler cap from the camshaft cover (twist it through a quarter-turn anti-clockwise and withdraw it) **(see illustration)**.

4 Using a spanner, or preferably a suitable

3.3 Removing the oil filler cap

socket and bar, slacken the drain plug about half a turn. Position the draining container under the drain plug, then remove the plug completely **(see Haynes Hint)**.

5 Allow some time for the oil to drain, noting that it may be necessary to reposition the container as the oil flow slows to a trickle.

6 The oil filter is located on the front left-hand

> **HAYNES HiNT**
>
> *As the drain plug releases from the threads, move it away quickly so that the stream of oil running out of the sump goes into the drain pan and not up your sleeve.*

3.8 Using an oil filter removal tool to slacken the canister-type filter – 1.8 litre engines

3.9a Separate the paper-element type filter from the cap . . .

side of the cylinder block, and two different types may be encountered. On all 2.2 litre engines, the oil filter is of the paper element type. On 1.8 litre engines the oil filter may be either a paper element type or a metal canister type. Proceed as described under the following sub-Sections, according to engine.

1.8 litre engines

7 Move the container into position under the oil filter.

8 Where a canister-type oil filter is fitted, use an oil filter removal tool to slacken the filter initially, then unscrew it by hand the rest of the way **(see illustration)**. Empty the oil from the old filter into the container. In order to ensure that all the old oil is removed, puncture the 'dome' of the filter in two places and allow the oil to drain from the filter completely.

9 Where a paper element-type oil filter is fitted, unscrew the filter cap and withdraw it, together with the element, then separate the element, and remove the O-ring seal from the cap **(see illustrations)**.

10 Use a clean rag to remove all oil, dirt and sludge from the filter sealing area on the block. Where a paper element-type oil filter is used, if required, the oil filter housing can be removed from the cylinder block by unscrewing the retaining bolt. The housing can then be thoroughly cleaned and refitted

3.9b . . . then remove the O-ring seal – 1.8 litre engines

3.10 The oil filter housing can be removed from the cylinder block by unscrewing the retaining bolt – 1.8 litre engines

to the block with a new sealing ring **(see illustration)**. Tighten the retaining bolt to the specified torque.

11 On the canister-type filter, apply a light coating of clean engine oil to the sealing ring on the new filter, then screw the filter into position on the engine. Tighten the filter firmly by hand only – **do not** use any tools. If a genuine filter is being fitted and the special oil filter tool (a socket which fits over the end of the filter) is available, tighten the filter to the specified torque.

12 On the paper element-type filter, locate a new O-ring seal in the groove on the retaining

cap, then locate the new element in the cap and insert them both in the filter housing. Screw on the cap and tighten to the specified torque.

2.2 litre engines

13 Move the container into position under the oil filter.

14 Unscrew the filter cap and withdraw it, together with the element, then separate the element, and remove the O-ring seal from the cap **(see illustrations)**.

15 Use a clean rag to remove all oil, dirt and sludge from the oil filter housing and cap.

3.14a Unscrew the filter cap . . .

3.14b . . . and withdraw it together with the element . . .

3.14c . . . then separate the element from the cap – 2.2 litre engines

16 Locate a new O-ring seal in the groove on the retaining cap, then locate the new element in the cap and insert them both in the filter housing. Screw on the cap and tighten to the specified torque.

All engines

17 After all the oil has drained, wipe the drain plug and the sealing washer/O-ring with a clean rag. Examine the condition of the sealing washer/O-ring, and renew it if it shows signs of damage which may prevent an oil-tight seal. Clean the area around the drain plug opening, and refit the plug complete with the washer/O-ring. Tighten the plug to the specified torque, using a torque wrench.

18 Remove the old oil and all tools from under the vehicle then lower the vehicle to the ground.

19 Fill the engine through the filler hole in the camshaft cover, using the correct grade and type of oil (refer to *Weekly checks* for details of topping-up). Pour in half the specified quantity of oil first, then wait a few minutes for the oil to drain into the sump. Continue to add oil, a small quantity at a time, until the level is up to the lower mark on the dipstick. Adding approximately a further 1.0 litre will bring the level up to the upper mark on the dipstick.

20 Start the engine and run it until it reaches normal operating temperature. While the engine is warming-up, check for leaks around the oil filter and the sump drain plug.

21 Stop the engine, and wait at least five minutes for the oil to settle in the sump once more. With the new oil circulated and the filter now completely full, recheck the level on the dipstick, and add more oil as necessary.

22 Dispose of the used engine oil and filter safely, with reference to *General repair procedures* in the Reference Chapter of this manual. Do not discard the old filter with domestic household waste. The facility for waste oil disposal provided by many local council refuse tips and/or recycling centres generally has a filter receptacle alongside.

Every 18 000 miles or 12 months

4 Hose and fluid leak check

1 Visually inspect the engine joint faces, gaskets and seals for any signs of water or oil leaks. Pay particular attention to the areas around the camshaft cover, cylinder head, oil filter and sump joint faces. Similarly, check the transmission and (where applicable) the air conditioning compressor for oil leakage. Bear in mind that, over a period of time, some very slight seepage from these areas is to be expected; what you are really looking for is any indication of a serious leak. Should a leak be found, renew the offending gasket or oil seal by referring to the appropriate Chapters in this manual.

2 Also check the security and condition of all the engine-related pipes and hoses. Ensure that all cable ties or securing clips are in place, and in good condition. Clips which are broken or missing can lead to chafing of the hoses pipes or wiring, which could cause more serious problems in the future.

3 Carefully check the radiator hoses and heater hoses along their entire length. Renew any hose which is cracked, swollen or deteriorated. Cracks will show up better if the hose is squeezed. Pay close attention to the hose clips that secure the hoses to the cooling system components. Hose clips can pinch and puncture hoses, resulting in cooling system leaks. If wire-type hose clips are used, it may be a good idea to update them with screw-type clips.

4 Inspect all the cooling system components (hoses, joint faces, etc) for leaks. Where any problems of this nature are found on system components, renew the component or gasket with reference to Chapter 3 **(see Haynes Hint 1)**.

5 Where applicable, inspect the automatic transmission fluid cooler hoses for leaks or deterioration.

6 With the vehicle raised, inspect the petrol tank and filler neck for punctures, cracks and other damage. The connection between the filler neck and tank is especially critical. Sometimes, a rubber filler neck or connecting hose will leak due to loose retaining clamps or deteriorated rubber.

7 Carefully check all rubber hoses and metal fuel lines leading away from the petrol tank. Check for loose connections, deteriorated hoses, crimped lines and other damage. Pay particular attention to the vent pipes and hoses, which often loop up around the filler neck and can become blocked or crimped. Follow the lines to the front of the vehicle, carefully inspecting them all the way. Renew damaged sections as necessary. Similarly, whilst the vehicle is raised, take the opportunity to inspect all underbody brake fluid pipes and hoses.

8 From within the engine compartment, check the security of all fuel hose attachments and pipe unions, and inspect the fuel hoses and vacuum hoses for kinks, chafing and deterioration.

5 Brake pad and disc check

1 Firmly apply the handbrake, then jack up the front and rear of the vehicle and support it securely on axle stands (see *Jacking and vehicle support*). Remove the roadwheels.

2 For a quick check, the pad thickness can be carried out via the inspection hole on the caliper **(see Haynes Hint 2)**. Using a steel rule, measure the thickness of the pad lining including the backing plate. This must not be less than that indicated in the Specifications.

3 The view through the caliper inspection hole gives a rough indication of the state of the brake pads. For a comprehensive check, the brake pads should be removed and cleaned. The operation of the caliper can then also be checked, and the condition of the brake disc itself can be fully examined on both sides. Chapter 9 contains a detailed description of how the brake disc should be checked for wear and/or damage.

Haynes hint 1: A leak in the cooling system will usually show up as white- or antifreeze-coloured deposits on the area adjoining the leak.

Haynes hint 2: For a quick check, the thickness of friction material remaining on the inner brake pad can be measured through the aperture in the caliper body.

7.4 Check for wear in the hub bearings by grasping the wheel and trying to rock it

8.2 Check the condition of the driveshaft gaiters (1) and the retaining clips (2)

4 If any pad's friction material is worn to the specified thickness or less, *all four pads must be renewed as a set.* Refer to Chapter 9 for details.

5 On completion, refit the roadwheels and lower the vehicle to the ground.

6 Brake fluid pipe and hose check

1 The brake hydraulic system includes a number of metal pipes, which run from the master cylinder to the hydraulic modulator of the anti-lock braking system (ABS) and then to the front and rear brake assemblies. Flexible hoses are fitted between the pipes and the front and rear brake assemblies, to allow for steering and suspension movement.

2 When checking the system, first look for signs of leakage at the pipe or hose unions, then examine the flexible hoses for signs of cracking, chafing or deterioration of the rubber. Bend the hoses between the fingers (but do not actually bend them double, or the casing may be damaged) and check that this does not reveal previously-hidden cracks, cuts or splits. Check that the pipes and hoses are securely fastened in their clips.

3 Carefully working along the length of the metal pipes, look for dents, kinks, damage of any sort, or corrosion. Light corrosion can be polished off, but if the depth of pitting is significant, the pipe must be renewed.

7 Front suspension and steering check

1 Apply the handbrake, then raise the front of the vehicle and securely support it on axle stands (see *Jacking and vehicle support*).

2 Inspect the balljoint dust covers and the steering gear gaiters for splits, chafing or deterioration.

3 Any wear of these components will cause loss of lubricant, and may allow water to enter the components, resulting in rapid deterioration of the balljoints or steering gear.

4 Grasp each roadwheel at the 12 o'clock and 6 o'clock positions, and try to rock it **(see illustration).** Very slight free play may be felt, but if the movement is appreciable, further investigation is necessary to determine the source. Continue rocking the wheel while an assistant depresses the footbrake. If the movement is now eliminated or significantly reduced, it is likely that the hub bearings are at fault. If the free play is still evident with the footbrake depressed, then there is wear in the suspension joints or mountings.

5 Now grasp each wheel at the 9 o'clock and 3 o'clock positions, and try to rock it as before. Any movement felt now may again be caused by wear in the hub bearings or the steering track rod end balljoints. If the track rod end balljoint is worn, the visual movement will be obvious.

6 Using a large screwdriver or flat bar, check for wear in the suspension mounting bushes by levering between the relevant suspension component and its attachment point. Some movement is to be expected, as the mountings are made of rubber, but excessive wear should be obvious. Also check the condition of any visible rubber bushes, looking for splits, cracks or contamination of the rubber.

7 Check for any signs of fluid leakage around the suspension struts, or from the rubber gaiters around the piston rods. Should any fluid be noticed, the suspension strut is defective internally, and should be renewed. **Note:** *Suspension struts should always be renewed in pairs on the same axle.*

8 With the vehicle standing on its wheels, have an assistant turn the steering wheel back-and-forth about an eighth of a turn each way. There should be very little, if any, lost movement between the steering wheel and roadwheels. If this is not the case, closely observe the joints and mountings previously described. In addition, check the steering column universal joints for wear, and also check the rack-and-pinion steering gear itself.

9 The efficiency of each suspension strut may be checked by bouncing the vehicle at each front corner. Generally speaking, the body will return to its normal position and stop after being depressed. If it rises and returns on a rebound, the suspension strut is probably suspect. Also examine the suspension strut upper mountings for any signs of wear.

8 Driveshaft check

1 Firmly apply the handbrake, then jack up the front of the car and support it securely on axle stands (see *Jacking and vehicle support*).

2 Turn the steering onto full lock then slowly rotate the roadwheel. Inspect the condition of the outer constant velocity (CV) joint rubber gaiters while squeezing the gaiters to open out the folds **(see illustration).** Check for signs of cracking, splits or deterioration of the rubber which may allow the grease to escape and lead to water and grit entry into the joint. Also check the security and condition of the retaining clips. Repeat these checks on the inner CV joints. If any damage or deterioration is found, the gaiters should be renewed as described in Chapter 8.

3 At the same time, check the general condition of the CV joints themselves by first holding the driveshaft and attempting to rotate the wheel. Repeat this check by holding the inner joint and attempting to rotate the driveshaft. Any appreciable movement indicates wear in the joints, wear in the driveshaft splines or loose driveshaft retaining nut.

9.3 Exhaust mountings

9 Exhaust system check

1 With the engine cold (at least an hour after the vehicle has been driven), check the complete exhaust system from the engine to the end of the tailpipe. The exhaust system is most easily checked with the vehicle raised on a hoist, or suitably-supported on axle stands, so that the exhaust components are readily visible and accessible (see *Jacking and vehicle support*).
2 Check the exhaust pipes and connections for evidence of leaks, severe corrosion and damage. Make sure that all brackets and mountings are in good condition, and that all relevant nuts and bolts are tight. Leakage at any of the joints or in other parts of the system will usually show up as a black sooty stain in the vicinity of the leak.
3 Rattles and other noises can often be traced to the exhaust system, especially the brackets and mountings **(see illustration)**. Try to move the pipes and silencers. If the components are able to come into contact with the body or suspension parts, secure the system with new mountings. Otherwise separate the joints (if possible) and twist the pipes as necessary to provide additional clearance.

10 Rear suspension check

1 Chock the front wheels, then jack up the rear of the vehicle and support securely on axle stands (see *Jacking and vehicle support*).
2 Inspect the rear suspension components for any signs of obvious wear or damage. Pay particular attention to the rubber mounting bushes, and renew if necessary (see Chapter 10).
3 Grasp each roadwheel at the 12 o'clock and 6 o'clock positions **(see illustration 7.4)**, and try to rock it. Any excess movement indicates wear in the wheel bearings. Wear may also be accompanied by a rumbling sound when the wheel is spun, or a noticeable roughness if the wheel is turned slowly. The wheel bearing can be renewed as described in Chapter 10.

4 Check for any signs of fluid leakage around the shock absorber bodies. Should any fluid be noticed, the shock absorber is defective internally, and should be renewed. **Note:** *Shock absorbers should always be renewed in pairs on the same axle.*
5 With the vehicle standing on its wheels, the efficiency of each shock absorber may be checked by bouncing the vehicle at each rear corner. Generally speaking, the body will return to its normal position and stop after being depressed. If it rises and returns on a rebound, the shock absorber is probably suspect.

11 Bodywork and underbody condition check

Note: *This work should be carried out by a Vauxhall/Opel dealer in order to validate the vehicle warranty. The work includes a thorough inspection of the vehicle paintwork and underbody for damage and corrosion.*

Damage/corrosion check

1 Once the car has been washed, and all tar spots and other surface blemishes have been cleaned off, carefully check all paintwork, looking closely for chips or scratches. Pay particular attention to vulnerable areas such as the front panels (bonnet and spoiler), and around the wheel arches. Any damage to the paintwork must be rectified as soon as possible, to comply with the terms of the manufacturer's anti-corrosion warranties; check with a Vauxhall/Opel dealer for details.
2 If a chip or light scratch is found which is recent and still free from rust, it can be touched-up using the appropriate touch-up stick which can be obtained from Vauxhall/Opel dealers. Any more serious damage, or rusted stone chips, can be repaired as described in Chapter 11, but if damage or corrosion is so severe that a panel must be renewed, seek professional advice as soon as possible.
3 Always check that the door and ventilation opening drain holes and pipes are completely clear, so that water can drain out.

Corrosion protection check

4 The wax-based underbody protective coating should be inspected annually, preferably just prior to Winter, when the underbody should be washed down as thoroughly as possible without disturbing the protective coating. Any damage to the coating should be repaired using a suitable wax-based sealer. If any of the body panels are disturbed for repair or renewal, do not forget to re-apply the coating. Wax should be injected into door cavities, sills and box sections, to maintain the level of protection provided by the vehicle manufacturer – seek the advice of a Vauxhall/Opel dealer.

12 Roadwheel bolt tightness check

1 Where applicable, remove the wheel trims from the wheels.
2 Using a torque wrench on each wheel bolt in turn, ensure that the bolts are tightened to the specified torque.
3 Where applicable, refit the wheel trims on completion, making sure they are fitted correctly.

13 Hinge and lock lubrication

1 Work around the vehicle and lubricate the hinges of the bonnet, doors, boot lid and tailgate with a light machine oil.
2 Lightly lubricate the bonnet release mechanism and exposed section of inner cable with a smear of grease.
3 Check the security and operation of all hinges, latches and locks, adjusting them where required. Check the operation of the central locking system.
4 Check the condition and operation of the tailgate struts, renewing them both if either is leaking or no longer able to support the tailgate securely when raised.

14 Electrical systems check

1 Check the operation of all the electrical equipment, ie, lights, direction indicators, horn, etc. Refer to the appropriate sections of Chapter 12 for details if any of the circuits are found to be inoperative.
2 Note that the stop-light switch is described in Chapter 9.
3 Check all accessible wiring connectors, harnesses and retaining clips for security, and for signs of chafing or damage. Rectify any faults found.

15 Headlight beam alignment check

1 Accurate adjustment of the headlight beam is only possible using optical beam-setting equipment, and this work should therefore be carried out by a Vauxhall/Opel dealer or service station with the necessary facilities. Refer to Chapter 12 for further information.

16 Road test

Instruments/ electrical equipment

1 Check the operation of all instruments, warning lights and electrical equipment.
2 Make sure that all instruments read correctly, and switch on all electrical equipment in turn, to check that it functions properly.

Steering and suspension

3 Check for any abnormalities in the steering, suspension, handling or road 'feel'.
4 Drive the vehicle, and check that there are no unusual vibrations or noises.
5 Check that the steering feels positive, with no excessive 'sloppiness', or roughness, and check for any suspension noises when cornering and driving over bumps.

Drivetrain

6 Check the performance of the engine, clutch, transmission and driveshafts.
7 Listen for any unusual noises from the engine, clutch and transmission.
8 Make sure that the engine runs smoothly when idling, and that there is no hesitation when accelerating.
9 Check that, where applicable, the clutch action is smooth and progressive, that the drive is taken up smoothly, and that the pedal travel is not excessive. Also listen for any noises when the clutch pedal is depressed.

10 Check that all gears can be engaged smoothly without noise, and that the gear lever action is smooth and not abnormally vague or 'notchy'.
11 On automatic transmission models, make sure that all gearchanges occur smoothly, without snatching, and without an increase in engine speed between changes. Check that all of the gear positions can be selected with the vehicle at rest. If any problems are found, they should be referred to a Vauxhall/Opel dealer.
12 Listen for a metallic clicking sound from the front of the vehicle, as the vehicle is driven slowly in a circle with the steering on full-lock. Carry out this check in both directions. If a clicking noise is heard, this indicates wear in a driveshaft joint (see Chapter 8).

Braking system

13 Make sure that the vehicle does not pull to one side when braking, and that the wheels do not lock when braking hard.
14 Check that there is no vibration through the steering when braking.
15 Check that the handbrake operates correctly, without excessive movement of the lever, and that it holds the vehicle stationary on a slope.
16 Test the operation of the brake servo unit as follows. Depress the footbrake four or five times to exhaust the vacuum, then start the engine. As the engine starts, there should be a noticeable 'give' in the brake pedal as vacuum builds-up. Allow the engine to run for at least two minutes, and then switch it off. If the brake pedal is now depressed again, it should

be possible to detect a hiss from the servo as the pedal is depressed. After about four or five applications, no further hissing should be heard, and the pedal should feel considerably harder.

17 Service interval indicator reset

1 With the ignition switched off, depress and hold the trip odometer reset button located on the instrument panel.
2 With the reset button depressed, switch on the ignition, wait until the service interval display changes, then keep the reset button depressed for at least a further 3 seconds.
3 After approximately 3 seconds the display will show the service symbol and the maximum mileage before the next required service. Release the reset button and switch off the ignition. When the button is released, the odometer reading will appear again.
4 This procedure resets the service interval indicator back to the ECOService-Flex flexible maintenance interval. If the standard maintenance schedule described in this Chapter is being used, then the interval until the next service, which will be shown on the display, is irrelevant. If it is wished to have the service interval indicator altered to show the standard maintenance intervals described in this Chapter, it will be necessary to have the system reprogrammed using dedicated Vauxhall/Opel diagnostic equipment or a compatible alternative.

Every 18 000 miles or 2 years

18 Pollen filter renewal

1 Open the bonnet, and pull up the rubber weatherseal from the flange at the rear of the engine compartment (see illustration).
2 Open the cover in the water deflector for access to the pollen filter (see illustration).
3 Release the clips from each end, then lift out the filter (see illustrations).
4 Fit the new filter using a reversal of the removal procedure; make sure that the filter is fitted the correct way up as indicated on the edge of the filter.

18.1 Pull up the rubber weatherseal . . .

18.2 . . . then open the cover

18.3a Release the clips at each end . . .

18.3b . . . and lift out the pollen filter

Every 36 000 miles or 2 years

19 Auxiliary drivebelt check and renewal

Checking

1 Due to their function and material make-up, drivebelts are prone to failure after a long period of time and should therefore be inspected regularly.

2 Apply the handbrake, then jack up the front of the vehicle and support it on axle stands (see *Jacking and vehicle support*). Remove the right-hand front roadwheel and the wheel arch liner inner cover for access to the right-hand side of the engine.

3 With the engine stopped, inspect the full length of the drivebelt for cracks and separation of the belt plies. It will be necessary to turn the engine (using a spanner or socket and bar on the crankshaft pulley bolt) so that the belt can be inspected thoroughly. Twist the belt between the pulleys so that both sides can be viewed. Also check for fraying, and glazing which gives the belt a shiny appearance. Check the pulleys for nicks, cracks, distortion and corrosion. If the belt shows signs of wear or damage, it should be renewed as a precaution against breakage in service.

4 On 2.2 litre engines also check the position of the drivebelt tensioner assembly arm. The mark on the underside of the moveable arm should be in between the two marks on the tensioner body, and the arm should be free to move.

Renewal

Note: *The manufacturers recommend that the tensioner pulley is checked and if necessary renewed at the same time as the drivebelt.*

5 If not already done, apply the handbrake, then jack up the front of the vehicle and support it on axle stands (see *Jacking and vehicle support*). Remove the right-hand front roadwheel and the wheel arch liner inner cover for access to the right-hand side of the engine.

6 For additional working clearance, remove the air cleaner housing as described in Chapter 4A.

7 If the drivebelt is to be re-used, mark it to indicate its normal running direction.

1.8 litre models

8 On 1.8 litre models, note the routing of the drivebelt then, using a spanner on the pulley centre bolt, turn the tensioner anti-clockwise against the spring tension. Hold the tensioner in this position by inserting a suitable locking pin/bolt through the special hole provided **(see illustration)**. Slip the auxiliary drivebelt off of the pulleys.

9 Locate the auxiliary drivebelt onto the pulleys in the correct routing. If the drivebelt is being re-used, make sure it is fitted the correct way around.

10 Turn back the tensioner and remove the locking pin/bolt then release it, making sure that the drivebelt ribs locate correctly on each of the pulley grooves.

11 Refit the air cleaner housing (if removed), then refit the wheel arch liner inner cover and roadwheel, and lower the vehicle to the ground.

2.2 litre models

12 Note the routing of the drivebelt, then insert a socket bar or similar tool into the square hole on the tensioner arm. Turn the tensioner anti-clockwise against the spring tension and slip the auxiliary drivebelt off of the pulleys **(see illustration)**. Release the tensioner arm.

13 Turn the tensioner anti-clockwise and locate the auxiliary drivebelt onto the pulleys in the correct routing. If the drivebelt is being re-used, make sure it is fitted the correct way around. With the belt in position, slowly release the tensioner arm making sure that the drivebelt ribs locate correctly on each of the pulley grooves.

14 Refit the air cleaner housing (if removed), then refit the wheel arch liner inner cover and roadwheel, and lower the vehicle to the ground.

J44721

19.8 Auxiliary drivebelt tensioner details – 1.8 litre engines

1 *Locking pin/bolt*
2 *Turn the tensioner as indicated to release the tension*

H46357

19.12 Auxiliary drivebelt tensioner details – 2.2 litre engines

Turn the tensioner as indicated to release the tension

20.1a Prise off the battery cover . . .

20.1b . . . and remove the circular battery

Every 2 years, regardless of mileage

20 Remote control battery renewal

1 Using a screwdriver, prise the battery cover from the ignition key fob **(see illustrations)**.
2 Note how the circular battery is fitted, then carefully remove it from the contacts.
3 Fit the new battery (type CR 20 32) and refit the cover making sure that it clips fully onto the base.
4 After changing the battery, lock and unlock the driver's door with the key in the lock to synchronise the remote control unit.

21 Hydraulic fluid renewal

⚠️ **Warning: Hydraulic fluid can harm your eyes and damage painted surfaces, so use extreme caution when handling and pouring it. Do not use fluid that has been standing open for some time, as it absorbs moisture from the air. Excess moisture can cause a dangerous loss of braking effectiveness.**
Note: *The brake and clutch hydraulic systems share a common reservoir.*
1 The procedure is similar to that for the bleeding of the hydraulic system as described in Chapters 9 (brake) and 6 (clutch).
2 Working as described in Chapter 9, open the first bleed screw in the sequence, and pump the brake pedal gently until nearly all the old fluid has been emptied from the master cylinder reservoir. Top-up to the MAX level with new fluid, and continue pumping until only the new fluid remains in the reservoir and new fluid can be seen emerging from the bleed screw. Tighten the screw, and top the reservoir level up to the MAX level line.

 Old hydraulic fluid is invariably much darker in colour than the new, making it easy to distinguish the two.

3 Work through all the remaining bleed screws in the sequence until new fluid can be seen at all of them. Be careful to keep the master cylinder reservoir topped-up to above the MIN level at all times, or air may enter the system and greatly increase the length of the task.
4 Bleed the fluid from the clutch hydraulic system as described in Chapter 6.
5 When the operation is complete, check that all bleed screws are securely tightened, and that their dust caps are refitted. Wash off all traces of spilt fluid, and recheck the master cylinder reservoir fluid level.
6 Check the operation of the brakes and clutch before taking the car on the road.

22 Coolant renewal

Note: *Vauxhall/Opel do not specify renewal intervals for the antifreeze mixture, as the mixture used to fill the system when the vehicle is new is designed to last the lifetime of the vehicle. However, it is strongly recommended that the coolant is renewed at the intervals specified in the 'Maintenance schedule', as a precaution against possible engine corrosion problems. This is particularly advisable if the coolant has been renewed using an antifreeze other than that specified by Vauxhall/Opel. With many antifreeze types, the corrosion inhibitors become progressively less effective with age. It is up to the individual owner whether or not to follow this advice.*

⚠️ **Warning: Wait until the engine is cold before starting this procedure. Do not allow**
antifreeze to come in contact with your skin, or with the painted surfaces of the vehicle. Rinse off spills immediately with plenty of water. Never leave antifreeze lying around in an open container, or in a puddle in the driveway or on the garage floor. Children and pets are attracted by its sweet smell, but antifreeze can be fatal if ingested.

Cooling system draining

1 To drain the cooling system, first cover the expansion tank cap with a wad of rag, and slowly turn the cap anti-clockwise to relieve the pressure in the cooling system (a hissing sound will normally be heard). Wait until any pressure remaining in the system is released, then continue to turn the cap until it can be removed.
2 The coolant drain plug is located at the bottom of the radiator right-hand end tank. Position a container beneath the radiator then unscrew the drain plug and allow the coolant to drain. On 2.2 litre engines, also unscrew the drain plug from under the coolant pump housing **(see illustration)**.
3 When the flow of coolant stops, refit and tighten the drain plug(s).

22.2 Removing the coolant drain plug located under the coolant pump housing – 2.2 litre engines

22.17 Lift up the wire clip and disconnect the left-hand heater hose from the heater matrix pipe stub

4 As no cylinder block drain plug is fitted, it is not possible to drain all of the coolant. Due consideration must be made for this when refilling the system, in order to maintain the correct concentration of antifreeze.

5 If the coolant has been drained for a reason other than renewal, then provided it is clean and less than two years old, it can be re-used.

Cooling system flushing

6 If coolant renewal has been neglected, or if the antifreeze mixture has become diluted, then in time, the cooling system may gradually lose efficiency, as the coolant passages become restricted due to rust, scale deposits, and other sediment. The cooling system efficiency can be restored by flushing the system clean.

7 The radiator should be flushed independently of the engine, to avoid unnecessary contamination.

Radiator flushing

8 Disconnect the top and bottom hoses and any other relevant hoses from the radiator, with reference to Chapter 3.

9 Insert a garden hose into the radiator top inlet. Direct a flow of clean water through the radiator, and continue flushing until clean water emerges from the radiator bottom outlet.

10 If after a reasonable period, the water still does not run clear, the radiator can be flushed with a good proprietary cleaning agent. It is important that the manufacturer's instructions are followed carefully. If the contamination is particularly bad, remove the radiator, insert the hose in the radiator bottom outlet, and reverse-flush the radiator.

Engine flushing

11 To flush the engine, the thermostat must be removed, because it will be shut, and would otherwise prevent the flow of water around the engine. The thermostat can be removed as described in Chapter 3. Take care not to introduce dirt or debris into the system if this approach is used.

12 With the bottom hose disconnected from the radiator, insert a garden hose into the thermostat opening. Direct a clean flow of water through the engine, and continue flushing until clean water emerges from the radiator bottom hose.

13 On completion of flushing, refit the thermostat with reference to Chapter 3, and reconnect the hoses.

Cooling system filling

14 Before attempting to fill the cooling system, make sure that all hoses and clips are in good condition, and that the clips are tight. Note that an antifreeze mixture must be used all year round, to prevent corrosion of the engine components.

15 Remove the expansion tank filler cap.

16 Fill the system by slowly pouring the coolant into the expansion tank until it is up to the filler neck.

17 Using a small screwdriver, lift up the wire clip securing the left-hand heater hose to the heater matrix pipe stub, and disconnect the hose from the stub (see illustration).

18 As soon as coolant begins to run from the heater matrix, push the securing wire clip back into position on the heater hose end fitting, then push the hose back onto the matrix pipe stub. Ensure that the wire clip securely locks the hose in position.

19 Top-up the expansion tank until the coolant level is up to the KALT/COLD mark on the side of the tank.

20 Refit and tighten the expansion tank filler cap.

21 Start the engine and run it at 2000 to 2500 rpm for 30 seconds, allow it to idle for 5 seconds, then run it at 2000 to 2500 rpm again for a further 30 seconds.

22 Continue running the engine at idling speed and allow it to warm-up. When the cooling fan cuts-in, run the engine again at 2000 to 2500 rpm for 30 seconds, allow it to idle for 5 seconds, then run it at 2000 to 2500 rpm again for a further 30 seconds.

23 Stop the engine, and allow it to cool, then recheck the coolant level with reference to *Weekly checks*. Top-up the level if necessary and refit the expansion tank filler cap.

Antifreeze mixture

24 Always use an ethylene-glycol based antifreeze which is suitable for use in mixed-metal cooling systems. **Note:** *Vauxhall/ Opel recommend the use of silicate-free 'red' coolant (09 194 431/19 40 650). The quantity of antifreeze and levels of protection are given in the Specifications.*

25 Before adding antifreeze, the cooling system should be completely drained, preferably flushed, and all hoses checked for condition and security.

26 After filling with antifreeze, a label should be attached to the expansion tank, stating the type and concentration of antifreeze used, and the date installed. Any subsequent topping-up should be made with the same type and concentration of antifreeze.

27 Do not use engine antifreeze in the windscreen/tailgate washer system, as it will cause damage to the vehicle paintwork. A screenwash additive should be added to the washer system in the quantities stated on the bottle.

23 Exhaust emission check

1 The exhaust emission check is carried out initially after 3 years, then every 2 years, however, on vehicles which are subject to intensive use (eg, taxis/hire cars/ambulances) it must be carried out annually. The check involves checking the engine management system operation by plugging an electronic tester into the system diagnostic socket to check the electronic control unit (ECU) memory for faults (see Chapter 4A).

2 In reality, if the vehicle is running correctly and the engine management warning light in the instrument panel is functioning normally, then this check need not be carried out.

24.2 Slacken the retaining clip and disconnect the air intake duct from the airflow meter

24.3 Disconnect the wiring connector from the airflow meter

Every 36 000 miles or 4 years

24 Air cleaner element renewal

1 The air cleaner is located in the front right-hand corner of the engine compartment.
2 Slacken the retaining clip and disconnect the air intake duct from the airflow meter **(see illustration)**.
3 Disconnect the wiring connector from the side of the airflow meter **(see illustration)**.
4 Undo the screws and lift off the air cleaner cover, then lift out the filter element **(see illustrations)**.
5 Wipe out the casing and the cover.
6 Fit the new filter, noting that the rubber locating flange should be uppermost, and secure the cover with the screws.
7 Reconnect the airflow meter wiring connector and the air intake duct.

25 Spark plug renewal

1 The correct functioning of the spark plugs is vital for the correct running and efficiency of the engine. It is essential that the plugs fitted are appropriate for the engine; suitable types are specified at the beginning of this Chapter, or in the vehicle's Owner's Handbook. If the correct type is used and the engine is in good condition, the spark plugs should not need attention between scheduled renewal intervals. Spark plug cleaning is rarely necessary, and should not be attempted unless specialised equipment is available, as damage can easily be caused to the firing ends.
2 Where applicable, remove the engine top cover after removing the oil filler cap. Refit the cap.
3 Remove the ignition module from the spark plugs with reference to Chapter 5B.

4 It is advisable to remove the dirt from the spark plug recesses using a clean brush, vacuum cleaner or compressed air before removing the plugs, to prevent dirt dropping into the cylinders.
5 Unscrew the spark plugs from the cylinder head using a spark plug spanner, suitable box spanner or a deep socket and extension bar **(see illustration)**. Keep the socket aligned with the spark plug – if it is forcibly moved to one side, the ceramic insulator may be broken off.
6 Examination of the spark plugs will give a good indication of the condition of the engine. As each plug is removed, examine it as follows. If the insulator nose of the spark plug is clean and white, with no deposits, this is indicative of a weak mixture or too hot a plug (a hot plug transfers heat away from the electrode slowly, a cold plug transfers heat away quickly).
7 If the tip and insulator nose are covered with hard black-looking deposits, then this is indicative that the mixture is too rich. Should the plug be black and oily, then it is likely that the engine is fairly worn, as well as the mixture being too rich.

24.4a Undo the retaining screws . . .

24.4b . . . lift off the air cleaner cover . . .

24.4c . . . then lift out the filter element

25.5 Removing the spark plugs – 2.2 litre engines

25.9 The gap of the multi-electrode plugs (where fitted) should not be adjusted

25.11a If single electrode plugs are fitted, check the electrode gap using a feeler gauge . . .

25.11b . . . or a wire gauge . . .

25.12 . . . and if necessary adjust the gap by bending the electrode

8 If the insulator nose is covered with light tan to greyish-brown deposits, then the mixture is correct and it is likely that the engine is in good condition.

9 Some engines are fitted with multi-electrode plugs as standard **(see illustration)**. On these plugs, the electrode gaps are all preset and no attempt should be made to bend the electrodes.

10 If single electrode plugs are to be installed, the spark plug electrode gap is of considerable importance. If the gap is too large or too small,

HAYNES HINT

It is very often difficult to insert spark plugs into their holes without cross-threading them. To avoid this possibility, fit a short length of rubber hose over the end of the spark plug. The flexible hose acts as a universal joint to help align the plug with the plug hole. Should the plug begin to cross-thread, the hose will slip on the spark plug, preventing thread damage to the aluminium cylinder head.

the size of the spark and its efficiency will be seriously impaired and it will not perform correctly under all engine speed and load conditions. For the best results, the spark plug gap should be set in accordance with the Specifications at the beginning of this Chapter.

11 To set the gap, measure it with a feeler blade or spark plug gap gauge and then carefully bend the outer plug electrode until the correct gap is achieved. The centre electrode should never be bent, as this may crack the insulator and cause plug failure, if nothing worse. If using feeler blades, the gap is correct when the appropriate-size blade is a firm sliding fit **(see illustrations)**.

12 Special spark plug electrode gap adjusting tools are available from most motor accessory shops, or from some spark plug manufacturers **(see illustration)**.

13 Before fitting the spark plugs, check that the threaded connector sleeves on the top of

27.1 The fuel filter is clipped to the side of the fuel tank

the plug are tight, and that the plug exterior surfaces and threads are clean.

14 Screw in the spark plugs by hand where possible, then tighten them to the specified torque. Take extra care to enter the plug threads correctly, as the cylinder head is of light alloy construction **(see Haynes Hint)**.

15 On completion, refit the ignition module as described in Chapter 5B then, where applicable, refit the engine top cover.

26 Timing belt, tensioner and idler pulley renewal

Refer to the procedures contained in Chapter 2A.

27 Fuel filter renewal

1 The fuel filter is located under the rear of the vehicle where it is clipped onto the side of the fuel tank **(see illustration)**.

2 Depressurise the fuel system as described in Chapter 4A.

3 Chock the front wheels, then jack up the rear of the vehicle and support on axle stands (see *Jacking and vehicle support*).

4 Position a suitable container below the fuel filter, to catch spilt fuel.

5 Disconnect the quick-release fittings and remove the fuel hoses from the fuel filter, noting their locations to ensure correct refitting. A Vauxhall/Opel special tool is available to disconnect the hose connectors, but provided care is taken, the connections can be released using a pair of long-nosed pliers, or a similar tool, to depress the retaining tangs. Be prepared for fuel spillage, and take adequate precautions. Vauxhall/Opel recommend that the connecting clips of the quick-release connectors are renewed whenever removed.

6 Lift the retaining tab and push the filter forwards, out of the mounting bracket. Note the orientation of the fuel flow direction arrow.

7 Fitting the new filter is a reversal of removal, bearing in mind the following points:

a) Ensure that the filter is fitted with the flow direction arrow on the filter body pointing in the direction of fuel flow.

b) Ensure that the hoses are reconnected to their correct locations, as noted before removal.

c) On completion, run the engine and check for leaks. If leakage is evident, stop the engine immediately and rectify the problem without delay.

28 Automatic transmission fluid renewal

Refer to the procedures contained in Chapter 7B.

Chapter 1 Part B:
Routine maintenance and servicing – diesel models

Contents

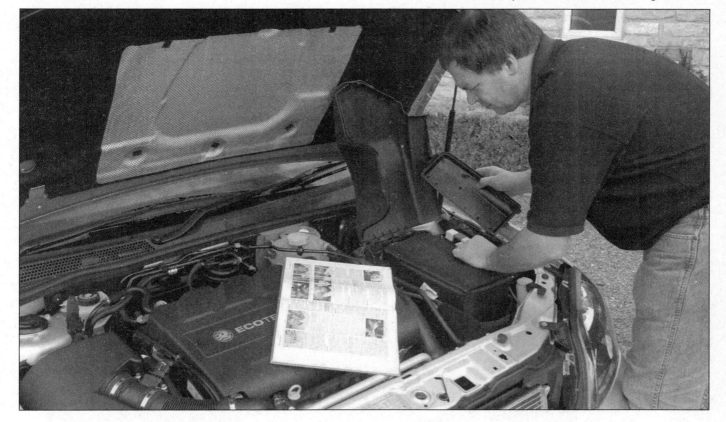

Degrees of difficulty

Easy, suitable for novice with little experience | **Fairly easy,** suitable for beginner with some experience | **Fairly difficult,** suitable for competent DIY mechanic | **Difficult,** suitable for experienced DIY mechanic | **Very difficult,** suitable for expert DIY or professional

Lubricants and fluids.................................... Refer to *Weekly checks*

Capacities

Engine oil (including oil filter)
1.9 litre engines .... 4.3 litres
2.0 and 2.2 litre engines.................................. 5.5 litres
Difference between MIN and MAX dipstick marks............... 1.0 litre

Cooling system
1.9 litre engines .... 7.5 litres
2.0 and 2.2 litre engines:
    Manual transmission without air conditioning .... 7.3 litres
    Manual transmission with air conditioning.................. 7.6 litres
    Automatic transmission with or without air conditioning .... 7.8 litres

Transmission
Manual transmission:
    F23 transmission .... 1.55 litres
    F35 transmission .... 1.9 litres
    F40 transmission .... 3.2 litres
Automatic transmission (at fluid change)..................... 3.0 to 3.5 litres (approximately)

Washer fluid reservoir
Without headlight washers................................. 2.9 litres
With headlight washers .... 5.6 litres

Fuel tank
Saloon and Hatchback models .... 60 litres
Estate models.. 61 litres

Cooling system
Antifreeze mixture:
    40% antifreeze .... Protection down to -28°C
    50% antifreeze .... Protection down to -40°C

Brakes
Friction material minimum thickness (including backing plate):
    Front brake pads .... 9.0 mm
    Rear brake pads....................................... 8.0 mm

Torque wrench settings

	Nm	lbf ft
Engine oil filter:		
1.9 litre engines	15	11
2.0 and 2.2 litre engines	25	18
Fuel filter housing cover retaining ring (1.9 litre engines)	30	22
Fuel filter housing cover centre bolt (2.0 and 2.2 litre engines)	6	4
Roadwheel bolts	110	81
Sump drain plug:		
1.9 litre engines	20	15
2.0 and 2.2 litre engines	10	7

Maintenance schedule

The maintenance intervals in this manual are provided with the assumption that you, not the dealer, will be carrying out the work. These are the minimum maintenance intervals based on the standard service schedule recommended by the manufacturer for vehicles driven daily. If you wish to keep your vehicle in peak condition at all times, you may wish to perform some of these procedures more often. We encourage frequent maintenance, because it enhances the efficiency, performance and resale value of your vehicle.

If the vehicle is driven in dusty areas, used to tow a trailer, or driven frequently at slow speeds (idling in traffic) or on short journeys, more frequent maintenance intervals are recommended.

When the vehicle is new, it should be serviced by a dealer service department (or other workshop recognised by the vehicle manufacturer as providing the same standard of service) in order to preserve the warranty. The vehicle manufacturer may reject warranty claims if you are unable to prove that servicing has been carried out as and when specified, using only original equipment parts or parts certified to be of equivalent quality.

Flexible maintenance intervals

All Vectra models covered by this manual are also capable of operating under the flexible maintenance interval plan known as Vauxhall/Opel ECOService-Flex. Under this flexible maintenance plan, a maximum service interval of 2 years or 30 000 miles can be achieved under ideal conditions.

Information on a number of variables such as distance driven, driving cycles, engine operating conditions, coolant temperature and oil temperature are obtained and stored in the engine management ECU. Based on this information, the ECU calculates the remaining distance until the next service is due and displays this distance on the service interval indicator.

The ECOService-Flex plan is entirely dependant on the exclusive use of specially developed 'long-life' engine oils meeting Vauxhall/Opel specification GM-LL-B-025. If any other type of oil is used (such as engine oils meeting the conventional ACEA specifications) then the shorter maintenance intervals shown in the following schedule must be adhered to.

As stated earlier, it is our philosophy that frequent maintenance is always the preferred option, however it is up to the individual owner as to the course of action to be adopted.

Every 250 miles or weekly
☐ Refer to *Weekly checks*

Every 9000 miles or 6 months – whichever comes first
☐ Renew the engine oil and filter (Section 3)*
* Note: *Vauxhall/Opel recommend that the engine oil and filter are changed every 18 000 miles or 12 months if the vehicle is being operated under the standard service schedule. However, oil and filter changes are good for the engine and we recommend that the oil and filter are renewed more frequently, especially if the vehicle is used on a lot of short journeys.*

Every 18 000 miles or 12 months – whichever comes first
☐ Check all underbonnet and underbody components, pipes and hoses for leaks (Section 4)
☐ Drain the water from the fuel filter (Section 5)
☐ Check the condition of the brake pads (renew if necessary), the calipers and discs (Section 6)
☐ Check the condition of all brake fluid pipes and hoses (Section 7)
☐ Check the condition of the front suspension and steering components, particularly the rubber gaiters and seals (Section 8)
☐ Check the condition of the driveshaft joint gaiters, and the driveshaft joints (Section 9)
☐ Check the condition of the exhaust system components (Section 10)
☐ Check the condition of the rear suspension components (Section 11)
☐ Check the bodywork and underbody for damage and corrosion, and check the condition of the underbody corrosion protection (Section 12)
☐ Check the tightness of the roadwheel bolts (Section 13)
☐ Lubricate all door, bonnet and tailgate hinges and locks (Section 14)
☐ Check the operation of the horn, all lights, and the wipers and washers (Section 15)
☐ Check the headlight beam alignment (Section 16)
☐ Carry out a road test (Section 17)
☐ Reset the service interval indicator (Section 18)

Every 18 000 miles or 2 years – whichever comes first
☐ Renew the pollen filter (Section 19)
☐ Renew the fuel filter (Section 20)

Every 36 000 miles or 2 years – whichever comes first
☐ Check the auxiliary drivebelt and tensioner (Section 21)
☐ Check, and if necessary adjust, the valve clearances – 1.9 litre Z19DT engines (Section 22)

Every 2 years, regardless of mileage
☐ Renew the battery for the remote control handset (Section 23)
☐ Renew the brake and clutch fluid (Section 24)
☐ Renew the coolant (Section 25)*
☐ Exhaust emission test (Section 26)
* Note: *Vauxhall/Opel do not specify renewal intervals for the antifreeze mixture, as the mixture used to fill the system when the vehicle is new is designed to last the lifetime of the vehicle. See Section 25.*

Every 36 000 miles or 4 years – whichever comes first
☐ Renew the air cleaner filter element (Section 27)
☐ Renew the timing belt, tensioner and idler pulleys – 1.9 litre engines (Section 28)*
☐ Renew the automatic transmission fluid – 2.2 litre engines (Section 29)
* Note: *The normal interval for timing belt renewal is 72 000 miles or 6 years for the Z19DT engines, and 90 000 miles or 10 years for the Z19DTH engines. However, it is strongly recommended that the interval used is 36 000 miles on vehicles which are subjected to intensive use, ie, mainly short journeys or a lot of stop-start driving. The actual belt renewal interval is therefore very much up to the individual owner, but bear in mind that severe engine damage will result if the belt breaks.*

Every 48 000 miles or 6 years – whichever comes first
☐ Renew the automatic transmission fluid – 1.9 litre engines (Section 30)

Underbonnet view of a 1.9 litre SOHC engine model

1 Engine oil level dipstick
2 Engine oil filler cap
3 Air cleaner assembly
4 Front suspension strut upper mounting
5 Screen washer fluid reservoir
6 Airflow meter
7 Brake (and clutch) fluid reservoir
8 Fuel filter
9 Coolant expansion tank
10 Battery
11 Fuse/relay box
12 ABS hydraulic modulator

Underbonnet view of a 1.9 litre DOHC engine model

1 Engine oil level dipstick
2 Engine oil filler cap
3 Air cleaner assembly
4 Front suspension strut upper mounting
5 Screen washer fluid reservoir
6 Airflow meter
7 Brake (and clutch) fluid reservoir
8 Fuel filter
9 Coolant expansion tank
10 Battery
11 Fuse/relay box
12 ABS hydraulic modulator

Underbonnet view of a 2.0 litre engine model

1 Engine oil level dipstick
2 Engine oil filler cap
3 Air cleaner assembly
4 Front suspension strut upper mounting
5 Screen washer fluid reservoir
6 Airflow meter
7 Brake (and clutch) fluid reservoir
8 Fuel filter
9 Coolant expansion tank
10 Battery
11 Fuse/relay box
12 ABS hydraulic modulator

Front underbody view

1 Exhaust front pipe
2 Steering track rods
3 Front suspension lower arms
4 Front brake calipers
5 Engine mounting front torque link
6 Engine mounting rear torque link
7 Right-hand driveshaft
8 Manual transmission
9 Engine oil drain plug
10 Air conditioning compressor
11 Electric cooling fan
12 Front subframe

Rear underbody view

1   Handbrake cable
2   Exhaust tailpipe and silencer
3   Exhaust heat shield
4   Rear axle body
5   Rear hub carrier
6   Lower control arm
7   Upper control arm
8   Auxiliary control arm
9   Shock absorber
10 Rear anti-roll bar
11 Rear suspension trailing arm
12 Fuel tank

Maintenance procedures

1 General information

1 This Chapter is designed to help the home mechanic maintain his/her vehicle for safety, economy, long life and peak performance.
2 The Chapter contains a master maintenance schedule, followed by Sections dealing specifically with each task in the schedule. Visual checks, adjustments, component renewal and other helpful items are included. Refer to the accompanying illustrations of the engine compartment and the underside of the vehicle for the locations of the various components.
3 Servicing your vehicle in accordance with the mileage/time maintenance schedule and the following Sections will provide a planned maintenance programme, which should result in a long and reliable service life. This is a comprehensive plan, so maintaining some items but not others at the specified service intervals will not produce the same results.
4 As you service your vehicle, you will discover that many of the procedures can – and should – be grouped together, because of the particular procedure being performed, or because of the proximity of two otherwise-unrelated components to one another. For example, if the vehicle is raised for any reason, the exhaust can be inspected at the same time as the suspension and steering components.
5 The first step in this maintenance programme is to prepare yourself before the

actual work begins. Read through all the Sections relevant to the work to be carried out, then make a list and gather all the parts and tools required. If a problem is encountered, seek advice from a parts specialist, or a dealer service department.

2 Regular maintenance

1 If, from the time the vehicle is new, the routine maintenance schedule is followed closely, and frequent checks are made of fluid levels and high-wear items, as suggested throughout this manual, the engine will be kept in relatively good running condition, and the need for additional work will be minimised.
2 It is possible that there will be times when the engine is running poorly due to the lack of regular maintenance. This is even more likely if a used vehicle, which has not received regular and frequent maintenance checks, is purchased. In such cases, additional work may need to be carried out, outside of the regular maintenance intervals.
3 If engine wear is suspected, a compression test (refer to the appropriate part of Chapter 2) will provide valuable information regarding the overall performance of the main internal components. Such a test can be used as a basis to decide on the extent of the work to be carried out. If, for example, a compression test indicates serious internal engine wear, conventional

maintenance as described in this Chapter will not greatly improve the performance of the engine, and may prove a waste of time and money, unless extensive overhaul work is carried out first.
4 The following series of operations are those most often required to improve the performance of a generally poor-running engine:

Primary operations
a) Clean, inspect and test the battery (refer to Weekly checks).
b) Check all the engine-related fluids (refer to Weekly checks).
c) Check the condition and tension of the auxiliary drivebelt (Section 21).
d) Check the condition of the air filter, and renew if necessary (Section 27).
e) Renew the fuel filter (Section 20).
f) Check the condition of all hoses, and check for fluid leaks (Section 4).
5 If the above operations do not prove fully effective, carry out the following secondary operations:

Secondary operations
All items listed under *Primary operations*, plus the following:
a) Check the charging system (refer to Chapter 5A).
b) Check the pre/post-heating system (refer to Chapter 5A).
c) Check the fuel, exhaust and emission control systems (refer to the appropriate Parts of Chapter 4).

3.3 Removing the oil filler cap – 1.9 litre Z19DT engines

3.4 Engine oil drain plug location (arrowed)

Every 9000 miles or 6 months

3 Engine oil and filter renewal

> **HAYNES HINT**
> *Frequent oil and filter changes are the most important preventative maintenance procedures which can be undertaken by the DIY owner. As engine oil ages, it becomes diluted and contaminated, which leads to premature engine wear.*

1 Before starting this procedure, gather together all the necessary tools and materials. Also make sure that you have plenty of clean rags and newspapers handy, to mop-up any spills. Ideally, the engine oil should be warm, as it will drain more easily, and more built-up sludge will be removed with it. Take care not to touch the exhaust or any other hot parts of the engine when working under the vehicle. To avoid any possibility of scalding, and to protect yourself from possible skin irritants and other harmful contaminants in used engine oils, it is advisable to wear gloves when carrying out this work.

2 Access to the underside of the vehicle will be greatly improved if it can be raised on a lift, driven onto ramps, or jacked up and supported on axle stands (see *Jacking and vehicle support*). Whichever method is chosen, make sure that the vehicle remains level, or if it is at an angle, that the drain plug is at the lowest point. Remove the engine undertray for access.

3 Remove the oil filler cap from the camshaft cover (twist it through a quarter-turn anti-clockwise and withdraw it) **(see illustration)**.

4 Using a spanner, or preferably a suitable socket and bar, slacken the drain plug about half a turn **(see illustration)**. Position the draining container under the drain plug, then remove the plug completely **(see Haynes Hint)**.

5 Allow some time for the oil to drain, noting that it may be necessary to reposition the container as the oil flow slows to a trickle.

6 Position another container under the oil filter. On 1.9 litre engines, the oil filter is located at the rear of the engine and is accessible from under the car. On 2.0 and 2.2 litre engines the oil filter is located at the front of the engine and is accessible from above. Proceed as described under the following sub-Sections, according to engine.

> **HAYNES HINT**
> *As the drain plug releases from the threads, move it away quickly so that the stream of oil running out of the sump goes into the drain pan and not up your sleeve.*

1.9 litre engines

7 Unscrew the filter housing cap and withdraw it, together with the element, then separate the element, and remove the two O-ring seals from the cap **(see illustrations)**.

8 Use a clean rag to remove all oil, dirt and sludge from the oil filter housing and cap.

9 Locate the new O-ring seals in their grooves on the housing cap, then locate the new element in the cap and insert them both in the

3.7a Unscrew the filter cap and withdraw it together with the element . . .

3.7b . . . then separate the element from the cap . . .

3.7c . . . and remove the two O-ring seals – 1.9 litre engines

3.10 Remove the plastic cover from the top of the engine – 2.0 and 2.2 litre engines

3.11a Unscrew the oil filter housing cap . . .

3.11b . . . and lift out the old filter element – 2.0 and 2.2 litre engines

3.14 Fit new sealing rings to the cap recesses (arrowed) and refit the cap to the housing – 2.0 and 2.2 litre engines

filter housing. Screw on the cap and tighten to the specified torque.

2.0 and 2.2 litre engines

10 To gain access to the oil filter housing, undo the retaining screws and remove the plastic cover from the top of the engine (see illustration).

11 Unscrew the filter housing cap and remove

it from the top of the oil filter housing. Lift out the old filter element (see illustrations).

12 Use a clean rag to remove all oil, dirt and sludge from the oil filter housing and cap.

13 Fit the new filter element to the housing.

14 Renew the sealing rings then refit the filter housing cap and tighten it to the specified torque (see illustration). Refit the plastic cover to the engine and securely tighten its screws.

All engines

15 After all the oil has drained, wipe the drain plug and the sealing washer/O-ring with a clean rag. Examine the condition of the sealing washer/O-ring, and renew it if it shows signs of damage which may prevent an oil-tight seal. Clean the area around the drain plug opening, and refit the plug complete with the washer/O-ring. Tighten the plug to the specified torque, using a torque wrench.

16 Remove the old oil and all tools from under the vehicle then lower the vehicle to the ground.

17 Fill the engine through the filler hole in the camshaft cover, using the correct grade and type of oil (refer to *Weekly checks* for details of topping-up). Pour in half the specified quantity of oil first, then wait a few minutes for the oil to drain into the sump. Continue to add oil, a small quantity at a time, until the level is up to the lower mark on the dipstick. Adding approximately a further 1.0 litre will bring the level up to the upper mark on the dipstick.

18 Start the engine and run it until it reaches normal operating temperature. While the engine is warming-up, check for leaks around the oil filter and the sump drain plug.

19 Stop the engine, and wait at least five minutes for the oil to settle in the sump once more. With the new oil circulated and the filter now completely full, recheck the level on the dipstick, and add more oil as necessary.

20 Dispose of the used engine oil and filter safely, with reference to *General repair procedures* in the Reference Chapter of this manual. Do not discard the old filter with domestic household waste. The facility for waste oil disposal provided by many local council refuse tips and/or recycling centres generally has a filter receptacle alongside.

Every 18 000 miles or 12 months

4 Hose and fluid leak check

1 Visually inspect the engine joint faces, gaskets and seals for any signs of water or oil leaks. Pay particular attention to the areas around the camshaft cover, cylinder head, oil filter and sump joint faces. Similarly, check the transmission and (where applicable) the air conditioning compressor for oil leakage. Bear in mind that, over a period of time, some very slight seepage from these areas is to be expected; what you are really looking for is any indication of a serious leak. Should a leak be found, renew the offending gasket or oil seal by referring to the appropriate Chapters in this manual.

2 Also check the security and condition of all the engine-related pipes and hoses. Ensure that all cable ties or securing clips are in place, and in good condition. Clips which are broken or missing can lead to chafing of

the hoses pipes or wiring, which could cause more serious problems in the future.

3 Carefully check the radiator hoses and heater hoses along their entire length. Renew any hose which is cracked, swollen

HAYNES HINT

A leak in the cooling system will usually show up as white- or antifreeze-coloured deposits on the area adjoining the leak.

or deteriorated. Cracks will show up better if the hose is squeezed. Pay close attention to the hose clips that secure the hoses to the cooling system components. Hose clips can pinch and puncture hoses, resulting in cooling system leaks. If wire-type hose clips are used, it may be a good idea to update them with screw-type clips.

4 Inspect all the cooling system components (hoses, joint faces, etc) for leaks. Where any problems of this nature are found on system components, renew the component or gasket with reference to Chapter 3 (see Haynes Hint).

5 Where applicable, inspect the automatic transmission fluid cooler hoses for leaks or deterioration.

6 With the vehicle raised, inspect the fuel tank and filler neck for punctures, cracks and other damage. The connection between the filler neck and tank is especially critical. Sometimes, a rubber filler neck or connecting hose will leak due to loose retaining clamps or deteriorated rubber.

5.2a Disconnect the heater element wiring connector from the fuel filter cover . . .

5.2b . . . and the water level sensor wiring connector from the base of the filter housing – 1.9 litre engines

5.3 Depress the retaining clip and lift the filter from the crash box – 1.9 litre engines

7 Carefully check all rubber hoses and metal fuel lines leading away from the fuel tank. Check for loose connections, deteriorated hoses, crimped lines and other damage. Pay particular attention to the vent pipes and hoses, which often loop up around the filler neck and can become blocked or crimped. Follow the lines to the front of the vehicle, carefully inspecting them all the way. Renew damaged sections as necessary. Similarly, whilst the vehicle is raised, take the opportunity to inspect all underbody brake fluid pipes and hoses.

8 From within the engine compartment, check the security of all fuel hose attachments and pipe unions, and inspect the fuel hoses and vacuum hoses for kinks, chafing and deterioration.

5 Fuel filter water draining

Caution: Before starting any work on the fuel filter, wipe clean the filter assembly and the area around it; it is essential that no dirt or other foreign matter is allowed into the system. Obtain a suitable container into which the filter can be drained and place rags or similar material under the filter assembly to catch any spillages. Do not allow diesel fuel to contaminate components such as the alternator and starter motor, the coolant hoses and engine mountings, and any wiring.

1.9 litre engines

1 The fuel filter is located at the rear of the engine compartment, in the centre of the bulkhead.
2 Disconnect the heater element wiring connector from the fuel filter cover, and the water level sensor wiring connector from the base of the filter housing **(see illustrations)**.
3 Using a screwdriver inserted from the right-hand side, depress the retaining clip and lift the filter from the crash box **(see illustration)**.
4 In addition to taking the precautions noted above to catch any fuel spillages, connect a tube to the drain screw on the base of the fuel filter **(see illustration)**. Place the other end of the tube in a clean jar or can.

5.4 Fuel filter drain screw (arrowed) – 1.9 litre engines

5 Loosen the drain screw approximately one complete turn and allow the filter to drain until clean fuel, free of dirt or water, emerges from the tube (approximately 100 cc is usually sufficient).
6 Remove the drain tube, then tighten the drain screw securely.
7 Insert the filter in the crash box making sure that the retaining clip engages.
8 Reconnect the wiring.
9 On completion, dispose of the drained fuel safely. Check all disturbed components to ensure that there are no leaks (of air or fuel) when the engine is restarted.

2.0 and 2.2 litre engines

10 The fuel filter is located at the rear of the engine compartment, adjacent to the coolant expansion tank.
11 In addition to taking the precautions noted above to catch any fuel spillages, connect a tube to the drain screw on the base of the fuel filter housing. Place the other end of the tube in a clean jar or can.
12 Unscrew the drain screw and allow the filter to drain until clean fuel, free of dirt or water, emerges from the tube (approximately 100 cc is usually sufficient) **(see illustration)**. Note that it maybe necessary to slacken the filter housing cover bolt to allow the fuel to drain.
13 Securely close the drain screw and remove the tube, containers and rag, mopping-up any spilt fuel. Where necessary, securely tighten the housing cover screw.
14 On completion, dispose of the drained fuel safely. Check carefully all disturbed

5.12 Draining the water from the fuel filter – 2.0 and 2.2 litre engines

components to ensure that there are no leaks (of air or fuel) when the engine is restarted.
15 If necessary, bleed the fuel system as described in Chapter 4B.

6 Brake pad and disc check

1 Firmly apply the handbrake, then jack up the front and rear of the vehicle and support it securely on axle stands (see *Jacking and vehicle support*). Remove the roadwheels.
2 For a quick check, the pad thickness can be carried out via the inspection hole on the caliper **(see Haynes Hint)**. Using a steel rule, measure the thickness of the pad lining

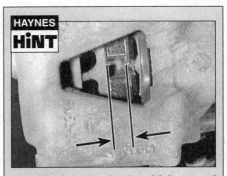

For a quick check, the thickness of friction material remaining on the inner brake pad can be measured through the aperture in the caliper body.

8.4 Check for wear in the hub bearings by grasping the wheel and trying to rock it

including the backing plate. This must not be less than that indicated in the Specifications.

3 The view through the caliper inspection hole gives a rough indication of the state of the brake pads. For a comprehensive check, the brake pads should be removed and cleaned. The operation of the caliper can then also be checked, and the condition of the brake disc itself can be fully examined on both sides. Chapter 9 contains a detailed description of how the brake disc should be checked for wear and/or damage.

4 If any pad's friction material is worn to the specified thickness or less, *all four pads must be renewed as a set*. Refer to Chapter 9 for details.

5 On completion, refit the roadwheels and lower the vehicle to the ground.

7 Brake fluid pipe and hose check

1 The brake hydraulic system includes a number of metal pipes, which run from the master cylinder to the hydraulic modulator of the anti-lock braking system (ABS) and then to the front and rear brake assemblies. Flexible hoses are fitted between the pipes and the front and rear brake assemblies, to allow for steering and suspension movement.

2 When checking the system, first look for signs of leakage at the pipe or hose unions, then examine the flexible hoses for signs of cracking, chafing or deterioration of the rubber. Bend the hoses between the fingers

9.2 Check the condition of the driveshaft gaiters (1) and the retaining clips (2)

(but do not actually bend them double, or the casing may be damaged) and check that this does not reveal previously-hidden cracks, cuts or splits. Check that the pipes and hoses are securely fastened in their clips.

3 Carefully working along the length of the metal pipes, look for dents, kinks, damage of any sort, or corrosion. Light corrosion can be polished off, but if the depth of pitting is significant, the pipe must be renewed.

8 Front suspension and steering check

1 Apply the handbrake, then raise the front of the vehicle and securely support it on axle stands (see *Jacking and vehicle support*).

2 Inspect the balljoint dust covers and the steering gear gaiters for splits, chafing or deterioration.

3 Any wear of these components will cause loss of lubricant, and may allow water to enter the components, resulting in rapid deterioration of the balljoints or steering gear.

4 Grasp each roadwheel at the 12 o'clock and 6 o'clock positions, and try to rock it **(see illustration)**. Very slight free play may be felt, but if the movement is appreciable, further investigation is necessary to determine the source. Continue rocking the wheel while an assistant depresses the footbrake. If the movement is now eliminated or significantly reduced, it is likely that the hub bearings are at fault. If the free play is still evident with the footbrake depressed, then there is wear in the suspension joints or mountings.

5 Now grasp each wheel at the 9 o'clock and 3 o'clock positions, and try to rock it as before. Any movement felt now may again be caused by wear in the hub bearings or the steering track rod end balljoints. If the track rod end balljoint is worn, the visual movement will be obvious.

6 Using a large screwdriver or flat bar, check for wear in the suspension mounting bushes by levering between the relevant suspension component and its attachment point. Some movement is to be expected, as the mountings are made of rubber, but excessive wear should be obvious. Also check the condition of any visible rubber bushes, looking for splits, cracks or contamination of the rubber.

7 Check for any signs of fluid leakage around the suspension struts, or from the rubber gaiters around the piston rods. Should any fluid be noticed, the suspension strut is defective internally, and should be renewed. **Note:** *Suspension struts should always be renewed in pairs on the same axle.*

8 With the vehicle standing on its wheels, have an assistant turn the steering wheel back-and-forth about an eighth of a turn each way. There should be very little, if any, lost movement between the steering wheel and roadwheels. If this is not the case, closely observe the joints and mountings

previously described. In addition, check the steering column universal joints for wear, and also check the rack-and-pinion steering gear itself.

9 The efficiency of each suspension strut may be checked by bouncing the vehicle at each front corner. Generally speaking, the body will return to its normal position and stop after being depressed. If it rises and returns on a rebound, the suspension strut is probably suspect. Also examine the suspension strut upper mountings for any signs of wear.

9 Driveshaft check

1 Firmly apply the handbrake, then jack up the front of the car and support it securely on axle stands (see *Jacking and vehicle support*).

2 Turn the steering onto full lock then slowly rotate the roadwheel. Inspect the condition of the outer constant velocity (CV) joint rubber gaiters while squeezing the gaiters to open out the folds **(see illustration)**. Check for signs of cracking, splits or deterioration of the rubber which may allow the grease to escape and lead to water and grit entry into the joint. Also check the security and condition of the retaining clips. Repeat these checks on the inner CV joints. If any damage or deterioration is found, the gaiters should be renewed as described in Chapter 8.

3 At the same time, check the general condition of the CV joints themselves by first holding the driveshaft and attempting to rotate the wheel. Repeat this check by holding the inner joint and attempting to rotate the driveshaft. Any appreciable movement indicates wear in the joints, wear in the driveshaft splines or loose driveshaft retaining nut.

10 Exhaust system check

1 With the engine cold (at least an hour after the vehicle has been driven), check the complete exhaust system from the engine to the end of the tailpipe. The exhaust system is most easily checked with the vehicle raised on a hoist, or suitably-supported on axle stands, so that the exhaust components are readily visible and accessible (see *Jacking and vehicle support*).

2 Check the exhaust pipes and connections for evidence of leaks, severe corrosion and damage. Make sure that all brackets and mountings are in good condition, and that all relevant nuts and bolts are tight. Leakage at any of the joints or in other parts of the system will usually show up as a black sooty stain in the vicinity of the leak.

3 Rattles and other noises can often be traced to the exhaust system, especially the brackets

and mountings **(see illustration)**. Try to move the pipes and silencers. If the components are able to come into contact with the body or suspension parts, secure the system with new mountings. Otherwise separate the joints (if possible) and twist the pipes as necessary to provide additional clearance.

11 Rear suspension check

1 Chock the front wheels, then jack up the rear of the vehicle and support securely on axle stands (see *Jacking and vehicle support*).
2 Inspect the rear suspension components for any signs of obvious wear or damage. Pay particular attention to the rubber mounting bushes, and renew if necessary (see Chapter 10).
3 Grasp each roadwheel at the 12 o'clock and 6 o'clock positions **(see illustration 8.4)**, and try to rock it. Any excess movement indicates wear in the wheel bearings. Wear may also be accompanied by a rumbling sound when the wheel is spun, or a noticeable roughness if the wheel is turned slowly. The wheel bearing can be renewed as described in Chapter 10.
4 Check for any signs of fluid leakage around the shock absorber bodies. Should any fluid be noticed, the shock absorber is defective internally, and should be renewed. **Note:** *Shock absorbers should always be renewed in pairs on the same axle.*
5 With the vehicle standing on its wheels, the efficiency of each shock absorber may be checked by bouncing the vehicle at each rear corner. Generally speaking, the body will return to its normal position and stop after being depressed. If it rises and returns on a rebound, the shock absorber is probably suspect.

12 Bodywork and underbody condition check

Note: *This work should be carried out by a Vauxhall/Opel dealer in order to validate the vehicle warranty. The work includes a thorough inspection of the vehicle paintwork and underbody for damage and corrosion.*

Damage/corrosion check

1 Once the car has been washed, and all tar spots and other surface blemishes have been cleaned off, carefully check all paintwork, looking closely for chips or scratches. Pay particular attention to vulnerable areas such as the front panels (bonnet and spoiler), and around the wheel arches. Any damage to the paintwork must be rectified as soon as possible, to comply with the terms of the manufacturer's anti-corrosion warranties; check with a Vauxhall/Opel dealer for details.
2 If a chip or light scratch is found which

10.3 Exhaust mountings

is recent and still free from rust, it can be touched-up using the appropriate touch-up stick which can be obtained from Vauxhall/Opel dealers. Any more serious damage, or rusted stone chips, can be repaired as described in Chapter 11, but if damage or corrosion is so severe that a panel must be renewed, seek professional advice as soon as possible.
3 Always check that the door and ventilation opening drain holes and pipes are completely clear, so that water can drain out.

Corrosion protection check

4 The wax-based underbody protective coating should be inspected annually, preferably just prior to Winter, when the underbody should be washed down as thoroughly as possible without disturbing the protective coating. Any damage to the coating should be repaired using a suitable wax-based sealer. If any of the body panels are disturbed for repair or renewal, do not forget to re-apply the coating. Wax should be injected into door cavities, sills and box sections, to maintain the level of protection provided by the vehicle manufacturer – seek the advice of a Vauxhall/Opel dealer.

13 Roadwheel bolt tightness check

1 Where applicable, remove the wheel trims from the wheels.
2 Using a torque wrench on each wheel bolt in turn, ensure that the bolts are tightened to the specified torque.
3 Where applicable, refit the wheel trims on completion, making sure they are fitted correctly.

14 Hinge and lock lubrication

1 Work around the vehicle and lubricate the hinges of the bonnet, doors, boot lid and tailgate with a light machine oil.
2 Lightly lubricate the bonnet release mechanism and exposed section of inner cable with a smear of grease.
3 Check the security and operation of all

hinges, latches and locks, adjusting them where required. Check the operation of the central locking system.
4 Check the condition and operation of the tailgate struts, renewing them both if either is leaking or no longer able to support the tailgate securely when raised.

15 Electrical systems check

1 Check the operation of all the electrical equipment, ie, lights, direction indicators, horn, etc. Refer to the appropriate sections of Chapter 12 for details if any of the circuits are found to be inoperative.
2 Note that the stop-light switch is described in Chapter 9.
3 Check all accessible wiring connectors, harnesses and retaining clips for security, and for signs of chafing or damage. Rectify any faults found.

16 Headlight beam alignment check

1 Accurate adjustment of the headlight beam is only possible using optical beam-setting equipment, and this work should therefore be carried out by a Vauxhall/Opel dealer or service station with the necessary facilities. Refer to Chapter 12 for further information.

17 Road test

Instruments/ electrical equipment

1 Check the operation of all instruments, warning lights and electrical equipment.
2 Make sure that all instruments read correctly, and switch on all electrical equipment in turn, to check that it functions properly.

Steering and suspension

3 Check for any abnormalities in the steering, suspension, handling or road 'feel'.
4 Drive the vehicle, and check that there are no unusual vibrations or noises.
5 Check that the steering feels positive, with no excessive 'sloppiness', or roughness, and check for any suspension noises when cornering and driving over bumps.

Drivetrain

6 Check the performance of the engine, clutch, transmission and driveshafts.
7 Listen for any unusual noises from the engine, clutch and transmission.
8 Make sure that the engine runs smoothly when idling, and that there is no hesitation when accelerating.

9 Check that, where applicable, the clutch action is smooth and progressive, that the drive is taken up smoothly, and that the pedal travel is not excessive. Also listen for any noises when the clutch pedal is depressed.

10 Check that all gears can be engaged smoothly without noise, and that the gear lever action is smooth and not abnormally vague or 'notchy'.

11 On automatic transmission models, make sure that all gearchanges occur smoothly, without snatching, and without an increase in engine speed between changes. Check that all of the gear positions can be selected with the vehicle at rest. If any problems are found, they should be referred to a Vauxhall/Opel dealer.

12 Listen for a metallic clicking sound from the front of the vehicle, as the vehicle is driven slowly in a circle with the steering on full-lock. Carry out this check in both directions. If a clicking noise is heard, this indicates wear in a driveshaft joint (see Chapter 8).

Braking system

13 Make sure that the vehicle does not pull to one side when braking, and that the wheels do not lock prematurely when braking hard.

14 Check that there is no vibration through the steering when braking.

15 Check that the handbrake operates correctly, without excessive movement of the lever, and that it holds the vehicle stationary on a slope.

16 Test the operation of the brake servo unit as follows. Depress the footbrake four or five times to exhaust the vacuum, then start the engine. As the engine starts, there should be a noticeable 'give' in the brake pedal as vacuum builds-up. Allow the engine to run for at least two minutes, and then switch it off. If the brake pedal is now depressed again, it should be possible to detect a hiss from the servo as the pedal is depressed. After about four or five applications, no further hissing should be heard, and the pedal should feel considerably harder.

18 Service interval indicator reset

1 With the ignition switched off, depress and hold the trip odometer reset button located on the instrument panel.

2 With the reset button depressed, switch on the ignition, wait until the service interval display changes, then keep the reset button depressed for at least a further 3 seconds.

3 After approximately 3 seconds the display will show the service symbol and the maximum mileage before the next required service. Release the reset button and switch off the ignition. When the button is released, the odometer reading will appear again.

4 This procedure resets the service interval indicator back to the ECOService-Flex flexible maintenance interval. If the standard maintenance schedule described in this Chapter is being used, then the interval until the next service, which will be shown on the display, is irrelevant. If it is wished to have the service interval indicator altered to show the standard maintenance intervals described in this Chapter, it will be necessary to have the system reprogrammed using dedicated Vauxhall/Opel diagnostic equipment or a compatible alternative.

Every 18 000 miles or 2 years

19 Pollen filter renewal

1 Open the bonnet, and pull up the rubber weatherseal from the flange at the rear of the engine compartment (see illustration).

2 Open the cover in the water deflector for access to the pollen filter (see illustration).

3 Release the clips from each end, then lift out the filter (see illustrations).

4 Fit the new filter using a reversal of the removal procedure; make sure that the filter is fitted the correct way up as indicated on the edge of the filter.

20 Fuel filter renewal

Caution: Before starting any work on the fuel filter, wipe clean the filter assembly and the area around it; it is essential that no dirt or other foreign matter is allowed into the system. Obtain a suitable container into which the filter can be drained and place rags or similar material under the filter assembly to catch any spillages. Do not allow diesel fuel to contaminate components such as the starter motor, the coolant hoses and engine mountings, and any wiring.

1.9 litre engines

Note: Vauxhall/Opel special tool EN-46784-010, or a suitable alternative will be required to unscrew the filter housing cover retaining ring.

1 The fuel filter is located at the rear of the engine compartment, in the centre of the bulkhead.

2 Disconnect the heater element wiring connector from the fuel filter cover, and the water level sensor wiring connector from the base of the filter housing (see illustrations 5.2a and 5.2b).

3 Detach the two fuel hose quick-release connectors and remove the hoses from the

19.1 Pull up the rubber weatherseal . . .

19.2 . . . then open the cover

19.3a Release the clips at each end . . .

19.3b . . . and lift out the pollen filter

20.3a Depress the quick-release connector retaining tangs . . .

20.3b . . . and remove the hoses from the fuel filter housing cover – 1.9 litre engines

20.7 Using a home-made tool to slacken the filter housing cover retaining ring – 1.9 litre engines

20.9a Unscrew and remove the cover retaining ring . . .

20.9b . . . then lift the cover together with the filter element . . .

20.9c . . . and recover the O-ring seal – 1.9 litre engines

fuel filter housing and cover. A Vauxhall/Opel special tool (KM-796-A) is available to disconnect the hose connectors, but provided care is taken, the connections can be released using two screwdrivers, a pair of long-nosed pliers, or similar, to depress the retaining tangs **(see illustrations)**. Suitably cover or plug the open hose connections to prevent dirt entry.
4 Using a screwdriver inserted from the right-hand side, depress the retaining clip and lift the filter housing from the crash box.
5 Loosen the drain screw on the base of the filter housing one complete turn and drain the fuel into a suitable container. Tighten the drain screw securely once the filter has drained.
6 Lay the filter on its side and clamp the two filter housing mounting lugs in a soft-jawed

vice. Take great care not to damage the lugs and only tighten the vice sufficiently to hold the housing while the cover retaining ring is slackened.
7 Slacken the filter housing cover retaining ring using the Vauxhall/Opel special tool or a suitable alternative **(see illustration)**.
8 Reposition the filter housing vertically in the vice and tighten the vice lightly.
9 Fully unscrew the cover retaining ring, then lift the cover together with the filter element from the housing. Recover the O-ring seal **(see illustrations)**.
10 Turn the filter element approximately 50° anti-clockwise to release it from the cover **(see illustration)**.
11 Empty the fuel from the filter housing, then

thoroughly clean the housing and cover with a lint-free cloth.
12 Align the arrow on the new filter element with the corresponding arrow on the cover then push the filter onto the cover until it locks in position **(see illustrations)**.
13 Locate a new O-ring seal on the filter housing, then fit the element and cover to the housing **(see illustrations)**.
14 Lubricate the threads of the retaining ring with a little diesel fuel then screw the ring onto the housing. Reposition the housing horizontally in the vice as before, and tighten the retaining ring to the specified torque using the special tool or an alternative.
15 Insert the filter assembly into the crash box, making sure that the retaining clip

20.10 Turn the filter element approximately 50° anti-clockwise to release it from the cover – 1.9 litre engines

20.12a Align the arrow on the new filter element with the corresponding arrow on the cover . . .

20.12b . . . then push the filter onto the cover until it locks in position – 1.9 litre engines

20.13a Locate a new O-ring seal on the filter housing . . .

20.13b . . . then fit the element and cover to the housing – 1.9 litre engines

engages. Reconnect the fuel hoses and the wiring connectors.

16 Bleed the fuel system as described in Chapter 4B and check all disturbed components to ensure that there are no leaks (of air or fuel) when the engine is restarted.

17 On completion, safely dispose of the drained fuel.

2.0 and 2.2 litre engines

Note: *After fitting a new fuel filter, it will be necessary to prime and bleed the fuel system using the Vauxhall/Opel bleeder unit (KM-948) or a suitable alternative. Refer to the information contained in the Section 'Fuel system – priming and bleeding' in Chapter 4B, before proceeding.*

18 The fuel filter is located at the rear of the engine compartment, adjacent to the coolant expansion tank.

19 Disconnect the heater element wiring connector from the fuel filter cover **(see illustration)**.

20 Tilt the coolant expansion tank upwards at the front and release it from its mounting bracket. Place the tank to one side.

21 Release the two fuel hoses from their retaining clips on the bulkhead.

22 Depress the retaining clip and lift the filter housing from the crash box.

20.19 Disconnect the heater element wiring connector (arrowed) from the fuel filter cover – 2.0 and 2.2 litre engines

23 Suitably identify the fitted position of the fuel hoses at their filter attachments to avoid confusion when refitting. Detach the two fuel hose quick-release connectors and remove the hoses from the filter housing cover. A Vauxhall/Opel special tool (KM-796-A) is available to disconnect the hose connectors, but provided care is taken, the connections can be released using two screwdrivers, a pair of long-nosed pliers, or similar, to depress the retaining tangs **(see illustration 20.3a)**. Suitably cover or plug the open hose connections to prevent dirt entry.

24 Unscrew the centre bolt and remove the cover from the filter housing **(see illustration)**. Collect the cover sealing ring.

25 Remove the filter element, then empty the fuel from the filter housing. Thoroughly clean the housing and cover with a lint-free cloth.

26 Fit a new sealing ring to the centre bolt and filter housing, then place the new element in the housing.

27 Fill the filter housing with fresh diesel fuel until the level is just below the rim of the housing.

28 Refit the cover to the housing then refit the centre bolt, tightening it to the specified torque. **Do not** overtighten the cover screw as the housing is easily damaged.

29 Insert the filter assembly into the crash box, making sure that the retaining clip engages. Reconnect the fuel hoses in their correct locations as noted during removal, and reconnect the heater element wiring connector.

30 Reattach the two fuel hoses to their retaining clips on the bulkhead, then refit the coolant expansion tank to its mounting bracket.

31 Bleed the fuel system as described in Chapter 4B and check all disturbed components to ensure that there are no leaks (of air or fuel) when the engine is restarted.

32 On completion, safely dispose of the drained fuel.

H46358

20.24 Fuel filter and housing components – 2.0 and 2.2 litre engines

1 Centre bolt
2 Centre bolt sealing ring
3 Filter housing cover
4 Filter housing cover sealing ring
5 Filter element
6 Filter housing

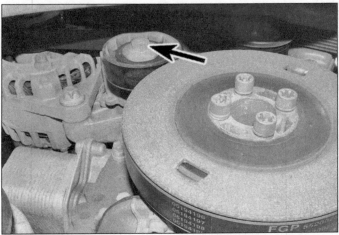

21.7a Turn the drivebelt tensioner clockwise using a spanner on the pulley centre bolt (arrowed) . . .

21.7b . . . then lock the tensioner by inserting a locking pin or drill bit (arrowed) through the special hole – 1.9 litre engines

Every 36 000 miles or 2 years

21 Auxiliary drivebelt check and renewal

Checking

1 Due to their function and material make-up, drivebelts are prone to failure after a long period of time and should therefore be inspected regularly.

2 Apply the handbrake, then jack up the front of the vehicle and support it on axle stands (see *Jacking and vehicle support*). Remove the right-hand front roadwheel and the engine undertray.

3 With the engine stopped, inspect the full length of the drivebelt for cracks and separation of the belt plies. It will be necessary to turn the engine (using a spanner or socket and bar on the crankshaft pulley bolt) so that the belt can be inspected thoroughly. Twist the belt between the pulleys so that both sides can be viewed. Also check for fraying, and glazing which gives the belt a shiny appearance. Check the pulleys for nicks, cracks, distortion and corrosion. If the belt shows signs of wear or damage, it should be renewed as a precaution against breakage in service.

Renewal

4 If not already done, apply the handbrake, then jack up the front of the vehicle and support it on axle stands (see *Jacking and vehicle support*). Remove the right-hand front roadwheel and the engine undertray.

5 For additional working clearance, remove the air cleaner housing as described in Chapter 4B.

6 If the drivebelt is to be re-used, mark it to indicate its normal running direction.

1.9 litre engines

7 Using a spanner on the pulley centre bolt, turn the tensioner clockwise against the spring tension. Hold the tensioner in this position by inserting a suitable locking pin or drill bit through the special hole provided **(see illustrations)**.

8 Slip the drivebelt from the pulleys.

9 Locate the new drivebelt on the pulleys in the correct routing **(see illustrations)**. If the drivebelt is being re-used, make sure it is fitted the correct way around.

10 Turn back the tensioner and remove the locking pin/drill bit, then release it, making sure that the drivebelt ribs locate correctly on each of the pulley grooves.

11 Refit the air cleaner housing (if removed), then refit the engine undertray and roadwheel, and lower the vehicle to the ground.

H46359

21.9a Auxiliary drivebelt configuration on models without air conditioning . . .

H46360

21.9b . . . and on models with air conditioning – 1.9 litre engines

21.12 Turn the drivebelt tensioner backplate anti-clockwise and slip the belt off the pulleys – 2.0 and 2.2 litre engines

2.0 and 2.2 litre engines

12 Using a suitable spanner or socket fitted to the special hexagonal section on the tensioner pulley backplate, lever the tensioner anti-clockwise away from the belt until there is sufficient slack to enable the belt to be slipped off the pulleys (see illustration). Carefully release the tensioner pulley until it is against its stop then remove the belt from the vehicle.
13 Locate the new drivebelt on the pulleys in the correct routing (see illustrations). If the drivebelt is being re-used, make sure it is fitted the correct way around.

H32957

21.13a Auxiliary drivebelt configuration on models without air conditioning . . .

14 Lever the tensioner roller back against spring tension, and seat the belt on the pulleys. Ensure the belt is centrally located on all pulleys then slowly release the tensioner pulley until the belt is correctly tensioned.
15 Refit the air cleaner housing (if removed), then refit the engine undertray and roadwheel, and lower the vehicle to the ground.

H32958

21.13b . . . and on models with air conditioning – 2.0 and 2.2 litre engines

22 Valve clearance check and adjustment – 1.9 litre Z19DT engines

Refer to the procedures contained in Chapter 2C.

Every 2 years, regardless of mileage

23 Remote control battery renewal

1 Using a screwdriver, prise the battery cover from the ignition key fob (see illustrations).
2 Note how the circular battery is fitted, then carefully remove it from the contacts.
3 Fit the new battery (type CR 20 32) and refit the cover making sure that it clips fully onto the base.
4 After changing the battery, lock and unlock the driver's door with the key in the lock to synchronise the remote control unit.

23.1a Prise off the battery cover . . .

24 Hydraulic fluid renewal

⚠ *Warning: Hydraulic fluid can harm your eyes and damage painted surfaces, so use extreme caution when handling and pouring it. Do not use fluid that has been standing open for some time, as it absorbs moisture from the air. Excess moisture can cause a dangerous loss of braking effectiveness.*
Note: *The brake and clutch hydraulic systems share a common reservoir.*

23.1b . . . and remove the circular battery

1 The procedure is similar to that for the bleeding of the hydraulic system as described in Chapters 9 (brake) and 6 (clutch).
2 Working as described in Chapter 9, open the first bleed screw in the sequence, and pump the brake pedal gently until nearly all the old fluid has been emptied from the master cylinder reservoir. Top-up to the MAX level with new fluid, and continue pumping until only the new fluid remains in the reservoir, and new fluid can be seen emerging from the bleed screw. Tighten the screw, and top the reservoir level up to the MAX level line.

 HAYNES HINT *Old hydraulic fluid is invariably much darker in colour than the new, making it easy to distinguish the two.*

3 Work through all the remaining bleed screws in the sequence until new fluid can be seen at all of them. Be careful to keep the master cylinder reservoir topped-up to above the MIN level at all times, or air may enter the system and greatly increase the length of the task.
4 Bleed the fluid from the clutch hydraulic system as described in Chapter 6.
5 When the operation is complete, check that all bleed screws are securely tightened, and that their dust caps are refitted. Wash off all

traces of spilt fluid, and recheck the master cylinder reservoir fluid level.

6 Check the operation of the brakes and clutch before taking the car on the road.

25 Coolant renewal

Note: *Vauxhall/Opel do not specify renewal intervals for the antifreeze mixture, as the mixture used to fill the system when the vehicle is new is designed to last the lifetime of the vehicle. However, it is strongly recommended that the coolant is renewed at the intervals specified in the 'Maintenance schedule', as a precaution against possible engine corrosion problems. This is particularly advisable if the coolant has been renewed using an antifreeze other than that specified by Vauxhall/Opel. With many antifreeze types, the corrosion inhibitors become progressively less effective with age. It is up to the individual owner whether or not to follow this advice.*

⚠️ *Warning: Wait until the engine is cold before starting this procedure. Do not allow antifreeze to come in contact with your skin, or with the painted surfaces of the vehicle. Rinse off spills immediately with plenty of water. Never leave antifreeze lying around in an open container, or in a puddle in the driveway or on the garage floor. Children and pets are attracted by its sweet smell, but antifreeze can be fatal if ingested.*

Cooling system draining

1 To drain the cooling system, first cover the expansion tank cap with a wad of rag, and slowly turn the cap anti-clockwise to relieve the pressure in the cooling system (a hissing sound will normally be heard). Wait until any pressure remaining in the system is released, then continue to turn the cap until it can be removed.

2 Remove the engine undertray, then position a suitable container beneath the right-hand side of the radiator.

3 The coolant drain plug is located at the bottom of the radiator right-hand end tank. Unscrew the drain plug and allow the coolant to drain..

4 When the flow of coolant stops, refit and tighten the drain plugs.

5 As no cylinder block drain plug is fitted, it is not possible to drain all of the coolant. Due consideration must be made for this when refilling the system, in order to maintain the correct concentration of antifreeze.

6 If the coolant has been drained for a reason other than renewal, then provided it is clean and less than two years old, it can be re-used.

Cooling system flushing

7 If coolant renewal has been neglected, or if the antifreeze mixture has become diluted,

25.18a Lift up the wire clip and disconnect the left-hand heater hose from the heater matrix pipe stub . . .

then in time, the cooling system may gradually lose efficiency, as the coolant passages become restricted due to rust, scale deposits, and other sediment. The cooling system efficiency can be restored by flushing the system clean.

8 The radiator should be flushed independently of the engine, to avoid unnecessary contamination.

Radiator flushing

9 Disconnect the top and bottom hoses and any other relevant hoses from the radiator, with reference to Chapter 3.

10 Insert a garden hose into the radiator top inlet. Direct a flow of clean water through the radiator, and continue flushing until clean water emerges from the radiator bottom outlet.

11 If after a reasonable period, the water still does not run clear, the radiator can be flushed with a good proprietary cleaning agent. It is important that the manufacturer's instructions are followed carefully. If the contamination is particularly bad, remove the radiator, insert the hose in the radiator bottom outlet, and reverse-flush the radiator.

Engine flushing

12 To flush the engine, the thermostat must be removed, because it will be shut, and would otherwise prevent the flow of water around the engine. The thermostat can be removed as described in Chapter 3. Take care not to introduce dirt or debris into the system if this approach is used.

13 With the bottom hose disconnected from the radiator, insert a garden hose into the thermostat opening. Direct a clean flow of water through the engine, and continue flushing until clean water emerges from the radiator bottom hose.

14 On completion of flushing, refit the thermostat with reference to Chapter 3, and reconnect the hoses.

Cooling system filling

15 Before attempting to fill the cooling system, make sure that all hoses and clips are in good condition, and that the clips are tight. Note that an antifreeze mixture must be used all year round, to prevent corrosion of the engine components.

25.18b On 1.9 litre engines, open the bleed screw (arrowed) in the coolant pipe above the exhaust manifold

16 Remove the expansion tank filler cap.

17 Fill the system by slowly pouring the coolant into the expansion tank until it is up to the filler neck.

18 Using a small screwdriver, lift up the wire clip securing the left-hand heater hose to the heater matrix pipe stub, and disconnect the hose from the stub. Additionally, on 1.9 litre engines, open the bleed screw in the coolant pipe above the exhaust manifold **(see illustrations)**.

19 As soon as coolant begins to run from the heater matrix, push the securing wire clip back into position on the heater hose end fitting, then push the hose back onto the matrix pipe stub. Ensure that the wire clip securely locks the hose in position. On 1.9 litre engines, close the coolant pipe bleed screw as soon as coolant emerges.

20 Top-up the expansion tank until the coolant level is up to the KALT/COLD mark on the side of the tank.

21 Refit and tighten the expansion tank filler cap.

22 Start the engine and run it at 2000 to 2500 rpm for 30 seconds, allow it to idle for 5 seconds, then run it at 2000 to 2500 rpm again for a further 30 seconds.

23 Continue running the engine at idling speed and allow it to warm-up. When the cooling fan cuts-in, run the engine again at 2000 to 2500 rpm for 30 seconds, allow it to idle for 5 seconds, then run it at 2000 to 2500 rpm again for a further 30 seconds.

24 Stop the engine, and allow it to cool, then recheck the coolant level with reference to *Weekly checks*. Top-up the level if necessary and refit the expansion tank filler cap. Refit the engine undertray.

Antifreeze mixture

25 Always use an ethylene-glycol based antifreeze which is suitable for use in mixed-metal cooling systems. **Note:** *Vauxhall/Opel recommend the use of silicate-free 'red' coolant (09 194 431/19 40 650). The quantity of antifreeze and levels of protection are given in the Specifications.*

26 Before adding antifreeze, the cooling system should be completely drained, preferably flushed, and all hoses checked for condition and security.

27.2 Slacken the retaining clip and disconnect the air intake duct from the airflow meter

27.3 Disconnect the wiring connector from the airflow meter

27.4a Undo the retaining screws . . .

27.4b . . . lift off the air cleaner cover . . .

27.4c . . . then lift out the filter element

27 After filling with antifreeze, a label should be attached to the expansion tank, stating the type and concentration of antifreeze used, and the date installed. Any subsequent topping-up should be made with the same type and concentration of antifreeze.

28 Do not use engine antifreeze in the windscreen/tailgate washer system, as it will cause damage to the vehicle paintwork. A screenwash additive should be added to the washer system in the quantities stated on the bottle.

26 Exhaust emission check

1 The exhaust emission check is carried out initially after 3 years, then every 2 years, however, on vehicles which are subject to intensive use (eg, taxis/hire cars/ambulances) it must be carried out annually. The check involves checking the engine management system operation by plugging an electronic tester into the system diagnostic socket to check the electronic control unit (ECU) memory for faults (see Chapter 4B).

2 In reality, if the vehicle is running correctly and the engine management warning light in the instrument panel is functioning normally, then this check need not be carried out.

Every 36 000 miles or 4 years

27 Air cleaner element renewal

1 The air cleaner is located in the front right-hand corner of the engine compartment.

2 Slacken the retaining clip and disconnect the air intake duct from the airflow meter **(see illustration)**.

3 Disconnect the wiring connector from the side of the airflow meter **(see illustration)**.

4 Undo the screws and lift off the air cleaner cover, then lift out the filter element **(see illustrations)**.

5 Wipe out the casing and the cover.

6 Fit the new filter, noting that the rubber locating flange should be uppermost, and secure the cover with the screws.

7 Reconnect the airflow meter wiring connector and the air intake duct.

28 Timing belt, tensioner and idler pulley renewal – 1.9 litre engines

Refer to Chapter 2C or 2D.

29 Automatic transmission fluid renewal – 2.2 litre engines

Refer to Chapter 7B.

Every 48 000 miles or 6 years

30 Automatic transmission fluid renewal – 1.9 litre engines

Refer to Chapter 7B.

Chapter 2 Part A:
1.8 litre petrol engine in-car repair procedures

Contents

Degrees of difficulty

| Easy, suitable for novice with little experience | | Fairly easy, suitable for beginner with some experience | | Fairly difficult, suitable for competent DIY mechanic | | Difficult, suitable for experienced DIY mechanic | | Very difficult, suitable for expert DIY or professional | |

Specifications

General

Engine type	Four-cylinder, in-line, water-cooled. Double overhead camshafts, belt-driven
Manufacturer's engine codes*	Z18XE and Z18XEL
Bore	80.5 mm
Stroke.	88.2 mm
Capacity.	1796 cc
Compression ratio	10.5:1
Firing order.	1-3-4-2 (No 1 cylinder at timing belt end)
Direction of crankshaft rotation	Clockwise (viewed from timing belt end of engine)

* For details of engine code location, see 'Vehicle identification' in the Reference Chapter.

Compression pressures

Standard	14 to 16 bar
Maximum difference between any two cylinders.	1 bar

Lubrication system

Minimum oil pressure at 80°C	1.4 bar at idle speed
Oil pump type	Rotor-type, driven directly from crankshaft
Rotor-to-housing clearance (endfloat)	0.03 to 0.10 mm

Torque wrench settings

	Nm	lbf ft
Camshaft bearing cap bolts	8	6
Camshaft cover bolts	8	6
Camshaft sprocket bolt:*		
Stage 1	50	37
Stage 2	Angle-tighten a further 60°	
Stage 3	Angle-tighten a further 15°	
Connecting rod big-end bearing cap bolt:*		
Stage 1	25	18
Stage 2	Angle-tighten a further 30°	
Crankshaft pulley bolt:*		
Stage 1	95	70
Stage 2	Angle-tighten a further 30°	
Stage 3	Angle-tighten a further 15°	
Crankshaft sensor mounting bracket bolt	8	6
Cylinder head bolts:*		
Stage 1	25	18
Stage 2	Angle-tighten a further 90°	
Stage 3	Angle-tighten a further 90°	
Stage 4	Angle-tighten a further 90°	
Stage 5	Angle-tighten a further 45°	
Engine mountings:		
Front mounting/torque link bracket to transmission	80	59
Front mounting/torque link to subframe	80	59
Left-hand:		
Mounting-to-body bolts	20	15
Mounting bracket to transmission bracket	55	41
Transmission bracket to transmission	80	59
Rear mounting/torque link bracket to transmission	80	59
Rear mounting/torque link to subframe	60	44
Rear mounting/torque link to transmission bracket	80	59
Right-hand:		
Engine bracket-to-engine bolts:*		
Stage 1	65	48
Stage 2	Angle-tighten a further 45°	
Mounting-to-body bolts/nut	55	41
Mounting-to-engine bracket bolts	55	41
Engine-to-transmission bolts	60	44
Flywheel bolts:*		
Stage 1	35	26
Stage 2	Angle-tighten a further 30°	
Stage 3	Angle-tighten a further 15°	
Main bearing cap bolts:*		
Stage 1	50	37
Stage 2	Angle-tighten a further 45°	
Stage 3	Angle-tighten a further 15°	
Oil pump:		
Retaining bolts	6	4
Pump cover screws	6	4
Oil pressure relief valve bolt	50	37
Oil pump pick-up/strainer and baffle bolts	8	6
Roadwheel bolts	110	81
Sump bolts:		
Sump-to-cylinder block/oil pump bolts	10	7
Sump flange-to-transmission bolts	40	30
Drain plug	14	10
Timing belt cover bolts:		
Upper and lower covers	4	3
Rear cover	6	4
Timing belt idler pulley bolt	25	18
Timing belt tensioner bolt	20	15

* Use new fasteners

1 General information

How to use this Chapter

This Part of Chapter 2 describes the repair procedures which can reasonably be carried out on the engine while it remains in the vehicle. If the engine has been removed from the vehicle and is being dismantled as described in Chapter 2F, any preliminary dismantling procedures can be ignored.

Note that, while it may be possible physically to overhaul items such as the piston/connecting rod assemblies while the engine is in the vehicle, such tasks are not usually carried out as separate operations, and usually require the execution of several additional procedures (not to mention the cleaning of components and of oilways); for this reason, all such tasks are classed as major overhaul procedures, and are described in Chapter 2F.

Chapter 2F describes the removal of the engine/transmission unit from the vehicle, and the full overhaul procedures which can then be carried out.

Engine description

The engine is a double overhead camshaft, four-cylinder, in-line unit, mounted transversely at the front of the car, with the transmission attached to its left-hand end.

The crankshaft is supported within the cylinder block on five shell-type main bearings. Thrustwashers are fitted to number 3 main bearing, to control crankshaft endfloat.

The connecting rods are attached to the crankshaft by horizontally-split shell-type big-end bearings, and to the pistons by interference-fit gudgeon pins. The aluminium alloy pistons are of the slipper type, and are fitted with three piston rings, comprising two compression rings and a scraper-type oil control ring.

The camshafts run directly in the cylinder head, and are driven by the crankshaft via a toothed composite rubber timing belt (which also drives the coolant pump). The camshafts operate each valve via a hydraulic self-adjusting camshaft follower. One camshaft operates the inlet valves, and the other operates the exhaust valves.

Lubrication is by pressure-feed from a rotor-type oil pump, which is mounted on the right-hand end of the crankshaft. The pump draws oil through a strainer located in the sump, and then forces it through an externally mounted full-flow oil filter. The oil flows into galleries in the main bearing cap bridge arrangement and cylinder block/ crankcase, from where it is distributed to the crankshaft (main bearings) and camshafts. The big-end bearings are supplied with oil via internal drillings in the crankshaft, while the camshaft bearings also receive a pressurised supply. The camshaft lobes and valves are lubricated by splash, as are all other engine components.

A semi-closed crankcase ventilation system is employed; crankcase fumes are drawn from cylinder head cover, and passed via a hose to the inlet manifold.

Operations with engine in car

The following operations can be carried out without having to remove the engine from the car.
a) Removal and refitting of the cylinder head.
b) Removal and refitting of the timing belt, tensioner and sprockets.
c) Renewal of the camshaft oil seals.
d) Removal and refitting of the camshafts and followers.
e) Removal and refitting of the sump.
f) Removal and refitting of the connecting rods and pistons.*
g) Removal and refitting of the oil pump.
h) Renewal of the crankshaft oil seals.
i) Renewal of the engine mountings.
j) Removal and refitting of the flywheel.
* Although the operation marked with an asterisk can be carried out with the engine in the car (after removal of the sump), it is preferable for the engine to be removed, in the interests of cleanliness and improved access. For this reason, the procedure is described in Chapter 2F.

2 Compression test – general information

1 When engine performance is down, or if misfiring occurs which cannot be attributed to the ignition or fuel systems, a compression test can provide diagnostic clues as to the engine's condition. If the test is performed regularly, it can give warning of trouble before any other symptoms become apparent.

2 Due to the electronic throttle control system used on these engines, a compression test can only be carried out with the engine management electronic control unit connected to Vauxhall/Opel diagnostic test equipment, or a compatible alternative unit. Without the test equipment, the throttle valve cannot be opened (as there is no accelerator cable) and the test will be inconclusive. Note that even with the accelerator pedal fully depressed, the engine management ECU will only control the throttle valve position when the engine is actually running. The test equipment independently actuates the throttle valve (irrespective of ECU commands) and opens the throttle valve fully.

3 As the equipment needed for the compression test is unlikely to be available to the home mechanic, it is recommended that the test is performed by a Vauxhall/Opel dealer, or suitably-equipped garage.

3 Top dead centre (TDC) for No 1 piston – locating

1 Top dead centre (TDC) is the highest point in the cylinder that a piston reaches as the crankshaft turns. Each piston reaches TDC at the end of the compression stroke, and again at the end of the exhaust stroke. For the purpose of timing the engine, TDC refers to the position of No 1 piston at the end of its compression stroke. No 1 piston and cylinder are at the timing belt end of the engine.

2 Disconnect the battery negative terminal (refer to *Disconnecting the battery* in the Reference Chapter).

3 Remove the upper timing belt cover as described in Section 6.

4 Apply the handbrake, then jack up the front of the vehicle and support it on axle stands (see *Jacking and vehicle support*). Remove the right-hand front roadwheel, then remove the wheel arch liner inner cover for access to the crankshaft pulley.

5 Using a suitable spanner or socket on the crankshaft pulley bolt, rotate the crankshaft to bring No 1 piston to TDC. Note that turning the engine will be made much easier if the spark plugs are removed first (see Chapter 1A).

6 The timing marks must be aligned as follows (see illustrations).
a) The timing marks on the camshaft sprockets must be directly opposite each other, and aligned with the top edge of the cylinder head.
b) The timing mark on the crankshaft pulley

3.6a Camshaft sprocket timing marks (A) aligned with top edge of cylinder head (B)

3.6b Crankshaft sprocket timing mark (A) aligned with mark (B) on timing belt inner cover (crankshaft pulley removed)

4.3 Disconnect the breather hoses from the camshaft cover

4.5 Remove the bolt supporting the coolant pipe across the camshaft cover

4.9 Carefully fit the camshaft cover seal

must be aligned with the pointer (raised line) on the timing belt lower cover. Note that if the crankshaft pulley and lower timing belt cover have been removed, the timing mark on the crankshaft sprocket can be used instead of the mark on the pulley. The mark on the crankshaft sprocket must align with the corresponding mark on the rear timing belt cover (there may be two marks on the sprocket, in which case ignore the mark with a cross stamped across it).

4 Camshaft cover – removal and refitting

Removal

1 Remove the oil filler cap, then undo the retaining screws, and remove the plastic cover from the top of the engine. Refit the oil filler cap.

2 Remove the ignition module from the spark plugs with reference to Chapter 5B.

3 Slacken the retaining clips and disconnect the breather hoses from the left-hand rear of the cover **(see illustration)**.

4 Disconnect the wiring plug from the coolant temperature sensor and camshaft sensor.

5 Disconnect the coolant pipe from the thermostat housing. Unbolt the retaining bracket from the camshaft cover and inlet manifold, release the retaining clips and move the pipe to one side **(see illustration)**. Be prepared for coolant spillage.

6 Unclip the oxygen sensor wiring from the camshaft cover.

7 Evenly and progressively slacken and remove the camshaft cover retaining bolts.

8 Lift the camshaft cover away from the cylinder head and recover the rubber seal. Examine the seal for signs of wear or damage and renew if necessary.

Refitting

9 Ensure the cover and cylinder head surfaces are clean and dry then fit the rubber seal securely to the cover groove **(see illustration)**.

10 Apply a smear of suitable sealant to areas of the cylinder head surface around the right-hand end inlet and exhaust camshaft bearing caps.

11 Carefully manoeuvre the camshaft cover into position, taking great care to ensure the seal remains correctly seated. Refit the cover retaining bolts and tighten the retaining bolts to the specified torque, working in a spiral pattern from the centre outwards.

12 Reconnect the coolant pipe to the thermostat housing, making sure it is secured by the retaining bracket on the camshaft cover and inlet manifold.

13 Refit the wiring plugs to the coolant temperature sensor and camshaft sensor. Clip the oxygen sensor wiring back into position in the camshaft cover.

14 Reconnect the breather hoses, securing them in position with the retaining clips.

15 Refit the ignition module with reference to Chapter 5B.

16 Refit the engine cover, then top-up the cooling system as described in Chapter 1A.

5 Crankshaft pulley – removal and refitting

Note: *A new pulley retaining bolt will be required on refitting.*

Removal

1 Firmly apply the handbrake, then jack up the front of the car and support it securely on axle stands (see *Jacking and vehicle support*). Remove the right-hand roadwheel.

2 Remove the auxiliary drivebelt as described

5.5 Align the pulley cut-out with the raised notch

in Chapter 1A. Prior to removal, mark the direction of rotation on the belt to ensure the belt is refitted the same way around.

3 Slacken the crankshaft pulley retaining bolt. To prevent crankshaft rotation, have an assistant select top gear and apply the brakes firmly.

4 Unscrew the retaining bolt and washer and remove the crankshaft pulley from the end of the crankshaft.

Refitting

5 Refit the crankshaft pulley, aligning the pulley cut-out with the raised notch on the timing belt sprocket, then fit the washer and new retaining bolt **(see illustration)**.

6 Lock the crankshaft by the method used on removal, and tighten the pulley retaining bolt to the specified Stage 1 torque setting, then angle-tighten the bolt through the specified Stage 2 angle, using a socket and extension bar, and finally through the specified Stage 3 angle. It is recommended that an angle-measuring gauge is used during the final stages of the tightening, to ensure accuracy. If a gauge is not available, use white paint to make alignment marks between the bolt head and pulley prior to tightening; the marks can then be used to check that the bolt has been rotated through the correct angle.

7 Refit the auxiliary drivebelt as described in Chapter 1A using the mark made prior to removal to ensure the belt is fitted the correct way around.

8 Refit the roadwheel then lower the car to the ground and tighten the wheel bolts to the specified torque.

6 Timing belt covers – removal and refitting

Upper cover

1 Remove the oil filler cap, then undo the retaining screws, and remove the plastic cover from the top of the engine. Refit the oil filler cap.

2 For improved access, remove the air cleaner housing as described in Chapter 4A.

3 Undo the three retaining screws then unclip the upper cover from the rear cover and

6.3 Undo the three screws and remove the timing belt upper cover

6.7 Remove the auxiliary drivebelt tensioner

6.8 Timing belt lower cover retaining bolt

remove it from the engine compartment (see illustration).

4 Refitting is the reverse of removal, tighten the retaining bolts to the specified torque.

Lower cover

5 Remove the upper cover as described in paragraphs 1 to 3.

6 Remove the crankshaft pulley as described in Section 5.

7 Undo the retaining bolt and remove the auxiliary drivebelt tensioner (see illustration).

8 Undo the retaining bolt then unclip the lower cover from the rear cover and manoeuvre it out of position (see illustration).

9 Refitting is the reverse of removal, clip the cover into position and tighten the cover bolts to the specified torque.

Rear cover

10 Remove the timing belt as described in Section 7.

11 Remove the camshaft sprockets, crankshaft sprocket, timing belt tensioner, front idler pulley and the rear idler pulley as described in Section 8.

12 Slacken and remove the three retaining bolts, and withdraw the engine mounting bracket bolted to the cylinder block (see illustration).

13 Undo the four retaining bolts and remove the rear cover upwards and away from the engine (see illustration).

14 Refitting is the reverse of removal. Refit and tighten the cover bolts to the specified torque.

7 Timing belt –
removal and refitting

Note: *The timing belt must be removed and refitted with the engine cold.*

Removal

1 Position No 1 cylinder at TDC on its compression stroke as described in Section 3.

2 Remove the timing belt upper and lower covers as described in Section 6.

3 Check the camshaft sprocket timing marks are correctly aligned with the cylinder head surface and the crankshaft sprocket timing

mark is aligned with the mark on the rear timing belt cover (see Section 3). Undo the two bolts securing the camshaft sensor to the cylinder head and position it clear of the engine (see illustration).

4 Remove the right-hand engine mounting as described in Section 16.

5 Slacken the timing belt tensioner bolt. Using an Allen key, rotate the tensioner arm clockwise to its stop to relieve the tension in the timing belt, hold it in position and securely tighten the retaining bolt (see illustration).

6 Slide the timing belt from its sprockets and remove it from the engine (see illustration). If the belt is to be re-used, use white paint or similar to mark the direction of rotation on the belt. **Do not** rotate the crankshaft or camshafts until the timing belt has been refitted.

7 Check the timing belt carefully for any signs of uneven wear, splitting or oil contamination,

6.12 Engine mounting bracket-to-cylinder block retaining bolts

7.3 Unbolt the camshaft sensor and position it clear of the timing belt

and renew it if there is the slightest doubt about its condition. If the engine is undergoing an overhaul and is approaching the specified interval for belt renewal (see Chapter 1A) renew the belt as a matter of course, regardless of its apparent condition. If signs of oil contamination are found, trace the source

6.13 Lift the rear cover away from the engine

7.5 Slacken the timing belt tensioner bolt (1) and rotate the tensioner clockwise using an Allen key in the arm cut-out (2)

7.6 Removing the timing belt

of the oil leak and rectify it, then wash down the engine timing belt area and all related components to remove all traces of oil.

Refitting

8 On reassembly, thoroughly clean the timing belt sprockets and tensioner/idler pulleys.

9 Check that the camshaft and crankshaft sprocket timing marks are still correctly aligned as described in Section 3.

10 Fit the timing belt over the crankshaft and camshaft sprockets and around the idler pulleys, ensuring that the belt front run is taut (ie, all slack is on the tensioner side of the belt), then fit the belt over the coolant pump sprocket and tensioner pulley. Do not twist the belt sharply while refitting it. Ensure that the belt teeth are correctly seated centrally in the sprockets, and that the timing marks remain in alignment. If a used belt is being refitted, ensure that the arrow mark made on removal points in the normal direction of rotation, as before.

11 Slacken the timing belt tensioner bolt to release the tensioner spring. Rotate the tensioner arm anti-clockwise until the tensioner pointer is positioned just before the left stop, without exerting any excess strain on the belt. Hold the tensioner in position and securely tighten its retaining bolt.

12 Check the sprocket timing marks are still correctly aligned. If adjustment is necessary, release the tensioner again then disengage the belt from the sprockets and make any necessary adjustments.

13 Using a socket on the crankshaft pulley bolt, rotate the crankshaft smoothly through

8.3 Counterholding the inlet camshaft using a spanner on the flats in front of No 1 cam lobe

USED NEW BELT

J44606

7.15 Align the pointer (1) with the relevant mark on the tensioner backplate (2)

two complete turns (720°) in the normal direction of rotation to settle the timing belt in position.

14 Check that both the camshaft and crankshaft sprocket timing marks are correctly realigned then slacken the tensioner bolt again.

15 If a new timing belt is being fitted, adjust the tensioner so that the pointer is aligned with the cut-out on the backplate **(see illustration)**. Hold the tensioner in the correct position and tighten its retaining bolt to the specified torque. Rotate the crankshaft smoothly through another two complete turns in the normal direction of rotation, to bring the sprocket timing marks back into alignment. Check that the tensioner pointer is still aligned with the backplate cut-out.

16 If the original belt is being refitted, adjust the tensioner so that the pointer is positioned 4 mm to the left of the cut-out on

8.8 Ensure the camshaft sprocket cut-out (arrowed) is correctly engaged with the locating pin

the backplate **(see illustration 7.15)**. Hold the tensioner in the correct position and tighten its retaining bolt to the specified torque. Rotate the crankshaft smoothly through another two complete turns in the normal direction of rotation, to bring the sprocket timing marks back into alignment. Check that the tensioner pointer is still correctly positioned in relation to the backplate cut-out.

17 If the tensioner pointer is not correctly positioned in relation to the backplate, repeat the procedure in paragraph 15 (new belt) or 16 (original belt) (as applicable).

18 Once the tensioner pointer and backplate remain correctly aligned, refit the camshaft sensor, then refit the timing belt covers as described in Section 6.

19 Refit the right-hand engine mounting as described in Section 16, then refit the crankshaft pulley as described in Section 5.

<table>
<tr><td>**8**</td><td>**Timing belt sprockets, tensioner and idler pulleys –** removal and refitting</td><td></td></tr>
</table>

Camshaft sprockets

Note: *New sprocket retaining bolt(s) will be required on refitting.*

Removal

1 Remove the camshaft cover as described in Section 4.

2 Remove the timing belt as described in Section 7.

3 The camshaft must be prevented from turning as the sprocket bolt is unscrewed, and this can be achieved in one of two ways as follows:

  a) *Make up a sprocket-holding tool using two lengths of steel strip (one long, the other short), and three nuts and bolts; one nut and bolt forms the pivot of a forked tool, with the remaining two nuts and bolts at the tips of the 'forks' to engage with the sprocket holes.*

  b) *Hold the camshaft with an open-ended spanner on the flats provided **(see illustration)**.*

4 Unscrew the retaining bolt and washer and remove the sprocket from the end of the camshaft. If the sprocket locating pin is a loose fit in the camshaft end, remove it and store it with the sprocket for safe-keeping.

5 If necessary, remove the remaining sprocket using the same method. The inlet and exhaust sprockets are different; the exhaust camshaft sprocket can be easily identified by the lugs which activate the camshaft position sensor.

Refitting

6 Prior to refitting check the oil seal(s) for signs of damage or leakage. If necessary, renew as described in Section 9.

7 Ensure the locating pin is in position in the camshaft end.

8 Refit the sprocket to the camshaft end, aligning its cut-out with the locating pin, and

8.13 Refit the crankshaft sprocket with the locating flange and pulley locating lug outermost

8.17 Engage the tensioner backplate lug with the locating hole in the oil pump housing

8.20 Idler pulley retaining bolt

fit the washer and new retaining bolt **(see illustration)**. If both sprockets have been removed, ensure each sprocket is fitted to the correct shaft; the exhaust camshaft sprocket can be identified by the lugs on the sprocket outer face which trigger the camshaft position sensor.

9 Retain the sprocket by the method used on removal, and tighten the pulley retaining bolt to the specified Stage 1 torque setting then angle-tighten the bolt through the specified Stage 2 angle, using a socket and extension bar, and finally through the specified Stage 3 angle. It is recommended that an angle-measuring gauge is used during the final stages of the tightening, to ensure accuracy. If a gauge is not available, use white paint to make alignment marks between the bolt head and pulley prior to tightening; the marks can then be used to check that the bolt has been rotated through the correct angle.

10 Refit the timing belt as described in Section 7, then refit the camshaft cover as described in Section 4.

Crankshaft sprocket

Removal

11 Remove the timing belt as described in Section 7.
12 Slide the sprocket off from the end of the crankshaft, noting which way around it is fitted.

Refitting

13 Align the sprocket locating key with the crankshaft groove then slide the sprocket into position, making sure its timing mark is facing outwards **(see illustration)**.
14 Refit the timing belt as described in Section 7.

Tensioner assembly

Removal

15 Remove the timing belt as described in Section 7.
16 Slacken and remove the retaining bolt and remove the tensioner assembly from the engine.

Refitting

17 Fit the tensioner to the engine, making

sure that the lug on the backplate is correctly located in the oil pump housing hole **(see illustration)**. Ensure the tensioner is correctly seated then refit the retaining bolt. Using an Allen key, rotate the tensioner arm clockwise to its stop then securely tighten the retaining bolt.
18 Refit the timing belt as described in Section 7.

Idler pulleys

Removal

19 Remove the timing belt as described in Section 7.
20 Slacken and remove the retaining bolt(s) and remove the idler pulley(s) from the engine **(see illustration)**.

Refitting

21 Refit the idler pulley(s) and tighten the retaining bolt(s) to the specified torque.
22 Refit the timing belt as described in Section 7.

9 Camshaft oil seals – renewal

1 Remove the relevant camshaft sprocket as described in Section 8.
2 Carefully punch or drill two small holes opposite each other in the oil seal. Screw a self-tapping screw into each, and pull on the screws with pliers to extract the seal **(see illustration)**.

9.2 Camshaft oil seal removal method

3 Clean the seal housing, and polish off any burrs or raised edges which may have caused the seal to fail in the first place.
4 Lubricate the lips of the new seal with clean engine oil, and press it into position using a suitable tubular drift (such as a socket) which bears only on the hard outer edge of the seal **(see illustration)**. Take care not to damage the seal lips during fitting; note that the seal lips should face inwards.
5 Refit the camshaft sprocket as described in Section 8.

10 Camshaft and followers – removal, inspection and refitting

Note: *New timing belt end oil seals, and a tube of suitable sealant will be required when refitting.*

Removal

1 Remove the timing belt as described in Section 7.
2 Remove the camshaft sprockets as described in Section 8.
3 Unbolt the timing belt rear cover from the cylinder head and block.
4 Starting on the inlet camshaft, working in a spiral pattern from the outside inwards, slacken the camshaft bearing cap retaining bolts by half a turn at a time, to relieve the pressure of the valve springs on the bearing caps gradually and evenly **(the reverse of illustration 10.16)**. Once the valve spring

9.4 Using the old camshaft sprocket bolt and a socket to fit the new camshaft oil seal

10.4a Camshaft bearing cap numbering sequence (No 1 at timing belt end)

10.4b Camshaft bearing cap numbers (exhaust camshaft shown)

pressure has been relieved, the bolts can be fully unscrewed and removed along with the caps; the bearing caps and the cylinder head locations are numbered (inlet camshaft 1 to 5, exhaust camshaft 6 to 10) to ensure the caps are correctly positioned on refitting **(see illustrations)**. Take care not to loose the locating dowels (where fitted).

Caution: If the bearing cap bolts are carelessly slackened, the bearing caps might break. If any bearing cap breaks then the complete cylinder head assembly must be renewed; the bearing caps are matched to the head and are not available separately.

5 Lift the camshaft out of the cylinder head and slide off the oil seal.

6 Repeat the operations described in paragraphs 4 and 5 and remove the exhaust camshaft.

7 Obtain sixteen small, clean plastic containers, and label them for identification. Alternatively, divide a larger container into compartments. Using a rubber sucker tool, lift the followers out from the top of the cylinder head and store each one in its respective fitted position **(see illustration)**. **Note:** *Store all the followers the correct way up, with the oil groove at the bottom, to prevent the oil draining from the hydraulic valve adjustment mechanisms.*

Inspection

8 Examine the camshaft bearing surfaces and cam lobes for signs of wear ridges and scoring. Renew the camshaft if any of these conditions are apparent. Examine the condition of the bearing surfaces both on the camshaft journals and in the cylinder head. If the head bearing surfaces are worn excessively, the cylinder head will need to be renewed.

9 Examine the follower bearing surfaces which contact the camshaft lobes for wear ridges and scoring. Check the followers and their bores in the cylinder head for signs of wear or damage. If any follower is thought to be faulty or is visibly worn it should be renewed.

Refitting

10 Commence refitting by turning the crankshaft anti-clockwise by 60°. This will position Nos 1 and 4 pistons a third of the way down the bore, and prevent any chance of the valves touching the piston crowns as the camshafts are being fitted. This could happen if any of the cam followers have excessive oil in them before the pressure of the valve springs forces it out.

11 Where removed, lubricate the followers with clean engine oil and carefully insert each

one into its original location in the cylinder head.

12 Lubricate the camshaft followers with molybdenum disulphide paste (or clean engine oil) then lay the camshafts in position.

13 Ensure the mating surfaces of the bearing caps and cylinder head are clean and dry and lubricate the camshaft journals and lobes with clean engine oil.

14 Apply a smear of sealant to the mating surfaces of both the inlet (No 1) and exhaust (No 6) camshaft right-hand bearing caps **(see illustration)**.

15 Ensure the locating dowels (where fitted) are in position then refit the camshaft bearing caps and the retaining bolts in their original locations on the cylinder head. The caps are numbered (inlet camshaft 1 to 5, exhaust camshaft 6 to 10) from right to left, and the corresponding numbers are marked on the cylinder head upper surface. All bearing cap numbers should be the right way up when viewed from the front of the engine.

16 Working on the inlet camshaft, tighten the bearing cap bolts by hand only then, working in a spiral pattern from the centre outwards, tighten the bolts by half a turn at a time to gradually impose the pressure of the valve springs on the bearing caps **(see illustration)**. Repeat this sequence until all bearing caps are in contact with the cylinder head then go around and tighten the camshaft bearing cap bolts to the specified torque.

Caution: If the bearing cap bolts are carelessly tightened, the bearing caps might break. If any bearing cap breaks then the complete cylinder head assembly must be renewed; the bearing caps are matched to the head and are not available separately.

17 Tighten the exhaust camshaft bearing cap bolts as described in paragraph 16.

18 Fit new camshaft oil seals as described in Section 9.

19 Refit and tighten the timing belt rear cover bolts.

10.7 Remove the followers from the cylinder head, and store with the oil groove (arrowed) at the bottom

10.14 Apply a smear of sealant to the right-hand bearing caps

10.16 Camshaft bearing cap tightening sequence (exhaust camshaft shown – inlet identical)

11.20 Cylinder head bolt loosening sequence

20 Refit the camshaft sprockets as described in Section 8.

21 Align all the sprocket timing marks to bring the camshafts and crankshaft back to TDC then refit the timing belt as described in Section 7.

11 Cylinder head – removal and refitting

Note: *The engine must be cold when removing the cylinder head. A new cylinder head gasket and new cylinder head bolts must be used on refitting.*

Removal

1 Depressurise the fuel system as described in Chapter 4A.

2 Disconnect the battery negative terminal (refer to *Disconnecting the battery* in the Reference Chapter).

3 Apply the handbrake, then jack up the front of the vehicle and support it on axle stands (see *Jacking and vehicle support*). Remove the right-hand front roadwheel and the wheel arch liner inner cover for access to the right-hand side of the engine.

4 Drain the cooling system as described in Chapter 1A.

5 Remove the spark plugs as described in Chapter 1A.

6 Remove the camshaft cover as described in Section 4.

7 Remove the timing belt as described in Section 7.

8 Remove the camshaft sprockets, timing belt tensioner, and the timing belt idler rollers, as described in Section 8.

9 Remove the rear timing belt cover with reference to Section 6.

10 Refer to Chapter 4A and unbolt the exhaust front pipe from the exhaust manifold, taking care to support the flexible section. **Note:** *Angular movement in excess of 10° can cause permanent damage to the flexible section.*

Release the mounting rubbers and support the front of the exhaust pipe to one side.

11 Disconnect the engine management wiring loom from the following, noting its routing:

a) *Crankshaft speed/position sensor.*
b) *Oil pressure switch.*
c) *Oil level sensor.*

12 Release the cable ties and place the wiring loom to one side.

13 Unscrew the securing bolts, and remove the upper alternator mounting bracket. Pivot the alternator rearwards away from the manifold as far as it will go.

14 Remove the inlet and exhaust manifolds as described in Chapter 4A.

15 Referring to Chapter 3, unclip the coolant hoses from the heater matrix unions on the engine compartment bulkhead to drain the coolant from the cylinder block. Once the flow of coolant has stopped, reconnect both hoses and mop up any spilt coolant.

16 Loosen the clips and remove the upper hose from the radiator and thermostat housing.

17 Loosen the clips and disconnect the two heater hoses from the left-hand end of the cylinder head.

18 Undo the bolt and free the oil dipstick guide tube from the cylinder head.

19 Make a final check to ensure that all relevant hoses, pipes and wires have been disconnected.

20 Working in sequence, progressively loosen the cylinder head bolts **(see illustration)**. First loosen all the bolts by quarter of a turn, then loosen all the bolts by half a turn, then finally slacken all the bolts fully and withdraw them from the cylinder head. Recover the washers.

21 Lift the cylinder head from the cylinder block. If necessary, tap the cylinder head gently with a soft-faced mallet to free it from the block, but **do not** lever at the mating faces. Note that the cylinder head is located on dowels.

22 Recover the cylinder head gasket, and discard it.

Preparation for refitting

23 The mating faces of the cylinder head and block must be perfectly clean before refitting the head. Use a scraper to remove all traces of gasket and carbon, and also clean the tops of the pistons. Take particular care with the aluminium surfaces, as the soft metal is damaged easily. Also, make sure that debris is not allowed to enter the oil and water channels – this is particularly important for the oil circuit, as carbon could block the oil supply to the camshaft or crankshaft bearings. Using adhesive tape and paper, seal the water, oil and bolt holes in the cylinder block. To prevent carbon entering the gap between the pistons and bores, smear a little grease in the gap. After cleaning the piston, rotate the crankshaft so that the piston moves down the bore, then wipe out the grease and carbon with a cloth rag. Clean the other piston crowns in the same way.

24 Check the block and head for nicks, deep scratches and other damage. If slight, they may be removed carefully with a file. More serious damage may be repaired by machining, but this is a specialist job.

25 If warpage of the cylinder head is suspected, use a straight-edge to check it for distortion. Refer to Chapter 2F if necessary.

26 Ensure that the cylinder head bolt holes in the crankcase are clean and free of oil. Syringe or soak up any oil left in the bolt holes. This is most important in order that the correct bolt tightening torque can be applied and to prevent the possibility of the block being cracked by hydraulic pressure when the bolts are tightened.

27 Renew the cylinder head bolts regardless of their apparent condition.

Refitting

28 Ensure that the two locating dowels are in position at each end of the cylinder block/crankcase surface.

29 Fit the new cylinder head gasket to the block, making sure it is fitted with the correct

11.29 Ensure the head gasket is fitted with its OBEN/TOP marking uppermost

11.32a Cylinder head bolt tightening sequence

way up with its OBEN/TOP mark uppermost **(see illustration)**.

30 Carefully refit the cylinder head, locating it on the dowels.

31 Fit the washers to the new cylinder head bolts then carefully insert them into position **(do not drop)**, tightening them finger-tight only at this stage.

32 Working progressively and in sequence, first tighten all the cylinder head bolts to the Stage 1 torque setting **(see illustrations)**.

33 Once all bolts have been tightened to the Stage 1 torque, again working in sequence, tighten each bolt through its specified Stage 2 angle, using a socket and extension bar. It is recommended that an angle-measuring gauge is used during this stage of the tightening, to ensure accuracy **(see illustration)**.

34 Working in the specified sequence, go around again and tighten all bolts through the specified Stage 3 angle.

35 Working again in sequence, go around and tighten all bolts through the specified Stage 4 angle.

36 Finally go around in the specified sequence again and tighten all bolts through the specified Stage 5 angle.

37 Refit the exhaust manifold as described in Chapter 4A.

38 Reconnect the two heater hoses to the left-hand end of the cylinder head and tighten the clips.

39 Refit the upper hose to the radiator and thermostat housing and tighten the clips.

40 Refit the inlet manifold as described in Chapter 4A.

41 Refit the alternator upper mounting bracket and tighten the bolts.

42 Reconnect the wiring to the components listed in paragraph 11, then secure the wiring with cable ties.

43 Refer to Chapter 4A and refit the exhaust front pipe to the exhaust manifold. Refit the mounting rubbers.

44 Refit the rear timing belt cover with reference to Section 6.

45 Refit the camshaft sprockets, timing belt tensioner, and the timing belt idler rollers, with reference to Section 8.

46 Refit the timing belt as described in Section 7.

47 Refit the spark plugs as described in Chapter 1A.

48 Refit the camshaft cover as described in Section 4.

49 Refit the wheel arch liner inner cover and front roadwheel, then lower the vehicle to the ground.

50 Reconnect the battery negative terminal.

51 Check that all relevant hoses, pipes and wires, etc, have been reconnected. Check the security of the fuel hose connections.

52 Refill and bleed the cooling system with reference to Chapter 1A.

53 When the engine is started, check for signs of oil or coolant leakage.

12 Sump – removal and refitting

Removal

1 Disconnect the battery negative terminal (refer to *Disconnecting the battery* in the Reference Chapter).

2 Apply the handbrake, then jack up the front of the vehicle and support it on axle stands (see *Jacking and vehicle support*). Remove the right-hand front roadwheel and the wheel arch liner inner cover for access to the right-hand side of the engine.

3 Drain the engine oil as described in Chapter 1A, then fit a new sealing washer and refit the drain plug, tightening it to the specified torque.

4 Remove the exhaust system as described in Chapter 4A.

5 Disconnect the wiring connector from the oil level sensor.

6 Slacken and remove the bolts securing the sump flange to the transmission housing.

7 Remove the rubber plugs from the transmission end of the sump flange to gain access to the sump end retaining bolts.

8 Progressively slacken and remove the bolts securing the sump to the base of the cylinder block/oil pump. Using a wide-bladed scraper or similar tool inserted between the sump and baseplate, carefully break the joint, then remove the sump from under the car.

9 While the sump is removed, take the opportunity to check the oil pump pick-up/

11.32b Tighten the cylinder head bolts to the specified Stage 1 torque setting . . .

11.33 . . . and then through the various specified angles as described in the text

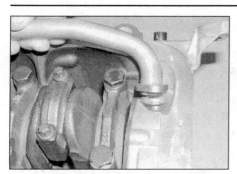

12.11 Fit new seal/gasket to the oil pump pick-up pipe

12.13 Apply sealant to the oil pump and rear main bearing cap joints (arrowed) before the sump is refitted

12.14 Apply a 2.5mm thick bead of sealant to the sump sealing surface – increase the thickness to 3.5mm around the No 5 main bearing cap area

strainer for signs of clogging or splitting. If necessary, unbolt the pick-up/strainer and remove it from the engine along with its sealing ring. The strainer can then be cleaned easily in solvent or renewed.

Refitting

10 Remove all traces of sealer and oil from the mating surfaces of the sump and cylinder block and (where removed) the pick-up/strainer. Also remove all traces of locking compound from the pick-up bolts (where removed).

11 Where necessary, position a new gasket/seal on top of the oil pump pick-up/strainer and fit the strainer (see illustration). Apply locking compound to the threads of the retaining bolts then fit the bolts and tighten to the specified torque.

12 Ensure the sump and cylinder block mating surfaces are clean and dry and remove all traces of locking compound from the sump bolts.

13 Apply a smear of suitable sealant (available form Vauxhall/Opel dealers) to the areas of the cylinder block mating surface around the areas of the of the oil pump housing and rear main bearing cap joints (see illustration).

14 Apply a bead of suitable sealant (available from Vauxhall/Opel dealers) approximately 2.5 mm thick to the sealing surface of the sump. Around the No 5 main bearing cap area, increase the thickness of the bead to 3.5 mm (see illustration).

15 Offer up the sump, and loosely refit all the retaining bolts. Working out from the centre in a diagonal sequence, progressively tighten the bolts securing the sump to the cylinder block/oil pump to their specified torque setting.

16 Tighten the bolts securing the sump flange to the transmission housing to their specified torque settings. Refit the rubber plugs to the sump flange cut-outs.

17 Refit the exhaust system (see Chapter 4A) and reconnect the oil level sender wiring connector.

18 Refit the wheel arch liner inner cover and front roadwheel, then lower the vehicle to the ground. Fill the engine with fresh oil, with reference to Chapter 1A.

13 Oil pump –
removal, overhaul and refitting

Note: *The pressure relief valve can be removed with pump in position on the engine unit, although on some models it will be necessary to unbolt the mounting bracket assembly from the block to allow the valve to be removed.*

Removal

1 Remove the timing belt as described in Section 7.

2 Remove the rear timing belt cover as described in Section 6.

3 Remove the sump and oil pump pick-up/strainer as described in Section 12.

4 Disconnect the wiring connector from the oil pressure switch.

5 Slacken and remove the retaining bolts then slide the oil pump housing assembly off of the end of the crankshaft, taking great care not to lose the locating dowels.

6 Remove the housing gasket and discard it.

Overhaul

7 Undo the retaining screws and lift off the pump cover from the rear of the housing.

8 Check the inner and outer rotors for identification dots indicating which way round they are fitted. If no marks are visible, use a suitable marker pen to mark the surface of both the pump inner and outer rotors.

13.9 Removal of the pump outer rotor – outer face identification punch mark arrowed

9 Lift out the inner and outer rotors from the pump housing (see illustration).

10 Unscrew the oil pressure relief valve bolt from the front of the housing and withdraw the spring and plunger from the housing, noting which way around the plunger is fitted. Remove the sealing washer from the valve bolt (see illustration).

11 Clean the components, and carefully examine the rotors, pump body and relief valve plunger for any signs of scoring or wear. Renew any component which shows signs of wear or damage; if the rotors or pump housing are marked then the complete pump assembly should be renewed.

12 If the components appear serviceable, measure the rotor endfloat using feeler blades, and check the flatness of the end cover (see illustrations). If the clearances exceed the specified tolerances the pump must be renewed.

13 If the pump is satisfactory, reassemble the components in the reverse order of removal, noting the following.

a) Ensure both rotors are fitted the correct way around.

b) Fit a new sealing ring to the pressure relief valve bolt and tighten the bolt to the specified torque.

c) Apply a little locking compound to the threads, and tighten the pump cover screws to the specified torque.

d) On completion prime the oil pump by filling it with clean engine oil whilst rotating the inner rotor.

13.10 Oil pressure relief valve components

1 *Plunger*
2 *Spring*
3 *Sealing washer*
4 *Valve bolt*

13.12a Using a feeler blade to check rotor clearance

13.12b Using a straight-edge and feeler blade to measure rotor endfloat

14 Flywheel –
removal, inspection
and refitting

Note: *New flywheel retaining bolts will be required on refitting.*

Removal

1 Remove the transmission as described in Chapter 7A, then remove the clutch assembly as described in Chapter 6.
2 Prevent the flywheel from turning by locking the ring gear teeth with a similar arrangement to that shown **(see illustration)**. Alternatively, bolt a strap between the flywheel and the cylinder block/crankcase. Make alignment marks between the flywheel and crankshaft using paint or a suitable marker pen.
3 Slacken and remove the retaining bolts and remove the flywheel. Do not drop it, as it is very heavy.

13.14 Fitting a new crankshaft oil seal to the oil pump housing

13.17 Take care not to damage the oil seal on the crankshaft lip (1) and engage the inner gear with the crankshaft flats (2)

Inspection

4 Examine the flywheel for scoring of the clutch face. If the clutch face is scored, the flywheel may be surface-ground, but renewal is preferable. Also check for wear or chipping of the ring gear teeth.
5 If there is any doubt about the condition of the flywheel, seek the advice of a Vauxhall/ Opel dealer or engine reconditioning specialist. They will be able to advise if it is possible to recondition it or whether renewal is necessary.

Refitting

14 Prior to refitting, carefully lever out the crankshaft oil seal using a flat-bladed screwdriver. Fit the new oil seal, ensuring its sealing lip is facing inwards, and press it squarely into the housing using a tubular drift which bears only on the hard outer edge of the seal **(see illustration)**. Press the seal into position so that it is flush with the housing and lubricate the oil seal lip with clean engine oil.
15 Ensure the mating surfaces of the oil pump and cylinder block are clean and dry and the locating dowels are in position.
16 Fit a new gasket to the cylinder block.
17 Carefully manoeuvre the oil pump into position and engage the inner gear with the crankshaft end **(see illustration)**. Locate the

pump on the dowels, taking great care not damage the oil seal lip.
18 Refit the pump housing retaining bolts in their original locations and tighten them to the specified torque.
19 Reconnect the oil pressure sensor wiring connector.
20 Refit the oil pump pick-up/strainer and sump as described in Section 12.
21 Refit the rear timing belt cover to the engine, tightening its retaining bolts to the specified torque.
22 Refit the timing belt sprockets, idler pulleys and tensioner then refit the belt as described in Sections 8 and 7.
23 On completion, fit a new oil filter and fill the engine with clean oil as described in Chapter 1A.

6 Clean the mating surfaces of the flywheel and crankshaft.
7 Offer up the flywheel and fit the new retaining bolts. If the original is being refitted align the marks made prior to removal.
8 Lock the flywheel by the method used on removal, and tighten the retaining bolts to the specified Stage 1 torque setting then angle-tighten the bolts through the specified Stage 2 angle, using a socket and extension bar, and finally through the specified Stage 3 angle. It is recommended that an angle-measuring gauge is used during the final stages of the tightening, to ensure accuracy **(see illustrations)**.

14.2 Prevent the flywheel from turning by locking the ring gear teeth with a suitable tool

14.8a Tighten the flywheel bolts to the specified torque using a torque wrench . . .

14.8b . . . then through the specified angle using an angle tightening gauge

15.2 Removing the crankshaft oil seal

15.4 Fitting a new crankshaft oil seal

15.7 Left-hand crankshaft oil seal –
transmission and flywheel removed

If a gauge is not available, use white paint to make alignment marks between the bolt head and flywheel prior to tightening; the marks can then be used to check that the bolt has been rotated through the correct angle.

9 Refit the clutch as described in Chapter 6 then remove the locking tool, and refit the transmission as described in Chapter 7A.

15 Crankshaft oil seals – renewal

Right-hand (timing belt end)

1 Remove the crankshaft sprocket as described in Section 8.
2 Carefully punch or drill two small holes opposite each other in the oil seal. Screw a self-tapping screw into each and pull on the screws with pliers to extract the seal (see illustration).
Caution: Great care must be taken to avoid damage to the oil pump.
3 Clean the seal housing and polish off any burrs or raised edges which may have caused the seal to fail in the first place.
4 Lubricate the lips of the new seal with clean engine oil and ease it into position on the end of the shaft. Press the seal squarely into position until it is flush with the housing. If necessary, a suitable tubular drift, such as a socket, which bears only on the hard outer edge of the seal can be used to tap the seal into position (see illustration). Take great care

not to damage the seal lips during fitting and ensure that the seal lips face inwards.
5 Wash off any traces of oil, then refit the crankshaft sprocket as described in Section 8.

Left-hand (flywheel end)

6 Remove the flywheel as described in Section 14.
7 Renew the seal as described in paragraphs 2 to 4 (see illustration).
8 Refit the flywheel as described in Section 14.

16 Engine/transmission mountings – inspection and renewal

Inspection

1 If improved access is required, firmly apply the handbrake, then jack up the front of the car and support it securely on axle stands (see *Jacking and vehicle support*).
2 Check the mounting rubber to see if it is cracked, hardened or separated from the metal at any point; renew the mounting if any such damage or deterioration is evident.
3 Check that all the mounting's fasteners are securely tightened; use a torque wrench to check if possible.
4 Using a large screwdriver or a pry bar, check for wear in the mounting by carefully levering against it to check for free play; where this is not possible, enlist the aid of an assistant to move the engine/transmission unit back-and-forth, or from side-to-side, while you watch the mounting. While some free play is to be expected even from new components, excessive wear should be obvious. If excessive free play is found, check first that the fasteners are correctly secured, then renew any worn components as described below.

Renewal

Note: *Before slackening any of the engine mounting bolts/nuts, the relative positions of the mountings to their various brackets should be marked to ensure correct alignment upon refitting.*

Front mounting/torque link

5 Apply the handbrake, then jack up the front

of the vehicle and support it on axle stands (see *Jacking and vehicle support*).
6 Slacken and remove the nut securing the mounting to the subframe bracket. Withdraw the through-bolt (see illustration).
7 Undo the bolts securing the mounting bracket to the transmission, then manoeuvre the mounting and bracket out of position.
8 Check all components for signs of wear or damage, and renew as necessary.
9 Locate the mounting in the subframe, refit the through-bolt and nut, then tighten the nut finger-tight at this stage.
10 Refit the mounting bracket to the transmission and tighten its bolts to the specified torque.
11 Tighten the through-bolt nut to the specified torque.
12 On completion, lower the vehicle to the ground.

Rear mounting/torque link

13 Apply the handbrake, then jack up the front of the vehicle and support it on axle stands (see *Jacking and vehicle support*).
14 Undo the three bolts securing the mounting bracket to the transmission and the through-bolt securing the mounting to the bracket (see illustration).
15 Undo the nuts and remove the two bolts securing the mounting to the subframe (see illustration). Manoeuvre the mounting and bracket out from under the car.
16 Refit the bracket to the transmission and tighten the bolts to the specified torque.
17 Locate the new mounting in position.

16.6 Front mounting/torque link
through-bolt (A) and mounting bracket-to-transmission bolts (B)

16.14 Rear mounting/torque link
through-bolt (arrowed)

16.15 Rear mounting/torque link bracket-to-subframe mounting bolt nuts (arrowed)

16.22a Right-hand mounting bracket-to-engine bracket bolts (arrowed) . . .

16.22b . . . and mounting-to-body retaining bolts (A) and nut (B)

16.28 Left-hand mounting bracket-to-transmission bracket retaining bolts (arrowed) – diesel model shown, petrol similar

16.29 Left-hand mounting-to-body retaining bolts (arrowed) – shown with engine/transmission removed

Insert the bolts and tighten the bolt/nuts to the specified torque.

18 On completion, lower the vehicle to the ground.

Right-hand mounting

19 Apply the handbrake, then jack up the front of the vehicle and support it on axle stands (see *Jacking and vehicle support*).

20 Remove the air cleaner as described in Chapter 4A.

21 Attach a suitable hoist and lifting tackle to the engine lifting brackets on the cylinder head, and support the weight of the engine.

22 Mark the position of the three bolts securing the mounting bracket to the engine bracket and undo the bolts. Undo the two bolts and one nut securing the mounting to the body and remove the mounting assembly **(see illustrations)**.

23 Place the mounting assembly in position and refit the two bolts and the nut securing the mounting to the body. Tighten the bolts/nut to the specified torque. Align the mounting in its original position, then tighten the three mounting bracket bolts to the specified torque.

24 Remove the hoist, then refit the air cleaner as described in Chapter 4A.

25 On completion, lower the vehicle to the ground.

Left-hand mounting

26 Remove the battery and battery box as described in Chapter 5A.

27 Attach a suitable hoist and lifting tackle to the engine lifting brackets on the cylinder head, and support the weight of the engine.

28 Using a Torx socket, unscrew the three bolts securing the mounting bracket to the transmission bracket **(see illustration)**.

29 Undo the four bolts securing the mounting to the body and the three bolts securing the transmission bracket to the transmission **(see illustration)**. Remove the mounting assembly from the car.

30 Locate the mounting brackets in position then insert the bolts and tighten them to the specified torque.

31 Disconnect the hoist and lifting tackle.

32 Refit the battery box and battery as described in Chapter 5A.

Chapter 2 Part B:
2.2 litre petrol engine in-car repair procedures

Contents

Degrees of difficulty

Easy, suitable for novice with little experience	Fairly easy, suitable for beginner with some experience	Fairly difficult, suitable for competent DIY mechanic 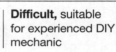	Difficult, suitable for experienced DIY mechanic	Very difficult, suitable for expert DIY or professional

Specifications

General

Engine type.	Four-cylinder, in-line, water-cooled. Double overhead camshafts, chain-driven
Manufacturer's engine codes*	Z22SE and Z22YH
Bore	86.0 mm
Stroke.	94.6 mm
Capacity	2198 cc
Compression ratio:	
Z22SE engines	10.0:1
Z22YH engines	12.0:1
Firing order	1-3-4-2 (No 1 cylinder at timing chain end of engine)
Direction of crankshaft rotation	Clockwise (viewed from timing chain end of engine)

* For details of engine code location, see 'Vehicle identification' in the Reference Chapter.

Compression pressures

Standard:	
Z22SE engines	12 to 15 bar
Z22YH engines	16 to 20 bar
Maximum difference between any two cylinders.	1 bar

Lubrication system

Minimum oil pressure at 80°C	1.5 bar at idle speed
Oil pump type.	Rotor-type, driven by crankshaft pulley/vibration damper from crankshaft
Oil pump clearances:	
Between outer rotor and oil pump housing	0.350 mm (max)
Between inner and outer rotor	0.150 mm (max)
Indentation/endfloat (rotor to upper edge of timing case cover)	0.080 mm (max)

Torque wrench settings

	Nm	lbf ft
Auxiliary drivebelt tensioner mounting bolt	42	31
Balance shaft retaining bracket bolts	10	7
Balance shaft sprocket bolts:*		
Stage 1	8	6
Stage 2	Angle-tighten a further 30°	
Camshaft bearing cap bolts:		
Bearing caps 1 to 10	10	7
Bearing cap 11 (intake camshaft, flywheel/driveplate end)	22	16
Bearing cap 11 cover plate	23	17
Camshaft cover bolts	10	7
Camshaft sprocket bolt:*		
Stage 1	85	63
Stage 2	Angle-tighten a further 30°	
Stage 3	Angle-tighten a further 15°	
Connecting rod big-end bearing cap bolt:*		
Stage 1	25	18
Stage 2	Angle-tighten a further 50°	
Stage 3	Angle-tighten a further 50°	
Stage 4	Angle-tighten a further 15°	
Coolant drain bolt in coolant pump	20	15
Coolant pump sprocket access cover bolts	7	5
Coolant pump sprocket bolts	8	6
Coolant pump-to-cylinder block bolts	23	17
Crankshaft pulley/vibration damper bolt:*		
Stage 1	100	74
Stage 2	Angle-tighten a further 75°	
Stage 3	Angle-tighten a further 15°	
Cylinder block lower casing to cylinder block :		
M8 bolts	25	18
M10 bolts (main bearing bolts):*		
Stage 1	20	15
Stage 2	Angle-tighten a further 70°	
Stage 3	Angle-tighten a further 15°	
Cylinder head x10 (main) bolts:*		
Stage 1	30	22
Stage 2	Angle-tighten a further 90°	
Stage 3	Angle-tighten a further 60°	
Stage 4	Angle-tighten a further 15°	
Cylinder head x4 (timing chain end) bolts	35	26
Driveplate bolts:*		
Stage 1	53	39
Stage 2	Angle-tighten a further 25°	
Engine mountings:		
Front mounting/torque link bracket to transmission	80	59
Front mounting/torque link to subframe	80	59
Left-hand:		
Mounting-to-body bolts	20	15
Mounting bracket to transmission bracket	55	41
Transmission bracket to transmission	55	41
Rear mounting/torque link bracket to transmission	80	59
Rear mounting/torque link to subframe	60	44
Rear mounting/torque link to transmission bracket	80	59
Right-hand:		
Engine bracket-to-engine bolts	55	41
Mounting-to-body bolts/nut	55	41
Mounting-to-engine bracket bolts	55	41
Engine-to-transmission bolts	60	44
Exhaust system front pipe to catalytic converter	20	15
Flywheel bolts:*		
Z22SE engines:		
Stage 1	53	39
Stage 2	Angle-tighten a further 25°	
Z22YH engines:		
Stage 1	60	44
Stage 2	Angle-tighten a further 30°	
Stage 3	Angle-tighten a further 15°	
Oil dipstick tube to inlet manifold	10	7

Torque wrench settings (continued)

	Nm	lbf ft
Oil level sensor bolts	10	7
Oil pump:		
Oil pressure control valve plug	40	30
Oil pump cover plate-to-timing cover bolts	6	4
Roadwheel bolts	110	81
Sump drain plug	25	18
Sump-to-cylinder block lower casing bolts	23	17
Sump-to-transmission bolts	40	30
Timing chain cover bolts	21	15
Timing chain guide rail bolt access plug	65	48
Timing chain guide rail bolts	10	7
Timing chain oil spray/injector nozzle	10	7
Timing chain sliding rail bolt*	10	7
Timing chain tensioner:		
Balance shafts	10	7
Camshaft	75	55
Timing chain tensioner rail pivot bolt	10	7

* Use new fasteners

1 General information

This Part of Chapter 2 describes the repair procedures which can reasonably be carried out on the engine while it remains in the vehicle. If the engine has been removed from the vehicle and is being dismantled as described in Chapter 2F, any preliminary dismantling procedures can be ignored.

Note that, while it may be possible physically to overhaul items such as the piston/connecting rod assemblies while the engine is in the vehicle, such tasks are not usually carried out as separate operations, and usually require the execution of several additional procedures (not to mention the cleaning of components and of oilways); for this reason, all such tasks are classed as major overhaul procedures, and are described in Chapter 2F.

Chapter 2F describes the removal of the engine/transmission unit from the vehicle, and the full overhaul procedures which can then be carried out.

Engine description

The engine is of the sixteen-valve, in-line four-cylinder, double overhead camshaft (DOHC) type, mounted transversely at the front of the car with the transmission attached to its left-hand end.

The aluminium alloy cylinder block is of the dry-liner type. The crankshaft is supported within the cylinder block on five shell-type main bearings. Thrustwashers are fitted to number 2 main bearing, to control crankshaft endfloat.

The connecting rods rotate on horizontally-split bearing shells at their big-ends. The pistons are attached to the connecting rods by gudgeon pins, which are retained by circlips. The aluminium-alloy pistons are fitted with three piston rings – two compression rings and scraper-type oil control ring.

The inlet and exhaust valves are each closed by coil springs, and operate in guides pressed into the cylinder head.

The camshafts are driven by the crankshaft via a timing chain arrangement; there is also a lower timing chain which links the crankshaft to the balance shafts and coolant pump. The camshafts rotate directly in the head and operate the sixteen valves via followers and hydraulic tappets. The followers are situated directly below the camshafts, each one operating a separate valve. Valve clearances are automatically adjusted by the hydraulic tappets.

Lubrication is by means of an oil pump, which is driven off the right-hand end of the crankshaft. It draws oil from the sump, and then forces it through an externally-mounted filter into galleries in the cylinder block/crankcase. From there, the oil is distributed to the crankshaft (main bearings) and camshafts. The big-end bearings are supplied with oil via internal drillings in the crankshaft, while the camshaft bearings also receive a pressurised supply. The camshaft lobes and valves are lubricated by splash, as are all other engine components. The timing chain is lubricated by an oil spray nozzle.

A semi-closed crankcase ventilation system is employed; crankcase fumes are drawn from camshaft cover, and passed via a hose to the inlet manifold.

Operations with engine in car

The following operations can be carried out without having to remove the engine from the car.

a) Compression pressure – testing.
b) Camshaft cover – removal and refitting.
c) Timing chain cover – removal and refitting.
d) Timing chains – removal and refitting.
e) Timing chain tensioners, guides and sprockets – removal and refitting.
f) Camshaft and followers – removal, inspection and refitting.
g) Cylinder head – removal and refitting.
h) Connecting rods and pistons – removal and refitting.*
i) Sump – removal and refitting.
j) Oil pump – removal, overhaul and refitting.
k) Crankshaft oil seals – renewal.
l) Engine/transmission mountings – inspection and renewal.
m) Flywheel/driveplate – removal, inspection and refitting.

* Although the operation marked with an asterisk can be carried out with the engine in the car (after removal of the sump), it is better for the engine to be removed, in the interests of cleanliness and improved access. For this reason, the procedure is described in Chapter 2F.

2 Compression test – general information

Refer to Chapter 2A, Section 2.

3 Valve timing – checking and adjustment

Note: *To check the valve timing, it will be necessary to use the following Vauxhall/Opel special tool (or suitable equivalent); the camshaft locking tool number is KM-6148 (see illustration). If access to this tool cannot*

3.0 Vauxhall/Opel camshaft locking tool (KM-6148)

A Camshaft sprocket locating pins

3.4 Crankshaft pulley and timing chain cover timing marks (arrowed)

3.6 Locking the camshaft sprockets in position using the Vauxhall/Opel tool KM-6148

be gained, this task must be entrusted to a Vauxhall/Opel dealer. The camshaft locking tool has locating pins that locate in the holes in the camshaft sprockets, to ensures that the camshafts remain correctly positioned.

1 The valve timing is checked and, if necessary adjusted, with No 4 piston at top dead centre (TDC) on its compression stroke. No 4 piston and cylinder are at the flywheel/driveplate end of the engine.

2 Remove the camshaft cover as described in Section 4.

3 Apply the handbrake, then jack up the front of the vehicle and support it on axle stands (see *Jacking and vehicle support*). Remove the right-hand front roadwheel and the wheel arch liner inner cover for access to the crankshaft pulley.

4 Using a socket and extension bar on the crankshaft pulley bolt, rotate the crankshaft clockwise (when viewed from the right-hand side of the car) until the notch on the crankshaft pulley rim is aligned with the pointer on the timing chain cover **(see illustration)**. The engine is now positioned with No 1 and 4 pistons at TDC.

5 To determine which piston is on its compression stroke, check the position of the camshaft lobes. When No 4 piston is at TDC on its compression stroke, No 4 cylinder

camshaft lobes will be pointing upwards. If No 4 cylinder camshaft lobes are pointing downwards, rotate the crankshaft through a further complete turn (360°) to bring No 4 cylinder to TDC on its compression stroke.

6 With the notch on the crankshaft pulley rim aligned with the pointer on the timing chain cover, insert the camshaft locking tool into position on the camshaft sprockets **(see illustration)**.

7 If the locking tool can be correctly fitted the valve timing is correctly set and no adjustment is necessary.

8 Refit the camshaft cover as described In Section 4, then refit the wheel arch liner inner cover and roadwheel, and lower the vehicle to the ground.

9 If the camshaft tool cannot be inserted correctly into the camshaft sprockets, the timing will need to be reset. Refer to Section 8 for the removal, inspection and refitting of the timing chain and sprockets.

---

4 Camshaft cover – removal and refitting

Removal

1 Unclip and remove the plastic cover from the top of the engine **(see illustration)**.

2 Remove the air cleaner assembly and air intake duct as described in Chapter 4A.

3 Remove the ignition module as described in Chapter 5B.

4 Disconnect the breather hose from the front of the camshaft cover **(see illustration)**.

5 Unscrew the nut securing the coolant pipe to the stud at the left-hand end of the camshaft cover.

6 Disconnect the wiring connectors from the EGR (exhaust gas recirculation) valve and the oxygen sensors.

7 Undo the two retaining bolts and release the

wiring bracket from the left-hand side of the camshaft cover. With the bracket removed, undo the right-hand stud to release the earth strap.

8 Undo the two retaining bolts from the timing chain end of the camshaft cover to release the hoses and pipe supports.

9 Free the wiring harness from its clips/brackets at the front and side of the camshaft cover as necessary.

10 Slacken and remove the camshaft cover retaining bolts along with their sealing washers (where fitted) then lift the camshaft cover and gasket/seals away from the cylinder head. Renew the cover gasket/seals and retaining bolt sealing washers, as applicable.

Refitting

11 Refitting is a reversal of removal noting the following points:
a) *Use new camshaft cover gasket/seals.*
b) *Once the cover is in position, first tighten all the bolts hand-tight, then go around and tighten them all to the specified torque setting.*
c) *Refit the ignition module as described in Chapter 5B.*
d) *Refit the air cleaner and intake duct as described in Chapter 4A.*

4.1 Remove the plastic cover from the top of the engine

4.4 Disconnect the breather hose (arrowed) from the camshaft cover

5.5a Turn the pulley until the flat on the centre hub locates with the oil pump drive . . .

5.5b . . . then fit a new securing bolt to the pulley

5.6 Using an angle-measuring gauge to tighten the crankshaft pulley whilst preventing pulley rotation with a suitable tool

5 Crankshaft pulley/vibration damper – removal and refitting

Note 1: *Vauxhall/Opel special tools KM-956-1 and KM-J-38122 or suitable alternatives will be required to prevent crankshaft rotation whilst the retaining bolt is slackened/tightened.*
Note 2: *A new pulley retaining bolt will be required on refitting.*

Removal

1 Apply the handbrake, then jack up the front of the vehicle and support it on axle stands (see *Jacking and vehicle support*). Remove the right-hand front roadwheel and the wheel arch liner inner cover for access to the crankshaft pulley.
2 Remove the auxiliary drivebelt as described in Chapter 1A. Prior to removal, mark the direction of rotation on the belt to ensure the belt is refitted the same way around.
3 Slacken the crankshaft pulley retaining bolt. To prevent crankshaft rotation whilst the retaining bolt is slackened, it will be necessary to hold the crankshaft pulley with the Vauxhall/Opel tool or a suitable alternative **(see illustration 5.6)**.
4 Unscrew the retaining bolt and washer and remove the crankshaft pulley from the end of the crankshaft. Whilst the pulley is removed check the oil seal for signs of wear or damage and, if necessary, renew as described in Section 14.

Refitting

5 Carefully locate the crankshaft pulley on the crankshaft end. Align the flats on the pulley with the oil pump, then turn the pulley to align the slot in the pulley with the crankshaft key. Slide the pulley fully into position, taking great care not to damage the oil seal, then fit the washer and new retaining bolt **(see illustrations)**.
6 Lock the crankshaft by the method used on removal, and tighten the pulley retaining bolt to the specified Stage 1 torque setting then angle-tighten the bolt through the specified Stage 2 angle, using a socket and extension bar, and finally through the specified Stage 3

angle. It is recommended that an angle-measuring gauge is used during the final stages of the tightening, to ensure accuracy **(see illustration)**. If a gauge is not available, use white paint to make alignment marks between the bolt head and pulley prior to tightening; the marks can then be used to check that the bolt has been rotated through the correct angle.
7 Refit the auxiliary drivebelt as described in Chapter 1A using the mark made prior to removal to ensure the belt is fitted the correct way around.
8 Refit the wheel arch liner inner cover and roadwheel, and lower the vehicle to the ground.

6 Timing chain cover – removal and refitting

Removal

1 Unclip and remove the plastic cover from the top of the engine **(see illustration 4.1)**.
2 Disconnect the battery negative terminal (refer to *Disconnecting the battery* in the Reference Chapter).
3 Remove the air cleaner assembly and air intake duct as described in Chapter 4A.
4 Apply the handbrake, then jack up the front of the vehicle and support it on axle stands (see *Jacking and vehicle support*). Remove the right-hand front roadwheel and the wheel arch liner inner cover.

6.9 Rear engine mounting/torque link through-bolt (arrowed)

5 Drain the engine oil as described in Chapter 1A. When the oil has completely drained, refit the drain plug with new sealing washer, and tighten to the specified torque.
6 Remove the crankshaft pulley/vibration damper as described in Section 5.
7 On Z22SE engines, carry out the following:
a) *Depressurise the fuel system as described in Chapter 4A.*
b) *Unscrew the union nut and disconnect the fuel supply pipe from the fuel rail. Plug or tape over the end of the pipe and the fuel rail to prevent dirt entry.*
c) *Disconnect the evaporative emission control purge valve hose at the quick-release fitting on the inlet manifold.*
8 Undo the three nuts securing the exhaust system front pipe to the catalytic converter, taking care to support the flexible section. **Note:** *Angular movement in excess of 10° can cause permanent damage to the flexible section.* Separate the flange joint and recover the gasket.
9 Undo the through-bolt securing the rear engine mounting/torque link to the mounting bracket, and the three bolts securing the mounting bracket to the transmission **(see illustration)**. Remove the mounting bracket from under the car.
10 Unscrew the nut and remove the through-bolt securing the front engine mounting/torque link to the subframe **(see illustration)**.
11 Connect a suitable hoist and lifting tackle to the right-hand end of the engine and support its weight. If available, the type of support bar

6.10 Front engine mounting/torque link through-bolt (arrowed)

6.12a Undo the three bolts (arrowed) securing the right-hand engine mounting to the engine bracket . . .

6.12b . . . and the two bolts (A) and one nut (B) securing the mounting to the body

which locates in the engine compartment side channels is to be preferred.

12 Mark the bolt positions for correct refitting, then undo the three bolts securing the right-hand engine mounting to the engine bracket, and the two bolts and one nut securing the mounting to the body (**see illustrations**). Remove the mounting.

13 Using the hoist, carefully raise the right-hand end of the engine until the bolts securing the engine mounting bracket to the cylinder head are accessible. Undo the three bolts and remove the engine bracket.

14 Reposition the hoist as necessary, then undo the drivebelt tensioner central mounting

bolt. Remove the tensioner assembly from the engine (**see illustration**).

15 Noting each bolt's correct fitted location (one bolt also secures the coolant pump), slacken and remove all the bolts securing the timing chain cover to the cylinder block (**see illustration**). It may be necessary to raise or lower the engine using the hoist to enable all the bolts to be removed.

16 Carefully ease the timing cover squarely away from the cylinder block and manoeuvre it out of position, noting the correct fitted positions of its locating dowels. If the locating dowels are a loose fit, remove them and store with the cover for safe-keeping.

17 Remove the gasket and ensure the mating surfaces are clean. Obtain a new gasket for refitting.

Refitting

18 Prior to refitting the cover, it is recommended that the crankshaft oil seal should be renewed. Carefully lever the old seal out of the cover using a large flat-bladed screwdriver. Fit the new seal to the cover, making sure its sealing lip is facing inwards. Press/tap the seal into position until it is flush with the cover, using a suitable tubular drift, such as a socket, which bears only on the hard outer edge of the seal (**see illustrations**).

19 Ensure the mating surfaces of the cover and cylinder block are clean and dry and the locating dowels are in position.

20 Manoeuvre the new gasket into position and locate it on the dowels.

21 Manoeuvre the timing cover into position, locating it on the dowels. Refit the cover retaining bolts, ensuring each one is fitted in its original location, and tighten them evenly and progressively to the specified torque.

22 Place the auxiliary drivebelt tensioner assembly in position ensuring that the locating peg on the tensioner mounting surface engages correctly with the corresponding hole in the timing chain cover. Tighten the tensioner central mounting bolt to the specified torque.

23 Refit the engine mounting bracket to the cylinder head and tighten the three retaining bolts to the specified torque.

24 Locate the right-hand engine mounting in position, then refit the three bolts securing the mounting to the engine bracket and the two bolts and one nut securing the mounting to the body. Align the mounting in its original position, then tighten the bolts and nut to the specified torque.

25 Remove the hoist and lifting tackle from the engine.

26 Refit the through-bolt and nut securing the front engine mounting/torque link to the subframe. Tighten the nut to the specified torque.

6.14 Undo the central mounting bolt and remove the auxiliary drivebelt tensioner

6.15 Note retaining bolt (arrowed) on the inner part of the timing chain cover casing

6.18a Carefully lever the old crankshaft oil seal out of the cover . . .

6.18b . . . then using a suitable drift tap in the new oil seal

27 Place the rear engine mounting/torque link mounting bracket in position and refit the three bolts securing the bracket to the transmission. Tighten the bolts to the specified torque.

28 Refit the rear engine mounting/torque link through-bolt and tighten the bolt to the specified torque.

29 Using a new gasket, refit the exhaust front pipe flange joint to the catalytic converter and tighten the three retaining nuts to the specified torque.

30 Refit the crankshaft pulley/vibration damper as described in Section 5.

31 Refit the auxiliary drivebelt as described in Chapter 1A.

32 Refit the wheel arch liner inner cover and roadwheel, and lower the vehicle to the ground.

33 On Z22SE engines, reconnect the purge valve hose to the inlet manifold and the fuel supply pipe to the fuel rail. Tighten the fuel pipe union nut to the specified torque (see Chapter 4A).

34 Refer to Chapter 4A if necessary and refit the air cleaner assembly and air intake duct.

35 Refill the engine with oil as described in Chapter 1A.

36 On completion, reconnect the battery negative terminal and refit the engine cover. Start the engine and check for signs of oil leaks.

7 Timing chain tensioners – removal and refitting

Camshaft chain tensioner

Note: *If a new camshaft timing chain tensioner is being fitted, then a new tension rail should be fitted at the same time. Under no circumstances should the old tension rail be fitted with a new tensioner.*

Removal

1 Remove the camshaft cover as described in Section 4.

2 Apply the handbrake, then jack up the front of the vehicle and support it on axle stands (see *Jacking and vehicle support*). Remove the right-hand front roadwheel and the wheel arch liner inner cover.

3 Refer to the information contained in Section 3, and set No 4 piston at approximately 10° BTDC on its compression stroke.

4 Unscrew the camshaft timing chain tensioner from the rear of the cylinder head, and remove the inner piston assembly **(see illustration)**. Remove the sealing rings and discard them, new ones should be used on refitting.

Caution: Do not rotate the engine whilst the tensioner is removed.

5 Dismantle the tensioner, and inspect the tensioner piston for signs of wear or damage and renew if necessary **(see illustration)**.

Refitting

6 Pretension the timing chain tensioner,

7.4 Removing the timing chain tensioner assembly

7.5 Inner piston removed to check for wear or damage

7.6a Turn the inner piston screw clockwise until it locks in position . . .

7.6b . . . then fit the inner piston to the outer tensioner assembly

by turning the inner piston clockwise **(see illustrations)** and allow it to lock in position. Lubricate the inner piston, then reassemble the timing chain tensioner.

7 Fit the sealing rings, then lubricate the timing chain tensioner/piston with clean engine oil and insert it into the cylinder head. **Note:** *Check the threads are clean on the tensioner and in the cylinder head before refitting.*

8 Tighten the tensioner to the specified torque.

9 Release the tensioner, by pressing on the tension rail/timing chain with a rounded bar **(see illustration)**. This will press against the inner piston of the tensioner to unlock it, when it releases, the spring-loaded piston will take up the slack in the timing chain.

Caution: This procedure must be carried out correctly, otherwise the chain may be left slack and skip a tooth on the sprockets. This will result in engine damage.

10 Rotate the crankshaft through two complete rotations (720°) in the correct direction of rotation and recheck the valve timing as described in Section 3.

11 Refit the camshaft cover as described in Section 4.

7.9 Press the bar against the tension rail to release the tensioner inner piston

7.16 1.0 mm drill bit (arrowed) used to lock the tensioner piston in place

7.18 Removing the locking pin to release the tensioner

12 Refit the wheel arch liner inner cover and roadwheel, and lower the vehicle to the ground.

Balance shaft chain tensioner

Removal

13 Remove the timing chain cover as described in Section 6.

14 Undo the two retaining bolts and remove the balance shaft chain tensioner from the cylinder block.

Caution: Do not rotate the engine whilst the tensioner is removed.

15 Inspect the tensioner piston for signs of wear or damage and renew if necessary.

Refitting

16 Pretension the balance shaft chain tensioner, by turning the piston clockwise

8.0a Align the silver link (arrowed) with the triangular timing mark on the exhaust sprocket . . .

8.0c . . . and the second silver-coloured link (arrowed) with the timing mark (white dot) on the crankshaft sprocket

approximately 45° and push it back into the tensioner housing. Insert a 1.0 mm locking pin or drill bit into the hole in the piston housing, which will lock the piston in position **(see illustration)**.

17 Lubricate the tensioner piston with clean engine oil, then refit it onto the cylinder block tightening the bolts to their specified torque.

18 Once the tensioner is in position, remove the locking pin to release the tensioner piston **(see illustration)**. Make sure the piston engages with the tension rail correctly and takes up any slack in the balancer shaft timing chain.

Caution: This procedure must be carried out correctly, otherwise the chain may be left slack and skip a tooth on the sprockets. This could result in engine vibration or damage.

8.0b . . . the copper-coloured link (arrowed) with the diamond timing mark on the intake sprocket . . .

8.6 Undo the two retaining bolts (arrowed) from the chain sliding rail

19 Refit the timing chain cover as described in Section 6.

Chain tensioner and guide rails

20 Tensioner and guide rail removal and refitting is part of the timing chain and sprockets removal and refitting procedure (see Section 8). They must be renewed if they show signs of wear or damage on their chain surfaces.

8 Timing chains and sprockets – removal, inspection and refitting

Note: In order to set the valve timing accurately at TDC, a Vauxhall/Opel special tool (or suitable alternative) is required (see Section 3). If the timing chain and sprockets are to be completely removed or refitted, then this task can be carried out without the tool. The timing can be re-aligned using the coloured links on the timing chain and the alignment marks on the sprockets (see illustrations).

Caution: Prior to removal, ensure the camshaft sprockets are suitably marked as they are identical and can be refitted to either camshaft.

Note: If there is any wear on the camshaft timing chain, tension rails, guides and crankshaft sprocket the components must always be renewed as a complete assembly.

Removal

Camshaft chain and sprockets

Note: New camshaft sprocket retaining bolts and new timing chain sliding rail retaining bolts will be required on refitting.

1 Disconnect the battery negative terminal (refer to *Disconnecting the battery* in the Reference Chapter), then remove the camshaft cover (see Section 4).

2 Position No 4 piston at TDC on its compression stroke, as described in Section 3.

3 Remove the timing chain cover as described in Section 6.

4 Remove the camshaft timing chain tensioner as described in Section 7.

5 On Z22YH engines, disconnect the wiring plug, then undo the retaining bolt and remove the camshaft position sensor from the cylinder head.

6 Undo the two retaining bolts from the camshaft timing chain sliding rail on the top of the cylinder head **(see illustration)**.

7 Remove the access plug from the cylinder head and undo the upper securing bolt for the timing chain guide rail **(see illustrations)**.

8 Undo the lower securing bolt for the timing chain guide rail and remove downwards out from the engine **(see illustration)**.

9 Hold the camshafts in turn using an open-ended spanner on the flats provided, then slacken and remove the camshaft sprocket retaining bolts **(see illustration)**.

10 Remove the exhaust camshaft sprocket, making sure it is identified for refitting.

8.7a Remove the access plug from the cylinder head . . .

8.7b . . . and remove the guide rail upper securing bolt

8.8 Undo the lower guide rail securing bolt (arrowed) and remove the guide rail downwards

11 Undo the lower securing bolt from the timing chain tension rail, then remove it downwards and out from the engine **(see illustration)**.

12 Lift the timing chain off the crankshaft sprocket and remove the intake camshaft sprocket complete with timing chain out through the top of the cylinder head.

13 Slide the crankshaft drivegear/sprocket (and spring washer, where fitted) off the Woodruff key on the crankshaft. **Note:** *FRONT is marked on the outer face of the gear.*

Balance shaft chain and sprockets

Note: *If there is any wear on the balance shaft timing chain, tension rail and guides, balance shaft chain tensioner or drivegears/sprockets the components must always be renewed as a complete assembly.*

14 Remove the camshaft timing chain and sprockets as described in paragraphs 1 to 13.

15 Undo the two retaining bolts and remove the balance shaft chain tensioner from the cylinder block.

16 Undo the securing bolts and remove the tension rail and the two guide rails from the cylinder block **(see illustration)**.

17 Lift the balance shaft timing chain from the sprockets and remove.

8.9 Undo the camshaft sprocket retaining bolts – hold the camshafts using an open-ended spanner

18 Using a suitable drift, lock the balance shaft sprockets and undo the retaining bolts, then remove the sprocket from the balance shaft **(see illustration)**. Use new bolts when refitting.

19 Slide the crankshaft drivegear/sprocket (and spring washer, where fitted) off the Woodruff key on the crankshaft. **Note:** *FRONT is marked on the outer face of the gear.*

20 Lock the coolant pump drivegear with a suitable screwdriver, and undo the three securing bolts. Remove the drivegear from the coolant pump.

8.11 Undo the retaining bolt and remove the tension rail from the engine

Inspection

21 Examine the teeth on the sprockets for any sign of wear or damage such as chipped, hooked or missing teeth. If there is any sign of wear or damage on any sprocket/gear, all the sprockets/gears and the relevant chain should be renewed as a set.

22 Inspect the links of each timing chain for signs of wear or damage on the rollers. The extent of wear can be judged by checking the amount by which the chain can be bent sideways; a new chain will have very little

8.16 Undo the retaining bolts and remove the tension rail and guide rails

A Tension rail   *B Guide rails*

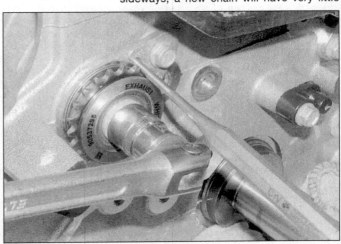

8.18 Using a drift to lock the balance shaft sprocket

8.27 Refit the timing chain crankshaft sprocket, noting FRONT is marked on the outer face

8.30 Turning the camshaft slightly using an open-ended spanner to locate the sprocket in the correct position

sideways movement. If there is an excessive amount of side play in a timing chain, it must be renewed.

23 Note that it is a sensible precaution to renew the timing chains, regardless of their apparent condition, if the engine has covered a high mileage, or if it has been noted that the chain(s) have sounded noisy when the engine running. It is advised renewing the chains and sprockets as a matched set, since it is false economy to run a new chain on worn sprockets and *vice versa*. If there is any doubt about the condition of the timing chains and sprockets, seek the advice of a Vauxhall/Opel dealer service department, who will be able to advise you as to the best course of action, based on their previous knowledge of the engine.

24 Examine the chain guide(s) and tensioner rail(s) for signs of wear or damage to their chain contact faces, renewing any which are badly marked.

Refitting

Camshaft chain and sprockets

25 If any new components are being fitted, transfer any alignment marks you have made from the original components to aid refitting. Ensure the crankshaft is still at the TDC position.

26 If not already fitted, refit the balance shaft timing chain and sprockets as described in paragraphs 42 to 49.

27 Slide the crankshaft drive sprocket (and spring washer, where fitted) onto the Woodruff

key on the crankshaft. **Note:** *FRONT is marked on the outer face of the sprocket* **(see illustration)**.

28 Refit the intake camshaft sprocket complete with timing chain down through the top of the cylinder head. The copper-coloured link should line up with the INT mark on the intake sprocket (a cable tie can be used to keep the chain in position – **see illustration 8.0b**). Attach the sprocket to the camshaft using a new securing bolt, tightening it hand-tight at this stage.

29 Insert the timing chain tension rail up through the engine casing into position for the tensioner. (Do not refit the lower securing bolt until the timing chain is in position.)

30 Insert the exhaust camshaft sprocket into the timing chain, making sure the silver link on the timing chain lines up with the EXH mark on the sprocket (a cable tie can be used to keep the chain in position – **see illustration 8.0a**). Attach the sprocket to the camshaft using a new securing bolt, tightening it hand-tight at this stage. **Note:** *One or both of the camshafts may have moved slightly, due to valve spring pressure. It may be necessary to turn the camshafts slightly to locate the sprockets in the correct position, use an open-ended spanner on the camshaft if required* **(see illustration)**. *Do not turn the camshafts too far as the engine is set at TDC and the valves could hit the pistons.*

31 Locate the timing chain onto the crankshaft drive sprocket, aligning the silver link with the mark on the sprocket **(see illustration 8.0c)**.

32 The lower securing bolt can now be fitted to the tension rail and tightened to its specified torque.

33 Insert the guide rail and fit lower securing bolt, tightening it to its specified torque.

34 Refit the guide rail upper securing bolt and access bolt in the cylinder head, tightening them to their specified torque.

Caution: All the timing marks (coloured chain links) must be aligned with the corresponding marks on the sprockets. This procedure must be carried out correctly, otherwise the timing being offset by one tooth will result in engine damage.

35 Refit the timing chain cover as described in Section 6.

36 Remove the cable ties from camshaft sprockets. Hold the camshafts in turn with an open-ended spanner on the flats provided and tighten the sprocket bolts to the specified Stage 1 torque setting, then tighten the bolts through the specified Stage 2 and Stage 3 angles. It is recommended that an angle-measuring gauge is used during the final stages of the tightening, to ensure accuracy. If a gauge is not available, use white paint to make alignment marks prior to tightening; the marks can then be used to check that the bolts have been rotated through the correct angle.

37 Attach the sliding rail for the camshaft timing chain to the top of the cylinder head, using new retaining bolts tighten them to the specified torque **(see illustration)**.

38 Refit the camshaft timing chain tensioner as described in Section 7.

39 On Z22YH engines, refit the camshaft position sensor and reconnect the wiring plug.

40 Rotate the crankshaft through two complete revolutions (720°) in the correct direction of rotation (to bring number 4 piston back to TDC on its compression stroke). If the special tool is available, check the valve timing as described in Section 3.

41 Refit the camshaft cover as described in Section 4, then reconnect the battery negative terminal.

Balance shaft chain and sprockets

42 Refit the drivegear to the coolant pump, and tighten the three securing bolts to the specified torque.

43 Slide the crankshaft drivegear/sprocket (and spring washer, where fitted) onto the Woodruff key on the crankshaft. **Note:** *FRONT is marked on the outer face of the gear* **(see illustration)**. The timing mark on the drivegear should be pointing downwards to align with the silver-coloured link on the timing chain.

44 Refit the exhaust sprocket to the balance shaft, using a new securing bolt **(see illustration)**. The sprocket is marked EXHAUST and has an arrow which points downwards to align with the silver-coloured link on the timing chain. Tighten the bolts to the specified torque, locking the balance shaft sprockets as on removal.

8.37 Use new retaining bolts when refitting the sliding rail

8.43 Refit the balance shaft crankshaft sprocket, noting FRONT is marked on the outer face

8.44 **Refit the balance shaft sprockets using new securing bolts**

8.45 **The arrow points upwards on the intake sprocket**

45 Refit the intake sprocket to the balance shaft, using a new securing bolt. The sprocket is marked INTAKE and has an arrow which points upwards to align with the copper-coloured link on the timing chain (see illustration). Tighten the bolts to the specified torque, locking the balance shaft sprockets as on removal.
46 Refit the balance shaft timing chain to the sprockets/gears and align the timing marks (coloured chain links) with the marks on the appropriate sprockets as described above (see illustration).
47 Refit the tension rail and two guide rails to the cylinder block, tightening the securing bolts to the specified torque.
48 Refit the balance shaft chain tensioner as described in Section 7.
49 Refit the camshaft timing chain and sprockets as described above.

9 Camshaft and followers – removal, inspection and refitting

Note: New camshaft sprocket retaining bolts and new timing chain sliding rail retaining bolts will be required on refitting.

Removal

1 Disconnect the battery negative terminal (refer to Disconnecting the battery in the Reference Chapter).
2 On Z22YH engines, remove the high-pressure fuel pump as described in Chapter 4A.
3 Remove the camshaft cover as described in Section 4.
4 Position No 4 piston at TDC on its compression stroke, as described in Section 3.
5 Undo the two retaining bolts and remove the camshaft timing chain sliding rail on the top of the cylinder head (see illustration 8.6).
6 Check that No 4 piston is still positioned at TDC on its compression stroke then cable tie the timing chain to the camshaft sprockets and mark the sprockets in relation to the cylinder head (see illustration).
7 If the vehicle is still on axle stands, lower it back onto the ground making sure the handbrake is on and a gear is engaged. This is to prevent the engine being turned once TDC has been aligned.
8 Remove the camshaft timing chain tensioner as described in Section 7.
9 On Z22YH engines, disconnect the wiring plug, then undo the retaining bolt and remove the camshaft position sensor from the cylinder head.

10 Hold the camshafts, using an open-ended spanner on the flats provided, then slacken and remove the camshaft sprocket retaining bolts (see illustration 8.9).
11 Disengage the camshaft sprockets (complete with chain) from the camshafts, keeping the chain under tension. Use a suitable screwdriver, bar or bolt to pass through the sprockets and rest on the upper surface of the cylinder head, to prevent the timing chain falling down and coming off the crankshaft drivegear/sprocket.
12 Note the identification markings on the camshaft bearing caps. The caps are numbered 1 to 10 with all numbers being the right way up when viewed from the driver's seat; numbers 1 to 5 on the exhaust camshaft starting from the timing chain end of the engine, and numbers 6 to 10 on the intake camshaft starting at the timing chain end.
Note: There is also an 11th cap on the intake camshaft, at the flywheel/driveplate end of the cylinder head. If the markings are not clearly visible, make identification marks to ensure each cap is fitted correctly on refitting.
13 On Z22SE engines, undo the two bolts and remove the cover plate from No 11 bearing cap.
14 Working in a spiral pattern from the outside inwards, slacken the camshaft bearing cap retaining bolts by half a turn at a time, to relieve the pressure of the valve springs on the bearing caps gradually and evenly. Once the valve spring pressure has been relieved, the bolts can be fully unscrewed and removed, along with the caps. Take care not to loose any locating dowels which may be fitted to some of the bearing caps and lift the camshaft out of the head.
Caution: If the bearing cap bolts are carelessly slackened, the bearing caps might break. If any bearing cap breaks then the complete cylinder head assembly must be renewed; the bearing caps are

8.46 **Balance shaft timing chain layout**

A Silver-coloured chain links aligned with timing marks
B Copper-coloured chain link aligned with timing mark

9.6 **Alignment marks made on camshaft sprockets for refitting**

9.15 Use a container to keep the followers and hydraulic tappets in order

9.16 Keep the hydraulic tappets in labelled containers with clean engine oil

9.20 Lubricate the tappets with clean engine oil before refitting

matched to the head and are not available separately.

15 Obtain 16 small, clean plastic containers, and label them for identification. Alternatively, divide a larger container into compartments. Lift the followers out from the top of the cylinder head and store each one in its respective fitted position **(see illustration)**.
16 If the hydraulic tappets are also to be removed, withdraw each hydraulic tappet and place them in small containers with clean engine oil. This will keep them primed ready for refitting **(see illustration)**.

Inspection

17 Examine the camshaft bearing surfaces and cam lobes for signs of wear ridges and scoring. Renew the camshaft if any of these conditions are apparent. Examine the condition of the bearing surfaces both on the camshaft journals and in the cylinder head. If the head

bearing surfaces are worn excessively, the cylinder head will need to be renewed.
18 Examine the follower bearing surfaces which contact the camshaft lobes for wear ridges and scoring. Renew any followers on which these conditions are apparent.
19 Check the hydraulic tappets (where removed) and their bores in the cylinder head for signs of wear or damage. If any tappet is thought to be faulty it should be renewed.

Refitting

20 Where removed, lubricate the hydraulic tappets with clean engine oil and carefully insert each one into its original location in the cylinder head **(see illustration)**.
21 Refit the camshaft followers to the cylinder head, ensuring each follower is fitted in its original location **(see illustration)**.
22 Lubricate the camshaft followers with clean engine oil then lay the camshafts into

position. Ensure the crankshaft is still set at TDC, and position the camshafts so that the lobes of No 4 cylinder are pointing upward.
23 Ensure the mating surfaces of the bearing caps and cylinder head are clean and dry and lubricate the camshaft journals and lobes with clean engine oil.
24 Apply a smear of sealant to the cylinder head mating surface at the flywheel/driveplate end of the intake camshaft (No 11) bearing cap **(see illustration)**. Refit the cap locating dowels to the cap if they have been removed.
25 Refit the camshaft bearing caps and the retaining bolts in their original locations on the cylinder head. The caps are numbered 1 to 10 with all numbers being the right way up when viewed from the driver's seat; numbers 1 to 5 on the exhaust camshaft starting from the timing chain end of the engine, and numbers 6 to 10 on the intake camshaft starting at the timing chain end. Refit the 11th cap on the intake camshaft, at the flywheel/driveplate end of the cylinder head **(see illustration)**.
26 Tighten all bolts by hand only then, working in a spiral pattern from the centre outwards, tighten the bolts by half a turn at a time to gradually impose the pressure of the valve springs on the bearing caps. Repeat this sequence until all bearing caps are in contact with the cylinder head then go around and tighten the camshaft bearing cap bolts to the specified torque. When all the caps have been tightened, refit the cover plate to No 11 bearing cap (Z22SE engines), using a new gasket, and tighten the two bolts to the specified torque.
Caution: If the bearing cap bolts are carelessly tightened, the bearing caps might break. If any bearing cap breaks then the complete cylinder head assembly must be renewed; the bearing caps are matched to the head and are not available separately.
27 Using the marks made on removal, ensure that the timing chain is still correctly engaged with the sprockets then refit the camshaft sprockets to the camshafts. It may be necessary to turn the camshafts slightly to locate the sprockets in the correct position, use an open-ended spanner on the camshaft if required. Fit the new retaining bolts hand-tight at this stage **(see illustration)**. Remove the cable ties from the timing chain and sprockets.

9.21 Refit the camshaft followers in their original position

9.24 Apply silicone sealing compound thinly to the surface areas arrowed

9.25 Refitting No 11 cap to the flywheel/driveplate end of the intake camshaft

9.27 Refit new retaining bolts to the camshaft sprockets

28 Refit the camshaft timing chain tensioner as described in Section 7.

29 If the special tool is available, check that No 4 cylinder is correctly set at TDC on compression as described in Section 3. If the special tool is not available, make sure the marks made on the sprockets prior to removal are correctly aligned.

30 Hold the camshafts in turn with an open-ended spanner on the flats provided and tighten the sprocket bolts to the specified Stage 1 torque setting, then tighten the bolts through the specified Stage 2 and Stage 3 angles. It is recommended that an angle-measuring gauge is used during the final stages of the tightening, to ensure accuracy. If a gauge is not available, use white paint to make alignment marks prior to tightening; the marks can then be used to check that the bolts have been rotated through the correct angle.

31 Refit the camshaft timing chain sliding rail using new retaining bolts, then tighten to the specified torque.

32 Rotate the crankshaft through two complete revolutions (720°) in the correct direction of rotation (to bring number 4 piston back to TDC on its compression stroke). If the special tool is available, check the valve timing as described in Section 4. If the special tool is not available, check that the marks made on the sprockets prior to removal are correctly aligned.

33 On Z22YH engines, refit the camshaft position sensor and reconnect the wiring plug.

34 Refit the camshaft cover as described in Section 4.

35 On Z22YH engines, refit the high-pressure fuel pump as described in Chapter 4A.

36 Reconnect the battery negative terminal and lower the vehicle to the ground (where applicable)

10 Cylinder head – removal and refitting

Note: New cylinder head bolts, camshaft timing chain sliding rail bolts and camshaft sprocket retaining bolts will be required on refitting.

Removal

1 Drain the cooling system as described in Chapter 1A.

2 Remove the camshaft timing chain and sprockets as described in Section 8.

3 Remove the inlet and exhaust manifolds as described in Chapter 4A.

4 Release the retaining clips and disconnect the coolant hoses from the front of the right-hand end of the cylinder head **(see illustration)**.

5 Slacken and remove the four retaining bolts from the timing chain end of the cylinder head **(see illustration 10.21)**.

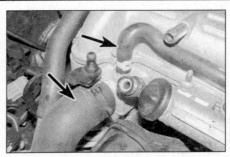

10.4 Remove the two coolant hoses (arrowed) from the front of the cylinder head

6 Working in the **reverse** of the tightening sequence shown in illustration 10.21, progressively slacken the ten main cylinder head bolts by half a turn at a time, until all bolts can be unscrewed by hand.

7 Lift out the cylinder head bolts and where applicable recover the washers.

8 Lift the cylinder head away; seek assistance if possible, as it is a heavy assembly.

9 Remove the gasket, noting the locating dowels fitted to the top of the cylinder block. If they are a loose fit, remove the locating dowels and store them with the head for safe-keeping.

Caution: Do not lay the head on its lower mating surface; support the head on wooden blocks as it may be damaged if the head is placed directly onto a bench.

10 If the cylinder head is to be dismantled for overhaul, then refer to Part F of this Chapter.

Preparation for refitting

11 The mating faces of the cylinder head and cylinder block/crankcase must be perfectly clean before refitting the head. Use a hard plastic or wood scraper to remove all traces of gasket and carbon; also clean the piston crowns. Take particular care, as the surfaces are damaged easily. Also, make sure that the carbon is not allowed to enter the oil and water passages – this is particularly important for the lubrication system, as carbon could block the oil supply to any of the engine's components. Using adhesive tape and paper, seal the water, oil and bolt holes in the cylinder block/crankcase. To prevent carbon entering the gap between the pistons and bores, smear

10.16 Using a tap to clean out the threads in the cylinder block

a little grease in the gap. After cleaning each piston, use a small brush to remove all traces of grease and carbon from the gap, then wipe away the remainder with a clean rag. Clean all the pistons in the same way.

12 Check the mating surfaces of the cylinder block/crankcase and the cylinder head for nicks, deep scratches and other damage. If slight, they may be removed carefully with a file, but if excessive, machining may be the only alternative to renewal (see your local specialist for machining).

13 Ensure that the cylinder head bolt holes in the crankcase are clean and free of oil. Syringe or soak up any oil left in the bolt holes. This is most important in order that the correct bolt tightening torque can be applied and to prevent the possibility of the block being cracked by hydraulic pressure when the bolts are tightened.

14 The cylinder head bolts must be discarded and renewed, regardless of their apparent condition.

15 If warpage of the cylinder head gasket surface is suspected, use a straight-edge to check it for distortion. Refer to Part F of this Chapter if necessary.

Refitting

16 Using a tap, clean out the thread in the four bolt holes at the timing chain end of the cylinder block **(see illustration)**. Wipe clean the mating surfaces of the cylinder head and cylinder block/crankcase.

17 Check that the locating dowels are in position then fit the new gasket to the cylinder block **(see illustrations)**.

10.17a Check the dowels are in position to locate the cylinder head gasket . . .

10.17b . . . ensuring the gasket is fitted with its OBEN/TOP marking uppermost

10.21 Cylinder head bolt tightening sequence

18 Ensure the crankshaft is positioned approx 60° BTDC (this is to prevent any damage to the valves or pistons when refitting the cylinder head).

19 With the aid of an assistant, carefully refit the cylinder head assembly to the block, aligning it with the locating dowels.

20 Apply a smear of oil to the threads and the underside of the heads of the new cylinder head bolts and carefully enter each bolt into its relevant hole (*do not drop them in*). Screw all bolts in, by hand only, until finger-tight.

21 Working progressively and in sequence, tighten the cylinder head bolts to their Stage 1 torque setting, using a torque wrench and suitable socket **(see illustration)**.

22 Once all bolts have been tightened to the Stage 1 torque, working again in sequence, go around and tighten all bolts through the specified Stage 2 angle. It is recommended

that an angle-measuring gauge is used to ensure accuracy **(see illustration)**. If a gauge is not available, use white paint to make alignment marks prior to tightening; the marks can then be used to check that the bolt has been rotated through the correct angle.

23 Go around again in the specified sequence and angle tighten the bolts through the specified Stage 3 angle.

24 Finally go around in sequence and angle tighten the bolts through the specified Stage 4 angle.

25 Refit the four bolts securing the right-hand end of the cylinder head to the block (timing chain end) and tighten them to the specified torque setting **(see illustrations)**.

26 Turn the crankshaft carefully in the direction of engine rotation, to bring No 4 cylinder back to TDC.

27 Reconnect the coolant hoses to the

cylinder head and secure them in position with the retaining clips.

28 Refit the inlet and exhaust manifolds and associated components as described in Chapter 4A.

29 Refit the camshaft timing chain and sprockets as described in Section 8.

30 On completion, refill the cooling system and refill the engine with oil as described in Chapter 1A.

11 Sump – removal and refitting

Removal

1 Disconnect the battery negative terminal (refer to *Disconnecting the battery* in the Reference Chapter).

2 Apply the handbrake, then jack up the front of the vehicle and support it on axle stands (see *Jacking and vehicle support*). Remove the right-hand front roadwheel and the wheel arch liner inner cover.

3 Remove the auxiliary drivebelt as described in Chapter 1A. Prior to removal, mark the direction of rotation on the belt to ensure the belt is refitted the same way around.

4 Drain the engine oil as described in Chapter 1A. When the oil has completely drained, refit the drain plug with new sealing washer, and tighten to the specified torque.

5 Disconnect the wiring connector from the oil level sensor (see Chapter 5A).

6 Undo the bolt securing the oil dipstick guide tube to the inlet manifold, then withdraw the guide tube from the sump.

7 Remove the lower mounting bolt for the air conditioning compressor. Slacken (do not remove) the upper two mounting bolts and use a block of wood (or similar) to wedge the compressor away from the sump. **Note:** *Take care not to damage the bolts or alloy mounting point when inserting the wedge; do not use excessive force.*

8 Slacken and remove the bolts securing the sump flange to the transmission housing **(see illustration)**.

9 Progressively slacken and remove the bolts securing the sump to the base of the cylinder

10.22 Tightening the cylinder head down through its stages, using an angle gauge

10.25a Fit four new retaining bolts to the timing chain end of the cylinder head . . .

10.25b . . . two of the bolts are inside the timing chain housing (bolt arrowed on exhaust side of head)

11.8 Undo the two sump-to-transmission bolts (A) and also the sump-to-lower cylinder block bolt (B)

11.12a Apply a continuous bead of silicone sealer around the sump . . .

block lower casing (there is one long bolt at the transmission end of the sump – see illustration 11.8). To break the sump joint it may be necessary to cut the silicone sealer using a suitable knife, taking care not to damage any surfaces. Lower the sump away from the engine.
10 While the sump is removed, take the opportunity to check the oil pump pick-up/strainer (if possible) for signs of clogging or splitting. Note: The pick-up/strainer cannot be removed from the sump as it is riveted in position.

Refitting

11 Remove all traces of silicone sealer and oil from the mating surfaces of the sump and cylinder block.
12 Apply a continuous bead of silicone sealing compound (available from your Vauxhall/Opel dealer) at approximately 1.0 mm from the inner edge of the sump. The bead of sealant should be between 2.0 and 2.5 mm in diameter. Also apply a bead of sealant (2.0 to 2.5 mm) around the oil intake pipe area of the sump mating surface (see illustrations).
13 Offer up the sump to the cylinder block and loosely refit all the retaining bolts.
14 Working out from the centre in a diagonal sequence, progressively tighten the bolts securing the sump to the cylinder block lower casing. Tighten all the bolts to their specified torque setting.
15 Tighten the bolts securing the sump flange to the transmission housing to their specified torque settings.
16 Remove the wedge-shaped block from the air conditioning compressor and refit the lower mounting bolt. Tighten the three compressor mounting bolts to their specified torque (see Chapter 3).
17 Refit the oil dipstick guide tube and securely tighten the retaining bolt.
18 Reconnect the oil level sensor wiring connector.
19 Refit the auxiliary drivebelt as described

in Chapter 1A using the mark made prior to removal to ensure the belt is fitted the correct way around.
20 Refit the wheel arch liner inner cover and roadwheel, and lower the vehicle to the ground.
21 Fill the engine with fresh engine oil as described in Chapter 1A.

12 Oil pump – removal, inspection and refitting

Note: The oil pump pressure control valve can be removed with the timing chain cover in position on the engine (see paragraph 5 below).

Removal

1 The oil pump assembly is built into the timing chain cover. Removal and refitting of the cover is as described in Section 6.

Inspection

2 Undo the retaining screws and lift off the pump cover plate from the inside of the timing chain cover (see illustration).
3 Note any marks identifying the outer faces of the pump rotors. If none can be seen, use a suitable marker pen and mark the surface

11.12b . . . and also around the oil intake pipe area

of both the pump inner and outer rotors; the marks can then be used to ensure the rotors are refitted the correct way around.
4 Lift out the inner and outer rotors from the cover (see illustration).
5 Unscrew the oil pressure control valve plug from the timing chain cover and withdraw the spring and plunger, noting which way around the plunger is fitted. Remove the sealing ring from the valve bolt (see illustrations).
6 Clean the components, and carefully examine the rotors, pump body and valve plungers for any signs of scoring or wear. Renew any component which shows signs of wear or damage; if the rotors or pump housing

12.2 Undo the retaining screws and remove the pump cover plate

12.4 Removing the inner and outer rotors

12.5a Undo and remove the oil pressure control valve plug . . .

12.5b . . . and remove the oil pressure valve spring and plunger

12.7a Using a feeler blade to check the inner-to-outer rotor clearance . . .

12.7b . . . the outer rotor-to-oil pump housing . . .

12.7c . . . and also using a straight-edge to check the endfloat

are marked then the complete pump assembly should be renewed.

7 If the components appear serviceable, measure the clearances (using feeler blades) between:

a) *The inner rotor and the outer rotor.*
b) *The outer rotor and oil pump housing.*
c) *The rotor endfloat.*
d) *The flatness of the end cover.*

If the clearances exceed the specified tolerances (see Specifications at the beginning of this Chapter), the pump must be renewed **(see illustrations)**.

8 If the pump is satisfactory, reassemble the components in the reverse order of removal, noting the following.

a) *Ensure both rotors and the valve plunger are fitted the correct way around.*
b) *Fit new sealing rings to the pressure control valve and tighten to the specified torque setting.*

c) *Refit the pump cover tightening the cover screws to the specified torque.*
d) *On completion prime the oil pump by filling it with clean engine oil whilst rotating the inner rotor.*

Refitting

9 Refit the timing chain cover as described in Section 6.

13 Balance shaft – removal and refitting

Removal

1 Remove the balance shaft timing chain and sprockets as described in Section 8.
2 If the balance shaft sprockets are removed, mark the shafts to identify the intake shaft from the exhaust shaft for refitting.

3 Undo the securing bolt from the balance shaft retaining plate and slide the balance shaft out from the cylinder block **(see illustrations)**.

Refitting

4 Refitting is the reverse of removal, tighten the retaining plate bolts to their specified torque.
5 Refit the balance shaft timing chain and sprockets as described in Section 8.

14 Crankshaft oil seals – renewal

Right-hand (timing chain end)

1 Remove the crankshaft pulley as described in Section 5.
2 Using a large flat-bladed screwdriver, carefully lever the seal out from the timing chain cover.
3 Clean the seal housing and polish off any burrs or raised edges which may have caused the seal to fail in the first place.
4 Lubricate the lips of the new seal with clean engine oil and press/tap it squarely into position until it sits into the recess in the cover **(see illustration)**. If necessary, a suitable tubular drift, such as a socket, which bears only on the hard outer edge of the seal can be used to tap the seal into position. Take great care not to damage the seal lips during fitting and ensure that the seal lips face inwards.

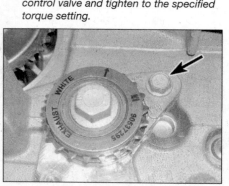

13.3a Undo the retaining bolt (arrowed) . . .

13.3b . . . and withdraw the balance shaft assembly

14.4 Make sure the seal seats squarely into the timing chain cover

14.7 Removing a crankshaft left-hand oil seal, using a pair of pliers and a screw

14.9 Carefully ease the oil seal over the end of the crankshaft and tap/press it squarely into position

15.2 Lock the flywheel/driveplate ring gear

5 Wash off any traces of oil, then refit the crankshaft pulley as described in Section 5.

Left-hand (flywheel/driveplate end)

6 Remove the flywheel/driveplate as described in Section 15.

7 Carefully punch or drill two small holes opposite each other in the oil seal. Screw a self-tapping screw into each and pull on the screws with pliers to extract the seal **(see illustration)**.

8 Clean the seal housing and polish off any burrs or raised edges which may have caused the seal to fail in the first place. **Note:** *Insulation tape can be put around the crankshaft flange to help fit the oil seal.*

9 Lubricate the lips of the new seal with clean engine oil and ease it into position on the end of the crankshaft. Press the seal squarely into position until it is flush with the bearing cap. If necessary, a suitable tubular drift, such as a socket, which bears only on the hard outer edge of the seal can be used to tap the seal into position. Take great care not to damage the seal lips during fitting and ensure that the seal lips face inwards **(see illustration)**.

10 If insulation tape was used around the crankshaft flange, remove it, taking care not to damage the oil seal. Refit the flywheel as described in Section 15.

15 Flywheel/driveplate – removal, inspection and refitting

Note: *New flywheel/driveplate retaining bolts will be required on refitting.*

Removal

Manual transmission models

1 Remove the transmission as described in Chapter 7A then remove the clutch assembly as described in Chapter 6.

2 Prevent the flywheel from turning by locking the ring gear teeth with a similar arrangement to that shown **(see illustration)**. Alternatively, bolt a strap between the flywheel and the cylinder block/crankcase. Make alignment marks between the flywheel and crankshaft using paint or a suitable marker pen.

3 Slacken and remove the retaining bolts and remove the flywheel. Do not drop it, as it is very heavy.

Automatic transmission models

4 Remove the transmission as described in Chapter 7B then remove the driveplate as described in paragraphs 2 and 3.

Inspection

5 On manual transmission models, examine the flywheel for scoring of the clutch face. If the clutch face is scored, the flywheel may be surface-ground, but renewal is preferable.

6 On automatic transmission models closely examine the driveplate and ring gear teeth for signs of wear or damage and check the driveplate surface for any signs of cracks.

7 If there is any doubt about the condition of the flywheel/driveplate, seek the advice of a Vauxhall/Opel dealer or engine reconditioning specialist. They will be able to advise if it is possible to recondition it or whether renewal is necessary.

Refitting

Manual transmission models

8 Clean the mating surfaces of the flywheel and crankshaft.

9 Apply a drop of locking compound to each of the new retaining bolt threads then offer up the flywheel, if the original is being refitted align the marks made prior to removal. Screw in the retaining bolts.

10 Lock the flywheel by the method used on removal, and tighten the retaining bolts to the specified Stage 1 torque setting then angle-tighten the bolts through the specified

Stage 2 angle, using a socket and extension bar, and finally (on Z22YH engines) through the specified Stage 3 angle. It is recommended that an angle-measuring gauge is used during the final stages of the tightening, to ensure accuracy. If a gauge is not available, use white paint to make alignment marks between the bolt head and flywheel prior to tightening; the marks can then be used to check that the bolt has been rotated through the correct angle.

11 Refit the clutch as described in Chapter 6 then remove the locking tool, and refit the transmission as described in Chapter 7A.

Automatic transmission models

12 Clean the mating surfaces of the drive-plate and crankshaft and remove all traces of locking compound from the driveplate retaining bolt threads.

13 Apply a drop of locking compound to each of the new retaining bolt threads then offer up the driveplate, if the original is being refitted align the marks made prior to removal. Screw in the retaining bolts.

14 Lock the driveplate by the method used on removal, and tighten the retaining bolts to the specified Stage 1 torque setting then angle-tighten the bolts through the specified Stage 2 angle, using a socket and extension bar. It is recommended that an angle-measuring gauge is used during the final stages of the tightening, to ensure accuracy. If a gauge is not available, use white paint to make alignment marks between the bolt head and flywheel prior to tightening; the marks can then be used to check that the bolt has been rotated through the correct angle.

15 Remove the locking tool and refit the transmission as described in Chapter 7B.

16 Engine/transmission mountings – inspection and renewal

Refer to Chapter 2A, Section 16.

Chapter 2 Part C:
1.9 litre SOHC diesel engine in-car repair procedures

Contents

Degrees of difficulty

| **Easy,** suitable for novice with little experience | | **Fairly easy,** suitable for beginner with some experience | | **Fairly difficult,** suitable for competent DIY mechanic | | **Difficult,** suitable for experienced DIY mechanic | | **Very difficult,** suitable for expert DIY or professional | |

Specifications

General

Engine type.	Four-cylinder, in-line, water-cooled. Single overhead camshaft, belt-driven
Manufacturer's engine code*	Z19DT
Bore	82.0 mm
Stroke.	90.4 mm
Capacity.	1910 cc
Compression ratio	18.0:1
Firing order.	1-3-4-2 (No 1 cylinder at timing belt end of engine)
Direction of crankshaft rotation	Clockwise (viewed from timing belt end of engine)

* For details of engine code location, see 'Vehicle identification' in the Reference Chapter.

Compression pressures

Maximum difference between any two cylinders.	1.5 bar

Valve clearances

Engine cold (inlet and exhaust)	0.30 to 0.40 mm

Lubrication system

Minimum oil pressure at 100ºC	1.0 bar at idle speed
Oil pump type.	Rotor-type, driven by crankshaft pulley/vibration damper from crankshaft

Torque wrench settings

	Nm	lbf ft
Air conditioning compressor mounting bracket to cylinder block/sump	50	37
Auxiliary drivebelt idler pulley bolt	50	37
Auxiliary drivebelt tensioner assembly bolts	50	37
Camshaft bearing cap bolts	15	11
Camshaft cover bolts	10	7
Camshaft sprocket bolt*	120	89
Connecting rod big-end bearing cap bolt:*		
Stage 1	25	18
Stage 2	Angle-tighten a further 60°	
Crankshaft oil seal housing	9	7
Crankshaft pulley/vibration damper bolts	25	18
Crankshaft sprocket bolt*†	360	266
Cylinder head bolts:*		
Stage 1	20	15
Stage 2	65	48
Stage 3	Angle-tighten a further 90°	
Stage 4	Angle-tighten a further 90°	
Stage 5	Angle-tighten a further 90°	
Engine mountings:		
Front mounting/torque link bracket to transmission	80	59
Front mounting/torque link to subframe	80	59
Left-hand:		
Mounting-to-body bolts	20	15
Mounting bracket to transmission bracket	55	41
Transmission bracket to transmission	55	41
Rear mounting/torque link bracket to transmission	80	59
Rear mounting/torque link to subframe	60	44
Rear mounting/torque link to transmission bracket	80	59
Right-hand:		
Engine bracket-to-engine bolts	55	41
Lower bolts (M8)	25	18
Upper bolts (M10)	50	37
Mounting-to-body bolts/nut	55	41
Mounting-to-engine bracket bolts	55	41
Engine-to-transmission unit bolts:		
M10 bolts	40	30
M12 bolts	60	44
Flywheel bolts*	160	118
High-pressure fuel pump sprocket nut*	50	37
Intermediate shaft bearing housing support bracket bolts	55	41
Main bearing cap bolts:*		
Stage 1	25	18
Stage 2	Angle-tighten a further 100°	
Oil filter housing to cylinder block	50	37
Oil pump housing to cylinder block	9	7
Oil pump pick-up/strainer bolts	9	7
Roadwheel bolts	110	81
Sump bolts:		
M6 bolts	9	7
M8 bolts	25	18
M10 bolts	40	30
Sump drain plug	20	15
Timing belt idler pulley bolt	50	37
Timing belt tensioner bolt	30	22
Timing belt upper cover bolts:		
M6 bolts	9	7
M8 bolts	25	18

* Use new nuts/bolts
† Left-hand thread

1 General information

How to use this Chapter

This Part of Chapter 2 describes the repair procedures which can reasonably be carried out on the engine while it remains in the vehicle. If the engine has been removed from the vehicle and is being dismantled as described in Chapter 2F, any preliminary dismantling procedures can be ignored.

Note that, while it may be possible physically to overhaul items such as the piston/connecting rod assemblies while the engine is in the vehicle, such tasks are not usually carried out as separate operations, and usually require the execution of several additional procedures (not to mention the cleaning of components and of oilways); for this reason, all such tasks are classed as major overhaul procedures, and are described in Chapter 2F.

Chapter 2F describes the removal of the engine/transmission unit from the vehicle, and the full overhaul procedures which can then be carried out.

Engine description

The 1.9 litre SOHC diesel engine is of the eight-valve, in-line four-cylinder, single overhead camshaft type, mounted transversely at the front of the car, with the transmission on its left-hand end.

The crankshaft is supported within the cylinder block on five shell-type main bearings. Thrustwashers are fitted to number 3 main bearing, to control crankshaft endfloat.

The connecting rods rotate on horizontally-split bearing shells at their big-ends. The pistons are attached to the connecting rods by gudgeon pins, which are retained by circlips. The aluminium-alloy pistons are fitted with three piston rings – two compression rings and scraper-type oil control ring.

The camshaft runs directly in the cylinder head, and is driven by the crankshaft via a toothed composite rubber timing belt (which also drives the high-pressure fuel pump and the coolant pump). The camshaft operates each valve via a camshaft follower with adjustment shim.

Lubrication is by pressure-feed from a rotor-type oil pump, which is mounted on the right-hand end of the crankshaft. The pump draws oil through a strainer located in the sump, and then forces it through an externally mounted full-flow cartridge-type filter. The oil flows into galleries in the cylinder block/crankcase, from where it is distributed to the crankshaft (main bearings) and camshaft. The big-end bearings are supplied with oil via internal drillings in the crankshaft, while the camshaft bearings also receive a pressurised supply. The camshaft lobes and valves are lubricated by splash, as are all other engine components.

A semi-closed crankcase ventilation system is employed; crankcase fumes are drawn from the oil separator (integral with the camshaft cover), and passed via a hose to the inlet manifold.

Operations with engine in car

The following operations can be carried out without having to remove the engine from the car.

a) Removal and refitting of the camshaft cover.
b) Adjustment of the valve clearances.
c) Removal and refitting of the cylinder head.
d) Removal and refitting of the timing belt, tensioner, idler pulleys and sprockets.
e) Renewal of the camshaft oil seal.
f) Removal and refitting of the camshaft and followers.
g) Removal and refitting of the sump.
h) Removal and refitting of the connecting rods and pistons.*
i) Removal and refitting of the oil pump.
j) Removal and refitting of the oil filter housing.
k) Renewal of the crankshaft oil seals.
l) Renewal of the engine mountings.
m) Removal and refitting of the flywheel.

* Although the operation marked with an asterisk can be carried out with the engine in the car (after removal of the sump), it is preferable for the engine to be removed, in the interests of cleanliness and improved access. For this reason, the procedure is described in Chapter 2F.

2 Compression and leakdown tests – description and interpretation

Compression test

Note 1: *A compression tester specifically designed for diesel engines must be used for this test.*

Note 2: *The battery must be in a good state of charge, the air filter must be clean, and the engine should be at normal operating temperature.*

1 When engine performance is down, or if misfiring occurs which cannot be attributed to the fuel system, a compression test can provide diagnostic clues as to the engine's condition. If the test is performed regularly, it can give warning of trouble before any other symptoms become apparent.

2 A compression tester specifically intended for diesel engines must be used, because of the higher pressures involved. The tester is connected to an adapter which screws into the injector holes. It is unlikely to be worthwhile buying such a tester for occasional use, but it may be possible to borrow or hire one – if not, have the test performed by a Vauxhall/Opel dealer, or suitably-equipped garage. If the necessary equipment is available, proceed as follows.

3 Remove the fuel injectors as described in Chapter 4B.

4 Screw the compression tester adapter in to the fuel injector hole of No 1 cylinder.

5 With the help of an assistant, crank the engine on the starter motor; after one or two revolutions, the compression pressure should build-up to a maximum figure, and then stabilise. Record the highest reading obtained.

6 Repeat the test on the remaining cylinders, recording the pressure in each.

7 All cylinders should produce very similar pressures; any difference greater than the maximum figure given in the Specifications indicates the existence of a fault. Note that the compression should build-up quickly in a healthy engine; low compression on the first stroke, followed by gradually-increasing pressure on successive strokes, indicates worn piston rings. A low compression reading on the first stroke, which does not build-up during successive strokes, indicates leaking valves or a blown head gasket (a cracked head could also be the cause). **Note:** *The cause of poor compression is less easy to establish on a diesel engine than on a petrol one. The effect of introducing oil into the cylinders ('wet' testing) is not conclusive, because there is a risk that the oil will sit in the recess on the piston crown instead of passing to the rings.*

8 On completion of the test, refit the fuel injectors as described in Chapter 4B.

Leakdown test

9 A leakdown test measures the rate at which compressed air fed into the cylinder is lost. It is an alternative to a compression test, and in many ways it is better, since the escaping air provides easy identification of where pressure loss is occurring (piston rings, valves or head gasket).

10 The equipment needed for leakdown testing is unlikely to be available to the home mechanic. If poor compression is suspected, have the test performed by a Vauxhall/Opel dealer, or suitably-equipped garage.

3 Top dead centre (TDC) for No 1 piston – locating

Note: *To accurately determine the TDC position for No 1 piston, it will be necessary to use Vauxhall/Opel special tool EN-46788 (or suitable equivalent) to set the crankshaft at the TDC position (see illustration).*

1 In its travel up and down its cylinder bore, Top Dead Centre (TDC) is the highest point that each piston reaches as the crankshaft rotates. While each piston reaches TDC both at the top of the compression stroke and again at the top of the exhaust stroke, for the

3.0 Vauxhall/Opel special tool EN-46788 (or equivalent) is required to set the TDC position for No 1 piston

3.3a Remove the engine oil filler cap . . .

3.3b . . . undo the two retaining bolts (arrowed) . . .

3.3c . . . release the hose support clip . . .

3.3d . . . then lift off the plastic cover over the top of the engine

3.5 Undo the central mounting bolt (arrowed), and remove the auxiliary drivebelt tensioner assembly

purpose of timing the engine, TDC refers to the piston position of No 1 cylinder at the top of its compression stroke.

2 Number 1 piston (and cylinder) is at the right-hand (timing belt) end of the engine, and its TDC position is located as follows. Note that the crankshaft rotates clockwise when viewed from the right-hand side of the car.

3 Remove the engine oil filler cap, undo the two retaining bolts, release the hose support clip, then lift off the plastic cover over the top of the engine **(see illustrations)**. Refit the oil filler cap.

4 Remove the crankshaft pulley/vibration damper as described in Section 6.

5 Undo the central mounting bolt, and remove the auxiliary drivebelt tensioner assembly from the engine **(see illustration)**.

6 Remove the air cleaner assembly and air intake duct as described in Chapter 4B.

7 Place a trolley jack beneath the right-hand end of the engine with a block of wood on the jack head. Raise the jack until it is supporting the weight of the engine.

8 Mark the bolt positions for correct refitting, then undo the three bolts securing the

right-hand engine mounting to the engine bracket, and the two bolts and one nut securing the mounting to the body. Remove the mounting **(see illustration)**.

9 Unclip the wiring harness from the top and side of the upper timing belt cover. Unscrew the six retaining bolts and lift off the upper timing belt cover **(see illustration)**.

10 Using a socket and extension bar on the crankshaft sprocket bolt, rotate the crankshaft in the normal direction of rotation until the mark on the camshaft sprocket is aligned with the pointer on the camshaft cover **(see illustration)**.

3.8 Undo the retaining nut and bolts and remove the right-hand engine mounting

3.9 Upper timing belt cover retaining bolts (arrowed)

3.10 Rotate the crankshaft to align the mark on the camshaft sprocket (arrowed) with the pointer on the camshaft cover

3.11 Screw the fastening stud of special tool EN-46788 into the oil pump housing

3.12 Positioning ring of tool EN-46788 (arrowed) attached to the fastening stud and crankshaft sprocket

11 Unscrew the bolt from the lower left-hand side of the oil pump housing and screw in the fastening stud of Vauxhall/Opel special tool EN-46788 **(see illustration)**.

12 Fit the positioning ring of tool EN-46788 over the fastening stud and engage it with the crankshaft sprocket. Ensure that the hole in the positioning ring engages with the lug on the sprocket. Secure the tool in position with the retaining bolt and nut **(see illustration)**.

13 With the crankshaft positioning ring in place and the mark on the camshaft sprocket aligned with the pointer on the camshaft cover, the engine is positioned with No 1 piston at TDC on compression.

4 Valve timing – checking and adjustment

1 Position No 1 cylinder at TDC on its compression stroke as described in Section 3.

2 With the crankshaft positioning ring in place, check that the mark on the camshaft sprocket is aligned with the pointer on the camshaft cover; if so, the valve timing is correct.

3 If the mark on the camshaft sprocket is not aligned with the pointer on the camshaft cover, readjust the timing belt position as described in Section 7.

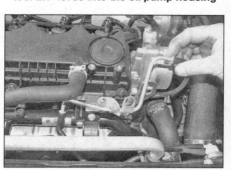

5.2 Undo the retaining bolt(s) to release the vacuum lines from the camshaft cover

5 Camshaft cover – removal and refitting

Removal

1 Remove the engine oil filler cap, undo the two retaining bolts, release the hose support clip, then undo the two bolts and lift off the plastic cover over the top of the engine **(see illustrations 3.3a to 3.3d)**. Refit the oil filler cap.

2 Undo the retaining bolt(s) to release the

5.3a Release the retaining clips and disconnect the breather hoses from the front . . .

vacuum lines running over the top of the camshaft cover **(see illustration)**.

3 Release the retaining clips and disconnect the breather hoses from the front and rear of the camshaft cover **(see illustrations)**.

4 Disconnect the fuel leak-off hose connection at No 2 and No 3 injector by extracting the locking clip and lifting out the hose fitting. Refit the locking clips to the injectors after disconnecting the hose fitting.

5 Undo the seven retaining bolts securing the camshaft cover to the cylinder head **(see illustration)**.

5.3b . . . and rear of the camshaft cover

5.5 Undo the seven bolts (arrowed) securing the camshaft cover to the cylinder head

5.6 Move the leak-off hose assembly rearward, then lift the camshaft cover from the cylinder head

5.7 Fit the seal to the camshaft cover groove

6.3 Crankshaft pulley/vibration damper retaining bolts (arrowed)

6 Carefully move the disconnected leak-off hose assembly rearward, then lift the camshaft cover from the cylinder head (**see illustration**).

Refitting

7 Ensure the cover and cylinder head surfaces are clean and dry then fit the seal to the cover groove (**see illustration**).
8 Move the leak-off hose assembly to the rear and carefully lower the cover into position. Screw in the retaining bolts and lightly tighten them. Once all bolts are hand-tight, go around and tighten them all to the specified torque setting.
9 Reconnect the leak-off hose fittings to the injectors by pushing in the locking clip, attaching the fitting, then releasing the locking clip. Ensure that each fitting is securely connected and retained by the clip.

10 Reconnect the breather hoses to the cover.
11 Refit and tighten the bolts securing the vacuum lines.
12 Refit the plastic cover to the top of the engine, tighten the two retaining bolts and resecure the hose.

6 Crankshaft pulley/ vibration damper – removal and refitting

Removal

1 Apply the handbrake, then jack up the front of the vehicle and support it on axle stands (see *Jacking and vehicle support*). Remove the right-hand front roadwheel, then undo the ten bolts and remove the engine undertray for access to the crankshaft pulley.

2 Remove the auxiliary drivebelt as described in Chapter 1B. Prior to removal, mark the direction of rotation on the belt to ensure the belt is refitted the same way around.
3 Undo the four bolts securing the pulley to the crankshaft sprocket and remove the pulley from the sprocket (**see illustration**).

Refitting

4 Locate the crankshaft pulley on the sprocket, ensuring that the hole on the rear face of the pulley engages with the lug on the sprocket.
5 Refit the four retaining bolts and tighten them progressively to the specified torque.
6 Refit the auxiliary drivebelt as described in Chapter 1B using the mark made prior to removal to ensure the belt is fitted the correct way around.
7 Refit the roadwheel and engine undertray, then lower the car to the ground and tighten the wheel bolts to the specified torque.

7 Timing belt – removal and refitting

Note: *The timing belt must be removed and refitted with the engine cold.*

Removal

1 Position No 1 cylinder at TDC on its compression stroke as described in Section 3.
2 Undo the retaining bolt and remove the auxiliary drivebelt idler pulley from the engine bracket (**see illustration**).
3 Undo the two lower bolts, and the three upper bolts, and remove the engine bracket from the engine (**see illustrations**).
4 Undo the nut and bolt and remove the crankshaft positioning tool (EN-46788) from the crankshaft sprocket.
5 Slacken the timing belt tensioner retaining bolt and allow the tensioner to retract, relieving the tension on the timing belt.
6 Slide the timing belt from its sprockets and remove it from the engine. If the belt is to be re-used, use white paint or similar to mark the direction of rotation on the belt. **Do not** rotate the crankshaft or camshafts until the timing belt has been refitted.

7.2 Undo the bolt (arrowed) and remove the auxiliary drivebelt idler pulley from the engine bracket

7.3a Undo the two lower bolts (arrowed) . . .

7.3b . . . and the three upper bolts (arrowed) . . .

7.3c . . . and remove the engine bracket from the engine

7 Check the timing belt carefully for any signs of uneven wear, splitting or oil contamination, and renew it if there is the slightest doubt about its condition. If the engine is undergoing an overhaul and is approaching the specified interval for belt renewal (see Chapter 1B) renew the belt as a matter of course, regardless of its apparent condition. If signs of oil contamination are found, trace the source of the oil leak and rectify it, then wash down the engine timing belt area and all related components to remove all traces of oil.

Refitting

8 On reassembly, thoroughly clean the timing belt sprockets and tensioner/idler pulleys.

9 Place the timing belt in position over the crankshaft sprocket. If the original belt is being refitted, ensure that the arrow mark made on removal points in the normal direction of rotation, as before.

10 Check that the camshaft and crankshaft are still correctly positioned with No 1 piston at TDC on compression as described in Section 3, and refit the crankshaft positioning tool.

11 Fit the timing belt over the crankshaft, camshaft and fuel pump sprockets and around the idler pulleys, ensuring that the belt front run is taut (ie, all slack is on the tensioner side of the belt), then fit the belt over the coolant pump sprocket and tensioner pulley. Do not twist the belt sharply while refitting it. Ensure that the belt teeth are correctly seated centrally in the sprockets, and that the timing mark on the camshaft sprocket remain in alignment.

12 Screw in a suitable bolt, approximately 50 mm in length, into the threaded hole directly below the timing belt tensioner. Using a screwdriver resting on the bolt as a pivot, move the adjusting lever on the tensioner until the tensioner pointer is aligned with the mark on the backplate. Hold the tensioner in this position and tighten the tensioner retaining bolt (see illustrations).

13 Remove the crankshaft positioning tool.

14 Using a socket on the crankshaft sprocket bolt, rotate the crankshaft smoothly through two complete turns (720°) in the normal direction of rotation to settle the timing belt in position. At the end of the second turn, align the mark on the camshaft sprocket with the pointer on the camshaft cover.

15 Refit the positioning ring of tool EN-46788 over the fastening stud and engage it with the crankshaft sprocket. Ensure that the hole in the positioning ring engages with the lug on the sprocket. Secure the tool in position with the retaining bolt and nut.

16 Slacken the timing belt tensioner retaining bolt and, using a screwdriver resting on the pivot bolt as before, move the adjusting lever on the tensioner until the tensioner pointer is once again aligned with the mark on the backplate. Hold the tensioner in this position and tighten the tensioner retaining bolt to the specified torque.

17 Remove all the positioning tools and

7.12a Using a screwdriver resting on a pivot bolt (arrowed), move the adjusting lever on the tensioner . . .

7.12b . . . until the tensioner pointer (arrowed) is aligned with the mark on the backplate

again rotate the crankshaft smoothly through two complete turns (720°) in the normal direction of rotation. Check that the timing belt tensioner pointer is still aligned with the mark on the backplate. If not, repeat the procedure described in paragraph 16.

18 When all is correct, remove the tensioner position pivot bolt. Refit the bolt removed from the oil pump housing and tighten it to the specified torque.

19 Place the engine bracket in position and refit the two lower bolts, and the three upper bolts. Tighten the bolts to the specified torque. Refit the auxiliary drivebelt idler pulley to the engine bracket and tighten the retaining bolt to the specified torque.

20 Refit the upper timing belt cover and tighten the retaining bolts to the specified torque. Clip the wiring harness back into position.

21 Place the right-hand engine mounting assembly in position and refit the two bolts and the nut securing the mounting to the body. Tighten the bolts/nut to the specified torque.

TOOL TiP

To make a sprocket holding tool, obtain two lengths of steel strip about 6 mm thick by about 30 mm wide or similar, one 600 mm long, the other 200 mm long (all dimensions are approximate). Bolt the two strips together to form a forked end, leaving the bolt slack so that the shorter strip can pivot freely. At the other end of each 'prong' of the fork, drill a suitable hole and fit a nut and bolt to allow the tool to engage with the spokes in the sprocket.

Align the mounting in its original position, then tighten the three mounting bracket bolts to the specified torque. Remove the jack from under the engine.

22 Refit the air cleaner assembly and air intake duct as described in Chapter 4B.

23 Place the auxiliary drivebelt tensioner assembly in position ensuring that the locating peg on the tensioner mounting surface engages correctly with the corresponding hole in the mounting bracket. Tighten the tensioner central mounting bolt to the specified torque.

24 Refit the crankshaft pulley/vibration damper as described in Section 6, then refit the auxiliary drivebelt as described in Chapter 1B.

25 Refit the plastic cover to the top of the engine and tighten the retaining bolts.

26 Refit the roadwheel and engine undertray, then lower the car to the ground and tighten the wheel bolts to the specified torque.

8 Timing belt sprockets, tensioner and idler pulley – removal and refitting

Note: *Certain special tools will be required for the removal and refitting of the sprockets. Read through the entire procedure to familiarise yourself with the work involved, then either obtain the manufacturer's special tools, or use the alternatives described.*

Camshaft sprocket

Note: *A new sprocket retaining bolt will be required for refitting.*

Removal

1 Remove the timing belt as described in Section 7.

2 It will now be necessary to hold the camshaft sprocket to enable the retaining bolt to be removed. Vauxhall/Opel special tools EN-46787 and KM-956-1 are available for this purpose, however, a home-made tool can easily be fabricated (see Tool Tip).

3 Engage the tool with the holes in the camshaft sprocket, taking care not to damage the camshaft sensor located behind the sprocket

4 Unscrew the retaining bolt and remove the sprocket from the end of the camshaft.

8.12a Remove the bolt and washer . . .

8.12b . . . and slide the sprocket off the end of the crankshaft

8.18 Engage the holding tool with the holes in the fuel pump sprocket and undo the retaining nut

Refitting

5 Prior to refitting check the oil seal for signs of damage or leakage. If necessary, renew as described in Section 9.

6 Refit the sprocket to the camshaft end, aligning its cut-out with the locating peg, and fit the new retaining bolt.

7 Retain the sprocket using the holding tool, and tighten the retaining bolt to the specified torque.

8 Refit the timing belt as described in Section 7.

Crankshaft sprocket

Note 1: *The crankshaft sprocket retaining bolt is extremely tight. Ensure that the holding tool used to prevent rotation as the bolt is slackened is of sturdy construction and securely attached.*

Note 2: *A new sprocket retaining bolt will be required for refitting.*

Removal

9 Remove the timing belt as described in Section 7.

10 It will now be necessary to hold the crankshaft sprocket to enable the retaining bolt to be removed. Vauxhall special tools EN-47630 and KM-956-1 are available for this purpose, however, a home-made tool similar to that described in paragraph 2, can easily be fabricated.

11 Using the crankshaft pulley retaining bolts, securely attach the tool to the crankshaft sprocket. With the help of an assistant, hold

the sprocket stationary and unscrew the retaining bolt. **Note:** *The sprocket retaining bolt has a **left-hand thread** and is unscrewed by turning it clockwise.*

12 Remove the bolt and washer and slide the sprocket off the end of the crankshaft **(see illustrations)**. Note that a new bolt will be required for refitting.

Refitting

13 Align the sprocket location key with the crankshaft groove and slide the sprocket into position. Fit the new retaining bolt and washer.

14 Hold the sprocket stationary using the holding tool and tighten the retaining bolt to the specified torque. Remove the holding tool.

15 Refit the timing belt as described in Section 7.

High-pressure fuel pump sprocket

Note: *A new sprocket retaining nut will be required for refitting.*

Removal

16 Remove the timing belt as described in Section 7.

17 It will now be necessary to hold the fuel pump sprocket to enable the retaining nut to be removed. Vauxhall special tools KM-6347 and KM-956-1 are available for this purpose, however, a home-made tool similar to that described in paragraph 2, can easily be fabricated.

18 Engage the tool with the holes in the fuel pump sprocket and undo the sprocket retaining nut **(see illustration)**.

19 Attach a suitable puller to the threaded holes in the fuel pump sprocket using bolts and washers similar to the arrangement shown **(see illustration)**.

20 Tighten the puller centre bolt to release the sprocket from the taper on the pump shaft. Once the taper releases, remove the puller and withdraw the sprocket. Collect the Woodruff key from the pump shaft **(see illustrations)**.

Refitting

21 Clean the fuel pump shaft and the sprocket hub ensuring that all traces of oil or grease are removed.

22 Refit the Woodruff key to the pump shaft, then locate the sprocket in position. Fit the new retaining nut.

23 Hold the sprocket stationary using the holding tool and tighten the retaining nut to the specified torque. Remove the holding tool.

24 Refit the timing belt as described in Section 7.

Tensioner assembly

Removal

25 Remove the timing belt as described in Section 7.

26 Slacken and remove the retaining bolt and remove the tensioner assembly from the engine **(see illustration)**.

8.19 Use a suitable puller to release the fuel pump sprocket taper

8.20a Once the taper releases, withdraw the sprocket . . .

8.20b . . . and collect the Woodruff key from the pump shaft

Refitting

27 Fit the tensioner to the engine, making sure that the slot on the tensioner backplate is correctly located over the peg on the engine bracket **(see illustration)**.

28 Clean the threads of the retaining bolt and apply thread locking compound to the bolt threads. Screw in the retaining bolt, set the tensioner in the retracted position and tighten the retaining bolt.

29 Refit the timing belt as described in Section 7.

Idler pulley

Removal

30 Remove the timing belt as described in Section 7.

31 Slacken and remove the retaining bolt and remove the idler pulley from the engine.

Refitting

32 Refit the idler pulley and tighten the retaining bolt to the specified torque.

33 Refit the timing belt as described in Section 7.

9 Camshaft oil seal – renewal

1 Remove the camshaft sprocket as described in Section 8.

2 Carefully punch or drill a small hole in the oil seal. Screw in a self-tapping screw, and pull on the screw with pliers to extract the seal.

3 Clean the seal housing, and polish off any burrs or raised edges which may have caused the seal to fail in the first place.

4 Lubricate the lips of the new seal with clean engine oil, and press it into position using a suitable tubular drift (such as a socket) which bears only on the hard outer edge of the seal. Take care not to damage the seal lips during fitting; note that the seal lips should face inwards.

5 Refit the camshaft sprocket as described in Section 8.

10 Valve clearances – checking and adjustment

Note: *Vauxhall/Opel special tools EN-46797 and EN-46799 (or suitable equivalents) will be required if adjustment is necessary.*

Checking

1 The importance of having the valve clearances correctly adjusted cannot be overstressed, as they vitally affect the performance of the engine. The engine must be cold for the check to be accurate. The clearances are checked as follows.

2 Apply the handbrake, then jack up the front of the vehicle and support it on axle stands (see *Jacking and vehicle support*). Remove

8.26 Slacken and remove the retaining bolt and remove the timing belt tensioner assembly

the right-hand front roadwheel, then undo the ten bolts and remove the engine undertray for access to the crankshaft pulley.

3 Remove the camshaft cover as described in Section 5.

4 Using a socket and extension on the crankshaft pulley bolt, rotate the crankshaft in the normal direction of rotation (clockwise when viewed from the right-hand end of the engine) until camshaft lobes 1 and 6 are pointing upward **(see illustration)**.

5 On a piece of paper, draw the outline of the engine with the cylinders numbered from the timing belt end. Show the position of each valve, together with the specified valve clearance. Note that the clearance for both the inlet and exhaust valves is the same.

6 With the cam lobes positioned as described in paragraph 4, using feeler blades, measure the clearance between the base of camshaft lobes 1 and 6 and the adjustment shim located on the top of the camshaft follower **(see illustration)**. Record the clearances on the paper.

7 Rotate the crankshaft until camshaft lobes 5 and 8 are pointing upward. Measure the clearance between the base of the camshaft lobes and the shims on their followers and record the clearances on the paper.

8 Rotate the crankshaft until camshaft lobes 4 and 7 are pointing upward. Measure the clearance between the base of the camshaft lobes and the shims on their followers and record the clearances on the paper.

9 Rotate the crankshaft until camshaft lobes 2 and 3 are pointing upward. Measure the clearance between the base of the camshaft

10.6 Valve clearance measurement

8.27 The slot on the tensioner backplate must locate over the peg (arrowed) on the engine bracket

lobes and the shims on their followers and record the clearances on the paper.

10 If all the clearances are correct, refit the camshaft cover as described in Section 5. Refit the roadwheel and engine undertray, then lower the car to the ground and tighten the wheel bolts to the specified torque.

11 If any clearance measured is not correct, adjustment must be carried out as described in the following paragraphs.

Adjustment

12 Rotate the crankshaft clockwise until camshaft lobes 1 and 6 are once again pointing upward. With the camshaft in this position, valve No 1 and valve No 6 can be adjusted as follows.

13 Rotate the follower until the groove on its upper edge is facing towards the front of the engine **(see illustration)**.

14 Insert Vauxhall/Opel special tool EN-46797

10.4 Camshaft positioned with No 1 and No 6 cam lobes (arrowed) pointing upward

10.13 Rotate the follower until the groove (arrowed) is facing towards the front of the engine

10.16 The thickness of each shim should be stamped on one of its surfaces

between the base of the camshaft lobe and the shim and lever downward to open the valve. Now insert Vauxhall/Opel special tool EN-46799 between the edge of the follower and the base of the camshaft to hold the valve open. Take care when doing this as it is possible for the valve to contact the piston. If any resistance is felt as the valve is opened, remove the tool and rotate the crankshaft slightly to move the piston down its bore.

15 Using a small screwdriver inserted in the groove on the edge of the follower, lift up the shim, then slide it out from between the follower and camshaft.

16 Clean the shim, and measure its thickness with a micrometer. The shims carry thickness markings, but wear may have reduced the original thickness, so be sure to double-check **(see illustration)**.

17 Add the measured clearance of the valve to the thickness of the original shim then subtract the specified valve clearance from this figure. This will give you the thickness of the shim required. For example:

Measured valve clearance	0.45 mm
Plus thickness of the original shim	2.70 mm
Equals	3.15 mm
Minus clearance required	0.35 mm
Thickness of shim required	2.80 mm

18 Obtain the correct thickness of shim required and lubricate it with clean engine oil. With the valve still held open with the special tool, slide the shim into position, with the thickness number downwards, ensuring it is correctly located.

19 Using the first special tool, lever down on the shim and remove the second special tool.

Allow the valve to close and remove the first special tool. Check that the valve clearance is within limits.

 It may be possible to correct the clearances by moving the shims around between the valves, but don't rotate the crankshaft with any shims missing. Keep a note of all the shim thicknesses to assist valve clearance adjustment when they need to be done again.

20 Rotate the crankshaft clockwise until camshaft lobes 5 and 8 are once again pointing upward. Adjust No 5 and No 8 valve clearances as described in paragraphs 13 to 19.

21 Rotate the crankshaft clockwise until camshaft lobes 4 and 7 are once again pointing upward. Adjust No 4 and No 7 valve clearances as described in paragraphs 13 to 19.

22 Rotate the crankshaft clockwise until camshaft lobes 2 and 3 are once again pointing upward. Adjust No 2 and No 3 valve clearances as described in paragraphs 13 to 19.

23 On completion, refit the camshaft cover as described in Section 5. Refit the roadwheel and engine undertray, then lower the car to the ground and tighten the wheel bolts to the specified torque.

11 Camshaft and followers – removal, inspection and refitting

Removal

1 Remove the timing belt as described in Section 7.

2 Remove the camshaft sprocket as described in Section 8.

3 Remove the camshaft cover as described in Section 5.

4 Remove the braking system vacuum pump as described in Chapter 9.

5 Check for identification markings on the camshaft bearing caps. If no markings can be seen, make suitable identification marks on the caps, to indicate their number and which way round they are fitted.

6 Working in a spiral pattern from the outside inwards, slacken the twelve camshaft bearing cap retaining bolts by half a turn at a time, to relieve the pressure of the valve springs on the bearing caps gradually and evenly **(see illustration)**. Once the valve spring pressure has been relieved, the bolts can be fully unscrewed and removed.

Caution: If the bearing cap bolts are carelessly slackened, the bearing caps might break. If any bearing cap breaks then the complete cylinder head assembly must be renewed; the bearing caps are matched to the head and are not available separately.

7 Carefully release the oil supply pipe from its location in the cylinder head, then lift the pipe off the bearing caps **(see illustration)**.

8 Remove the bearing caps, then lift the camshaft out of the cylinder head and slide off the oil seal.

9 Obtain eight small, clean plastic containers, and label them for identification. Alternatively, divide a larger container into compartments. Lift the followers and shims out from the top of the cylinder head and store each one in its respective fitted position. Make sure the followers and shims are not mixed up, to ensure the valve clearances remain correct on refitting.

Inspection

10 Examine the camshaft bearing surfaces and cam lobes for signs of wear ridges and scoring. Renew the camshaft if any of these conditions are apparent. Examine the condition of the bearing surfaces both on the camshaft journals and in the cylinder head. If the head bearing surfaces are worn excessively, the cylinder head will need to be renewed.

11 Check the camshaft followers and their bores in the cylinder head for signs of wear or damage. If any follower is thought to be faulty or is visibly worn it should be renewed.

Refitting

12 Commence refitting by turning the crankshaft anti-clockwise by 90°. This will position all the pistons half way down their bores, and prevent any chance of the valves touching the piston crowns as the camshaft is being fitted.

13 Lubricate the camshaft followers with clean engine oil and carefully insert each one (together with its adjusting shim) into its original location in the cylinder head.

14 Lubricate the camshaft follower shims, and the bearing journals with clean engine oil, then lay the camshaft in position.

15 Apply a smear of sealant to the mating surfaces of both the No 1 and No 5 camshaft bearing caps. Using the marks made on removal as a guide, refit the camshaft bearing caps in their original locations on the cylinder head.

16 Carefully engage the oil supply pipe into its location in the cylinder head, then place the pipe in position on the bearing caps.

17 Refit the bearing cap retaining bolts and

11.6 Camshaft bearing cap retaining bolts (arrowed)

11.7 Carefully release the oil pipe (arrowed) from its location in the cylinder head

tighten them by hand until they just contact the bearing caps.

18 Working in a spiral pattern from the centre outwards, tighten the bolts by half a turn at a time to gradually impose the pressure of the valve springs on the bearing caps. Repeat this sequence until all bearing caps are in contact with the cylinder head then go around and tighten the camshaft bearing cap bolts to the specified torque.

Caution: If the bearing cap bolts are carelessly tightened, the bearing caps might break. If any bearing cap breaks then the complete cylinder head assembly must be renewed; the bearing caps are matched to the head and are not available separately.

19 Fit a new camshaft oil seal as described in Section 9.

20 Refit the braking system vacuum pump as described in Chapter 9.

21 Refit the camshaft cover as described in Section 5.

22 Refit the camshaft sprocket as described in Section 8. Rotate the camshaft until the mark on the camshaft sprocket is aligned with the pointer on the camshaft cover (see Section 3).

23 Turn the crankshaft clockwise by 90° to bring No 1 and 4 pistons to approximately the TDC position.

24 Refit the timing belt as described in Section 7.

25 If any new components have been fitted, check, and if necessary adjust, the valve clearances as described in Section 10.

---

12 Cylinder head – removal and refitting

Note: *New cylinder head bolts will be required on refitting.*

Removal

1 Disconnect the battery negative terminal (refer to *Disconnecting the battery* in the Reference Chapter).

2 Drain the cooling system as described in Chapter 1B.

3 Remove the timing belt as described in Section 7.

4 Disconnect the wiring harness connectors from the following components with reference to the Chapters indicated:

a) *Coolant temperature sensor (Chapter 3).*
b) *Fuel pressure sensor (Chapter 4B).*
c) *Fuel pressure regulating valve (Chapter 4B).*
d) *Throttle valve module (Chapter 4B).*
e) *Fuel injectors (Chapter 4B).*
f) *Air conditioning compressor (Chapter 3).*
g) *EGR valve (Chapter 4C).*
h) *Inlet manifold pressure sensor (Chapter 4B).*
i) *High-pressure fuel pump (Chapter 4B).*
j) *Camshaft sensor (Chapter 4B).*

5 Undo the wiring harness support bracket bolts, release the retaining clips and move the

harness to one side **(see illustration)**.

6 Remove the inlet and exhaust manifolds as described in Chapter 4B.

7 Remove the camshaft cover as described in Section 5.

8 Remove the braking system vacuum pump as described in Chapter 9.

9 Make a final check to ensure that all relevant hoses, pipes and wires have been disconnected.

10 Working in the **reverse** of the tightening sequence **(see illustration 12.28)**, progressively slacken the cylinder head bolts by half a turn at a time, until all bolts can be unscrewed by hand. Note that an M14 RIBE socket bit will be required to unscrew the bolts. Remove the cylinder head bolts and recover the washers.

11 Engage the help of an assistant and lift the cylinder head from the cylinder block. Take care as it is a bulky and heavy assembly.

Caution: Do not lay the head on its lower mating surface; support the head on wooden blocks, ensuring each block only contacts the head mating surface.

12 Remove the gasket and keep it for identification purposes (see paragraph 19).

13 If the cylinder head is to be dismantled for overhaul, then refer to Part F of this Chapter.

Preparation for refitting

14 The mating faces of the cylinder head and cylinder block/crankcase must be perfectly clean before refitting the head. Use a hard plastic or wood scraper to remove all traces of gasket and carbon; also clean the piston crowns. Take particular care, as the surfaces are damaged easily. Also, make sure that the carbon is not allowed to enter the oil and water passages – this is particularly important for the lubrication system, as carbon could block the oil supply to any of the engine's components. Using adhesive tape and paper, seal the water, oil and bolt holes in the cylinder block/crankcase. To prevent carbon entering the gap between the pistons and bores, smear a little grease in the gap. After cleaning each piston, use a small brush to remove all traces of grease and carbon from the gap, then wipe away the remainder with a clean rag. Clean all the pistons in the same way.

15 Check the mating surfaces of the cylinder block/crankcase and the cylinder head for nicks, deep scratches and other damage. If slight, they may be removed carefully with a file, but if excessive, machining may be the only alternative to renewal.

16 Ensure that the cylinder head bolt holes in the crankcase are clean and free of oil. Syringe or soak up any oil left in the bolt holes. This is most important in order that the correct bolt tightening torque can be applied and to prevent the possibility of the block being cracked by hydraulic pressure when the bolts are tightened.

17 The cylinder head bolts must be discarded and renewed, regardless of their apparent condition.

18 If warpage of the cylinder head gasket

12.5 Undo the support bracket bolts (arrowed), release the retaining clips and move the wiring harness to one side

surface is suspected, use a straight-edge to check it for distortion. Refer to Part F of this Chapter if necessary.

19 On this engine, the cylinder head-to-piston clearance is controlled by fitting different thickness head gaskets. The gasket thickness can be determined by looking at the holes stamped on the edge of the gasket **(see illustration)**.

Number of holes	Gasket thickness
No holes	0.77 to 0.87 mm
One hole	0.87 to 0.97 mm
Two holes	0.97 to 1.07 mm

The correct thickness of gasket required is selected by measuring the piston protrusions as follows.

20 Mount a dial test indicator securely on the block so that its pointer can be easily pivoted between the piston crown and block mating surface. Turn the crankshaft to bring No 1 piston roughly to the TDC position. Move the dial test indicator probe over and in contact with No 1 piston. Turn the crankshaft back-and-forth slightly until the highest reading is shown on the gauge, indicating that the piston is at TDC.

21 Zero the dial test indicator on the gasket surface of the cylinder block then carefully move the indicator over No 1 piston. Measure its protrusion at the highest point between the valve cut-outs, and then again at its highest point between the valve cut-outs at 90° to the first measurement **(see illustration)**. Repeat this procedure with No 4 piston.

22 Rotate the crankshaft half a turn (180°) to bring No 2 and 3 pistons to TDC. Ensure

12.19 Cylinder head gasket thickness identification hole (arrowed)

12.21 Using a dial test indicator to measure piston protrusion

12.24 Place the new gasket in position with the words ALTO/TOP uppermost

13 Sump – removal and refitting

the crankshaft is accurately positioned then measure the protrusions of No 2 and 3 pistons at the specified points. Once all pistons have been measured, rotate the crankshaft to position all the pistons at their mid-stroke.

23 Select the correct thickness of head gasket required by determining the largest amount of piston protrusion, and using the following table.

Piston protrusion measurement (mm)	Gasket thickness required (mm)
0.020 to 0.100	0.77 to 0.87 (no holes)
0.101 to 0.200	0.87 to 0.97 (one hole)
0.201 to 0.295	0.97 to 1.07 (two holes)

Refitting

24 Wipe clean the mating surfaces of the cylinder head and cylinder block/crankcase. Place the new gasket in position with the words ALTO/TOP uppermost **(see illustration)**.

25 If not already done, rotate the crankshaft to position all the pistons at their mid-stroke.

26 With the aid of an assistant, carefully refit the cylinder head assembly to the block, aligning it with the locating dowels.

27 Apply a thin film of engine oil to the bolt threads and the underside of the bolt heads. Carefully enter each new cylinder head bolt into its relevant hole (*do not drop them in*). Screw all bolts in, by hand only, until finger-tight.

28 Working progressively in the sequence shown, tighten the cylinder head bolts to their Stage 1 torque setting, using a torque wrench and suitable socket **(see illustration)**. Working again in the same sequence, go around and tighten all bolts through the specified Stage 2 torque setting.

29 Once all bolts have been tightened to the Stage 2 torque, working again in the same sequence, go around and tighten all bolts through the specified Stage 3 angle, then through the specified Stage 4 angle, and finally through the specified Stage 5 angle using an angle-measuring gauge.

30 Refit the braking system vacuum pump as described in Chapter 9.

31 Refit the camshaft cover as described in Section 5.

32 Refit the inlet and exhaust manifolds as described in Chapter 4B.

33 Reconnect the wiring harness connectors to the components listed in paragraph 4, then refit the wiring harness support bracket bolts, and secure the harness with the retaining clips.

34 Refit the timing belt as described in Section 7.

35 On completion, reconnect the battery negative terminal, then refill the cooling system as described in Chapter 1B.

Removal

1 Disconnect the battery negative terminal (refer to *Disconnecting the battery* in the Reference Chapter).

2 Apply the handbrake, then jack up the front of the vehicle and support it on axle stands (see *Jacking and vehicle support*). Remove the right-hand front roadwheel, then undo the ten bolts and remove the engine undertray.

3 Remove the right-hand driveshaft and the intermediate shaft as described in Chapter 8.

4 Undo the three bolts securing the intermediate shaft bearing housing support bracket to the cylinder block and remove the support bracket **(see illustration)**.

5 Remove the exhaust system as described in Chapter 4B.

6 Undo the three bolts and remove the support bracket from the catalytic converter and sump.

7 Remove the crankshaft pulley/vibration damper as described in Section 6.

8 Disconnect the wiring connector from the air conditioning compressor. Undo the three bolts securing the air conditioning compressor to the mounting bracket and suitably support the compressor on the front subframe.

9 Undo the four bolts securing the compressor mounting bracket to the cylinder block and sump **(see illustration)**. Unclip the wiring harness and remove the mounting bracket.

10 Drain the engine oil as described in Chapter 1B. When the oil has completely drained, refit the drain plug with new sealing washer, and tighten to the specified torque.

11 Undo the upper bolt securing the oil dipstick guide tube to the coolant pipe. Undo the lower bolt securing the guide tube to the sump flange, then unclip the wiring harness

12.28 Cylinder head bolt tightening sequence

13.4 intermediate shaft bearing housing support bracket retaining bolts (arrowed)

13.9 Air conditioning compressor mounting bracket retaining bolts (arrowed)

13.17 Removing the oil baffle plate from inside the sump

13.18 Renew the pick-up/strainer sealing ring prior to refitting

and withdraw the tube from the sump flange sealing grommet.

12 Disconnect the wiring connector from the oil level sensor, then release the retaining clip and disconnect the oil return hose.

13 Undo the two bolts securing the sump flange to the transmission bellhousing.

14 Using a socket and extension on the crankshaft pulley bolt, rotate the crankshaft in the normal direction of rotation (clockwise when viewed from the right-hand end of the engine) until the opening in the flywheel is positioned to allow access to one of the rear sump retaining bolts. Undo and remove the bolt, then rotate the crankshaft again until the flywheel allow access to the second rear retaining bolt. Undo and remove the bolt.

15 Progressively slacken and remove the remaining twelve bolts securing the sump to the base of the cylinder block and oil pump housing. Using a wide-bladed scraper or similar tool inserted between the sump and cylinder block, carefully break the joint to release the sump.

16 Manoeuvre the sump out from under the car. Clearance is extremely limited between the sump and subframe, and it may be necessary to release the oil pump pick-up/strainer, by undoing its two retaining bolts, to enable the sump to be removed.

17 If required, undo the retaining bolts and remove the oil baffle plate from inside the sump **(see illustration)**.

18 While the sump is removed, take the opportunity to check the oil pump pick-up/strainer for signs of clogging or splitting. If not already done, unbolt the oil pump pick-up/strainer and remove it from the engine along with its sealing ring. The strainer can then be cleaned easily in solvent or renewed. Renew the pick-up/strainer sealing ring prior to refitting **(see illustration)**.

Refitting

19 Thoroughly clean the sump and remove all traces of silicone sealer and oil from the mating surfaces of the sump and cylinder block. If removed, refit the oil baffle plate and tighten its retaining bolts securely.

20 If clearance allows, refit the oil pump pick-up/strainer using a new sealing ring, and tighten its two retaining bolts securely.

If it was necessary to unbolt the pick-up/strainer to allow the sump to be removed, place the unit in position and loosely screw in the bolt securing it to the main bearing cap. It must still be possible for the forward end of the pipe to be moved to the rear as the sump is refitted.

21 Apply a continuous bead of silicone sealing compound (available from your Vauxhall/Opel dealer) at approximately 1.0 mm from the inner edge of the sump **(see illustration)**. The bead of sealant should be between 2.0 and 2.5 mm in diameter.

22 Locate the sump over the pick-up/strainer then, where applicable, fit the forward end of the pick-up/strainer to the oil pump housing and fit the retaining bolt. Tighten both retaining bolts securely.

23 Engage the sump with the cylinder block and loosely refit all the retaining bolts.

24 Working out from the centre in a diagonal sequence, progressively tighten the bolts securing the sump to the cylinder block and oil pump housing. Tighten all the bolts to their specified torque setting.

25 Tighten the two bolts securing the sump flange to the transmission bellhousing to their specified torque settings.

26 Reconnect the wiring connector to the oil level sensor, then refit the oil return hose and secure with the retaining clip.

27 Refit the oil dipstick guide tube and secure with the two bolts tightened securely.

28 Locate the air conditioning compressor mounting bracket in position and refit the four retaining bolts. Tighten the bolts to the

13.21 Apply a continuous bead of silicone sealing compound to the sump flange

specified torque. Clip the wiring harness back into position on the bracket.

29 Position the air conditioning compressor on the mounting bracket. Fit and tighten the three retaining bolts to the specified torque (see Chapter 3), then reconnect the compressor wiring connector.

30 Refit the crankshaft pulley/vibration damper as described in Section 6.

31 Refit the catalytic converter support bracket and securely tighten the three bolts.

32 Refit the exhaust system as described in Chapter 4B.

33 Position the intermediate shaft bearing housing support bracket on the cylinder block and secure with the three retaining bolts tightened to the specified torque.

34 Refit the intermediate shaft and right-hand driveshaft as described in Chapter 8.

35 Refit the roadwheel and engine undertray, then lower the car to the ground and tighten the wheel bolts to the specified torque.

36 Fill the engine with fresh engine oil as described in Chapter 1B.

37 On completion, reconnect the battery negative terminal.

14 Oil pump – removal, overhaul and refitting

Removal

1 Remove the timing belt as described in Section 7.

2 Remove the crankshaft sprocket as described In Section 8.

3 Remove the sump and oil pump pick-up/strainer as described in Section 13.

4 Slacken and remove the seven retaining bolts then slide the oil pump housing assembly off of the end of the crankshaft **(see illustration)**. Remove the housing gasket and discard it.

Overhaul

5 Undo the retaining screws and lift off the pump cover from the rear of the housing **(see illustration)**.

6 Check the inner and outer rotors for identification dots indicating which way round they are fitted **(see illustration)**. If no marks

14.4 Oil pump housing retaining bolts (arrowed)

14.5 Undo the retaining screws and lift off the oil pump cover

14.6 Oil pump inner and outer rotor identification dots (arrowed)

14.8a Unscrew the oil pressure relief valve bolt . . .

14.8b . . . and withdraw the spring . . .

14.8c . . . and plunger

are visible, use a suitable marker pen to mark the surface of both the pump inner and outer rotors.

7 Lift out the inner and outer rotors from the pump housing.

8 Unscrew the oil pressure relief valve bolt from the base of the housing and withdraw the spring and plunger, noting which way around the plunger is fitted **(see illustrations)**. Remove the sealing washer from the valve bolt.

9 Clean the components, and carefully examine the rotors, pump body and relief valve plunger for any signs of scoring or wear. If any damage or wear is noticed, it will be necessary to renew the complete pump assembly.

10 If the pump is satisfactory, reassemble the components in the reverse order of removal, noting the following.

a) *Ensure both rotors are fitted the correct way around.*
b) *Fit a new sealing ring to the pressure relief valve bolt and securely tighten the bolt.*
c) *Apply a little locking compound to the threads, and securely tighten the pump cover screws.*
d) *On completion prime the oil pump by filling it with clean engine oil whilst rotating the inner rotor (see illustration).*

Refitting

11 Prior to refitting, carefully lever out the crankshaft oil seal using a flat-bladed screwdriver. Fit the new oil seal, ensuring its sealing lip is facing inwards, and press it squarely into the housing using a tubular drift which bears only on the hard outer edge of the seal. Press the seal into position so that it

is flush with the housing and lubricate the oil seal lip with clean engine oil.

12 Ensure the mating surfaces of the oil pump and cylinder block are clean and dry.

13 Fit a new gasket to the oil pump housing and bend down the tabs on the edge of the gasket to retain it on the pump housing **(see illustration)**.

14 Locate the pump housing over the end of the crankshaft and into position on the cylinder block.

15 Refit the pump housing retaining bolts and tighten them to the specified torque.

16 Refit the oil pump pick-up/strainer and sump as described in Section 13.

17 Refit the crankshaft sprocket as described in Section 8.

18 Refit the timing belt as described in Section 7.

19 On completion, fit a new oil filter and fill the engine with clean oil as described in Chapter 1B.

15 Oil filter housing – removal and refitting

Removal

1 The oil filter housing with integral oil cooler is located at the rear of the cylinder block, above the right-hand driveshaft.

2 Disconnect the battery negative terminal (refer to *Disconnecting the battery* in the Reference Chapter).

3 Apply the handbrake, then jack up the front

14.10 Prime the oil pump by filling it with clean engine oil whilst rotating the inner rotor

14.13 Bend down the tabs on the edge of the gasket to retain it on the oil pump housing

15.10 Oil filter housing retaining bolts (arrowed)

15.11a Fit a new sealing ring to the oil filter housing supply channel . . .

of the vehicle and support it on axle stands (see *Jacking and vehicle support*). Remove the right-hand front roadwheel, then undo the ten bolts and remove the engine undertray.

4 Drain the cooling system as described in Chapter 1B.

5 Remove the engine oil filter element as described in Chapter 1B.

6 Remove the right-hand driveshaft and the intermediate shaft as described in Chapter 8.

7 Undo the three bolts securing the intermediate shaft bearing housing support bracket to the cylinder block and remove the support bracket **(see illustration 13.4)**.

8 Disconnect the wiring connector from the oil pressure switch.

9 Release the retaining clips and disconnect the two coolant hoses from the oil cooler on the oil filter housing.

10 Undo the three retaining bolts and remove the oil filter housing from the cylinder block **(see illustration)**. Recover the two rubber seals from the rear of the housing. Note that new seals will be required for refitting.

Refitting

11 Thoroughly clean the oil filter housing, then fit the two new sealing rings **(see illustrations)**.

12 Position the oil filter housing on the cylinder block and refit the retaining bolts. Tighten the bolts to the specified torque.

13 Refit the two coolant hoses and secure with their retaining clips. Reconnect the oil pressure switch wiring connector.

14 Position the intermediate shaft bearing housing support bracket on the cylinder block and secure with the three retaining bolts tightened to the specified torque.

15 Refit the intermediate shaft and right-hand driveshaft as described in Chapter 8.

16 Fit a new oil filter element as described in Chapter 1B.

17 Refit the roadwheel and engine undertray, then lower the car to the ground and tighten the wheel bolts to the specified torque.

18 Refill the cooling system as described in Chapter 1B.

19 Check, and if necessary, top-up the engine oil as described in *Weekly checks*.

20 On completion, reconnect the battery negative terminal.

16 Crankshaft oil seals – renewal

Right-hand (timing belt end)

1 Remove the crankshaft sprocket as described in Section 8.

2 Carefully punch or drill a small hole in the oil seal. Screw in a self-tapping screw and pull on the screw with pliers to extract the seal **(see illustration)**.

3 Clean the seal housing and polish off any burrs or raised edges which may have caused the seal to fail in the first place.

4 Lubricate the lips of the new seal with clean engine oil and ease it into position on the end of the shaft. Press the seal squarely into position until it is flush with the housing. If necessary, a suitable tubular drift which bears only on the hard outer edge of the seal can be used to tap the seal into position **(see illustration)**. Take great care not to damage

15.11b . . . and to the return channel

the seal lips during fitting and ensure that the seal lips face inwards.

5 Wash off any traces of oil, then refit the crankshaft sprocket as described in Section 8.

Left-hand (flywheel end)

6 Remove the flywheel as described in Section 17.

7 Remove the sump as described in Section 13.

8 Undo the five bolts and remove the oil seal housing. Note that the oil seal and the housing are a single assembly.

9 Clean the crankshaft and polish off any

16.2 Screw in a self-tapping screw and pull on the screw with pliers to extract the oil seal

16.4 Using a socket as a tubular drift to fit the new oil seal

16.10 Fitting the new oil seal housing, with integral oil seal over the crankshaft

burrs or raised edges which may have caused the seal to fail in the first place.

10 Position the new oil seal housing, complete with seal over the crankshaft and into position on the cylinder block **(see illustration)**. Note that the new oil seal housing is supplied with a protector sleeve over the oil seal. Leave the sleeve in position as the housing is fitted.

11 Refit the five retaining bolts and tighten to the specified torque.

12 Remove the protector sleeve from the housing **(see illustration)**.

13 Refit the sump as described in Section 13.

14 Refit the flywheel as described in Section 17.

17.2 Prevent the flywheel from turning by locking the ring gear teeth

16.12 After fitting, remove the protector sleeve from the housing

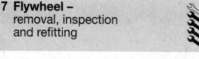

17 Flywheel –
removal, inspection and refitting

Note: *New flywheel retaining bolts will be required on refitting.*

Removal

1 Remove the transmission as described in Chapter 7A, then remove the clutch assembly as described in Chapter 6.

2 Prevent the flywheel from turning by locking the ring gear teeth with a similar arrangement to that shown **(see illustration)**.

3 Slacken and remove the retaining bolts and remove the flywheel **(see illustration)**. Do not drop it, as it is very heavy.

Inspection

4 If there is any doubt about the condition of the flywheel, seek the advice of a Vauxhall/Opel dealer or engine reconditioning specialist. They will be able to advise if it is possible to recondition it or whether renewal is necessary.

Refitting

5 Clean the mating surfaces of the flywheel and crankshaft.

6 Offer up the flywheel and engage it over the

positioning dowel on the crankshaft. Apply a drop of locking compound to the threads of each new flywheel retaining bolt (unless they are precoated) and install the new bolts.

7 Lock the flywheel by the method used on removal then, working in a diagonal sequence, evenly and progressively tighten the retaining bolts to the specified torque.

8 Refit the clutch as described in Chapter 6 then remove the locking tool, and refit the transmission as described in Chapter 7A.

18 Engine/transmission mountings –
inspection and renewal

Inspection

1 If improved access is required, firmly apply the handbrake, then jack up the front of the car and support it securely on axle stands (see *Jacking and vehicle support*).

2 Check the mounting rubber to see if it is cracked, hardened or separated from the metal at any point; renew the mounting if any such damage or deterioration is evident.

3 Check that all the mounting's fasteners are securely tightened; use a torque wrench to check if possible.

4 Using a large screwdriver or a pry bar, check for wear in the mounting by carefully levering against it to check for free play; where this is not possible, enlist the aid of an assistant to move the engine/transmission unit back-and-forth, or from side-to-side, while you watch the mounting. While some free play is to be expected even from new components, excessive wear should be obvious. If excessive free play is found, check first that the fasteners are correctly secured, then renew any worn components as described below.

Renewal

Note: *Before slackening any of the engine mounting bolts/nuts, the relative positions of the mountings to their various brackets should*

17.3 Flywheel retaining bolts (arrowed)

18.6 Front mounting/torque link through-bolt (A) and mounting bracket-to-transmission bolts (B)

18.14 Rear mounting/torque link through-bolt (arrowed)

18.15 Rear mounting/torque link bracket-to-subframe mounting bolt nuts (arrowed)

18.22a Right-hand mounting bracket-to-engine bracket bolts (arrowed) . . .

18.22b . . . and mounting-to-body retaining bolts (A) and nut (B)

18.28 Left-hand mounting bracket-to-transmission bracket retaining bolts (arrowed)

18.29 Left-hand mounting-to-body retaining bolts (arrowed) – shown with engine/transmission removed

be marked to ensure correct alignment upon refitting.

Front mounting/torque link

5 Apply the handbrake, then jack up the front of the vehicle and support it on axle stands (see *Jacking and vehicle support*).
6 Slacken and remove the nut securing the mounting to the subframe bracket. Withdraw the through-bolt (see illustration).
7 Undo the bolts securing the mounting bracket to the transmission, then manoeuvre the mounting and bracket out of position.
8 Check all components for signs of wear or damage, and renew as necessary.
9 Locate the mounting in the subframe, refit the through-bolt and nut, then tighten the nut finger tight at this stage.
10 Refit the mounting bracket to the transmission and tighten its bolts to the specified torque.
11 Tighten the through-bolt nut to the specified torque.
12 On completion, lower the vehicle to the ground.

Rear mounting/torque link

13 Apply the handbrake, then jack up the front of the vehicle and support it on axle stands (see *Jacking and vehicle support*).
14 Undo the three bolts securing the mounting bracket to the transmission and

the through-bolt securing the mounting to the bracket (see illustration).
15 Undo the nuts and remove the two bolts securing the mounting to the subframe (see illustration). Manoeuvre the mounting and bracket out from under the car.
16 Refit the bracket to the transmission and tighten the bolts to the specified torque.
17 Locate the new mounting in position. Insert the bolts and tighten the bolt/nuts to the specified torque.
18 On completion, lower the vehicle to the ground.

Right-hand mounting

19 Apply the handbrake, then jack up the front of the vehicle and support it on axle stands (see *Jacking and vehicle support*).
20 Remove the air cleaner as described in Chapter 4B.
21 Place a trolley jack beneath the right-hand end of the engine with a block of wood on the jack head. Raise the jack until it is supporting the weight of the engine.
22 Mark the position of the three bolts securing the mounting bracket to the engine bracket and undo the bolts. Undo the two bolts and one nut securing the mounting to the body and remove the mounting assembly (see illustrations).
23 Place the mounting assembly in position and refit the two bolts and the nut securing

the mounting to the body. Tighten the bolts/nut to the specified torque. Align the mounting in its original position, then tighten the three mounting bracket bolts to the specified torque.
24 Remove the support jack, then refit the air cleaner as described in Chapter 4B.
25 On completion, lower the vehicle to the ground.

Left-hand mounting

26 Remove the battery and battery box as described in Chapter 5A.
27 Place a trolley jack beneath the transmission with a block of wood on the jack head. Raise the jack until it is supporting the weight of the engine/transmission unit.
28 Using a Torx socket, unscrew the three bolts securing the mounting bracket to the transmission bracket (see illustration).
29 Undo the four bolts securing the mounting to the body and the three bolts securing the transmission bracket to the transmission (see illustration). Remove the mounting assembly from the car.
30 Locate the mounting brackets in position then insert the bolts and tighten them to the specified torque.
31 Remove the support jack from under the transmission.
32 Refit the battery box and battery as described in Chapter 5A.

Chapter 2 Part D:
1.9 litre DOHC diesel engine in-car repair procedures

Contents

Degrees of difficulty

Easy, suitable for novice with little experience | **Fairly easy,** suitable for beginner with some experience | **Fairly difficult,** suitable for competent DIY mechanic | **Difficult,** suitable for experienced DIY mechanic | **Very difficult,** suitable for expert DIY or professional

Specifications

General

Engine type. . . . . Four-cylinder, in-line, water-cooled. Double overhead camshaft, belt-driven
Manufacturer's engine code* Z19DTH
Bore . . . . 82.0 mm
Stroke. . . . . 90.4 mm
Capacity . . . . 1910 cc
Compression ratio 17.5:1
Firing order . . . . 1-3-4-2 (No 1 cylinder at timing belt end of engine)
Direction of crankshaft rotation . . . . Clockwise (viewed from timing belt end of engine)
For details of engine code location, see 'Vehicle identification' in the Reference Chapter.

Compression pressures

Maximum difference between any two cylinders. . . . . 1.5 bar

Lubrication system

Minimum oil pressure at 100°C . . . . 1.0 bar at idle speed
Oil pump type. . . . . Rotor-type, driven by crankshaft pulley/vibration damper from crankshaft

Torque wrench settings

	Nm	lbf ft
Air conditioning compressor mounting bracket to cylinder block/sump	50	37
Auxiliary drivebelt idler pulley bolt	50	37
Auxiliary drivebelt tensioner assembly bolts	50	37
Camshaft drivegear bolts	120	89
Camshaft housing bolts	25	18
Camshaft housing closure bolt	16	12
Camshaft sprocket bolt*	120	89
Connecting rod big-end bearing cap bolt:*		
Stage 1	25	18
Stage 2	Angle-tighten a further 60°	
Crankshaft oil seal housing	9	7
Crankshaft pulley/vibration damper bolts	25	18
Crankshaft sprocket bolt*†	360	266
Cylinder head bolts:*		
Stage 1	20	15
Stage 2	65	48
Stage 3	Angle-tighten a further 90°	
Stage 4	Angle-tighten a further 90°	
Stage 5	Angle-tighten a further 90°	
Driveplate bolts*	160	118
Engine mountings:		
Front mounting/torque link bracket to transmission	80	59
Front mounting/torque link to subframe	80	59
Left-hand:		
Mounting-to-body bolts	20	15
Mounting bracket to transmission bracket	55	41
Transmission bracket to transmission	55	41
Rear mounting/torque link bracket to transmission	80	59
Rear mounting/torque link to subframe	60	44
Rear mounting/torque link to transmission bracket	80	59
Right-hand:		
Engine bracket-to-engine bolts	55	41
Lower bolts (M8)	25	18
Upper bolts (M10)	50	37
Mounting-to-body bolts/nut	55	41
Mounting-to-engine bracket bolts	55	41
Engine-to-transmission unit bolts:		
M10 bolts	40	30
M12 bolts	60	44
Flywheel bolts*	160	118
High-pressure fuel pump sprocket nut*	50	37
Intermediate shaft bearing housing support bracket bolts	55	41
Main bearing cap bolts:*		
Stage 1	25	18
Stage 2	Angle-tighten a further 100°	
Oil filler housing bolts	9	7
Oil filter housing to cylinder block	50	37
Oil pump housing to cylinder block	9	7
Oil pump pick-up/strainer bolts	9	7
Roadwheel bolts	110	81
Sump bolts:		
M6 bolts	9	7
M8 bolts	25	18
M10 bolts	40	30
Sump drain plug	20	15
Timing belt idler pulley bolt	50	37
Timing belt tensioner bolt	30	22
Timing belt upper cover bolts:		
M6 bolts	9	7
M8 bolts	25	18

Use new nuts/bolts

† Left-hand thread

1 General information

How to use this Chapter

This Part of Chapter 2 describes the repair procedures which can reasonably be carried out on the engine while it remains in the vehicle. If the engine has been removed from the vehicle and is being dismantled as described in Chapter 2F, any preliminary dismantling procedures can be ignored.

Note that, while it may be possible physically to overhaul items such as the piston/connecting rod assemblies while the engine is in the vehicle, such tasks are not usually carried out as separate operations, and usually require the execution of several additional procedures (not to mention the cleaning of components and of oilways); for this reason, all such tasks are classed as major overhaul procedures, and are described in Chapter 2F.

Chapter 2F describes the removal of the engine/transmission unit from the vehicle, and the full overhaul procedures which can then be carried out.

Engine description

The 1.9 litre DOHC diesel engine is of the sixteen-valve, in-line four-cylinder, double overhead camshaft type, mounted transversely at the front of the car, with the transmission on its left-hand end.

The crankshaft is supported within the cylinder block on five shell-type main bearings. Thrustwashers are fitted to number 3 main bearing, to control crankshaft endfloat.

The connecting rods rotate on horizontally-split bearing shells at their big-ends. The pistons are attached to the connecting rods by gudgeon pins, which are retained by circlips. The aluminium-alloy pistons are fitted with three piston rings – two compression rings and scraper-type oil control ring.

The camshafts are situated in a separate housing bolted to the top of the cylinder head. The exhaust camshaft is driven by the crankshaft via a toothed composite rubber timing belt (which also drives the high-pressure fuel pump and the coolant pump). The exhaust camshaft drives the inlet camshaft via a spur gear. Each cylinder has four valves (two inlet and two exhaust), operated via followers which are supported at their pivot ends by hydraulic self-adjusting tappets. One camshaft operates the inlet valves, and the other operates the exhaust valves.

The inlet and exhaust valves are each closed by a single valve spring, and operate in guides pressed into the cylinder head.

Lubrication is by pressure-feed from a rotor-type oil pump, which is mounted on the right-hand end of the crankshaft. The pump draws oil through a strainer located in the sump, and then forces it through an externally mounted full-flow cartridge-type filter. The oil flows into galleries in the cylinder block/crankcase, from where it is distributed to the crankshaft (main bearings) and camshafts. The big-end bearings are supplied with oil via internal drillings in the crankshaft, while the camshaft bearings also receive a pressurised supply. The camshaft lobes and valves are lubricated by splash, as are all other engine components.

A semi-closed crankcase ventilation system is employed; crankcase fumes are drawn from the oil separator attached to the cylinder block via a hose to the camshaft housing. The fumes are then passed via a hose to the inlet manifold.

Operations with engine in car

The following operations can be carried out without having to remove the engine from the car.
a) Removal and refitting of the cylinder head.
b) Removal and refitting of the timing belt, tensioner, idler pulleys and sprockets.
c) Renewal of the camshaft oil seal.
d) Removal and refitting of the camshaft housing.
e) Removal and refitting of the camshafts and followers.
f) Removal and refitting of the sump.
g) Removal and refitting of the connecting rods and pistons.*
h) Removal and refitting of the oil pump.
i) Removal and refitting of the oil filter housing.
j) Renewal of the crankshaft oil seals.
k) Renewal of the engine mountings.
l) Removal and refitting of the flywheel/driveplate.

* Although the operation marked with an asterisk can be carried out with the engine in the car (after removal of the sump), it is preferable for the engine to be removed, in the interests of cleanliness and improved access. For this reason, the procedure is described in Chapter 2F.

2 Compression and leakdown tests – description and interpretation

Compression test

Note 1: *A compression tester specifically designed for diesel engines must be used for this test.*
Note 2: *The battery must be in a good state of charge, the air filter must be clean, and the engine should be at normal operating temperature.*

1 When engine performance is down, or if misfiring occurs which cannot be attributed to the fuel system, a compression test can provide diagnostic clues as to the engine's condition. If the test is performed regularly, it can give warning of trouble before any other symptoms become apparent.

2 A compression tester specifically intended for diesel engines must be used, because of the higher pressures involved. The tester is connected to an adapter which screws into the glow plug holes. It is unlikely to be worthwhile buying such a tester for occasional use, but it may be possible to borrow or hire one – if not, have the test performed by a Vauxhall/Opel dealer, or suitably-equipped garage. If the necessary equipment is available, proceed as follows.

3 Remove the glow plugs as described in Chapter 5A, then disconnect the wiring connector from the fuel pressure regulating valve on the fuel rail (see Chapter 4B) to prevent the engine from running or fuel from being discharged.

4 Screw the compression tester adapter in to the glow plug hole of No 1 cylinder.

5 With the help of an assistant, crank the engine on the starter motor; after one or two revolutions, the compression pressure should build-up to a maximum figure, and then stabilise. Record the highest reading obtained.

6 Repeat the test on the remaining cylinders, recording the pressure in each.

7 All cylinders should produce very similar pressures; any difference greater than the maximum figure given in the Specifications indicates the existence of a fault. Note that the compression should build-up quickly in a healthy engine; low compression on the first stroke, followed by gradually-increasing pressure on successive strokes, indicates worn piston rings. A low compression reading on the first stroke, which does not build-up during successive strokes, indicates leaking valves or a blown head gasket (a cracked head could also be the cause). **Note:** *The cause of poor compression is less easy to establish on a diesel engine than on a petrol one. The effect of introducing oil into the cylinders ('wet' testing) is not conclusive, because there is a risk that the oil will sit in the recess on the piston crown instead of passing to the rings.*

8 On completion of the test refit the glow plugs as described in Chapter 5A, and reconnect the wiring connector to the fuel pressure regulating valve.

Leakdown test

9 A leakdown test measures the rate at which compressed air fed into the cylinder is lost. It is an alternative to a compression test, and in many ways it is better, since the escaping air provides easy identification of where pressure loss is occurring (piston rings, valves or head gasket).

10 The equipment needed for leakdown testing is unlikely to be available to the home mechanic. If poor compression is suspected, have the test performed by a Vauxhall/Opel dealer, or suitably-equipped garage.

3.0a Vauxhall/Opel special tool EN-46788 (or equivalent) is required to set the TDC position for No 1 piston . . .

3.0b . . . together with Vauxhall/Opel special tool EN-46789 (or equivalent) to set the camshaft position

3.5 Undo the central mounting bolt (arrowed), and remove the auxiliary drivebelt tensioner assembly

3 Top dead centre (TDC) for No 1 piston – locating

Note: *To accurately determine the TDC position for No 1 piston, it will be necessary to use Vauxhall/Opel special tool EN-46788 (or suitable equivalent) to set the crankshaft at the TDC position, together with the camshaft positioning tool, Vauxhall/Opel special tool EN-46789 (or suitable equivalent)* **(see illustrations).**

1 In its travel up and down its cylinder bore, Top Dead Centre (TDC) is the highest point that each piston reaches as the crankshaft rotates. While each piston reaches TDC both at the top of the compression stroke and again at the top of the exhaust stroke, for the purpose of timing the engine, TDC refers to the piston position of No 1 cylinder at the top of its compression stroke.

2 Number 1 piston (and cylinder) is at the right-hand (timing belt) end of the engine, and its TDC position is located as follows. Note that the crankshaft rotates clockwise when viewed from the right-hand side of the car.

3 Disconnect the battery negative terminal (refer to *Disconnecting the battery* in the Reference Chapter), then lift off the plastic cover over the top of the engine.

4 Remove the crankshaft pulley/vibration damper as described in Section 5.

5 Undo the central mounting bolt, and remove the auxiliary drivebelt tensioner assembly from the engine **(see illustration).**

6 Remove the air cleaner assembly and air intake duct as described in Chapter 4B.

7 Place a trolley jack beneath the right-hand end of the engine with a block of wood on the jack head. Raise the jack until it is supporting the weight of the engine.

8 Mark the bolt positions for correct refitting, then undo the three bolts securing the right-hand engine mounting to the engine bracket, and the two bolts and one nut securing the mounting to the body. Remove the mounting **(see illustration).**

9 Release the retaining clip securing the engine breather hose to the breather pipe adjacent to the engine oil dipstick. Undo the two bolts securing the breather pipe to the cylinder head, and disconnect the pipe from the hose **(see illustration).**

10 Undo the bolt and release the engine oil dipstick guide tube from the coolant pipe **(see illustration).**

11 Unscrew the closure bolt from the valve timing checking hole in the camshaft housing **(see illustration).**

12 Screw the camshaft positioning tool (Vauxhall/Opel special tool EN-46789) into the valve timing checking hole.

13 Using a socket and extension bar on the crankshaft sprocket bolt, rotate the crankshaft in the normal direction of rotation until the spring-loaded plunger of the positioning tool slides into engagement with the slot in the camshaft. There will be an audible click from the tool when this happens.

14 Unscrew the bolt from the lower left-hand side of the oil pump housing and screw in the fastening stud of Vauxhall/Opel special tool EN-46788 **(see illustration).**

15 Fit the positioning ring of tool EN-46788 over the fastening stud and engage it with the

3.8 Undo the retaining nut and bolts (arrowed) and remove the right-hand engine mounting

3.9 Engine breather pipe retaining bolts (arrowed)

3.10 Undo the bolt (arrowed) and release the engine oil dipstick guide tube from the coolant pipe

3.11 Unscrew the closure bolt from the valve timing checking hole in the camshaft housing

3.14 Screw the fastening stud of special tool EN-46788 into the oil pump housing

crankshaft sprocket. Ensure that the hole in the positioning ring engages with the lug on the sprocket. Secure the tool in position with the retaining bolt and nut **(see illustration)**.

16 With the crankshaft positioning ring in place and the camshaft positioning tool engaged with the slot in the camshaft, the engine is positioned with No 1 piston at TDC on compression.

4 Valve timing – checking and adjustment

Note: *To check and adjust the valve timing, it will be necessary to use Vauxhall/Opel special tool EN-46788 (or suitable equivalent) to set the crankshaft at the TDC position. Additionally, it will be necessary to use Vauxhall/Opel special tools EN-46789 and EN46789-100 (or suitable equivalents) to lock the camshafts in the TDC position.*

Checking

1 Disconnect the battery negative terminal (refer to *Disconnecting the battery* in the Reference Chapter), then lift off the plastic cover over the top of the engine.

2 Release the retaining clip securing the engine breather hose to the breather pipe adjacent to the engine oil dipstick. Undo the two bolts securing the breather pipe to the cylinder head, and disconnect the pipe from the hose **(see illustration 3.9)**.

3 Undo the bolt and release the engine oil dipstick guide tube from the coolant pipe **(see illustration 3.10)**.

4 Unscrew the closure bolt from the valve timing checking hole in the exhaust side of camshaft housing **(see illustration 3.11)**.

5 Screw the exhaust camshaft positioning tool (Vauxhall/Opel special tool EN-46789) into the valve timing checking hole.

6 Unscrew the closure bolt from the valve timing checking hole in the inlet side of the camshaft housing. The closure bolt is located below the fuel pressure regulating valve on the fuel rail.

7 Screw the inlet camshaft positioning tool (Vauxhall/Opel special tool EN-46789-100) into the valve timing checking hole.

8 Using a socket and extension bar on the crankshaft sprocket bolt, rotate the crankshaft in the normal direction of rotation until the spring-loaded plungers of the positioning tools slide into engagement with the slots in the camshafts. There will be an audible click from the tools when this happens.

9 Remove the crankshaft pulley/vibration damper as described in Section 5.

10 Unscrew the bolt from the lower left-hand side of the oil pump housing and screw in the fastening stud of Vauxhall/Opel special tool EN-46788 **(see illustration 3.14)**.

11 Fit the positioning ring of tool EN-46788 over the fastening stud and engage it with the crankshaft sprocket. Ensure that the hole in the positioning ring engages with the lug on the

3.15 Positioning ring of tool EN-46788 (arrowed) attached to the fastening stud and crankshaft sprocket

sprocket. Secure the tool in position with the retaining bolt and nut **(see illustration 3.15)**.

12 If it is not possible to fit the positioning ring of tool EN-46788 as described, or if the camshaft positioning tools did not engage with the camshaft slots, adjust the valve timing as follows.

Adjustment

13 Remove the timing belt as described in Section 6.

14 Using a socket and extension bar on the crankshaft sprocket bolt, rotate the crankshaft anti-clockwise by 90°. This will position all the pistons half-way down their bores, and prevent any chance of the valves touching the piston crowns during the following procedure.

15 Remove the inlet and exhaust camshaft positioning tools from the valve timing checking holes.

16 Using a suitable tool engaged with the timing belt sprocket on the exhaust camshaft, rotate the sprocket approximately 90° clockwise. Vauxhall/Opel special tools EN-46787 and KM-956-1 are available for this purpose, however, a home-made tool can easily be fabricated **(see Tool Tip in Section 7)**. Take care not to damage the camshaft sensor with the tool as the sprocket is rotated.

17 Screw the inlet camshaft positioning tool (Vauxhall/Opel special tool EN-46789-100) into the valve timing checking hole.

18 Rotate the camshaft sprocket clockwise until the spring-loaded plunger of the positioning tool slides into engagement with the slot in the inlet camshaft. There will be an audible click from the tool when this happens.

5.3 Crankshaft pulley/vibration damper retaining bolts (arrowed)

19 Release the two retaining clips and disconnect the charge air hose from the throttle body/housing, and intercooler charge air pipe.

20 Release the clip and disconnect the crankcase ventilation hose from the engine oil filler housing.

21 Disconnect the wiring connector from the coolant temperature sensor, then undo the three retaining bolts and remove the oil filler housing.

22 Remove the braking system vacuum pump as described in Chapter 9.

23 Working through the oil filler housing aperture, and using the holding tool to prevent rotation of the camshaft, slacken the inlet camshaft drivegear retaining bolt. Working through the vacuum pump aperture, slacken the exhaust camshaft drivegear retaining bolt in the same way.

24 Screw the exhaust camshaft positioning tool (Vauxhall/Opel special tool EN-46789) into the valve timing checking hole.

25 Rotate the camshaft sprocket clockwise until the spring-loaded plunger of the positioning tool slides into engagement with the slot in the exhaust camshaft. There will be an audible click from the tool when this happens.

26 Hold the camshaft sprocket with the tool and tighten both drivegear retaining bolts to the specified torque.

27 Remove the positioning tool from the inlet camshaft and refit the closure bolt. Tighten the bolt to the specified torque.

28 Refit the oil filler housing to the camshaft housing using a new gasket, refit the retaining bolts and tighten the bolts to the specified torque. Reconnect the coolant temperature sensor wiring connector, and reconnect the crankcase ventilation hose.

29 Refit the braking system vacuum pump as described in Chapter 9.

30 Refit the charge air hose to the throttle body/housing, and intercooler charge air pipe and secure with the retaining clips.

31 Refit the timing belt as described in Section 6.

5 Crankshaft pulley/ vibration damper – removal and refitting

Removal

1 Apply the handbrake, then jack up the front of the vehicle and support it on axle stands (see *Jacking and vehicle support*). Remove the right-hand front roadwheel, then undo the ten bolts and remove the engine undertray for access to the crankshaft pulley.

2 Remove the auxiliary drivebelt as described in Chapter 1B. Prior to removal, mark the direction of rotation on the belt to ensure the belt is refitted the same way around.

3 Undo the four bolts securing the pulley to the crankshaft sprocket and remove the pulley from the sprocket **(see illustration)**.

6.2 Upper timing belt cover retaining bolts (arrowed)

6.3 Undo the bolt (arrowed) and remove the auxiliary drivebelt idler pulley from the engine bracket

6.4a Undo the two lower bolts (arrowed) . . .

6.4b . . . and the three upper bolts (arrowed) . . .

6.4c . . . and remove the engine bracket from the engine

Refitting

4 Locate the crankshaft pulley on the sprocket, ensuring that the hole on the rear face of the pulley engages with the lug on the sprocket.

5 Refit the four retaining bolts and tighten them progressively to the specified torque.

6 Refit the auxiliary drivebelt as described in Chapter 1B using the mark made prior to removal to ensure the belt is fitted the correct way around.

7 Refit the roadwheel and engine undertray, then lower the car to the ground and tighten the wheel bolts to the specified torque.

6 Timing belt – removal and refitting

Note: *The timing belt must be removed and refitted with the engine cold.*

Removal

1 Position No 1 cylinder at TDC on its compression stroke as described in Section 3.

2 Unclip the wiring harness from the side of the upper timing belt cover. Unscrew the seven retaining bolts and lift off the upper timing belt cover **(see illustration)**.

3 Undo the retaining bolt and remove the auxiliary drivebelt idler pulley from the engine bracket **(see illustration)**.

4 Undo the two lower bolts, and the three upper bolts, and remove the engine bracket from the engine **(see illustrations)**.

5 Undo the nut and bolt and remove the crankshaft positioning tool (EN-46788) from the crankshaft sprocket.

6 Slacken the timing belt tensioner retaining bolt and allow the tensioner to retract, relieving the tension on the timing belt.

7 Slide the timing belt from its sprockets and remove it from the engine. If the belt is to be

re-used, use white paint or similar to mark the direction of rotation on the belt. **Do not** rotate the crankshaft or camshafts until the timing belt has been refitted.

8 Check the timing belt carefully for any signs of uneven wear, splitting or oil contamination, and renew it if there is the slightest doubt about its condition. If the engine is undergoing an overhaul and is approaching the manufacturer's specified interval for belt renewal (see Chapter 1B) renew the belt as a matter of course, regardless of its apparent condition. If signs of oil contamination are found, trace the source of the oil leak and rectify it, then wash down the engine timing belt area and all related components to remove all traces of oil.

Refitting

9 On reassembly, thoroughly clean the timing belt sprockets and tensioner/idler pulleys.

10 Place the timing belt in position over the crankshaft sprocket. If the original belt is being refitted, ensure that the arrow mark made on removal points in the normal direction of rotation, as before.

11 Check that the camshaft and crankshaft are still positioned with No 1 piston at TDC on compression as described in Section 3, and with the camshaft positioning tool still in place. Now refit the crankshaft positioning tool.

12 Fit the timing belt over the crankshaft, camshaft and fuel pump sprockets and around the idler pulleys, ensuring that the belt front run is taut (ie, all slack is on the tensioner side of the belt), then fit the belt over the coolant pump sprocket and tensioner pulley. Do not twist the belt sharply while refitting it. Ensure that the belt teeth are correctly seated centrally in the sprockets.

13 Screw in a suitable bolt, approximately 50 mm in length, into the threaded hole directly below the timing belt tensioner. Using a screwdriver resting on the bolt as a pivot, move the adjusting lever on the tensioner until the tensioner pointer is aligned with the mark on the backplate. Hold the tensioner in this position and tighten the tensioner retaining bolt **(see illustrations)**.

14 Remove the crankshaft and camshaft positioning tools.

15 Using a socket on the crankshaft sprocket

6.13a Using a screwdriver resting on a pivot bolt (arrowed), move the adjusting lever on the tensioner . . .

6.13b . . . until the tensioner pointer (arrowed) is aligned with the mark on the backplate

bolt, rotate the crankshaft smoothly through two complete turns (720°) in the normal direction of rotation to settle the timing belt in position. Stop rotating the crankshaft just before completing the second turn.

16 Refit the camshaft positioning tool and continue turning the crankshaft until the camshaft positioning tool engages.

17 Refit the positioning ring of tool EN-46788 over the fastening stud and engage it with the crankshaft sprocket. Ensure that the hole in the positioning ring engages with the lug on the sprocket. Secure the tool in position with the retaining bolt and nut.

18 Slacken the timing belt tensioner retaining bolt and, using a screwdriver resting on the pivot bolt as before, move the adjusting lever on the tensioner until the tensioner pointer is once again aligned with the mark on the backplate. Hold the tensioner in this position and tighten the tensioner retaining bolt to the specified torque.

19 Remove all the positioning tools and again rotate the crankshaft smoothly through two complete turns (720°) in the normal direction of rotation. Check that the timing belt tensioner pointer is still aligned with the mark on the backplate. If not, repeat the procedure described in paragraph 18.

20 When all is correct, remove the tensioner position pivot bolt. Refit the bolt removed from the oil pump housing and tighten it to the specified torque. Refit the closure plug to the camshaft housing and tighten to the specified torque.

21 Place the engine bracket in position and refit the two lower bolts, and the three upper bolts. Tighten the bolts to the specified torque. Refit the auxiliary drivebelt idler pulley to the engine bracket and tighten the retaining bolt to the specified torque.

22 Refit the upper timing belt cover and tighten the retaining bolts to the specified torque. Clip the wiring harness back into position.

23 Place the right-hand engine mounting assembly in position and refit the two bolts and the nut securing the mounting to the body. Tighten the bolts/nut to the specified torque. Align the mounting in its original position, then tighten the three mounting bracket bolts to the specified torque. Remove the jack from under the engine.

24 Refit the air cleaner assembly and air intake duct as described in Chapter 4B.

25 Place the auxiliary drivebelt tensioner assembly in position ensuring that the locating peg on the tensioner mounting surface engages correctly with the corresponding hole in the mounting bracket. Tighten the tensioner central mounting bolt to the specified torque.

26 Refit the crankshaft pulley/vibration damper as described in Section 5, then refit the auxiliary drivebelt as described in Chapter 1B.

27 Move the engine oil dipstick guide tube back into position. Refit the bolt securing the guide tube to the coolant pipe and tighten the bolt securely.

28 Attach the engine breather hose to the breather pipe and secure with the retaining clip. Secure the breather pipe to the cylinder head with the two bolts securely tightened.

29 Refit the plastic cover to the top of the engine.

30 Refit the roadwheel and engine undertray, then lower the car to the ground and tighten the wheel bolts to the specified torque.

7 Timing belt sprockets, tensioner and idler pulley – removal and refitting

Note: *Certain special tools will be required for the removal and refitting of the sprockets. Read through the entire procedure to familiarise yourself with the work involved, then either obtain the manufacturer's special tools, or use the alternatives described.*

Camshaft sprocket

Note: *A new sprocket retaining bolt will be required for refitting.*

Removal

1 Remove the timing belt as described in Section 6, then remove camshaft positioning tool from the valve timing checking hole.

2 It will now be necessary to hold the camshaft sprocket to enable the retaining bolt to be removed. Vauxhall/Opel special tools EN-46787 and KM-956-1 are available for this purpose, however, a home-made tool can easily be fabricated **(see Tool Tip)**.

3 Engage the tool with the holes in the camshaft sprocket, taking care not to damage the camshaft sensor located behind the sprocket

4 Unscrew the retaining bolt and remove the sprocket from the end of the camshaft.

Refitting

5 Prior to refitting check the oil seal for signs of damage or leakage. If necessary, renew as described in Section 8.

6 Refit the sprocket to the camshaft end, aligning its cut-out with the locating peg, and fit the new retaining bolt finger-tight only at this stage. Final tightening is carried out after the timing belt has been fitted and tensioned.

7 Refit the camshaft positioning tool to the valve timing checking hole. If necessary, rotate the camshaft slightly, by means of the sprocket, until the tool audibly engages.

8 Proceed with the timing belt refitting procedure as described in Section 6, paragraphs 9 to 14.

9 Retain the camshaft sprocket using the holding tool, and tighten the retaining bolt to the specified torque.

10 Continue with the timing belt refitting procedure as described in Section 6, paragraphs 15 to 30.

Crankshaft sprocket

Note 1: *The crankshaft sprocket retaining bolt is extremely tight. Ensure that the holding tool used to prevent rotation as the bolt*

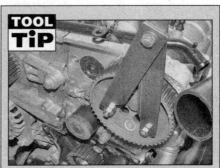

To make a sprocket holding tool, obtain two lengths of steel strip about 6 mm thick by about 30 mm wide or similar, one 600 mm long, the other 200 mm long (all dimensions are approximate). Bolt the two strips together to form a forked end, leaving the bolt slack so that the shorter strip can pivot freely. At the other end of each 'prong' of the fork, drill a suitable hole and fit a nut and bolt to allow the tool to engage with the spokes in the sprocket.

is slackened is of sturdy construction and securely attached.

Note 2: *A new sprocket retaining bolt will be required for refitting.*

Removal

11 Remove the timing belt as described in Section 6.

12 It will now be necessary to hold the crankshaft sprocket to enable the retaining bolt to be removed. Vauxhall special tools EN-47630 and KM-956-1 are available for this purpose, however, a home-made tool similar to that described in paragraph 2, can easily be fabricated.

13 Using the crankshaft pulley retaining bolts, securely attach the tool to the crankshaft sprocket. With the help of an assistant, hold the sprocket stationary and unscrew the retaining bolt. **Note:** *The sprocket retaining bolt has a **left-hand thread** and is unscrewed by turning it clockwise.*

14 Remove the bolt and washer and slide the sprocket off the end of the crankshaft **(see illustrations)**. Note that a new bolt will be required for refitting.

7.14a Remove the bolt and washer . . .

7.14b ... and slide the sprocket off the end of the crankshaft

7.20 Engage the holding tool with the holes in the fuel pump sprocket and undo the retaining nut

7.21 Use a suitable puller to release the fuel pump sprocket taper

Refitting

15 Align the sprocket location key with the crankshaft groove and slide the sprocket into position. Fit the new retaining bolt and washer.

16 Hold the sprocket stationary using the holding tool and tighten the retaining bolt to the specified torque. Remove the holding tool.

17 Refit the timing belt as described in Section 6.

High-pressure fuel pump sprocket

Note: *A new sprocket retaining nut will be required for refitting.*

Removal

18 Remove the timing belt as described in Section 6.

19 It will now be necessary to hold the fuel

pump sprocket to enable the retaining nut to be removed. Vauxhall special tools KM-6347 and KM-956-1 are available for this purpose, however, a home-made tool similar to that described in paragraph 2, can easily be fabricated.

20 Engage the tool with the holes in the fuel pump sprocket and undo the sprocket retaining nut **(see illustration)**. Note that a new nut will be required for refitting.

21 Attach a suitable puller to the threaded holes in the fuel pump sprocket using bolts and washers similar to the arrangement shown **(see illustration)**.

22 Tighten the puller centre bolt to release the sprocket from the taper on the pump shaft. Once the taper releases, remove the puller and withdraw the sprocket. Collect the Woodruff key from the pump shaft **(see illustrations)**.

Refitting

23 Clean the fuel pump shaft and the sprocket hub ensuring that all traces of oil or grease are removed.

24 Refit the Woodruff key to the pump shaft, then locate the sprocket in position. Fit the new retaining nut.

25 Hold the sprocket stationary using the holding tool and tighten the retaining nut to the specified torque. Remove the holding tool.

26 Refit the timing belt as described in Section 6.

Tensioner assembly

Removal

27 Remove the timing belt as described in Section 6.

28 Slacken and remove the retaining bolt and remove the tensioner assembly from the engine **(see illustrations)**.

Refitting

29 Fit the tensioner to the engine, making sure that the slot on the tensioner backplate is correctly located over the peg on the engine bracket **(see illustration)**.

30 Clean the threads of the retaining bolt and apply thread-locking compound to the bolt threads. Screw in the retaining bolt, set the tensioner in the retracted position and tighten the retaining bolt.

31 Refit the timing belt as described in Section 6.

7.22a Once the taper releases, withdraw the sprocket ...

7.22b ... and collect the Woodruff key from the pump shaft

7.28a Slacken and remove the retaining bolt ...

7.28b ... and remove the timing belt tensioner assembly

7.29 The slot on the tensioner backplate must locate over the peg (arrowed) on the engine bracket

7.33 Slacken and remove the retaining bolt and remove the idler pulley from the engine

Idler pulley

Removal

32 Remove the timing belt as described in Section 6.
33 Slacken and remove the retaining bolt and remove the idler pulley from the engine **(see illustration)**.

Refitting

34 Refit the idler pulley and tighten the retaining bolt to the specified torque.
35 Refit the timing belt as described in Section 6.

8 Camshaft oil seal – renewal

1 Remove the camshaft sprocket as described in Section 7.
2 Carefully punch or drill a small hole in the oil seal. Screw in a self-tapping screw, and pull on the screw with pliers to extract the seal.
3 Clean the seal housing, and polish off any burrs or raised edges which may have caused the seal to fail in the first place.
4 Lubricate the lips of the new seal with clean engine oil, and press it into position using a suitable tubular drift (such as a socket) which bears only on the hard outer edge of the seal. Take care not to damage the seal lips during fitting; note that the seal lips should face inwards.
5 Refit the camshaft sprocket as described in Section 7.

9 Camshaft housing – removal and refitting

Removal

1 Remove the timing belt as described in Section 6.
2 Disconnect the wiring harness connectors from the following components **(see illustrations)**:
a) Fuel injectors.
b) Fuel pressure regulating valve.
c) Fuel pressure sensor.

9.2a Disconnect the wiring connectors at the fuel injectors . . .

9.2c . . . fuel pressure sensor . . .

d) Camshaft sensor.
e) Air conditioning compressor.
3 Release the air conditioning compressor wiring harness from the clip on the oil dipstick guide tube. Undo the two bolts securing the plastic wiring harness guide to the camshaft

9.2e . . . and air conditioning compressor (arrowed)

9.3b . . . and move the disconnected wiring harness to one side

9.2b . . . fuel pressure regulating valve . . .

9.2d . . . camshaft sensor . . .

housing and move the disconnected wiring harness to one side **(see illustrations)**.
4 Disconnect the two vacuum hoses from the vacuum pipe assembly on top of the camshaft housing. Undo the two retaining bolts and move the pipe assembly to one side **(see illustration)**.

9.3a Undo the two bolts (arrowed) securing the wiring harness guide to the camshaft housing . . .

9.4a Disconnect the two vacuum hoses from the vacuum pipe assembly . . .

9.4b ... then undo the two retaining bolts (arrowed) and move the pipe assembly to one side

9.6 Release the retaining clips and remove the charge air hose

9.7 Disconnect the vacuum hose quick-release fitting from the braking system vacuum pump

9.8 Disconnect the crankcase ventilation hose from the engine oil filler housing

9.11 Lift the camshaft housing off the cylinder head and recover the gasket

5 Remove the fuel injectors and the fuel rail as described in Chapter 4B.

6 Release the two retaining clips and disconnect the charge air hose from the throttle body/housing, and intercooler charge air pipe (see illustration).

7 Disconnect the vacuum hose quick-release fitting from the braking system vacuum pump (see illustration).

8 Release the clip and disconnect the crankcase ventilation hose from the engine oil filler housing (see illustration).

9 Undo the retaining bolts and remove the two engine lifting brackets from the left-hand end of the camshaft housing. Undo the bolt securing the turbocharger charge air pipe to the right-hand end of the camshaft housing

10 Working in a spiral pattern from the outside inwards, progressively slacken, then remove, the sixteen bolts securing the camshaft housing to the cylinder head. Ensure that the housing releases evenly from the cylinder block.

11 Lift the camshaft housing off the cylinder head and recover the gasket (see illustration).

12 Thoroughly clean the mating faces of the cylinder head, camshaft housing and vacuum pump and obtain a new gasket for refitting.

Refitting

13 Check that all the hydraulic tappets and rocker arms are correctly positioned in the cylinder head and none have been disturbed.

14 Commence refitting by turning the crankshaft anti-clockwise by 90°. This will

position all the pistons half-way down their bores, and prevent any chance of the valves touching the piston crowns as the camshaft housing is being fitted.

15 Place a new gasket on the cylinder head, then locate the camshaft housing in position aligning it with the locating dowels.

16 Refit the sixteen camshaft housing retaining bolts. Progressively screw in the bolts to gradually draw the housing down and into contact with the cylinder head.

17 Working in a spiral pattern from the inside outwards, progressively tighten the sixteen bolts to the specified torque.

18 Refit the two engine lifting brackets to the left-hand end of the camshaft housing and tighten the retaining bolts securely. Refit and tighten the charge air pipe retaining bolt.

19 Reconnect the crankcase ventilation hose to the engine oil filler housing.

20 Reconnect the vacuum hose quick-release

10.3 Undo the three retaining bolts and remove the oil filler housing

fitting to the braking system vacuum pump ensuring that the fitting audibly engages.

21 Refit the charge air hose to the throttle body/housing, and intercooler charge air pipe and secure with the retaining clips.

22 Refit the fuel rail and fuel injectors as described in Chapter 4B.

23 Place the vacuum pipe assembly in position on the top of the camshaft housing and refit the two retaining bolts. Tighten the bolts securely, then reconnect the two vacuum hoses.

24 Lay the plastic wiring harness guide in position on the camshaft housing, then refit and tighten the two retaining bolts.

25 Reconnect the wiring harness connectors to the components listed in paragraph 2, ensuring that the harness is secured by all the relevant retaining clips.

26 Turn the crankshaft clockwise by 90° to bring No 1 and 4 pistons to approximately the TDC position.

27 Refit the timing belt as described in Section 6.

10 Camshafts –
removal, inspection
and refitting

Note: *An additional camshaft positioning tool Vauxhall/Opel special tool EN-46789 (or suitable equivalent) will be required for this operation – two in total (see Section 3).*

Removal

1 Carry out the operations described in Section 9, paragraphs 1 to 8.

2 Remove the braking system vacuum pump as described in Chapter 9.

3 Disconnect the wiring connector from the coolant temperature sensor, then undo the three retaining bolts and remove the oil filler housing (see illustration).

4 Undo the retaining bolt and remove the camshaft sensor from the right-hand end of the camshaft housing.

5 Before removing the camshaft housing completely, the retaining bolts for the camshaft drivegears and sprocket should be slackened as follows.

6 Remove the exhaust camshaft positioning tool from the valve timing checking hole.

10.8a Slacken the inlet camshaft drivegear retaining bolt . . .

10.8b . . . and the exhaust camshaft drivegear retaining bolt

10.12a Unscrew and remove the two previously-slackened retaining bolts . . .

7 It will be necessary to hold the camshaft sprocket to enable the drivegear and sprocket retaining bolts to be slackened. Vauxhall special tools EN-46787 and KM-956-1 are available for this purpose, however, a home-made tool can easily be fabricated **(see Tool Tip in Section 7).**

8 Working through the oil filler housing aperture, and using the holding tool to prevent rotation of the camshaft, slacken the inlet camshaft drivegear retaining bolt. Working through the vacuum pump aperture, slacken the exhaust camshaft drivegear retaining bolt in the same way **(see illustrations).**

9 Again, using the holding tool, slacken the camshaft sprocket retaining bolt.

10 Continue with the camshaft housing removal procedure as described in Section 9, paragraphs 9 to 11.

11 With the camshaft housing placed upside down on the bench, unscrew and remove the previously-slackened retaining bolt, and remove the timing belt sprocket from the exhaust camshaft.

12 At the other end of the housing, unscrew and remove the two previously-slackened retaining bolts, and lift off the drivegears from the inlet and exhaust camshafts **(see illustrations).**

13 Carefully prise out the exhaust camshaft oil seal with a screwdriver or similar hooked tool. Carefully withdraw the exhaust camshaft out from the timing belt end of the camshaft housing **(see illustration).**

14 Using a wooden dowel or similar, carefully tap the end of the inlet camshaft toward the timing belt end of the housing, to release the blanking cap. Remove the cap, then carefully

10.12b . . . then lift out the exhaust camshaft drivegear . . .

withdraw the inlet camshaft from the housing **(see illustration).**

Inspection

15 Examine the camshaft bearing surfaces and cam lobes for signs of wear ridges and scoring. Renew the camshaft(s) if any of these conditions are apparent. Examine the condition of the bearing surfaces in the camshaft housing. If the any wear or scoring is evident, the camshaft housing will need to be renewed.

16 If either camshaft is being renewed, it will be necessary to renew all the rocker arms and tappets for that particular camshaft also (see Section 11).

17 Check the condition of the camshaft drivegears and sprocket for chipped or damaged teeth, wear ridges and scoring. Renew any components as necessary.

Refitting

18 Prior to refitting, thoroughly clean all

10.12c . . . and the inlet camshaft drivegear

components and dry with a lint-free cloth. Ensure that all traces of oil and grease are removed from the contact faces of the drivegears, sprocket and camshafts.

19 Lubricate the camshaft bearing journals in the camshaft housing and carefully insert the inlet and exhaust camshafts.

20 Ensuring that the contact faces are clean and dry, refit the drivegear to each camshaft. Note that the gear with the vacuum pump drive dogs is fitted to the exhaust camshaft, and the plain gear is fitted to the inlet camshaft.

21 Screw in a new drivegear retaining bolt for each camshaft and tighten both bolts finger tight only at this stage.

22 Refit the camshaft positioning tool to the valve timing checking hole of the exhaust camshaft. If necessary, rotate the exhaust camshaft slightly, until the tool audibly engages **(see illustration).**

23 Unscrew and remove the closure bolt

10.13 Withdraw the exhaust camshaft . . .

10.14 . . . and inlet camshaft from the camshaft housing

10.22 Refit the camshaft positioning tool to the valve timing checking hole of the exhaust camshaft

10.23a Unscrew the closure bolt from the inlet camshaft side of the camshaft housing . . .

10.23b . . . and fit a camshaft positioning tool for the inlet camshaft

10.24 With both camshafts locked, tighten both drivegear retaining bolts to the specified torque

10.26a Fit a new inlet camshaft blanking cap to the camshaft housing . . .

10.26b . . . and tap it into position until it is flush with the outer face of the housing

10.27 Similarly, fit a new exhaust camshaft oil seal to the camshaft housing

from the inlet camshaft side of the camshaft housing and fit a second camshaft positioning tool (see illustrations). If necessary, rotate the camshaft slightly, until the tool audibly engages.

24 With both camshafts locked by means of the positioning tools, tighten both drivegear retaining bolts to the specified torque (see illustration). It may be beneficial to have an assistant securely support the camshaft housing as the bolts are tightened.

25 Remove the positioning tool from the inlet camshaft and refit the closure bolt. Tighten the bolt to the specified torque.

26 Fit a new inlet camshaft blanking cap to the timing belt end of the camshaft housing and tap it into position until it is flush with the outer face of the housing, using a suitable socket or tube, or a wooden block (see illustrations).

27 Similarly, fit a new exhaust camshaft oil

seal to the timing belt end of the camshaft housing and tap it into position until it is flush with the outer face of the housing, using a suitable socket or tube, or a wooden block (see illustration).

28 Refit the timing belt sprocket to the exhaust camshaft, aligning its cut-out with the locating peg, and fit the new retaining bolt finger-tight only at this stage. Final tightening is carried out after the timing belt has been fitted and tensioned.

29 Refit the camshaft sensor to the camshaft housing and tighten the retaining bolt securely.

30 Refit the oil filler housing to the camshaft housing using a new gasket, refit the retaining bolts and tighten the bolts to the specified torque. Reconnect the coolant temperature sensor wiring connector.

31 Refit the braking system vacuum pump as described in Chapter 9.

32 Thoroughly clean the mating faces of the cylinder head and camshaft housing.

33 Refit the camshaft housing to the cylinder head as described in Section 9, paragraphs 13 to 26.

34 Commence refitting of the timing belt as described in Section 6, paragraphs 9 to 14.

35 Retain the camshaft sprocket using the holding tool, and tighten the retaining bolt to the specified torque.

36 Continue refitting of the timing belt as described in Section 6, paragraphs 15 to 30.

11 Camshaft followers and hydraulic tappets – removal, inspection and refitting

Removal

1 Remove the camshaft housing as described in Section 9.

2 Obtain sixteen small, oil-tight clean plastic containers, and number them inlet 1 to 8 and exhaust 1 to 8; alternatively, divide a larger container into sixteen compartments and number each compartment accordingly.

3 Withdraw each camshaft follower and hydraulic tappet in turn, unclip the follower from the tappet, and place them in their respective container (see illustrations). Do not interchange the followers and tappets, or the rate of wear will be much increased. Fill each container with clean engine oil and ensure that the tappet is submerged.

11.3a Withdraw each camshaft follower . . .

11.3b . . . and hydraulic tappet in turn, and place them in their respective container

Inspection

4 Examine the followers and hydraulic tappet bearing surfaces for wear ridges and scoring. Renew any follower or tappet on which these conditions are apparent.

5 If any new hydraulic tappets are obtained, they should be immersed in a container of clean engine oil prior to refitting.

Refitting

6 Liberally oil the cylinder head hydraulic tappet bores and the tappets. Working on one assembly at a time, clip the follower back onto the tappet, then refit the tappet to the cylinder head, ensuring that it is refitted to its original bore. Lay the follower over its respective valve (**see illustrations**).

7 Refit the remaining tappets and followers in the same way.

8 With all the tappets and followers in place, refit the camshaft housing as described in Section 9.

12 Cylinder head – removal and refitting

Note: New cylinder head bolts will be required for refitting.

Removal

1 Disconnect the battery negative terminal (refer to Disconnecting the battery in the Reference Chapter).

2 Drain the cooling system as described in Chapter 1B.

3 Remove the camshaft housing as described in Section 9.

4 Remove the camshaft followers and hydraulic tappets as described in Section 11.

5 Remove the inlet and exhaust manifolds as described in Chapter 4B.

6 Release the clips and disconnect the remaining two coolant hoses at the thermostat housing, and the coolant hose at the EGR valve heat exchanger (**see illustration**).

7 Release the coolant pipe from the stud at the base of the thermostat housing (**see illustration**).

8 Undo the bolt securing the high-pressure fuel pump mounting bracket to the cylinder head (**see illustration**).

9 Make a final check to ensure that all relevant hoses, pipes and wires have been disconnected.

10 Working in the **reverse** of the tightening sequence (**see illustration 12.27**), progressively slacken the cylinder head bolts by half a turn at a time, until all bolts can be unscrewed by hand. Note that an M14 RIBE socket bit will be required to unscrew the bolts. Remove the cylinder head bolts and recover the washers.

11 Engage the help of an assistant, if necessary, and lift the cylinder head from the cylinder block (**see illustration**).

Caution: Do not lay the head on its lower

11.6a Clip the follower back onto the tappet . . .

11.6b . . . then refit the tappet to its original bore, and lay the follower over its respective valve

mating surface; support the head on wooden blocks, ensuring each block only contacts the head mating surface.

12 Remove the gasket and keep it for identification purposes (see paragraph 19).

13 If the cylinder head is to be dismantled for overhaul, then refer to Part F of this Chapter.

Preparation for refitting

14 The mating faces of the cylinder head and cylinder block/crankcase must be perfectly clean before refitting the head. Use a hard plastic or wood scraper to remove all traces of gasket and carbon; also clean the piston crowns. Take particular care, as the surfaces are damaged easily. Also, make sure that the carbon is not allowed to enter the oil and water passages – this is particularly important for the lubrication system, as carbon could

12.6 Disconnect the coolant hoses at the thermostat housing (A), and at the EGR valve heat exchanger (B)

12.8 Undo the bolt (arrowed) securing the high-pressure fuel pump mounting bracket to the cylinder head

block the oil supply to any of the engine's components. Using adhesive tape and paper, seal the water, oil and bolt holes in the cylinder block/crankcase. To prevent carbon entering the gap between the pistons and bores, smear a little grease in the gap. After cleaning each piston, use a small brush to remove all traces of grease and carbon from the gap, then wipe away the remainder with a clean rag. Clean all the pistons in the same way.

15 Check the mating surfaces of the cylinder block/crankcase and the cylinder head for nicks, deep scratches and other damage. If slight, they may be removed carefully with a file, but if excessive, machining may be the only alternative to renewal.

16 Ensure that the cylinder head bolt holes in the crankcase are clean and free of oil. Syringe or soak up any oil left in the bolt holes.

12.7 Release the coolant pipe from the stud (arrowed) at the base of the thermostat housing

12.11 Lift the cylinder head from the cylinder block

12.19 Cylinder head gasket thickness identification hole (arrowed)

12.21 Using a dial test indicator to measure piston protrusion

This is most important in order that the correct bolt tightening torque can be applied and to prevent the possibility of the block being cracked by hydraulic pressure when the bolts are tightened.

17 The cylinder head bolts must be discarded and renewed, regardless of their apparent condition.

18 If warpage of the cylinder head gasket surface is suspected, use a straight-edge to check it for distortion. Refer to Part F of this Chapter if necessary.

19 On this engine, the cylinder head-to-piston clearance is controlled by fitting different thickness head gaskets. The gasket thickness can be determined by looking at the holes stamped on the edge of the gasket **(see illustration)**.

Number of holes	Gasket thickness
No holes	0.77 to 0.87 mm
One hole	0.87 to 0.97 mm
Two holes	0.97 to 1.07 mm

The correct thickness of gasket required is selected by measuring the piston protrusions as follows.

20 Mount a dial test indicator securely on the block so that its pointer can be easily pivoted between the piston crown and block mating surface. Turn the crankshaft to bring No 1 piston roughly to the TDC position. Move the dial test indicator probe over and in contact with No 1 piston. Turn the crankshaft back-and-forth slightly until the highest reading is shown on the gauge, indicating that the piston is at TDC.

21 Zero the dial test indicator on the gasket surface of the cylinder block then carefully move the indicator over No 1 piston. Measure its protrusion at the highest point between the valve cut-outs, and then again at its highest point between the valve cut-outs at 90° to the first measurement **(see illustration)**. Repeat this procedure with No 4 piston.

22 Rotate the crankshaft half a turn (180°) to bring No 2 and 3 pistons to TDC. Ensure the crankshaft is accurately positioned then measure the protrusions of No 2 and 3 pistons at the specified points. Once all pistons have been measured, rotate the crankshaft to position all the pistons at their mid-stroke.

23 Select the correct thickness of head gasket required by determining the largest amount of piston protrusion, and using the following table.

Piston protrusion measurement (mm)	Gasket thickness required (mm)
0.020 to 0.100	0.77 to 0.87 (no holes)
0.101 to 0.200	0.87 to 0.97 (one hole)
0.201 to 0.295	0.97 to 1.07 (two holes)

Refitting

24 Wipe clean the mating surfaces of the cylinder head and cylinder block/crankcase. Place the new gasket in position with the words ALTO/TOP uppermost **(see illustration)**.

25 Carefully refit the cylinder head assembly to the block, aligning it with the locating dowels.

26 Apply a thin film of engine oil to the bolt threads and the underside of the bolt heads. Carefully enter each new cylinder head bolt into its relevant hole (*do not drop them in*). Screw all bolts in, by hand only, until finger-tight.

27 Working progressively in the sequence shown, tighten the cylinder head bolts to their Stage 1 torque setting, using a torque wrench and suitable socket **(see illustration)**. Working again in the same sequence, go around and tighten all bolts through the specified Stage 2 torque setting.

28 Once all bolts have been tightened to the Stage 2 torque, working again in the same sequence, go around and tighten all bolts through the specified Stage 3 angle, then through the specified Stage 4 angle, and finally through the specified Stage 5 angle using an angle-measuring gauge.

29 Refit the bolt securing the high-pressure fuel pump mounting bracket to the cylinder head and tighten the bolt securely.

30 Engage the coolant pipe with the stud on the thermostat housing, then reconnect the coolant hoses to the thermostat housing and EGR valve heat exchanger.

31 Refit the inlet and exhaust manifolds as described in Chapter 4B.

32 Refit the camshaft followers and hydraulic tappets as described in Section 11.

33 Refit the camshaft housing as described in Section 9.

34 On completion, reconnect the battery negative terminal, then refill the cooling system as described in Chapter 1B.

12.24 Place the new gasket in position with the words ALTO/TOP uppermost

12.27 Cylinder head bolt tightening sequence

13.4 intermediate shaft bearing housing support bracket retaining bolts (arrowed)

13.9 Air conditioning compressor mounting bracket retaining bolts (arrowed)

13.17 Removing the oil baffle plate from inside the sump

13 Sump – removal and refitting

Removal

1 Disconnect the battery negative terminal (refer to *Disconnecting the battery* in the Reference Chapter).

2 Apply the handbrake, then jack up the front of the vehicle and support it on axle stands (see *Jacking and vehicle support*). Remove the right-hand front roadwheel, then undo the ten bolts and remove the engine undertray.

3 Remove the right-hand driveshaft and the intermediate shaft as described in Chapter 8.

4 Undo the three bolts securing the intermediate shaft bearing housing support bracket to the cylinder block and remove the support bracket **(see illustration)**.

5 Remove the exhaust system as described in Chapter 4B.

6 Undo the three bolts and remove the support bracket from the catalytic converter and sump.

7 Remove the crankshaft pulley/vibration damper as described in Section 5.

8 Disconnect the wiring connector from the air conditioning compressor. Undo the three bolts securing the air conditioning compressor to the mounting bracket and suitably support the compressor on the front subframe.

9 Undo the four bolts securing the compressor mounting bracket to the cylinder block and sump **(see illustration)**. Unclip the wiring harness and remove the mounting bracket.

10 Drain the engine oil as described in Chapter 1B. When the oil has completely drained, refit the drain plug with new sealing washer, and tighten to the specified torque.

11 Undo the upper bolt securing the oil dipstick guide tube to the coolant pipe. Undo the lower bolt securing the guide tube to the sump flange, then unclip the wiring harness and withdraw the tube from the sump flange sealing grommet.

12 Disconnect the wiring connector from the oil level sensor, then release the retaining clip and disconnect the oil return hose.

13 Undo the two bolts securing the sump flange to the transmission bellhousing.

14 Using a socket and extension on the crankshaft pulley bolt, rotate the crankshaft in the normal direction of rotation (clockwise when viewed from the right-hand end of the engine) until the opening in the flywheel is positioned to allow access to one of the rear sump retaining bolts. Undo and remove the bolt, then rotate the crankshaft again until the flywheel allow access to the second rear retaining bolt. Undo and remove the bolt.

15 Progressively slacken and remove the remaining twelve bolts securing the sump to the base of the cylinder block and oil pump housing. Using a wide-bladed scraper or similar tool inserted between the sump and cylinder block, carefully break the joint to release the sump.

16 Manoeuvre the sump out from under the car. Clearance is extremely limited between the sump and subframe, and it may be necessary to release the oil pump pick-up/strainer, by undoing its two retaining bolts, to enable the sump to be removed.

17 If required, undo the retaining bolts and remove the oil baffle plate from inside the sump **(see illustration)**.

18 While the sump is removed, take the opportunity to check the oil pump pick-up/strainer for signs of clogging or splitting. If not already done, unbolt the oil pump pick-up/strainer and remove it from the engine along with its sealing ring. The strainer can then be cleaned easily in solvent or renewed. Renew the pick-up/strainer sealing ring prior to refitting **(see illustration)**.

Refitting

19 Thoroughly clean the sump and remove all traces of silicone sealer and oil from the mating surfaces of the sump and cylinder block. If removed, refit the oil baffle plate and tighten its retaining bolts securely.

20 If clearance allows, refit the oil pump pick-up/strainer using a new sealing ring, and tighten its two retaining bolts securely. If it was necessary to unbolt the pick-up/strainer to allow the sump to be removed, place the unit in position and loosely screw in the bolt securing it to the main bearing cap. It must still be possible for the forward end of the pipe to be moved to the rear as the sump is refitted.

21 Apply a continuous bead of silicone sealing compound (available from your Vauxhall/Opel dealer) at approximately 1.0 mm from the inner edge of the sump **(see illustration)**. The bead of sealant should be between 2.0 and 2.5 mm in diameter.

22 Locate the sump over the pick-up/strainer then, where applicable, fit the forward end of the pick-up/strainer to the oil pump housing and fit the retaining bolt. Tighten both retaining bolts securely.

23 Engage the sump with the cylinder block and loosely refit all the retaining bolts.

24 Working out from the centre in a diagonal sequence, progressively tighten the bolts securing the sump to the cylinder block and oil pump housing. Tighten all the bolts to their specified torque setting.

25 Tighten the two bolts securing the sump

13.18 Renew the pick-up/strainer sealing ring prior to refitting

13.21 Apply a continuous bead of silicone sealing compound to the sump flange

14.4 Oil pump housing retaining bolts (arrowed)

14.5 Undo the retaining screws and lift off the oil pump cover

14.6 Oil pump inner and outer rotor identification dots (arrowed)

14.8a Unscrew the oil pressure relief valve bolt . . .

14.8b . . . and withdraw the spring . . .

14.8c . . . and plunger

flange to the transmission bellhousing to their specified torque settings.

26 Reconnect the wiring connector to the oil level sensor, then refit the oil return hose and secure with the retaining clip.

27 Refit the oil dipstick guide tube and secure with the two bolts tightened securely.

28 Locate the air conditioning compressor mounting bracket in position and refit the four retaining bolts. Tighten the bolts to the specified torque. Clip the wiring harness back into position on the bracket.

29 Position the air conditioning compressor on the mounting bracket. Fit and tighten the three retaining bolts to the specified torque (see Chapter 3), then reconnect the compressor wiring connector.

30 Refit the crankshaft pulley/vibration damper as described in Section 5.

31 Refit the catalytic converter support bracket and securely tighten the three bolts.

32 Refit the exhaust system as described in Chapter 4B.

33 Position the intermediate shaft bearing housing support bracket on the cylinder block and secure with the three retaining bolts tightened to the specified torque.

34 Refit the intermediate shaft and right-hand driveshaft as described in Chapter 8.

35 Refit the roadwheel and engine undertray, then lower the car to the ground and tighten the wheel bolts to the specified torque.

36 Fill the engine with fresh engine oil as described in Chapter 1B.

37 On completion, reconnect the battery negative terminal.

14 Oil pump –
removal, overhaul and refitting

Removal

1 Remove the timing belt as described in Section 6.

2 Remove the crankshaft sprocket as described In Section 7.

3 Remove the sump and oil pump pick-up/strainer as described in Section 13.

4 Slacken and remove the seven retaining bolts then slide the oil pump housing assembly off of the end of the crankshaft **(see illustration)**. Remove the housing gasket and discard it.

Overhaul

5 Undo the retaining screws and lift off the

14.10 Prime the oil pump by filling it with clean engine oil whilst rotating the inner rotor

pump cover from the rear of the housing **(see illustration)**.

6 Check the inner and outer rotors for identification dots indicating which way round they are fitted **(see illustration)**. If no marks are visible, use a suitable marker pen to mark the surface of both the pump inner and outer rotors.

7 Lift out the inner and outer rotors from the pump housing.

8 Unscrew the oil pressure relief valve bolt from the base of the housing and withdraw the spring and plunger, noting which way around the plunger is fitted **(see illustrations)**. Remove the sealing washer from the valve bolt.

9 Clean the components, and carefully examine the rotors, pump body and relief valve plunger for any signs of scoring or wear. If any damage or wear is noticed, it will be necessary to renew the complete pump assembly.

10 If the pump is satisfactory, reassemble the components in the reverse order of removal, noting the following:

a) Ensure both rotors are fitted the correct way around.

b) Fit a new sealing ring to the pressure relief valve bolt and securely tighten the bolt.

c) Apply a little locking compound to the threads, and securely tighten the pump cover screws.

d) On completion prime the oil pump by filling it with clean engine oil whilst rotating the inner rotor **(see illustration)**.

Refitting

11 Prior to refitting, carefully lever out the crankshaft oil seal using a flat-bladed screwdriver. Fit the new oil seal, ensuring its sealing lip is facing inwards, and press it squarely into the housing using a tubular drift which bears only on the hard outer edge of the seal. Press the seal into position so that it is flush with the housing and lubricate the oil seal lip with clean engine oil.

12 Ensure the mating surfaces of the oil pump and cylinder block are clean and dry.

13 Fit a new gasket to the oil pump housing and bend down the tabs on the edge of the gasket to retain it on the pump housing **(see illustration)**.

14 Locate the pump housing over the end of the crankshaft and into position on the cylinder block.

15 Refit the pump housing retaining bolts and tighten them to the specified torque.

16 Refit the oil pump pick-up/strainer and sump as described in Section 13.

17 Refit the crankshaft sprocket as described in Section 7.

18 Refit the timing belt as described in Section 6.

19 On completion, fit a new oil filter and fill the engine with clean oil as described in Chapter 1B.

15 Oil filter housing – removal and refitting

Removal

1 The oil filter housing with integral oil cooler is located at the rear of the cylinder block, above the right-hand driveshaft.

2 Disconnect the battery negative terminal (refer to *Disconnecting the battery* in the Reference Chapter).

3 Apply the handbrake, then jack up the front of the vehicle and support it on axle stands (see *Jacking and vehicle support*). Remove the right-hand front roadwheel, then undo the ten bolts and remove the engine undertray.

4 Drain the cooling system as described in Chapter 1B.

5 Remove the engine oil filter element as described in Chapter 1B.

6 Remove the right-hand driveshaft and the intermediate shaft as described in Chapter 8.

7 Undo the three bolts securing the intermediate shaft bearing housing support bracket to the cylinder block and remove the support bracket **(see illustration 13.4)**.

8 Disconnect the wiring connector from the oil pressure switch.

9 Release the retaining clips and disconnect the two coolant hoses from the oil cooler on the oil filter housing.

10 Undo the three retaining bolts and remove the oil filter housing from the cylinder block **(see illustration)**. Recover the two rubber

14.13 Bend down the tabs on the edge of the gasket to retain it on the oil pump housing

seals from the rear of the housing. Note that new seals will be required for refitting.

Refitting

11 Thoroughly clean the oil filter housing, then fit the two new sealing rings **(see illustrations)**.

12 Position the oil filter housing on the cylinder block and refit the retaining bolts. Tighten the bolts to the specified torque.

13 Refit the two coolant hoses and secure with their retaining clips. Reconnect the oil pressure switch wiring connector.

14 Position the intermediate shaft bearing housing support bracket on the cylinder block and secure with the three retaining bolts tightened to the specified torque.

15 Refit the intermediate shaft and right-hand driveshaft as described in Chapter 8.

16 Fit a new oil filter element as described in Chapter 1B.

17 Refit the roadwheel and engine undertray,

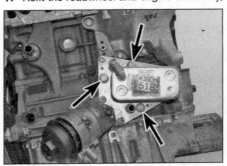

15.10 Oil filter housing retaining bolts (arrowed)

15.11b . . . and to the return channel

then lower the car to the ground and tighten the wheel bolts to the specified torque.

18 Refill the cooling system as described in Chapter 1B.

19 Top-up the engine oil as described in *Weekly checks*.

20 On completion, reconnect the battery negative terminal.

16 Crankshaft oil seals – renewal

Right-hand (timing belt end)

1 Remove the crankshaft sprocket as described in Section 7.

2 Carefully punch or drill a small hole in the oil seal. Screw in a self-tapping screw and pull on the screw with pliers to extract the seal **(see illustration)**.

3 Clean the seal housing and polish off any burrs or raised edges which may have caused the seal to fail in the first place.

4 Lubricate the lips of the new seal with clean engine oil and ease it into position on the end of the shaft. Press the seal squarely into position until it is flush with the housing. If necessary, a suitable tubular drift which bears only on the hard outer edge of the seal can be used to tap the seal into position **(see illustration)**. Take great care not to damage the seal lips during fitting and ensure that the seal lips face inwards.

5 Wash off any traces of oil, then refit the crankshaft sprocket as described in Section 7.

15.11a Fit a new sealing ring to the oil filter housing supply channel . . .

16.2 Screw in a self-tapping screw and pull on the screw with pliers to extract the oil seal

16.4 Using a socket as a tubular drift to fit the new oil seal

16.10 Fitting the new oil seal housing, with integral oil seal over the crankshaft

16.12 After fitting, remove the protector sleeve from the housing

17.2 Prevent the flywheel from turning by locking the ring gear teeth

17.3 Flywheel retaining bolts (arrowed)

Left-hand
(flywheel/driveplate end)

6 Remove the flywheel/driveplate as described in Section 17.

7 Remove the sump as described in Section 13.

8 Undo the five bolts and remove the oil seal housing. Note that the oil seal and the housing are a single assembly.

9 Clean the crankshaft and polish off any burrs or raised edges which may have caused the seal to fail in the first place.

10 Position the new oil seal housing, complete with seal over the crankshaft and into position on the cylinder block **(see illustration)**. Note that the new oil seal housing is supplied with a protector sleeve over the oil seal. Leave the sleeve in position as the housing is fitted.

11 Refit the five retaining bolts and tighten to the specified torque.

12 Remove the protector sleeve from the housing **(see illustration)**.

13 Refit the sump as described in Section 13.

14 Refit the flywheel/driveplate as described in Section 17.

17 Flywheel/driveplate –
removal, inspection and refitting

Note: *New flywheel/driveplate retaining bolts will be required on refitting.*

Removal

Manual transmission models

1 Remove the transmission as described in Chapter 7A, then remove the clutch assembly as described in Chapter 6.

2 Prevent the flywheel from turning by locking the ring gear teeth with a similar arrangement to that shown **(see illustration)**.

3 Slacken and remove the retaining bolts and remove the flywheel **(see illustration)**. Do not drop it, as it is very heavy.

Automatic transmission models

4 Remove the transmission as described in Chapter 7B then remove the driveplate as described in paragraphs 2 and 3.

Inspection

5 If there is any doubt about the condition of the flywheel/driveplate, seek the advice of a Vauxhall/Opel dealer or engine reconditioning specialist. They will be able to advise if it is possible to recondition it or whether renewal is necessary.

Refitting

Manual transmission models

6 Clean the mating surfaces of the flywheel and crankshaft.

7 Offer up the flywheel and engage it over the positioning dowel on the crankshaft. Apply a drop of locking compound to the threads of each new flywheel retaining bolt (unless they are precoated) and install the new bolts.

8 Lock the flywheel by the method used on removal then, working in a diagonal sequence, evenly and progressively tighten the retaining bolts to the specified torque.

9 Refit the clutch as described in Chapter 6 then remove the locking tool, and refit the transmission as described in Chapter 7A.

Automatic transmission models

10 Refit the driveplate as described in paragraphs 6 to 8.

11 Remove the locking tool, and refit the transmission as described in Chapter 7B.

18 Engine/transmission mountings –
inspection and renewal

Refer to Chapter 2C, Section 18.

Chapter 2 Part E:
2.0 and 2.2 litre diesel engine in-car repair procedures

Contents

Degrees of difficulty

Easy, suitable for novice with little experience	**Fairly easy,** suitable for beginner with some experience	**Fairly difficult,** suitable for competent DIY mechanic	**Difficult,** suitable for experienced DIY mechanic	**Very difficult,** suitable for expert DIY or professional

Specifications

General

Engine type	Four-cylinder, in-line, water-cooled. Single overhead camshaft, chain-driven
Manufacturer's engine code:*	
2.0 litre engines	Y20DTH
2.2 litre engines	Y22DTR
Bore	84.0 mm
Stroke:	
2.0 litre engines	90.0 mm
2.2 litre engines	98.0 mm
Capacity:	
2.0 litre engines	1994 cc
2.2 litre engines	2171 cc
Compression ratio	18.5:1
Firing order	1-3-4-2 (No 1 cylinder at timing chain end of engine)
Direction of crankshaft rotation	Clockwise (viewed from timing chain end of engine)

* For details of engine code location, see 'Vehicle identification' in the Reference Chapter.

Compression pressures

Standard	25.0 to 28.0 bar
Maximum difference between any two cylinders	1.0 bar

Lubrication system

Minimum oil pressure at 100°C	1.5 bar at idle speed
Oil pump type	Rotor-type, driven directly from crankshaft

Torque wrench settings	Nm	lbf ft
Auxiliary drivebelt tensioner assembly bolts:		
M8 bolt	20	15
M10 bolt	42	31
Balancer shaft to cylinder block:*		
Centre bolts:		
Stage 1	20	15
Stage 2	Angle-tighten a further 60°	
Outer bolts:		
Stage 1	20	15
Stage 2	Angle-tighten a further 30°	
Balancer shaft chain tensioner bolt	9	7
Balancer shaft sprocket bolt:*		
Stage 1	90	66
Stage 2	Angle-tighten a further 30°	
Camshaft bearing cap bolts.................................	15	11
Camshaft cover bolts......................................	8	6
Camshaft sprocket bolt:*		
Stage 1	90	66
Stage 2	Angle-tighten a further 60°	
Stage 3	Angle-tighten a further 30°	
Connecting rod big-end bearing cap bolt:*		
Stage 1	35	26
Stage 2	Angle-tighten a further 45°	
Stage 2	Angle-tighten a further 15°	
Crankshaft pulley bolt:*		
Stage 1	150	111
Stage 2	Angle-tighten a further 45°	
Stage 3	Angle-tighten a further 15°	
Cylinder block oil spray nozzle bolts	22	16
Cylinder head bolts:*		
Stage 1	25	18
Stage 2	Angle-tighten a further 65°	
Stage 3	Angle-tighten a further 65°	
Stage 4	Angle-tighten a further 65°	
Stage 5	Angle-tighten a further 65°	
Stage 6	Angle-tighten a further 15°	
Cylinder head-to-timing chain cover/block bolts:*		
Stage 1	20	15
Stage 2	Angle-tighten a further 30°	
Stage 3	Angle-tighten a further 5°	
Driveplate bolts:*		
Stage 1	45	33
Stage 2	Angle-tighten a further 30°	
Stage 3	Angle-tighten a further 15°	
Engine mountings:		
Front mounting/torque link bracket to transmission	80	59
Front mounting/torque link to subframe.......................	80	59
Left-hand:		
Mounting-to-body bolts	20	15
Mounting bracket to transmission bracket....................	55	41
Rear mounting/torque link bracket to transmission	80	59
Rear mounting/torque link to subframe	60	44
Rear mounting/torque link to transmission bracket	80	59
Right-hand:		
Engine bracket-to-engine bolts	55	41
Mounting-to-body bolts/nut	55	41
Mounting-to-engine bracket bolts	55	41
Engine-to-transmission unit bolts:		
M8 bolts	20	15
M10 bolts	40	30
M12 bolts	60	44
Flywheel bolts:*		
Stage 1	45	33
Stage 2	Angle-tighten a further 30°	
Stage 3	Angle-tighten a further 15°	
Injection pump sprocket bolts	28	21
Injection pump sprocket cover bolts	6	4

Torque wrench settings (continued)	Nm	lbf ft
Main bearing cap bolts:*		
Stage 1	90	66
Stage 2	Angle-tighten a further 60°	
Stage 3	Angle-tighten a further 15°	
Main bearing cap bridge bolts	20	15
Oil cooler-to-oil filter housing bolts	20	15
Oil filter housing cover	25	18
Oil pump:		
Oil pressure relief valve bolt	60	44
Pump cover screws	8	6
Pump pick-up/strainer bolts	8	6
Safety valve bolt	45	33
Roadwheel bolts	110	81
Sump bolts:		
Sump to cylinder block/timing chain cover bolts	20	15
Sump flange-to-transmission bolts:		
M8 bolts	20	15
M10 bolts	40	30
Drain plug	10	7
Timing chain cover bolts	20	15
Timing chain guide bolts*	8	6
Timing chain tensioner blade pivot bolt	20	15
Timing chain tensioner cap	60	44

* Use new nuts/bolts

1 General information

How to use this Chapter

This Part of Chapter 2 describes the repair procedures which can reasonably be carried out on the engine while it remains in the vehicle. If the engine has been removed from the vehicle and is being dismantled as described in Chapter 2F, any preliminary dismantling procedures can be ignored.

Note that, while it may be possible physically to overhaul items such as the piston/connecting rod assemblies while the engine is in the vehicle, such tasks are not usually carried out as separate operations, and usually require the execution of several additional procedures (not to mention the cleaning of components and of oilways); for this reason, all such tasks are classed as major overhaul procedures, and are described in Chapter 2F.

Chapter 2F describes the removal of the engine/transmission unit from the vehicle, and the full overhaul procedures which can then be carried out.

Engine description

The engines are of the sixteen-valve, in-line four-cylinder, single overhead camshaft (SOHC) type, mounted transversely at the front of the car with the transmission attached to its left-hand end.

The crankshaft runs in five main bearings. Thrustwashers are fitted to No 3 main bearing to control crankshaft endfloat.

The connecting rods rotate on horizontally-split bearing shells at their big-ends. The pistons are attached to the connecting rods by gudgeon pins, which are a sliding fit in the connecting rod small-end eyes being retained by circlips. The aluminium-alloy pistons are fitted with three piston rings – two compression rings and an oil control ring.

The cylinder block is made of cast iron and the cylinder bores are an integral part of the block. On this type of engine the cylinder bores are sometimes referred to as having dry liners.

The inlet and exhaust valves are each closed by coil springs, and operate in guides pressed into the cylinder head.

The camshaft is driven by the crankshaft via a dual timing chain arrangement; the lower timing chain links the crankshaft to the fuel injection pump and the upper chain links the injection pump to the camshaft. The camshaft rotates directly in the head and operates the sixteen valves via followers and hydraulic tappets. The followers are situated directly below the camshaft, each one operating two valves. Valve clearances are automatically adjusted by the hydraulic tappets.

Lubrication is by means of an oil pump, which is driven off the right-hand end of the crankshaft. It draws oil through a strainer located in the sump, and then forces it through an externally-mounted filter into galleries in the cylinder block/crankcase. From there, the oil is distributed to the crankshaft (main bearings) and camshaft. The big-end bearings are supplied with oil via internal drillings in the crankshaft, while the camshaft bearings also receive a pressurised supply. The camshaft lobes and valves are lubricated by splash, as are all other engine components. An oil cooler is fitted to keep the oil temperature stable under arduous operating conditions.

A balancer unit is fitted to the 2.2 litre engine, consisting of two balancer shafts which are driven via a chain from the crankshaft. The balancer shafts rotate in opposite directions at double the crankshaft speed. This unit is to help provide a vibration and noise-free running of the engine.

Operations with engine in car

The following operations can be carried out without having to remove the engine from the car.

a) Compression pressure – testing.
b) Camshaft cover – removal and refitting.
c) Timing chain cover – removal and refitting.
d) Timing chains – removal and refitting.
e) Timing chain tensioners, guides and sprockets – removal and refitting.
f) Camshaft and followers – removal, inspection and refitting.
g) Cylinder head – removal and refitting.
h) Connecting rods and pistons – removal and refitting.*
i) Sump – removal and refitting.
j) Oil pump – removal, overhaul and refitting.
k) Oil cooler – removal and refitting.
l) Crankshaft oil seals – renewal.
m) Engine/transmission mountings – inspection and renewal.
n) Flywheel/driveplate – removal, inspection and refitting.
o) Balancer unit – removal and refitting.

* Although the operation marked with an asterisk can be carried out with the engine in the car after removal of the sump, it is better for the engine to be removed, in the interests of cleanliness and improved access. For this reason, the procedure is described in Chapter 2F.

3.7a When No 1 cylinder is at TDC on its compression stroke, its camshaft lobes (arrowed) will be pointing upwards . . .

3.7b . . . and the timing hole (arrowed) on the left-hand end of the camshaft will be at the top

2 Compression and leakdown tests – general information

Compression test

1 When engine performance is down, or if misfiring occurs which cannot be attributed to the fuel system, a compression test can provide diagnostic clues as to the engine's condition. If the test is performed regularly, it can give warning of trouble before any other symptoms become apparent.

2 Due to the design of the fuel injection pump electronic control system used on these engines, a compression test can only be carried out with the engine management electronic control unit connected to Vauxhall/Opel diagnostic test equipment, or a compatible alternative unit. Without the test equipment, it is not possible to prevent the injection pump from supplying fuel to the injectors when the engine is cranking. When connected, the test equipment communicates with the engine management ECU to inhibit fuel supply to the injectors.

3 As the equipment needed for the compression test is unlikely to be available to the home mechanic, it is recommended that the test is performed by a Vauxhall/Opel dealer, or suitably-equipped garage.

Leakdown test

4 A leakdown test measures the rate at which compressed air fed into the cylinder is lost. It is an alternative to a compression test, and in many ways it is better, since the escaping air provides easy identification of where pressure loss is occurring (piston rings, valves or head gasket).

5 As the equipment needed for the compression test is also unlikely to be available to the home mechanic, it is recommended that the test is performed by a Vauxhall/Opel dealer, or suitably-equipped garage.

3 Top dead centre (TDC) for No 1 piston – locating

1 In its travel up and down its cylinder bore, Top Dead Centre (TDC) is the highest point that each piston reaches as the crankshaft rotates. While each piston reaches TDC both at the top of the compression stroke and again at the top of the exhaust stroke, for the purpose of timing the engine, TDC refers to the piston position (usually number 1) at the top of its compression stroke.

2 Number 1 piston (and cylinder) is at the right-hand (timing chain) end of the engine, and its TDC position is located as follows. Note that the crankshaft rotates clockwise when viewed from the right-hand side of the car.

3 Disconnect the battery negative terminal (refer to *Disconnecting the battery* in the Reference Chapter).

4 Apply the handbrake, then jack up the front of the vehicle and support it on axle stands (see *Jacking and vehicle support*). Remove the right-hand front roadwheel, then undo the ten bolts and remove the engine undertray for access to the crankshaft pulley.

5 To check the position of the camshaft either remove the camshaft cover (Section 5), so that the position of the cam lobes can be seen, or remove the braking system vacuum pump (Chapter 9) so the timing hole on the camshaft end can be seen.

6 Using a socket and extension bar on the crankshaft pulley bolt, rotate the crankshaft until the notch on the crankshaft pulley rim is aligned with the mark on the timing chain cover. Once the mark is correctly aligned, No 1 and 4 pistons are at TDC.

7 To determine which piston is at TDC on its com- pression stroke, check the position of the camshaft lobes/timing hole (as applicable). When No 1 piston is at TDC on its compression stroke, No 1 cylinder cam- shaft lobes will be pointing upwards and the timing hole on the left-hand of the camshaft will be at the top (12 o'clock position) with the camshaft slot parallel with the head surface **(see illustrations)**. If No 1 cylinder camshaft lobes are pointing downwards and the camshaft end timing mark is at the bottom (6 o'clock position) then No 4 cylinder is at TDC on its compression stroke; rotate the crankshaft through a further complete turn (360°) to bring No 1 cylinder to TDC on its compression stroke.

8 With No 1 piston at TDC on its compression stroke, the crankshaft can be locked in position by inserting a pin in through the crankshaft sensor bore on the front of the cylinder block. If access to the special Vauxhall/Opel tool (KM-929) cannot be gained, a home-made alternative will have to be manufactured (see Section 4). Remove the crankshaft sensor (see Chapter 4B) and insert the pin, making sure it is correctly located in the crankshaft web slot **(see illustrations)**.

3.8a Remove the crankshaft sensor from the cylinder block and insert the locking pin . . .

3.8b . . . making sure it is correctly engaged with the crankshaft cut-out (arrowed – shown with sump removed)

4.0a Home-made tools necessary to check/adjust the valve timing

   A   *Crankshaft locking pin*
   B   *Injection pump flange locking pin*
   C   *Camshaft locking tool*

4.0b Crankshaft locking pin dimensions (in mm)

4.0c Injection pump flange locking pin dimensions (in mm)

4.8a Insert the locking pin in through the flange cut-out and engage it in the pump body hole

4 Valve timing – checking and adjustment

Note: To check the valve (and fuel injection pump) timing, it will be necessary to use the following Vauxhall/Opel special tools (or suitable equivalents); the camshaft locking tool (KM-932), the injection pump flange locking pin (KM-927), the crankshaft locking pin (KM-929) and the camshaft sprocket wrench (KM-933). If access to these tools cannot be gained, this task must be entrusted to a Vauxhall/Opel dealer. If the necessary facilities are available to manufacture home-made tools, the dimensions of the locking pins are given in the accompanying illustrations (see illustrations). The camshaft locking tool ensures that the camshaft remains correctly positioned by keeping the camshaft slot parallel to the cylinder head surface.

1 Remove the air cleaner assembly and air intake duct as described in Chapter 4B.
2 Remove the auxiliary drivebelt as described

in Chapter 1B. Undo the auxiliary drivebelt tensioner pulley strut lower mounting bolt and the pulley backplate pivot bolt and remove the tensioner assembly from the engine. **Note:** *Store the assembly so the tensioner strut is the correct way up; if the strut is not stored properly it will have to be primed once it is refitted.*
3 Remove the braking system vacuum pump as described in Chapter 9.
4 Remove the camshaft cover and position No 1 cylinder at TDC on it compression stroke as described in Section 3.
5 Remove the crankshaft sensor as described in Chapter 4B.
6 Undo the retaining screws securing the injection pump sprocket cover to the timing chain cover. Using a wide spatula, carefully separate the sprocket cover from the timing chain cover. Take great care not to distort the sprocket cover during removal.
7 Ensure the crankshaft pulley notch is correctly aligned with the timing chain cover mark then insert the crankshaft locking pin into the crankshaft sensor aperture and

engage it with the slot in the crankshaft web **(see illustrations 3.8a and 3.8b)**.
8 With the crankshaft locked in position, insert the injection pump flange locking pin into the hole in the flange and engage it with hole in the pump body, then slide the camshaft locking tool into position on the left-hand end of the camshaft **(see illustrations)**.
9 If all the locking tools can be correctly fitted the valve timing is correctly set and

4.8b Engage the camshaft locking tool with the camshaft cut-out (arrowed)

4.14 Ensure the pump sprocket timing mark (arrowed) is correctly positioned then tighten the sprocket bolts

4.18 Adjust the upper timing chain tension as described then tighten the camshaft sprocket bolt to the Stage 1 torque setting

4.21 Apply a bead of sealant to the mating surface of the injection pump sprocket cover mating surface

no adjustment is necessary, proceed as described in paragraphs 21 to 26. If either of the tools can not be inserted, adjust the timing as follows, noting that a new camshaft sprocket bolt and tensioner bolt sealing ring will be required.

10 Remove the camshaft/injection pump sprocket locking tool (as applicable).

11 Unscrew the upper timing chain tensioner cap from the rear of the cylinder head and remove the plunger, noting which way around it is fitted. Remove the sealing ring from the cap and discard it, a new one should be used on refitting.

12 Hold the camshaft, using an open-ended spanner on the flats provided, then slacken and remove the camshaft sprocket retaining bolt. Fit the new bolt, tightening it finger-tight only at this stage.

13 Slacken the bolts securing the injection pump sprocket to the pump flange.

14 With the crankshaft locked in position, ensure the timing mark on the injection pump upper timing chain sprocket is correctly aligned with the pump flange timing hole. Insert the flange locking pin, making sure it is correctly seated, then tighten the sprocket retaining bolts to the specified torque **(see illustration)**.

15 Slide the camshaft locking tool into position making sure its pin engages centrally in the camshaft bore.

16 With all locking tools in position, fit the sprocket wrench to the camshaft sprocket; in the absence of the special wrench, pass two bolts through the sprocket holes and use

a screwdriver to lever on the bolts. Have an assistant keep the timing chain taut on its guide (upper) side by applying **slight** pressure to the sprocket; this will ensure all slack in the chain is on the tensioner side of chain.

17 With the upper timing chain tensioned as described, check that the injection pump locking pin slides in and out of position with only a slight amount of drag. If excessive force is needed to move the pin, have your assistant decrease the pressure on the sprocket or, if the pin moves easily, increase the pressure.

18 Once the upper timing chain is correctly tensioned, retain the camshaft with an open-ended spanner and tighten the camshaft sprocket retaining bolt to the specified Stage 1 torque setting **(see illustration)**. Check the injection pump pin action then tighten the bolt through the specified Stage 2 angle and finally through the specified Stage 3 angle. It is recommended that an angle-measuring gauge is used during the final stages of the tightening, to ensure accuracy. If a gauge is not available, use white paint to make alignment marks between the bolt head and pulley prior to tightening; the marks can then be used to check that the bolt has been rotated through the correct angle.

19 Remove all the locking tools and fit a new sealing ring to the upper timing chain tensioner cap. Insert the plunger into the cylinder head, ensuring its closed end is facing the timing chain, then install the cap and tighten it to the specified torque. **Note:** *If a new tensioner is being fitted, release it by pushing the cap centre pin fully in until it is heard to 'click', the*

tensioner pin should then be able to be easily depressed and return smoothly.

20 Rotate the crankshaft through two complete rotations (720°) in the correct direction of rotation (to bring number 1 piston back to TDC on its compression stroke) and check that all the locking tools can be inserted correctly.

21 Ensure the mating surfaces of the pump sprocket cover and timing chain cover are clean and dry, with all traces of old sealant removed. Apply a bead of sealant (approximately 2 mm thick) to the cover mating surface then refit the cover and tighten its retaining bolts to the specified torque **(see illustration)**.

22 Refit the auxiliary drivebelt tensioner assembly to the engine unit, tightening the strut and backplate pivot bolts to their specified torque settings. If a new tensioner strut is being fitted, or the original was not stored properly, prime the strut by repeatedly compressing it using a socket on the backplate hexagonal section. Once the strut is functioning correctly, refit the auxiliary drivebelt as described in Chapter 1B.

23 Refit the camshaft cover (see Section 5).

24 Refit the air cleaner assembly and intake duct as described in the Chapter 4B.

25 Refit the vacuum pump to the cylinder head (see Chapter 9).

26 Fit the crankshaft sensor to the cylinder block (see Chapter 4B) and reconnect the battery.

5 Camshaft cover – removal and refitting

Removal

1 Undo the three bolts and lift off the plastic cover over the top of the engine **(see illustration)**.

2 Undo the two bolts securing the charge air pipe to the camshaft cover **(see illustration)**. Slacken the retaining clip and disconnect the charge air pipe connecting hose from the turbocharger elbow. Move the charge air pipe to one side.

3 Slacken the retaining clip and disconnect the breather hose from the rear of the cover.

5.1 Undo the three bolts and lift off the plastic cover over the top of the engine

5.2 Undo the two bolts (arrowed) securing the charge air pipe to the camshaft cover

5.4 Unclip the two fuel hoses (arrowed) and vacuum hose from the right-hand end of the camshaft cover

5.8 Disconnect the charge (boost) pressure sensor wiring connector (arrowed)

5.9 Slacken and remove the camshaft cover retaining bolts noting the sealing washer (arrowed) which is fitted to each bolt

5.10 Fit the seal to the camshaft cover groove

5.12a Apply a smear of sealant to the semi-circular cut-out on the right-hand end of the cylinder head . . .

5.12b . . . and to the areas of the cylinder head surface on each side of the left-hand end camshaft cap (arrowed)

4 Unclip the two fuel hoses and vacuum hose from the right-hand end of the cover **(see illustration)**.

5 Unscrew the two bolts and release the wiring harness trough from the rear of the cover.

6 With the engine cold, slowly unscrew the cooling system expansion tank cap, to release any pressure present in the cooling system, and remove the cap.

7 Place a suitable container beneath the expansion tank, then slacken the retaining clip and disconnect the upper coolant hose from the tank. Unscrew the two retaining bolts and move the hose clear of the camshaft cover.

8 Disconnect the charge (boost) pressure sensor wiring connector **(see illustration)**.

9 Slacken and remove the camshaft cover retaining bolts along with their sealing washers then lift the camshaft cover and seal away from the cylinder head **(see illustration)**. Examine the cover seal and retaining bolt sealing washers for signs of damage or deterioration and renew if necessary.

Refitting

10 Ensure the cover and cylinder head surfaces are clean and dry then fit the seal to the cover groove **(see illustration)**.

11 Fit the sealing washers to the retaining bolts, ensuring they are fitted the correct way up. Fit the retaining bolts to the cover making sure the cover seal is held firmly in position by the lower shoulder on each bolt.

12 Apply a smear of sealant to the circular cut-out on the right-hand end of the cylinder

head mating surface and the areas of the cylinder head mating surface on either side of the left-hand end of the camshaft **(see illustrations)**.

13 Carefully lower the cover into position and screw in the retaining bolts. Once all bolts are hand-tight, go around and tighten them all to the specified torque setting.

14 Reconnect the intake air pressure sensor wiring connector.

15 Reconnect the coolant hose to the expansion tank, and secure the hose with the two retaining bolts.

16 Refit and tighten the two bolts securing the wiring harness trough the rear of the camshaft cover.

17 Reposition the fuel hoses and vacuum hose into their retaining clips on the right-hand end of the cover. Reconnect the breather hose to the rear of the cover.

18 Place the charge air pipe in position and attach the connecting hose to the turbocharger elbow. Secure the pipe to the camshaft cover with the two bolts tightened securely.

19 Refit the plastic cover to the top of the engine and tighten the three retaining bolts.

20 Top-up the cooling system with reference to *Weekly checks*.

6 Crankshaft pulley – removal and refitting

Note 1: *Vauxhall/Opel special tools KM-977-1 or KM-6619, together with KM-956-1 or*

suitable alternative will be required to prevent crankshaft rotation whilst the retaining bolt is slackened/tightened.

Note 2: *A new pulley retaining bolt will be required on refitting.*

Removal

1 Apply the handbrake, then jack up the front of the vehicle and support it on axle stands (see *Jacking and vehicle support*). Remove the right-hand front roadwheel, then undo the ten bolts and remove the engine undertray for access to the crankshaft pulley.

2 Undo the three bolts and lift off the plastic cover over the top of the engine.

3 Remove the auxiliary drivebelt as described in Chapter 1B. Prior to removal, mark the direction of rotation on the belt to ensure the belt is refitted the same way around.

4 Slacken the crankshaft pulley retaining bolt. To prevent crankshaft rotation whilst the retaining bolt is slackened, it will be necessary to hold the crankshaft pulley with the Vauxhall/ Opel tool or a suitable alternative.

5 Undo the two bolts securing the charge air pipe to the camshaft cover **(see illustration 5.2)**. Slacken the retaining clip and disconnect the charge air pipe connecting hose from the turbocharger elbow. Move the charge air pipe to one side.

6 Remove the air cleaner assembly and air intake duct as described in Chapter 4B.

7 Unclip the two fuel hoses and vacuum hose from the right-hand end of the cover **(see illustration 5.4)**.

6.12a Slide the crankshaft pulley carefully into position engaging its slot (arrowed) with the Woodruff key . . .

6.12b . . . then fit the retaining bolt and washer

8 Connect a suitable hoist and lifting tackle to the right-hand end of the engine and support its weight. If available, the type of support bar which locates in the engine compartment side channels is to be preferred.

9 Mark the bolt positions for correct refitting, then undo the three bolts securing the right-hand engine mounting to the engine bracket, and the two bolts and one nut securing the mounting to the body **(see illustrations 17.25a and 17.25b)**. Remove the mounting.

10 Taking care not to place undue strain on any of the engine attachments, carefully lower the right-hand side of the engine by approximately 20 mm.

11 Unscrew the retaining bolt and washer and remove the crankshaft pulley from the end of the crankshaft. Whilst the pulley is removed check the oil seal for signs of wear or damage and, if necessary, renew as described in Section 15.

Refitting

12 Carefully locate the crankshaft pulley on the crankshaft end, aligning the pulley slot with the crankshaft key. Slide the pulley fully into position, taking great care not to damage the oil seal, then fit the washer and new retaining bolt **(see illustrations)**.

13 Raise the engine and locate the right-hand engine mounting in position. Refit the three bolts securing the mounting to the engine

bracket and the two bolts and one nut securing the mounting to the body. Align the mounting in its original position, then tighten the bolts and nut to the specified torque.

14 Remove the hoist and lifting tackle from the engine.

15 Reposition the fuel hoses into their retaining clips on the right-hand end of the cover.

16 Lock the crankshaft by the method used on removal, and tighten the pulley retaining bolt to the specified Stage 1 torque setting then angle-tighten the bolt through the specified Stage 2 angle, using a socket and extension bar, and finally through the specified Stage 3 angle. It is recommended that an angle-measuring gauge is used during the final stages of the tightening, to ensure accuracy. If a gauge is not available, use white paint to make alignment marks between the bolt head and pulley prior to tightening; the marks can then be used to check that the bolt has been rotated through the correct angle.

17 Refit the auxiliary drivebelt as described in Chapter 1B using the mark made prior to removal to ensure the belt is fitted the correct way around.

18 Place the charge air pipe in position and attach the connecting hose to the turbocharger elbow. Secure the pipe to the camshaft cover with the two bolts tightened securely.

19 Refit the air cleaner assembly and air intake duct as described in Chapter 4B.

20 Refit the plastic cover to the top of the engine and tighten the three retaining bolts.

21 Refit the roadwheel and engine undertray, then lower the car to the ground and tighten the wheel bolts to the specified torque.

7 Timing chain cover – removal and refitting

Note 1: *Although it is just possible to remove the timing chain cover with the engine in the car, it is a very complicated and involved procedure, and access to the right-hand side of the engine is extremely limited. To perform this operation satisfactorily, it is strongly recommended that the engine/transmission unit is removed first, as described in Chapter 2F.*

Note 2: *The following procedure is based on the engine being removed from the car.*

Removal

1 Remove the upper timing chain and sprockets as described in Section 9.

2 Remove the cylinder head as described in Section 11.

3 Remove the coolant pump as described in Chapter 3.

4 Remove the crankshaft pulley as described in Section 6. Prior to slackening the pulley bolt, temporarily remove the locking pin from the crankshaft to prevent damage. Refit the pin once the bolt is loose.

5 Remove the sump as described in Section 12.

6 Remove the alternator as described in Chapter 5A.

7 Unscrew the lower timing chain tensioner cap from the rear of the timing chain cover and remove the tensioner plunger, noting which way around it is fitted. Remove the sealing ring from the cap and discard it, a new one should be used on refitting.

8 Noting each bolt's correct fitted location (the bolts are not all the same length), slacken and remove all the bolts securing the timing chain cover to the cylinder block **(see illustration)**.

9 Carefully ease the timing cover squarely

7.8 Timing chain cover retaining bolt locations (arrowed)

7.10 Unscrew the pivot bolt and remove the upper (1) and lower (2) timing chain tensioner blades

away from the cylinder block and manoeuvre it out of position, noting the correct fitted positions of its locating dowels. If the locating dowels are a loose fit, remove them and store with the cover for safe-keeping.

10 Undo the pivot bolt and remove the upper and lower timing chain tensioner blades from the cylinder block **(see illustration)**.

11 Undo the retaining bolts and remove the lower timing chain guide from the cylinder block, noting which way around the guide is fitted **(see illustration)**.

12 Temporarily free the lower timing chain sprocket from the injection pump and manoeuvre the timing chain cover gasket away from the cylinder block. Once the gasket has been removed, seat the sprocket back on the injection pump flange **(see illustration)**.

Refitting

13 Prior to refitting the cover, it is recommended that the crankshaft oil seal should be renewed. Carefully lever the old seal out of the cover using a large flat-bladed screwdriver. Fit the new seal to the cover, making sure its sealing lip is facing inwards. Press/tap the seal into position until it is flush with the cover, using a suitable tubular drift, such as a socket, which bears only on the hard outer edge of the seal.

14 Ensure the mating surfaces of the cover and cylinder block are clean and dry and the locating dowels are in position.

15 Temporarily free the sprocket from the injection pump flange then manoeuvre the gasket into position and locate it on the dowels. Locate the sprocket back on the injection pump flange.

16 Refit the lower timing chain guide to the cylinder block and tighten its new retaining bolts to the specified torque. Ensure the guide is fitted the correct way around with its stepped face on the inside **(see illustration)**.

17 Manoeuvre the timing chain tensioner blades into position and refit the pivot bolt, tightening it to the specified torque setting **(see illustration)**.

18 Manoeuvre the timing cover into position. Align the oil pump drivegear with the crankshaft sprocket and slide the cover into position, locating it on the dowels.

19 Refit the timing chain cover retaining bolts, ensuring each one is fitted in its original location, and tighten them evenly and progressively to the specified torque.

20 Fit a new sealing ring to the lower timing chain tensioner cap. Insert the plunger, ensuring its closed end is facing the timing chain, then fit the cap to the timing chain cover and tighten to the specified torque. **Note:** *If a new tensioner is being fitted, release it by pushing the cap centre pin fully in until it is heard to 'click', the tensioner pin should then be able to be easily depressed and return smoothly.*

21 Refit the cylinder head as described in Section 11.

22 Refit the upper timing chain and sprockets as described in Section 9.

23 Refit the sump as described in Section 12.

7.11 Undo the retaining bolts (arrowed) and remove the lower timing chain guide

7.16 Refit the lower timing chain guide and tighten its retaining bolts to the specified torque

24 Refit the crankshaft pulley as described in Section 6.

25 Refit the coolant pump and alternator (see Chapters 3 and 5A) and refit the auxiliary drivebelt (see Chapter 1B).

26 On completion refill the engine with oil and coolant as described in Chapter 1B. Start the engine and check for signs of oil leaks.

8	Timing chain tensioners – removal and refitting

Upper chain tensioner

Removal

1 Remove the air cleaner assembly and air intake duct as described in Chapter 4B.

8.2a Unscrew the tensioner cap from the rear of the cylinder head . . .

7.12 Free the sprocket from the injection pump and remove the timing chain cover gasket

7.17 Refit the pivot bolt to the tensioner blades and tighten to the specified torque

2 Unscrew the tensioner cap from the rear of the cylinder head and remove the plunger, noting which way around it is fitted **(see illustrations)**. Remove the sealing ring from the cap and discard it, a new one should be used on refitting.

Caution: Do not rotate the engine whilst the tensioner is removed.

3 Inspect the tensioner plunger for signs of wear or damage and renew if necessary.

Refitting

4 Lubricate the tensioner plunger with clean engine oil and insert it into the cylinder head. Ensure the plunger is fitted the correct way around with its closed end facing the timing chain.

5 Fit a new sealing ring to the tensioner cap then fit the cap to the cylinder head, tightening it to the specified torque. **Note:** *If a new*

8.2b . . . and withdraw the plunger, noting which way around it is fitted

8.5a Insert the plunger, ensuring its closed end faces the timing chain, then fit the tensioner cap and sealing washer (arrowed)

8.5b If a new tensioner is being fitted, release it by depressing the cap centre pin until it is heard to click

8.8a Slacken and remove the lower timing chain tensioner cap and sealing washer from the rear of the timing chain cover . . .

8.8b . . . then withdraw the tensioner plunger

8.10 Ensure the plunger is fitted the correct way around with its closed end (arrowed) facing the timing chain

8.11 If a new tensioner is being fitted, release it by depressing the centre pin until it is heard to click

tensioner is being fitted, release it by pushing the cap centre pin fully in until it is heard to 'click', the tensioner pin should then be able to be easily depressed and return smoothly **(see illustrations)**.

6 Refit the air cleaner assembly and air intake duct as described in Chapter 4B.

Lower chain tensioner

Removal

7 Apply the handbrake, then jack up the front of the vehicle and support it on axle stands (see *Jacking and vehicle support*). Undo the ten bolts and remove the engine undertray.

8 Unscrew the tensioner cap from the rear of the timing chain cover and remove the plunger, noting which way around it is fitted. Remove the sealing ring from the cap and discard it, a new one should be used on refitting.

Caution: Do not rotate the engine whilst the tensioner is removed.

9 Inspect the tensioner plunger for signs of wear or damage and renew if necessary.

Refitting

10 Lubricate the tensioner plunger with clean engine oil and insert it into the timing chain cover. Ensure the plunger is fitted the correct way around with its closed end facing the timing chain **(see illustration)**.

11 Fit a new sealing ring to the tensioner cap then fit the cap to the cover, tightening it to the specified torque. **Note:** *If a new tensioner is being fitted, release it by pushing the cap centre pin fully in until it is heard to 'click',*

the tensioner pin should then be able to be easily depressed and return smoothly **(see illustration)**.

12 Refit the undertray then lower the vehicle to the ground.

Tensioner blades

13 Tensioner blade removal and refitting is part of the timing chain cover removal and refitting procedure (see Section 7). The blades must be renewed if they show signs of wear or damage on their chain surfaces.

---

9 Timing chains and sprockets – removal, inspection and refitting

Note: *In order to set the valve timing accurately, several special Vauxhall/Opel service tools (or suitable alternatives) are required (see Section 4). If access to suitable tools cannot be gained then it is recommended that this task is entrusted to a Vauxhall/Opel dealer or suitably-equipped garage. If the task is to be carried out without the tools then accurate alignment marks must be made between the sprocket(s), chain(s) and the shaft(s) prior to removal to ensure the valve timing is correctly set on refitting.*

Removal

Upper chain and sprockets

Note: *A new camshaft sprocket bolt and*

new timing chain guide retaining bolts will be required on refitting.

1 Disconnect the battery negative terminal (refer to *Disconnecting the battery* in the Reference Chapter).

2 Remove the air cleaner assembly and air intake duct as described in Chapter 4B.

3 Remove the auxiliary drivebelt as described in Chapter 1B. Undo the auxiliary drivebelt tensioner pulley strut lower mounting bolt and the pulley backplate pivot bolt and remove the tensioner assembly from the engine. **Note:** *Store the assembly so the tensioner strut is the correct way up; if the strut is not stored properly it will have to be primed once it is refitted.*

4 Remove the braking system vacuum pump as described in Chapter 9.

5 Remove the camshaft cover as described in Section 5.

6 Position No 1 cylinder at TDC on its compression stroke as described in Section 3 and lock the crankshaft in position.

7 Undo the retaining screws securing the injection pump sprocket cover to the timing chain cover. Using a wide spatula, carefully separate the sprocket cover from the timing chain cover **(see illustrations)**. Take great care not to distort the sprocket cover during removal.

8 Remove both the upper and lower timing chain tensioners as described in Section 8.

9 If the special locking tools are available, lock the injection pump sprockets and camshaft in position (see Section 4). If the tools are not

9.7a Undo the retaining screws . . .

9.7b . . . and remove the injection pump sprocket cover from the engine

9.10a To ease removal, heat the upper timing chain guide bolts with a hot air gun prior to removal

9.10b Unscrew both retaining bolts . . .

9.10c . . . and lift the upper guide out from the top of the cylinder head

9.11 Retain the camshaft with an open-ended spanner and unscrew the sprocket retaining bolt

being used, make accurate alignment marks between the chain and sprockets, and the sprockets and the camshaft/pump flange.

10 Undo the retaining bolts then lift the upper chain guide out from the top of the cylinder head. **Note:** *The upper timing chain guide bolts should be heated with a hot air gun prior to removal; this loosens the locking compound on the bolt head and significantly eases removal of the bolts* **(see illustrations)**.

11 Hold the camshaft using an open-ended spanner on the flats provided, then slacken and remove the camshaft sprocket retaining bolt **(see illustration)**. To ensure the camshaft sprocket and chain remain correctly mated, cable tie the chain to the sprocket. **Note:** *If the locking tools are being used, remove them prior to slackening the sprocket bolt and refit them once the bolt is loose.*

12 Remove the injection pump locking tool (where fitted) then slacken and remove the bolts securing the injection pump sprockets to the pump flange. Manoeuvre the injection pump upper chain sprocket out of position then free the camshaft sprocket from the camshaft end and lift the sprocket and upper timing chain out from the top of the cylinder head **(see illustration)**.

Lower chain and sprockets

Note: *Refer to the notes at the beginning of Section 7 before starting this procedure.*

13 Remove the upper timing chain and sprockets as described in paragraphs 1 to 12.

14 Remove the timing chain cover as described in Section 7.

15 Make alignment marks between the chain and sprockets and the injection pump sprocket and pump flange.

16 Free the pump sprocket from its flange and remove the sprocket and timing chain

9.12 Unbolt the sprocket from the injection pump then free it from the chain and remove it through the cover aperture

9.17a Slide the sprocket off from the end of the crankshaft . . .

from the engine, noting which way around the sprocket is fitted **(see illustration)**.

17 Slide the crankshaft sprocket off from the crankshaft end and recover the Woodruff key from the crankshaft groove **(see illustrations)**.

9.16 Free the sprocket from the injection pump flange and remove it complete with the lower timing chain

9.17b . . . and remove the Woodruff key

9.26 Align the injection pump sprocket timing mark (arrowed) with the pump flange hole and refit the retaining bolts

9.27 Fit the new camshaft sprocket retaining bolt and tighten it by hand only

9.29 Refit the upper timing chain guide to the cylinder head making sure its locating lug (arrowed) is uppermost

Inspection

18 Examine the teeth on the sprockets for any sign of wear or damage such as chipped, hooked or missing teeth. If there is any sign of wear or damage on either sprocket, both sprockets and the relevant chain should be renewed as a set.

19 Inspect the links of each timing chain for signs of wear or damage on the rollers. The extent of wear can be judged by checking the amount by which the chain can be bent sideways; a new chain will have very little sideways movement. If there is an excessive amount of side play in a timing chain, it must be renewed.

20 Note that it is a sensible precaution to renew the timing chains, regardless of their apparent condition, if the engine has covered a high mileage, or if it has been noted that the chain(s) have sounded noisy when the engine running. Although not strictly necessary, it is always worth renewing the chains and sprockets as a matched set, since it is false economy to run a new chain on worn sprockets and *vice versa*. If there is any doubt about the condition of the timing chains and sprockets, seek the advice of a Vauxhall/Opel dealer service department, who will be able to advise you as to the best course of action, based on their previous knowledge of the engine.

21 Examine the chain guide(s) and tensioner blade(s) for signs of wear or damage to their chain contact faces, renewing any which are badly marked.

Refitting

Upper chain and sprockets

22 If any new components are being fitted, transfer the alignment marks from the original components to aid refitting. Ensure the crankshaft is still locked in the TDC position.

23 Engage the camshaft sprocket with the chain and lower the assembly into position.

24 Manoeuvre the injection pump sprocket into position and engage it with the timing chain.

25 Ensure the marks made prior to removal are all correctly aligned then engage the sprockets with the camshaft and injection pump flange. Where necessary, remove the cable tie from camshaft sprocket.

26 Align the injection pump sprocket timing mark with the hole in the pump flange then refit the retaining bolts tightening them by hand only at this stage **(see illustration)**.

27 Fit the new sprocket retaining bolt to the camshaft end, tightening by hand only at this stage **(see illustration)**.

28 Refit the lower timing chain tensioner as described in Section 8.

29 Slide the upper timing chain guide into position, ensuring its locating lug is uppermost, then fit the new retaining bolts and tighten them to the specified torque **(see illustration)**.

30 If the special tools are available, fit all the tools to ensure the pump, camshaft and crankshaft are correctly positioned. If the tools are not being used, ensure the marks made prior to removal are realigned.

31 If the special tools are available, adjust the valve timing as described in Section 4, paragraphs 14 to 18. Remove all the locking tools.

32 If the tools are not available, align the marks made prior to removal then tighten the injection pump sprocket bolts to the specified torque. Tighten the camshaft sprocket bolt to the specified Stage 1 torque setting, whilst preventing the camshaft from rotating. Ensure the marks remain in alignment then tighten the bolt through the specified Stage 2 angle and finally through the specified Stage 3 angle. It is recommended that an angle-measuring gauge is used during the final stages of the tightening, to ensure accuracy. If a gauge is not available, use white paint to make alignment marks prior to tightening; the marks can then be used to check that the bolt has been rotated through the correct angle.

33 Refit the upper timing chain tensioner as described in Section 8.

34 Ensure the mating surfaces of the pump sprocket cover and timing chain cover are clean and dry, with all traces of old sealant removed. Apply a bead of sealant (approximately 2 mm thick) to the cover mating surface then refit the cover and tighten its retaining bolts to the specified torque **(see illustration 4.21)**.

35 Refit the auxiliary drivebelt tensioner assembly to the engine unit, tightening

the strut and backplate pivot bolts to their specified torque settings. If a new tensioner strut is being fitted, or the original was not stored properly, prime the strut by repeatedly compressing it using a socket on the backplate hexagonal section. Once the strut is functioning correctly, refit the auxiliary drivebelt as described in Chapter 1B.

36 Refit the camshaft cover as described in Section 5.

37 Refit the braking system vacuum pump as described in Chapter 9.

38 Refit the crankshaft sensor, air cleaner assembly and air intake duct as described in Chapter 4B.

Lower chain and sprockets

39 If any new components are being fitted transfer the alignment marks from the original components to aid refitting.

40 Refit the Woodruff key to the crankshaft then slide on the crankshaft sprocket, aligning the sprocket groove with the key.

41 Ensure the injection pump flange is still correctly positioned with the flange timing cut-out aligned with the hole in the pump body and the crankshaft is still locked at TDC.

42 Aligning the marks made prior to removal, engage the pump sprocket with the chain and manoeuvre the assembly into position. Engage the chain with the crankshaft sprocket and seat the pump sprocket on the flange, ensuring the sprocket is fitted the correct way around. Check that all the marks made prior to removal are correctly aligned and that the injection pump flange timing cut-out is correctly position in the oblong slot in the sprocket.

43 Refit the timing cover as described in Section 7 then refit the upper timing chain as described earlier in this Section.

10 Camshaft and followers – removal, inspection and refitting

Note: *A new camshaft sprocket retaining bolt and new upper timing chain guide retaining bolts will be required on refitting.*

Removal

1 Disconnect the battery negative terminal

(refer to *Disconnecting the battery* in the Reference Chapter).

2 Remove the air cleaner assembly and air intake duct as described in Chapter 4B.

3 Remove the auxiliary drivebelt as described in Chapter 1B. Undo the auxiliary drivebelt tensioner pulley strut lower mounting bolt and the pulley backplate pivot bolt and remove the tensioner assembly from the engine. **Note:** *Store the assembly so the tensioner strut is the correct way up; if the strut is not stored properly it will have to be primed once it is refitted.*

4 Remove the braking system vacuum pump as described in Chapter 9.

5 Remove the camshaft cover as described in Section 5.

6 Position No 1 cylinder at TDC on its compression stroke as described in Section 3 and lock the crankshaft in position.

7 Remove the upper timing chain tensioner as described in Section 8.

8 Undo the retaining screws securing the injection pump sprocket cover to the timing chain cover. Using a wide spatula, carefully separate the sprocket cover from the timing chain cover. Take great care not to distort the sprocket cover during removal.

9 Make accurate alignment marks between the upper timing chain and sprockets, and the camshaft sprocket and camshaft.

10 Undo the retaining bolts then lift the upper chain guide out from the top of the cylinder head **(see illustration)**. **Note:** *The upper timing chain guide bolts should be heated with a hot air gun prior to removal; this loosens the locking compound on the bolt head and significantly eases removal of the bolts.*

11 Hold the camshaft, using an open-ended spanner on the flats provided, then slacken and remove the camshaft sprocket retaining bolt. Remove the crankshaft locking tool prior to slackening the sprocket bolt and refit it once the bolt is loose.

12 Disengage the camshaft sprocket from the upper timing chain and remove it from the engine. Pass a screwdriver or extension bar through the upper chain, to prevent it falling down into the cylinder head, and rest it on the head upper surface **(see illustrations)**.

13 Note the identification markings on the camshaft bearing caps. The caps are numbered 1 to 5 with all numbers being the right way up when viewed from the front of the engine; number 1 cap being at the timing chain end of the engine and number 5 at the flywheel end **(see illustration)**. If the markings are not clearly visible, make identification marks to ensure each cap is fitted correctly on refitting.

14 Working in a spiral pattern from the outside inwards, slacken the camshaft bearing cap retaining bolts by half a turn at a time, to relieve the pressure of the valve springs on the bearing caps gradually and evenly. Once the valve spring pressure has been relieved, the bolts can be fully unscrewed and removed,

10.10 Remove the retaining bolts (arrowed) and lift out the upper timing chain guide

10.12b . . . then pass a screwdriver or extension bar through the chain to prevent it falling down into the engine

along with the caps. Take care not to lose the locating dowels which are fitted to left-hand end (No 5) bearing cap and lift the camshaft out from the head.

Caution: If the bearing cap bolts are carelessly slackened, the bearing caps might break. If any bearing cap breaks then the complete cylinder head assembly must be renewed; the bearing caps are matched to the head and are not available separately.

15 Obtain eight (twenty-four if the tappets are also to be removed) small, clean plastic containers, and label them for identification. Alternatively, divide a larger container into compartments. Lift the followers out from the top of the cylinder head and store each one in its respective fitted position **(see illustration)**.

16 If the hydraulic tappets are also to be removed, remove the injector crosspipes as described in Chapter 4B. Using a rubber sucker or magnet, withdraw each hydraulic tappet and place it in its container.

Inspection

17 Examine the camshaft bearing surfaces and cam lobes for signs of wear ridges and scoring. Renew the camshaft if any of these conditions are apparent. Examine the condition of the bearing surfaces both on the camshaft journals and in the cylinder head. If the head bearing surfaces are worn excessively, the cylinder head will need to be renewed.

18 Examine the follower bearing surfaces

10.12a Free the camshaft sprocket from the timing chain . . .

10.13 Each camshaft bearing cap should be stamped with an identification number (arrowed)

which contact the camshaft lobes for wear ridges and scoring. Renew any followers on which these conditions are apparent.

19 Check the hydraulic tappets (where removed) and their bores in the cylinder head for signs of wear or damage. If any tappet is thought to be faulty it should be renewed.

Refitting

20 Remove the crankshaft locking tool and turn the crankshaft back (anti-clockwise) approximately 60°. This is to prevent any possibility of the valves contacting the pistons when the camshaft is refitted.

21 Where removed, lubricate the hydraulic tappets with clean engine oil and carefully insert each one into its original location in the cylinder head **(see illustration)**. Refit the injector crosspipes as described in Chapter 4B.

22 Refit the camshaft followers to the cylinder

10.15 Removing a camshaft follower

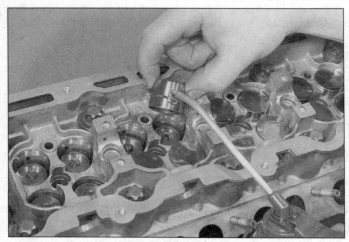

10.21 Lubricate the hydraulic tappets with clean engine oil and install them in the cylinder head

10.22 On refitting ensure that all followers are correctly positioned and that the punch marks (A) are facing towards the injector crosspipe (B)

head. Ensure each follower is fitted in its original location and the punch marks on the follower upper surface are facing the injector crosspipe **(see illustration)**.

23 Lubricate the camshaft followers with clean engine oil then lay the camshaft in position. Turn the camshaft so that the lobes of No 1 cylinder are pointing upwards and the slot on the left-hand end of the camshaft is parallel with the cylinder head surface (timing hole at the top) **(see illustrations)**.

24 Ensure the mating surfaces of the bearing caps and cylinder head are clean and dry and lubricate the camshaft journals and lobes with clean engine oil.

25 Apply a smear of sealant to the cylinder head mating surface of the left-hand (No 5) bearing cap and fit the cap locating dowels to the cylinder head **(see illustration)**.

26 Refit the camshaft bearing caps and the retaining bolts in their original locations on the cylinder head **(see illustration)**. The caps are numbered 1 to 5 from timing chain end of the cylinder head and all numbers should be the right way up when viewed from the front of the engine.

27 Tighten all bolts by hand only then, working in a spiral pattern from the centre outwards, tighten the bolts by one turn at a time to gradually impose the pressure of the valve springs on the bearing caps. Repeat this sequence until all bearing caps are in contact with the cylinder head then go around and tighten the camshaft bearing cap bolts to the specified torque **(see illustration)**.

Caution: If the bearing cap bolts are carelessly tightened, the bearing caps might break. If any bearing cap breaks then the complete cylinder head assembly must be renewed; the bearing caps are matched to the head and are not available separately.

28 Turn the crankshaft clockwise to bring No 1 cylinder back to TDC on its compression stroke as described in Section 3 and lock the crankshaft in position.

29 Using the marks made on removal, ensure that the upper timing chain is still correctly engaged with the injection pump sprocket then refit the camshaft sprocket to the chain. Seat the sprocket on the end of the camshaft and fit the new retaining bolt **(see illustration)**.

10.23a Refit the camshaft, positioning it so that No 1 cylinder lobes are pointing upwards (arrowed) . . .

10.23b . . . and the slot in its left-hand end is parallel to the cylinder head with the timing hole (arrowed) at the top

10.25 Apply sealant to the areas shown on the left-hand end of the cylinder head (arrowed)

10.26 Refit the camshaft bearing caps using the identification markings to ensure each one is correctly positioned

10.27 Working as described in text, tighten the bearing cap bolts to the specified torque

10.29 Refit the camshaft sprocket and install the new retaining bolt

10.32a If the timing tools are not available, align the marks made prior to removal then tighten the sprocket bolt to the Stage 1 torque setting . . .

10.32b . . . and then through the specified Stage 2 and 3 angles

30 Slide the upper timing chain guide into position, ensuring its locating lug is uppermost, then fit the new retaining bolts and tighten them to the specified torque.

31 If the special tools are available, adjust the valve timing as described in Section 4, paragraphs 14 to 18. Remove all the locking tools.

32 If the tools are not available, align the marks made prior to removal on the camshaft and sprocket. Hold the camshaft with an open-ended spanner and tighten the sprocket bolt to the specified Stage 1 torque setting. Ensure the marks have remained in alignment then tighten the bolt through the specified Stage 2 angle and finally through the specified Stage 3 angle. It is recommended that an angle-measuring gauge is used during the final stages of the tightening, to ensure accuracy **(see illustrations)**. If a gauge is not available, use white paint to make alignment marks prior to tightening; the marks can then be used to check that the bolt has been rotated through the correct angle.

33 Refit the upper timing chain tensioner as described in Section 8.

34 Ensure the mating surfaces of the pump sprocket cover and timing chain cover are clean and dry, with all traces of old sealant removed. Apply a bead of sealant (approximately 2 mm thick) to the cover mating surface then refit the cover and tighten its retaining bolts to the specified torque.

35 Refit the auxiliary drivebelt tensioner assembly to the engine unit, tightening the strut and backplate pivot bolts to their specified torque settings. If a new tensioner strut is being fitted, or the original was not stored properly, prime the strut by repeatedly compressing it using a socket on the backplate hexagonal section. Once the strut is functioning correctly, refit the auxiliary drivebelt as described in Chapter 1B.

36 Refit the camshaft cover as described in Section 5.

37 Refit the vacuum pump as described in Chapter 9.

38 Refit the crankshaft sensor, air cleaner assembly and air intake duct as described in Chapter 4B.

11 Cylinder head –
removed and refitting

Caution: Be careful not to allow dirt into the fuel injection pump or injector pipes during this procedure.

Note: New cylinder head bolts, upper timing chain guide bolts and a camshaft sprocket retaining bolt will be required on refitting.

Removal

1 Drain the cooling system as described in Chapter 1B.

2 Remove the complete exhaust system as described in Chapter 4B.

3 Carry out the operations described in paragraphs 1 to 12 of Section 10.

4 Wipe clean the area around the fuel hose unions on the injection pump then slacken and remove the union bolts and sealing washers. Disconnect the return pipe from the pump union then release the hoses from their retaining clips, and position them clear of the cylinder head **(see illustrations)**.

5 Remove the inlet and exhaust manifolds as described in Chapter 4B. If no work is to be carried out on the cylinder head, the head can be removed complete with manifolds once the following operations have been carried out.

a) *Remove the air intake ducts and connection hoses from the turbocharger and inlet manifold.*

b) *Unbolt the wiring harness tray from the top of the inlet manifold, disconnect the wiring connectors and position it clear of the engine. Unclip the crankshaft sensor wiring from the manifold.*

c) *Disconnect the intake air pressure sensor wiring connector, then undo the four bolts and remove the air intake elbow from the top of the inlet manifold. Recover the gasket.*

d) *Remove the injector pipes linking the pump to the injectors.*

e) *Disconnect the vacuum hoses from the inlet manifold switchover valve.*

f) *Disconnect the coolant hoses and wiring connector from the EGR valve.*

g) *Disconnect/unbolt the wiring connectors from the glow plugs then remove the turbocharger heat shields.*

h) *Disconnect the turbocharger oil pipes from the cylinder block. Disconnect the wastegate diaphragm vacuum hose.*

i) *Remove the starter motor heat shield and unbolt the wiring harness guide and exhaust manifold support bracket from the rear of the block.*

6 Release the retaining clips and disconnect the coolant hoses from the front and rear of the right-hand end of the cylinder head **(see illustrations)**.

7 Disconnect the alternator wiring connectors and the oil pressure switch wiring connector. Undo the retaining bolts and release the alternator wiring trough. Slacken the alternator lower mounting nut and bolt and remove the

11.4a Unscrew the union bolts (arrowed) then disconnect the fuel feed and return hose unions from the injection pump . . .

11.4b . . . and disconnect the return pipe

11.6a Disconnect the coolant hoses (arrowed) from the front of the cylinder head . . .

11.6b . . . and the hose from the rear of the cylinder head

11.10 Unscrew the bolts (arrowed) securing the right-hand end of the cylinder head to the timing chain cover/block

alternator upper mounting bolt. Pivot the alternator to the rear to position it clear of the cylinder head.

8 Place a trolley jack beneath the right-hand of the engine with a block of wood on the jack head. Raise the jack until it is supporting the weight of the engine.

9 Mark the bolt positions for correct refitting, then undo the three bolts securing the right-hand engine mounting to the engine bracket, and the two bolts and one nut securing the mounting to the body. Remove the mounting.

10 Slacken and remove the three bolts securing the right-hand end of the cylinder head to the top of the timing chain cover and the single bolt securing the head to the block **(see illustration)**.

11 Working in the **reverse** of the sequence shown in illustration 11.30, progressively slacken the ten main cylinder head bolts by half a turn at a time, until all bolts can be unscrewed by hand.

12 Lift out the cylinder head bolts and recover the washers.

13 Lift the cylinder head away; seek assistance if possible, as it is a heavy assembly (especially if complete with manifolds). Remove the gasket, noting the two locating dowels fitted to the top of the cylinder block. If they are a loose fit, remove the locating dowels and store them with the head for safe-keeping. Keep the head gasket for identification purposes (see paragraph 20). *Caution: Do not lay the head on its lower mating surface; support the head on*

11.20 Cylinder head gasket thickness identification cut-outs (arrowed)

wooden blocks, ensuring each block only contacts the head mating surface not the glow plugs or injector nozzles. The glow plugs and injector nozzles protrude out the bottom of the head and they will be damaged if the head is placed directly onto a bench.

14 If the cylinder head is to be dismantled for overhaul, then refer to Part F of this Chapter.

Preparation for refitting

15 The mating faces of the cylinder head and cylinder block/crankcase must be perfectly clean before refitting the head. Use a hard plastic or wood scraper to remove all traces of gasket and carbon; also clean the piston crowns. Take particular care, as the surfaces are damaged easily. Also, make sure that the carbon is not allowed to enter the oil and water passages – this is particularly important for the lubrication system, as carbon could block the oil supply to any of the engine's components. Using adhesive tape and paper, seal the water, oil and bolt holes in the cylinder block/crankcase. To prevent carbon entering the gap between the pistons and bores, smear a little grease in the gap. After cleaning each piston, use a small brush to remove all traces of grease and carbon from the gap, then wipe away the remainder with a clean rag. Clean all the pistons in the same way.

16 Check the mating surfaces of the cylinder block/crankcase and the cylinder head for nicks, deep scratches and other damage. If slight, they may be removed carefully with a

11.21 Measuring piston protrusion using a dial gauge

file, but if excessive, machining may be the only alternative to renewal.

17 Ensure that the cylinder head bolt holes in the crankcase are clean and free of oil. Syringe or soak up any oil left in the bolt holes. This is most important in order that the correct bolt tightening torque can be applied and to prevent the possibility of the block being cracked by hydraulic pressure when the bolts are tightened.

18 The cylinder head bolts must be discarded and renewed, regardless of their apparent condition.

19 If warpage of the cylinder head gasket surface is suspected, use a straight-edge to check it for distortion. Refer to Part F of this Chapter if necessary.

20 On this engine, the cylinder head-to-piston clearance is controlled by fitting different thickness head gaskets. The gasket thickness can be determined by looking at the tab situated directly in front of No 1 cylinder **(see illustration)**.

Notches on tab	Gasket thickness
One notch	1.3 mm
Two notches	1.4 mm

The correct thickness of gasket required is selected by measuring the piston protrusions as follows.

21 Ensure that the crankshaft is still locked in the TDC position. Mount a dial test indicator securely on the block so that its pointer can be easily pivoted between the piston crown and block mating surface. Zero the dial test indicator on the gasket surface of the cylinder block then carefully move the indicator over No 1 piston and measure its protrusion **(see illustration)**. Repeat this procedure on No 4 piston.

22 Remove the crankshaft locking tool and rotate the crankshaft half a turn (180º) to bring No 2 and 3 pistons to TDC. Ensure the crankshaft is accurately positioned then measure the protrusions of No 2 and 3 pistons. Once both pistons have been measured, rotate the crankshaft through a further one and a half turns (540º) to bring No 1 and 4 pistons back to TDC and lock the crankshaft in position again. *Caution: When rotating the crankshaft, keep the upper timing chain taut to prevent the chain jamming around the injection pump sprocket.*

11.26 Ensure the locating dowels are in position (arrowed) and fit the new gasket

11.30 Cylinder head bolt tightening sequence

23 Using the largest protrusion measurement of the four pistons, select the correct thickness of head gasket required using the following table.

Piston protrusion measurement	Gasket thickness required
0.51 to 0.60 mm	1.3 mm
0.61 to 0.70 mm	1.4 mm

Refitting

24 Remove the crankshaft locking tool and turn the crankshaft back (anti-clockwise) approximately 60°. This is to prevent any possibility of the valves contacting the pistons when the cylinder head is refitted.
25 Wipe clean the mating surfaces of the cylinder head and cylinder block/crankcase.
26 Check that the two locating dowels are in position then fit a new gasket to the cylinder block **(see illustration)**.
27 Ensure the camshaft is correctly positioned with the lobes of No 1 cylinder pointing upwards and the slot on the left-hand end of the camshaft parallel with the cylinder head surface (timing hole at the top).
28 With the aid of an assistant, carefully refit the cylinder head assembly to the block, aligning it with the locating dowels. As the head is fitted, pass the upper timing chain up through the cylinder head, holding it in position by passing a screwdriver through the upper chain and resting it on the head upper surface.
29 Apply a smear of oil to the threads and the underside of the heads of the new cylinder head bolts and carefully enter each bolt into its relevant hole (*do not drop them in*). Screw all bolts in, by hand only, until finger-tight.
30 Working progressively and in the sequence shown, tighten the cylinder head bolts to their Stage 1 torque setting, using a torque wrench and suitable socket **(see illustration)**.
31 Once all bolts have been tightened to the Stage 1 torque, working again in the specified sequence, go around and tighten all bolts

through the specified Stage 2 angle. It is recommended that an angle-measuring gauge is used to ensure accuracy. If a gauge is not available, use white paint to make alignment marks prior to tightening; the marks can then be used to check that the bolt has been rotated through the correct angle.
32 Go around again in the specified sequence and angle tighten the bolts through the specified Stage 3 angle.
33 Working again in the specified sequence, go around and tighten all bolts through the specified Stage 4 angle.
34 Go around again in the specified sequence and angle tighten the bolts through the specified Stage 5 angle.
35 Finally go around in the specified sequence and angle tighten the bolts through the specified Stage 6 angle.
36 Refit the bolts securing the right-hand end of the cylinder head to the block/timing cover and tighten them to the specified torque/angle setting.
37 Turn the crankshaft clockwise to bring No 1 cylinder back to TDC on its compression stroke as described in Section 3 and lock the crankshaft in position.
38 Raise the engine and locate the right-hand engine mounting in position. Refit the three bolts securing the mounting to the engine bracket and the two bolts and one nut securing the mounting to the body. Align the mounting in its original position, then tighten the bolts and nut to the specified torque.
39 Pivot the alternator back into position and tighten its upper mounting bolt to the specified torque (Chapter 5A).
40 Reconnect the coolant hoses to the cylinder head and secure them in position with the retaining clips.
41 Refit/reconnect the inlet and exhaust manifolds and associated components as described in Chapter 4B.
42 Refit the camshaft sprocket to the camshaft as described in paragraphs 29 to 38 of Section 10.

43 Position a new sealing washer on each side of the injection pump fuel hose unions then refit both union bolts and tighten them to the specified torque (Chapter 4B).
44 Refit the exhaust system as described in Chapter 4B.
45 On completion refill the cooling system as described in Chapter 1B.

12 Sump – removal and refitting

Removal

1 Disconnect the battery negative terminal (refer to *Disconnecting the battery* in the Reference Chapter).
2 Apply the handbrake, then jack up the front of the vehicle and support it on axle stands (see *Jacking and vehicle support*). Undo the ten bolts and remove the engine undertray.
3 Drain the engine oil as described in Chapter 1B, then fit a new sealing washer and refit the drain plug, tightening it to the specified torque.
4 Disconnect the wiring connectors from the oil temperature sensor and the oil level sensor **(see illustration)**.

12.4 Disconnect the wiring connector from the oil temperature sensor (arrowed)

12.5 Slacken and remove the bolts securing the sump flange to the transmission housing (lower bolts arrowed)

12.7 Oil pump pick-up/strainer retaining bolts (arrowed)

12.10a Apply a smear of sealant to the areas of the cylinder block/timing chain cover joints . . .

12.10b . . . and the rear main bearing cap/ cylinder block joints

12.11 Fit a new gasket to the sump and manoeuvre it up into position

14 Reconnect the oil temperature/level sensor wiring connectors. Refit the engine undertray.

15 Lower the vehicle to the ground then fill the engine with fresh oil (see Chapter 1B).

 13 Oil pump – removal, inspection and refitting

Note: *The oil pump safety valve can be removed with the timing chain cover in position on the engine and the pressure relief valve can be removed once the sump has been removed (see below).*

Removal

1 The oil pump assembly is built into the timing chain cover. Removal and refitting is as described in Section 7.

Inspection

2 Undo the retaining screws and lift off the pump cover from the inside of the timing chain cover **(see illustration)**.

3 Using a suitable marker pen, mark the surface of both the pump inner and outer rotors; the marks can then be used to ensure the rotors are refitted the correct way around.

4 Lift out the inner and outer rotors from the cover **(see illustrations)**.

5 Unscrew the oil pressure relief valve bolt from the base of the timing chain cover and withdraw the spring, spring sleeve and

5 Slacken and remove the bolts securing the sump flange to the transmission housing **(see illustration)**.

6 Progressively slacken and remove the bolts securing the sump to the base of the cylinder block/oil pump. Break the sump joint by striking the sump with the palm of the hand, then lower the sump away from the engine and withdraw it. Remove the gasket and discard it.

7 While the sump is removed, take the opportunity to check the oil pump pick-up/ strainer for signs of clogging or splitting. If necessary, unbolt the pick-up/strainer and remove it from the sump along with its sealing ring **(see illustration)**. The strainer can then be cleaned easily in solvent or renewed.

Refitting

8 Remove all traces of dirt and oil from the

mating surfaces of the sump and cylinder block and (where removed) the pick-up/strainer.

9 Where necessary, position a new sealing ring on the oil pump pick-up/strainer flange and fit the strainer to the sump, tightening its retaining bolts to the specified torque.

10 Apply a smear of suitable sealant to the areas of the cylinder block mating surface around the oil pump housing and rear main bearing cap joints **(see illustrations)**.

11 Fit a new gasket to the sump then offer up the sump to the cylinder block and loosely refit all the retaining bolts **(see illustration)**.

12 Working out from the centre in a diagonal sequence, progressively tighten the bolts securing the sump to the cylinder block/oil pump to their specified torque setting.

13 Tighten the bolts securing the sump flange to the transmission housing to their specified torque settings.

13.2 Remove the oil pump cover from the rear of the timing chain cover . . .

13.4a . . . then lift out the pump inner . . .

13.4b . . . and outer rotors

13.5a Unscrew the oil pressure relief valve bolt and sealing washer . . .

13.5b . . . and withdraw the spring, spring sleeve (arrowed) . . .

13.5c . . . and plunger from the timing chain cover

13.6a Unscrew the safety valve bolt and washer . . .

13.6b . . . then remove the spring and valve plunger from the timing chain cover

13.8 On refitting tighten the pump cover screws to the specified torque

plunger, noting which way around the plunger is fitted. Remove the sealing ring from the valve bolt **(see illustrations)**.

6 Unscrew the safety valve bolt from the rear of the timing chain cover, the safety valve is the uppermost of the three bolts on the rear of the cover. Withdraw the spring and plunger from the cover, noting which way around the plunger is fitted **(see illustrations)**. Remove the sealing ring from the valve bolt.

7 Clean the components, and carefully examine the rotors, pump body and valve plungers for any signs of scoring or wear. Renew any component which shows signs of wear or damage; if the rotors or pump housing are marked then the complete pump assembly should be renewed.

8 If the pump is satisfactory, reassemble the components in the reverse order of removal, noting the following.

  a) *Ensure both rotors and the valve plungers are fitted the correct way around.*

  b) *Fit new sealing rings to the pressure relief valve and safety valve bolts and tighten both bolts to their specified torque settings.*

  c) *Refit the pump cover tightening the cover screws to the specified torque (see illustration).*

  d) *On completion prime the oil pump by filling it with clean engine oil whilst rotating the inner rotor.*

Refitting

9 Refit the timing chain cover as described in Section 7.

14 Oil cooler – removal and refitting

Removal

1 The oil cooler/filter assembly is mounted onto the front, left-hand end of cylinder block and the cooler is bolted onto the front of the oil filter housing. To improve access, apply the handbrake, then jack up the front of the vehicle and support it on axle stands (see *Jacking and vehicle support*). Undo the ten bolts and remove the engine undertray.

2 Undo the three bolts and lift off the plastic cover over the top of the engine.

3 Remove the engine oil filter element as described in Chapter 1B.

4 Disconnect the wiring connector at the EGR valve adjacent to the oil filter housing.

5 Release the three clips and detach the wiring trough from the front of the oil cooler.

6 To minimise coolant loss, clamp the coolant hoses on either side of the oil cooler then release the retaining clips and detach both hoses. Be prepared for some coolant loss and mop-up any spilt coolant.

7 Wipe clean the area around the oil cooler then undo the retaining bolts and remove the cooler and sealing rings from the oil filter housing **(see illustration)**. Be prepared for oil spillage as the oil cooler is removed.

Refitting

8 Refitting is the reverse of removal, using

14.7 Undo the three retaining screws (arrowed) and remove the oil cooler from the oil filter housing

1 Cooler-to-oil filter housing oil seal

15.2 Lever the right-hand crankshaft oil seal out from the timing chain cover

15.4 Press/tap the new seal squarely into position until it is flush with the cover

15.7 Removing the crankshaft left-hand oil seal

15.9 Carefully ease the new seal over the end of the crankshaft and tap/press it squarely into position

new sealing rings. Fit a new oil filter element, then check and top-up the engine oil and coolant as described in Chapter 1B.

15 Crankshaft oil seals – renewal

Right-hand (timing chain end)

1 Remove the crankshaft pulley as described in Section 6.
2 Using a large flat-bladed screwdriver, carefully lever the seal out from the timing chain cover (see illustration).
3 Clean the seal housing and polish off any burrs or raised edges which may have caused the seal to fail in the first place.
4 Lubricate the lips of the new seal with clean engine oil and press/tap it squarely into position until it is flush with the cover (see illustration). If necessary, a suitable tubular drift, such as a socket, which bears only on the hard outer edge of the seal can be used to tap the seal into position. Take great care not to damage the seal lips during fitting and ensure that the seal lips face inwards.
5 Wash off any traces of oil, then refit the crankshaft pulley as described in Section 6.

Left-hand (flywheel/driveplate end)

6 Remove the flywheel/driveplate as described in Section 16.
7 Carefully punch or drill two small holes

opposite each other in the oil seal. Screw a self-tapping screw into each and pull on the screws with pliers to extract the seal (see illustration).
8 Clean the seal housing and polish off any burrs or raised edges which may have caused the seal to fail in the first place.
9 Lubricate the lips of the new seal with clean engine oil and ease it into position on the end of the crankshaft. Press the seal squarely into position until it is flush with the bearing cap. If necessary, a suitable tubular drift, such as a socket, which bears only on the hard outer edge of the seal can be used to tap the seal into position. Take great care not to damage the seal lips during fitting and ensure that the seal lips face inwards (see illustration).
10 Refit the flywheel/driveplate as described in Section 16.

16.2 Lock the flywheel ring gear with a suitable tool

16 Flywheel/driveplate – removal, inspection and refitting

Note: New flywheel/driveplate retaining bolts will be required on refitting.

Removal

Manual transmission models

1 Remove the transmission as described in Chapter 7A then remove the clutch assembly as described in Chapter 6.
2 Prevent the flywheel from turning by locking the ring gear teeth with a similar arrangement to that shown (see illustration). Alternatively, bolt a strap between the flywheel and the cylinder block/crankcase. Make alignment marks between the flywheel and crankshaft using paint or a suitable marker pen.
3 Slacken and remove the retaining bolts and remove the flywheel. Do not drop it, as it is very heavy.

Automatic transmission models

4 Remove the transmission as described in Chapter 7B then remove the driveplate as described in paragraphs 2 and 3.

Inspection

5 On manual transmission models, examine the flywheel for scoring of the clutch face. If the clutch face is scored, the flywheel may be surface-ground, but renewal is preferable.
6 On automatic transmission models closely examine the driveplate and ring gear teeth for signs of wear or damage and check the driveplate surface for any signs of cracks.
7 If there is any doubt about the condition of the flywheel/driveplate, seek the advice of a Vauxhall/Opel dealer or engine reconditioning specialist. They will be able to advise if it is possible to recondition it or whether renewal is necessary.

Refitting

Manual transmission models

8 Clean the mating surfaces of the flywheel and crankshaft.
9 Apply a drop of locking compound to each of the new retaining bolt threads then offer up the flywheel, if the original is being refitted align the marks made prior to removal. Screw in the retaining bolts.
10 Lock the flywheel by the method used on removal, and tighten the retaining bolts to the specified Stage 1 torque setting then angle-tighten the bolts through the specified Stage 2 and Stage 3 angle, using a socket and extension bar. It is recommended that an angle-measuring gauge is used during the final stages of the tightening, to ensure accuracy. If a gauge is not available, use white paint to make alignment marks between the bolt head and flywheel prior to tightening; the marks can then be used to check that the bolt has been rotated through the correct angle.

11 Refit the clutch as described in Chapter 6 then remove the locking tool, and refit the transmission as described in Chapter 7A.

Automatic transmission models

12 Clean the mating surfaces of the drive-plate and crankshaft and remove all traces of locking compound from the driveplate retaining bolt threads.

13 Apply a drop of locking compound to each of the new retaining bolt threads then offer up the driveplate, if the original is being refitted align the marks made prior to removal. Screw in the retaining bolts.

14 Lock the driveplate by the method used on removal, and tighten the retaining bolts to the specified Stage 1 torque setting then angle-tighten the bolts through the specified Stage 2 and Stage 3 angle, using a socket and extension bar. It is recommended that an angle-measuring gauge is used during the final stages of the tightening, to ensure accuracy. If a gauge is not available, use white paint to make alignment marks between the bolt head and driveplate prior to tightening; the marks can then be used to check that the bolt has been rotated through the correct angle.

15 Remove the locking tool and refit the transmission as described in Chapter 7B.

---

17 Engine/transmission mountings – inspection and renewal

Inspection

1 If improved access is required, firmly apply the handbrake, then jack up the front of the car and support it securely on axle stands (see *Jacking and vehicle support*). If necessary, undo the ten bolts and remove the engine undertray.

2 Check the mounting rubber to see if it is cracked, hardened or separated from the metal at any point; renew the mounting if any such damage or deterioration is evident.

3 Check that all the mounting's fasteners are securely tightened; use a torque wrench to check if possible.

4 Using a large screwdriver or a pry bar, check for wear in the mounting by carefully levering against it to check for free play; where this is not possible, enlist the aid of an assistant to move the engine/transmission unit back-and-forth, or from side-to-side, while you watch the mounting. While some free play is to be expected even from new components, excessive wear should be obvious. If excessive free play is found, check first that the fasteners are correctly secured, then renew any worn components as described below.

Renewal

Note: *Before slackening any of the engine mounting bolts/nuts, the relative positions of the mountings to their various brackets should be marked to ensure correct alignment upon refitting.*

17.7 Front mounting/torque link through-bolt (A) and mounting bracket-to-transmission bolts (B)

Front mounting/torque link

5 Apply the handbrake, then jack up the front of the vehicle and support it on axle stands (see *Jacking and vehicle support*). Undo the ten bolts and remove the engine undertray.

6 Undo the retaining bolt and detach the coolant pipe from the mounting.

7 Slacken and remove the nut securing the mounting to the subframe bracket. Withdraw the through-bolt **(see illustration)**.

8 Undo the bolts securing the mounting bracket to the transmission, then manoeuvre the mounting and bracket out of position.

9 Check all components for signs of wear or damage, and renew as necessary.

10 Locate the mounting in the subframe, refit the through-bolt and nut, then tighten the nut finger tight at this stage.

11 Refit the mounting bracket to the transmission and tighten its bolts to the specified torque.

12 Tighten the through-bolt nut to the specified torque then refit the coolant pipe.

13 On completion, lower the vehicle to the ground.

Rear mounting/torque link

14 Apply the handbrake, then jack up the front of the vehicle and support it on axle stands (see *Jacking and vehicle support*).

15 Undo the three nuts securing the exhaust system front pipe to the catalytic converter, taking care to support the flexible section. **Note:** *Angular movement in excess of 10° can cause permanent damage to the flexible section.* Separate the flange joint and recover the gasket.

17.17 Rear mounting/torque link bracket-to-subframe mounting bolt nuts (arrowed)

17.16 Rear mounting/torque link through-bolt (arrowed)

16 Undo the three bolts securing the mounting bracket to the transmission and the through-bolt securing the mounting to the bracket **(see illustration)**.

17 Undo the nuts and remove the two bolts securing the mounting to the subframe **(see illustration)**. Manoeuvre the mounting and bracket out from under the car.

18 Refit the bracket to the transmission and tighten the bolts to the specified torque.

19 Locate the new mounting in position. Insert the bolts and tighten the bolt/nuts to the specified torque.

20 Using a new gasket, refit the exhaust front pipe flange joint to the catalytic converter and tighten the three retaining nuts to the specified torque.

21 On completion, lower the vehicle to the ground.

Right-hand mounting

22 Apply the handbrake, then jack up the front of the vehicle and support it on axle stands (see *Jacking and vehicle support*).

23 Remove the air cleaner assembly as described in Chapter 4B.

24 Attach a suitable hoist and lifting tackle to the engine lifting brackets on the cylinder head, and support the weight of the engine.

25 Mark the position of the three bolts securing the mounting bracket to the engine bracket and undo the bolts. Undo the two bolts and one nut securing the mounting to the body and remove the mounting assembly **(see illustrations)**.

26 Place the mounting assembly in position and refit the two bolts and the nut securing

17.25a Right-hand mounting bracket-to-engine bracket bolts (arrowed) . . .

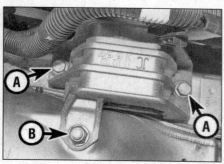

17.25b ... and mounting-to-body retaining bolts (A) and nut (B)

the mounting to the body. Tighten the bolts/nut to the specified torque. Align the mounting in its original position, then tighten the three mounting bracket bolts to the specified torque.

27 Remove the hoist, then refit the air cleaner as described in Chapter 4B.

28 On completion, lower the vehicle to the ground.

Left-hand mounting

29 Remove the battery and battery box as described in Chapter 5A.

30 Attach a suitable hoist and lifting tackle to the engine lifting brackets on the cylinder head, and support the weight of the engine.

31 Using a Torx socket, unscrew the three bolts securing the mounting bracket to the transmission bracket.

32 Undo the four bolts securing the mounting to the body and remove the mounting assembly from the car.

33 Locate the mounting brackets in position then insert the bolts and tighten them to the specified torque.

34 Disconnect the hoist and lifting tackle.

35 Refit the battery box and battery as described in Chapter 5A.

18 Balancer unit (2.2 litre engines) – removal and refitting

Note 1: *Two special tools are required for the removal and refitting of the balancer unit. In order to carry out the procedure, Vauxhall/Opel tool No KM-979 must be used to lock the balancer shafts in the TDC position and tool No KM-978 to lock the chain tensioner.*

Note 2: *New balancer unit retaining bolts and sprocket retaining bolts will be required for refitting.*

Removal

1 A balancer unit is fitted to 2.2 litre engines, to help provide a vibration and noise-free running of the engine. It consists of two balancer shafts which are driven via a chain from the crankshaft, the chain is kept under tension by a hydraulic chain tensioner located inside the balancer unit housing **(see illustration)**. The balancer shafts rotate in opposite directions at double the crankshaft speed.

2 The balancer unit is mounted on the 2nd and 3rd crankshaft main bearings, and the oil supply to the balancer unit is also via these two main bearings.

3 Position No 1 cylinder at TDC on its compression stroke as described in Section 3 and lock the crankshaft in position.

4 Remove the sump as described in Section 12.

5 Undo the four bolts and remove the cover from the front of the balancer unit.

6 Insert Vauxhall/Opel special tool KM-979 into the side of the balancer unit, to lock the balancer shafts.

7 Push the chain tensioner back into its bore and lock it in the retracted position using Vauxhall/Opel special tool KM-978.

8 Undo the balancer shaft sprocket retaining bolt and withdraw the sprocket from the balancer shaft. Disengage the chain and remove the sprocket.

9 Starting with the outer bolts and working towards the centre, slacken and remove the seven balancer unit retaining bolts and withdraw the unit from the crankcase.

Refitting

10 Ensure that the unit is still locked in position with Vauxhall/Opel tools KM-979 and KM-978.

11 Locate the unit on the crankcase and refit the seven new retaining bolts.

12 Tighten the two centre retaining bolts to the specified Stage 1 torque setting, then tighten the bolts through the specified Stage 2 angle. Now tighten the outer bolts to the specified Stage 1 torque setting, then through the specified Stage 2 angle. It is recommended that an angle-measuring gauge is used during the final stages of the tightening, to ensure accuracy. If a gauge is not available, use white paint to make alignment marks prior to tightening; the marks can then be used to check that the bolt has been rotated through the correct angle.

13 Engage the balancer shaft sprocket with the chain, then refit the sprocket to the balancer unit shaft. Fit the new retaining bolt and tighten to the specified Stage 1 torque setting, then through the specified Stage 2 angle. It is recommended that an angle-measuring gauge is used during the final stages of the tightening, to ensure accuracy. If a gauge is not available, use white paint to make alignment marks prior to tightening; the marks can then be used to check that the bolt has been rotated through the correct angle.

14 Remove the locking tools and refit the cover to the front of the unit. Tighten the cover retaining bolts securely

15 Refit the sump as described in Section 12.

16 Refit the crankshaft sensor as described in Chapter 4B.

18.1 Balancer unit layout – 2.2 litre engines

1 Balancer unit
2 Crankshaft sprocket
3 Chain tensioner
4 Drive sprocket for balancer shaft

Chapter 2 Part F:
Engine removal and overhaul procedures

Contents

Degrees of difficulty

Easy, suitable for novice with little experience	**Fairly easy,** suitable for beginner with some experience	**Fairly difficult,** suitable for competent DIY mechanic	**Difficult,** suitable for experienced DIY mechanic	**Very difficult,** suitable for expert DIY or professional

Specifications

Engine identification

Engine type	Manufacturer's engine code
1.8 litre (1796 cc) DOHC 16-valve petrol engine	Z18XE and Z18XEL
2.2 litre (2198 cc) DOHC 16-valve petrol engine	Z22SE and Z22YH
1.9 litre (1910 cc) diesel engine:	
SOHC 8-valve	Z19DT
DOHC 16-valve	Z19DTH
2.0 litre (1994 cc) SOHC 16-valve diesel engine	Y20DTH
2.2 litre (2171 cc) SOHC 16-valve diesel engine	Y22DTR

1.8 litre petrol engines (Z18XE and Z18XEL)

Cylinder head

Maximum gasket face distortion	0.05 mm
Cylinder head height	135.85 to 136.00 mm
Valve seat angle in cylinder head	90° 30'
Valve seat width in cylinder head:	
Inlet	1.0 to 1.4 mm
Exhaust	1.4 to 1.8 mm

Valves and guides

Stem diameter:	
Inlet valve	4.955 to 4.970 mm
Exhaust valve	4.935 to 4.950 mm
Valve head diameter:	
Inlet valve	31.10 to 31.30 mm
Exhaust valve	27.40 to 27.60 mm
Valve length:	
Inlet valve	101.20 to 101.60 mm
Exhaust valve	100.56 to 100.96 mm
Maximum permissible valve stem play in guide:	
Inlet	0.030 to 0.057 mm
Exhaust	0.050 to 0.077 mm
Valve clearances	Automatic adjustment by hydraulic cam followers

1.8 litre petrol engines (Z18XE and Z18XEL) (continued)

Cylinder block

Maximum gasket face distortion	0.05 mm
Cylinder bore diameter	80.485 to 80.555 mm (nominal)
Maximum cylinder bore ovality and taper	0.013 mm

Crankshaft and bearings

Number of main bearings	5
Main bearing journal diameter	54.980 to 54.997 mm
Big-end bearing journal diameter	42.971 to 42.987 mm
Crankshaft endfloat	0.100 to 0.202 mm

Pistons

Piston diameter	80.455 to 80.525 mm (nominal)

Piston rings

Number of rings (per piston)	2 compression, 1 oil control
Ring end gap:	
Compression	0.30 to 0.50 mm
Oil control	0.40 to 1.40 mm

Torque wrench settings

Refer to Chapter 2A Specifications

2.2 litre petrol engines (Z22SE and Z22YH)

Cylinder head

Maximum gasket face distortion	0.05 mm
Cylinder head height	129.00 mm
Valve seat angle in cylinder head	90°
Valve seat width in cylinder head:	
Inlet valve	1.1 to 1.3 mm
Exhaust valve	1.4 to 1.8 mm

Valves and guides

Stem diameter:	
Inlet valve	5.955 to 5.970 mm
Exhaust valve	5.945 to 5.960 mm
Valve head diameter:	
Inlet valve	34.95 to 35.25 mm
Exhaust valve	29.95 to 30.25 mm
Valve length:	
Inlet valve	101.995 to 102.545 mm
Exhaust valve	100.685 to 101.235 mm
Maximum permissible valve stem play in guide:	
Inlet	0.042 to 0.045 mm
Exhaust	0.052 to 0.055 mm
Valve clearances	Automatic adjustment by hydraulic cam followers

Cylinder block

Maximum gasket face distortion	0.05 mm
Cylinder bore diameter	85.992 to 86.008 mm
Maximum cylinder bore ovality and taper	0.013 mm

Crankshaft and bearings

Number of main bearings	5
Main bearing journal diameter	55.994 to 56.008 mm
Big-end bearing journal diameter	49.000 to 49.014 mm
Crankshaft endfloat	0.04 to 0.292 mm

Pistons

Piston diameter	85.967 to 85.982 mm

Piston rings

Number of rings (per piston)	2 compression, 1 oil control
Ring end gap:	
Top compression	0.20 to 0.40 mm
Second compression	0.35 to 0.55 mm
Oil control	0.25 to 0.76 mm

Torque wrench settings

Refer to Chapter 2B Specifications

1.9 litre SOHC diesel engines (Z19DT)

Note: *Where specifications are given as N/A, no information was available at the time of writing. Refer to your Vauxhall/Opel dealer for the latest information available.*

Cylinder head
Maximum gasket face distortion	0.10 mm
Cylinder head height	140.85 to 141.15 mm
Valve seat angle in cylinder head	N/A
Valve seat width in cylinder head	N/A

Valves and guides
Stem diameter (inlet and exhaust)	7.974 to 7.992 mm
Valve head diameter	N/A
Valve length	N/A
Maximum permissible valve stem play in guide	N/A
Valve clearances (cold):	
Inlet valve	0.25 to 0.35 mm
Exhaust valve	0.30 to 0.40 mm

Cylinder block
Maximum gasket face distortion	0.15 mm
Cylinder bore diameter	82.000 to 82.030 mm
Maximum cylinder bore ovality	0.050 mm
Maximum cylinder bore taper	0.005 mm

Crankshaft and bearings
Number of main bearings	5
Main bearing journal diameter	59.855 to 60.000 mm
Big-end bearing journal diameter	50.660 to 50.805 mm
Crankshaft endfloat	0.049 to 0.211 mm

Pistons
Piston diameter	81.920 to 81.950 mm

Piston rings
Number of rings (per piston)	2 compression, 1 oil control
Ring end gap:	
Top compression	0.25 to 0.40 mm
Second compression	0.25 to 0.50 mm
Oil control	0.25 to 0.50 mm

Torque wrench settings
Refer to Chapter 2C Specifications

1.9 litre DOHC diesel engines (Z19DTH)

Note: *Where specifications are given as N/A, no information was available at the time of writing. Refer to your Vauxhall/Opel dealer for the latest information available.*

Cylinder head
Maximum gasket face distortion	0.10 mm
Cylinder head height	106.95 to 107.05 mm
Valve seat angle in cylinder head	N/A
Valve seat width in cylinder head	N/A

Valves and guides
Stem diameter:	
Inlet valve	5.982 to 6.000 mm
Exhaust valve	5.972 to 5.990 mm
Valve head diameter	N/A
Valve length	N/A
Maximum permissible valve stem play in guide	N/A
Valve clearances	Automatic adjustment by hydraulic cam followers

Cylinder block
Maximum gasket face distortion	0.15 mm
Cylinder bore diameter	82.000 to 82.030 mm
Maximum cylinder bore ovality	0.050 mm
Maximum cylinder bore taper	0.005 mm

Crankshaft and bearings
Number of main bearings	5
Main bearing journal diameter	59.855 to 60.000 mm
Big-end bearing journal diameter	50.660 to 50.805 mm
Crankshaft endfloat	0.049 to 0.211 mm

1.9 litre DOHC diesel engines (Z19DTH) (continued)

Pistons

Piston diameter . . . . 81.920 to 81.950 mm

Piston rings

Number of rings (per piston) . . . . 2 compression, 1 oil control

Ring end gap:
    Top compression . . . . 0.20 to 0.35 mm
    Second compression . . . . 0.60 to 0.80 mm
    Oil control . . . . 0.25 to 0.50 mm

Torque wrench settings

Refer to Chapter 2D Specifications

2.0 and 2.2 litre diesel engines (Y20DTH and Y22DTR)

Note: *Where specifications are given as N/A, no information was available at the time of writing. Refer to your Vauxhall/Opel dealer for the latest information available.*

Cylinder head

Maximum gasket face distortion . . . . N/A
Cylinder head height . . . . 140.00 mm
Valve seat angle in cylinder head . . . . 90°
Valve seat width in cylinder head . . . . 1.4 to 1.8 mm

Valves and guides

Stem diameter:
    Inlet valve . . . . 5.955 to 5.970 mm
    Exhaust valve . . . . 5.945 to 5.960 mm
Valve head diameter:
    Inlet valve . . . . 29.00 mm
    Exhaust valve . . . . 26.00 mm
Valve length . . . . 96.90 to 97.30 mm
Maximum permissible valve stem play in guide:
    Inlet . . . . 0.030 to 0.057 mm
    Exhaust . . . . 0.040 to 0.067 mm
Valve clearances . . . . Automatic adjustment by hydraulic cam followers

Cylinder block

Maximum gasket face distortion . . . . N/A
Cylinder bore diameter . . . . 83.975 to 84.025 mm
Maximum cylinder bore ovality and taper . . . . N/A

Crankshaft and bearings

Number of main bearings 5
Main bearing journal diameter . . . . 67.966 to 67.982 mm
Big-end bearing journal diameter . . . . 48.971 to 48.990 mm
Crankshaft endfloat . . . . 0.01 to 0.02 mm

Pistons

Piston diameter . . . . 83.930 to 83.980 mm

Piston rings

Number of rings (per piston) . . . . 2 compression, 1 oil control

Ring end gap:
    Top compression . . . . 0.20 to 0.45 mm
    Second compression . . . . 0.25 to 0.50 mm
    Oil control . . . . 0.25 to 0.50 mm

Torque wrench settings

Refer to Chapter 2E Specifications

1 General information

Included in this Part of Chapter 2 are details of removing the engine/transmission from the car and general overhaul procedures for the cylinder head, cylinder block/crankcase and all other engine internal components.

The information given ranges from advice concerning preparation for an overhaul and the purchase of parts, to detailed step-by-step procedures covering removal, inspection, renovation and refitting of engine internal components.

After Section 5, all instructions are based on the assumption that the engine has been removed from the car. For information concerning in-car engine repair, as well as the removal and refitting of those external components necessary for full overhaul, refer to Part A, B, C, D or E of this Chapter (as applicable) and to Section 5. Ignore any preliminary dismantling operations described in Part A, B, C, D or E that are no longer relevant once the engine has been removed from the car.

Apart from torque wrench settings, which are given at the beginning of Part A, B, C, D or E (as applicable), all specifications relating to engine overhaul are at the beginning of this Part of Chapter 2.

2 Engine overhaul – general information

It is not always easy to determine when, or if, an engine should be completely overhauled, as a number of factors must be considered.

High mileage is not necessarily an indication that an overhaul is needed, while low mileage does not preclude the need for an overhaul. Frequency of servicing is probably the most important consideration. An engine which has had regular and frequent oil and filter changes, as well as other required maintenance, should give many thousands of miles of reliable service. Conversely, a neglected engine may require an overhaul very early in its life.

Excessive oil consumption is an indication that piston rings, valve seals and/or valve guides are in need of attention. Make sure that oil leaks are not responsible before deciding that the rings and/or guides are worn. Have a compression test performed (refer to Part A or B of this Chapter for petrol engines and to Part C, D or E for diesel engines), to determine the likely cause of the problem.

Check the oil pressure with a gauge fitted in place of the oil pressure switch, and compare it with that specified. If it is extremely low, the main and big-end bearings, and/or the oil pump, are probably worn out.

Loss of power, rough running, knocking or metallic engine noises, excessive valve gear noise, and high fuel consumption may also point to the need for an overhaul, especially if they are all present at the same time. If a complete service does not cure the situation, major mechanical work is the only solution.

A full engine overhaul involves restoring all internal parts to the specification of a new engine. During a complete overhaul, the pistons and the piston rings are renewed, and the cylinder bores are reconditioned. New main and big-end bearings are generally fitted; if necessary, the crankshaft may be reground, to compensate for wear in the journals. The valves are also serviced as well, since they are usually in less-than-perfect condition at this point. Always pay careful attention to the condition of the oil pump when overhauling the engine, and renew it if there is any doubt as to its serviceability. The end result should be an as-new engine that will give many trouble-free miles.

Critical cooling system components such as the hoses, thermostat and coolant pump should be renewed when an engine is overhauled. The radiator should also be checked carefully, to ensure that it is not clogged or leaking.

Before beginning the engine overhaul, read through the entire procedure, to familiarise yourself with the scope and requirements of the job. Check on the availability of parts and make sure that any necessary special tools and equipment are obtained in advance. Most work can be done with typical hand tools, although a number of precision measuring tools are required for inspecting parts to determine if they must be renewed.

The services provided by an engineering machine shop or engine reconditioning specialist will almost certainly be required, particularly if major repairs such as crankshaft regrinding or cylinder reboring are necessary. Apart from carrying out machining operations, these establishments will normally handle the inspection of parts, offer advice concerning reconditioning or renewal and supply new components such as pistons, piston rings and bearing shells. It is recommended that the establishment used is a member of the Federation of Engine Re-Manufacturers, or a similar society.

Always wait until the engine has been completely dismantled, and until all components (especially the cylinder block/crankcase and the crankshaft) have been inspected, before deciding what service and repair operations must be performed by an engineering works. The condition of these components will be the major factor to consider when determining whether to overhaul the original engine, or to buy a reconditioned unit. Do not, therefore, purchase parts or have overhaul work done on other components until they have been thoroughly inspected. As a general rule, time is the primary cost of an overhaul, so it does not pay to fit worn or sub-standard parts.

As a final note, to ensure maximum life and minimum trouble from a reconditioned engine, everything must be assembled with care, in a spotlessly-clean environment.

3 Engine removal – methods and precautions

If you have decided that the engine must be removed for overhaul or major repair work, several preliminary steps should be taken.

Engine/transmission removal is extremely complicated and involved on these vehicles. It must be stated, that unless the vehicle can be positioned on a ramp, or raised and supported on axle stands over an inspection pit, it will be very difficult to carry out the work involved.

Cleaning the engine compartment and engine/transmission before beginning the removal procedure will help keep tools clean and organised.

An engine hoist will also be necessary. Make sure the equipment is rated in excess of the combined weight of the engine and transmission. Safety is of primary importance, considering the potential hazards involved in removing the engine/transmission from the car.

The help of an assistant is essential. Apart from the safety aspects involved, there are many instances when one person cannot simultaneously perform all of the operations required during engine/transmission removal.

Plan the operation ahead of time. Before starting work, arrange for the hire of or obtain all of the tools and equipment you will need. Some of the equipment necessary to perform engine/transmission removal and installation safely (in addition to an engine hoist) is as follows: a heavy duty trolley jack, complete sets of spanners and sockets as described in the rear of this manual, wooden blocks, and plenty of rags and cleaning solvent for mopping-up spilled oil, coolant and fuel. If the hoist must be hired, make sure that you arrange for it in advance, and perform all of the operations possible without it beforehand. This will save you money and time.

Plan for the car to be out of use for quite a while. An engineering machine shop or engine reconditioning specialist will be required to perform some of the work which cannot be accomplished without special equipment. These places often have a busy schedule, so it would be a good idea to consult them before removing the engine, in order to accurately estimate the amount of time required to rebuild or repair components that may need work.

During the engine/transmission removal procedure, it is advisable to make notes of the locations of all brackets, cable ties, earthing points, etc, as well as how the wiring harnesses, hoses and electrical connections are attached and routed around the engine and engine compartment. An effective way of doing this is to take a series of photographs of the various components before they are disconnected or removed; the resulting photographs will prove invaluable when the engine/transmission is refitted.

Always be extremely careful when removing and refitting the engine/transmission. Serious injury can result from careless actions. Plan ahead and take your time, and a job of this nature, although major, can be accomplished successfully.

On all Vectra models, the engine must be removed complete with the transmission as an assembly. There is insufficient clearance in the engine compartment to remove the engine leaving the transmission in the vehicle. The assembly is removed by raising the front of the vehicle, and lowering the assembly from the engine compartment.

4 Engine and transmission unit – removal, separation and refitting

Note 1: *The engine can be removed from the car only as a complete unit with the transmission; the two are then separated for overhaul. The engine/transmission unit is lowered out of position, and withdrawn from under the vehicle. Bearing this in mind, and*

4.8a Unscrew the bolts (arrowed) securing the fuse/relay box upper and lower sections and the wiring harness block connectors . . .

4.8b . . . depress the tabs at each end and lift the upper section off the lower section . . .

also bearing in mind the information contained in Section 3, ensure the vehicle is raised sufficiently so that there is enough clearance between the front of the vehicle and the floor to allow the engine/transmission unit to be slid out once it has been lowered out of position.

Note 2: *Such is the complexity of the power unit arrangement on these vehicles, and the variations that may be encountered according to model and optional equipment fitted, that the following should be regarded as a guide to the work involved, rather than a step-by-step*

4.8c . . . while at the same time disconnecting the wiring harness block connectors

4.9b . . . then release the disconnected wiring harness from the fuse/relay box lower section so that it is free to be removed with the engine

procedure. Where differences are encountered, or additional component disconnection or removal is necessary, make notes of the work involved as an aid to refitting.

Removal

1 On models equipped with air conditioning, have the air conditioning system fully discharged by an air conditioning specialist.

2 Position the vehicle as described in Section 3, paragraph 2, and remove both front roadwheels. On petrol engine models, remove the right-hand

4.9a Undo the nut securing the earth lead to the stud in front of the battery box (arrowed) . . .

4.10 Disconnect the wiring block connector from the cooling fan module above the cooling fans

wheel arch liner inner cover. On diesel engine models, remove the engine undertray

3 Remove the bonnet and the front bumper as described in Chapter 11.

4 Remove the plastic cover from the top of the engine.

5 Remove the battery and battery box as described in Chapter 5A.

6 Carry out the following operations as described in Chapter 1A or 1B, as applicable:
  a) Drain the engine oil.
  b) Drain the cooling system.
  c) Remove the auxiliary drivebelt.

7 Remove the air cleaner assembly and intake ducts as described in Chapter 4A or 4B, as applicable.

8 Lift off the cover from the engine compartment fuse/relay box, and unscrew the two bolts securing the upper section of the fuse/relay box to the lower section. Undo the three bolts securing the engine wiring harness block connectors to the fuse/relay box upper section. Depress the tabs at each end and lift the upper section off the lower section, while at the same time disconnecting the three block connectors **(see illustrations)**.

9 Undo the nut securing the earth lead to the stud in front of the battery box location. Release the disconnected wiring harness from the fuse/ relay box lower section so that it is free to be removed with the engine **(see illustrations)**.

10 Disconnect the wiring block connector from the cooling fan module above the cooling fans **(see illustration)**. Release the wiring harness from the retaining clips so that it is free to be removed with the engine.

11 Remove the air conditioning system compressor as described in Chapter 3.

Petrol engine models

12 Depressurise the fuel system with reference to Chapter 4A, then disconnect the fuel supply pipe from the fuel rail and support bracket. Be prepared for fuel spillage, and take adequate precautions. Clamp or plug the open unions, to minimise further fuel loss.

4.14 Detach the additional relay box at the left-hand side of the engine compartment – diesel engines

4.16a Disconnect the heater element wiring connector from the fuel filter cover . . .

4.16b . . . and the water level sensor wiring connector from the base of the filter housing

13 Disconnect the brake vacuum servo hose, and fuel evaporation purge hose.

Diesel engine models

14 Detach the additional relay box at the left-hand side of the engine compartment and free the wiring harness so that it can be removed with the engine **(see illustration)**.
15 Disconnect the brake vacuum servo hose from the vacuum pump.
16 Disconnect the heater element wiring connector from the fuel filter cover, and the water level sensor wiring connector from the base of the filter housing **(see illustrations)**.
17 On 1.9 litre engines, detach the two fuel hose quick-release connectors and remove the hoses from the fuel filter housing and cover. A Vauxhall/Opel special tool (KM-796-A) is available to disconnect the hose connectors, but provided care is taken, the connections can be released using two screwdrivers, a pair of long-nosed pliers, or similar, to depress the retaining tangs **(see illustrations)**. Suitably cover or plug the open hose connections to prevent dirt entry.
18 On 2.0 and 2.2 litre engines, detach the fuel feed hose quick-release connector (see paragraph 17) then slacken the retaining clip and disconnect the fuel return hose.
19 Working under the front, right-hand side of the car, release the locking lever catch, then lift the locking levers and disconnect the two wiring connectors from the engine management system ECU **(see illustrations)**.

All models

20 Loosen the clips and remove the upper and lower radiator hoses.
21 Release the retaining clips and disconnect the coolant hoses at the cooling system expansion tank. Disconnect the wiring connector then remove the expansion tank from its mounting bracket.
22 Using a small screwdriver, lift up the wire clips securing the two heater hoses to the heater matrix pipe stubs, and disconnect the hoses from the stubs **(see illustration)**.
23 On manual transmission models, using a suitable forked tool, release the gearchange selector cable end fittings from the transmission selector levers. Pull back the retaining sleeves and detach the outer cables

4.17a Depress the retaining tangs and detach the two fuel hose quick-release connectors . . .

4.17b . . . then remove the hoses from the fuel filter housing and cover – 1.9 litre diesel engines

from the mounting bracket on the transmission **(see illustrations)**.
24 On automatic transmission models, use

a forked tool or flat-bladed screwdriver, and carefully lever the gear selector inner cable end fitting off the balljoint on the selector lever

4.19a Release the locking lever catch . . .

4.19b . . . then lift the locking levers . . .

4.19c . . . and disconnect the two wiring connectors from the ECU – diesel engines

4.22 Lift up the wire clips and disconnect the heater hoses from the matrix pipe stubs

4.23a Release the selector inner cable end fittings from the transmission selector levers . . .

4.23b . . . then pull back the retaining sleeves and detach the outer cables from the transmission mounting bracket

4.28 Unscrew the nut and remove the bolt (arrowed) securing the steering column intermediate shaft to the steering gear pinion shaft

position switch. Pull back the retaining sleeve and detach the outer cable from the mounting bracket on the transmission.

25 Drain the manual transmission oil or automatic transmission fluid as described in Chapter 7A or 7B, as applicable.

26 Remove both driveshafts as described in Chapter 8.

27 Position the steering with the front roadwheels straight-ahead, and lock the steering by removing the ignition key.

28 Unscrew the nut and remove the bolt securing the steering column intermediate shaft to the steering gear pinion shaft. Separate the intermediate shaft from the pinion shaft by pulling the intermediate shaft upwards **(see illustration)**.

Caution: To prevent damage to the airbag wiring contact unit, the steering lock must remain locked until the intermediate shaft is re-attached to the pinion shaft.

29 On manual transmission models, remove the filler cap from the brake/clutch fluid reservoir on the bulkhead, then tighten it onto a piece of polythene. This will reduce the loss of fluid when the clutch hydraulic hose is disconnected. Alternatively, fit a hose clamp to the flexible hose next to the clutch hydraulic connection on the transmission housing.

30 Place some cloth rags beneath the hose, then prise out the retaining clip securing the clutch hydraulic hose to the end fitting on top of the transmission bellhousing. Detach the hose from the end fitting **(see illustrations)**.

Gently squeeze the two legs of the retaining clip together and re-insert the retaining clip back into position in the end fitting. Discard the sealing ring from the hose end; a new sealing ring must be used on refitting. Plug/cover both the end fitting and hose end to minimise fluid loss and prevent the entry of dirt into the hydraulic system. **Note:** *Whilst the hose is disconnected, do not depress the clutch pedal.*

31 On automatic transmission models, unscrew the central retaining bolt (or nut) and detach the fluid cooler pipes from the transmission. Suitably cover the pipe ends and plug the transmission orifices to prevent dirt entry.

32 Attach a suitable hoist and lifting tackle to the engine lifting brackets on the cylinder head, and support the weight of the engine/transmission.

33 Remove the front subframe as described in Chapter 10.

34 Mark the position of the three bolts securing the right-hand engine mounting bracket to the engine bracket and undo the bolts. **(see illustration)**. **Note:** *There is no need to remove the mounting, since the engine/transmission is lowered from the engine compartment.*

35 Mark the position of the three bolts securing the left-hand engine mounting to the transmission bracket **(see illustration)**.

36 Make a final check to ensure that all relevant pipes, hoses, wires, etc, have been disconnected, and that they are positioned clear of the engine and transmission.

37 With the help of an assistant, carefully lower the engine/transmission assembly to the ground. Make sure that the surrounding components in the engine compartment are not damaged. Ideally, the assembly should be lowered onto a trolley jack or low platform with castors, so that it can easily be withdrawn from under the car.

38 Ensure that the assembly is adequately supported, then disconnect the engine hoist and lifting tackle, and withdraw the engine/transmission assembly from under the front of the vehicle.

39 Clean away any external dirt using paraffin or a water-soluble solvent and a stiff brush.

4.30a Prise out the clip securing the clutch hydraulic hose to the end fitting on the transmission bellhousing . . .

4.30b . . . then detach the hose from the end fitting

4.34 Right-hand engine mounting bracket-to-engine bracket retaining bolts (arrowed)

4.35 Left-hand engine mounting-to-transmission bracket retaining bolts (arrowed)

40 With reference to Chapter 7A or 7B, unbolt the transmission from the engine. Carefully withdraw the transmission from the engine. On manual transmission models, ensure that its weight is not allowed to hang on the input shaft while engaged with the clutch friction disc. On automatic transmission models, ensure that the torque converter is removed together with the transmission so that it remains engaged with the oil pump. Note that the transmission locates on dowels positioned in the rear of the cylinder block.

Refitting

41 With reference to Chapter 7A or 7B, refit the transmission to the engine and tighten the bolts to the specified torque.
42 With the front of the vehicle raised and supported on axle stands, move the engine/transmission assembly under the vehicle, ensuring that the assembly is adequately supported.
43 Reconnect the hoist and lifting tackle to the engine lifting brackets, and carefully raise the engine/transmission assembly up into the engine compartment with the help of an assistant.
44 Reconnect the right- and left-hand engine/transmission mountings and tighten the bolts to the specified torque given in Chapter 2A, 2B, 2C, 2D or 2E, as applicable. Ensure that the marks made on removal are correctly aligned when tightening the retaining bolts.
45 Refit the front subframe as described in Chapter 10.
46 Disconnect the hoist and lifting tackle from the engine lifting brackets.
47 Refit the driveshafts as described in Chapter 8.
48 On manual transmission models, refill the transmission with correct quantity and type of oil, as described in Chapter 7A.
49 Reconnect the steering column intermediate shaft to the steering gear pinion shaft and tighten the bolt and nut with reference to Chapter 10.
50 On automatic transmission models, reconnect the fluid cooler pipes together with new O-ring seals to the transmission.
51 On manual transmission models, reconnect and bleed the clutch hydraulic connection at the transmission with reference to Chapter 6.
52 Refit the gearchange/selector outer cable(s) to the mounting bracket on the transmission. Engage the inner cable end fitting(s) with the selector lever balljoint, squeezing them together with pliers if necessary.
53 Push the securing wire clip back into position on the heater hose end fittings, then push the hoses back onto the matrix pipe stubs. Ensure that the wire clips securely lock the hoses in position.
54 Refit the cooling system expansion tank, and reconnect the wiring connector and the coolant hoses.
55 Reconnect the upper and lower radiator hoses.

Petrol engine models

56 Reconnect the brake vacuum servo hose, and fuel evaporation purge hose and fuel supply pipe.

Diesel engine models

57 Reconnect the two vacuum hoses at the solenoid valve located above the radiator.
58 Reconnect the brake vacuum servo hose to the vacuum pump, and the fuel hoses and wiring connectors at the fuel filter.
59 Refit the additional relay box to its location at the left-hand side of the engine compartment and secure the wiring harness.
60 Reconnect the two wiring connectors to the engine management system ECU.

All models

61 Refit the air conditioning system compressor as described in Chapter 3, then refit the auxiliary drivebelt as described in Chapter 1A or 1B, as applicable.
62 Reconnect the wiring block connector to the cooling fan module.
63 Locate the engine wiring harness block connectors back into position in the fuse/relay box lower section. Refit the upper section to the lower section ensuring that the block connectors are properly engaged. Refit and tighten the three bolts securing the block connectors, and the two bolts securing the upper section to the lower section.
64 Reconnect the earth lead to the stud in front of the battery box location and secure with the retaining nut.
65 Refit the air cleaner assembly and intake ducts as described in Chapter 4A or 4B, as applicable.
66 Refit the battery box and battery as described in Chapter 5A.
67 Refit the bonnet and the front bumper as described in Chapter 11.
68 Refit the right-hand wheel arch liner inner cover, or engine undertray, and both front roadwheels, then lower the vehicle to the ground.
69 Make a final check to ensure that all relevant hoses, pipes and wires have been correctly reconnected.
70 Refill the engine with oil with reference to Chapter 1A or 1B, as applicable.
71 Refill the transmission with correct quantity and type of fluid, as described in Chapter 7A or 7B.
72 Refill and bleed the cooling system with reference to Chapter 1A or 1B, as applicable.
73 On models equipped with air conditioning, have the air conditioning system evacuated, charged and leak-tested by the specialist who discharged it.

5 Engine overhaul – dismantling sequence

1 It is much easier to dismantle and work on the engine if it is mounted on a portable engine stand. These stands can often be hired

from a tool hire shop. Before the engine is mounted on a stand, the flywheel/driveplate should be removed, so that the stand bolts can be tightened into the end of the cylinder block/crankcase.
2 If a stand is not available, it is possible to dismantle the engine with it blocked up on a sturdy workbench, or on the floor. Be extra careful not to tip or drop the engine when working without a stand.
3 If you are going to obtain a reconditioned engine, all the external components must be removed first, to be transferred to the new engine (just as they will if you are doing a complete engine overhaul yourself). These components include the following:
 a) Engine wiring harness and supports.
 b) Alternator and air conditioning compressor mounting brackets (as applicable).
 c) Coolant pump (where applicable) and inlet/outlet housings.
 d) Dipstick tube.
 e) Fuel system components.
 f) All electrical switches and sensors.
 g) Inlet and exhaust manifolds and, where fitted, the turbocharger.
 h) Oil filter and oil cooler/heat exchanger.
 i) Flywheel/driveplate.
Note: When removing the external components from the engine, pay close attention to details that may be helpful or important during refitting. Note the fitted position of gaskets, seals, spacers, pins, washers, bolts, and other small items.
4 If you are obtaining a 'short' engine (which consists of the engine cylinder block/crankcase, crankshaft, pistons and connecting rods all assembled), then the cylinder head, sump, oil pump, and timing belt/chains (as applicable) will have to be removed also.
5 If you are planning a complete overhaul, the engine can be dismantled, and the internal components removed, in the order given below.

Petrol engines
 a) Inlet and exhaust manifolds (see Chapter 4A).
 b) Timing belt/chain, sprockets, tensioner and idler pulleys (see Chapter 2A or 2B).
 c) Coolant pump (see Chapter 3).
 d) Cylinder head (see Chapter 2A or 2B).
 e) Flywheel/driveplate (see Chapter 2A or 2B).
 f) Sump (see Chapter 2A or 2B).
 g) Oil pump (see Chapter 2A or 2B).
 h) Pistons/connecting rod assemblies (see Section 9).
 i) Crankshaft (see Section 10).

Diesel engines
 a) Inlet and exhaust manifolds (see Chapter 4B).
 b) Timing belt, sprockets, tensioner and idler pulleys – 1.9 litre engines (see Chapter 2C or 2D).
 c) Coolant pump – 1.9 litre engines (see Chapter 3).

6.2 Using a valve spring compressor, compress the valve spring to relieve the pressure on the collets

6.4 Extract the two split collets by hooking them out using a small screwdriver

6.5a Remove the valve spring cap . . .

6.5b . . . and the spring . . .

6.5c . . . then withdraw the valve through the combustion chamber

6.5d Using pliers, remove the valve stem oil seal, which also incorporates the spring seat on most engines

d) *Cylinder head (see Chapter 2C, 2D or 2E).*
e) *Flywheel/driveplate (see Chapter 2C, 2D or 2E).*
f) *Sump (see Chapter 2C, 2D or 2E).*
g) *Oil pump (see Chapter 2C, 2D or 2E).*
h) *Timing chains and sprockets – 2.0 and 2.2 litre engines (see Chapter 2E).*
i) *Coolant pump – 2.0 and 2.2 litre engines (see Chapter 3).*
j) *Piston/connecting rod assemblies (see Section 9).*
k) *Crankshaft (see Section 10).*

6 Before beginning the dismantling and overhaul procedures, make sure that you have all of the correct tools necessary. See *Tools and working facilities* for further information.

6 Cylinder head – dismantling

Note: *New and reconditioned cylinder heads are available from the manufacturer, and from engine overhaul specialists. Due to the fact that some specialist tools are required for the dismantling and inspection procedures, and new components may not be readily available, it may be more practical and economical for the home mechanic to purchase a reconditioned head rather than to dismantle, inspect and recondition the original head. A valve spring compressor tool will be required for this operation.*

1 With the cylinder head removed as described in the relevant Part of this Chapter,

clean away all external dirt, and remove the following components as applicable, if not already done:
a) *Manifolds (see Chapter 4A or 4B).*
b) *Spark plugs (petrol engines – see Chapter 1A).*
c) *Glow plugs (diesel engines – see Chapter 5A).*
d) *Camshafts and and associated valve train components (see Chapter 2A, 2B, 2C, 2D or 2E).*
e) *Fuel injectors (diesel engines – see Chapter 4B).*
f) *Engine lifting brackets.*

2 To remove a valve, fit a valve spring compressor tool. Ensure that the arms of the compressor tool are securely positioned on the head of the valve and the spring cap **(see illustration)**. The valves are deeply-recessed on petrol engines, and a suitable

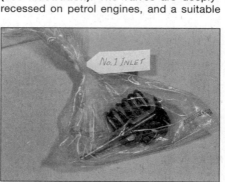

6.6 Place each valve assembly in a labelled polythene bag or similar container

extension piece may be required for the spring compressor.

3 Compress the valve spring to relieve the pressure of the spring cap acting on the collets.

> **HAYNES HiNT** *If the spring cap sticks to the valve stem, support the compressor tool, and give the end a light tap with a soft-faced mallet to help free the spring cap.*

4 Extract the two split collets by hooking them out using a small screwdriver, then slowly release the compressor tool **(see illustration)**.

5 Remove the valve spring cap and the spring, then withdraw the valve through the combustion chamber. Using pliers, remove the valve stem oil seal, which also incorporates the spring seat on most engines **(see illustrations)**. If the spring seat is not part of the valve stem oil seal, hook it out using a small screwdriver.

6 Repeat the procedure for the remaining valves, keeping all components in strict order so that they can be refitted in their original positions, unless all the components are to be renewed. If the components are to be kept and used again, place each valve assembly in a labelled polythene bag or a similar small container **(see illustration)**. Note that as with cylinder numbering, the valves are normally numbered from the timing chain (or timing belt) end of the engine. Make sure that the valve components are identified as inlet and exhaust, as well as numbered.

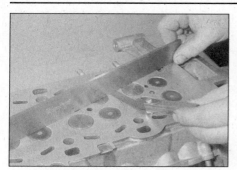

7.6 Using a straight-edge and feeler gauge to check cylinder head surface distortion

7.11 Using a micrometer to measure valve stem diameter

7.14 Grinding-in a valve

7 Cylinder head and valves – cleaning and inspection

1 Thorough cleaning of the cylinder head and valve components, followed by a detailed inspection, will enable you to decide how much valve service work must be carried out during the engine overhaul. **Note:** *If the engine has been severely overheated, it is best to assume that the cylinder head is warped – check carefully for signs of this.*

Cleaning

2 Scrape away all traces of old gasket material from the cylinder head.
3 Scrape away the carbon from the combustion chambers and ports, then wash the cylinder head thoroughly with paraffin or a suitable solvent.
4 Scrape off any heavy carbon deposits that may have formed on the valves, then use a power-operated wire brush to remove deposits from the valve heads and stems.

Inspection

Note: *Be sure to perform all the following inspection procedures before concluding that the services of a machine shop or engine overhaul specialist are required. Make a list of all items that require attention.*

Cylinder head

5 Inspect the head very carefully for cracks, evidence of coolant leakage, and other damage. If cracks are found, a new cylinder head should be obtained.
6 Use a straight-edge and feeler gauge blade to check that the cylinder head surface is not distorted **(see illustration)**. If it is, it may be possible to resurface it, provided that the cylinder head is not reduced to less than the minimum specified height.
7 Examine the valve seats in each of the combustion chambers. If they are severely pitted, cracked or burned, then they will need to be recut by an engine overhaul specialist. If they are only slightly pitted, this can be removed by grinding-in the valve heads and seats with fine valve-grinding compound, as described below.
8 If the valve guides are worn, indicated by

a side-to-side motion of the valve, oversize valve guides are available, and valves with oversize stems can be fitted. This work is best carried out by an engine overhaul specialist. A dial gauge may be used to determine whether the amount of side play of a valve exceeds the specified maximum.
9 Check the tappet bores in the cylinder head for wear. If excessive wear is evident, the cylinder head must be renewed. Also check the tappet oil holes in the cylinder head for obstructions.

Valves

10 Examine the head of each valve for pitting, burning, cracks and general wear, and check the valve stem for scoring and wear ridges. Rotate the valve, and check for any obvious indication that it is bent. Look for pitting and excessive wear on the tip of each valve stem. Renew any valve that shows any such signs of wear or damage.
11 If the valve appears satisfactory at this stage, measure the valve stem diameter at several points using a micrometer **(see illustration)**. Any significant difference in the readings obtained indicates wear of the valve stem. Should any of these conditions be apparent, the valve(s) must be renewed.
12 If the valves are in satisfactory condition, they should be ground (lapped) into their respective seats, to ensure a smooth gas-tight seal. If the seat is only lightly pitted, or if it has been recut, fine grinding compound **only** should be used to produce the required finish. Coarse valve-grinding compound should **not** be used unless a seat is badly burned or deeply pitted; if this is the case, the cylinder head and valves should be inspected by an expert to decide whether seat recutting, or even the renewal of the valve or seat insert, is required.
13 Valve grinding is carried out as follows. Place the cylinder head upside-down on a bench, with a block of wood at each end to give clearance for the valve stems.
14 Smear a trace of the appropriate grade of valve-grinding compound on the seat face, and press a suction grinding tool onto the valve head. With a semi-rotary action, grind the valve head to its seat, lifting the valve occasionally to redistribute the grinding compound **(see illustration)**. A light spring

placed under the valve head will greatly ease this operation.
15 If coarse grinding compound is being used, work only until a dull, matt even surface is produced on both the valve seat and the valve, then wipe off the used compound and repeat the process with fine compound. When a smooth unbroken ring of light grey matt finish is produced on both the valve and seat, the grinding operation is complete. **Do not** grind in the valves any further than absolutely necessary, or the seat will be prematurely sunk into the cylinder head.
16 When all the valves have been ground-in, carefully wash off all traces of grinding compound using paraffin or a suitable solvent before reassembly of the cylinder head.

Valve components

17 Examine the valve springs for signs of damage and discoloration; if possible; also compare the existing spring free length with new components.
18 Stand each spring on a flat surface, and check it for squareness. If any of the springs are damaged, distorted or have lost their tension, obtain a complete new set of springs.

8 Cylinder head – reassembly

1 Lubricate the stems of the valves, and insert them into their original locations **(see illustration)**. If new valves are being fitted, insert them into the locations to which they have been ground.

8.1 Lubricate the valve stem with engine oil and insert the valve into the correct guide

8.2a Fit the spring seat . . .

8.2b . . . then fit the seal protector (where supplied) to the valve . . .

8.2c . . . and install the new valve stem oil seal . . .

8.2d . . . pressing it onto the valve guide with a suitable socket

8.3 Refit the valve spring and fit the spring cap

8.4 Compress the valve and locate the collets in the recess on the valve stem

2 Working on the first valve, refit the spring seat if it is not an integral part of the valve stem oil seal. Dip the new valve stem seal in fresh engine oil, then carefully locate it over the valve and onto the guide. Take care not to damage the seal as it is passed over the valve stem. Use a suitable socket or metal tube to press the seal firmly onto the guide. **Note:** *If genuine seals are being fitted, use the oil seal protector which is supplied with the seals; the protector fits over the valve stem and prevents the oil seal lip being damaged on the valve (see illustrations).*

3 Locate the spring on the seat and fit the spring cap **(see illustration).**

4 Compress the valve spring, and locate the split collets in the recess in the valve stem

(see illustration and Haynes Hint). Release the compressor, then repeat the procedure on the remaining valves.

5 With all the valves installed, support the cylinder head on blocks on the bench and, using a hammer and interposed block of wood, tap the end of each valve stem to settle the components.

6 Refit the components removed in Section 6, paragraph 1.

9 Pistons/connecting rods – removal

Note : *New connecting rod big-end cap bolts will be needed on refitting.*

1 Referring to the relevant Part of this Chapter, remove the cylinder head and sump. Where fitted, unbolt the pick-up/strainer from the base of the oil pump. On 2.2 litre diesel engines, remove the balancer unit as described in Part E of this Chapter.

2 On all models, if there is a pronounced wear ridge at the top of any bore, it may be necessary to remove it with a scraper or ridge reamer, to avoid piston damage during removal. Such a ridge indicates excessive wear of the cylinder bore.

3 If the connecting rods and big-end caps are not marked to indicate their positions in the cylinder block (ie, marked with cylinder numbers), suitably mark both the rod and cap with quick-drying paint or similar. Note which side of the engine the marks face and accurately record this also. There may not be

any other way of identifying which way round the cap fits on the rod, when refitting.

4 Turn the crankshaft to bring pistons 1 and 4 to BDC (bottom dead centre).

5 Unscrew the bolts from No 1 piston big-end bearing cap, then take off the cap and recover the bottom half-bearing shell. If the bearing shells are to be re-used, tape the cap and the shell together.

Caution: On some engines, the connecting rod/bearing cap mating surfaces are not machined flat; the big-end bearing caps are 'cracked' off from the rod during production and left untouched to ensure the cap and rod mate perfectly. Where this type of connecting rod is fitted, great care must be taken to ensure the mating surfaces of the cap and rod are not marked or damaged in anyway. Any damage to the mating surfaces will adversely affect the strength of the connecting rod and could lead to premature failure.

6 Using a hammer handle, push the piston up through the bore, and remove it from the top of the cylinder block. Recover the bearing shell, and tape it to the connecting rod for safe-keeping.

7 Loosely refit the big-end cap to the connecting rod, and secure with the nuts/bolts – this will help to keep the components in their correct order.

8 Remove No 4 piston assembly in the same way.

9 Turn the crankshaft through 180° to bring pistons 2 and 3 to BDC, and remove them in the same way.

HAYNES HINT

Use a little dab of grease to hold the collets in position on the valve stem while the spring compressor is released.

10.3 Check the crankshaft endfloat using a dial gauge . . .

10.4 . . . or a feeler gauge

10.5 Main bearing cap identification markings (arrowed) – 1.8 litre petrol engines

10 Crankshaft – removal

Note: *New main bearing cap bolts will be required on refitting.*

1.8 litre petrol engines

1 Working as described in Part A of this Chapter, remove the flywheel and the oil pump.

2 Remove the piston and connecting rod assemblies as described in Section 9. If no work is to be done on the pistons and connecting rods, unbolt the caps and push the pistons far enough up the bores that the connecting rods are positioned clear of the crankshaft journals.

3 Before removing the crankshaft, check the endfloat using a dial gauge in contact with the end of the crankshaft. Push the crankshaft fully one way, and then zero the gauge. Push the crankshaft fully the other way, and check the endfloat **(see illustration)**. The result should be compared with the specified limit, and will give an indication as to the size of the main bearing shell thrust journal width which will be required for reassembly.

4 If a dial gauge is not available, a feeler gauge can be used to measure crankshaft endfloat. Push the crankshaft fully towards one end of the crankcase, and insert a feeler gauge between the thrust flange of the main bearing shell and the machined surface of the crankshaft web **(see illustration)**. Before measuring, ensure that the crankshaft is fully forced towards one end of the crankcase, to give the widest possible gap at the measuring location. **Note:** *Measure at the bearing with the thrustwasher (see Section 17).*

5 The main bearing caps should be numbered 1 to 5 from the timing belt end of the engine and all identification numbers should be the right way up when read from the rear of the cylinder block **(see illustration)**. If the bearing caps are not marked, using a hammer and punch or a suitable marker pen, number the caps from 1 to 5 from the timing belt end and mark each cap to indicate its correct fitted direction to avoid confusion on refitting.

6 Working in a diagonal sequence, evenly and progressively slacken the ten main bearing cap retaining bolts by half a turn at a time until all bolts are loose. Remove all the bolts.

7 Carefully remove each cap from the cylinder block, ensuring that the lower main bearing shell remains in position in the cap.

8 Carefully lift out the crankshaft, taking care not to displace the upper main bearing shells **(see illustration)**. Remove the oil seal and discard it.

9 Recover the upper bearing shells from the cylinder block, and tape them to their respective caps for safe-keeping.

2.2 litre petrol engines

10 Working as described in Part B of this Chapter, remove the flywheel/driveplate and the timing chains and sprockets.

11 Remove the piston and connecting rod assemblies as described in Section 9. If no work is to be done on the pistons and connecting rods, unbolt the caps and push the pistons far enough up the bores that the connecting rods are positioned clear of the crankshaft journals.

12 Before removing the crankshaft, check the endfloat as described in paragraph 3 or 4.

13 Evenly and progressively slacken the cylinder block lower casing retaining bolts and remove the casing from the cylinder block **(see illustration)**. If the locating dowels are a loose fit, remove them and store them with the casing for safe-keeping.

14 Carefully lift out the crankshaft, taking care not to displace the upper main bearing shells. Remove the oil seal and discard it.

15 Recover the upper bearing shells from the cylinder block, and tape them to their respective positions in the lower casing for safe-keeping.

1.9 litre diesel engines

16 Working as described in Part C or D of this Chapter (as applicable), remove the flywheel/ driveplate, oil pump and the crankshaft left-hand oil seal housing.

17 Remove the piston and connecting rod assemblies as described in Section 9. If no work is to be done on the pistons and connecting rods, unbolt the caps and push the pistons far enough up the bores that the connecting rods are positioned clear of the crankshaft journals.

18 Before removing the crankshaft, check the endfloat as described in paragraphs 3 and 4.

19 Check the main bearing caps for identification markings. Normally, No 1 bearing cap (timing belt end) is not marked and the remaining caps are numbered I, II, III, IIII. The lug at the base of the cap is used to identify the inlet manifold side of the engine **(see illustrations)**. If the bearing caps are not marked, using a hammer and punch or a suitable marker pen, number the caps from 1 to 5 from the timing belt end of the engine and mark each cap to indicate its correct fitted direction to avoid confusion on refitting.

20 Working in a diagonal sequence, evenly and progressively slacken the ten main bearing cap retaining bolts by half a turn at a time until all bolts are loose. Remove all the bolts.

10.8 Removing the crankshaft – 1.8 litre petrol engines

10.13 Lifting the cylinder block lower casing from the cylinder block – 2.2 litre petrol engines

10.19a Main bearing cap identification marks (arrowed) . . .

10.19b . . . and the lug at the base of the cap (arrowed) is used to identify the inlet manifold side of the engine – 1.9 litre diesel engines

10.27 No 1 and 2 main bearing cap identification marks (arrowed) – 2.0 and 2.2 litre diesel engines

21 Carefully remove each cap from the cylinder block, ensuring that the lower main bearing shell remains in position in the cap.
22 Carefully lift out the crankshaft, taking care not to displace the upper main bearing shells.
23 Recover the upper bearing shells and the thrustwashers from the cylinder block, and tape them to their respective caps for safe-keeping.

2.0 and 2.2 litre diesel engines

24 Working as described in Part E of this Chapter, remove the flywheel/driveplate and the timing chains and sprockets. On 2.0 litre engines, remove the main bearing ladder casting from the base of the bearing caps, noting which way around it is fitted.
25 Remove the piston and connecting rod assemblies as described in Section 9. If no work is to be done on the pistons and connecting rods, unbolt the caps and push the pistons far enough up the bores that the connecting rods are positioned clear of the crankshaft journals.
26 Before removing the crankshaft, check the endfloat as described in paragraphs 3 and 4.
27 It will be necessary to make identification markings on each main bearing cap as only caps number 1 and 2 are marked by the manufacturer **(see illustration)**. Using a hammer and punch or a suitable marker pen, number the caps from 1 to 5 from the timing chain end of the engine and mark each cap

11.3 On diesel engines unscrew the retaining bolts and remove the piston oil spray nozzles from the cylinder block

to indicate its correct fitted direction to avoid confusion on refitting.
28 Working in a diagonal sequence, evenly and progressively slacken the ten main bearing cap retaining bolts by half a turn at a time until all bolts are loose. Remove all the bolts.
29 Carefully remove each cap from the cylinder block, ensuring that the lower main bearing shell remains in position in the cap.
30 Carefully lift out the crankshaft, taking care not to displace the upper main bearing shells. Remove the oil seal and discard it. On 2.2 litre engines, remove the balancer unit chain.
31 Recover the upper bearing shells from the cylinder block, and tape them to their respective caps for safe-keeping.

11 Cylinder block – cleaning and inspection

Cleaning

1 For complete cleaning, remove all external components (senders, sensors, brackets, oil pipes, coolant pipes, etc) from the cylinder block.
2 Scrape all traces of gasket and/or sealant from the cylinder block and lower casing (where applicable), taking particular care not to damage the cylinder head and sump mating faces.
3 Remove all oil gallery plugs, where fitted. The plugs are usually very tight – they may have to be drilled out and the holes retapped. Use new plugs when the engine is reassembled. On diesel engines, undo the retaining bolts and remove the piston oil spray nozzles from inside the cylinder block **(see illustration)**.
4 If the block and lower casing (where applicable) are extremely dirty, they should be steam-cleaned.
5 If the components have been steam-cleaned, clean all oil holes and oil galleries one more time on completion. Flush all internal passages with warm water until the water runs clear. Dry the block and, where necessary, the lower casing thoroughly and

wipe all machined surfaces with a light oil. If you have access to compressed air, use it to speed-up the drying process, and to blow out all the oil holes and galleries.

> **Warning: Wear eye protection when using compressed air.**

6 If the block and lower casing are relatively clean, an adequate cleaning job can be achieved with hot soapy water and a stiff brush. Take plenty of time, and do a thorough job. Regardless of the cleaning method used, be sure to clean all oil holes and galleries very thoroughly, dry everything completely, and coat all cast-iron machined surfaces with light oil.
7 The threaded holes in the cylinder block must be clean, to ensure accurate torque readings when tightening fixings during reassembly. Run the correct-size tap (which can be determined from the size of the relevant bolt) into each of the holes to remove rust, corrosion, thread sealant or other contamination, and to restore damaged threads. If possible, use compressed air to clear the holes of debris produced by this operation. Do not forget to clean the threads of all bolts and nuts which are to be re-used, as well.
8 Where applicable, apply suitable sealant to the new oil gallery plugs, and insert them into the relevant holes in the cylinder block. Tighten the plugs securely. On diesel engines, refit the oil spray nozzles into the block and secure with the retaining bolts tightened securely.
9 If the engine is to be left dismantled for some time, cover the cylinder block with a large plastic bag to keep it clean and prevent corrosion. Where applicable, refit the lower casing and tighten the bolts finger-tight.

Inspection

10 Visually check the block for cracks, rust and corrosion. Look for stripped threads in the threaded holes. It's also a good idea to have the block checked for hidden cracks by an engine reconditioning specialist that has the equipment to do this type of work, especially if the vehicle had a history of overheating or using coolant. If defects are found, have the block repaired, if possible, or renewed.

11 If in any doubt as to the condition of the cylinder block, have it inspected and measured by an engine reconditioning specialist. If the bores are worn or damaged, they will be able to carry out any necessary reboring (where possible), and supply appropriate oversized pistons, etc.

12 Pistons/connecting rods – inspection

1 Before the inspection process can begin, the piston/connecting rod assemblies must be cleaned, and the original piston rings removed from the pistons. **Note:** *Always use new piston rings when the engine is reassembled.*
2 Carefully expand the old rings over the top of the pistons. The use of two or three old feeler gauges will be helpful in preventing the rings dropping into empty grooves **(see illustration)**. Take care, however, as piston rings are sharp.
3 Scrape away all traces of carbon from the top of the piston. A hand-held wire brush, or a piece of fine emery cloth, can be used once the majority of the deposits have been scraped away.
4 Remove the carbon from the ring grooves in the piston, using an old ring. Break the ring in half to do this (be careful not to cut your fingers – piston rings are sharp). Be very careful to remove only the carbon deposits – do not remove any metal, and do not nick or scratch the sides of the ring grooves.
5 Once the deposits have been removed, clean the piston/connecting rod assembly with paraffin or a suitable solvent, and dry thoroughly. Make sure that the oil return holes in the ring grooves are clear.
6 If the pistons and cylinder bores are not damaged or worn excessively, and if the cylinder block does not need to be rebored, the original pistons can be refitted. Normal piston wear shows up as even vertical wear on the piston thrust surfaces, and slight looseness of the top ring in its groove. New piston rings should always be used when the engine is reassembled.
7 Carefully inspect each piston for cracks around the skirt, at the gudgeon pin bosses, and at the piston ring lands (between the ring grooves).
8 Look for scoring and scuffing on the thrust faces of the piston skirt, holes in the piston crown, and burned areas at the edge of the crown. If the skirt is scored or scuffed, the engine may have been suffering from overheating, and/or abnormal combustion ('pinking') which caused excessively-high operating temperatures. The cooling and lubrication systems should be checked thoroughly. A hole in the piston crown, or burned areas at the edge of the piston crown indicates that abnormal combustion (pre-ignition, 'pinking', knocking or detonation) has been occurring. If any of the above problems exist, the causes must be

investigated and corrected, or the damage will occur again.
9 Corrosion of the piston, in the form of pitting, indicates that coolant has been leaking into the combustion chamber and/or the crankcase. Again, the cause must be corrected, or the problem may persist in the rebuilt engine.
10 If in any doubt as to the condition of the pistons and connecting rods, have them inspected and measured by an engine reconditioning specialist. If new parts are required, they will be able to supply and fit appropriate-sized pistons/rings, and rebore (where possible) or hone the cylinder block.

13 Crankshaft – inspection

1 Clean the crankshaft using paraffin or a suitable solvent, and dry it, preferably with compressed air if available. Be sure to clean the oil holes with a pipe cleaner or similar probe, to ensure that they are not obstructed.

⚠ **Warning: Wear eye protection when using compressed air.**

2 Check the main and big-end bearing journals for uneven wear, scoring, pitting and cracking.
3 Big-end bearing wear is accompanied by distinct metallic knocking when the engine is running (particularly noticeable when the engine is pulling from low revs), and some loss of oil pressure.
4 Main bearing wear is accompanied by severe engine vibration and rumble – getting progressively worse as engine revs increase – and again by loss of oil pressure.
5 Check the bearing journal for roughness by running a finger lightly over the bearing surface. Any roughness (which will be accompanied by obvious bearing wear) indicates that the crankshaft requires regrinding.
6 If the crankshaft has been reground, check for burrs around the crankshaft oil holes (the holes are usually chamfered, so burrs should not be a problem unless regrinding has been carried out carelessly). Remove any burrs with a fine file or scraper, and thoroughly clean the oil holes as described previously.
7 Have the crankshaft journals measured by an engine reconditioning specialist. If the crankshaft is worn or damaged, they may be able to regrind the journals and supply suitable undersize bearing shells. If no undersize shells are available and the crankshaft has worn beyond the specified limits, it will have to be renewed. Consult your Vauxhall/Opel dealer or engine reconditioning specialist for further information on parts availability.
8 If a new crankshaft is to be fitted, undo the screws securing the crankshaft speed/position sensor pulse pick-up ring to the crankshaft, and transfer the ring to the new crankshaft **(see illustration)**.

12.2 Using a feeler blade to remove a piston ring

14 Main and big-end bearings – inspection

1 Even though the main and big-end bearings should be renewed during the engine overhaul, the old bearings should be retained for close examination, as they may reveal valuable information about the condition of the engine.
2 Bearing failure occurs because of lack of lubrication, the presence of dirt or other foreign particles, overloading the engine, or corrosion **(see illustration overleaf)**. If a bearing fails, the cause must be found and eliminated before the engine is reassembled, to prevent the failure from happening again.
3 To examine the bearing shells, remove them from the cylinder block, the main bearing caps or cylinder block lower casing, the connecting rods and the big-end bearing caps, and lay them out on a clean surface in the same order as they were fitted to the engine. This will enable any bearing problems to be matched with the corresponding crankshaft journal.
4 Dirt and other foreign particles can enter the engine in a variety of ways. Contamination may be left in the engine during assembly, or it may pass through filters or the crankcase ventilation system. Normal engine wear produces small particles of metal, which can eventually cause problems. If particles find their way into the lubrication system, it is likely that they will eventually be carried to the bearings. Whatever the source, these foreign particles often end up embedded in the soft

13.8 Transfer the crankshaft speed/position sensor pulse pick-up ring to the new crankshaft

FATIGUE FAILURE   IMPROPER SEATING

CRATERS OR POCKETS   BRIGHT (POLISHED) SECTIONS

SCRATCHED BY DIRT   LACK OF OIL

DIRT EMBEDDED INTO BEARING MATERIAL   OVERLAY WIPED OUT

EXCESSIVE WEAR   TAPERED JOURNAL

OVERLAY WIPED OUT   RADIUS RIDE

H 28395

14.2 Typical bearing failures

bearing material, and are easily recognised. Large particles will not embed in the bearing, and will score or gouge the bearing and journal. To prevent possible contamination, clean all parts thoroughly, and keep everything spotlessly-clean during engine assembly. Once the engine has been installed in the vehicle, ensure that engine oil and filter changes are carried out at the recommended intervals.

5 Lack of lubrication (or lubrication breakdown) has a number of interrelated causes. Excessive heat (which thins the oil), overloading (which squeezes the oil from the bearing face), and oil leakage (from excessive bearing clearances, worn oil pump or high engine speeds) all contribute to lubrication breakdown. Blocked oil passages, which may be the result of misaligned oil holes in a bearing shell, will also starve a bearing of oil and destroy it. When lack of lubrication is the cause of bearing failure, the bearing material is wiped or extruded from the steel backing of the bearing. Temperatures may increase to the point where the steel backing turns blue from overheating.

6 Driving habits can have a definite effect on bearing life. Full-throttle, low-speed operation (labouring the engine) puts very high loads on bearings, which tends to squeeze out the oil film. These loads cause the bearings to flex, which produces fine cracks in the bearing face (fatigue failure). Eventually the bearing material will loosen in places, and tear away from the steel backing. Regular short journeys can lead to corrosion of bearings, because insufficient engine heat is produced to drive off the condensed water and corrosive gases which form inside the engine. These products collect in the engine oil, forming acid and sludge. As the oil is carried to the bearings, the acid attacks and corrodes the bearing material.

7 Incorrect bearing installation during engine assembly will also lead to bearing failure.

Tight-fitting bearings leave insufficient bearing lubrication clearance, and will result in oil starvation. Dirt or foreign particles trapped behind a bearing shell results in high spots on the bearing which can lead to failure.

8 *Do not* touch any shell's bearing surface with your fingers during reassembly; there is a risk of scratching the delicate surface, or of depositing particles of dirt on it.

9 As mentioned at the beginning of this Section, the bearing shells should be renewed as a matter of course during engine overhaul; to do otherwise is false economy.

15 Engine overhaul – reassembly sequence

1 Before reassembly begins, ensure that all necessary new parts have been obtained (particularly gaskets, and various bolts which must be renewed), and that all the tools required are available. Read through the entire procedure to familiarise yourself with the work involved, and to ensure that all items necessary for reassembly of the engine are to hand. In addition to all normal tools and materials, a thread-locking compound will be required. A tube of suitable sealant will be required to seal certain joint faces which are not fitted with gaskets.

2 In order to save time and avoid problems, engine reassembly can be carried out in the following order:

1.8 litre petrol engines

a) *Piston rings (see Section 16).*
b) *Crankshaft (see Section 17).*
c) *Piston/connecting rod assemblies (see Section 18).*
d) *Oil pump (see Chapter 2A).*
e) *Sump (see Chapter 2A).*
f) *Flywheel (see Chapter 2A).*
g) *Cylinder head (see Chapter 2A).*
h) *Coolant pump (see Chapter 3).*
i) *Timing belt and sprockets (see Chapter 2A).*
j) *Inlet and exhaust manifolds (see Chapter 4A).*

2.2 litre petrol engines

a) *Piston rings (see Section 16).*
b) *Crankshaft (see Section 17).*
c) *Piston/connecting rod assemblies (see Section 18).*
d) *Sump (see Chapter 2B).*
e) *Flywheel/driveplate (see Chapter 2B).*
f) *Cylinder head (see Chapter 2B).*
g) *Coolant pump (see Chapter 3).*
h) *Timing chains and sprockets (see Chapter 2B).*
i) *Timing chain cover (see Chapter 2B).*
j) *Inlet and exhaust manifolds (see Chapter 4A).*

1.9 litre diesel engines

a) *Piston rings (see Section 16).*
b) *Crankshaft (see Section 17).*

c) *Pistons/connecting rod assemblies (see Section 18).*
d) *Cylinder head (see Chapter 2C or 2D).*
e) *Oil pump (see Chapter 2C or 2D).*
f) *Sump (see Chapter 2C or 2D).*
g) *Flywheel/driveplate (see Chapter 2C or 2D).*
h) *Coolant pump (see Chapter 3).*
i) *Timing belt, sprockets, tensioner and idler pulleys (see Chapter 2C or 2D).*
j) *Inlet and exhaust manifolds (see Chapter 4B).*

2.0 and 2.2 litre diesel engines

a) *Piston rings (see Section 16).*
b) *Crankshaft (see Section 17).*
c) *Pistons/connecting rod assemblies (see Section 18).*
d) *Cylinder head (see Chapter 2E).*
e) *Coolant pump (see Chapter 3).*
f) *Timing chains and sprockets (see Chapter 2E).*
g) *Oil pump (see Chapter 2E).*
h) *Sump (see Chapter 2E).*
i) *Flywheel/driveplate (see Chapter 2E).*
j) *Inlet and exhaust manifolds (see Chapter 4B).*

3 At this stage, all engine components should be absolutely clean and dry, with all faults repaired. The components should be laid out (or in individual containers) on a completely clean work surface.

16 Piston rings – refitting

1 Before refitting the new piston rings, the ring end gaps must be checked as follows.

2 Lay out the piston/connecting rod assemblies and the new piston ring sets, so that the ring sets will be matched with the same piston and cylinder during the end gap measurement and subsequent engine reassembly.

3 Insert the top ring into the first cylinder, and push it down the bore slightly using the top of the piston. This will ensure that the ring remains square with the cylinder walls. Push the ring down into the bore until it is positioned 15 to 20 mm down from the top edge of the bore, then withdraw the piston.

4 Measure the end gap using feeler gauges,

16.4 Measuring a piston ring end gap using a feeler gauge

and compare the measurements with the figures given in the Specifications (see illustration).

5 If the gap is too small (unlikely if genuine Vauxhall/Opel parts are used), it must be enlarged or the ring ends may contact each other during engine operation, causing serious damage. Ideally, new piston rings providing the correct end gap should be fitted, but as a last resort, the end gap can be increased by filing the ring ends very carefully with a fine file. Mount the file in a vice equipped with soft jaws, slip the ring over the file with the ends contacting the file face, and slowly move the ring to remove material from the ends – take care, as piston rings are sharp, and are easily broken.

6 With new piston rings, it is unlikely that the end gap will be too large. If they are too large, check that you have the correct rings for your engine and for the particular cylinder bore size.

7 Repeat the checking procedure for each ring in the first cylinder, and then for the rings in the remaining cylinders. Remember to keep rings, pistons and cylinders matched up.

8 Once the ring end gaps have been checked and if necessary corrected, the rings can be fitted to the pistons.

9 The oil control ring (lowest one on the piston) is composed of three sections, and should be installed first. Fit the lower steel ring, then the spreader ring, followed by the upper steel ring (see illustration).

10 With the oil control ring components installed, the second (middle) ring can be fitted. It is usually stamped with a mark (TOP) which must face up, towards the top of the piston. Note: *Always follow the instructions supplied with the new piston ring sets – different manufacturers may specify different procedures. Do not mix up the top and middle rings, as they have different cross-sections.* Using two or three old feeler blades, as for removal of the old rings, carefully slip the ring into place in the middle groove.

11 Fit the top ring in the same manner, ensuring that, where applicable, the mark on the ring is facing up. If a stepped ring is being fitted, fit the ring with the smaller diameter of the step uppermost.

12 Repeat the procedure for the remaining pistons and rings.

17 Crankshaft – refitting

Note: *It is recommended that new main bearing shells are fitted regardless of the condition of the original ones.*

1 Refitting the crankshaft is the first step in the engine reassembly procedure. It is assumed at this point that the cylinder block, cylinder block lower casing (where applicable) and crankshaft have been cleaned, inspected and repaired or reconditioned as necessary.

16.9 Fitting the oil control spreader ring

2 Position the cylinder block with the sump/lower casing mating face uppermost.

3 Clean the bearing shells and the bearing recesses in both the cylinder block and the lower casing/caps. If new shells are being fitted, ensure that all traces of the protective grease are cleaned off using paraffin. Wipe the shells dry with a clean lint-free cloth.

4 Note that the crankshaft endfloat is controlled by thrustwashers located on one of the main bearing shells. The thrustwashers may be separate or incorporated into, or attached to, the bearing shells themselves.

5 If the original bearing shells are being re-used, they must be refitted to their original locations in the block and lower casing, or caps.

6 Fit the upper main bearing shells in place in the cylinder block, ensuring that the tab on

17.6 Fitting a main bearing shell to the cylinder block

17.10 Lubricate the crankshaft journals then refit bearing caps Nos 1 to 4 – 1.8 litre petrol engines

each shell engages in the notch in the cylinder block (see illustration). Where separate thrustwashers are fitted, use a little grease to stick them to each side of their respective bearing upper location; ensure that the oilway grooves on each thrustwasher face outwards (away from the block).

1.8 litre petrol engines

7 Liberally lubricate each bearing shell in the cylinder block, and lower the crankshaft into position (see illustration).

8 If necessary, seat the crankshaft using light taps from a soft-faced mallet on the crankshaft balance webs.

9 Fit the bearing shells into the bearing caps.

10 Lubricate the bearing shells in the bearing caps, and the crankshaft journals, then fit Nos 1 to 4 bearing caps, and tighten the new bolts as far as possible by hand (see illustration).

11 Ensure the No 5 bearing cap is clean and dry then fill the groove on each side of the cap with sealing compound (Vauxhall/Opel recommend the use of sealant part No 90485251, available from your dealer) (see illustration). Fit the bearing cap to the engine, ensuring it is fitted the correct way around, and tighten the new bolts as far as possible by hand.

12 Working in a diagonal sequence from the centre outwards, tighten the main bearing cap bolts to the specified Stage 1 torque setting (see illustration).

13 Once all bolts are tightened to the specified Stage 1 torque, go around again

17.7 Lubricate the upper bearing shells with clean engine oil then fit the crankshaft – 1.8 litre petrol engines

17.11 Fill the side grooves of the No 5 bearing cap with sealant prior to refitting it to the engine – 1.8 litre petrol engines

17.12 Tighten the bolts to the specified Stage 1 torque setting . . .

17.13 . . . and then through the specified Stages 2 and 3 angles – 1.8 litre petrol engines

and tighten all bolts through the specified Stage 2 angle then go around for once more and tighten all bolts through the specified Stage 3 angle. It is recommended that an angle-measuring gauge is used during the final stages of the tightening, to ensure accuracy **(see illustration)**. If a gauge is not available, use white paint to make alignment marks between the bolt head and cap prior to tightening; the marks can then be used to check that the bolt has been rotated through the correct angle.

14 Once all the bolts have been tightened, inject more sealant down the grooves in the No 5 main bearing cap until sealant is seen to be escaping through the joints. Once you are sure the cap grooves are full of sealant, wipe off all excess sealant using a clean cloth.

15 Check that the crankshaft is free to rotate smoothly; if excessive pressure is required to turn the crankshaft, investigate the cause before proceeding further.

16 Check the crankshaft endfloat with reference to Section 10.

17 Refit/reconnect the piston connecting rod assemblies to the crankshaft as described in Section 18.

18 Referring to Part A of this Chapter, fit a new left-hand crankshaft oil seal, then refit the oil pump, sump, flywheel, cylinder head, timing belt sprocket(s) and fit a new timing belt.

2.2 litre petrol engines

19 Liberally lubricate each bearing shell in the cylinder block, and lower the crankshaft into position.

20 If necessary, seat the crankshaft using light taps from a soft-faced mallet on the crankshaft balance webs.

21 Fit the bearing shells into the cylinder block lower casing.

22 Ensure that the cylinder block and lower casing mating surfaces are clean and dry, then apply a 2 to 5 mm diameter bead of sealant to the groove in the cylinder block **(see illustration)**. Vauxhall/Opel recommend the use of sealant part No 90543772, available from your dealer.

23 Locate the lower casing over the crankshaft and onto the cylinder block.

24 Fit the twenty new M10 bolts and the ten M8 bolts and tighten the bolts as far as possible by hand.

25 Working in a diagonal sequence from the centre outwards, tighten the twenty M10 lower casing bolts to the specified Stage 1 torque setting.

26 Once all M10 bolts are tightened to the specified Stage 1 torque, go around again and tighten them through the specified Stage 2 angle then go around once more and tighten them through the specified Stage 3 angle. It is recommended that an angle-measuring gauge is used during the final stages of the tightening,

to ensure accuracy **(see illustration)**. If a gauge is not available, use white paint to make alignment marks between the bolt head and casing prior to tightening; the marks can then be used to check that the bolt has been rotated through the correct angle.

27 After tightening all the M10 bolts, tighten the M8 bolts to the specified torque, working in a diagonal sequence from the centre outwards.

28 Check that the crankshaft is free to rotate smoothly; if excessive pressure is required to turn the crankshaft, investigate the cause before proceeding further.

29 Check the crankshaft endfloat with reference to Section 10.

30 Refit/reconnect the piston connecting rod assemblies to the crankshaft as described in Section 18.

31 Referring to Part B of this Chapter, fit a new left-hand crankshaft oil seal, then refit the sump, flywheel/driveplate, cylinder head, and the timing chains and sprockets.

1.9 litre diesel engines

32 Liberally lubricate each bearing shell in the cylinder block, and lower the crankshaft into position.

33 If necessary, seat the crankshaft using light taps from a soft-faced mallet on the crankshaft balance webs.

34 Fit the bearing shells into the bearing caps.

35 Lubricate the bearing shells in the bearing caps, and the crankshaft journals, then fit the caps ensuring they are fitted to their correct locations and the right way around. Fit and tighten the new bolts as far as possible by hand.

36 Working in a spiral pattern from the centre outwards, tighten the main bearing cap bolts to the specified Stage 1 torque setting.

37 Once all bolts are tightened to the specified Stage 1 torque, go around again and tighten all bolts through the specified Stage 2 angle. It is recommended that an angle-measuring gauge is used during the final stages of the tightening, to ensure accuracy. If a gauge is not available, use white paint to make alignment marks between the bolt head and cap prior to tightening; the marks can then be used to check that the bolt has been rotated through the correct angle.

38 Check that the crankshaft is free to rotate smoothly; if excessive pressure is required to turn the crankshaft, investigate the cause before proceeding further.

39 Check the crankshaft endfloat with reference to Section 10.

40 Refit/reconnect the piston connecting rod assemblies to the crankshaft as described in Section 18.

41 Referring to Part C of this Chapter, fit a new left-hand crankshaft oil seal/housing, then refit the oil pump, sump, flywheel/driveplate, cylinder head, timing belt sprocket(s) and fit a new timing belt.

17.22 Apply a continuous bead of sealant (arrowed) to the groove in the cylinder block – 2.2 litre petrol engines

17.26 Tightening the cylinder block lower casing bolts through the specified angles – 2.2 litre petrol engines

2.0 and 2.2 litre diesel engines

42 Liberally lubricate each bearing shell in the cylinder block, and lower the crankshaft into position. On 2.2 litre engines, ensure the balancer chain is in position on the crankshaft.

43 If necessary, seat the crankshaft using light taps from a soft-faced mallet on the crankshaft balance webs.

44 Fit the bearing shells into the bearing caps.

45 Lubricate the bearing shells in the bearing caps, and the crankshaft journals, then fit Nos 1 to 4 bearing caps, and tighten the new bolts as far as possible by hand.

46 Ensure the No 5 bearing cap is clean and dry then fill the groove on each side of the cap with sealing compound (Vauxhall/Opel recommend the use of sealant part No 90485251, available from your dealer). Fit the bearing cap to the engine, ensuring it is fitted the correct way around, and tighten the new bolts as far as possible by hand.

47 Working in a diagonal sequence from the centre outwards, tighten the main bearing cap bolts to the specified Stage 1 torque setting.

48 Once all bolts are tightened to the specified Stage 1 torque, go around again and tighten all bolts through the specified Stage 2 angle then go around for once more and tighten all bolts through the specified Stage 3 angle. It is recommended that an angle-measuring gauge is used during the final stages of the tightening, to ensure accuracy. If a gauge is not available, use white paint to make alignment marks between the bolt head and cap prior to tightening; the marks can then be used to check that the bolt has been rotated through the correct angle.

49 Once all the bolts have been tightened, inject more sealant down the grooves in the No 5 main bearing cap until sealant is seen to be escaping through the joints **(see illustrations)**. Once you are sure the cap grooves are full of sealant, wipe off all excess sealant using a clean cloth.

50 Check that the crankshaft is free to rotate smoothly; if excessive pressure is required to turn the crankshaft, investigate the cause before proceeding further.

51 Check the crankshaft endfloat with reference to Section 10.

52 Refit/reconnect the piston connecting rod assemblies to the crankshaft as described in Section 18.

53 On 2.0 litre engines, ensure the bearing cap and main bearing ladder casting surfaces are clean and dry. Refit the casting to the engine ensuring that the arrow on the casting is pointing towards the timing chain end of the engine, then refit the retaining bolts and tighten them to the specified torque, working in a diagonal sequence from the centre outwards **(see illustrations)**.

54 Referring to Part E of this Chapter, fit a new left-hand crankshaft oil seal, then refit the cylinder head, timing chains and sprockets, oil pump, sump and the flywheel/driveplate.

17.49a With the No 5 bearing cap in position, inject sealant down the groove . . .

17.49b . . . until it is seen to be forced out through the hole in the cap (arrowed) – 2.0 and 2.2 litre diesel engines

17.53a Refit the main bearing ladder casting . . .

17.53b . . . ensuring the arrow points towards the timing chain end of the engine, then tighten the bolts to the specified torque – 2.0 litre diesel engines

18 Pistons/connecting rods – refitting

Note: *It is recommended that new big-end bearing shells are fitted regardless of the condition of the original ones.*

1 Clean the backs of the big-end bearing shells and the recesses in the connecting rods and big-end caps. If new shells are being fitted, ensure that all traces of the protective grease are cleaned off using paraffin. Wipe the shells, caps and connecting rods dry with a lint-free cloth.

2 Press the bearing shells into their locations, ensuring that the tab on each shell engages in the notch in the connecting rod and cap **(see illustration)**. If there is no tab on the bearing

shell (and no notch in the rod or cap) position the shell equidistant from each side of the rod and cap. If the original bearing shells are being used ensure they are refitted in their original locations.

3 Lubricate the bores, the pistons and piston rings then lay out each piston/connecting rod assembly in its respective position **(see illustration)**.

Petrol engines

4 Lubricate No 1 piston and piston rings, and check that the ring gaps are correctly positioned. The gaps in the upper and lower steel rings of the oil control ring should be offset by 25 to 50 mm to the right and left of the spreader ring gap. The two upper

18.2 Fit the bearing shells making sure their tabs are correctly located in the connecting rod/cap groove (arrowed)

18.3 Lubricate the piston rings with clean engine oil

**18.4 Piston ring end gap positions –
petrol engines**

*I Top and second compression rings
II Oil control ring side rails*

compression ring gaps should be offset by
180° to each other **(see illustration)**.
5 Fit a ring compressor to No 1 piston, then
insert the piston and connecting rod into
the cylinder bore so that the base of the
compressor stands on the block. With the
crankshaft big-end bearing journal positioned
at its lowest point, tap the piston carefully
into the cylinder bore with the wooden handle
of a hammer, and at the same time guide
the connecting rod onto the bearing journal.
Note that the arrow on the piston crown must
point towards the timing chain/belt end of the
engine **(see illustrations)**.
6 Liberally lubricate the bearing journals and
bearing shells, and fit the bearing cap in its
original location (the lug on the bearing cap
base should be facing the flywheel/driveplate
end of the engine) **(see illustration)**.

**18.11 Piston ring end gap positions –
diesel engines**

*I Top compression ring
II Second compression ring
III Oil control ring*

**18.5a Ensure the piston ring end gaps
are correctly spaced then fit the ring
compressor – petrol engines**

**18.5c Tap the piston gently into the bore
using handle of a hammer – petrol engines**

7 Screw in the new bearing cap retaining
bolts, and tighten both bolts to the specified
Stage 1 torque setting then tighten them
through the specified Stage 2 angle, and
finally through the specified Stage 3 angle.
It is recommended that an angle-measuring
gauge is used during the final stages of the
tightening, to ensure accuracy. If a gauge
is not available, use white paint to make
alignment marks between the bolt head and
cap prior to tightening; the marks can then be
used to check that the bolt has been rotated
through the correct angle.
8 Refit the remaining three piston and
connecting rod assemblies in the same way.
9 Rotate the crankshaft, and check that it
turns freely, with no signs of binding or tight
spots.
10 Refit the oil pump pick-up/strainer, sump
and the cylinder head as described in Part A
or B (as applicable) of this Chapter.

Diesel engines

11 Lubricate No 1 piston and piston rings,
and space the ring gaps uniformly around the
piston at 120° intervals **(see illustration)**.
12 Fit a ring compressor to No 1 piston,
then insert the piston and connecting rod
into the cylinder bore so that the base of
the compressor stands on the block. Ensure
that the piston/connecting rod assembly is
positioned as follows:
*a) On 1.9 litre engines, the cut-out on the
piston skirt must be on the same side as
the the oil spray jet, and the lugs on the*

**18.5b Ensuring the arrow on the piston
crown (circled) is pointing towards the
timing belt end of the engine – petrol engines**

**18.6 Make sure the lug (arrowed) is facing
the flywheel/driveplate end of the engine –
petrol engines**

*cap and rod must be toward the timing
belt end of the engine **(see illustration)**.
b) On 2.0 and 2.2 litre engines, the arrow on
the piston crown must point towards the
timing chain end of the engine, and the
lugs on the cap and rod must be toward
the flywheel/driveplate end of the engine
(see illustration 18.6).*
13 With the crankshaft big-end bearing
journal positioned at its lowest point, tap the

**18.12 The cut-out on the piston skirt (A)
must be on the same side as the oil spray
jet, and the lugs on the cap and rod (B)
must be toward the timing belt end of the
engine – 1.9 litre diesel engines**

piston carefully into the cylinder bore with the wooden handle of a hammer, and at the same time guide the connecting rod onto the bearing journal.

14 Liberally lubricate the bearing journals and bearing shells, and fit the bearing cap in its original location.

15 Screw in the new bearing cap retaining bolts, and tighten both bolts to the specified Stage 1 torque setting then tighten them through the specified Stage 2 angle. On 2.0 and 2.2 litre engines additionally tighten the bolts through the specified Stage 3 angle. It is recommended that an angle-measuring gauge is used during the final stages of the tightening, to ensure accuracy. If a gauge is not available, use white paint to make alignment marks between the bolt head and cap prior to tightening; the marks can then be used to check that the bolt has been rotated through the correct angle.

16 Refit the remaining three piston and connecting rod assemblies in the same way.

17 Rotate the crankshaft, and check that it turns freely, with no signs of binding or tight spots.

18 Refit the oil pump pick-up/strainer, balancer unit (2.2.litre engines), sump and the cylinder head as described in Part C, D or E (as applicable) of this Chapter.

19 Engine –
initial start-up after overhaul

1 With the engine refitted in the vehicle, double-check the engine oil and coolant levels. Make a final check that everything has been reconnected, and that there are no tools or rags left in the engine compartment.

2 Start the engine, noting that this may take a little longer than usual. Make sure that the oil pressure warning light goes out. Note that on 2.0 and 2.2 litre diesel engines it will be necessary to bleed the fuel system as described in Chapter 4B before starting the engine.

3 While the engine is idling, check for fuel, water and oil leaks. Don't be alarmed if there are some odd smells and smoke from parts getting hot and burning off oil deposits.

4 Assuming all is well, run the engine until it reaches normal operating temperature, then switch off the engine.

5 After a few minutes, recheck the oil and coolant levels as described in *Weekly checks*, and top-up as necessary.

6 Note that there is no need to retighten the cylinder head bolts once the engine has first run after reassembly.

7 If new pistons, rings or crankshaft bearings have been fitted, the engine must be treated as new, and run-in for the first 600 miles. *Do not* operate the engine at full-throttle, or allow it to labour at low engine speeds in any gear. It is recommended that the oil and filter be changed at the end of this period.

Notes

Chapter 3
Cooling, heating and air conditioning systems

Contents

Degrees of difficulty

Easy, suitable for novice with little experience	Fairly easy, suitable for beginner with some experience	Fairly difficult, suitable for competent DIY mechanic	Difficult, suitable for experienced DIY mechanic	Very difficult, suitable for expert DIY or professional

Specifications

Thermostat

Opening temperatures:
  Petrol engines:
    1.8 litre engines... 92°C
    2.2 litre engines... 82°C
  Diesel engines .... 92°C

Air conditioning compressor

Lubricant capacity:
  Petrol engines... 120 cc
  Diesel engines:
    2.0 and 2.2 litre engines .... 120 cc
    1.9 litre engines.. 135 cc
Lubricant type (synthetic PAG fluid) .... Vauxhall part number 90 509 933/19 49 873

Torque wrench settings

	Nm	lbf ft
Petrol engine models		
Air conditioning compressor mounting bolts.....................	20	15
Air conditioning refrigerant pipe block connections................	20	15
Coolant pump retaining bolts:		
1.8 litre engines	8	6
2.2 litre engines	23	17
Coolant pump sprocket bolts (2.2 litre engines).................	8	6
Coolant temperature sensor.................................	20	15
Radiator mounting brackets to subframe......................	15	11
Thermostat housing/cover:		
1.8 litre engines	20	15
2.2 litre engines	10	7
Diesel engine models		
Air conditioning compressor mounting bolts.....................	20	15
Air conditioning refrigerant pipe block connections................	20	15
Coolant pump pulley bolts (2.0 and 2.2 litre engines)	20	15
Coolant pump retaining bolts:		
1.9 litre engines	25	18
2.0 and 2.2 litre engines	20	15
Coolant temperature sensor:		
1.9 litre engines	20	15
2.0 and 2.2 litre engines.................................	10	7
Radiator mounting brackets to subframe......................	15	11
Thermostat housing/cover:		
1.9 litre engines	25	18
2.0 and 2.2 litre engines	8	6

1 General information and precautions

General information

The cooling system is of pressurised type, comprising a coolant pump, a crossflow radiator, electric cooling fan(s), and thermostat. On 1.8 litre petrol engines and 1.9 litre diesel engines, the coolant pump is driven by the timing belt. On the 2.2 litre petrol engine, the coolant pump is driven by the balancer shaft drive chain. On 2.0 and 2.2 litre diesel engines the coolant pump is driven by the auxiliary drivebelt.

The system functions as follows. Cold coolant from the radiator passes through the bottom hose to the coolant pump, where it is pumped around the cylinder block, head passages and heater matrix. After cooling the cylinder bores, combustion surfaces and valve seats, the coolant reaches the underside of the thermostat, which is initially closed. The coolant passes through the heater, and is returned to the coolant pump.

When the engine is cold, the coolant circulates only through the cylinder block, cylinder head and heater. When the coolant reaches a predetermined temperature, the thermostat opens and the coolant also passes through to the radiator. As the coolant circulates through the radiator, it is cooled by the inrush of air when the car is in forward motion. Airflow is supplemented by the action of the electric cooling fan when necessary. Once the coolant has passed through the radiator, and has cooled, the cycle is repeated.

The electric cooling fan, mounted on the rear of the radiator, is controlled by the engine management system electronic control unit, in conjunction with a cooling fan module. At a predetermined coolant temperature, the fan is actuated. An auxiliary electric cooling fan is fitted to models with air conditioning.

An expansion tank is fitted to the left-hand side of the engine compartment to accommodate expansion of the coolant when hot. The expansion tank is connected to the top of the radiator.

Precautions

⚠️ **Warning: Do not attempt to remove the expansion tank filler cap, or disturb any part of the cooling system, while the engine is hot; there is a high risk of scalding. If the cap must be removed before the engine and radiator have fully cooled (even though this is not recommended) the pressure in the cooling system must first be relieved. Cover the cap with a thick layer of cloth, to avoid scalding, and slowly unscrew the filler cap until a hissing sound can be heard. When the hissing has stopped, indicating that the pressure has reduced, slowly unscrew the**

filler cap until it can be removed; if more hissing sounds are heard, wait until they have stopped before unscrewing the cap completely. At all times, keep well away from the filler cap opening.

⚠️ **Warning: Do not allow antifreeze to come into contact with the skin, or with the painted surfaces of the vehicle. Rinse off spills immediately, with plenty of water. Never leave antifreeze lying around in an open container, or in a puddle on the driveway or garage floor. Children and pets are attracted by its sweet smell, but antifreeze can be fatal if ingested.**

⚠️ **Warning: If the engine is hot, the electric cooling fan may start rotating even if the engine is not running; be careful to keep hands, hair and loose clothing well clear when working in the engine compartment.**

⚠️ **Warning: Refer to Section 10 for precautions to be observed when working on models equipped with air conditioning.**

2 Cooling system hoses – disconnection and renewal

Note: *Refer to the warnings given in Section 1 of this Chapter before proceeding. Do not attempt to disconnect any hose while the system is still hot.*

1 If the checks described in Chapter 1A or 1B reveal a faulty hose, it must be renewed as follows.

2 First drain the cooling system (see Chapter 1A or 1B). If the coolant is not due for renewal, it may be re-used if it is collected in a clean container.

3 Before disconnecting a hose, first note its routing in the engine compartment, and whether it is secured by any additional retaining clips or cable ties. Use a pair of pliers to release the clamp-type clips, or a screwdriver to slacken the screw-type clips, then move the clips along the hose, clear of the relevant inlet/outlet union. Carefully work the hose free.

4 Note that the radiator inlet and outlet unions are fragile; do not use excessive force when attempting to remove the hoses. If a hose proves to be difficult to remove, try to release it by rotating the hose ends before attempting to free it.

5 When fitting a hose, first slide the clips onto the hose, then work the hose into position. If clamp-type clips were originally fitted, it is a good idea to use screw-type clips when refitting the hose. If the hose is stiff, use a little soapy water (washing-up liquid is ideal) as a lubricant, or soften the hose by soaking it in hot water.

6 Work the hose into position, checking that it is correctly routed and secured. Slide each clip along the hose until it passes over the

flared end of the relevant inlet/outlet union, before tightening the clips securely.

7 Refill the cooling system with reference to Chapter 1A or 1B.

8 Check thoroughly for leaks as soon as possible after disturbing any part of the cooling system.

3 Radiator – removal, inspection and refitting

Note: *The radiator is removed from below, complete with the cooling fan assembly.*

Removal

Petrol engine

1 Disconnect the battery negative terminal (refer to *Disconnecting the battery* in the Reference Chapter).

2 Remove the plastic cover from the top of the engine.

3 Apply the handbrake, then jack up the front of the vehicle and support it on axle stands (see *Jacking and vehicle support*).

4 Remove the front bumper as described in Chapter 11.

5 Drain the cooling system as described in Chapter 1A.

6 Remove the air cleaner assembly and air intake duct as described in Chapter 4A.

7 Release the retaining clip and disconnect the expansion tank hose from the top of the radiator.

8 Release the retaining clip and disconnect the top hose from the radiator.

9 Pull out the locking bar and disconnect the wiring harness connector from the cooling fan module at the top of the fan housing **(see illustration)**. Free the wiring harness from the cable ties.

10 Slacken (but do not remove) the two bolts securing the radiator left-hand and right-hand mounting brackets to the subframe **(see illustrations)**.

11 Release the radiator upper rubber mounting bushes on each side from their guides, and carefully move the top of the radiator forward.

3.9 Pull out the locking bar and disconnect the wiring harness connector from the cooling fan module

3.10a Slacken the bolt (arrowed) securing the radiator left-hand . . .

3.10b . . . and right-hand mounting brackets to the subframe

3.16 Carefully lower the radiator down and out from under the car

12 Release the clamp and disconnect the bottom hose from the radiator.

13 On models with air conditioning, undo the bolt each side securing the condenser upper mounting brackets to the radiator. Carefully lift up or remove the plastic panels on each side of the radiator for improved access, if necessary. Suitably secure the condenser to the upper body panel using cable ties or similar, to retain it in place when the radiator is removed.

14 On models with automatic transmission, detach the protective ring (where fitted) over the fluid cooler pipe unions at the radiator. Using a small screwdriver, release the quick-release fitting retaining lugs and disconnect the fitting from the radiator. Suitably cover the open unions after disconnection.

15 Check that all hoses, and connections are released from the radiator in the engine compartment, then engage the help of an assistant to support the radiator.

16 Remove the two bolts securing the radiator left-hand and right-hand mounting brackets to the subframe and carefully lower the radiator down and out from under the car **(see illustration)**. Disengage the condenser lower mounting lugs from the radiator as the radiator is lowered.

Diesel engine

17 Disconnect the battery negative terminal (refer to *Disconnecting the battery* in the Reference Chapter).

18 Remove the plastic cover from the top of the engine

19 Apply the handbrake, then jack up the front of the vehicle and support it on axle stands (see *Jacking and vehicle support*). Undo the ten bolts and remove the engine undertray.

20 Remove the front bumper as described in Chapter 11.

21 Remove the headlights as described in Chapter 12.

22 Drain the cooling system as described in Chapter 1B.

23 Remove the air cleaner assembly and air intake duct as described in Chapter 4B.

24 Release the retaining clip and disconnect the expansion tank hose from the top of the radiator **(see illustration)**.

3.24 Release the retaining clip (arrowed) and disconnect the expansion tank hose from the top of the radiator

25 Release the two retaining clips and disconnect the top hose from the radiator and thermostat housing.

26 Pull out the locking bar and disconnect the wiring harness connector from the cooling fan module at the top of the fan housing **(see illustration 3.9)**. Free the wiring harness from the cable ties.

27 Slacken the two retaining clips and remove the upper charge air hose from the turbocharger, and intercooler right-hand charge air pipe.

28 Slacken the two retaining clips and disconnect the upper charge air hose from the throttle body/housing, and intercooler left-hand charge air pipe.

29 Undo the intercooler left-hand charge air pipe upper retaining bolt **(see illustration)**.

3.29 Undo the intercooler left-hand charge air pipe upper retaining bolt (arrowed)

30 Slacken the retaining clips and remove the left-hand and right-hand lower charge air hoses from the intercooler and charge air pipes **(see illustrations)**.

31 Slacken (but do not remove) the two bolts securing the radiator left-hand and right-hand mounting brackets to the subframe **(see illustrations 3.10a and 3.10b)**.

32 Release the radiator upper rubber mounting bushes on each side from their guides, and carefully move the top of the radiator forward.

33 Undo the bolt securing the intercooler right-hand charge air pipe upper mounting to the radiator **(see illustration)**.

34 Undo the bolt each side securing the intercooler left-hand and right-hand charge air pipe lower mountings to the radiator **(see illustrations)**.

3.30a Slacken the retaining clips (arrowed) and remove the left-hand . . .

3.30b . . . and right-hand lower charge air hoses from the intercooler and charge air pipes

3.33 Undo the bolt (arrowed) securing the intercooler right-hand charge air pipe upper mounting to the radiator

3.34a Undo the bolt (arrowed) securing the intercooler left-hand . . .

3.34b . . . and right-hand charge air pipe lower mountings to the radiator

35 Release the clamp and disconnect the bottom hose from the radiator.

36 On models with air conditioning, undo the two bolts securing the receiver-dryer to the right-hand side of the radiator **(see illustration)**.

37 Undo the bolt each side securing the intercooler upper mounting brackets to the radiator **(see illustration)**. Carefully lift up or remove the plastic panels on each side of the radiator for improved access, if necessary. Suitably secure the intercooler to the upper body panel using cable ties or similar, to retain it in place when the radiator is removed.

38 On models with automatic transmission, detach the protective ring (where fitted) over the fluid cooler pipe unions at the radiator. Using a small screwdriver, release the quick-release fitting retaining lugs and disconnect the fitting from the radiator. Suitably cover the open unions after disconnection.

39 Check that all hoses, and connections are released from the radiator in the engine compartment, then engage the help of an assistant to support the radiator.

40 Remove the two bolts securing the radiator left-hand and right-hand mounting brackets to the subframe and carefully lower the radiator down and out from under the car **(see illustration 3.16)**. Disengage the intercooler lower mounting lugs from the radiator as the radiator is lowered.

Inspection

41 If the radiator has been removed due

to suspected blockage, reverse-flush it as described in Chapter 1A or 1B.

42 Clean dirt and debris from the radiator fins, using an airline (in which case, wear eye protection) or a soft brush.

Caution: Be careful, as the fins are easily damaged, and are sharp.

43 If necessary, a radiator specialist can perform a 'flow test' on the radiator, to establish whether an internal blockage exists.

44 A leaking radiator must be referred to a specialist for permanent repair. Do not attempt to weld or solder a leaking radiator.

45 In an emergency, minor leaks from the radiator can be cured by using a suitable radiator sealant (in accordance with its manufacturer's instructions) with the radiator fitted in the vehicle.

46 Inspect the radiator mounting rubbers, and renew them if necessary.

Refitting

47 Refitting is a reversal of removal, bearing in mind the following points.
 a) *Ensure that the intercooler or condenser (as applicable) lower mountings are correctly engaged with the radiator when refitting.*
 b) *Ensure that all hoses are correctly reconnected, and their retaining clips securely tightened.*
 c) *On completion, refill the cooling system as described in Chapter 1A or 1B.*
 d) *On models with automatic transmission, check and if necessary top-up the*

automatic transmission fluid level with reference to the 'Transmission fluid – draining and refilling' procedures contained in Chapter 7B.

4 Thermostat – removal and refitting

Removal

1.8 litre petrol engine

1 The thermostat is located on the front right-hand side of the cylinder head, and is integral with its housing.

2 Disconnect the battery negative terminal (refer to *Disconnecting the battery* in the Reference Chapter).

3 Apply the handbrake, then jack up the front of the vehicle and support it on axle stands (see *Jacking and vehicle support*). Remove the plastic cover from the top of the engine.

4 Drain the cooling system as described in Chapter 1A.

5 Loosen the clips and disconnect the top hose, expansion tank hose and throttle housing coolant hose from the thermostat housing.

6 Disconnect the wiring connector from the coolant temperature sensor on the housing.

7 Unbolt and remove the housing from the cylinder head, then remove the gasket. Thoroughly clean the contact surfaces of the housing and cylinder head.

2.2 litre petrol engine

8 The thermostat is located on the left-hand rear of the cylinder head, over the transmission.

9 Disconnect the battery negative terminal (refer to *Disconnecting the battery* in the Reference Chapter).

10 Apply the handbrake, then jack up the front of the vehicle and support it on axle stands (see *Jacking and vehicle support*).

11 Drain the cooling system as described in Chapter 1A.

12 Release the clip and disconnect the top hose from the thermostat cover.

13 Unscrew the bolts and remove the cover from the thermostat housing **(see illustration)**.

14 Lift the thermostat from the housing **(see**

3.36 On models with air conditioning, undo the two bolts (arrowed) securing the receiver-dryer to the radiator

3.37 Undo the bolt (arrowed) each side securing the intercooler upper mounting brackets to the radiator

4.13 Removing the thermostat housing cover

4.14 Removing the thermostat from the housing

4.20 Disconnect the charge air hose from the throttle body/housing, and intercooler charge air pipe

illustration). Remove the seal from the rim of the thermostat and discard it. Obtain a new one. Clean the contact surfaces of the cover and housing.

1.9 litre diesel engine

15 The thermostat is located on the left-hand end of the cylinder head, and is integral with the housing.

16 Remove the plastic cover over the top of the engine.

17 Remove the battery and battery box as described in Chapter 5A.

18 Apply the handbrake, then jack up the front of the vehicle and support it on axle stands (see *Jacking and vehicle support*).

19 Drain the cooling system as described in Chapter 1B.

20 Release the two retaining clips and disconnect the charge air hose from the throttle body/housing, and intercooler charge air pipe **(see illustration)**.

21 Release the clips and disconnect the hoses from the thermostat housing.

22 Disconnect the coolant temperature sensor wiring connector.

23 Unscrew the nut and release the coolant pipes from the stud at the base of the thermostat housing.

24 Unbolt the thermostat housing from the cylinder head. Clean away all traces of gasket from the housing and cylinder head.

2.0 and 2.2 litre diesel engine

25 The thermostat is located on the front right-hand end of the cylinder head, and is integral with the housing.

4.28 Undo the three bolts and lift off the plastic cover over the top of the engine

26 Disconnect the battery negative terminal (refer to *Disconnecting the battery* in the Reference Chapter).

27 Apply the handbrake, then jack up the front of the vehicle and support it on axle stands (see *Jacking and vehicle support*).

28 Undo the three bolts and lift off the plastic cover over the top of the engine **(see illustration)**.

29 Slacken the retaining clip and disconnect the charge air pipe connecting hose from the pipe. Move the hose to one side **(see illustration)**.

30 Drain the cooling system as described in Chapter 1B.

31 Release the clips and disconnect the hoses from the thermostat housing **(see illustration)**.

32 Unbolt the thermostat housing from the cylinder head **(see illustrations)**. Clean away all traces of gasket from the housing and cylinder head.

4.29 Slacken the retaining clip (arrowed) and disconnect the charge air pipe connecting hose from the pipe

Refitting

33 Refitting is a reversal of removal, but fit a new gasket/seal and tighten the mounting bolts to the specified torque (where given). Refill the cooling system as described in Chapter 1A or 1B as applicable.

---

5 Electric cooling fan – removal and refitting

⚠️ *Warning: If the engine is hot, the cooling fan may start up at any time. Take extra precautions when working in the vicinity of the fan.*

Removal

1.8 litre petrol engine

1 Disconnect the battery negative terminal

4.31 Disconnect the hoses from the thermostat housing

4.32a Unscrew the mounting bolts . . .

4.32b . . . then remove the thermostat housing from the cylinder head

5.16 Undo the three retaining bolts (arrowed) and remove the fan from the housing

5.19 Unscrew the two retaining bolts (arrowed) and lift the fan housing from the lower guides on the radiator

(refer to *Disconnecting the battery* in the Reference Chapter).

2 Remove the plastic cover over the top of the engine.

3 Unclip the radiator hose and detach the plastic panel at the front of the battery box.

4 Pull out the locking bar and disconnect the wiring harness connector from the cooling fan module at the side of the fan housing. Free the wiring harness from the cable ties.

5 Firmly apply the handbrake, then jack up the front of the car and support it securely on axle stands (see *Jacking and vehicle support*).

6 Release the four retaining clips and detach the front bumper lower panel from the subframe.

7 Unscrew the two bolts securing the fan housing to the radiator; one at each upper corner of the housing.

8 Carefully lift the fan housing upwards to disengage it from the lower guides on the radiator, and remove the housing from the engine compartment.

9 To remove the fan motor, disconnect the wiring connector and unclip the wiring harness from the fan housing. Undo the three retaining bolts and remove the fan from the housing.

10 To remove the cooling fan module, undo the retaining screw and unclip the unit from the fan housing.

2.2 litre petrol engine

11 Remove the battery and battery box as described in Chapter 5A.

12 Undo the retaining bolt and unclip the air intake resonator from above the radiator.

13 Pull out the locking bar and disconnect the wiring harness connector from the cooling fan module at the top of the fan housing. Free the wiring harness from the cable ties.

14 Unscrew the two bolts securing the fan housing to the radiator; one at each upper corner of the housing.

15 Carefully lift the fan housing upwards to disengage it from the lower guides on the radiator, and remove the housing from the engine compartment.

16 To remove the fan motor(s), disconnect the wiring connector at the relevant motor and unclip the wiring harness from the fan housing. Undo the three retaining bolts and remove the fan from the housing (see illustration).

17 To remove the cooling fan module, undo the retaining screw and unclip the unit from the fan housing.

Diesel engine

18 Remove the radiator as described in Section 3.

19 Unscrew the two retaining bolts and lift

the fan housing from the lower guides on the radiator (see illustration).

20 To remove the fan motor(s), disconnect the wiring connector at the relevant motor and unclip the wiring harness from the fan housing. Undo the three retaining bolts and remove the fan from the housing (see illustration 5.16).

21 To remove the cooling fan module, undo the retaining screw and unclip the unit from the fan housing (see illustration).

Refitting

22 Refitting is a reversal of removal.

---

6 Coolant temperature sensor – testing, removal and refitting

Testing

1 Testing of the coolant temperature sensor must be entrusted to a Vauxhall/Opel dealer, who will have the necessary specialist diagnostic equipment.

Removal

Petrol engine

2 Partially drain the cooling system with reference to Chapter 1A. Alternatively, it is possible to change the sensor quickly with minimal loss of coolant by first releasing any pressure from the cooling system. With the engine cold, temporarily remove the expansion tank cap.

3 Remove the plastic cover from the top of the engine.

4 Disconnect the wiring from the coolant temperature sensor. On 1.8 litre engines the sensor is located on the thermostat housing on the right-hand end of the cylinder head. On 2.2 litre engines, the sensor is located on the thermostat housing at the left-hand end of the cylinder head (see illustration).

5 Unscrew and remove the sensor.

6 Fit the new sensor using a reversal of the

5.21 Undo the retaining screw (arrowed) and unclip the cooling fan module from the fan housing

6.4 Coolant temperature sensor located on the thermostat housing – 2.2 litre petrol engine models

removal procedure, but tighten the sensor to the specified torque and refill the cooling system with reference to Chapter 1A.

Diesel engine

7 Partially drain the cooling system with reference to Chapter 1B. Alternatively, it is possible to change the sensor quickly with minimal loss of coolant by first releasing any pressure from the cooling system. With the engine cold, temporarily remove the expansion tank cap.

8 Remove the plastic cover from the top of the engine.

9 On 1.9 litre engines, slacken the two retaining clips and disconnect the upper charge air hose from the throttle body/ housing, and intercooler left-hand charge air pipe.

10 Disconnect the wiring connector from the sensor. On 1.9 litre engines the sensor is located on the thermostat housing on the left-hand end of the cylinder head. On 2.0 and 2.2 litre engines, the sensor is located on the right-hand end of the cylinder head, adjacent to the thermostat housing **(see illustrations)**.

11 Unscrew and remove the sensor.

Refitting

12 Fit the new sensor using a reversal of the removal procedure, but tighten the sensor to the specified torque and refill the cooling system with reference to Chapter 1A or 1B.

7 Coolant pump – removal and refitting

Removal

1.8 litre petrol engine

1 Disconnect the battery negative terminal (refer to *Disconnecting the battery* in the Reference Chapter).

2 Remove the plastic cover from the top of the engine.

3 Drain the cooling system as described in Chapter 1A.

4 Remove the timing belt and timing belt rear cover as described in Chapter 2A. **Note:** *The timing belt must not come into contact with*

6.10a Coolant temperature sensor (arrowed) located on the thermostat housing – 1.9 litre diesel engine models

coolant.

5 Unscrew and remove the three coolant pump securing bolts.

6 Withdraw the coolant pump from the cylinder block, noting that it may be necessary to tap the pump lightly with a soft-faced mallet to free it from the cylinder block.

7 Recover the pump sealing ring, and discard it; a new one must be used on refitting.

8 Note that it is not possible to overhaul the pump. If it is faulty, the unit must be renewed complete.

2.2 litre petrol engine

9 Disconnect the battery negative terminal (refer to *Disconnecting the battery* in the Reference Chapter).

10 Remove the plastic cover from the top of the engine.

11 Remove the air cleaner assembly and air intake duct as described in Chapter 4A.

12 Apply the handbrake, then jack up the front of the vehicle and support it on axle stands (see *Jacking and vehicle support*).

13 Disconnect the two oxygen sensor wiring connectors at the right-hand end of the cylinder head. Unclip the wiring harness from the support bracket.

14 Undo the nut and bolt and remove the right-hand engine lifting eye from the cylinder head.

15 Unbolt the heat shield from the exhaust manifold.

16 Drain the cooling system as described in Chapter 1A. Refit and tighten the coolant pump drain plug on completion.

6.10b Coolant temperature sensor (arrowed) located on the cylinder head – 2.0 and 2.2 litre diesel engine models

17 Loosen the clip and disconnect the hose from the thermostat housing cover. Also disconnect the heater hoses from the thermostat housing and heater matrix. Remove the hoses.

18 Unclip the coolant temperature sensor wiring from the thermostat housing cover, then disconnect the wiring from the sensor.

19 Unscrew and remove the coolant temperature sensor from the thermostat housing.

20 Unscrew the bolts and remove the thermostat housing and coolant pipe from the cylinder block and coolant pump. Note the lower bolt is a stud bolt, and note the location of the O-ring seal in the pump housing **(see illustrations)**.

21 Unbolt the coolant pump drive sprocket access cover from the timing cover on the right-hand side of the engine **(see illustration)**.

22 Vauxhall/Opel technicians use a special tool (KM-J-43651) to hold the sprocket stationary while the coolant pump is being removed. The tool consists of a flanged tube which is bolted to the sprocket and also to the timing housing, with holes to allow removal of the coolant pump bolts. It is possible to fabricate a simple home-made tool from a length of flat metal bar using two threaded rods screwed into the sprocket. First unscrew one of the pump mounting bolts from the sprocket taking care not to drop it into the timing case, then bolt the tool into position to hold the sprocket. With the tool in position,

7.20a Thermostat housing retaining bolts – 2.2 litre petrol engine models

7.20b Removing the coolant pipe from the pump housing – 2.2 litre petrol engine models

7.21 Coolant pump drive sprocket access cover – 2.2 litre petrol engine models

7.22a Home-made tool holding the coolant pump drive sprocket stationary – 2.2 litre petrol engine models

7.22b Unscrew the two remaining bolts securing the coolant pump to the sprocket – 2.2 litre petrol engine models

unscrew the two remaining bolts from the sprocket (see illustrations). To prevent losing any of the bolts, temporarily place a cloth rag beneath the sprocket in the timing case.

23 Unscrew the pump mounting bolts noting that if you are using the Vauxhall/Opel tool, one of the bolts cannot be removed completely. There are two bolts at the front and two at the rear. Remove the pump from the timing housing and withdraw upwards from the engine (see illustrations).

24 Recover the pump sealing ring, and discard it; a new one must be used on refitting.

25 Note that it is not possible to overhaul the pump. If it is faulty, the unit must be renewed complete.

1.9 litre diesel engine

26 Disconnect the battery negative terminal (refer to *Disconnecting the battery* in the Reference Chapter).

27 Remove the plastic cover from the top of the engine.

28 Drain the cooling system as described in Chapter 1B.

29 Remove the timing belt as described in Chapter 2C or 2D as applicable. **Note:** *The timing belt must not come into contact with coolant.*

30 Unscrew and remove the three coolant pump securing bolts (see illustration).

31 Withdraw the coolant pump from the cylinder block, noting that it may be necessary to tap the pump lightly with a soft-faced mallet to free it from the cylinder block (see illustration).

32 Recover the pump sealing ring, and discard it; a new one must be used on refitting.

33 Note that it is not possible to overhaul the pump. If it is faulty, the unit must be renewed complete.

7.22c Vauxhall tool KM-J-43651 retaining the coolant pump sprocket while the pump is being removed – 2.2 litre petrol engine models

1 Bolts holding the tool to the timing housing
2 Bolts holding the sprocket to the tool
Arrows indicate pump mounting bolts

7.23a Unscrew the rear bolts . . .

7.23b . . . and the front bolts . . .

7.23c . . . and withdraw the coolant pump from the timing housing – 2.2 litre petrol engine models

7.30 Undo the coolant pump retaining bolts (arrowed) . . .

7.31 . . . and remove the pump from the cylinder head – 1.9 litre diesel engine models

7.41 Undo the two bolts (arrowed) securing the charge air pipe to the camshaft cover – 2.0 and 2.2 litre diesel engine models

7.44 Unclip the two fuel hoses (arrowed) and vacuum hose from the camshaft cover – 2.0 and 2.2 litre diesel engine models

7.46a Right-hand mounting bracket-to-engine bracket bolts (arrowed) . . .

7.46b . . . and mounting-to-body retaining bolts (A) and nut (B) – 2.0 and 2.2 litre diesel engine models

2.0 and 2.2 litre diesel engine

34 Disconnect the battery negative terminal (refer to *Disconnecting the battery* in the Reference Chapter).

35 Remove the plastic cover from the top of the engine.

36 Apply the handbrake, then jack up the front of the vehicle and support it on axle stands (see *Jacking and vehicle support*). Remove the engine compartment undertray.

37 Drain the cooling system as described in Chapter 1B.

38 Remove the auxiliary drivebelt as described in Chapter 1B. Prior to removal, mark the direction of rotation on the belt to ensure the belt is refitted the same way around.

39 Refer to Chapter 4B and unbolt the exhaust front pipe from the exhaust manifold, taking care to support the flexible section. **Note:** *Angular movement in excess of 10° can cause permanent damage to the flexible section.* Release the mounting rubbers and support the front of the exhaust pipe to one side.

40 Undo the retaining bolt and detach the coolant pipe from the engine/transmission front mounting/torque link.

41 Undo the two bolts securing the charge air

pipe to the camshaft cover **(see illustration)**. Slacken the retaining clip and disconnect the charge air pipe connecting hose from the turbocharger elbow. Move the charge air pipe to one side.

42 Remove the air cleaner assembly and air intake duct as described in Chapter 4B.

43 Release the retaining clips and remove the radiator top hose.

44 Unclip the two fuel hoses and vacuum hose from the right-hand end of the camshaft cover **(see illustration)**.

45 Connect a suitable hoist and lifting tackle

7.49 Unscrew the mounting bolts . . .

to the right-hand end of the engine and support its weight. If available, the type of support bar which locates in the engine compartment side channels is to be preferred.

46 Mark the bolt positions for correct refitting, then undo the three bolts securing the right-hand engine mounting to the engine bracket, and the two bolts and one nut securing the mounting to the body **(see illustrations)**. Remove the mounting.

47 Taking care not to place undue strain on any of the engine attachments, carefully raise the right-hand side of the engine as far as possible.

48 Hold the coolant pump pulley stationary using an old auxiliary drivebelt or an oil filter strap wrench, then unscrew and remove the bolts and remove the pulley from the drive flange on the coolant pump.

49 Unscrew and remove the three coolant pump securing bolts **(see illustration)**.

50 Withdraw the coolant pump from the cylinder block, noting that it may be necessary to tap the pump lightly with a soft-faced mallet to free it from the cylinder block **(see illustration)**.

51 Recover the pump sealing ring, and discard it; a new one must be used on refitting **(see illustration)**.

7.50 ... withdraw the coolant pump from the cylinder block ...

7.51 ... and recover the sealing ring – 2.0 and 2.2 litre diesel engine models

52 Note that it is not possible to overhaul the pump. If it is faulty, the unit must be renewed complete.

Refitting

1.8 litre petrol engine

53 Ensure that the pump and cylinder block mating surfaces are clean and dry, and apply a smear of silicone grease to the pump mating surface in the cylinder block.
54 Fit a new sealing ring to the pump, and locate the pump in the cylinder block. Make sure that the lug on the oil pump housing engages in the groove of the pump.
55 Insert the securing bolts and tighten to the specified torque.
56 Refit the timing belt rear cover and timing belt as described in Chapter 2A.
57 Reconnect the battery negative terminal, then refill the cooling system as described in Chapter 1A.

2.2 litre petrol engine

58 Ensure that the pump and timing housing mating surfaces are clean and dry, and apply a smear of silicone grease to the pump mating surface.
59 Fit a new sealing ring to the groove in the pump, then locate the pump in the timing housing, making sure that the three bolt holes are aligned with the holes in the sprocket.
60 Insert the pump mounting bolts and two of the sprocket bolts hand-tight to start with, then tighten them to the specified torque.
61 Remove the holding tool and refit the final sprocket bolt, tightening it to the specified torque.
62 Refit the coolant pump drive sprocket access cover to the timing cover together with a new gasket, and tighten the bolts securely.
63 Refit the coolant pipe and thermostat housing together with new sealing rings, and tighten the bolts securely.
64 Refit the coolant temperature sensor to the thermostat housing and tighten to the specified torque, then reconnect the wiring and secure.
65 Refit the hoses to the thermostat housing cover and heater matrix and tighten the clips.
66 Refit the exhaust manifold heat shield and engine lifting eye.
67 Reconnect the two oxygen sensor wiring

connectors at the right-hand end of the cylinder head. Secure the wiring harness to the support bracket.
68 Lower the vehicle to the ground, then refit the air cleaner assembly and air intake duct as described in Chapter 4A.
69 Refit the plastic cover to the top of the engine.
70 Reconnect the battery negative terminal, then refill the cooling system as described in Chapter 1A.

1.9 litre diesel engine

71 Ensure that the pump and cylinder block mating surfaces are clean and dry, and apply a smear of silicone grease to the pump mating surface in the cylinder block.
72 Fit a new sealing ring to the pump, and locate the pump in the cylinder block.
73 Insert the securing bolts and tighten to the specified torque.
74 Refit the timing belt as described in Chapter 2C or 2D as applicable.
75 Reconnect the battery negative terminal, then refill the cooling system as described in Chapter 1B.

2.0 and 2.2 litre diesel engine

76 Ensure that the pump and cylinder block mating surfaces are clean and dry, and apply a smear of silicone grease to the pump mating surface in the cylinder block.
77 Fit a new sealing ring to the pump, and install the pump in the cylinder block.
78 Insert the securing bolts and tighten to the specified torque.
79 Refit the pulley and tighten the securing bolts to the specified torque.
80 Lower the engine and locate the right-hand engine mounting in position. Refit the three bolts securing the mounting to the engine bracket and the two bolts and one nut securing the mounting to the body. Align the mounting in its original position, then tighten the bolts and nut to the specified torque (See Chapter 2E).
81 Remove the hoist and lifting tackle from the engine.
82 Refer to Chapter 4B and refit the exhaust front pipe to the manifold.
83 Reposition the fuel hoses into their retaining clips on the right-hand end of the cover.

84 Refit the radiator top hose and secure with the retaining clips.
85 Refit the auxiliary drivebelt as described in Chapter 1B using the mark made prior to removal to ensure the belt is fitted the correct way around.
86 Refit and tighten the retaining bolt securing the coolant pipe to the engine/transmission front mounting/torque link.
87 Place the charge air pipe in position and attach the connecting hose to the turbocharger elbow. Secure the pipe to the camshaft cover with the two bolts tightened securely.
88 Refit the air cleaner assembly and air intake duct as described in Chapter 4B.
89 Refit the plastic cover to the top of the engine.
90 Reconnect the battery negative terminal, then refill the cooling system as described in Chapter 1B.

8 Heating and ventilation system – general information

The heater/ventilation system consists of a four-speed blower motor (housed behind the facia), face-level vents in the centre and at each end of the facia, and air ducts to the front and rear footwells.

The heater controls are located in the centre of the facia, and the controls operate flap valves to deflect and mix the air flowing through the various parts of the heater/ventilation system. The flap valves are contained in the air distribution housing, which acts as a central distribution unit, passing air to the various ducts and vents.

Cold air enters the system through the grille at the rear of the engine compartment. A pollen filter is fitted to the ventilation intake, to filter out dust, soot, pollen and spores from the air entering the vehicle.

The air (boosted by the blower fan if required) then flows through the various ducts, according to the settings of the controls. Stale air is expelled through ducts at the rear of the vehicle. If warm air is required, the cold air is passed through the heater matrix, which is heated by the engine coolant.

A recirculation switch enables the outside air supply to be closed off, while the air inside the vehicle is recirculated. This can be useful to prevent unpleasant odours entering from outside the vehicle, but should only be used briefly, as the recirculated air inside the vehicle will soon deteriorate.

9 Heater/ventilation system components – removal and refitting

Air vents

Removal

1 To remove the air vents from the centre of

9.1a Carefully release the facia decorative strip using a plastic spatula or similar . . .

9.1b . . . and remove the strip from the facia

9.2a Undo the four bolts (arrowed) . . .

9.2b . . . and withdraw the centre vent housing from the facia

9.3 Undo the four screws (arrowed) and remove the information display unit from the centre vent housing

9.4 Carefully release the driver's side facia decorative strip using a plastic spatula or similar

the facia, carefully release the facia decorative strip using a plastic spatula or similar tool **(see illustrations)**.

2 Undo the four bolts securing the centre vent housing to the facia and withdraw the housing from its location **(see illustrations)**. Lift the locking bar(s) and disconnect the wiring connector(s) from the rear of the information display unit.

3 If required, undo the four screws and remove the information display unit from the centre vent housing **(see illustration)**.

4 To remove the vent from the driver's side of the facia, carefully release the facia decorative strip using a plastic spatula or similar tool **(see illustration)**.

5 Undo the two screws securing the base of the vent to the facia. Pull the vent out at the bottom, disengage the two upper retaining lugs, and remove the vent from the facia **(see illustrations)**.

6 To remove the vent from the passenger's side of the facia, release the facia decorative strip as described in paragraph 1, then remove the vent as described in paragraph 5.

7 To remove the rear passenger's air vents, carefully prise them from their locations in the centre console using a plastic spatula inserted at the side of each vent.

Refitting

8 Refitting is a reversal of removal.

Heater blower motor

Removal

9 Remove the glovebox and the facia

footwell trim panel on the passenger's side as described in Chapter 11.

10 Undo the retaining bolt and detach the passenger's side footwell air duct **(see illustrations)**.

9.5a Undo the two screws (arrowed) . . .

9.10a Undo the retaining bolt (arrowed) . . .

11 Disconnect the wiring connector at the blower motor, and blower motor resistor at the base of the blower motor housing **(see illustration)**.

12 Undo the seven bolts securing the blower

9.5b . . . then pull the vent out at the bottom and disengage the two upper retaining lugs (arrowed)

9.10b . . . and detach the passenger's side footwell air duct

9.11 Disconnect the wiring connectors (arrowed) at the blower motor, and blower motor resistor

motor housing to the base of the recirculating air valve housing **(see illustration)**.

13 Release the three retaining tabs and remove the blower motor down and out from under the facia **(see illustration)**.

Refitting

14 Refitting is a reversal of removal.

Heater blower motor resistor

Removal

15 Carry out the operations described in paragraphs 9 and 10.

16 Disconnect the wiring connector at the blower motor resistor at the base of the blower motor housing **(see illustration 9.11)**.

17 Slide the resistor towards the centre of the car until its internal lugs align with the slots in the blower motor housing, then withdraw the resistor from the housing.

9.20 Disconnect the wiring connector (arrowed) from the recirculating air valve servo motor

9.27 Mixed air valve servo motor wiring connector (A) and retaining bolts (B)

9.12 Undo the bolts (arrowed) securing the blower motor to the base of the recirculating air valve housing

Refitting

18 Refitting is a reversal of removal.

Recirculating air valve housing

Removal

19 Remove the heater blower motor as described previously.

20 Disconnect the wiring connector from the recirculating air valve servo motor and release the wiring harness from the clip on the air valve housing **(see illustration)**.

21 Undo the retaining bolt and manoeuvre the housing out from under the facia.

Refitting

22 Refitting is a reversal of removal, ensuring that the housing air duct is correctly seated.

9.24 Recirculating air valve servo motor retaining bolts (arrowed)

9.32 Undo the three bolts (arrowed) and remove the heater matrix cover

9.13 Release the three retaining tabs and remove the blower motor down and out from under the facia

Recirculating air valve servo motor

Removal

23 Remove the recirculating air valve housing as described previously.

24 Undo the two retaining bolts and remove the motor from the housing **(see illustration)**. Disengage the servo lever from the air valve lever as the unit is removed.

Refitting

25 Refitting is a reversal of removal. Engage the servo lever with the air valve lever as the unit is refitted.

Mixed air valve servo motor

Removal

26 Remove the glovebox and the facia footwell trim panel on the passenger's side as described in Chapter 11.

27 Disconnect the wiring connector from the servo motor, then undo the two retaining bolts. Disengage the operating lever from the air valve and remove the servo motor **(see illustration)**.

Refitting

28 Refitting is a reversal of removal. Engage the servo lever with the air valve lever as the unit is refitted.

Heater matrix

Removal

29 Working in the engine compartment, use two hose clamps to clamp the hoses leading to the heater matrix. The hoses are located on the bulkhead, just above the steering gear. Alternatively, drain the cooling system completely as described in Chapter 1A or 1B.

30 Using a small screwdriver, lift up the wire clip securing the left-hand and right-hand heater hoses to the heater matrix pipe stubs, and disconnect the hoses from the stubs. Be prepared for some loss of coolant as the hoses are released, by placing cloth rags beneath them.

31 Remove the facia footwell trim panel on the driver's side as described in Chapter 11.

32 Undo the three bolts and remove the heater matrix cover **(see illustration)**.

33 Undo the two bolts and release the clamps

9.33 Undo the two bolts and release the clamps (arrowed) securing the heater pipes to the matrix

9.36 Carefully prise out the heater control assembly from the facia . . .

securing the heater pipes to the matrix **(see illustration)**. Be prepared for coolant spillage as the pipes are disconnected, and place some cloths or absorbent material over the carpet.

34 Pull the heater matrix from its location and remove it from the car.

Refitting

35 Refitting is a reversal of removal, bearing in mind the following:

a) *Push the securing wire clip back into position on the heater hose end fittings, then push the hoses back onto the matrix pipe stubs. Ensure that the wire clips securely lock the hoses in position.*

b) *If the cooling system was completely drained, refill as described in Chapter 1A or 1B. If the heater hoses were clamped prior to removal, top-up the cooling system as described in 'Weekly checks'.*

Heater control assembly

Removal

36 Using a small screwdriver, carefully prise out the heater control assembly from the facia **(see illustration)**.

37 Disconnect the wiring from the rear of the control assembly **(see illustration)**.

Refitting

38 Refitting is a reversal of removal.

Air distribution housing

Note: *On models with air conditioning, it is not possible to remove the air distribution housing without opening the refrigerant circuit (see Sections 10 and 11). Have the refrigerant discharged at a dealer service department or an automotive air conditioning repair facility before proceeding.*

Removal

39 Drain the cooling system as described in Chapter 1A or 1B.

40 Remove the complete facia assembly and the facia crossmember as described in Chapter 11.

41 Remove the windscreen wiper arms as described in Chapter 12.

42 Pull up the rubber weatherseal from the flange at the rear of the engine compartment. Carefully release the water deflector by pulling it away from the windscreen to release the retaining clips. Withdraw the water deflector and disconnect the washer hose.

43 Remove the pollen filter as described in Chapter 1A or 1B.

44 Using a small screwdriver, lift up the wire clip securing the left-hand and right-hand heater hoses to the heater matrix pipe stubs, and disconnect the hoses from the stubs. Be prepared for some loss of coolant as the hoses are released by placing cloth rags beneath them.

45 Release the matrix pipe stub rubber seal from the bulkhead by pushing it inward (the seal remains on the pipe stubs).

46 On models with air conditioning, undo the nut securing the refrigerant pipe block connection to the expansion valve and withdraw the refrigerant pipes from the valve **(see illustration)**. Note that new seals for the refrigerant pipes will be required for refitting. Suitably plug or cover the disconnected pipes.

47 Release the expansion valve rubber seal from the bulkhead by pushing it inward (the seal remains on the valve).

48 Disconnect the wiring connectors at the heater blower motor and blower motor resistor.

49 Working inside the vehicle withdraw the air distribution housing from the bulkhead. **Note:** *Keep the matrix unions uppermost as the housing is removed, to prevent coolant spillage.* Mop-up any spilt coolant immediately, and wipe the affected area with a damp cloth to prevent staining.

Refitting

50 Refitting is the reverse of removal. On completion, refill the cooling system as described in Chapter 1A or 1B. On models with air conditioning, have the system evacuated, charged and leak-tested by the specialist who discharged it.

10 Air conditioning system – general information and precautions

General information

1 Air conditioning is standard on top of the range models, and optional on certain other models. It enables the temperature of incoming air to be lowered, and also dehumidifies the air, which makes for rapid demisting and increased comfort.

9.37 . . . then disconnect the wiring from the rear of the control assembly

9.46 Undo the nut (arrowed) securing the refrigerant pipe block connection to the expansion valve

TOOL TIP

Many car accessory shops sell one-shot air conditioning recharge aerosols. These generally contain refrigerant, compressor oil, leak sealer and system conditioner. Some also have a dye to help pinpoint leaks.

⚠️ **Warning: These products must only be used as directed by the manufacturer, and do not remove the need for regular maintenance.**

2 The cooling side of the system works in the same way as a domestic refrigerator. Refrigerant gas is drawn into a belt-driven compressor, and passes into a condenser mounted in front of the radiator, where it loses heat and becomes liquid. The liquid passes through an expansion valve to an evaporator, where it changes from liquid under high pressure to gas under low pressure. This change is accompanied by a drop in temperature, which cools the evaporator. The refrigerant returns to the compressor, and the cycle begins again.

3 Air blown through the evaporator passes to the heater assembly, where it is mixed with hot air blown through the heater matrix, to achieve the desired temperature in the passenger compartment.

4 The heating side of the system works in the same way as on models without air conditioning (see Section 8).

5 The operation of the system is controlled electronically. Any problems with the system should be referred to a Vauxhall/Opel dealer or an air conditioning specialist **(see Tool tip)**.

10.6 Air conditioning system high-pressure service port (A) and low-pressure service port (B)

Air conditioning service ports

6 The high-pressure service port is located just in front of the air cleaner housing **(see illustration)**.

7 The low-pressure service port is located at the front right-hand side of the engine compartment, just behind the body front cross-panel.

Precautions

8 It is necessary to observe special precautions whenever dealing with any part of the system, its associated components, and any items which necessitate disconnection of the system.

⚠️ **Warning: The refrigeration circuit contains a liquid refrigerant. This refrigerant is potentially dangerous, and should only be handled by qualified persons. If it is splashed onto the skin, it can cause frostbite. It is not itself poisonous, but in the presence of a naked flame it forms a poisonous gas; inhalation of the vapour through a lighted cigarette could prove fatal. Uncontrolled discharging of the refrigerant is dangerous, and potentially damaging to the environment. Do not disconnect any part of the system unless it has been discharged by a Vauxhall/Opel dealer or an air conditioning specialist.**
Caution: Do not operate the air conditioning system if it is known to be short of refrigerant, as this may damage the compressor.

11 Air conditioning system components – removal and refitting

⚠️ **Warning: The air conditioning system is under high pressure. Do not loosen any fittings or remove any components until after the system has been discharged. Air conditioning refrigerant should be properly discharged into an approved type of container at a dealer service department or an automotive air conditioning repair facility capable of handling R134a refrigerant. Cap or plug the pipe lines as soon as they are disconnected, to prevent the entry of moisture. Always wear eye protection when disconnecting air conditioning system fittings.**
Note: This Section refers to the components of the air conditioning system itself – refer to Sections 8 and 9 for details of components common to the heating/ventilation system.

Compressor
Removal

1 Have the refrigerant discharged at a dealer service department or an automotive air conditioning repair facility.

2 Disconnect the battery negative terminal (refer to Disconnecting the battery in the Reference Chapter).

3 Firmly apply the handbrake, then jack up the front of the car and support it securely on axle stands (see Jacking and vehicle support).

4 Remove the auxiliary drivebelt as described in Chapter 1A or 1B.

5 With the system discharged, undo the retaining bolt(s) and disconnect the refrigerant pipes from the compressor. Discard the O-ring seals – new ones must be used when refitting. Suitably cap the open fittings immediately to keep moisture and contamination out of the system.

6 Disconnect the compressor wiring connector.

7 Unbolt the compressor from the cylinder block/crankcase/sump, then withdraw the compressor downwards from under the vehicle.

Refitting

8 Refit the compressor in the reverse order of removal; renew all seals disturbed.

9 If you are installing a new compressor, refer to the compressor manufacturer's instructions for adding refrigerant oil to the system.

10 Have the system evacuated, charged and leak-tested by the specialist that discharged it.

11 After installing a new compressor, always observe the following running-in procedure:
  1) Open all instrument panel air outlet flaps.
  2) Start vehicle engine and stabilise idle speed for approximately 5 seconds.
  3) Switch fan to maximum speed.
  4) Switch on the air conditioning and let it run for at least 2 minutes without interruption at engine speed under 1500 rpm.

Evaporator
Removal

12 Have the refrigerant discharged at a dealer service department or an automotive air conditioning repair facility.

13 Remove the windscreen wiper motor and linkage as described in Chapter 12.

14 Undo the nut securing the refrigerant pipe block connection to the expansion valve and withdraw the refrigerant pipes from the valve **(see illustration 9.46)**. Note that new seals for the refrigerant pipes will be required for refitting. Suitably plug or cover the disconnected pipes.

15 Undo the two retaining bolts and remove the expansion valve **(see illustrations)**.

16 Remove the two seals from the evaporator pipe stubs **(see illustration)**. Note that new seals will be required for refitting.

17 Rotate the evaporator pipe retaining plate to release it from one pipe stub, then slide the plate sideways off the other pipe stub **(see illustration)**.

18 Release the rubber seal from the bulkhead then remove the seal from the pipe stubs **(see illustration)**.

19 Insert a small screwdriver through the slots in the housing and depress the tabs of the evaporator pipe retaining plate. Lift up the

11.15a Undo the two retaining bolts (arrowed) . . .

11.15b . . . and remove the expansion valve

11.16 Remove the two seals from the evaporator pipe stubs

retaining plate and remove it from the housing **(see illustrations).**
20 Remove the recirculating air valve housing as described in Section 9.
21 Undo the eight retaining bolts and remove the evaporator cover from the side of the air distribution housing **(see illustration).**
22 Carefully pull the evaporator out of the air distribution housing **(see illustration).**

Refitting

23 Refitting is the reverse of removal ensuring that all disturbed pipe seals are renewed.
24 Have the system evacuated, charged and leak-tested by the specialist who discharged it.

Condenser

Removal – petrol engine

25 Have the refrigerant discharged at a dealer service department or an automotive air conditioning repair facility.
26 Disconnect the battery negative terminal (refer to *Disconnecting the battery* in the Reference Chapter).
27 Undo the retaining nuts and disconnect the refrigerant pipe connector blocks from the condenser and receiver-dryer. Discard the seals – new ones must be used when refitting. Suitably cap the open fittings immediately to keep moisture and contamination out of the system.
28 Slacken (but do not remove) the two bolts securing the radiator left-hand and right-hand mounting brackets to the subframe **(see illustrations 3.10a and 3.10b).**
29 Release the radiator upper rubber mounting bushes on each side from their guides, and carefully move the top of the radiator forward.
30 Undo the bolt each side securing the condenser upper mounting brackets to the radiator. Carefully lift up or remove the plastic panels on each side of the radiator for improved access, if necessary.
31 Carefully lift the condenser upwards, disengage the lower mounting lugs from the radiator and remove the condenser from the engine compartment.
32 If required, remove the receiver-dryer from the condenser as described in paragraphs 44 and 45.

11.17 Rotate the pipe retaining plate to release it from one pipe stub, then slide the plate off the other pipe stub

Removal – diesel engine

33 Have the refrigerant discharged at a dealer service department or an automotive air conditioning repair facility.

11.19a Depress the tabs of the evaporator pipe retaining plate with a screwdriver . . .

11.21 Undo the retaining bolts (arrowed) and remove the evaporator cover

11.18 Release the rubber seal from the bulkhead then remove the seal from the pipe stubs

34 Disconnect the battery negative terminal (refer to *Disconnecting the battery* in the Reference Chapter).
35 Apply the handbrake, then jack up the

11.19b . . . then lift up the retaining plate and remove it from the housing

11.22 Carefully pull the evaporator out of the air distribution housing

11.37 Lower refrigerant pipe connector block retaining nut (arrowed)

11.38 Condenser left-hand upper mounting bracket retaining bolt (arrowed)

11.39 Lift the condenser upwards and disengage the lower mounting lug (arrowed) on each side

front of the vehicle and support it on axle stands (see *Jacking and vehicle support*).

36 Remove the front bumper as described in Chapter 11.

37 Undo the retaining nuts and disconnect the upper and lower refrigerant pipe connector blocks from the condenser **(see illustration)**. Discard the seals – new ones must be used when refitting. Suitably cap the open fittings immediately to keep moisture and contamination out of the system.

38 Undo the bolt each side securing the condenser upper mounting brackets to the intercooler **(see illustration)**.

39 Carefully lift the condenser upwards, disengage the lower mounting lugs from the intercooler and remove the condenser from the engine compartment **(see illustration)**.

Refitting – all models

40 Refitting is the reverse of removal ensuring that all disturbed pipe seals are renewed.

41 Have the system evacuated, charged and leak-tested by the specialist who discharged it.

Receiver-dryer

Removal – petrol engine

42 Have the refrigerant discharged at a dealer service department or an automotive air conditioning repair facility.

43 Disconnect the battery negative terminal (refer to *Disconnecting the battery* in the Reference Chapter).

44 Undo the retaining nuts and disconnect the refrigerant pipe connector blocks from the condenser and receiver-dryer. Discard the seals – new ones must be used when refitting. Suitably cap the open fittings immediately to keep moisture and contamination out of the system.

45 Undo the two retaining bolts and remove the receiver-dryer from the condenser.

Removal – 1.9 litre diesel engine

46 Have the refrigerant discharged at a dealer service department or an automotive air conditioning repair facility.

47 Disconnect the battery negative terminal (refer to *Disconnecting the battery* in the Reference Chapter).

48 Apply the handbrake, then jack up the front of the vehicle and support it on axle stands (see *Jacking and vehicle support*). Undo the ten bolts and remove the engine undertray.

49 Remove the front bumper as described in Chapter 11.

50 Undo the retaining nut and disconnect the refrigerant pipe upper connector block from the condenser. Discard the seal – a new one must be used when refitting. Suitably cap the open fittings immediately to keep moisture and contamination out of the system.

51 Undo the bolt securing the intercooler right-hand charge air pipe upper mounting to the radiator **(see illustration 3.33)**.

52 Slacken the retaining clips and remove the right-hand lower charge air hose from the intercooler and charge air pipe **(see illustration 3.30b)**.

53 Undo the bolt securing the refrigerant pipe bracket and intercooler right-hand charge air pipe lower mounting to the radiator **(see illustration 3.34b)**.

54 Slacken (but do not remove) the two bolts securing the radiator left-hand and right-hand mounting brackets to the subframe **(see illustrations 3.10a and 3.10b)**.

55 Release the radiator upper rubber mounting bushes on each side from their

guides, and carefully move the top of the radiator forward.

56 Undo the retaining nuts and disconnect the refrigerant pipe connector blocks from the condenser and receiver-dryer. Discard the seals – new ones must be used when refitting. Suitably cap the open fittings immediately to keep moisture and contamination out of the system.

57 Undo the two retaining bolts and remove the receiver-dryer from the radiator. Withdraw the receiver-dryer downwards and remove it from under the car.

Removal – 2.0 & 2.2 litre diesel engine

58 Have the refrigerant discharged at a dealer service department or an automotive air conditioning repair facility.

59 Disconnect the battery negative terminal (refer to *Disconnecting the battery* in the Reference Chapter).

60 Apply the handbrake, then jack up the front of the vehicle and support it on axle stands (see *Jacking and vehicle support*).

61 Remove the front bumper as described in Chapter 11.

62 Undo the retaining nuts and disconnect the refrigerant pipe connector blocks from the condenser and receiver-dryer. Discard the seals – new ones must be used when refitting. Suitably cap the open fittings immediately to keep moisture and contamination out of the system.

Refitting – all models

63 Refitting is the reverse of removal ensuring that all disturbed pipe seals are renewed.

64 Have the system evacuated, charged and leak-tested by the specialist who discharged it.

Chapter 4 Part A:
Fuel and exhaust systems – petrol engines

Contents

Degrees of difficulty

Easy, suitable for novice with little experience	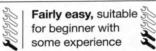	**Fairly easy,** suitable for beginner with some experience	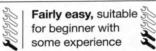	**Fairly difficult,** suitable for competent DIY mechanic	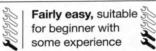	**Difficult,** suitable for experienced DIY mechanic	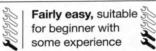	**Very difficult,** suitable for expert DIY or professional	

Specifications

System type
1.8 litre engines	Simtec 71.5 (multi-point injection)
2.2 litre engines:	
Z22SE	GMPT – E16 (multi-point injection)
Z22YH	Simtec 81.1 (high-pressure direct injection)

Fuel system data
All engines except 2.2 litre Z22YH:	
Fuel supply pump type	Electric, immersed in tank
Fuel pump regulated constant pressure	3.8 bar
Specified idle speed	Not adjustable – controlled by ECU
Idle mixture CO content	Not adjustable – controlled by ECU
2.2 litre Z22YH engines:	
Fuel pump type:	
Supply pump	Electric, immersed in tank
High-pressure pump	Mechanical, driven by inlet camshaft
Fuel supply pump delivery pressure	4.2 bar
Fuel system operating pressure	40 to 110 bar
Specified idle speed	Not adjustable – controlled by ECU
Idle mixture CO content	Not adjustable – controlled by ECU

Recommended fuel
Minimum octane rating	95 RON unleaded (UK premium unleaded)
	Leaded fuel or LRP must **NOT** be used

Torque wrench settings

	Nm	lbf ft
Accelerator pedal position sensor nuts	9	6
Camshaft sensor*	9	6
Crankshaft sensor bolt	10	7
Exhaust front pipe-to-manifold nuts*:		
1.8 litre engines	25	18
2.2 litre engines	20	15
Exhaust manifold nuts*	12	9
Exhaust manifold heat shield bolts/nuts:		
1.8 litre engines	8	6
2.2 litre engines:		
Heat shield stud bolts	23	17
Fuel pressure regulator to fuel rail	9	6
Fuel pressure sensor to fuel rail	25	18
Fuel rail bolts:		
1.8 litre engines	9	6
2.2 litre Z22SE engines	9	6
2.2 litre Z22YH engines:		
Fuel rail stud bolts	9	6
Fuel rail-to-injector bolts:		
Stage 1	4	3
Stage 2	9	6
Fuel tank retaining strap bolts	23	17
High-pressure fuel pipe union nuts	25	18
High-pressure fuel pump bolts	9	6
Inlet manifold nuts and bolts:		
1.8 litre engines:		
Manifold to cylinder head	22	16
Support bracket to manifold	20	15
Support bracket to cylinder block	35	26
2.2 litre Z22SE engines:		
Bolts	9	6
Nuts	6	4
2.2 litre Z22YH engines	9	6
Knock sensor bolt:		
1.8 litre engines	20	15
2.2 litre engines	23	17
Manifold absolute pressure sensor bolt	10	7
Throttle body/housing bolts	10	7

* Use new fasteners

1 General information and precautions

The fuel system consists of a fuel tank (which is mounted under the rear of the car, with an electric fuel pump immersed in it), a fuel filter and the fuel feed, and on some engines, return lines. On 1.8 litre and 2.2 litre Z22SE engines, the fuel pump supplies fuel to the fuel rail, which acts as a reservoir for the four fuel injectors which inject fuel into the inlet tracts. On 2.2 litre Z22YH engines, the tank-mounted fuel supply pump supplies fuel to the high-pressure pump mounted on the engine. The high-pressure pump supplies fuel to the fuel rail, which acts as a reservoir for the four fuel injectors which inject fuel directly into the combustion chambers in the cylinder head.

On all engines, the electronic control unit controls both the fuel injection system and the ignition system, integrating the two into a complete engine management system. Refer to Section 10 for further information on the operation of the fuel system and to Chapter 5B for details of the ignition side of the system.

Precautions

Note: *Refer to Part C of this Chapter for general information and precautions relating to the catalytic converter.*

• Before disconnecting any fuel lines, or working on any part of the fuel system, the system must be depressurised as described in Section 5.

• Care must be taken when disconnecting the fuel lines. When disconnecting a fuel union or hose, loosen the union or clamp screw slowly, to avoid sudden uncontrolled fuel spillage. Take adequate fire precautions.

• When working on fuel system components, scrupulous cleanliness must be observed, and care must be taken not to introduce any foreign matter into fuel lines or components.

• After carrying out any work involving disconnection of fuel lines, it is advisable to check the connections for leaks; pressurise the system by switching the ignition on and off several times.

• Electronic control units are very sensitive components, and certain precautions must be taken to avoid damage to these units as follows.

a) *When carrying out welding operations on the vehicle using electric welding equipment, the battery and alternator should be disconnected.*

b) *Although the underbonnet-mounted control units will tolerate normal underbonnet conditions, they can be adversely affected by excess heat or moisture. If using welding equipment or pressure-washing equipment in the vicinity of an electronic control unit, take care not to direct heat, or jets of water or steam, at the unit. If this cannot be avoided, remove the control unit from the vehicle, and protect its wiring plug with a plastic bag.*

c) *Before disconnecting any wiring, or removing components, always ensure that the ignition is switched off.*

d) *After working on fuel injection/engine management system components, ensure that all wiring is correctly reconnected before reconnecting the battery or switching on the ignition.*

⚠️ **Warning: Many of the procedures in this Chapter require the removal of fuel lines and connections, which may result in some fuel spillage. Before carrying out any operation on the fuel system, refer to the precautions given in 'Safety first!' at the beginning of this manual, and follow them implicitly. Petrol is a highly-dangerous and volatile liquid, and the precautions necessary when handling it cannot be overstressed.**

Note: *Residual pressure will remain in the fuel lines long after the vehicle was last used. Before disconnecting any fuel line, first depressurise the fuel system as described in Section 5.*

2 Air cleaner assembly and intake ducts – removal and refitting

Removal

1 Slacken the retaining clips securing the air intake duct to the airflow meter and throttle body/housing. Where applicable, release the clip and disconnect the crankcase ventilation hose from the camshaft cover. Detach the intake duct from the airflow meter and throttle body/housing, and remove the duct from the engine **(see illustration)**.

2 Disconnect the wiring connector from the side of the airflow meter **(see illustration)**.

3 Unclip the wiring harness from the side of the air cleaner housing.

4 Lift up the inner rear corner of the filter housing to release the mounting grommet. Move the filter housing toward the engine to disengage the front and rear mounting rubbers, then release the air intake duct at the front **(see illustrations)**. Lift the filter housing out from the engine compartment.

5 The various air intake pipes/ducts can be disconnected and removed once the retaining clips have been slackened. In some cases it will be necessary to disconnect breather hoses, vacuum pipes and wiring connectors to allow the pipe/duct to be removed; the pipe/duct may also be bolted to a support bracket

Refitting

6 Refitting is the reverse of removal, making sure all the air intake ducts/hoses are securely reconnected.

3 Accelerator pedal/ position sensor – removal and refitting

Removal

1 Disconnect the battery negative terminal (refer to *Disconnecting the battery* in the Reference Chapter).

2 Remove the driver's side lower facia panel as described in Chapter 11.

2.1 Detach the intake duct from the airflow meter and throttle body/housing, and remove the duct from the engine

2.4a Lift up the housing to release the mounting grommet (1) then move the housing toward the engine to disengage the rear mounting rubber (2) ...

3 Working in the driver's footwell under the facia, disconnect the wiring from the top of the accelerator pedal/position sensor **(see illustration)**.

4 Unscrew the three mounting nuts, and withdraw the sensor from the bulkhead.

Refitting

5 Refitting is a reversal of removal.

4 Unleaded petrol – general information and usage

Note: *The information given in this Chapter is correct at the time of writing. If updated information is thought to be required, check with a Vauxhall/Opel dealer. If travelling abroad,*

3.3 Accelerator pedal/position sensor wiring connector (A) and mounting nuts (B)

2.2 Disconnect the wiring connector (arrowed) from the side of the airflow meter

2.4b ... and front mounting rubber (arrowed)

consult one of the motoring organisations (or a similar authority) for advice on the fuel available.

All petrol models are designed to run on fuel with a minimum octane rating of 95 RON. However, if unavailable, 91 octane may be used on 1.8 litre engines and 2.2 litre Z22SE engines. The 2.2 litre Z22YH must not be run on 91 octane fuel.

All models have a catalytic converter, and so must be run on unleaded fuel only. Under no circumstances should leaded fuel or LRP be used, as this will damage the converter.

Super unleaded petrol (98 octane) can also be used in all models if wished, though there is no advantage in doing so.

5 Fuel injection system – depressurisation

⚠️ **Warning: Refer to the warning note in Section 1 before proceeding. The following procedure will merely relieve the pressure in the fuel system – remember that fuel will still be present in the system components, and take precautions accordingly before disconnecting any of them.**

1 The fuel system referred to in this Section is defined as the tank-mounted fuel pump, the fuel filter, the fuel injectors, and the metal pipes and flexible hoses of the fuel lines between these components. All these contain

5.3 Fuel pressure connection valve (arrowed) – 2.2 litre Z22YH engines

5.4 Unscrew the cap, and depress the valve core. Catch all the expelled fuel using a rag

Note 1: *Vauxhall/Opel special tool KM-797 (or suitable alternative) will be required to remove and refit the fuel pump cover locking ring.*
Note 2: *A new fuel pump cover sealing ring will be required on refitting.*

Removal

1 Disconnect the battery negative terminal (refer to *Disconnecting the battery* in the Reference Chapter).
2 Depressurise the fuel system as described in Section 5.
3 Fold the rear seat cushion forwards or alternatively remove the cushion as described in Chapter 11.
4 Lift up the flap in the carpet to reveal the fuel tank access cover **(see illustration)**.
5 Using a screwdriver, carefully prise the plastic access cover from the floor **(see illustration)**.
6 Disconnect the wiring connector from the fuel supply pump cover, and tape the connector to the vehicle body, to prevent it disappearing behind the tank **(see illustration)**.
7 Mark the fuel hoses for identification purposes. The hoses are equipped with quick-release fittings to ease removal. To disconnect each hose, compress the clips located on each side of the fitting and ease the fitting off of its union **(see illustration)**. Plug the hose ends to minimise fuel loss.
8 Using the Vauxhall/Opel special tool, unscrew the locking ring and remove it from the tank **(see illustration)**.
9 Make identification marks on the fuel pump cover and the body to ensure that the cover is refitted in its original position. There may be an arrow stamped on the cover; if so note its direction.
10 Carefully lift the fuel pump cover away from tank until the wiring connectors can be disconnected from its underside **(see illustration)**.
11 Release the retaining clip and disconnect the fuel supply hose from the underside of the fuel pump cover. Where fitted, also disconnect the fuel return hose quick-release fitting from the underside of the cover **(see illustration)**. Remove the fuel pump cover and collect the sealing ring from the top of the tank.
12 The fuel gauge sender unit is clipped to

fuel which will be under pressure while the engine is running, and/or while the ignition is switched on. The pressure will remain for some time after the ignition has been switched off, and it must be relieved in a controlled fashion when any of these components are disturbed for servicing work.
2 Remove the plastic cover over the top of the engine.
3 Locate the fuel pressure connection valve which is fitted to the fuel rail. On 1.8 litre engines it can be found on the top, left-hand end of the fuel rail. On 2.2 litre Z22SE engines the fuel pressure connection valve is located in the fuel line adjacent to the air cleaner housing. On 2.2 litre Z22YH engines the fuel pressure connection valve is located on the fuel inlet pipe connection on the high-pressure fuel pump **(see illustration)**.

6.4 Lift up the flap in the carpet to reveal the fuel tank access cover

4 Unscrew the cap from the valve and position a container beneath the valve. Hold a wad of rag over the valve and relieve the pressure in the fuel system by depressing the valve core with a suitable screwdriver **(see illustration)**. Be prepared for the squirt of fuel as the valve core is depressed and catch it with the rag. Hold the valve core down until no more fuel is expelled from the valve.
5 Once all pressure is relieved, securely refit the valve cap.

6 Fuel gauge sender unit – removal and refitting

⚠️ **Warning: Refer to the warning note in Section 1 before proceeding.**

6.5 Carefully prise the plastic access cover from the floor

6.6 Disconnect the wiring connector from the fuel pump cover

6.7 Compress the clips located on each side of the fuel hose fitting and ease the fitting off of its union

6.8 Using the Vauxhall/Opel special tool, unscrew the locking ring and remove it from the tank

the side of the fuel supply pump. Depress the retaining clip then slide the sender unit upwards to release it from the pump **(see illustrations)**.

13 Manoeuvre the sender unit through the fuel tank aperture, taking great care not damage the float arm.

Refitting

14 Place a new sealing ring in position on the top of the fuel tank.

15 Manoeuvre the sender unit carefully in through the tank aperture and slide it into position on the side of the fuel supply pump. Ensure the sender unit is clipped securely in position.

16 Reconnect the fuel supply hose and, where fitted, the return hose to the fuel pump cover.

17 Reconnect the fuel pump and sender unit wiring connectors to the fuel pump cover. Locate the cover in position on the tank and align the marks, or direction arrow in the position noted during removal.

18 Refit the locking ring and tighten it with the special tool until it locks in place.

19 Reconnect the fuel hoses to the pump cover, using the marks made on removal, then reconnect the wiring connector.

20 Reconnect the battery then start the engine and check for fuel leaks. If all is well, refit the access cover then refit or fold the seat cushion back into position.

7 Fuel supply pump – removal and refitting

> ⚠ **Warning: Refer to the warning note in Section 1 before proceeding.**

Removal

1 Remove the fuel gauge sender unit as described in Section 6.

2 Release the three retaining clips by pressing them inwards then lift the fuel supply pump out of the fuel tank, taking great care not to spill fuel onto the interior of the vehicle. **(see illustrations)**.

3 Inspect the fuel filter for signs of damage or deterioration and renew if necessary **(see illustration)**.

7.2a Release the three retaining clips (arrowed) by pressing them inwards . . .

6.10 Lift the fuel pump cover away from tank until the wiring connectors can be disconnected from its underside

6.12a Depress the retaining clip . . .

Refitting

4 Ensure the filter is securely fitted to the base of the pump then carefully manoeuvre the pump assembly into position, making sure it clips securely into position.

5 Refit the fuel gauge sender unit as described in Section 6.

8 Fuel tank – removal and refitting

> ⚠ **Warning: Refer to the warning note in Section 1 before proceeding.**

Removal

1 Disconnect the battery negative terminal (refer to *Disconnecting the battery* in the Reference Chapter).

7.2b . . . then lift the fuel supply pump out of the fuel tank

6.11 Disconnect the fuel supply hose from the fuel pump cover and, where fitted, disconnect the fuel return hose

6.12b . . . then slide the sender unit upwards to release it from the fuel supply pump

2 Depressurise the fuel system as described in Section 5.

3 Before removing the fuel tank, all fuel must be drained from the tank. Since a fuel tank drain plug is not provided, it is therefore preferable to carry out the removal operation when the tank is nearly empty. The remaining fuel can then be syphoned or hand-pumped from the tank.

4 Remove the exhaust system and relevant heat shield(s) as described in Section 17.

5 Unclip the handbrake cables from the underbody and fuel tank, then tie them to one side, away from the fuel tank.

6 Disconnect the wiring for the fuel pump and fuel gauge sender at the underbody connector in front of the left-hand side of the tank. Unclip the wiring harness from the two retaining clips.

7 Disconnect the fuel feed line, return line

7.3 Inspect the fuel filter for signs of damage or deterioration and renew if necessary

9.12 Disconnect the wiring connector(arrowed) from the throttle body/housing – 2.2 litre engines

(where applicable) and the evaporative vent line at the underbody quick-release connectors on the right-hand side of the tank. Be prepared for some loss of fuel. A Vauxhall/Opel special tool is available to release the fuel line connectors, but provided care is taken, the connectors can be released using a pair of long-nosed pliers, or a similar tool, to depress the retaining tangs. Suitably plug the disconnected fuel and vent hoses to prevent entry of dust and dirt.

8 Place a suitable container under the tank, then slacken the clip and disconnect the fuel filler hose from the fuel tank. Collect the escaping fuel in the container.

9 Support the weight of the fuel tank on a jack with interposed block of wood.

10 Undo the four bolts and remove the two securing straps from the fuel tank.

11 Taking care not to damage the charcoal canister, slowly lower the tank and move it forwards. When sufficient clearance exists, disconnect the charcoal canister vent hose quick-release fitting.

12 Continue to lower the tank until it can be removed from under the vehicle.

13 If necessary, remove the fuel lines and hoses, heat shield and wiring from the tank for transfer to the new tank. If a new tank is being fitted, it is recommended that the filter is renewed at the same time.

14 If the tank contains sediment or water, it may cleaned out with two or three rinses of clean fuel. Remove the fuel gauge sender unit and fuel supply pump as described in

9.14 Undo the four bolts (arrowed) and lift the throttle body off the inlet manifold – 2.2 litre engines

Sections 6 and 7 respectively. Shake the tank vigorously, and change the fuel as necessary to remove all contamination from the tank. *This procedure should be carried out in a well-ventilated area, and it is vital to take adequate fire precautions.*

15 Any repairs to the fuel tank should be carried out by a professional. Do not under any circumstances attempt any form of DIY repair to a fuel tank.

Refitting

16 Refitting is the reverse of the removal procedure, noting the following points:
  a) *When lifting the tank back into position, take care to ensure that none of the hoses become trapped between the tank and vehicle body. Refit the retaining straps and tighten the bolts to the specified torque.*
  b) *Ensure all pipes and hoses are correctly routed and all hoses unions are securely joined.*
  c) *On completion, refill the tank with a small amount of fuel, and check for signs of leakage prior to taking the vehicle out on the road.*

9 Throttle body/housing – removal and refitting

Removal

1.8 litre engines

1 Disconnect the battery negative terminal (refer to *Disconnecting the battery* in the Reference Chapter).

2 Remove the plastic cover over the top of the engine.

3 Slacken the retaining clips securing the air intake duct to the airflow meter and throttle body/housing. Release the clip and disconnect the crankcase ventilation hose from the camshaft cover. Detach the intake duct from the airflow meter and throttle body/housing, and remove the duct from the engine.

4 Disconnect the wiring connector from the throttle body/housing.

5 Release the retaining clips and disconnect the crankcase ventilation hose and the fuel evaporation hose from the throttle body/housing.

6 Clamp the two coolant hoses to minimise coolant loss, then release the retaining clips and disconnect the two coolant hoses from the rear of the throttle body/housing.

7 Undo the four bolts and lift the throttle body off the inlet manifold. Recover the gasket.

8 It is not possible to obtain the throttle valve control motor or throttle valve position sensor separately, so if either is faulty, the complete throttle body must be renewed.

2.2 litre engines

9 Disconnect the battery negative terminal (refer to *Disconnecting the battery* in the Reference Chapter).

10 Remove the plastic cover over the top of the engine.

11 Slacken the retaining clips securing the air intake duct to the airflow meter and throttle body/housing. On Z22SE engines, release the clip and disconnect the crankcase ventilation hose from the camshaft cover. Detach the intake duct from the airflow meter and throttle body/housing, and remove the duct from the engine **(see illustration 2.1)**.

12 Disconnect the wiring connector from the throttle body/housing **(see illustration)**.

13 On Z22SE engines, undo the retaining nut and release the wiring harness bracket from the throttle body/housing retaining stud bolt.

14 Undo the four bolts and lift the throttle body off the inlet manifold **(see illustration)**. Recover the gasket.

15 It is not possible to obtain the throttle valve control motor or throttle valve position sensor separately, so if either is faulty, the complete throttle body must be renewed.

Refitting

16 Refitting is a reversal of removal, but thoroughly clean the mating faces and use a new gasket. Tighten the bolts progressively and securely. On 1.8 litre engines, top-up the coolant level as described in *Weekly checks*.

10 Fuel injection systems – general information

Simtec 71.5 multi-point injection system

The Simtec 71.5 engine management (fuel injection/ignition) system incorporates a closed-loop catalytic converter, an evaporative emission control system, an exhaust gas recirculation system, and complies with the latest emission control standards. The fuel injection side of the system operates as follows; refer to Chapter 5B for information on the ignition system.

The fuel supply pump, immersed in the fuel tank, pumps fuel from the fuel tank to the fuel rail, via a filter mounted underneath the rear of the vehicle. Fuel supply pressure is controlled by the pressure regulator located in the fuel tank.

The electrical control system consists of the ECU, along with the following sensors.
  a) *Throttle potentiometer – informs the ECU of the throttle position, and the rate of throttle opening or closing.*
  b) *Accelerator pedal position sensor – informs the ECU of accelerator pedal position.*
  c) *Coolant temperature sensor – informs the ECU of engine temperature.*
  d) *Airflow meter – informs the ECU of the load on the engine (expressed in terms of the mass of air passing from the air cleaner to the throttle body/housing).*
  e) *Oxygen sensors (two) – inform the ECU of*

the oxygen content of the exhaust gases (explained in greater detail in Part C of this Chapter).

f) Crankshaft sensor – informs the ECU of engine speed and crankshaft position.

g) Camshaft sensor – informs the ECU of speed and position of the exhaust camshaft.

h) Knock sensor – informs the ECU when pre-ignition ('pinking') is occurring.

i) ABS control unit – informs the ECU of the vehicle speed.

All the above information is analysed by the ECU and, based on this, the ECU determines the appropriate ignition and fuelling requirements for the engine. The ECU controls the fuel injector by varying its pulse width – the length of time the injector is held open – to provide a richer or weaker mixture, as appropriate. The mixture is constantly varied by the ECU, to provide the best setting for cranking, starting (with either a hot or cold engine), warm-up, idle, cruising, and acceleration.

Idle speed and throttle position are controlled by an electronic accelerator (no accelerator cable), this consists of an accelerator pedal module and a throttle valve module. Each module has two potentiometers (sensors) which determine the position of the pedal, which then transmits a signal to the ECU.

Another additional feature of the Simtec system is that it incorporates a variable tract inlet manifold to help increase torque output at low engine speeds. Each inlet manifold tract is fitted with a valve. The valve is controlled by the ECU via a solenoid valve and vacuum diaphragm unit.

At low engine speeds (below approximately 3600 rpm) the valves remain closed. The air entering the engine is then forced to take the long inlet path through the manifold which leads to an increase in the engine torque output.

At higher engine speeds, the ECU switches the solenoid valve which then allows vacuum to act on the diaphragm unit. The diaphragm unit is linked to the valve assemblies and opens up each of the four valves allowing the air passing through the manifold to take the shorter inlet path which is more suited to higher engine speeds.

The ECU also controls the exhaust and evaporative emission control systems, which are described in detail in Part C of this Chapter.

If certain sensors fail, and send abnormal signals to the ECU, the ECU has a back-up programme. In this event, the abnormal signals are ignored, and a preprogrammed value is substituted for the sensor signal, allowing the engine to continue running, albeit at reduced efficiency. If the ECU enters its back-up mode, a warning light on the instrument panel will illuminate, and a fault code will be stored in the ECU memory. This fault code can be read using suitable specialist test equipment.

GMPT – E16 multi-point injection system

The GMPT – E16 engine management (fuel injection/ignition) system is very similar in operation to the Simtec 71.5 system described previously.

The only major differences are that a manifold absolute pressure sensor is used to inform the ECU of the engine load by monitoring the pressure in the inlet manifold, and special sensors are incorporated in the ignition module to replace the need for a camshaft sensor. The sensors read the injection impulse so as to determine the cylinder position.

Simtec 81.1 high-pressure direct injection system

The Simtec 81.1 engine management (fuel injection/ignition) system incorporates a closed-loop catalytic converter, an evaporative emission control system, an exhaust gas recirculation system, and complies with the latest emission control standards. The fuel injection side of the system operates as follows; refer to Chapter 5B for information on the ignition system.

The fuel supply pump, immersed in the fuel tank, pumps fuel from the fuel tank to the high-pressure fuel pump, via a filter mounted underneath the rear of the vehicle.

The high-pressure fuel pump is mounted on the left-hand end of the cylinder head and is driven directly by the inlet camshaft. The high-pressure pump supplies fuel at a variable pressure of between 40 and 110 bar to the fuel rail. The fuel pressure at the fuel rail is controlled by means of a fuel pressure sensor and fuel pressure regulator.

The electrical control system consists of the ECU, along with the following sensors.

a) Throttle potentiometer – informs the ECU of the throttle position, and the rate of throttle opening or closing.

b) Accelerator pedal position sensor – informs the ECU of accelerator pedal position.

c) Coolant temperature sensor – informs the ECU of engine temperature.

d) Airflow meter – informs the ECU of the load on the engine (expressed in terms of the mass of air passing from the air cleaner to the throttle body/housing).

e) Manifold absolute pressure sensor – informs the ECU of the engine load by monitoring the pressure in the inlet manifold.

f) Oxygen sensors (two) – inform the ECU of the oxygen content of the exhaust gases (explained in greater detail in Part C of this Chapter).

g) Crankshaft sensor – informs the ECU of engine speed and crankshaft position.

h) Camshaft sensor – informs the ECU of speed and position of the exhaust camshaft.

i) Knock sensor – informs the ECU when pre-ignition ('pinking') is occurring.

j) ABS control unit – informs the ECU of the vehicle speed.

All the above information is analysed by the ECU and, based on this, the ECU determines the appropriate ignition and fuelling requirements for the engine. The ECU controls the fuel injector by varying its pulse width – the length of time the injector is held open – to provide a richer or weaker mixture, as appropriate. The mixture is constantly varied by the ECU, to provide the best setting for cranking, starting (with either a hot or cold engine), warm-up, idle, cruising, and acceleration.

Idle speed and throttle position are controlled by an electronic accelerator (no accelerator cable), this consists of an accelerator pedal module and a throttle valve module. Each module has two potentiometers (sensors) which determine the position of the pedal, which then transmits a signal to the ECU.

The system incorporates a variable tract inlet manifold to help increase torque output at low engine speeds. Each inlet manifold tract is fitted with a valve. The valve is controlled by the ECU via a solenoid valve and vacuum diaphragm unit.

At low engine speeds (below approximately 3600 rpm) the valves remain closed. The air entering the engine is then forced to take the long inlet path through the manifold which leads to an increase in the engine torque output.

At higher engine speeds, the ECU switches the solenoid valve which then allows vacuum to act on the diaphragm unit. The diaphragm unit is linked to the valve assemblies and opens up each of the four valves allowing the air passing through the manifold to take the shorter inlet path which is more suited to higher engine speeds.

The ECU also controls the exhaust and evaporative emission control systems, which are described in detail in Part C of this Chapter.

If certain sensors fail, and send abnormal signals to the ECU, the ECU has a back-up programme. In this event, the abnormal signals are ignored, and a preprogrammed value is substituted for the sensor signal, allowing the engine to continue running, albeit at reduced efficiency. If the ECU enters its back-up mode, a warning light on the instrument panel will illuminate, and a fault code will be stored in the ECU memory. This fault code can be read using suitable specialist test equipment.

11 Fuel injection system components – testing

1 If a fault appears in the engine management system, first ensure that all the system wiring connectors are securely connected and free of corrosion. Ensure that the fault is not due to poor maintenance; ie, check that the air cleaner filter element is clean, the spark plugs are in

good condition and correctly gapped, the cylinder compression pressures are correct and that the engine breather hoses are clear and undamaged, referring to Chapters 1A, 2A and 2B for further information.

2 If these checks fail to reveal the cause of the problem, the vehicle should be taken to a suitably-equipped Vauxhall/Opel dealer or engine management diagnostic specialist for testing. A diagnostic socket is located in the centre console, beneath the ashtray insert, to which a fault code reader or other suitable test equipment can be connected **(see illustration)**. By using the code reader or test equipment, the engine management ECU can be interrogated, and any stored fault codes can be retrieved. Live data can also be captured from the various system sensors and actuators, indicating their operating parameters. This will allow the fault to be quickly and simply traced, alleviating the need to test all the system components individually, which is a time-consuming operation that carries a risk of damaging the ECU.

---

12 Simtec 71.5 injection system components – removal and refitting

Fuel rail and injectors

Note: *Before condemning an injector, if a faulty injector is suspected, it is worth trying the effect of one of the proprietary injector-cleaning treatments.*

1 Disconnect the battery negative terminal (refer to *Disconnecting the battery* in the Reference Chapter).

2 Remove the plastic cover over the top of the engine.

3 Depressurise the fuel system as described in Section 5.

4 Slacken the retaining clips securing the air intake duct to the airflow meter and throttle body/housing. Release the clip and disconnect the crankcase ventilation hose from the camshaft cover. Detach the intake duct from the airflow meter and throttle body/housing, and remove the duct from the engine.

5 Firmly apply the handbrake, then jack up the front of the car and support it securely on axle stands (see *Jacking and vehicle support*).

6 From under the rear of the engine, disconnect the wiring connectors for the oxygen sensor and oil pressure switch. Release the wiring harness from its clips.

7 From under the front of the engine disconnect the wiring connectors at the oil level sensor and crankshaft sensor. Release the wiring harness from its clips.

8 Working from above, disconnect the camshaft sensor wiring connector, then undo the nut and disconnect the earth lead from the alternator.

9 Release the clip and disconnect the remaining crankcase ventilation hose from the camshaft cover.

11.2 The diagnostic socket is located beneath the ashtray insert

10 Disconnect the wiring connectors from the following components, labelling each connector to avoid confusion when refitting:
 a) *Fuel injectors.*
 b) *Air conditioning compressor.*
 c) *Coolant temperature sensor.*
 d) *Air conditioning pressure switch.*
 e) *Throttle body/housing.*
 f) *Fuel injection ECU.*
 g) *Knock sensor.*
 h) *EGR valve.*
 i) *Ignition module.*
 j) *Oxygen sensor.*
 k) *Wiring harness block connector.*

11 Detach the knock sensor wiring harness plug bracket and the earth lead.

12 Release the wiring harness cable ties and unscrew the bolt securing the plastic wiring trough to the engine lifting eye. Lift up the disconnected harness and place it to one side.

13 Disconnect the fuel feed hose quick-release connector at the fuel rail. Be prepared for some loss of fuel. A Vauxhall/Opel special tool is available to release the connector, but provided care is taken, it can be released using a pair of long-nosed pliers, or a similar tool, to depress the retaining tangs. Suitably cover or plug the open unions, to prevent dirt ingress and further fuel spillage.

14 Unscrew the two mounting bolts, then lift the fuel rail complete with the injectors off of the inlet manifold.

15 To remove an injector from the fuel rail, prise out the metal securing clip using a screwdriver or a pair of pliers, and pull the injector from the fuel rail. Remove and discard

12.31 Undo the two retaining bolts and remove the camshaft sensor from the cylinder head – 1.8 litre engines

the injector sealing rings; new ones must be fitted on refitting.

16 Overhaul of the fuel injectors is not possible, as no spares are available. If faulty, an injector must be renewed.

17 Commence refitting by fitting new O-ring seals to both ends of the fuel injectors. Coat the seals with a thin layer of petroleum jelly before fitting.

18 Refitting is a reversal of removal, bearing in mind the following points:
 a) *When refitting the injectors to the fuel rail, note that the groove in the metal securing clip must engage with the lug on the injector body.*
 b) *Make sure that the quick-release connector audibly engages on the fuel rail.*
 c) *Ensure that all wiring connectors are securely reconnected, and that the wiring is secured in the relevant clips and brackets.*

Coolant temperature sensor

19 The coolant temperature sensor is located on the thermostat housing on the right-hand end of the cylinder head. Refer to Chapter 3 for removal and refitting details.

Airflow meter

20 Slacken the retaining clip securing the air intake duct to the airflow meter and disconnect the duct.

21 Disconnect the airflow meter wiring connector.

22 Slacken the retaining clip and remove the airflow meter from the air cleaner housing lid.

23 Refitting is a reversal of removal, but ensure that the arrow on the airflow meter points toward the throttle body/housing when fitted.

Crankshaft sensor

24 The crankshaft sensor is mounted on the front of the cylinder block below the oil filter.

25 Firmly apply the handbrake, then jack up the front of the car and support it securely on axle stands (see *Jacking and vehicle support*).

26 Disconnect the wiring connector, then unscrew the retaining bolt and remove the sensor from the front of the cylinder block. Discard the sealing ring, a new one should be used on refitting.

27 Refitting is the reverse of removal using a new sealing ring and tightening the sensor bolt to the specified torque.

Camshaft sensor

28 Remove the plastic cover over the top of the engine.

29 Undo the three retaining screws, then unclip the timing belt upper cover from the rear cover and remove it from the engine compartment.

30 Unscrew the nut from the fuel line bracket, then unscrew the stud bolt. Disconnect the camshaft sensor wiring connector, then unclip the wiring harness.

31 Undo the two retaining bolts and remove the sensor from the cylinder head **(see illustration)**.

32 Refitting is the reverse of removal, tightening the sensor retaining bolts to the specified torque.

Knock sensor

33 Firmly apply the handbrake, then jack up the front of the car and support it securely on axle stands (see *Jacking and vehicle support*).
34 Unscrew the two retaining bolts and remove the inlet manifold support bracket.
35 Undo the retaining bolt securing the knock sensor to the cylinder block and release the sensor from its location **(see illustration)**.
36 Trace the wiring back to the knock sensor wiring connector. Disconnect the connector, release the wiring harness and remove the sensor.
37 On refitting, ensure the mating surfaces are clean and dry then fit the sensor and tighten its retaining bolt to the specified torque. Ensure the wiring is correctly routed and securely reconnected.

Electronic control unit (ECU)

Note: *If a new ECU is to be fitted, this work must be entrusted to a Vauxhall/Opel dealer or suitably-equipped specialist as it is necessary to programme the new ECU after installation. This work requires the use of dedicated Vauxhall/Opel diagnostic equipment or a compatible alternative.*
38 Remove the plastic cover over the top of the engine.
39 Lift up the locking bars and disconnect the two ECU wiring connectors.
40 Disconnect the knock sensor wiring connector.
41 Undo the retaining bolt and detach the earth lead from the ECU.
42 Undo the two retaining bolts and remove the ECU from the engine.
43 Refitting is a reversal of removal.

13 GMPT – E16 injection system components – removal and refitting

Fuel rail and injectors

Note: *Before condemning an injector, it is worth trying the effect of one of the proprietary injector-cleaning treatments.*

13.18a Disconnect the wiring connector from the pressure sensor . . .

12.35 Undo the retaining bolt and release the knock sensor from the cylinder block – 1.8 litre engines

1 Disconnect the battery negative terminal (refer to *Disconnecting the battery* in the Reference Chapter).
2 Remove the plastic cover over the top of the engine.
3 Depressurise the fuel system as described in Section 5.
4 Slacken the retaining clips and disconnect the crankcase ventilation hose.
5 Unscrew the union nut and disconnect the fuel pipe from the fuel rail. Release the fuel pipe from the retaining clips and move to one side. Suitably cover or plug the open unions, to prevent dirt ingress and further fuel spillage.
6 Disconnect the four wiring connectors at the fuel injectors.
7 Unscrew the two mounting bolts, then lift the fuel rail complete with the injectors off of the inlet manifold.
8 To remove an injector from the fuel rail, prise out the metal securing clip using a screwdriver or a pair of pliers, and pull the injector from the fuel rail. Remove and discard the injector sealing rings; new ones must be fitted on refitting.
9 Overhaul of the fuel injectors is not possible, as no spares are available. If faulty, an injector must be renewed.
10 Commence refitting by fitting new O-ring seals to both ends of the fuel injectors. Coat the seals with a thin layer of petroleum jelly before fitting.
11 Refitting is a reversal of removal, bearing in mind the following points:
   a) When refitting the injectors to the fuel rail,

13.18b . . . and turn clockwise 1/4 of a turn to release from the manifold – 2.2 litre Z22SE engines

   note that the groove in the metal securing clip must engage with the lug on the injector body.
   b) Ensure that all wiring connectors are securely reconnected, and that the wiring is secured in the relevant clips and brackets.

Coolant temperature sensor

12 The coolant temperature sensor is located on the thermostat housing at the left-hand end of the cylinder head. Refer to Chapter 3 for removal and refitting details.

Airflow meter

13 Slacken the retaining clip securing the air intake duct to the airflow meter and disconnect the duct.
14 Disconnect the airflow meter wiring connector **(see illustration 2.2)**.
15 Slacken the retaining clip and remove the airflow meter from the air cleaner housing lid.
16 Refitting is a reversal of removal, but ensure that the arrow on the airflow meter points toward the throttle body/housing when fitted.

Manifold absolute pressure sensor

17 Remove the throttle body/housing as described in Section 9.
18 Disconnect the wiring connector from the manifold absolute pressure sensor, turn the pressure sensor 1/4 of a turn clockwise and carefully pull out of the inlet manifold **(see illustrations)**.
19 Refitting is the reverse of removal, using a new sealing ring.

Crankshaft sensor

20 Remove the starter motor as described in Chapter 5A.
21 Trace the wiring back from the sensor, releasing it from all the relevant clips and ties whilst noting its correct routing. Disconnect the wiring connector from the sensor.
22 Unscrew the retaining bolt and remove the sensor from the cylinder block **(see illustration)**.
23 Refitting is the reverse of removal, tightening the retaining bolt to the specified torque. Ensure the wiring is correctly routed and retained by all the necessary clips and ties.

13.22 Unbolt the crankshaft sensor (arrowed) – 2.2 litre Z22SE engines

13.26 Unbolt the knock sensor (arrowed) – 2.2 litre Z22SE engines

Knock sensor

24 Remove the starter motor as described in Chapter 5A.

25 Disconnect the wiring block connector, so the wiring is free to be removed with the sensor.

26 Unscrew the retaining bolt and remove the sensor from the cylinder block (see illustration).

27 On refitting ensure the mating surfaces are clean and dry then fit the sensor and tighten its retaining bolt to the specified torque. Ensure the wiring is correctly routed and retained by all the necessary clips and ties.

Electronic control unit (ECU)

Note: *If a new ECU is to be fitted, this work must be entrusted to a Vauxhall/Opel dealer or suitably-equipped specialist as it is necessary to program the new ECU after installation. This work requires the use of dedicated Vauxhall/Opel diagnostic equipment or a compatible alternative.*

28 Remove the plastic cover over the top of the engine.

29 Slacken the retaining clips securing the air intake duct to the airflow meter and throttle body/housing. Release the clip and disconnect the crankcase ventilation hose from the camshaft cover. Detach the intake duct from the airflow meter and throttle body/housing, and remove the duct from the engine (see illustration 2.1).

30 Lift up the locking bars and disconnect the two ECU wiring connectors.

31 Disconnect the harness multiplug adjacent to the ECU.

32 Undo the four bolts and remove the ECU from the inlet manifold.

33 Refitting is a reversal of removal.

14 Simtec 81.1 injection system components – removal and refitting

Fuel rail and injectors

Note 1: *Numerous special tools are required to remove and refit the injectors and fuel rail. Read through the entire procedure to familiarise yourself with the work involved, and ensure the special tools (or suitable alternatives) are available before proceeding.*

Note 2: *New sealing rings and retaining clips will be required for each injector for refitting.*

1 Disconnect the battery negative terminal (refer to *Disconnecting the battery* in the Reference Chapter).

2 Remove the plastic cover over the top of the engine.

3 Depressurise the fuel system as described in Section 5.

4 Slacken the retaining clips securing the air intake duct to the airflow meter and throttle body/housing. Detach the intake duct from the airflow meter and throttle body/housing, and remove the duct from the engine.

5 Release the clips securing the crankcase ventilation valve hoses to the camshaft cover and inlet manifold (see illustrations). Unclip the ventilation valve and remove it from the engine.

6 Remove the engine management electronic control unit as described later in this Section.

7 Disconnect the wiring connectors at the fuel pressure sensor and fuel pressure regulator (see illustrations).

8 Disconnect the fuel feed hose quick-release connector at the fuel pressure regulator (see illustration). Be prepared for some loss of fuel. A Vauxhall/Opel special tool is available to release the connector, but provided care is taken, it can be released using a pair of long-nosed pliers, or a similar tool, to depress the retaining tangs. Suitably cover or plug the open unions, to prevent dirt ingress and further fuel spillage. Release the disconnected hose from its retaining clips and move it to one side.

9 Disconnect the fuel return hose quick-release connectors at the fuel pressure regulator and high-pressure fuel pump (see illustrations). Be prepared for some loss of

14.5a Release the clips (arrowed) securing the crankcase ventilation valve hoses to the camshaft cover . . .

14.5b . . . and inlet manifold

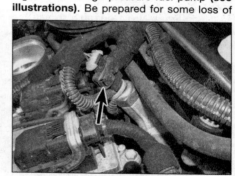

14.7a Disconnect the wiring connectors at the fuel pressure sensor (arrowed) . . .

14.7b . . . and fuel pressure regulator (arrowed)

14.8 Disconnect the fuel feed hose quick-release connector at the fuel pressure regulator (arrowed)

14.9a Disconnect the fuel return hose quick-release connectors at the fuel pressure regulator (arrowed) . . .

14.9b ... and high-pressure fuel pump (arrowed)

14.10 Unscrew the union nuts securing the fuel pipe to the fuel pump (A) and fuel rail (B)

fuel. Suitably cover or plug the open unions, to prevent dirt ingress and further fuel spillage. Release the retaining clips and remove the hose from the engine.

10 Thoroughly clean the fuel pipe unions on the high-pressure fuel pump and fuel rail. Using an open-ended spanner, unscrew the union nuts securing the fuel pipe to the fuel pump and fuel rail **(see illustration)**. Be prepared for some loss of fuel. Withdraw the high-pressure fuel pipe and plug or cover the open unions to prevent dirt entry.

11 Disconnect the wiring harness connectors at the evaporative emission control purge valve, manifold absolute pressure sensor and the inlet manifold switchover solenoid valve. Undo the two nuts and detach the wiring harness bracket. Unclip the wiring harness and move it to one side.

12 Unscrew the two stud bolts and the four mounting bolts securing the fuel rail and injectors to the cylinder head.

13 Screw the Vauxhall/Opel special tool KM-6359 into the stud bolt holes at each end of the fuel rail. Tighten both tools to draw the fuel rail and injectors out from the cylinder head. Take care not to tilt the fuel rail as it is being removed.

14 Detach the injector wiring harness, then remove the spring clip and plastic clip and withdraw each injector from the fuel rail. Note that new clips and new injector seals will be required for each injector for refitting.

15 If the injectors remained in place in the cylinder head when the fuel rail was removed, it will be necessary to use Vauxhall/Opel special tools KM-6360 and KM-328-B to remove them. Detach the sealing ring and support ring from the top of each injector. Attach KM-6360 to the injector and turn the tool back-and-forth to release the injector from its seat. Once the injector is free, use tool KM-328-B to pull the injector from the cylinder head. Remove the remaining injectors in the same way.

16 Clean the body of each injector with a soft

brass brush taking great care not to touch the injector nozzle.

17 Remove the combustion chamber sealing ring on each injector then fit a new sealing ring using the various components of Vauxhall/Opel special tool KM-6364. Place the new sealing ring on the fitting sleeve, then locate the fitting sleeve on the injector. Push the sealing ring into position on the injector using the cylindrical side of the fitting tool, until the seal reaches the groove in the injector. Smooth the sealing ring by turning it slightly with the conical side of the fitting tool, then leave the tool in position until the injectors are ready for refitting. Repeat this procedure for the remaining injectors.

18 Remove the old sealing ring and support ring from the top of each injector and clean the ring locations. Using the fitting sleeve of tool KM-6364, fit a new support ring, then fit a new sealing ring. Repeat this procedure for the remaining injectors.

19 Using a circular movement, fit the four injectors into the fuel rail and secure each one with a new spring clip and plastic clip.

20 Refit the injector wiring harness and reconnect the injectors, fuel pressure regulator and fuel pressure sensor.

21 Clean the injector locations in the cylinder head and remove the fitting tools from the injectors. Refit the injector and fuel rail assembly to the cylinder head.

22 Insert the four retaining bolts and tighten them in a spiral sequence, in two stages to the specified torque.

23 Refit the two stud bolts to the fuel rail and tighten to the specified torque.

24 The remainder of refitting is a reversal of removal, bearing in mind the following points:

a) *Ensure that all wiring connectors are securely reconnected, and that the wiring is secured in the relevant clips and brackets.*

b) *Tighten the high-pressure fuel pipe unions to the specified torque.*

c) *On completion, reconnect the battery,*

start the engine and check for fuel leaks. If satisfactory, refit the engine cover.

High-pressure fuel pump

25 Disconnect the battery negative terminal (refer to *Disconnecting the battery* in the Reference Chapter).

26 Remove the plastic cover over the top of the engine.

27 Depressurise the fuel system as described in Section 5.

28 Disconnect the fuel return hose quick-release connector at the high-pressure fuel pump **(see illustration 14.9b)**. Be prepared for some loss of fuel. A Vauxhall/Opel special tool is available to release the connector, but provided care is taken, it can be released using a pair of long-nosed pliers, or a similar tool, to depress the retaining tangs. Suitably cover or plug the open unions, to prevent dirt ingress and further fuel spillage.

29 Thoroughly clean the fuel pipe unions on the high-pressure fuel pump and fuel rail. Using an open-ended spanner, unscrew the union nuts securing the fuel pipe to the fuel pump and fuel rail **(see illustration 14.10)**. Be prepared for some loss of fuel. Withdraw the high-pressure fuel pipe and plug or cover the open unions to prevent dirt entry.

30 Undo the three retaining bolts and remove the high-pressure pump from the cylinder head. Collect the gasket.

31 Thoroughly clean the mating faces of the cylinder head and fuel pump and locate a new gasket on the pump.

32 Place the pump in position on the cylinder head and refit the three retaining bolts. Tighten the bolts to the specified torque.

33 Reconnect the fuel pipe to the pump and fuel rail and tighten the union nuts to the specified torque.

34 Reconnect the fuel return hose to the pump.

35 Reconnect the battery, then start the engine and check for fuel leaks.

36 Refit the engine cover on completion.

14.41 Undo the two retaining bolts (arrowed) and remove the fuel pressure regulator from the fuel rail

Fuel pressure regulator

37 Disconnect the battery negative terminal (refer to *Disconnecting the battery* in the Reference Chapter).

38 Remove the plastic cover over the top of the engine.

39 Depressurise the fuel system as described in Section 5.

40 Slacken the retaining clips securing the air intake duct to the airflow meter and throttle body/housing. Detach the intake duct from the airflow meter and throttle body/housing, and remove the duct from the engine.

41 Disconnect the wiring connector at the fuel pressure regulator, then undo the two retaining bolts and remove the regulator from the fuel rail **(see illustration)**. Be prepared for some loss of fuel. Remove the two sealing rings from the regulator.

42 Fit two new sealing rings to the regulator, then place the unit in position on the fuel rail. Refit and tighten the retaining bolts to the specified torque and reconnect the wiring connector.

43 Refit the air intake duct and securely tighten its retaining clips.

44 Refit the engine cover and reconnect the battery.

Fuel pressure sensor

45 Disconnect the battery negative terminal (refer to *Disconnecting the battery* in the Reference Chapter).

46 Remove the plastic cover over the top of the engine.

14.77 Lift up the locking bars and disconnect the two ECU wiring connectors

47 Depressurise the fuel system as described in Section 5.

48 Remove the cable tie, then disconnect the wiring connector at the fuel pressure sensor **(see illustration 14.7a)**. Unscrew the sensor and remove it from the fuel rail. Collect the sealing ring.

49 Refit the sensor to the fuel rail using a new sealing ring, and tighten the sensor to the specified torque.

50 Reconnect the wiring connector and secure with a new cable tie.

51 Reconnect the battery, then start the engine and check for fuel leaks.

52 Refit the engine cover on completion.

Coolant temperature sensor

53 The coolant temperature sensor is located on the thermostat housing at the left-hand end of the cylinder head. Refer to Chapter 3 for removal and refitting details.

Airflow meter

54 Slacken the retaining clip securing the air intake duct to the airflow meter and disconnect the duct.

55 Disconnect the airflow meter wiring connector **(see illustration 2.2)**.

56 Slacken the retaining clip and remove the airflow meter from the air cleaner housing lid.

57 Refitting is a reversal of removal, but ensure that the arrow on the airflow meter points toward the throttle body/housing when fitted.

Manifold absolute pressure sensor

58 Remove the plastic cover over the top of the engine.

59 Unclip the wiring harness connector located above the manifold absolute pressure sensor.

60 Disconnect the pressure sensor wiring connector, undo the retaining bolt and remove the sensor from the inlet manifold **(see illustration)**.

61 Refit the sensor to the manifold, refit the retaining bolt and tighten to the specified torque.

62 Reconnect the sensor wiring connector, secure the wiring harness connector, and refit the engine cover.

14.60 Disconnect the manifold absolute pressure sensor wiring connector (arrowed)

Crankshaft sensor

63 Remove the starter motor as described in Chapter 5A.

64 Trace the wiring back from the sensor, releasing it from all the relevant clips and ties whilst noting its correct routing. Disconnect the wiring connector from the sensor.

65 Unscrew the retaining bolt and remove the sensor from the cylinder block **(see illustration 13.22)**.

66 Refitting is the reverse of removal, tightening the retaining bolt to the specified torque. Ensure the wiring is correctly routed and retained by all the necessary clips and ties.

Camshaft sensor

67 Remove the plastic cover over the top of the engine.

68 Remove the air cleaner assembly and air intake duct as described in Section 2.

69 Disconnect the wiring connector, undo the retaining bolt and remove the sensor from the cylinder head.

70 Refitting is a reversal of removal.

Knock sensor

71 Remove the starter motor as described in Chapter 5A.

72 Disconnect the wiring block connector, so the wiring is free to be removed with the sensor.

73 Unscrew the retaining bolt and remove the sensor from the cylinder block **(see illustration 13.26)**.

74 On refitting ensure the mating surfaces are clean and dry then fit the sensor and tighten its retaining bolt to the specified torque. Ensure the wiring is correctly routed and retained by all the necessary clips and ties.

Electronic control unit (ECU)

Note: *If a new ECU is to be fitted, this work must be entrusted to a Vauxhall/Opel dealer or suitably-equipped specialist as it is necessary to programme the new ECU after installation. This work requires the use of dedicated Vauxhall/Opel diagnostic equipment or a compatible alternative.*

75 Disconnect the battery negative terminal (refer to *Disconnecting the battery* in the Reference Chapter).

76 Remove the plastic cover over the top of the engine.

77 Lift up the locking bars and disconnect the two ECU wiring connectors **(see illustration)**.

78 Undo the retaining bolt and disconnect the earth lead from the centre of the ECU.

79 Disconnect the wiring connector at the throttle body/housing and move the wiring harness clear of the ECU.

80 Undo the three retaining bolts and remove the ECU from the inlet manifold.

81 Refitting is a reversal of removal.

15 Inlet manifold –
removal and refitting

1.8 litre engines

Removal

1 Disconnect the battery negative terminal (refer to *Disconnecting the battery* in the Reference Chapter).
2 Remove the plastic cover over the top of the engine.
3 Drain the cooling system as described in Chapter 1A.
4 Remove the air cleaner assembly and air intake duct as described in Section 2.
5 Depressurise the fuel system as described in Section 5.
6 Remove the auxiliary drivebelt as described in Chapter 1A.
7 Remove the alternator as described in Chapter 5A.
8 Remove the fuel rail and injectors as described in Section 12.
9 Undo the two bolts and remove the inlet manifold support bracket.
10 Disconnect the remaining vacuum hoses, wiring connectors and auxiliary fittings to enable removal of the inlet manifold.
11 Slacken and remove the retaining nuts and manoeuvre the manifold assembly away from the engine. Remove the gasket and discard it. **Note:** *The manifold assembly must be treated as a sealed unit; do not attempt to dismantle it as no components, other than the switchover diaphragm and solenoid, are available separately.*

Refitting

12 Refitting is the reverse of removal noting the following.
   a) *Prior to refitting, check the manifold studs and renew any that are worn or damaged.*
   b) *Ensure the manifold and cylinder mating surfaces are clean and dry and fit the new gasket. Refit the manifold and tighten the retaining nuts evenly and progressively to the specified torque.*
   c) *Ensure that all relevant hoses are reconnected to their original positions, and are securely held (where necessary) by their retaining clips.*
   d) *On completion, top-up the coolant level as described in 'Weekly checks'.*

2.2 litre Z22SE engines

Removal

13 Disconnect the battery negative terminal (refer to *Disconnecting the battery* in the Reference Chapter).
14 Remove the plastic cover over the top of the engine.
15 Slacken the retaining clips securing the air intake duct to the airflow meter and throttle body/housing. Release the clip and disconnect the crankcase ventilation hose from the

camshaft cover. Detach the intake duct from the airflow meter and throttle body/housing, and remove the duct from the engine.
16 Remove the throttle body/housing as described in Section 9.
17 Remove the engine management electronic control unit as described in Section 13.
18 Unscrew the bolt securing the engine oil dipstick guide tube to the inlet manifold.
19 Remove the exhaust gas recirculation pipe by undoing the two nuts and detaching the engine cover bracket. Unscrew the two stud bolts, detach the retaining clip and remove the pipe. Recover the gasket.
20 Disconnect the brake servo vacuum pipe at the quick-release fitting.
21 Disconnect the wiring connector at the manifold absolute pressure sensor.
22 Undo the bolt and detach the engine management wiring harness bracket.
23 Disconnect any remaining wiring connectors and auxiliary fittings to enable removal of the inlet manifold.
24 Undo the five nuts and two bolts securing the inlet manifold to the cylinder head. Remove the manifold and recover the gaskets.

Refitting

25 Refitting is the reverse of removal noting the following.
   a) *Prior to refitting, check the manifold studs and renew any that are worn or damaged.*
   b) *Ensure the manifold and cylinder head mating surfaces are clean and dry and fit the new gasket. Refit the manifold and tighten the retaining nuts/bolts evenly and progressively to the specified torque.*
   c) *Renew all other disturbed gaskets and sealing rings.*
   d) *Ensure that all relevant hoses are reconnected to their original positions, and are securely held (where necessary) by their retaining clips.*

2.2 litre Z22YH engines

Removal

26 Disconnect the battery negative terminal (refer to *Disconnecting the battery* in the Reference Chapter).
27 Remove the plastic cover over the top of the engine.
28 Depressurise the fuel system as described in Section 5.
29 Slacken the retaining clips securing the air intake duct to the airflow meter and throttle body/housing. Detach the intake duct from the airflow meter and throttle body/housing, and remove the duct from the engine.
30 Remove the throttle body/housing as described in Section 9.
31 Remove the engine management electronic control unit as described in Section 14.
32 Unscrew the bolt securing the engine oil dipstick guide tube to the inlet manifold.
33 Remove the exhaust gas recirculation pipe by undoing the two nuts and detaching the engine cover bracket. Unscrew the two stud bolts, and undo the pipe support bracket bolt.

Undo the two bolts securing the pipe to the inlet manifold, and remove the pipe. Recover the gasket.
34 Release the clips securing the crankcase ventilation valve hoses to the camshaft cover and cylinder head **(see illustration 14.5a and 14.5b)**. Unclip the ventilation valve and remove it from the engine.
35 Disconnect the wiring harness connectors at the evaporative emission control purge valve, manifold absolute pressure sensor, inlet manifold switchover solenoid valve and the fuel pressure regulator. Unclip the wiring harness and move it to one side.
36 Firmly apply the handbrake, then jack up the front of the car and support it securely on axle stands (see *Jacking and vehicle support*).
37 Unclip the knock sensor wiring connector then remove the oil dipstick guide tube.
38 Undo the bolt securing the inlet manifold support bracket to the cylinder block.
39 Remove the auxiliary drivebelt as described in Chapter 1A.
40 Remove the alternator as described in Chapter 5A.
41 Disconnect the brake servo vacuum pipe at the quick-release fitting.
42 Undo the two retaining bolts and remove the fuel pressure regulator from the fuel rail **(see illustration 14.41)**. Be prepared for some loss of fuel. Remove the two sealing rings from the regulator.
43 Undo the seven bolts and two nuts securing the inlet manifold to the cylinder head. Remove the manifold from the cylinder head.
44 Remove the four switchover valves from the manifold ports, then remove the manifold gasket. Clean the mating surface and fit a new gasket, then refit the switchover valves.

Refitting

45 Refitting is the reverse of removal noting the following.
   a) *Ensure the cylinder head mating surface is clean and dry, refit the manifold and tighten the retaining bolts and nuts evenly and progressively to the specified torque.*
   b) *Renew the fuel pressure regulator sealing rings and the exhaust gas recirculation pipe gasket.*
   c) *Ensure that all relevant hoses are reconnected to their original positions, and are securely held (where necessary) by their retaining clips.*

16 Exhaust manifold –
removal and refitting

Note: *New manifold and exhaust front pipe retaining nuts will be required for refitting.*

1.8 litre engines

Removal

1 Disconnect the battery negative terminal (refer to *Disconnecting the battery* in the Reference Chapter).

17.7 Spray penetrating oil over the exhaust rubber mounting blocks in the area arrowed

2 Remove the plastic cover over the top of the engine.

3 Apply the handbrake, then jack up the front of the vehicle and support it on axle stands (see *Jacking and vehicle support*).

4 Undo the three retaining nuts and separate the exhaust front pipe from the exhaust manifold, taking care to support the flexible section. **Note:** *Angular movement in excess of 10° can cause permanent damage to the flexible section.* Recover the gasket.

5 Release the mounting rubbers and support the front of the exhaust front pipe to one side.

6 Trace the wiring back from the oxygen sensor (mixture regulation) and disconnect its wiring connector. Free the wiring from all the necessary clips and ties so the sensor is free to be removed with the manifold.

7 Drain the cooling system as described in Chapter 1A, or alternatively place a suitable container beneath the radiator top hose to collect escaping coolant. Release the retaining clip and disconnect the top hose from the thermostat housing.

8 Undo the three retaining bolts and remove the heat shield from the manifold.

9 Slacken and remove the ten retaining nuts, and manoeuvre the manifold out of the engine compartment. Recover the gasket.

Refitting

10 Examine all the exhaust manifold studs for signs of damage and corrosion; remove all traces of corrosion, and repair or renew any damaged studs.

17.8 Separate the exhaust front pipe from the exhaust manifold and recover the gasket

11 Ensure that the manifold and cylinder head sealing faces are clean and flat, and fit the new gasket.

12 Refit the manifold then fit the new retaining nuts and tighten them progressively, in a diagonal sequence, to the specified torque. Wait thirty seconds and tighten the nuts to the specified torque again.

13 Align the heat shield with the manifold, and tighten the screws to the specified torque.

14 Reconnect the exhaust front pipe, using a new gasket. Tighten the new nuts to the specified torque.

15 Reconnect the oxygen sensor wiring connector making sure the wiring is correctly routed and retained by all the necessary clips.

16 Refit the engine cover.

17 Reconnect the battery, then refill or top-up the cooling system as described in Chapter 1A, or *Weekly checks*, as applicable.

2.2 litre engines

Removal

18 Disconnect the battery negative terminal (refer to *Disconnecting the battery* in the Reference Chapter).

19 Remove the plastic cover over the top of the engine.

20 Apply the handbrake, then jack up the front of the vehicle and support it on axle stands (see *Jacking and vehicle support*).

21 Undo the three retaining nuts and separate the exhaust front pipe from the exhaust manifold, taking care to support the flexible section. **Note:** *Angular movement in excess of 10° can cause permanent damage to the flexible section.* Recover the gasket.

22 Release the mounting rubbers and support the front of the exhaust pipe to one side.

23 Disconnect the two oxygen sensor wiring connectors at the right-hand end of the cylinder head. Unclip the wiring harness from the support bracket.

24 Undo the nut and bolt and remove the right-hand engine lifting eye from the cylinder head.

25 Unbolt the heat shield from the exhaust manifold.

26 Slacken and remove the ten retaining nuts, and manoeuvre the manifold out of the engine compartment. Recover the gasket.

Refitting

27 Examine all the exhaust manifold studs for signs of damage and corrosion; remove all traces of corrosion, and repair or renew any damaged studs.

28 Ensure that the manifold and cylinder head sealing faces are clean and flat, and fit the new gasket.

29 Refit the manifold then fit the new retaining nuts and tighten them progressively, in a diagonal sequence, to the specified torque. Wait thirty seconds and tighten the nuts to the specified torque again.

30 Refit the heat shield and lifting eye, then reconnect the oxygen sensor wiring connectors.

31 Reconnect the exhaust front pipe, using a new gasket. Tighten the new nuts to the specified torque.

32 Refit the engine cover.

33 Lower the car to the ground and reconnect the battery.

---

17 Exhaust system – general information, removal and refitting

General information

1 The exhaust system consists of three sections: the front pipe which incorporates the oxygen sensor (catalytic converter control), the intermediate pipe and front silencer, and the tailpipe and rear silencer.

2 The front pipe is attached to the exhaust manifold (catalytic converter) by a flange joint secured by nuts. All other exhaust sections are joined by overlap joints which are secured by clamps. The system is suspended throughout its entire length by rubber mountings.

3 To remove an individual exhaust section, the complete system is first removed as a unit. The sections are then separated with the system off the car.

4 The manufacturers specify that if any of the exhaust sections are separated, the clamps must be renewed. As the clamps are attached to the exhaust sections by means of a spot weld at manufacture, it will be necessary to use a suitable grinder to remove the spot weld.

Complete system removal

5 To remove the system, first jack up the front and rear of the car and support it securely on axle stands. Alternatively, position the car over an inspection pit or on car ramps. The help of an assistant will be needed.

6 Trace the wiring back from the oxygen sensor, noting its correct routing, and disconnect its wiring connector. Free the wiring from any clips so the sensor is free to be removed with the system.

7 Spray some penetrating oil over the exhaust rubber mounting blocks so that the mounting blocks will slide easily on the exhaust and underbody hangers **(see illustration)**.

8 Undo the three retaining nuts and separate the exhaust front pipe from the exhaust manifold, taking care to support the flexible section. **Note:** *Angular movement in excess of 10° can cause permanent damage to the flexible section.* Recover the gasket **(see illustration)**.

9 Slide the front pipe rubber mounting blocks as far forward as possible. Move the exhaust system to the rear and disengage the front pipe hangers from the mounting blocks.

10 Move the exhaust system forward and disengage the intermediate pipe and tailpipe hangers from the rubber mounting blocks. Lower the system to the ground and slide it out from under the car.

Individual section removal

11 Remove the complete system as described previously.

12 Slacken and remove the nut from the relevant exhaust clamp retaining bolt. Apply liberal amounts of penetrating oil to the joint and tap around the joint and clamp with a hammer to free it. Twist the pipe to be removed in both directions while holding the adjacent pipe. Once the joint is free, pull the pipes apart.

13 Mark the position of the clamp on the pipe, so the new clamp can be fitted in the same position, then grind off the clamp retaining spot weld. Remove the clamp.

14 If the front pipe has been removed for renewal, refer to the procedures contained in Chapter 4C and transfer the oxygen sensor to the new pipe.

Catalytic converter removal

15 The catalytic converter is an integral part of the exhaust manifold and cannot be separated. Refer to Section 16 for exhaust manifold removal and refitting procedures.

Heat shield(s) removal

16 The heat shields are secured to the underside of the body by various nuts and threaded caps. Each shield can be removed once the relevant exhaust section has been removed. If a shield is being removed to gain access to a component located behind it, it may prove sufficient in some cases to remove the retaining nuts/caps, and simply lower the shield, without disturbing the exhaust system. If any of the threaded caps are damaged during removal, a suitable nut and washer can be used when refitting.

Refitting

17 Refitting is a reversal of the removal sequence, noting the following points:

a) *Ensure that all traces of corrosion have been removed from the system joints and renew all disturbed clamps.*

b) *Inspect the rubber mountings for signs of damage or deterioration, and renew as necessary.*

c) *When refitting the front pipe to the manifold (catalytic converter), use a new gasket and new retaining nuts, and tighten the nuts to the specified torque.*

d) *Prior to tightening the exhaust system clamps, ensure that all rubber mountings are correctly located, and that there is adequate clearance between the exhaust system and vehicle underbody. Tighten the clamp bolt retaining nuts securely.*

Notes

Chapter 4 Part B:
Fuel and exhaust systems – diesel engines

Contents

Degrees of difficulty

Easy, suitable for novice with little experience	**Fairly easy,** suitable for beginner with some experience	**Fairly difficult,** suitable for competent DIY mechanic	**Difficult,** suitable for experienced DIY mechanic	**Very difficult,** suitable for expert DIY or professional

Specifications

System type
1.9 litre engines . . . .   Bosch EDC 16C9 high-pressure direct injection 'common-rail' system, electronically-controlled
2.0 and 2.2 litre engines. . . . .   EDC PSG 16 direct injection system incorporating an electronically-controlled fuel injection pump

Fuel system data

1.9 litre engines
Firing order. . . . .   1–3–4–2 (No 1 at timing belt end of engine)
Fuel system operating pressure. . . . .   1400 bar at 2200 rpm
Idle speed. . . . .   Controlled by ECU
Maximum speed. . . . .   Controlled by ECU
High-pressure fuel pump:
    Type . . . .   Bosch CP1H
Fuel supply pump:
    Type . . . .   Electric, mounted in fuel tank
    Delivery pressure . . . .   3.3 bar (maximum)
Injectors:
    Type . . . .   Bosch CRIP 1-MI

2.0 and 2.2 litre engines
Firing order. . . . .   1–3–4–2 (No 1 at timing chain end of engine)
Idle speed. . . . .   Controlled by ECU
Maximum speed. . . . .   Controlled by ECU
Fuel injection pump:
    Type . . . .   Bosch VP44
    Pump timing (static) . . . .   Preset – controlled by ECU
Injectors:
    Opening pressure. . . . .   220 to 380 bar

Torque wrench settings

	Nm	lbf ft
1.9 litre engines		
Alternator and high-pressure fuel pump bracket bolts	25	18
Camshaft sensor retaining bolt(s).	9	7
Catalytic converter clamp bolt	20	15
Charge (boost) pressure sensor retaining bolts	9	7
Crankshaft sensor retaining bolt	9	7
ECU bracket lower mounting bolt:*		
Stage 1	80	59
Stage 2	Angle-tighten a further 120°	
Stage 3	Angle-tighten a further 15°	
EGR valve pipe to exhaust manifold	25	18
Exhaust manifold nuts*	25	18
Exhaust front pipe-to-catalytic converter nuts*	20	15
Fuel injector clamp bracket nuts:		
Z19DT engines	20	15
Z19DTH engines	25	18
Fuel pressure regulator to fuel rail	60	44
Fuel pressure sensor to fuel rail	70	52
Fuel rail retaining nuts/bolts	25	18
High-pressure fuel pipe unions:		
M12 union nuts	22	16
M14 union nuts	30	22
High-pressure fuel pump mounting bolts	25	18
Inlet manifold bolts	25	18
Injector clamp bracket nut	32	24
Throttle body/housing bolts:		
Z19DT engines	25	18
Z19DTH engines	9	7
Turbocharger oil return pipe bolts:		
M6 bolts	9	7
M8 bolts	25	18
Turbocharger oil supply pipe banjo union bolt	15	11
Vacuum reservoir to cylinder block	25	18
2.0 and 2.2 litre engines		
Auxiliary drivebelt tensioner assembly bolts:		
M8 bolt	20	15
M10 bolt	42	31
Camshaft sprocket bolt:*		
Stage 1	90	66
Stage 2	Angle-tighten a further 60°	
Stage 3	Angle-tighten a further 30°	
Charge (boost) pressure sensor bolt	8	6
Coolant temperature sensor	See Chapter 3	
Crankshaft sensor	8	6
Exhaust front pipe-to-turbocharger nuts	20	15
Exhaust manifold:		
Retaining nuts	22	16
Support bracket bolts	25	18
Fuel injection pump:		
Front mounting bolts	25	18
Fuel feed and return pipe union bolts	15	11
Rear mounting bracket bolts	20	15
Sprocket cover bolts	6	4
Sprocket retaining bolts	28	21
Fuel pipe union nuts	30	22
Inlet manifold:		
Lower section-to-cylinder head nuts*	22	16
Upper section-to-lower section bolts	8	6
Intake housing-to-inlet manifold bolts	8	6
Timing chain:		
Tensioner cap (upper and lower)	60	44
Upper chain guide bolts*	8	6

Torque wrench settings (continued)

	Nm	lbf ft
2.0 and 2.2 litre engines		
Turbocharger:		
Exhaust connection flange bolts	30	22
Oil feed pipe:		
Pipe-to-cylinder block union nut	20	15
Pipe-to-turbocharger union bolt...........................	20	15
Oil return pipe:		
Pipe-to-cylinder block union nut	20	15
Pipe-to-turbocharger bolts................................	8	6
Turbocharger-to-manifold bolts*...........................	30	22

* *Use new fasteners*

1 General information and precautions

General information

1.9 litre engines

1 1.9 litre engines are fitted with a high-pressure direct injection system which incorporates the very latest in diesel injection technology. On this system, a high-pressure fuel pump is used purely to provide the pressure required for the injection system and has no control over the injection timing (unlike conventional diesel injection systems). The injection timing is controlled by the electronic control unit (ECU) via the electrically-operated injectors. The system operates as follows.

2 The fuel system consists of a fuel tank (which is mounted under the rear of the car, with an electric fuel supply pump immersed in it), a fuel filter with integral water separator, a high-pressure fuel pump, injectors and associated components.

3 Fuel is supplied to the fuel filter housing which is located in the engine compartment. The fuel filter removes all foreign matter and water and ensures that the fuel supplied to the pump is clean. Excess fuel is returned from the outlet on the filter housing lid to the tank via the fuel cooler. The fuel cooler is fitted to the underside of the vehicle and is cooled by the passing airflow to ensure the fuel is cool before it enters the fuel tank.

4 The fuel is heated to ensure no problems occur when the ambient temperature is very low. This is achieved by an electrically-operated fuel heater incorporated in the filter housing, the heater is controlled by the ECU.

5 The high-pressure fuel pump is driven at half-crankshaft speed by the timing belt. The high pressure required in the system (up to 1350 bar) is produced by the three pistons in the pump. The high-pressure pump supplies high-pressure fuel to the fuel rail, which acts as a reservoir for the four injectors. Since the pump has no control over the injection timing, this means that there is no need to time the pump when installing the timing belt.

6 The electrical control system consists of the ECU, along with the following sensors:

 a) *Accelerator pedal position sensor –*
 informs the ECU of the accelerator pedal position, and the rate of throttle opening/ closing.
 b) *Coolant temperature sensor – informs the ECU of engine temperature.*
 c) *Airflow meter – informs the ECU of the amount of air passing through the intake duct.*
 d) *Crankshaft sensor – informs the ECU of the crankshaft position and speed of rotation.*
 e) *Camshaft sensor – informs the ECU of the positions of the pistons.*
 f) *Charge (boost) pressure sensor – informs ECU of the pressure in the inlet manifold.*
 g) *Fuel pressure sensor – informs the ECU of the fuel pressure present in the fuel rail.*
 h) *ABS control unit – informs the ECU of the vehicle speed.*

7 All the above signals are analysed by the ECU which selects the fuelling response appropriate to those values. The ECU controls the fuel injectors (varying the pulse width – the length of time the injectors are held open – to provide a richer or weaker mixture, as appropriate). The mixture is constantly varied by the ECU, to provide the best setting for cranking, starting (with either a hot or cold engine), warm-up, idle, cruising and acceleration.

8 The ECU also has full control over the fuel pressure present in the fuel rail via the high-pressure fuel regulator and third piston deactivator solenoid valve which are fitted to the high-pressure pump. To reduce the pressure, the ECU opens the high-pressure fuel regulator which allows the excess fuel to return direct to the tank from the pump. The third piston deactivator is used mainly to reduce the load on the engine, but can also be used to lower the fuel pressure. The deactivator solenoid valve relieves the fuel pressure from the third piston of the pump which results in only two of the pistons pressurising the fuel system.

9 The ECU also controls the exhaust gas recirculation (EGR) system, described in detail in Part C of this Chapter, the pre/post-heating system (see Chapter 5A), and the engine cooling fan.

10 The inlet manifold is fitted with a butterfly valve arrangement to improve efficiency at low engine speeds. Each cylinder has two intake tracts in the manifold, one of which is fitted with a valve; the operation of the valve is controlled by the ECU via an electric motor actuator drive arrangement. At low engine speeds (below approximately 1500 rpm) the valves remain closed, meaning that air entering each cylinder is passing through only one of the two manifold tracts. At higher engine speeds, the ECU opens up each of the four valves allowing the air passing through the manifold to pass through both inlet tracts.

11 A variable-vane turbocharger is fitted to increases engine efficiency. It does this by raising the pressure in the inlet manifold above atmospheric pressure. Instead of the air simply being sucked into the cylinders, it is forced in.

12 Between the turbocharger and the inlet manifold, the compressed air passes through an intercooler. This is an air-to-air heat exchanger and is mounted next to the radiator, and supplied with cooling air from the front of the vehicle. The purpose of the intercooler is to remove some of the heat gained in being compressed from the inlet air. Because cooler air is denser, removal of this heat further increases engine efficiency.

13 Energy for the operation of the turbocharger comes from the exhaust gas. The gas flows through a specially-shaped housing (the turbine housing) and in so doing, spins the turbine wheel. The turbine wheel is attached to a shaft, at the end of which is another vaned wheel known as the compressor wheel. The compressor wheel spins in its own housing, and compresses the inlet air on the way to the inlet manifold. The turbo shaft is pressure-lubricated by an oil feed pipe from the main oil gallery. The shaft 'floats' on a cushion of oil. A drain pipe returns the oil to the sump. Boost pressure (the pressure in the inlet manifold) is limited by a wastegate, which diverts the exhaust gas away from the turbine wheel in response to a pressure-sensitive actuator.

14 If certain sensors fail, and send abnormal signals to the ECU, the ECU has a back-up programme. In this event, the abnormal signals are ignored, and a preprogrammed value is substituted for the sensor signal, allowing the engine to continue running, albeit at reduced efficiency. If the ECU enters its back-up mode, a warning light on the instrument panel will illuminate, and a fault code will be stored in the ECU memory. This fault code can be read using suitable specialist test equipment plugged into the system's diagnostic socket.

1.14 The diagnostic socket is beneath the ashtray insert

The diagnostic socket is located in the centre console, beneath the ashtray insert **(see illustration)**.

2.0 and 2.2 litre engines

15 The fuel system consists of a rear-mounted fuel tank, a fuel filter with integral water separator, a fuel injection pump, injectors and associated components.

16 Fuel is drawn from the fuel tank by the fuel injection pump. Before reaching the pump, the fuel passes through a fuel filter, where foreign matter and water are removed. Excess fuel lubricates the moving components of the pump, and is then returned to the tank.

17 The fuel injection pump is driven at half crankshaft speed by the timing chain. The high pressure required to inject the fuel into the compressed air in the cylinder is achieved by a radial piston pump.

18 The injection pump is electronically-controlled to meet the latest emission standards. The system consists of the engine electronic control unit (ECU) and the following sensors.

a) *Accelerator pedal position sensor – informs the ECU of the accelerator pedal position.*

b) *Coolant temperature sensor – informs the ECU of engine temperature.*

c) *Intake air temperature sensor – informs the ECU of the temperature of the air passing through the intake duct. The sensor is integral with the airflow meter.*

d) *Oil temperature sensor – informs ECU of the temperature of the engine oil.*

e) *Airflow meter – informs the ECU of the amount of air passing through the intake duct.*

f) *Crankshaft sensor – informs the ECU of engine speed and crankshaft position.*

g) *Charge (boost) pressure sensor – informs ECU of the pressure in the inlet manifold.*

h) *ABS control unit – informs the ECU of the vehicle speed.*

i) *Atmospheric pressure sensor – informs the ECU of the atmospheric pressure.*

j) *Injection pump shaft sensor – used by the ECU to determine the exact injection timing.*

k) *Oil pressure switch – used by the engine ECU to control the instrument cluster oil warning lamp.*

19 All the above information is analysed by the ECU and, based on this, the ECU determines the appropriate injection requirements for the engine. The ECU controls the injection pump timing, to provide the best setting for cranking, starting (with either a hot or cold engine), warm-up, idle, cruising, and acceleration.

20 Basic injection timing is determined when the pump is fitted. When the engine is running, it is varied automatically to suit the prevailing engine speed by a mechanism which turns the cam plate or ring – controlled by the ECU.

21 The ECU also controls the exhaust gas recirculation (EGR) system (see Chapter 4C) and the preheating system (see Chapter 5A).

22 The four fuel injectors produce a spray of fuel directly into the cylinders. The injectors are calibrated to open and close at critical pressures to provide efficient and even combustion. Each injector needle is lubricated by fuel, which accumulates in the spring chamber and is channelled to the injection pump return hose by leak-off pipes.

23 The inlet manifold is fitted with a butterfly valve arrangement to improve efficiency at low engine speeds. Each cylinder has two intake tracts in the manifold, one of which is fitted with a valve; the operation of the valve is controlled by the ECU via a solenoid valve and vacuum diaphragm unit. At low engine speeds (below approximately 1500 rpm) the valves remain closed, meaning that air entering each cylinder is passing through only one of the two manifold tracts. At higher engine speeds, the ECU opens up each of the four valves allowing the air passing through the manifold to pass through both inlet tracts.

24 A variable-vane turbocharger is fitted to increase engine efficiency by raising the pressure in the inlet manifold above atmospheric pressure. Instead of the air simply being sucked into the cylinders, it is forced in. Additional fuel is supplied by the injection pump in proportion to the increased air intake.

25 Energy for the operation of the turbocharger comes from the exhaust gas. The gas flows through a specially-shaped housing (the turbine housing) and in so doing, spins the turbine wheel. The turbine wheel is attached to a shaft, at the end of which is another vaned wheel known as the compressor wheel. The compressor wheel spins in its own housing, and compresses the inlet air on the way to the inlet manifold.

26 Between the turbocharger and the inlet manifold, the compressed air passes through an intercooler. This is an air-to-air heat exchanger and is mounted next to the radiator, and supplied with cooling air from the front of the vehicle. The purpose of the intercooler is to remove some of the heat gained in being compressed from the inlet air. Because cooler air is denser, removal of this heat further increases engine efficiency.

27 Charge (boost) pressure which is the pressure in the inlet manifold, is limited by a wastegate. This diverts the exhaust gas away from the turbine wheel in response to a pressure-sensitive actuator.

28 The turbo shaft is pressure-lubricated by an oil feed pipe from the engine main oil so that the shaft 'floats' on a cushion of oil. A drain pipe returns the oil to the sump.

29 If certain sensors fail, and send abnormal signals to the ECU, the ECU has a back-up programme. In this event, the abnormal signals are ignored, and a preprogrammed value is substituted for the sensor signal, allowing the engine to continue running, albeit at reduced efficiency. If the ECU enters its back-up mode, a warning light on the instrument panel will illuminate, and a fault code will be stored in the ECU memory. This fault code can be read using suitable specialist test equipment plugged into the system's diagnostic socket. The diagnostic socket is located in the centre console, beneath the ashtray insert **(see illustration 1.14)**.

Precautions

⚠️ *Warning: It is necessary to take certain precautions when working on the fuel system components,* particularly the high-pressure side of the system. Before carrying out any operations on the fuel system, refer to the precautions given in 'Safety first!' at the beginning of this manual, and to any additional warning notes at the start of the relevant Sections. On 1.9 litre engines, also refer to the additional information contained in Section 2.

Caution: Do not operate the engine if any of air intake ducts are disconnected or the filter element is removed. Any debris entering the engine will cause severe damage to the turbocharger.

Caution: To prevent damage to the turbocharger, do not race the engine immediately after start-up, especially if it is cold. Allow it to idle smoothly to give the oil a few seconds to circulate around the turbocharger bearings. Always allow the engine to return to idle speed before switching it off – do not blip the throttle and switch off, as this will leave the turbo spinning without lubrication.

Caution: Observe the recommended intervals for oil and filter changing, and use a reputable oil of the specified quality. Neglect of oil changing, or use of inferior oil, can cause carbon formation on the turbo shaft, leading to subsequent failure.

2 High-pressure diesel injection system – special information

Warnings and precautions

1 On 1.9 litre engines, it is essential to observe strict precautions when working on the fuel system components, particularly the high-pressure side of the system. Before carrying out any operations on the fuel system, refer to the precautions given in *Safety first!* at the beginning of this manual, and to the following additional information.

• *Do not carry out any repair work on the high-pressure fuel system unless you are competent to do so, have all the necessary tools and equipment required, and are aware of the safety implications involved.*

• *Before starting any repair work on the fuel system, wait at least 30 seconds after switching off the engine to allow the fuel circuit to return to atmospheric pressure.*

• *Never work on the high-pressure fuel system with the engine running.*

• *Keep well clear of any possible source of fuel leakage, particularly when starting the engine after carrying out repair work. A leak in the system could cause an extremely high-pressure jet of fuel to escape, which could result in severe personal injury.*

• *Never place your hands or any part of your body near to a leak in the high-pressure fuel system.*

• *Do not use steam cleaning equipment or compressed air to clean the engine or any of the fuel system components.*

Repair procedures and general information

2 Strict cleanliness must be observed at all times when working on any part of the fuel system. This applies to the working area in general, the person doing the work, and the components being worked on.

3 Before working on the fuel system components, they must be thoroughly cleaned with a suitable degreasing fluid. Cleanliness is particularly important when working on the fuel system connections at the following components:

a) *Fuel filter.*
b) *High-pressure fuel pump.*
c) *Fuel rail.*
d) *Fuel injectors.*
e) *High-pressure fuel pipes.*

4 After disconnecting any fuel pipes or components, the open union or orifice must be immediately sealed to prevent the entry of dirt or foreign material. Plastic plugs and caps in various sizes are available in packs from motor factors and accessory outlets, and are particularly suitable for this application **(see illustration)**. Fingers cut from disposable rubber gloves should be used to protect components such as fuel pipes, fuel injectors and wiring connectors, and can be secured in place using elastic bands. Suitable gloves of this type are available at no cost from most petrol station forecourts.

5 Whenever any of the high-pressure fuel pipes are disconnected or removed, new pipe(s) must be obtained for refitting.

6 The torque wrench settings given in the Specifications must be strictly observed when tightening component mountings and connections. This is particularly important

2.4 Typical plastic plug and cap set for sealing disconnected fuel pipes and components

when tightening the high-pressure fuel pipe unions. To enable a torque wrench to be used on the fuel pipe unions, two crow-foot adapters are required. Suitable types are available from motor factors and accessory outlets **(see illustration)**.

3 Air cleaner assembly and intake ducts – removal and refitting

Removal

1 On 2.0 and 2.2 litre engines, detach the atmospheric pressure sensor and turbocharger wastegate solenoid mounting bracket from the rear of the air cleaner housing, by pulling it upwards.

2 Slacken the retaining clips securing the air intake duct to the airflow meter and

3.2 Slacken the clips (arrowed) securing the air intake duct to the airflow meter and turbocharger intake

3.4 Unclip the wiring harness from the side of the air cleaner housing

2.6 Two crow-foot adapters will be necessary for tightening the fuel pipe unions

turbocharger intake duct **(see illustration)**. Where applicable, release the clip and disconnect the crankcase ventilation hose from the camshaft cover. Detach the intake duct from the airflow meter and turbocharger intake duct and remove the duct from the engine.

3 Disconnect the wiring connector from the side of the airflow meter **(see illustration)**.

4 Unclip the wiring harness from the side of the air cleaner housing **(see illustration)**.

5 Lift up the inner rear corner of the filter housing to release the mounting grommet. Move the filter housing toward the engine to disengage the front and rear mounting rubbers, then release the air intake duct at the front **(see illustrations)**. Lift the filter housing out from the engine compartment.

6 The various air intake pipes/ducts linking the intercooler to the manifold and turbocharger

3.3 Disconnect the wiring connector from the airflow meter

3.5a Lift up the housing to release the mounting grommet (1) then move the housing to disengage the rear mounting rubber (2) . . .

3.5b ... and front mounting rubber (arrowed)

can be disconnected and removed once the retaining clips have been slackened. In some cases it will be necessary to disconnect breather hoses, vacuum pipes and wiring connectors to allow the pipe/duct to be removed; the pipe/duct may also be bolted to a support bracket

Refitting

7 Refitting is the reverse of removal, making sure all the air intake ducts/hoses are securely reconnected.

4 Accelerator pedal/ position sensor – removal and refitting

Refer to Chapter 4A, Section 3.

5 Fuel system – priming and bleeding

1 After disconnecting part of the fuel supply system or running out of fuel, it is necessary to prime the fuel system and bleed off any air which may have entered the system components, as follows.

1.9 litre engines

2 Operate the fuel supply pump by switching on the ignition three times for approximately 15 seconds. The engine should now start. If it doesn't, wait a few minutes and repeat the procedure.

9.2a Disconnect the heater element wiring connector from the fuel filter cover ...

2.0 and 2.2 litre engines

Note: *The Bosch VP44 fuel injection pump used on these engines is particularly susceptible to internal wear or damage if operated in a dry (unprimed) condition. The Vauxhall/Opel procedure for priming and bleeding is involved, and entails the use of the bleeder unit (KM-948). Theoretically, it should be possible to start the engine by cranking it on the starter motor in repeated short bursts, however internal damage **may** be caused to the pump. It is therefore up to the individual owner as to the course of action taken.*

3 To successfully prime and bleed the fuel system on these engines, the Vauxhall/Opel bleeder unit (KM-948) or a suitable alternative will be required. This unit is an electric pump with a series of adapters to enable it to be connected to the fuel return hose quick-release connectors. The unit is then connected to the battery and when switched on, draws fuel from the tank, through the filter and through the injection pump, before discharging the fuel back into the return line to the tank.

4 Assuming this equipment, or suitable alternative equipment is available, the procedure is as follows.

5 Disconnect the airflow meter wiring connector, then detach the atmospheric pressure sensor and turbocharger wastegate solenoid mounting bracket from the rear of the air cleaner housing by pulling it upwards. Move the sensor and solenoid valve to one side to gain access to the fuel pipe connectors.

6 Disconnect the fuel injection pump return pipe at the quick-release connector on the engine compartment bulkhead. Be prepared for some loss of fuel. A Vauxhall/Opel special tool is available to release the connector, but provided care is taken, it can be released using a pair of long-nosed pliers, or a similar tool, to depress the retaining tangs.

7 Attach the intake hose of KM-948 to the quick-release connector on the pump return pipe. Attach the delivery hose of KM-948 to the quick-release connector on the return pipe at the bulkhead.

8 Connect KM-948 to the battery, switch the unit on and allow it to run for approximately 3 minutes. This will provide a preliminary bleed of the system.

9 With KM-948 still connected and running, attempt to start the engine. Do not crank the engine for more than 40 seconds. If it doesn't start within this time, wait 20 seconds and try again. If the engine still doesn't start, wait a few minutes to allow the battery and starter motor to recuperate, then try again. Continue this process until the engine starts.

10 Once the engine starts, allow it to run for a few minutes, with KM-948 still connected and running.

11 Switch the engine off and switch KM-948 off. Disconnect KM-948 from the battery.

12 Disconnect the intake hose and delivery hose of KM-948 and reconnect the fuel

injection pump return pipe to the bulkhead connector.

13 Start the engine once more and check for fuel leaks.

14 On completion, refit the vacuum solenoid valve bracket and reconnect the airflow meter wiring connector.

6 Fuel gauge sender unit – removal and refitting

1 The fuel gauge sender unit can be removed as described in Chapter 4A, Section 6. **Note:** *On 2.0 and 2.2 litre engines, the fuel gauge sender unit does not have the fuel pump as part of the assembly, just a fuel pick-up filter.*

2 On completion, bleed the fuel system as described in Section 5.

7 Fuel supply pump (1.9 litre engines) – removal and refitting

1 On 1.9 litre engines, the diesel fuel supply pump is located in the same position as the fuel supply pump on petrol engine models, and the removal and refitting procedures are virtually identical. Refer to Chapter 4A, Section 7. On completion, bleed the fuel system as described in Section 5.

2 A fuel supply pump is not fitted to 2.0 and 2.2 litre engines.

8 Fuel tank – removal and refitting

1 Refer to Chapter 4A, Section 8, noting that there is no fuel filter clipped to the tank, and no charcoal canister.

2 On completion, bleed the fuel system as described in Section 5.

9 Fuel filter crash box – removal and refitting

1.9 litre engines

Removal

1 The fuel filter and crash box are located at the rear of the engine compartment, in the centre of the bulkhead.

2 Disconnect the heater element wiring connector from the fuel filter cover, and the water level sensor wiring connector from the base of the filter housing (see illustrations).

3 Using a screwdriver inserted from the right-hand side, depress the retaining clip and lift the filter from the crash box (see illustration).

4 Unclip the wiring harness from the side of the crash box.

5 Pull up the rubber weatherseal from the

9.2b . . . and the water level sensor wiring connector from the base of the filter housing

9.3 Lift the fuel filter from the crash box

9.5 Pull up the weatherseal from the flange at the rear of the engine compartment . . .

9.6 . . . then open the access cover in the water deflector

9.8 Remove the crash box from the bulkhead

9.11 Disconnect the heater element wiring connector (arrowed) from the fuel filter cover

flange at the rear of the engine compartment (see illustration).

6 Open the pollen filter access cover in the water deflector (see illustration).

7 Reach in through the pollen filter access cover and undo the three nuts securing the crash box to the bulkhead.

8 Remove the reinforcement plate and remove the crash box from the bulkhead (see illustration).

Refitting

9 Refitting is the reverse of the removal procedure.

2.0 and 2.2 litre engines

Removal

10 The fuel filter and crash box are located at the rear of the engine compartment, adjacent to the coolant expansion tank.

11 Disconnect the heater element wiring connector from the fuel filter cover (see illustration).

12 Tilt the coolant expansion tank upwards at the front and release it from its mounting bracket. Place the tank to one side.

13 Release the two fuel hoses from their retaining clips on the bulkhead.

14 Depress the retaining clip and lift the filter housing from the crash box.

15 Unclip the wiring harness from the side of the crash box.

16 Pull up the rubber weatherseal from the flange at the rear of the engine compartment (see illustration 9.5).

17 Open the pollen filter access cover in the water deflector (see illustration 9.6).

18 Reach in through the pollen filter access cover and undo the three nuts securing the crash box to the bulkhead.

19 Remove the reinforcement plate and remove the crash box from the bulkhead.

Refitting

20 Refitting is the reverse of the removal procedure.

---

10 Injection system electrical components (1.9 litre engines) – removal and refitting

Airflow meter

1 Slacken the retaining clip securing the air intake duct to the airflow meter and disconnect the duct (see illustration).

2 Disconnect the airflow meter wiring connector (see illustration 3.3).

10.1 Disconnect the air intake duct from the airflow meter

3 Slacken the retaining clip and remove the airflow meter from the air cleaner housing lid.

4 Refitting is a reversal of removal, but ensure that the arrow on the airflow meter points toward the throttle body/housing when fitted.

Throttle body/housing

Z19DT engines

5 Remove the plastic cover from the top of the engine.

6 Release the retaining clip and disconnect the charge air hose from the throttle body/housing.

7 Undo the four bolts and disconnect the metal EGR pipe from the EGR valve and throttle body/housing, noting its correct fitted position (see illustration). Recover the two gaskets.

8 Undo the three retaining bolts and remove the throttle body/housing from the inlet manifold. Note the location of any wiring

10.7 EGR pipe to EGR valve retaining bolts (arrowed)

10.11 Disconnect the charge air hose from the throttle body/housing, and intercooler charge air pipe

10.16 The crankshaft sensor (arrowed) is located below the starter motor

10.26 Camshaft sensor location (arrowed) – Z19DTH engines

harness support brackets also secured by the retaining bolts.

9 Refitting is a reversal of removal, but thoroughly clean the mating faces and use a new gasket/seal and new EGR pipe gaskets. Tighten the retaining bolts to the specified torque.

Z19DTH engines

10 Remove the plastic cover from the top of the engine.

11 Release the two retaining clips and disconnect the charge air hose from the throttle body/housing, and intercooler charge air pipe (see illustration).

12 Slacken the retaining clip and disconnect the crankcase ventilation hose from the oil filler housing.

13 Disconnect the wiring connector from the throttle body/housing.

14 Undo the three retaining bolts and remove the throttle body/housing from the inlet manifold. Note the location of any wiring harness support brackets also secured by the retaining bolts.

15 Refitting is a reversal of removal, but thoroughly clean the mating faces and use a new gasket/seal. Tighten the retaining bolts to the specified torque.

Crankshaft sensor

16 The sensor is located at the rear of the cylinder block, below the starter motor (see illustration). To gain access, firmly apply the handbrake, then jack up the front of the car and support it securely on axle stands (see *Jacking and vehicle support*).

17 Undo the ten retaining bolts and remove

the undertray from beneath the engine/transmission unit.

18 Wipe clean the area around the crankshaft sensor then disconnect the wiring connector.

19 Slacken and remove the retaining bolt and remove the sensor from the cylinder block. Recover the sealing ring.

20 Refitting is the reverse of removal, using a new sealing ring. Tighten the sensor retaining bolt to the specified torque.

Camshaft sensor

Z19DT engines

21 The camshaft sensor is located at the right-hand end of the cylinder head, behind the camshaft sprocket.

22 Remove the timing belt and camshaft sprocket as described in Chapter 2C.

23 Undo the two bolts securing the camshaft sensor bracket to the cylinder head.

24 Disconnect the sensor wiring connector, undo the two bolts and remove the sensor.

25 Refit the sensor using the reverse of removal, tightening the retaining bolts to the specified torque. Refit the camshaft sprocket and timing belt as described in Chapter 2C.

Z19DTH engines

26 The camshaft sensor is located at the right-hand end of the camshaft housing (see illustration). To gain access, remove the plastic cover from the top of the engine.

27 Wipe clean the area around the camshaft sensor then disconnect the wiring connector.

28 Slacken and remove the retaining bolt and remove the sensor from the camshaft cover. Recover the sealing ring.

29 Refitting is the reverse of removal, using a new sealing ring. Tighten the sensor retaining bolt to the specified torque.

Coolant temperature sensor

30 The coolant temperature sensor is located on the thermostat housing on the left-hand end of the cylinder head. Refer to Chapter 3 for removal and refitting details.

Charge (boost) pressure sensor

31 Remove the plastic cover from the top of the engine.

32 Disconnect the wiring connector from the charge pressure sensor located in the centre of the inlet manifold (see illustration).

33 Slacken and remove the retaining bolt and remove the sensor from the manifold. Recover the sealing ring.

34 Refitting is the reverse of removal, using a new sealing ring. Tighten the sensor retaining bolt to the specified torque.

Fuel pressure regulator

35 Disconnect the battery negative terminal (refer to *Disconnecting the battery* in the Reference Chapter).

36 Remove the plastic cover over the top of the engine.

37 On Z19DT engines, remove the fuel rail as described in Section 15.

38 On Z19DTH engines, disconnect the wiring connector from the fuel pressure regulator (see illustration).

39 Remove the regulator from the fuel rail by unscrewing the inner nut (nearest the fuel rail) while counterholding the regulator body with a second spanner. Be prepared for some fuel loss.

40 Refitting is the reverse of removal, tightening the regulator to the specified torque.

Fuel pressure sensor

41 Disconnect the battery negative terminal (refer to *Disconnecting the battery* in the Reference Chapter).

42 Remove the plastic cover over the top of the engine.

43 Disconnect the wiring connector at the fuel pressure sensor (see illustration).

44 Unscrew the sensor and remove it from the fuel rail. Be prepared for some loss of fuel.

45 Refitting is the reverse of removal, tightening the sensor to the specified torque.

10.32 Disconnect the wiring connector (arrowed) from the charge pressure sensor

10.38 Disconnect the wiring connector from the fuel pressure regulator – Z19DTH engines

10.43 Disconnect the fuel pressure sensor wiring connector

10.49a Undo the ECU mounting bracket lower retaining bolt . . .

10.49b . . . and upper retaining bolt (arrowed)

10.50a Release the locking clip . . .

10.50b . . . open the locking bar . . .

10.50c . . . and disconnect the ECU wiring connectors

Electronic control unit (ECU)

Note: *If a new ECU is to be fitted, this work must be entrusted to a Vauxhall/Opel dealer or suitably-equipped specialist as it is necessary to programme the new ECU after installation. This work requires the use of dedicated Vauxhall/Opel diagnostic equipment or a compatible alternative.*

46 Disconnect the battery negative terminal (refer to *Disconnecting the battery* in the Reference Chapter).

47 Firmly apply the handbrake, then jack up the front of the car and support it securely on axle stands (see *Jacking and vehicle support*).

48 Undo the three bolts and remove the access cover from under the front bumper on the right-hand side.

49 Undo the two ECU mounting bracket retaining bolts, noting that the larger bolt also secures the front subframe and must be renewed when refitting (**see illustrations**).

50 Release the locking clip, then open the locking bar and disconnect both wiring connectors from the ECU (**see illustrations**). Release the wiring harness from its cable ties and withdraw the ECU and mounting bracket from under the front wing.

51 Release the retaining catch and remove the ECU from the mounting bracket.

52 Refit the ECU to the mounting bracket, then locate the bracket in position under the front wing.

53 Refit the upper mounting bolt and the new lower mounting bolt. Tighten the upper mounting bolt securely, then tighten the lower mounting bolt to the specified torque, then through the specified angles.

54 Refit the access cover, then lower the car to the ground and reconnect the battery.

Turbocharger wastegate solenoid

55 The wastegate (charge pressure) solenoid valve is located at the front of the engine compartment above the radiator (**see illustration**).

56 Disconnect the wiring connector and the two vacuum hoses from the valve then undo the retaining nuts and remove the valve from its mounting bracket.

57 Refitting is the reverse of removal.

11 Injection system electrical components (2.0 and 2.2 litre engines) – removal and refitting

Airflow meter

1 Disconnect the wiring connector from the airflow meter (**see illustration**).

2 Slacken the retaining clip securing the air intake duct to the airflow meter and disconnect the duct (**see illustration**).

3 Slacken the retaining clip and remove the airflow meter from the air cleaner housing lid.

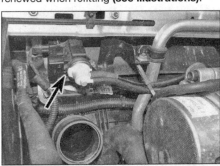

10.55 Turbocharger wastegate solenoid valve (arrowed)

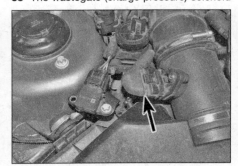

11.1 Disconnect the wiring connector (arrowed) from the airflow meter

11.2 Slacken the clip (arrowed) and disconnect the air intake duct from the airflow meter

11.9 Disconnect the wiring connector . . .

11.10 . . . then undo the bolt and remove the crankshaft sensor from the cylinder block (sealing ring arrowed)

11.14 Disconnect the wiring connector (arrowed) from the charge pressure sensor

11.20 Atmospheric pressure sensor location (arrowed)

11.25 The inlet manifold switchover solenoid (arrowed) is located above the radiator

11.28 Turbocharger wastegate solenoid valve location (arrowed)

4 Refitting is a reversal of removal, but ensure that the arrow on the airflow meter points toward the inlet manifold when fitted.

Crankshaft sensor

5 The crankshaft sensor is mounted on the front of the cylinder block below the oil filter.
6 Firmly apply the handbrake, then jack up the front of the car and support it securely on axle stands (see *Jacking and vehicle support*).
7 Undo the three retaining bolts and remove the plastic cover from the top of the engine.
8 Undo the retaining bolts and remove the undertray from beneath the engine/transmission unit.
9 Trace the wiring back from the crankshaft sensor to its wiring connector then free the connector from its bracket and disconnect it from the main harness (see illustration).
10 Wipe clean the area around the crankshaft sensor then slacken and remove the retaining bolt. Remove the sensor from the front of the cylinder block and recover the sealing ring (see illustration).
11 Refitting is the reverse of removal, using a new sealing ring. Tighten the sensor retaining bolt to the specified torque.

Coolant temperature sensor

12 The coolant temperature sensor is located on the right-hand end of the cylinder head, adjacent to the thermostat housing. Refer to Chapter 3 for removal and refitting details.

Charge (boost) pressure sensor

13 Undo the three retaining bolts and remove the plastic cover from the top of the engine.

14 Disconnect the wiring connector from the charge (boost) pressure sensor located in the intake housing on the inlet manifold (see illustration).
15 Slacken the clip and disconnect the charge air hose from the intake housing.
16 Disconnect the vacuum hose at the throttle valve vacuum unit (where fitted).
17 Undo the four bolts securing the intake housing to the top of the inlet manifold. Recover the engine cover bracket. Lift off the housing and remove the gasket.
18 Undo the retaining bolt and remove the sensor from the intake housing.
19 Refitting is the reverse of removal. Use a new gasket when refitting the intake housing and tighten the sensor and housing retaining bolts to the specified torque.

Atmospheric pressure sensor

20 The atmospheric pressure sensor is located in the right-hand rear corner of the engine compartment (see illustration).
21 Disconnect the wiring connector, then undo the retaining bolt and remove the sensor.
22 Refitting is the reverse of removal.

Oil temperature sensor

23 The oil temperature sensor is screwed into the front face of the sump. Refer to Chapter 5A for removal and refitting details.

Electronic control unit (ECU)

24 The control unit is an integral part of the injection pump and should not be disturbed. **Never** attempt to separate the control unit and pump.

Inlet manifold switchover solenoid

25 The switchover solenoid is located at the front of the engine compartment above the radiator (see illustration).
26 Disconnect the wiring connector and the two vacuum hoses from the valve then undo the retaining nuts and remove the valve from its mounting bracket.
27 Refitting is the reverse of removal.

Turbocharger wastegate solenoid

28 The wastegate (charge pressure) solenoid valve is located in the right-hand rear corner of the engine compartment (see illustration).
29 To gain access to the valve, slacken the clip and disconnect the intake duct from the airflow meter.
30 Disconnect the wiring connector and vacuum hoses from the valve then undo the retaining bolts and remove the valve from its mounting bracket.
31 Refitting is the reverse of removal.

---

12 High-pressure fuel pump (1.9 litre engines) – removal and refitting

⚠ *Warning: Refer to the information contained in Section 2 before proceeding.*

Z19DT engines

Note: *A complete new set of high-pressure fuel pipes will be required for refitting.*

Removal

1 Disconnect the battery negative terminal (refer to *Disconnecting the battery* in the Reference Chapter).
2 Remove the plastic cover over the top of the engine.
3 Remove the timing belt and the high-pressure fuel pump sprocket as described in Chapter 2C.
4 Remove the fuel rail as described in Section 15.
5 Disconnect the fuel return hose quick-release fitting on the top of the high-pressure fuel pump. Suitably plug or cover the open unions to prevent dirt entry.
6 Disconnect the wiring connector from the high-pressure fuel pump.
7 Unscrew the three retaining nuts and remove the pump from the engine bracket **(see illustrations)**.
Caution: The high-pressure fuel pump is manufactured to extremely close tolerances and must not be dismantled in any way. No parts for the pump are available separately and if the unit is in any way suspect, it must be renewed.

Refitting

8 Refit the pump to the engine bracket and tighten the retaining bolts to the specified torque.
9 Reconnect the pump wiring connector and the fuel return hose quick-release fitting.
10 Refit the fuel rail as described in Section 15.
11 Refit the high-pressure fuel pump sprocket and the timing belt as described in Chapter 2C.
12 Reconnect the battery negative terminal.
13 Observing the precautions listed in Section 2, prime the fuel system as described in Section 5, then start the engine and allow it to idle. Check for leaks at the high-pressure fuel pipe unions with the engine idling. If satisfactory, increase the engine speed to 4000 rpm and check again for leaks. Take the car for a short road test and check for leaks once again on return. If any leaks are detected, obtain and fit a new high-pressure fuel pipe.
14 Refit the engine cover on completion.

Z19DTH engines

Note: *A new fuel pump-to-fuel rail high-pressure fuel pipe will be required for refitting.*

Removal

15 Disconnect the battery negative terminal (refer to *Disconnecting the battery* in the Reference Chapter).
16 Remove the plastic cover over the top of the engine.
17 Remove the timing belt and the high-pressure fuel pump sprocket as described in Chapter 2D.
18 Release the retaining clips and disconnect the two fuel return hoses at the fuel return damping chamber **(see illustrations)**. Suitably plug or cover the open unions to prevent dirt entry.

12.7a Unscrew the three retaining nuts (arrowed) . . .

12.18a Release the clips and disconnect the upper (arrowed) . . .

19 Disconnect the injector leak-off pipe and the fuel return quick-release fitting, then undo the two bolts and remove the damping chamber. Suitably plug or cover the open unions to prevent dirt entry.
20 Disconnect the fuel return hose quick-release fitting on the top of the high-pressure fuel pump. Suitably plug or cover the open unions to prevent dirt entry.
21 Disconnect the wiring connector from the high-pressure fuel pump.
22 Thoroughly clean the fuel pipe unions on the fuel pump and fuel rail. Using an open-ended spanner, unscrew the union nuts securing the high-pressure fuel pipe to the fuel pump and fuel rail. Counterhold the union on the pump with a second spanner, while unscrewing the union nut **(see illustration)**. Withdraw the high-pressure fuel pipe and plug or cover the open unions to prevent dirt entry.
23 Unscrew the three retaining nuts and remove the pump from the engine bracket **(see illustrations 12.7a and 12.7b)**.
Caution: The high-pressure fuel pump is manufactured to extremely close tolerances and must not be dismantled in any way. No parts for the pump are available separately and if the unit is in any way suspect, it must be renewed.

Refitting

24 Refit the pump to the engine bracket and tighten the retaining bolts to the specified torque.
25 Remove the blanking plugs from the fuel pipe unions on the pump and fuel rail. Locate a new high-pressure fuel pipe over the unions

12.7b . . . and remove the high-pressure fuel pump from the engine bracket

12.18b . . . and lower (arrowed) fuel return hoses at the damping chamber

and screw on the union nuts finger-tight at this stage.
26 Using a torque wrench and crow-foot adapter, tighten the fuel pipe union nuts to the specified torque. Counterhold the unions on the pump with an open-ended spanner while tightening the union nuts.
27 Reconnect the pump wiring connector and the fuel return hose quick-release fitting.
28 Refit the damping chamber and tighten the retaining bolts securely. Reconnect the injector leak-off pipe, and the two remaining fuel return hoses.
29 Refit the high-pressure fuel pump sprocket and the timing belt as described in Chapter 2D.
30 Reconnect the battery negative terminal.
31 Observing the precautions listed in Section 2, prime the fuel system as described in Section 5, then start the engine and allow it to idle. Check for leaks at the high-pressure

12.22 Counterhold the fuel pipe union on the pump with a second spanner, while unscrewing the union nut

13.3 Undo the union bolts (arrowed) and disconnect the feed and return pipes from the pump

13.8 Slacken and remove the injection pump front mounting bolts (1) through the holes in the lower timing chain sprocket

fuel pipe unions with the engine idling. If satisfactory, increase the engine speed to 4000 rpm and check again for leaks. Take the car for a short road test and check for leaks once again on return. If any leaks are detected, obtain and fit a new high-pressure fuel pipe.

32 Refit the engine cover on completion.

13 Fuel injection pump (2.0 and 2.2 litre engines) – removal and refitting

Caution: Be careful not to allow dirt into the injection pump or injector pipes during this procedure.

Note 1: *Since it is necessary to remove the upper timing chain and sprockets to remove the injection pump, several special Vauxhall service tools (or suitable alternatives) will be required on refitting to enable the valve timing to be accurately adjusted (see Section 4 of Chapter 2E). If access to suitable tools cannot be gained then it is recommended that this task is entrusted to a Vauxhall/Opel dealer or suitably-equipped garage. If the task is to be carried out without the tools then accurate alignment marks must be made between the sprockets, camshaft and injection pump flange prior to removal. It is also likely that the special*

socket (MKM-604-30) will also be needed to unscrew the pump front mounting bolts.

Note 2: *A new camshaft sprocket bolt and upper timing chain guide bolts will be required on refitting.*

Note 3: *If a new pump is to be fitted, this work must be entrusted to a Vauxhall/Opel dealer or suitably-equipped specialist as it is necessary to programme the new ECU (integral with the pump) after installation. This work requires the use of dedicated Vauxhall/Opel diagnostic equipment or a compatible alternative.*

Removal

1 Remove the inlet manifold as described in Section 19.

2 Release the retaining clip, unclip the wiring harness and disconnect the coolant hose from the thermostat housing to the coolant pipe.

3 Remove all traces of dirt from around the injection pump fuel feed and return pipe unions. Disconnect the fuel leak-off hose, then slacken and remove the union bolts and sealing washers. Disconnect both pipes and position them clear of the pump **(see illustration)**.

4 Remove the upper timing chain and sprockets as described in Chapter 2E.

5 Unclip the wiring trough running along the front of the engine. Move the trough to one side.

6 Lift the locking levers and disconnect the two wiring connectors from the engine management ECU located on the injection pump. Disconnect the coolant temperature sensor wiring connector, unclip the wiring harness and move it to one side. Suitably cover the disconnected wiring connectors and the wiring sockets on the ECU.

7 Undo the two bolts and remove the wiring trough bracket from the oil filter housing.

8 Working through the holes in the lower timing chain sprocket, slacken and remove the pump front mounting bolts **(see illustration)**.

9 Slacken and remove the retaining bolts and remove the pump rear mounting bracket. Manoeuvre the pump out of position along with its sealing ring. Discard the sealing ring, a new one must be used on refitting **(see illustrations)**.

Caution: Never attempt to dismantle the pump assembly. If there is a problem, take the pump to a Vauxhall/Opel dealer or diesel injection specialist for testing/repair.

Refitting

10 Prior to refitting, ensure the timing cut-out in the pump sprocket flange is correctly aligned with the locating hole in the pump body and check that the camshaft and crankshaft are still correctly positioned.

11 Ensure the mating surfaces are clean and dry and fit a new sealing ring to the pump flange.

12 Manoeuvre the pump into position, engaging the lower timing chain sprocket with the pump flange. Refit the pump front mounting bolts and tighten them to the specified torque.

13 Refit the mounting bracket to the rear of the injection pump and tighten its retaining bolts to the specified torque.

14 Refit the wiring trough bracket, wiring trough and wiring connectors for the ECU and coolant temperature sensor.

15 Refit the upper timing chain and sprockets as described in Chapter 2E.

16 Position a new sealing washer on each

13.9a Slacken and remove the retaining bolts (arrowed – one hidden) and remove the rear mounting bracket . . .

13.9b . . . then remove the pump from the engine, noting the sealing ring

side of the injection pump feed and return pipe unions then refit the union bolts, tightening them to the specified torque.

17 Reconnect the coolant hose from the coolant pipe to the thermostat housing and clip the wiring harness back into position.

18 Refit the inlet manifold as described in Section 19.

19 Reconnect the battery then bleed the fuel system as described in Section 5.

20 Refill the cooling system as described in Chapter 1B.

14 Injection timing (2.0 and 2.2 litre engines) – checking methods and adjustment

1 The injection timing is determined by the ECU using the information supplied by the various sensors. Checking of the injection system can only be carried out using specialist diagnostic equipment.

15 Fuel rail (1.9 litre engines) – removal and refitting

⚠️ *Warning: Refer to the information contained in Section 2 before proceeding.*

Note: *A complete new set of high-pressure fuel pipes will be required for refitting.*

Z19DT engines

Removal

1 Disconnect the battery negative terminal (refer to *Disconnecting the battery* in the Reference Chapter).

2 Remove the plastic cover over the top of the engine.

3 Release the locking catches securing the wiring connectors to the four injectors, then disconnect the injector wiring.

4 Undo the two bolts at the top and the two bolts at the front securing the plastic wiring trough to the inlet manifold **(see illustrations)**. Move the wiring trough and injector wiring harness to one side.

5 Release the retaining clips and disconnect the two fuel return hoses at the fuel return damping chamber. Suitably plug or cover the open unions to prevent dirt entry.

6 Disconnect the injector leak-off pipe and the fuel return quick-release fitting, then undo the two bolts and remove the damping chamber. Suitably plug or cover the open unions to prevent dirt entry.

7 Thoroughly clean the fuel pipe unions on the fuel pump and fuel rail. Using an open-ended spanner, unscrew the union nuts securing the high-pressure fuel pipe to the fuel pump and fuel rail. Counterhold the unions on the pump with a second spanner, while unscrewing the union nuts. Withdraw the high-pressure fuel pipe and plug or cover the open unions to prevent dirt entry.

15.4a Undo the two bolts at the top (arrowed) . . .

8 Using two spanners, hold the unions and unscrew the union nuts securing the high-pressure fuel pipes to the fuel injectors. Unscrew the union nuts securing the high-pressure fuel pipes to the fuel rail, withdraw the pipes and plug or cover the open unions to prevent dirt entry.

9 Disconnect the wiring connectors at the fuel pressure regulator and fuel pressure sensor, then undo the two nuts and remove the fuel rail.

Refitting

10 Refit the fuel rail and tighten the retaining nuts to the specified torque. Reconnect the fuel pressure regulator and fuel pressure sensor wiring connectors.

11 Working on one fuel injector at a time, remove the blanking plugs from the fuel pipe unions on the fuel rail and the relevant injector. Locate the new high-pressure fuel pipe over the unions and screw on the union nuts finger-tight. Tighten the union nuts to the specified torque using a torque wrench and crow-foot adapter. Counterhold the union on the injector with an open-ended spanner, while tightening the union nut. Repeat this operation for the remaining three injectors.

12 Similarly, fit the new high-pressure fuel pipe to the fuel pump and fuel rail, and tighten the union nuts to the specified torque. Counterhold the union on the pump with an open-ended spanner, while tightening the union nut.

13 Refit the damping chamber and tighten the retaining bolts securely. Reconnect the injector leak-off pipe, and the fuel return hoses.

15.19 Unscrew the union nuts securing the high-pressure fuel pipes to the fuel rail and injectors

15.4b . . . and the two bolts at the front (arrowed) and move the wiring trough and harness to one side

14 Refit the wiring trough, and secure with the four retaining bolts. Reconnect the wiring connectors to the fuel injectors. Reconnect the battery negative terminal.

15 Observing the precautions listed in Section 2, prime the fuel system as described in Section 5, then start the engine and allow it to idle. Check for leaks at the high-pressure fuel pipe unions with the engine idling. If satisfactory, increase the engine speed to 4000 rpm and check again for leaks. Take the car for a short road test and check for leaks once again on return. If any leaks are detected, obtain and fit a new high-pressure fuel pipe.

16 Refit the engine cover on completion.

Z19DTH engines

Removal

17 Disconnect the battery negative terminal (refer to *Disconnecting the battery* in the Reference Chapter).

18 Remove the plastic cover over the top of the engine.

19 Thoroughly clean all the high-pressure fuel pipe unions on the fuel rail, fuel pump and injectors. Using two spanners, hold the unions and unscrew the union nuts securing the high-pressure fuel pipes to the fuel injectors. Unscrew the union nuts securing the high-pressure fuel pipes to the fuel rail, withdraw the pipes and plug or cover the open unions to prevent dirt entry **(see illustration)**.

20 Using an open-ended spanner, unscrew the union nuts securing the high-pressure fuel pipe to the fuel pump and fuel rail **(see illustration)**. Counterhold the unions on

15.20 Unscrew the union nuts securing the high-pressure fuel pipe to the fuel pump and fuel rail

15.21a Disconnect the fuel return hose . . .

15.21b . . . then undo the two bolts (arrowed) and remove the fuel rail

the pump with a second spanner, while unscrewing the union nuts. Withdraw the high-pressure fuel pipe and plug or cover the open unions to prevent dirt entry.

21 Disconnect the wiring connectors at the fuel pressure regulator and fuel pressure sensor, then release the clip and disconnect the fuel return hose. Undo the two bolts and remove the fuel rail **(see illustrations)**.

Refitting

22 Refit the fuel rail and tighten the retaining bolts to the specified torque. Reconnect the fuel pressure regulator and fuel pressure sensor wiring connectors, and reconnect the fuel return hose.

23 Working on one fuel injector at a time, remove the blanking plugs from the fuel pipe unions on the fuel rail and the relevant injector. Locate the new high-pressure fuel pipe over the unions and screw on the union nuts finger tight. Tighten the union nuts to the specified torque using a torque wrench and crow-foot adapter. Counterhold the union on the injector with an open-ended spanner while tightening the union nut. Repeat this operation for the remaining three injectors.

24 Similarly, fit the new high-pressure fuel pipe to the fuel pump and fuel rail, and tighten the union nuts to the specified torque. Counterhold the union on the pump with an open-ended spanner, while tightening the union nut.

25 Reconnect the battery negative terminal.

26 Observing the precautions listed in Section 2, prime the fuel system as described in Section 5, then start the engine and allow it

16.9 Remove the copper washer from the injector base

to idle. Check for leaks at the high-pressure fuel pipe unions with the engine idling. If satisfactory, increase the engine speed to 4000 rpm and check again for leaks. Take the car for a short road test and check for leaks once again on return. If any leaks are detected, obtain and fit a new high-pressure fuel pipe.

27 Refit the engine cover on completion.

16 Fuel injectors (1.9 litre engines) – removal and refitting

⚠ *Warning: Refer to the information contained in Section 2 before proceeding.*

Note 1: *A new copper washer, retaining nut and high-pressure fuel pipe will be required for each removed injector when refitting.*

Note 2: *The injector is an extremely tight fit in the cylinder head, and it is likely that the special Vauxhall/Opel puller (KM-328-B) and adapter (EN-46786) or suitable alternatives, will be needed.*

Z19DT engines

Removal

1 Disconnect the battery negative terminal (refer to *Disconnecting the battery* in the Reference Chapter).

2 Remove the plastic cover over the top of the engine.

3 Release the locking catches securing the wiring connectors to the four injectors, then disconnect the injector wiring.

4 Undo the two bolts at the top and the two bolts at the front securing the plastic wiring trough to the inlet manifold **(see illustrations 15.4a and 15.4b)**. Move the wiring trough and injector wiring harness to one side.

5 Thoroughly clean the fuel pipe unions on the fuel rail and injector. Using two spanners, hold the unions and unscrew the union nut securing the high-pressure fuel pipe to the fuel injector. Unscrew the union nut securing the high-pressure fuel pipe to the fuel rail, withdraw the pipe and plug or cover the open unions to prevent dirt entry.

6 Disconnect the fuel leak-off hose connection at each injector by pushing in the locking clip and lifting out the hose fitting. Suitably plug or cap the leak-off hose union on each injector,

and slip a plastic bag over the disconnected leak-off hose to prevent dirt entry.

7 Unscrew the retaining nut then remove the washer from the injector clamp bracket.

8 Withdraw the injector together with the clamp bracket from the cylinder head. If difficulty is experienced removing the injector, liberally apply penetrating oil to the base of the injector and allow time for the oil to penetrate. If the injector is still reluctant to free, it will be necessary to use a small slide hammer engaged under the flange of the injector body casting, and gently tap free. If available, use Vauxhall/Opel special tools EN-46786 and KM-328-B for this purpose. Note that it is not possible to twist the injector from side-to-side to free them due to the design of the clamp bracket.

9 Once the injector has been removed, separate it from the clamp bracket and remove the copper washer from the injector base **(see illustration)**. The copper washer may have remained in place at the base of the injector orifice in the cylinder head. If so, hook it out with a length of wire.

10 Remove the remaining injectors in the same way.

11 Examine the injector visually for any signs of obvious damage or deterioration. If any defects are apparent, renew the injector.

Caution: The injectors are manufactured to extremely close tolerances and must not be dismantled in any way. Do not unscrew the fuel pipe union on the side of the injector, or separate any parts of the injector body. Do not attempt to clean carbon deposits from the injector nozzle or carry out any form of ultrasonic or pressure testing.

12 If the injectors are in a satisfactory condition, plug the fuel pipe union (if not already done) and suitably cover the electrical element and the injector nozzle.

13 Prior to refitting, obtain a new copper washers a new retaining nut and new high-pressure fuel pipe for each injector.

Refitting

14 Thoroughly clean the injector seat in the cylinder head, ensuring all traces of carbon and other deposits are removed.

15 Locate a new copper washer on the base of the injector.

16 Place the injector clamp bracket in the slot on the injector body and refit the injector to the cylinder head.

17 Fit the washer and the new injector clamp bracket retaining nut and tighten the nut to the specified torque.

18 Remove the blanking plug from the fuel pipe union on the fuel rail and the injector. Locate the new high-pressure fuel pipe over the unions and screw on the union nuts. Take care not to cross-thread the nuts or strain the fuel pipe as it is fitted.

19 Tighten the fuel pipe union nuts to the specified torque using a torque wrench and crow-foot adapter **(see illustration 16.44)**.

16.28 Undo the two bolts (arrowed) and remove the breather pipe from the cylinder head

16.29a Release the locking catches . . .

16.29b . . . and disconnect the injector wiring connectors

16.30a Disconnect the fuel leak-off hose connection at each injector . . .

16.30b . . . then plug or cap the leak-off hose union on each injector

16.31 Counterhold the injector union when unscrewing the high-pressure fuel pipe unions

Counterhold the union on the injector with an open-ended spanner, while tightening the union nut.

20 Repeat this procedure for the remaining injectors.

21 Refit the wiring trough, and secure with the four retaining bolts. Reconnect the wiring connectors to the fuel injectors.

22 Reconnect the leak-off hose fittings to the injectors by pushing in the locking clip, attaching the fitting, then releasing the locking clip. Ensure that each fitting is securely connected and retained by the clip.

23 Reconnect the battery negative terminal.

24 Observing the precautions listed in Section 2, prime the fuel system as described in Section 5, then start the engine and allow it to idle. Check for leaks at the high-pressure fuel pipe unions with the engine idling. If satisfactory, increase the engine speed to 4000 rpm and check again for leaks. Take the car for a short road test and check for leaks once again on return. If any leaks are detected, obtain and fit a new high-pressure fuel pipe.

25 Refit the engine cover on completion.

Z19DTH engines

Removal

26 Disconnect the battery negative terminal (refer to *Disconnecting the battery* in the Reference Chapter).

27 Remove the plastic cover over the top of the engine.

28 Release the retaining clip securing the engine breather hose to the breather pipe

adjacent to the engine oil dipstick. Undo the two bolts securing the breather pipe to the cylinder head, and disconnect the pipe from the hose **(see illustration)**.

29 Release the locking catches securing the wiring connectors to the four injectors, then disconnect the injector wiring **(see illustrations)**.

30 Disconnect the fuel leak-off hose connection at each injector by pushing in the locking clip and lifting out the hose fitting. Suitably plug or cap the leak-off hose union on each injector, and slip a plastic bag over the disconnected leak-off hose to prevent dirt entry **(see illustrations)**.

31 Thoroughly clean the fuel pipe unions on the fuel rail and injector. Using two spanners, hold the unions and unscrew the union nut securing the high-pressure fuel pipe to the fuel injector **(see illustration)**. Unscrew the union nut securing the high-pressure fuel pipe

to the fuel rail, withdraw the pipe and plug or cover the open unions to prevent dirt entry.

32 Starting with injector No 1, unscrew the retaining nut then remove the washer from the injector clamp bracket **(see illustration)**.

33 Withdraw the injector together with the clamp bracket from the cylinder head. If difficulty is experienced removing the injector, liberally apply penetrating oil to the base of the injector and allow time for the oil to penetrate. If the injector is still reluctant to free, it will be necessary to use a small slide hammer engaged under the flange of the injector body casting, and gently tap it free **(see illustration)**. If available, use Vauxhall/Opel special tools EN-46786 and KM-328-B for this purpose. Note that it is not possible to twist the injector from side-to-side to free them due to the design of the clamp bracket.

34 Once the injector has been removed, separate it from the clamp bracket and remove

16.32 Unscrew the injector clamp bracket retaining nut then remove the washer

16.33 Using a small slide hammer to free the injector body from the cylinder head

16.34 Once the injector has been removed, separate it from the clamp bracket

16.42a Fit the washer . . .

16.42b . . . and the injector clamp bracket retaining nut

16.44 Tighten the fuel pipe union nuts to the specified torque using a torque wrench and crow-foot adapter

the copper washer from the injector base **(see illustration)**. The copper washer may have remained in place at the base of the injector orifice in the cylinder head. If so, hook it out with a length of wire.

35 Remove the remaining injectors in the same way.

36 Examine the injector visually for any signs of obvious damage or deterioration. If any defects are apparent, renew the injector.

Caution: The injectors are manufactured to extremely close tolerances and must not be dismantled in any way. Do not unscrew the fuel pipe union on the side of the injector, or separate any parts of the injector body. Do not attempt to clean carbon deposits from the injector nozzle or carry out any form of ultrasonic or pressure testing.

37 If the injectors are in a satisfactory

17.4 Remove the injector crossover pipe from the cylinder head (sealing ring arrowed) . . .

condition, plug the fuel pipe union (if not already done) and suitably cover the electrical element and the injector nozzle.

38 Prior to refitting, obtain a new set of copper washers, retaining nuts and high-pressure fuel pipes.

Refitting

39 Thoroughly clean the injector seat in the cylinder head, ensuring all traces of carbon and other deposits are removed.

40 Starting with injector No 4, locate a new copper washer on the base of the injector.

41 Place the injector clamp bracket in the slot on the injector body and refit the injector to the cylinder head.

42 Fit the washer and the injector clamp bracket retaining nut and tighten the nut to the specified torque **(see illustrations)**.

43 Remove the blanking plug from the fuel pipe union on the fuel rail and the injector. Locate the new high-pressure fuel pipe over the unions and screw on the union nuts. Take care not to cross-thread the nuts or strain the fuel pipe as it is fitted.

44 Tighten the fuel pipe union nuts to the specified torque using a torque wrench and crow-foot adapter **(see illustration)**. Counterhold the union on the injector with an open-ended spanner, while tightening the union nut.

45 Repeat this procedure for the remaining injectors.

46 Reconnect the leak-off hose fittings to the injectors by pushing in the locking clip, attaching the fitting, then releasing the locking

clip. Ensure that each fitting is securely connected and retained by the clip.

47 Reconnect the wiring connectors to the fuel injectors.

48 Attach the engine breather hose to the breather pipe and secure with the retaining clip. Secure the breather pipe to the cylinder head with the two bolts securely tightened.

49 Reconnect the battery negative terminal.

50 Observing the precautions listed in Section 2, prime the fuel system as described in Section 5, then start the engine and allow it to idle. Check for leaks at the high-pressure fuel pipe unions with the engine idling. If satisfactory, increase the engine speed to 4000 rpm and check again for leaks. Take the car for a short road test and check for leaks once again on return. If any leaks are detected, obtain and fit a new high-pressure fuel pipe.

51 Refit the engine cover on completion.

17 Fuel injectors (2.0 and 2.2 litre engines) – removal and refitting

⚠️ *Warning: Exercise extreme caution when working on the fuel injectors. Never expose the hands or any part of the body to injector spray, as the high working pressure can cause the fuel to penetrate the skin, with possibly fatal results. You are strongly advised to have any work which involves testing the injectors under pressure carried out by a dealer or fuel injection specialist.*

Caution: Be careful not to allow dirt into the injection pump, injectors or pipes during this procedure.

Caution: Take care not to drop the injectors, or allow the needles at their tips to become damaged. The injectors are precision-made to fine limits, and must not be handled roughly. In particular, never mount them in a bench vice.

Note: If the injector nozzle is to be removed from the cylinder head, it is likely that the special Vauxhall/Opel puller (KM-328-B) and adapter (KM-931) will be needed. New injector crossover pipe bolts should be used on refitting.

Removal

1 Remove the upper section of the inlet manifold as described in Section 19.

2 Remove the camshaft and followers as described in Chapter 2E.

3 Disconnect the return pipe from the injector crossover pipe.

4 Unscrew the retaining bolt then carefully free the crossover pipe from the top of the injector nozzle and ease it from the cylinder head **(see illustration)**.

5 Remove the sealing rings from the crossover pipe and the top of the injector nozzle and discard, new ones must be used on refitting **(see illustration)**.

6 Fit the adapter and puller (KM-328-B and

17.5 . . . then remove the sealing ring from the top of the injector nozzle

17.7a Fit a new sealing washer to the base of the nozzle . . .

17.7b . . . then refit the nozzle to the cylinder head, aligning its locating pin with the head cut-out (arrowed)

KM-931) to the top of the injector nozzle and carefully pull the nozzle squarely out of the top of the cylinder head. Recover the sealing washer which is fitted to the base of the nozzle and discard it.

Refitting

7 Fit a new sealing washer to the base of the injector nozzle then carefully ease the nozzle into position in the cylinder head, aligning its locating pin with the cylinder head cut-out **(see illustrations)**.

8 Ensure the injector nozzle is pushed fully into the cylinder head then fit a new sealing ring to its upper end.

9 Fit a new sealing ring to the crossover pipe recess. Ease the crossover pipe into position in the cylinder head, seating it correctly on the top of the injector nozzle, and fit the new retaining bolt. Tighten the retaining bolt as tight as possible by hand, then using a socket and extension bar, tighten it through a further complete rotation (360º).

10 Connect the return pipe to the crossover pipe then refit the inlet manifold section as described in Section 19.

11 Refit the camshaft and followers as described in Chapter 2E.

12 On completion bleed the fuel system as described in Section 5.

18 Inlet manifold (1.9 litre engines) – removal and refitting

Z19DT engines

Removal

1 Disconnect the battery negative terminal (refer to *Disconnecting the battery* in the Reference Chapter).

2 Remove the plastic cover over the top of the engine.

3 Drain the cooling system as described in Chapter 1B.

4 Remove the exhaust gas recirculation (EGR) valve as described in Chapter 4C.

5 Remove the high-pressure fuel pump as described in Section 12.

6 Undo the retaining bolt(s) to release the vacuum lines running over the top of the camshaft cover **(see illustration)**.

7 Remove the throttle body/housing as described in Section 10.

8 Disconnect the wiring connectors at the four glow plugs.

9 Undo the three retaining bolts and detach the vacuum reservoir from the rear of the cylinder block.

10 Release the retaining clips and disconnect the two coolant hoses at the EGR heat exchanger, and the adjacent hose at the thermostat housing.

11 Unscrew the nut and two bolts securing the coolant pipes to the starter motor bracket.

12 Release the clamp and disconnect the metal pipe from the EGR heat exchanger. Undo the retaining nut and bolt and remove the heat exchanger.

13 Remove the alternator as described in Chapter 5A.

14 Undo the six bolts securing the alternator and high-pressure fuel pump mounting bracket to the cylinder block and cylinder head. There are five bolts securing the bracket to the block at the rear, and one securing the bracket to the head at the front.

15 Undo the nine retaining nuts and remove the inlet manifold from the cylinder head studs. Recover the gasket.

Refitting

16 Thoroughly clean the inlet manifold and cylinder head mating faces, then locate a new gasket on the inlet manifold flange.

17 Locate the manifold in position and refit the retaining nuts. Diagonally and progressively, tighten the nuts to the specified torque.

18 Refit the alternator and high-pressure fuel pump bracket and tighten the retaining bolts to the specified torque.

19 Refit the alternator as described in Chapter 5A.

20 Refit the EGR heat exchanger and securely tighten the retaining nut and bolt. Reconnect the metal EGR pipe and secure with the retaining clamp.

21 Locate the coolant pipe on the starter motor bracket. Refit and securely tighten the retaining nut and bolts.

22 Reconnect the coolant hoses to the EGR heat exchanger and thermostat housing and secure with the retaining clips.

23 Attach the vacuum reservoir to the cylinder

block, refit the three retaining bolts and tighten to the specified torque.

24 Reconnect the wiring connectors to the glow plugs.

25 Refit the throttle body/housing as described in Section 10.

26 Refit the vacuum lines running over the top of the camshaft cover and reconnect the vacuum hoses.

27 Refit the high-pressure fuel pump as described in Section 12.

28 Refit the exhaust gas recirculation (EGR) valve as described in Chapter 4C.

29 Refill the cooling system as described in Chapter 1B.

30 Reconnect the battery negative terminal.

31 Observing the precautions listed in Section 2, prime the fuel system as described in Section 5, then start the engine and allow it to idle. Check for leaks at the high-pressure fuel pipe unions with the engine idling. If satisfactory, increase the engine speed to 4000 rpm and check again for leaks. Take the car for a short road test and check for leaks once again on return. If any leaks are detected, obtain and fit a new high-pressure fuel pipe.

32 Refit the engine cover on completion.

Z19DTH engines

Removal

33 Disconnect the battery negative terminal (refer to *Disconnecting the battery* in the Reference Chapter).

34 Remove the plastic cover over the top of the engine.

18.6 Undo the retaining bolt(s) to release the vacuum lines from the camshaft cover

18.39 Unscrew the two nuts and free the wiring harness and coolant pipes from the starter motor bracket

18.41a Undo the two nuts (arrowed) above the vacuum reservoir . . .

18.41b . . . the bolt at the base of the vacuum reservoir . . .

18.41c . . . and the bolt at the right-hand side of the oil separator . . .

18.41d . . . then remove the mounting bracket complete with oil separator and vacuum reservoir

18.43 Lock two nuts together and unscrew the fuel pump stud from the engine bracket

35 Remove the fuel filter crash box as described in Section 9.

36 Remove the high-pressure fuel pump as described in Section 12.

37 Remove the exhaust gas recirculation (EGR) valve as described in Chapter 4C.

38 Disconnect the four vacuum hoses then undo the bolt(s) and remove the two vacuum pipes over the top of the inlet manifold.

39 Unscrew the two nuts securing the wiring harness and coolant pipes to the starter motor bracket. Free the harness and pipes from the bracket **(see illustration)**.

40 Release the clips and disconnect the crankcase breather hoses from the top and bottom of the oil separator.

41 Remove the oil separator and vacuum reservoir mounting bracket by undoing the two nuts above the vacuum reservoir, the bolt at the base of the vacuum reservoir, and the

bolt at the right-hand side of the oil separator. Remove the mounting bracket complete with oil separator and vacuum reservoir **(see illustration)**.

42 Undo the three bolts, release the hose clip, free the wiring harness and detach the coolant pipe from the inlet manifold.

43 Screw two nuts onto the inner high-pressure fuel pump mounting stud. Lock the two nuts together and unscrew the stud from the engine bracket **(see illustration)**.

44 Disconnect the wiring connectors at the throttle body/housing and charge (boost) pressure sensor.

45 Undo the nine retaining nuts and remove the inlet manifold from the cylinder head studs **(see illustration)**. Recover the gasket.

46 With the manifold removed, if required, remove the throttle body/housing with reference to Section 10.

47 The changeover flap actuator drive can be removed by disconnecting the drive motor actuating rod ball socket, and undoing the two stud bolts.

Refitting

48 If removed, refit the throttle body/housing with reference to Section 10, then refit the changeover flap actuator drive.

49 Thoroughly clean the inlet manifold and cylinder head mating faces, then locate a new gasket on the inlet manifold flange.

50 Locate the manifold in position and refit the retaining nuts. Diagonally and progressively, tighten the nuts to the specified torque.

51 Reconnect the wiring connectors at the

18.45 Inlet manifold retaining nuts (arrowed)

throttle body/housing and charge (boost) pressure sensor.

52 Refit the high-pressure fuel pump mounting stud, then remove the two nuts used to remove/refit the stud.

53 Refit the coolant pipe to the manifold, and secure with the three bolts tightened securely. Reconnect the coolant pipe and attach the wiring harness.

54 Refit the oil separator and vacuum reservoir mounting bracket. Refit and tighten the two bolts and two nuts, then reconnect the crankcase breather hoses.

55 Refit the coolant pipe and wiring harness to the starter motor bracket, then refit and tighten the two nuts.

56 Refit the vacuum pipes over the manifold and reconnect the four vacuum pipes.

57 Refit the exhaust gas recirculation (EGR) valve as described in Chapter 4C.

58 Refit the high-pressure fuel pump as described in Section 12.

59 Refit the fuel filter crash box as described in Section 9.

60 Reconnect the battery negative terminal.

61 Observing the precautions listed in Section 2, prime the fuel system as described in Section 5, then start the engine and allow it to idle. Check for leaks at the high-pressure fuel pipe unions with the engine idling. If satisfactory, increase the engine speed to 4000 rpm and check again for leaks. Take the car for a short road test and check for leaks once again on return. If any leaks are detected, obtain and fit a new high-pressure fuel pipe.

62 Refit the engine cover on completion.

19.9a Slacken the union nuts securing the injector pipes to the injectors . . .

19.9b . . . and injection pump

19.11a Disconnect the vacuum pipe from the manifold switchover valve . . .

19 Inlet manifold (2.0 and 2.2 litre engines) – removal and refitting

Note: *New lower manifold section retaining nuts will be required on refitting.*

Removal

1 Disconnect the battery negative terminal (refer to *Disconnecting the battery* in the Reference Chapter).
2 Remove the plastic cover over the top of the engine.
3 Slacken the two retaining clips and disconnect the charge air hose from the intake housing on the inlet manifold and from the intercooler left-hand charge air pipe. Similarly slacken the clips and disconnect the charge air hose from the charge air pipe on the camshaft cover and from the intercooler right-hand charge air pipe.
4 Disconnect the wiring connector from the charge (boost) pressure sensor located in the intake housing on the inlet manifold **(see illustration 11.14)**.
5 Disconnect the vacuum hose at the throttle valve vacuum unit (where fitted).
6 Undo the four bolts securing the intake housing to the top of the inlet manifold. Recover the engine cover bracket. Lift off the housing and remove the gasket.
7 Disconnect the EGR valve wiring connector.
8 Place a suitable container beneath the EGR valve. Be prepared for coolant spillage, then slacken the retaining clips and disconnect the two coolant hoses from the EGR valve. Plug the valve and hoses to prevent further coolant loss.
9 Wipe clean the pipe unions then slacken the union nuts securing the injector pipes to the injectors and the four union nuts securing the pipes to the rear of the injection pump; as each pump union nut is slackened, retain the adapter with a suitable open-ended spanner to prevent it being unscrewed from the pump. With all the union nuts undone, remove the injector pipes from the engine unit and mop up any spilt fuel **(see illustrations)**. Seal the pipe end fittings to minimise fuel loss and prevent the entry of dirt.
10 Evenly and progressively slacken and

19.11b . . . then remove the bolt securing the crankshaft sensor wiring to the manifold lower section

remove the retaining bolts then lift off the upper part of the manifold. Recover the gasket and discard it.
11 To remove the lower section of the manifold, disconnect the vacuum pipe from the manifold switchover valve diaphragm unit and unbolt the wiring connector bracket from the manifold. Evenly and progressively slacken and remove the retaining nuts then remove the manifold lower section and gasket from the cylinder head **(see illustrations)**. Note that new retaining nuts will be required for refitting.

Refitting

12 Ensure that all mating surfaces are clean and dry.
13 Fit a new gasket to the cylinder head then refit the lower manifold section. Fit the new retaining nuts and, working in a diagonal sequence, evenly and progressively tighten them to the specified torque. Reconnect the switchover valve hose and refit the wiring bracket.
14 Fit a new gasket to the top of the manifold lower section then refit the upper section of the manifold, tightening its retaining bolts to the specified torque.
15 Refit the injector pipes, tightening the union nuts to the specified torque.
16 Reconnect the coolant hoses and wiring connector to the EGR valve.
17 Using a new gasket, refit the intake housing to the inlet manifold and tighten the retaining bolts to the specified torque. Where fitted, reconnect the vacuum hose to the throttle valve vacuum unit.

19.11c Unscrew the retaining nuts and remove the inlet manifold lower section from the engine

18 Reconnect the charge (boost) pressure sensor wiring connector.
19 Refit the two charge air hoses and tighten their retaining clips securely.
20 Refit the plastic cover to the cylinder head.
21 Top-up the cooling system as described in *Weekly checks*.
22 Reconnect the battery then bleed the fuel system as described in Section 5.

20 Inlet manifold changeover flap actuator drive (Z19DTH engines) – removal and refitting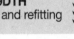

Removal

1 Disconnect the battery negative terminal (refer to *Disconnecting the battery* in the Reference Chapter).
2 Remove the plastic cover over the top of the engine.
3 Remove the fuel filter crash box as described in Section 9.
4 Disconnect the four vacuum hoses then undo the bolt(s) and remove the two vacuum pipes over the top of the inlet manifold.
5 Unscrew the two nuts securing the wiring harness and coolant pipes to the starter motor bracket. Free the harness and pipes from the bracket **(see illustration 18.39)**.
6 Release the clips and disconnect the crankcase breather hoses from the top and bottom of the oil separator.
7 Remove the oil separator and vacuum

20.8 Disconnect the actuating rod ball socket (A), undo the two stud bolts (B) and remove the actuator drive

reservoir mounting bracket by undoing the two nuts above the vacuum reservoir, the bolt at the base of the vacuum reservoir, and the bolt at the right-hand side of the oil separator. Remove the mounting bracket complete

with oil separator and vacuum reservoir **(see illustrations 18.41a to 18.41d)**.

8 Disconnect the drive motor actuating rod ball socket, and undoing the two stud bolts **(see illustration)**.

9 Withdraw the assembly from the inlet manifold and disconnect the wiring connector.

Refitting

10 Refitting is the reverse of removal.

21 Intercooler – removal and refitting

Removal

1 Disconnect the battery negative terminal (refer to *Disconnecting the battery* in the Reference Chapter).

2 Remove the plastic cover from the top of the engine.

3 Apply the handbrake, then jack up the front of the vehicle and support it on axle stands (see *Jacking and vehicle support*).

4 Remove the front bumper as described in Chapter 11.

5 Slacken (but do not remove) the two bolts securing the radiator left-hand and right-hand mounting brackets to the subframe **(see illustrations)**.

6 Release the radiator upper rubber mounting bushes on each side from their guides, and carefully move the top of the radiator forward.

7 On models with air conditioning, undo the bolt each side securing the condenser upper mounting brackets to the intercooler **(see illustration)**. Carefully lift up or remove the plastic panels on each side of the radiator for improved access, if necessary.

8 Carefully lift the condenser upwards, disengage the lower mounting lugs from the intercooler and secure the condenser to the upper body panel using cable ties or similar **(see illustration)**.

9 Slacken the retaining clips and remove the left-hand and right-hand lower charge air hoses from the intercooler and charge air pipes **(see illustrations)**.

10 Undo the bolt each side securing the intercooler upper mounting brackets to the radiator **(see illustration)**.

11 Carefully lift the intercooler upwards, disengage the lower mounting lugs from the radiator, then lower the intercooler down and remove it from under the car **(see illustration)**.

21.5a Slacken the bolt (arrowed) securing the radiator left-hand . . .

21.5b . . . and right-hand mounting brackets to the subframe

21.7 Undo the bolt (arrowed) each side securing the condenser upper mounting brackets to the intercooler

21.8 Lift the condenser upwards and disengage the lower mounting lug (arrowed) on each side

21.9a Slacken the retaining clips and remove the left-hand (arrowed) . . .

21.9b . . . and right-hand (arrowed) lower charge air hoses from the intercooler and charge air pipes

21.10 Undo the bolt (arrowed) each side securing the intercooler upper mounting brackets to the radiator

21.11 Lower the intercooler down and remove it from under the car

22.10 Release the retaining clip and disconnect the breather hose from the front of the camshaft cover

22.13a Undo the turbocharger charge air pipe upper retaining bolt (arrowed) . . .

22.13b . . . then slacken the clip (arrowed) and move the pipe to one side

Refitting

12 Refitting is the reverse of removal.

22 Exhaust manifold (1.9 litre engines) – removal and refitting

Note: *New manifold retaining nuts, new gaskets for all disturbed joints, and new copper washers for the turbocharger oil supply pipe banjo union will be required for refitting.*

Removal

1 Disconnect the battery negative terminal (refer to *Disconnecting the battery* in the Reference Chapter).
2 Remove the plastic cover from the top of the engine
3 Firmly apply the handbrake, then jack up the front of the car and support it securely on axle stands (see *Jacking and vehicle support*). Undo the ten bolts and remove the engine undertray.
4 Drain the cooling system as described in Chapter 1B.
5 Remove the complete exhaust system as described in Section 26.
6 Remove the air cleaner assembly and air intake duct as described in Section 3.
7 On Z19DT engines, undo the retaining bolt(s) to release the vacuum lines running over the top of the camshaft cover **(see illustration 18.6)**.
8 Release the retaining clips and remove the

charge air pipe above the right-hand side of the radiator. Suitably cover the turbocharger air inlet to prevent the entry of dirt and foreign material.
9 On Z19DTH engines, release the retaining clip securing the engine breather hose to the breather pipe adjacent to the engine oil dipstick. Undo the two bolts securing the breather pipe to the cylinder head, and disconnect the pipe from the hose **(see illustration 16.28)**.
10 On Z19DT engines, release the retaining clip and disconnect the breather hose from the front of the camshaft cover **(see illustration)**.
11 Release the two retaining clips and disconnect the charge air hose from the throttle body/housing, and intercooler charge air pipe **(see illustration 10.11)**.
12 Release the clip and disconnect the radiator top hose from the thermostat housing.
13 Undo the bolt securing the turbocharger charge air pipe to the right-hand end of the camshaft housing (Z19DTH engines) or support bracket (Z19DT engines). Slacken the retaining clip securing the charge air pipe to the turbocharger and move the pipe to one side **(see illustrations)**.
14 Undo the bolt and detach the engine oil dipstick guide tube upper mounting.
15 Release the retaining clip and disconnect the radiator hose from the coolant pipe, then undo the two bolts securing the coolant pipe flange to the right-hand end of the cylinder head.

16 Release the retaining clips securing the heater hose and EGR valve heat exchanger hose at the left-hand end of the pipe assembly. Undo the bolt securing the heater pipe to the left-hand end of the cylinder head, and the nut securing the pipe to the thermostat housing stud. Remove the pipe assembly from the engine and recover the flange gasket.
17 Undo the nut and bolt and remove the engine lifting eye from the cylinder head.
18 Undo the three nuts and three bolts securing the heat shield to the exhaust manifold and catalytic converter **(see illustration)**. Manipulate the heat shield off the studs and remove it from the engine.
19 Disconnect the vacuum hose from the turbocharger wastegate actuator.
20 Undo the retaining nut and bolt and release the metal EGR pipe clamp from the EGR valve heat exchanger. Separate the pipe from the heat exchanger and recover the gasket from the pipe fitting **(see illustration)**.
21 Undo the two bolts securing the other end of the pipe to the exhaust manifold. Remove the pipe and recover the gasket **(see illustration)**.
22 Unscrew the two bolts and one nut and remove the catalytic converter lower support bracket.
23 Disconnect the oxygen sensor wiring connector, unscrew the clamp bolt nut and remove the catalytic converter **(see illustrations)**.
24 Unscrew the four bolts securing the oil return pipe to the turbocharger and cylinder

22.18 Heat shield retaining nuts and bolts (arrowed)

22.20 Release the EGR pipe clamp from the heat exchanger, separate the pipe and recover the gasket

22.21 Disconnect the other end of the pipe from the exhaust manifold, then remove the pipe and recover the gasket

22.23a Unscrew the clamp bolt nut (arrowed) . . .

22.23b . . . and remove the catalytic converter

22.24 Unscrew the bolts (arrowed) securing the oil return pipe to the turbocharger and cylinder block

22.25 Unscrew the turbocharger oil supply pipe banjo union (arrowed) and collect the two copper washers

block **(see illustration)**. Remove the pipe and recover the gaskets.

25 Unscrew the turbocharger oil supply pipe banjo union from the cylinder block and collect the two copper washers **(see illustration)**.

26 Unscrew the eight nuts securing the exhaust manifold to the cylinder head **(see illustration)**. Note that new nuts will be required for refitting. Withdraw the manifold and turbocharger assembly from the mounting studs, manipulate it sideways, and remove from under the car. Recover the gasket.

Refitting

27 Refitting is the reverse of removal, noting the following points.

a) Ensure all mating surfaces are clean and dry and renew all gaskets, seals and copper washers.

b) Fit the new manifold nuts and tighten

23.7 Undo the two bolts (arrowed) securing the charge air pipe to the camshaft cover

22.26 Exhaust manifold retaining nuts (arrowed)

them evenly and progressively to the specified torque, working in a diagonal sequence.

c) Tighten all other retaining nuts and bolts to the specified torque (where given).

d) Refit the exhaust system as described in Section 26.

e) On completion refill the cooling system as described in Chapter 1B and, if necessary, top-up the oil level as described in 'Weekly checks'.

f) On starting the engine for the first time, allow the engine to idle for a few minutes before increasing the engine speed; this will allow oil to be circulated around the turbocharger bearings.

23 Exhaust manifold (2.0 and 2.2 litre engines) – removal and refitting

Note: New manifold retaining nuts and exhaust front pipe nuts will be required on refitting.

Removal

1 Disconnect the battery negative terminal (refer to Disconnecting the battery in the Reference Chapter).

2 Remove the plastic cover from the top of the engine

3 Firmly apply the handbrake, then jack up the front of the car and support it securely on axle stands (see Jacking and vehicle support). Undo the ten bolts and remove the engine undertray.

4 Drain the cooling system as described in Chapter 1B.

5 Remove the complete exhaust system as described in Section 26.

6 Remove the air cleaner assembly and air intake duct as described in Section 3.

7 Undo the two bolts securing the charge air pipe to the camshaft cover **(see illustration)**. Slacken the retaining clip and disconnect the charge air pipe connecting hose from the turbocharger elbow. Move the charge air pipe to one side.

8 Disconnect the brake servo vacuum hose at the quick-release fitting. Unclip the hose and move it to one side.

9 Working underneath the vehicle, undo the two retaining bolts, slacken the retaining nut and remove the heat shield from the rear of the starter motor.

10 Undo the retaining bolts and remove the wiring harness guide from the rear of the cylinder block.

11 Remove all traces of dirt from around the turbocharger oil feed and return pipe unions. Slacken the union nuts securing the pipes to the cylinder block and allow the oil to drain into a suitable container. Mop-up any spilt oil.

12 Disconnect the wiring connector from the top of the each glow plug. Undo the two bolts, unclip the wiring harness and position the harness and plastic guide to one side.

13 Undo the two bolts and release the wiring harness support bracket from the left-hand end of the cylinder head **(see illustration)**.

14 Undo the retaining screws and remove

23.13 Undo the bolts (arrowed) and release the wiring harness support bracket from the cylinder head the heat shields from the top of the manifold assembly **(see illustrations)**.

15 Slacken the retaining clamp and disconnect the breather hose from the camshaft cover.

16 Disconnect the vacuum hose from the turbocharger wastegate actuator.

17 Slacken and remove the retaining bolts and remove the manifold support bracket. Disconnect the vacuum hose from the turbocharger wastegate diaphragm.

18 Working in a diagonal sequence, evenly and progressively slacken and remove the exhaust manifold retaining nuts. Manoeuvre the manifold assembly out of position and recover the gasket. If necessary, separate the turbocharger from the manifold as described in Section 25.

Refitting

19 Refitting is the reverse of removal, noting the following points.

a) *Ensure all mating surfaces are clean and dry and renew all gaskets.*

b) *Fit the new manifold nuts and tighten them evenly and progressively to the specified torque, working in a diagonal sequence.*

c) *Tighten all other retaining nuts and bolts to the specified torque (where given).*

d) *Refit the exhaust system as described in Section 26.*

e) *On completion check and, if necessary, top-up the oil and coolant levels as described in 'Weekly checks'.*

f) *On starting the engine for the first time, allow the engine to idle for a few minutes before increasing the engine speed; this will allow oil to be circulated around the turbocharger bearings.*

24 Turbocharger –
description and precautions

Description

1 The turbocharger increases engine efficiency by raising the pressure in the inlet manifold above atmospheric pressure. Instead of the air simply being sucked into the cylinders, it is forced in.

2 Energy for the operation of the turbocharger comes from the exhaust gas. The gas flows through a specially-shaped housing (the turbine housing) and, in so doing, spins the turbine wheel. The turbine wheel is attached to a shaft, at the end of which is another vaned wheel known as the compressor wheel. The compressor wheel spins in its own housing, and compresses the inlet air on the way to the inlet manifold.

3 The turbochargers operate on the principle of variable vane geometry. At low engine speeds the vanes close to give less flow cross-section, then as the speed increases the vanes open to give an increased flow

23.14a Undo the retaining screws (arrowed) . . .

cross-section. This helps improve the efficiency of the turbocharger.

4 Boost pressure (the pressure in the inlet manifold) is limited by a wastegate, which diverts the exhaust gas away from the turbine wheel in response to a pressure-sensitive actuator.

5 The turbo shaft is pressure-lubricated by an oil feed pipe from the main oil gallery. The shaft 'floats' on a cushion of oil. A drain pipe returns the oil to the sump.

Precautions

6 The turbocharger operates at extremely high speeds and temperatures. Certain precautions must be observed to avoid premature failure of the turbo, or injury to the operator.

7 Do not operate the turbo with any of its parts exposed, or with any of its hoses removed. Foreign objects falling onto the rotating vanes could cause excessive damage, and (if ejected) personal injury.

8 Do not race the engine immediately after start-up, especially if it is cold. Give the oil a few seconds to circulate.

9 Always allow the engine to return to idle speed before switching it off – do not blip the throttle and switch off, as this will leave the turbo spinning without lubrication.

10 Allow the engine to idle for several minutes before switching off after a high-speed run.

11 Observe the recommended intervals for oil and filter changing, and use a reputable oil of the specified quality. Neglect of oil changing, or use of inferior oil, can cause carbon formation on the turbo shaft, leading to subsequent failure.

25 Turbocharger –
removal and refitting

Note: *On 1.9 litre engines, the turbocharger is an integral part of the exhaust manifold and cannot be separated. The following procedure is therefore only applicable to 2.0 and 2.2 litre engines.*

Removal

1 Remove the exhaust manifold and turbocharger assembly as described in Section 23.

23.14b . . . and remove the heat shields from the manifold assembly

2 With the assembly on the bench, undo the retaining bolts and remove the exhaust connection flange and gasket from the turbocharger.

3 Unscrew the union bolt and remove the oil feed pipe. Recover the sealing washers fitted on each side of the pipe union.

4 Undo the retaining bolts and remove the oil return pipe and gasket.

5 Slacken and remove the mounting bolts then remove the turbocharger and gasket from the manifold.

6 Do not attempt to dismantle the turbocharger any further. If the unit is thought to be faulty take it to a turbo specialist or Vauxhall/Opel dealer for testing and examination. They will be able to inform you if the unit can be overhauled or will need renewing.

Refitting

7 Refitting is the reverse of removal, using new gaskets/sealing washers, and tightening the fasteners to their specified torque settings (where given). Refit the manifold and turbocharger assembly as described in Section 23.

26 Exhaust system –
general information, removal and refitting

General information

1 The exhaust system consists of three sections: the front pipe with catalytic converter, the intermediate pipe and front silencer, and the tailpipe and rear silencer. On 1.9 litre models, an additional catalytic converter is fitted between the exhaust manifold and front pipe.

2 The front pipe is attached to the exhaust manifold/catalytic converter by a flange joint secured by nuts. All other exhaust sections are joined by overlap joints which are secured by clamps. The system is suspended throughout its entire length by rubber mountings.

3 To remove an individual exhaust section, the complete system is first removed as a unit. The sections are then separated with the system off the car.

4 The manufacturers specify that if any of the exhaust sections are separated, the clamps

26.6 Spray penetrating oil over the exhaust rubber mounting blocks in the area arrowed

26.8 Separate the exhaust front pipe from the manifold/catalytic converter and recover the gasket

must be renewed. As the clamps are attached to the exhaust sections by means of a spot weld at manufacture, it will be necessary to use a suitable grinder to remove the spot weld.

Complete system removal

5 To remove the system, first jack up the front and rear of the car and support it securely on axle stands. Alternatively, position the car over an inspection pit or on car ramps. The help of an assistant will be needed.
6 Spray some penetrating oil over the exhaust rubber mounting blocks so that the mounting blocks will slide easily on the exhaust and underbody hangers **(see illustration)**.
7 Undo the two bolts securing the front pipe support bracket to the transmission bracket.
8 Undo the three retaining nuts and separate the exhaust front pipe from the exhaust manifold/catalytic converter, taking care to support the flexible section. **Note:** *Angular movement in excess of 10° can cause permanent damage to the flexible section.* Recover the gasket **(see illustration)**. Note that new nuts will be required for refitting.
9 Slide the front pipe rubber mounting blocks

as far forward as possible. Move the exhaust system to the rear and disengage the front pipe hangers from the mounting blocks.
10 Move the exhaust system forward and disengage the intermediate pipe and tailpipe hangers from the rubber mounting blocks. Lower the system to the ground and slide it out from under the car.

Individual section removal

11 Remove the complete system as described previously.
12 Slacken and remove the nut from the relevant exhaust clamp retaining bolt. Apply liberal amounts of penetrating oil to the joint and tap around the joint and clamp with a hammer to free it. Twist the pipe to be removed in both directions while holding the adjacent pipe. Once the joint is free, pull the pipes apart.
13 Mark the position of the clamp on the pipe, so the new clamp can be fitted in the same position, then grind off the clamp retaining spot weld. Remove the clamp.

Catalytic converter removal

14 On 1.9 litre engines there are two catalytic

converters – one fitted between the exhaust manifold and the exhaust front pipe, and a second unit, integral with the exhaust front pipe. Refer to Section 22 for removal and refitting details for the converter fitted between the front pipe and manifold.
15 On all engines, a catalytic converter is integral with the exhaust front pipe.

Heat shield(s) removal

16 The heat shields are secured to the underside of the body by various nuts and threaded caps. Each shield can be removed once the relevant exhaust section has been removed. If a shield is being removed to gain access to a component located behind it, it may prove sufficient in some cases to remove the retaining nuts/caps, and simply lower the shield, without disturbing the exhaust system. If any of the threaded caps are damaged during removal, a suitable nut and washer can be used when refitting.

Refitting

17 Refitting is a reversal of the removal sequence, noting the following points:
a) *Ensure that all traces of corrosion have been removed from the system joints and renew all disturbed clamps.*
b) *Inspect the rubber mountings for signs of damage or deterioration, and renew as necessary.*
c) *When refitting the front pipe to the manifold/catalytic converter, use a new gasket and new retaining nuts, and tighten the nuts to the specified torque.*
d) *Prior to tightening the exhaust system clamps, ensure that all rubber mountings are correctly located, and that there is adequate clearance between the exhaust system and vehicle underbody. Tighten the clamp bolt retaining nuts securely.*

Chapter 4 Part C:
Emission control systems

Contents

Section number — Section number

Degrees of difficulty

Easy, suitable for novice with little experience	Fairly easy, suitable for beginner with some experience	Fairly difficult, suitable for competent DIY mechanic	Difficult, suitable for experienced DIY mechanic	Very difficult, suitable for expert DIY or professional

Specifications

Torque wrench settings	Nm	lbf ft
Petrol engines		
Exhaust gas recirculation (EGR) valve bolts:		
1.8 litre engines	20	15
2.2 litre engines	23	17
Oxygen sensor for catalytic converter (in front exhaust pipe):		
1.8 litre engines	30	22
2.2 litre engines	40	30
Oxygen sensor for mixture regulation (in exhaust manifold):		
1.8 litre engines	30	22
2.2 litre engines	40	30
Diesel engines		
Exhaust gas recirculation (EGR) pipe bolts	25	18
Exhaust gas recirculation (EGR) valve bolts/nuts:		
1.9 litre engines	25	18
2.0 and 2.2 litre engines	8	6
Oxygen sensor	55	41

1 General information

1 All petrol engine models use unleaded petrol and also have various other features built into the fuel system to help minimise harmful emissions. These include a crankcase emission control system, a catalytic converter, an exhaust gas recirculation (EGR) system (not all models) and an evaporative emission control system to keep fuel vapour/exhaust gas emissions down to a minimum.

2 All diesel engine models are also designed to meet strict emission requirements. All models are fitted with a crankcase emission control system and a catalytic converter to keep exhaust emissions down to a minimum. All models are also fitted with an exhaust gas recirculation (EGR) system to further decrease exhaust emissions.

3 The emission control systems function as follows.

Petrol engines

Crankcase emission control

4 To reduce the emission of unburned hydrocarbons from the crankcase into the atmosphere, the engine is sealed and the blow-by gases and oil vapour are drawn from inside the crankcase, through an oil separator, into the inlet tract to be burned by the engine during normal combustion.

5 Under all conditions the gases are forced out of the crankcase by the (relatively) higher crankcase pressure; if the engine is worn, the raised crankcase pressure (due to increased blow-by) will cause some of the flow to return under all manifold conditions.

Exhaust emission control

6 To minimise the amount of pollutants which escape into the atmosphere, all models are fitted with a catalytic converter in the exhaust system. The system is of the closed-loop type, in which the oxygen sensors in the exhaust system provides the fuel injection/ignition system ECU with constant feedback, enabling the ECU to adjust the mixture to provide the best possible conditions for the converter to operate.

7 Two heated oxygen sensors are fitted to the exhaust system. The sensor nearest the engine (before the catalytic converter) determines the residual oxygen content of the exhaust gases for mixture correction. The sensor in the exhaust front pipe (after the catalytic converter) monitors the function of the catalytic converter to give the driver a warning signal if there is a fault.

8 The oxygen sensor's tip is sensitive to oxygen and sends the ECU a varying voltage signal depending on the amount of oxygen in the exhaust gases. Peak conversion efficiency of all major pollutants occurs if the intake air/fuel mixture is maintained at the chemically-correct ratio for the complete combustion of petrol of 14.7 parts (by weight) of air to 1 part of fuel (the 'stoichiometric' ratio). The sensor output voltage alters in a large step at this point, the ECU using the signal change as a reference point and correcting the intake air/fuel mixture accordingly by altering the fuel injector pulse width.

2.8 Disconnect the wiring connector(arrowed) from the purge valve

Evaporative emission control

9 To minimise the escape into the atmosphere of unburned hydrocarbons, an evaporative emissions control system is also fitted to all models. The fuel tank filler cap is sealed and a charcoal canister is mounted on the fuel tank. The canister collects the petrol vapours generated in the tank when the car is parked and stores them until they can be cleared from the canister (under the control of the fuel injection/ignition system ECU) via the purge valve into the inlet tract to be burned by the engine during normal combustion.

10 To ensure that the engine runs correctly when it is cold and/or idling and to protect the catalytic converter from the effects of an over-rich mixture, the purge control valve is not opened by the ECU until the engine has warmed-up, and the engine is under load; the valve solenoid is then modulated on and off to allow the stored vapour to pass into the inlet tract.

Exhaust gas recirculation system

11 The EGR system is designed to recirculate small quantities of exhaust gas into the inlet tract, and therefore into the combustion process. This process reduces the level of unburnt hydrocarbons present in the exhaust gas before it reaches the catalytic converter. The system is controlled by the fuel injection/ignition ECU, using the information from its various sensors, via the electrically-operated EGR valve mounted on a housing bolted to the left-hand end of the cylinder head.

Diesel engines

Crankcase emission control

12 Refer to paragraphs 4 and 5.

Exhaust emission control

13 To minimise the level of exhaust pollutants released into the atmosphere, one or two catalytic converters are fitted in the exhaust system.

14 The catalytic converter consists of a canister containing a fine mesh impregnated with a catalyst material, over which the hot exhaust gases pass. The catalyst speeds up the oxidation of harmful carbon monoxide, unburned hydrocarbons and soot, effectively reducing the quantity of harmful products released into the atmosphere via the exhaust gases.

Exhaust gas recirculation system

15 The EGR system is designed to recirculate small quantities of exhaust gas into the inlet tract, and therefore into the combustion process. This process reduces the level of unburnt hydrocarbons present in the exhaust gas before it reaches the catalytic converter. The system is controlled by the injection system ECU, using the information from its various sensors, via the electrically-operated EGR valve.

2 Petrol engine emission control systems – testing and component renewal

Crankcase emission control

1 The components of this system require no attention other than to check that the hose(s) are clear and undamaged at regular intervals.

Evaporative emission control

Testing

2 If the system is thought to be faulty, disconnect the hoses from the charcoal canister and purge control valve and check that they are clear by blowing through them. Full testing of the system can only be carried out using specialist electronic equipment which is connected to the engine management system diagnostic connector. If the purge control valve or charcoal canister are thought to be faulty, they must be renewed.

Charcoal canister renewal

3 The charcoal canister is located on the fuel tank. To gain access to the canister, remove the fuel tank as described in Chapter 4A.

4 With the fuel tank removed, disconnect the vapour hose quick-release fittings at the charcoal canister.

5 Detach the locking clamp and release the canister from its mounting bracket on the fuel tank. Remove the canister from the tank.

6 Refitting is a reverse of the removal procedure, ensuring the hoses are correctly and securely reconnected.

Purge valve renewal

7 On 1.8 litre engines, the purge valve is mounted on the inlet manifold beneath the air cleaner intake duct. Remove the intake duct as

2.17 Oxygen sensor (arrowed) located in the exhaust manifold

described in Chapter 4A for access. On 2.2 litre engines the valve is mounted on the inlet manifold adjacent to the throttle body/housing.

8 To renew the valve, ensure the ignition is switched off then depress the retaining clip and disconnect the wiring connector from the valve (see illustration).

9 Disconnect the hoses from the valve, noting their correct fitted locations then unclip and remove the valve from the engine.

10 Refitting is a reversal of the removal procedure, ensuring the valve is fitted the correct way around and the hoses are securely connected.

Exhaust emission control

Testing

11 The performance of the catalytic converter can be checked only by measuring the exhaust gases using a good-quality, carefully-calibrated exhaust gas analyser.

12 If the CO level at the tailpipe is too high, the vehicle should be taken to a Vauxhall/Opel dealer or engine diagnostic specialist so that the complete fuel injection and ignition systems, including the oxygen sensors, can be thoroughly checked using diagnostic equipment. This equipment will give an indication as to where the fault lies and the necessary components can then be renewed.

Catalytic converter renewal

13 The catalytic converter is an integral part of the exhaust manifold. Exhaust manifold removal and refitting procedures are contained in Chapter 4A.

Oxygen sensor renewal

Note 1: *There are two heated oxygen sensors fitted to the exhaust system. The sensor in the exhaust manifold is for mixture regulation and the sensor in the exhaust front pipe is to check the operation of the catalytic converter (see Section 1).*

Note 2: *The oxygen sensor is delicate and will not work if it is dropped or knocked, if its power supply is disrupted, or if any cleaning materials are used on it.*

14 Warm the engine up to normal operating temperature then stop the engine and disconnect the battery negative terminal (refer to *Disconnecting the battery* in the Reference Chapter). Remove the plastic cover from the top of the engine.

15 For the sensor fitted in the exhaust front pipe, firmly apply the handbrake, then jack up the front of the car and support it securely on axle stands (see *Jacking and vehicle support*).

16 Trace the wiring back from the oxygen sensor which is to be renewed, and disconnect its wiring connector, freeing the wiring from any relevant retaining clips or ties and noting its correct routing.

Caution: Take great care not burn yourself on the hot manifold/sensor.

17 Unscrew the sensor and remove it from the exhaust system front pipe/manifold (see illustration). Where applicable recover the sealing washer and discard it; a new one should be used on refitting.

18 Refitting is a reverse of the removal procedure, using a new sealing washer (where applicable). Prior to installing the sensor, apply a smear of high temperature grease to the sensor threads (Vauxhall/Opel recommend the use of special grease 19 48 569, part No 90 513 210 – available from your dealer). Tighten the sensor to the specified torque and ensure that the wiring is correctly routed and in no danger of contacting either the exhaust system or engine.

Exhaust gas recirculation (EGR)

Testing

19 Comprehensive testing of the system can only be carried out using specialist electronic equipment which is connected to the engine management system diagnostic connector.

EGR valve renewal

Note: *On Z22SE engines, an EGR valve is only fitted to pre-2004 models.*

20 Ensure the ignition is switched off then disconnect the wiring connector from the EGR valve which mounted at the left-hand end of the cylinder head **(see illustration)**.

21 Undo the mounting bolts and remove the valve from its location. Recover the gasket.

22 Refitting is the reverse of removal using a new gasket and tightening the valve bolts to the specified torque.

---

3 Diesel engine emission control systems – testing and component renewal

---

Crankcase emission control

1 The components of this system require no attention other than to check that the hose(s) are clear and undamaged at regular intervals.

Exhaust emission control

Testing

2 The performance of the catalytic converter(s) can be checked only by measuring the exhaust gases using a good-quality, carefully-calibrated exhaust gas analyser.

3 If the catalytic converter(s) is thought to

2.20 Disconnect the wiring connector (arrowed) from the EGR valve

be faulty, before assuming a fault, it is worth checking the problem is not due to a faulty injector(s). Refer to your Vauxhall/Opel dealer for further information.

Catalytic converter renewal

4 On 1.9 litre engines there are two catalytic converters – one fitted between the exhaust manifold and the exhaust front pipe, and a second unit, integral with the exhaust front pipe. On 2.0 and 2.2 litre engines, a single catalytic converter is fitted, integral with the exhaust front pipe. Refer to Chapter 4B, Section 26, for removal and refitting details.

Oxygen sensor renewal – 1.9 litre engines

Note: *The oxygen sensor is delicate and will not work if it is dropped or knocked, if its power supply is disrupted, or if any cleaning materials are used on it.*

5 Warm the engine up to normal operating temperature then stop the engine and disconnect the battery negative terminal (refer to *Disconnecting the battery* in the Reference Chapter). Remove the plastic cover from the top of the engine.

6 Firmly apply the handbrake, then jack up the front of the car and support it securely on axle stands (see *Jacking and vehicle support*). Undo the ten bolts and remove the engine undertray.

7 Disconnect the oxygen sensor wiring connector, then unclip the wiring plug from the bracket on the front of the transmission.

Caution: Take great care not burn yourself on the hot manifold/sensor.

8 Unscrew the sensor and remove it from the exhaust manifold **(see illustration)**.

9 Refitting is a reverse of the removal procedure. Prior to installing the sensor, apply a smear of high temperature grease to the sensor threads (Vauxhall/Opel recommend the use of a special grease available from your dealer). Tighten the sensor to the specified torque and ensure that the wiring is correctly routed and in no danger of contacting either the exhaust system or engine.

Exhaust gas recirculation (EGR)

Testing

10 Comprehensive testing of the system can only be carried out using specialist electronic equipment which is connected to the injection system diagnostic wiring connector.

EGR valve renewal – 1.9 litre Z19DT engines

11 Disconnect the battery negative terminal (refer to *Disconnecting the battery* in the Reference Chapter). Remove the plastic cover over the top of the engine.

12 Disconnect the EGR valve wiring connector.

13 Undo the two bolts and disconnect the metal EGR pipe from the throttle body/ housing. Recover the gasket.

14 Undo the two bolts securing the EGR heat exchanger metal pipe to the base of the valve.

15 Undo the three bolts securing the EGR valve to the inlet manifold **(see illustration)**. Remove the valve together with the engine lifting eye bracket and recover the gasket fitted on each side of the lifting eye bracket.

16 Refitting is the reverse of removal using new gaskets and tightening the retaining bolts to the specified torque.

EGR valve renewal – 1.9 litre Z19DTH engines

17 Disconnect the battery negative terminal (refer to *Disconnecting the battery* in the Reference Chapter). Remove the plastic cover over the top of the engine.

18 Disconnect the EGR valve wiring connector.

19 Unscrew the two bolts on the top of the valve and detach the metal EGR pipe flange from the base of the valve. Recover the gasket **(see illustration)**.

3.8 Unscrew the oxygen sensor (arrowed) and remove it from the exhaust manifold

3.15 EGR valve retaining bolts (arrowed)

3.19 Unscrew the two bolts, detach the metal EGR pipe flange and recover the gasket

3.20 Unscrew the two nuts and two bolts (arrowed) securing the EGR valve to the inlet manifold

20 Unscrew the two nuts and two bolts securing the EGR valve to the inlet manifold and lift off the engine cover bracket **(see illustration)**.

21 To provide sufficient clearance to remove the valve, it will be necessary to unscrew the two mounting studs from the manifold. To do this, lock two nuts together on each stud and remove the studs by unscrewing the inner nut.

22 With the studs removed, lift off the valve and recover the gasket **(see illustration)**.

23 Refitting is the reverse of removal using new gaskets and tightening the retaining nuts and bolts to the specified torque.

EGR valve renewal – 2.0 and 2.2 litre engines

24 Disconnect the battery negative terminal (refer to *Disconnecting the battery* in the Reference Chapter). Remove the plastic cover over the top of the engine.

25 Disconnect the EGR valve wiring connector.

26 Place a suitable container beneath the EGR valve. Be prepared for coolant spillage, then slacken the retaining clips and disconnect the two coolant hoses from the EGR valve.

3.22 Lift off the valve and recover the gasket

Plug the valve and hoses to prevent further coolant loss.

27 Undo the three bolts securing the EGR valve to the inlet manifold. Remove the valve and recover the gasket.

28 Refitting is the reverse of removal using a new gasket and tightening the retaining bolts to the specified torque. On completion, top-up the cooling system as described in *Weekly checks*.

---

4 Catalytic converter – general information and precautions

1 The catalytic converter is a reliable and simple device which needs no maintenance in itself, but there are some facts of which an owner should be aware if the converter is to function properly for its full service life.

Petrol engines

a) *DO NOT use leaded petrol or LRP in a car equipped with a catalytic converter – the lead will coat the precious metals, reducing their converting efficiency and will eventually destroy the converter.*

b) *Always keep the ignition and fuel systems well-maintained in accordance with the manufacturer's schedule.*

c) *If the engine develops a misfire, do not drive the car at all (or at least as little as possible) until the fault is cured.*

d) *DO NOT push- or tow-start the car – this will soak the catalytic converter in unburned fuel, causing it to overheat when the engine does start.*

e) *DO NOT switch off the ignition at high engine speeds.*

f) *DO NOT use fuel or engine oil additives – these may contain substances harmful to the catalytic converter.*

g) *DO NOT continue to use the car if the engine burns oil to the extent of leaving a visible trail of blue smoke.*

h) *Remember that the catalytic converter operates at very high temperatures. DO NOT, therefore, park the car in dry undergrowth, over long grass or piles of dead leaves after a long run.*

i) *Remember that the catalytic converter is FRAGILE – do not strike it with tools during servicing work.*

j) *In some cases a sulphurous smell (like that of rotten eggs) may be noticed from the exhaust. This is common to many catalytic converter-equipped cars and once the car has covered a few thousand miles the problem should disappear. Sometimes the smell is caused by brand of fuel – try buying from a different filling station.*

k) *The catalytic converter, used on a well-maintained and well-driven car, should last for between 50 000 and 100 000 miles – if the converter is no longer effective it must be renewed.*

Diesel engines

2 Refer to the information given in parts f, g, h, i and k of the petrol engines information given above.

Chapter 5 Part A:
Starting and charging systems

Contents

Degrees of difficulty

Easy, suitable for novice with little experience	**Fairly easy,** suitable for beginner with some experience	**Fairly difficult,** suitable for competent DIY mechanic	**Difficult,** suitable for experienced DIY mechanic	**Very difficult,** suitable for expert DIY or professional

Specifications

General
Electrical system type . . . .   12 volt negative earth

Battery
Type . . . .   Lead-acid, 'maintenance-free' (sealed for life)
Charge condition:
  Poor . . . .   12.5 volts
  Normal . . . .   12.6 volts
  Good. . . . .   12.7 volts

Torque wrench settings	Nm	lbf ft
Alternator:		
Petrol engine models:		
1.8 litre engines	35	26
2.2 litre engines	20	15
Diesel engine models:		
1.9 litre engines	60	44
2.0 and 2.2 litre engines	35	26
Auxiliary drivebelt tensioner:		
Petrol engine models:		
1.8 litre engines	35	26
2.2 litre engines	43	32
Diesel engine models:		
1.9 litre engines	50	37
2.0 and 2.2 litre engines:		
M8 bolt	20	15
M10 bolt	42	31
Engine mountings (2.2 litre petrol engines):		
Front mounting/torque link bracket to transmission	80	59
Front mounting/torque link to subframe	80	59
Rear mounting/torque link bracket to transmission	80	59
Rear mounting/torque link to transmission bracket	80	59
Right-hand:		
Engine bracket-to-cylinder head bolts	55	41
Mounting-to-body bolts/nut	55	41
Mounting-to-engine bracket bolts	55	41
Exhaust system front pipe to catalytic converter (2.2 litre petrol engines)	20	15
Glow plugs	10	7
Oil pressure warning light switch:		
Petrol engine models:		
1.8 litre engines	30	22
2.2 litre engines	18	13
Diesel engine models:		
1.9 litre engines	22	16
2.0 and 2.2 litre engines	30	22
Oil temperature sensor	18	13
Roadwheel bolts	110	81
Starter motor:		
Petrol engine models:		
1.8 litre engines:		
Intake manifold support bracket to cylinder block	35	26
Intake manifold support bracket to manifold	20	15
Starter motor mounting bolts	25	18
2.2 litre engines:		
Starter motor mounting bolts	40	30
Diesel engine models:		
1.9 litre engines:		
Earth lead retaining nut	25	18
Starter motor mounting bolts	25	18
2.0 and 2.2 litre engines:		
Exhaust manifold support bracket bolts	25	18
Starter motor mounting bolts	40	30

1 General information, precautions and battery disconnection

General information

The engine electrical system consists mainly of the charging and starting systems, and the diesel engine pre/post-heating system. Because of their engine-related functions, these components are covered separately from the body electrical devices such as the lights, instruments, etc (which are covered in Chapter 12). On petrol engine models refer to Part B for information on the ignition system.

The electrical system is of 12 volt negative earth type.

The battery is of the maintenance-free (sealed for life) type, and is charged by the alternator, which is belt-driven from the crankshaft pulley.

The starter motor is of pre-engaged type incorporating an integral solenoid. On starting, the solenoid moves the drive pinion into engagement with the flywheel/driveplate ring gear before the starter motor is energised. Once the engine has started, a one-way clutch prevents the motor armature being driven by the engine until the pinion disengages.

Further details of the various systems are given in the relevant Sections of this Chapter. While some repair procedures are given, the usual course of action is to renew the component concerned. The owner whose interest extends beyond mere component renewal should obtain a copy of the *Automotive Electrical & Electronic Systems Manual*, available from the publishers of this manual.

Precautions

It is necessary to take extra care when

working on the electrical system to avoid damage to semi-conductor devices (diodes and transistors), and to avoid the risk of personal injury. In addition to the precautions given in *Safety first!* at the beginning of this manual, observe the following when working on the system:

• *Always remove rings, watches, etc before working on the electrical system. Even with the battery disconnected, capacitive discharge could occur if a component's live terminal is earthed through a metal object. This could cause a shock or nasty burn.*

• *Do not reverse the battery connections. Components such as the alternator, electronic control units, or any other components having semi-conductor circuitry could be irreparably damaged.*

• *If the engine is being started using jump leads and a slave battery, connect the batteries positive-to-positive and negative-to-negative (see 'Jump starting'). This also applies when connecting a battery charger but in this case both of the battery terminals should first be disconnected.*

• *Never disconnect the battery terminals, the alternator, any electrical wiring or any test instruments when the engine is running.*

• *Do not allow the engine to turn the alternator when the alternator is not connected.*

• *Never test for alternator output by flashing the output lead to earth.*

• *Never use an ohmmeter of the type incorporating a hand-cranked generator for circuit or continuity testing.*

• *Always ensure that the battery negative lead is disconnected when working on the electrical system.*

• *Before using electric-arc welding equipment on the car, disconnect the battery, alternator and components such as the fuel injection/ignition electronic control unit to protect them from the risk of damage.*

Battery disconnection

Refer to the precautions listed in *Disconnecting the battery* in the Reference Chapter.

2 Electrical fault finding – general information

Refer to Chapter 12.

3 Battery – testing and charging

Testing

Traditional and low maintenance battery

1 If the vehicle covers a small annual mileage, it is worthwhile checking the specific gravity

of the electrolyte every three months to determine the state of charge of the battery. Use a hydrometer to make the check and compare the results with the following table. Note that the specific gravity readings assume an electrolyte temperature of 15°C; for every 10°C below 15°C subtract 0.007. For every 10°C above 15°C add 0.007.

	Ambient temperature	
	Above 25°C	Below 25°C
Fully-charged	*1.210 to 1.230*	*1.270 to 1.290*
70% charged	*1.170 to 1.190*	*1.230 to 1.250*
Discharged	*1.050 to 1.070*	*1.110 to 1.130*

2 If the battery condition is suspect, first check the specific gravity of electrolyte in each cell. A variation of 0.040 or more between any cells indicates loss of electrolyte or deterioration of the internal plates.

3 If the specific gravity variation is 0.040 or more, the battery should be renewed. If the cell variation is satisfactory but the battery is discharged, it should be charged as described later in this Section.

Maintenance-free battery

4 Where a 'sealed for life' maintenance-free battery is fitted, topping-up and testing of the electrolyte in each cell is not possible. The condition of the battery can therefore only be tested using a battery condition indicator or a voltmeter.

5 Later models are fitted with a maintenance-free battery with a built-in 'magic-eye' charge condition indicator. The indicator is located in the top of the battery casing, and indicates the condition of the battery from its colour **(see illustration)**. If the indicator shows green, then the battery is in a good state of charge. If the indicator turns darker, eventually to black, then the battery requires charging, as described later in this Section. If the indicator shows clear/yellow, then the electrolyte level in the battery is too low to allow further use, and the battery should be renewed. Do not attempt to charge, load or jump start a battery when the indicator shows clear/yellow.

All battery types

6 If testing the battery using a voltmeter, connect the voltmeter across the battery and compare the result with those given in the Specifications under 'charge condition'. The test is only accurate if the battery has not been subjected to any kind of charge for the previous six hours. If this is not the case, switch on the headlights for 30 seconds, then wait four to five minutes before testing the battery after switching off the headlights. All other electrical circuits must be switched off, so check that the doors and tailgate are fully shut when making the test.

7 If the voltage reading is less than 12.2 volts, then the battery is discharged, whilst a reading of 12.2 to 12.4 volts indicates a partially-discharged condition.

8 If the battery is to be charged, remove it from the vehicle (Section 4) and charge it as described later in this Section.

3.5 Battery charge condition indicator – 'Delco' type battery

Charging

Note: *The following is intended as a guide only. Always refer to the manufacturer's recommendations (often printed on a label attached to the battery) before charging a battery.*

Traditional and low maintenance battery

9 Charge the battery at a rate of 3.5 to 4 amps and continue to charge the battery at this rate until no further rise in specific gravity is noted over a four hour period.

10 Alternatively, a trickle charger charging at the rate of 1.5 amps can safely be used overnight.

11 Specially rapid 'boost' charges which are claimed to restore the power of the battery in 1 to 2 hours are not recommended, as they can cause serious damage to the battery plates through overheating.

12 While charging the battery, note that the temperature of the electrolyte should never exceed 38°C.

Maintenance-free battery

13 This battery type takes considerably longer to fully recharge than the standard type, the time taken being dependent on the extent of discharge, but it will take anything up to three days.

14 A constant voltage type charger is required, to be set, when connected, to 13.9 to 14.9 volts with a charger current below 25 amps. Using this method, the battery should be usable within three hours, giving a voltage reading of 12.5 volts, but this is for a partially-discharged battery and, as mentioned, full charging can take considerably longer.

15 If the battery is to be charged from a fully-discharged state (condition reading less than 12.2 volts), have it recharged by your Vauxhall/Opel dealer or local automotive electrician, as the charge rate is higher and constant supervision during charging is necessary.

4 Battery and battery box – removal and refitting

Note: *Refer to 'Disconnecting the battery' in the Reference Chapter before proceeding.*

4.2 Lift open the battery box lid . . .

4.3 . . . then unclip the insulation jacket and lift open the jacket cover

4.4a Unscrew the battery negative (–) terminal retaining nut . . .

4.4b . . . then lift the terminal clamp off the battery post

4.10 Release the coolant hose from the clips on the side of the battery box

4.11 Depress the tab and release the positive cable terminal box from the side of the battery box

Battery

Removal

1 The battery is located at the front, left-hand side of the engine compartment, housed in a protective plastic box.

2 Open the battery box by releasing the lid at the front and pivoting it upwards (**see illustration**). If necessary, the lid can be removed completely by disengaging its hinges from the rear of the battery box.

3 Where fitted, unclip the insulation jacket and lift open the jacket cover (**see illustration**).

4 Disconnect the lead at the negative (–) terminal by unscrewing the retaining nut and removing the terminal clamp (**see illustrations**). Note that the battery negative (–) and positive (+) terminal connections are stamped on the battery case.

5 Disconnect the lead at the positive (+) terminal by unscrewing the retaining nut and

removing the terminal clamp. If necessary, the auxiliary lead may also be unbolted from the terminal.

6 On the inner side of the battery, unscrew the bolt and remove the retaining clamp.

7 Carefully lift the battery from its location and remove it from the car. Make sure the battery is kept upright at all times.

Refitting

Note: *As a precaution, before refitting the battery check that all doors are unlocked.*

8 Refitting is a reversal of removal, but smear petroleum jelly on the terminals after reconnecting the leads to reduce corrosion, and always reconnect the positive lead first, followed by the negative lead.

Battery box

Removal

9 Remove the battery as described previously.

10 Release the coolant expansion tank hose from the clips on the side of the battery box (**see illustration**).

11 Depress the plastic tab and release the positive cable terminal box from the side of the battery box (**see illustration**).

12 On diesel engine models, unclip the pre/post-heating system control unit from the side of the battery box (**see illustration**).

13 On 2.2 litre automatic transmission models, unclip the transmission electronic control unit mounting bracket and lift the control unit and bracket upwards and out of the battery box.

14 Depress the retaining tab and lift out the battery box corner panel (**see illustrations**).

15 Release the battery cable guides from the base of the battery box, by depressing the retaining tabs with a small screwdriver, and pulling outwards (**see illustration**).

16 Undo the three retaining bolts and lift

4.12 On diesel engine models, unclip the pre/post-heating system control unit from the side of the battery box

4.14a Depress the retaining tab . . .

4.14b . . . and lift out the battery box corner panel

the battery box up and out of the engine compartment **(see illustration)**.

Refitting

17 Refitting is a reversal of removal.

5 Charging system – testing

Note: *Refer to the precautions given in 'Safety first!' and in Section 1 of this Chapter before starting work.*

1 If the ignition no-charge warning light fails to illuminate when the ignition is switched on, first check the alternator wiring connections for security. If satisfactory, check the condition of all related fuses, fusible links, wiring connections and earthing points. If this fails to reveal the fault, the vehicle should be taken to a Vauxhall/Opel dealer or auto-electrician, as further testing entails the use of specialist diagnostic equipment.

2 If the ignition warning light illuminates when the engine is running, stop the engine and check the condition of the auxiliary drivebelt (see Chapter 1A or 1B) and the security of the alternator wiring connections. If satisfactory, have the alternator checked by a Vauxhall/Opel dealer or auto-electrician.

3 If the alternator output is suspect even though the warning light functions correctly, the regulated voltage may be checked as follows.

4 Connect a voltmeter across the battery terminals, and start the engine.

5 Increase the engine speed until the voltmeter reading remains steady; the reading should be approximately 12 to 13 volts, and no more than 14 volts.

6 Switch on as many electrical accessories (eg, the headlights, heated rear window and heater blower) as possible, and check that the alternator maintains the regulated voltage at around 13.5 to 14.5 volts.

7 If the regulated voltage is not as stated, the fault may be due to worn brushes, weak brush springs, a faulty voltage regulator, a faulty diode, a severed phase winding, or worn or damaged slip-rings. The alternator should be renewed or taken to a Vauxhall/Opel dealer or auto-electrician for testing and repair.

6 Auxiliary drivebelt – removal and refitting

Refer to Chapter 1A or 1B.

7 Auxiliary drivebelt tensioner – removal and refitting

Removal

1.8 litre petrol engines

1 Firmly apply the handbrake, then jack up

4.15 Depress the retaining tabs and release the battery cable guides by pulling outwards

the front of the car and support it securely on axle stands (see *Jacking and vehicle support*). Remove the right-hand front roadwheel.

2 Remove the auxiliary drivebelt as described in Chapter 1A.

3 Undo the central mounting bolt, and remove the tensioner assembly from the engine **(see illustration)**.

2.2 litre petrol engines

4 Disconnect the battery negative terminal (refer to *Disconnecting the battery* in the Reference Chapter).

5 Remove the air cleaner assembly and air intake duct as described in Chapter 4A.

6 On Z22SE engines, carry out the following:

a) *Depressurise the fuel system as described in Chapter 4A.*

b) *Unscrew the union nut and disconnect the fuel supply pipe from the fuel rail. Plug or tape over the end of the pipe and the fuel rail to prevent dirt entry.*

c) *Disconnect the evaporative emission control purge valve hose at the quick-release fitting on the intake manifold.*

7 Firmly apply the handbrake, then jack up the front of the car and support it securely on axle stands (see *Jacking and vehicle support*). Remove the right-hand front roadwheel.

7.3 Auxiliary drivebelt tensioner – 1.8 litre petrol engines

1 *Central mounting bolt*
2 *Locking tool*

4.16 Undo the three bolts (arrowed) and lift out the battery box

8 Remove the auxiliary drivebelt as described in Chapter 1A.

9 Undo the three nuts securing the exhaust system front pipe to the catalytic converter, taking care to support the flexible section. **Note:** *Angular movement in excess of 10° can cause permanent damage to the flexible section.* Separate the flange joint and recover the gasket.

10 Undo the through-bolt securing the rear engine mounting/torque link to the mounting bracket, and the three bolts securing the mounting bracket to the transmission. Remove the mounting bracket from under the car.

11 Unscrew the nut and remove the through-bolt securing the front engine mounting/torque link to the subframe.

12 Connect a suitable hoist and lifting tackle to the right-hand end of the engine and support its weight. If available, the type of support bar which locates in the engine compartment side channels is to be preferred.

13 Mark the bolt positions for correct refitting, then undo the three bolts securing the right-hand engine mounting to the engine bracket, and the two bolts and one nut securing the mounting to the body. Remove the mounting.

14 Using the hoist, carefully raise the right-hand end of the engine until the bolts securing the engine mounting bracket to the cylinder head are accessible. Undo the three bolts and remove the engine bracket.

15 Reposition the hoist as necessary, then undo the drivebelt tensioner central mounting bolt. Remove the tensioner assembly from the engine **(see illustration)**.

7.15 Removing the auxiliary drivebelt tensioner – 2.2 litre petrol engines

7.18 Undo the central mounting bolt (arrowed) and remove the tensioner assembly – 1.9 litre diesel engines

H32438

7.21 Tensioner arm pivot bolt (1) and damper strut lower mounting bolt (2) – 2.0 and 2.2 litre diesel engines

1.9 litre diesel engines

16 Firmly apply the handbrake, then jack up the front of the car and support it securely on axle stands (see *Jacking and vehicle support*). Remove the right-hand front roadwheel.

17 Remove the auxiliary drivebelt as described in Chapter 1B.

18 Undo the central mounting bolt, and remove the tensioner assembly from the engine **(see illustration)**.

2.0 and 2.2 litre diesel engines

19 Firmly apply the handbrake, then jack up the front of the car and support it securely on axle stands (see *Jacking and vehicle support*). Remove the right-hand front roadwheel.

20 Remove the auxiliary drivebelt as described in Chapter 1B.

21 Undo the tensioner arm pivot bolt, and the tensioner damper strut lower mounting bolt, then remove the tensioner assembly from the engine **(see illustration)**. With the tensioner removed, ensure that it is stored with the damper strut in an upright position.

Refitting

1.8 litre petrol engines

22 Place the tensioner assembly in position ensuring that the locating pegs on the tensioner mounting surface engage correctly with the corresponding holes in the mounting bracket. Tighten the tensioner central mounting bolt to the specified torque.

23 Refit the auxiliary drivebelt as described in Chapter 1A.

24 Refit the roadwheel then lower the car to the ground. Tighten the roadwheel bolts to the specified torque.

2.2 litre petrol engines

25 Place the tensioner assembly in position ensuring that the locating peg on the tensioner mounting surface engages correctly with the corresponding hole in the timing chain cover. Tighten the tensioner central mounting bolt to the specified torque.

26 Refit the engine mounting bracket to the cylinder head and tighten the three retaining bolts to the specified torque.

27 Locate the right-hand engine mounting in position, then refit the three bolts securing the mounting to the engine bracket and the two bolts and one nut securing the mounting to the body. Align the mounting in its original position, then tighten the bolts and nut to the specified torque.

28 Remove the hoist and lifting tackle from the engine.

29 Refit the through-bolt and nut securing the front engine mounting/torque link to the sub-frame. Tighten the nut to the specified torque.

30 Place the rear engine mounting/torque link mounting bracket in position and refit the three bolts securing the bracket to the transmission. Tighten the bolts to the specified torque.

31 Refit the rear engine mounting/torque link through-bolt and tighten the bolt to the specified torque.

32 Using a new gasket, refit the exhaust front pipe flange joint to the catalytic converter and tighten the three retaining nuts to the specified torque.

33 Refit the auxiliary drivebelt as described in Chapter 1A.

34 Refit the roadwheel then lower the car to the ground. Tighten the roadwheel bolts to the specified torque.

35 On Z22SE engines, reconnect the purge valve hose to the intake manifold and the fuel supply pipe to the fuel rail. Tighten the fuel pipe union nut to the specified torque (see Chapter 4A).

36 Refer to Chapter 4A if necessary and refit the air cleaner assembly and air intake duct.

37 On completion, reconnect the battery negative terminal.

1.9 litre diesel engines

38 Place the tensioner assembly in position ensuring that the locating peg on the tensioner mounting surface engages correctly with the corresponding hole in the mounting bracket.

Tighten the tensioner central mounting bolt to the specified torque.

39 Refit the auxiliary drivebelt as described in Chapter 1B.

40 Refit the roadwheel then lower the car to the ground. Tighten the roadwheel bolts to the specified torque.

2.0 and 2.2 litre diesel engines

41 If a new unit is being fitted, or if the damper strut was not stored in an upright position when removed, it must be bled by mounting it in a vice and operating it over five or more full strokes. Each stroke must be at constant load and speed to avoid damage to the unit.

42 Place the tensioner assembly in position on the engine and refit the pivot bolt and damper strut lower mounting bolt. Tighten the bolts to the specified torque.

43 Refit the auxiliary drivebelt as described in Chapter 1B.

44 Refit the roadwheel then lower the car to the ground. Tighten the roadwheel bolts to the specified torque.

8 Alternator – removal and refitting

Removal

1.8 litre petrol engines

1 Disconnect the battery negative terminal (refer to *Disconnecting the battery* in the Reference Chapter).

2 Firmly apply the handbrake, then jack up the front of the car and support it securely on axle stands (see *Jacking and vehicle support*). Remove the right-hand front roadwheel.

3 Remove the air cleaner assembly and air intake duct as described in Chapter 4A.

4 Release the quick-release fittings and disconnect the two evaporative emission control purge valve vacuum hoses. Disconnect the wiring connector, undo the retaining bolt and remove the purge valve.

5 Remove the auxiliary drivebelt as described in Chapter 1A.

6 Undo the central mounting bolt, and remove the auxiliary drivebelt tensioner assembly from the engine **(see illustration 7.3)**.

7 Remove the upper alternator mounting bolt.

8 Slacken the lower alternator bolt, and swing the alternator to the rear.

9 Disconnect the oil pressure switch wiring connector and move the cable to one side.

10 Remove the rubber covers (where fitted) from the alternator terminals, then unscrew the retaining nuts and disconnect the wiring from the rear of the alternator.

11 Slacken and remove the bolts securing the alternator mounting bracket to the cylinder block, then manoeuvre the alternator and bracket assembly upwards and out of position **(see illustration)**.

12 Undo the bolt securing the alternator to its mounting bracket and separate the two components **(see illustration)**.

2.2 litre petrol engines

13 Disconnect the battery negative terminal (refer to *Disconnecting the battery* in the Reference Chapter).

14 Firmly apply the handbrake, then jack up the front of the car and support it securely on axle stands (see *Jacking and vehicle support*). Remove the right-hand front roadwheel.

15 Remove the air cleaner assembly and air intake duct as described in Chapter 4A.

16 Remove the auxiliary drivebelt as described in Chapter 1A.

17 Drain the cooling system as described in Chapter 1A.

18 On Z22SE engines, disconnect the two wiring connectors from the engine management electronic control unit. Move the wiring harness to one side, undo the four retaining bolts and remove the control unit from the manifold. Note the location of the earth lead on one of the retaining bolts.

19 Release the retaining clip and disconnect the radiator top hose from the cylinder head.

20 Release the quick-release fittings and disconnect the two evaporative emission control purge valve vacuum hoses. Disconnect

8.11 Alternator mounting bracket bolts (arrowed) – 1.8 litre petrol engines

8.21a Undo the retaining nut . . .

the wiring connector, then unclip and remove the purge valve.

21 Unscrew the retaining nut and disconnect the wiring terminal **(see illustrations)**, then unplug the wiring block connector from the rear of the alternator.

22 Slacken and remove the four alternator mounting bolts, and manoeuvre the alternator out of position **(see illustration)**.

1.9 litre diesel engines

23 Disconnect the battery negative terminal (refer to *Disconnecting the battery* in the Reference Chapter).

24 Firmly apply the handbrake, then jack up the front of the car and support it securely on axle stands (see *Jacking and vehicle support*). Remove the right-hand front roadwheel.

25 Remove the auxiliary drivebelt as described in Chapter 1B.

26 Undo the alternator lower front mounting bolt **(see illustration)**.

8.12 Undo the bolt securing the alternator to its mounting bracket and separate the two components – 1.8 litre petrol engines

8.21b . . . and disconnect the wiring terminal – 2.2 litre petrol engines

27 Remove the fuel filter crash box as described in Chapter 4B.

28 On Z19DTH engines, undo the two bolts securing the wiring harness support bracket to the high-pressure fuel pump mounting bracket. Unclip the wiring harness as necessary and move it clear of the alternator.

29 Unscrew the two retaining nuts and disconnect the wiring connectors from the alternator terminals.

30 Undo the alternator upper rear mounting bolts and manoeuvre the alternator upwards and out of position **(see illustration)**.

2.0 and 2.2 litre diesel engines

31 Disconnect the battery negative terminal (refer to *Disconnecting the battery* in the Reference Chapter).

32 Firmly apply the handbrake, then jack up the front of the car and support it securely on axle stands (see *Jacking and vehicle support*). Remove the right-hand front roadwheel.

8.22 Alternator mounting bracket bolts arrowed – 2.2 litre petrol engines

8.26 Alternator lower front mounting bolt (arrowed) – 1.9 litre diesel engines

8.30 Alternator upper rear mounting bolts (arrowed) – 1.9 litre diesel engines

8.33 Undo the three bolts and lift off the plastic engine cover – 2.0 and 2.2 litre diesel engines

8.41 Lower alternator mounting bolt (3), upper mounting bolt (2), and coolant hose (1) – 2.0 and 2.2 litre diesel engines

33 Undo the three bolts and lift off the plastic cover over the top of the engine **(see illustration)**.

34 Remove the air cleaner assembly and air intake duct as described in Chapter 4B.

35 Remove the auxiliary drivebelt as described in Chapter 1B.

36 Remove the complete exhaust system as described in Chapter 4B.

37 Slacken the retaining nut, unscrew the two retaining bolts and remove the starter motor heat shield.

38 Unscrew the two retaining nuts and disconnect the wiring connectors from the alternator terminals.

39 Disconnect the oil pressure switch wiring connector and move the cable to one side.

40 Undo the lower retaining bolt and the two upper retaining bolts securing the alternator wiring trough in position.

41 Release the upper coolant hose from the support bracket on the alternator. Undo the alternator upper mounting nut and bolt and remove the coolant hose support bracket **(see illustration)**.

42 Where fitted, undo the three bolts and remove the steering gear heat shield.

43 Undo the alternator lower mounting nut and bolt, and manoeuvre the alternator downwards and out of position.

Refitting

1.8 litre petrol engines

44 Refit the mounting bracket to the alternator and secure with the mounting bolt, tightened finger-tight only at this stage.

45 Manoeuvre the alternator and mounting bracket assembly into position and refit the mounting bracket retaining bolts. Tighten the bolts to the specified torque.

46 Reconnect the wiring to the alternator terminals and tighten the retaining nuts securely. Where applicable, refit the rubber covers to the alternator terminals.

47 Reconnect the wiring to the oil pressure switch.

48 Refit the alternator upper mounting bolt, then tighten the upper and lower mounting bolts to the specified torque.

49 Place the auxiliary drivebelt tensioner assembly in position ensuring that the locating pegs on the tensioner mounting surface engage correctly with the corresponding holes in the mounting bracket. Tighten the tensioner central mounting bolt to the specified torque.

50 Refit the auxiliary drivebelt as described in Chapter 1A.

51 Refit the evaporative emission control purge valve and secure with the mounting bolt. Reconnect the two vacuum hose quick-release fittings.

52 Refit the air cleaner assembly and air intake duct as described in Chapter 4A.

53 Refit the roadwheel then lower the car to the ground. Tighten the roadwheel bolts to the specified torque.

54 On completion, reconnect the battery negative terminal.

2.2 litre petrol engines

55 Manoeuvre the alternator into position and refit the four retaining bolts. Tighten the bolts to the specified torque.

56 Reconnect the alternator wiring block connector and the terminal wiring, tightening the retaining nut securely.

57 Refit the evaporative emission control purge valve, then reconnect the wiring connector and the two vacuum hose quick-release fittings.

58 Reconnect the radiator top hose to the cylinder head.

59 On Z22SE engines, refit the engine management electronic control unit to the manifold and secure with the four bolts tightened securely. Ensure that the earth lead is correctly located on the relevant retaining bolt. Reconnect the two wiring connectors to the control unit.

60 Refit the auxiliary drivebelt as described in Chapter 1A.

61 Refit the air cleaner assembly and air intake duct as described in Chapter 4A.

62 Refit the roadwheel then lower the car to

the ground. Tighten the roadwheel bolts to the specified torque.

63 Reconnect the battery negative terminal, then refill the cooling system as described in Chapter 1A.

1.9 litre diesel engines

64 Manoeuvre the alternator into position and refit the upper rear retaining bolt(s). Tighten the bolt(s) finger-tight only at this stage.

65 Reconnect the wiring to the alternator terminals and tighten the retaining nuts securely.

66 On Z19DTH engines, refit the wiring harness support bracket to the fuel pump mounting bracket and secure with the two bolts. Clip the wiring harness back into position in the bracket.

67 Refit the alternator lower front mounting bolt, then tighten the upper and lower mounting bolts to the specified torque.

68 Refit the auxiliary drivebelt as described in Chapter 1B.

69 Refit the fuel filter crash box as described in Chapter 4B.

70 Refit the roadwheel then lower the car to the ground. Tighten the roadwheel bolts to the specified torque.

71 On completion, reconnect the battery negative terminal.

2.0 and 2.2 litre diesel engines

72 Manoeuvre the alternator into position and refit the lower mounting bolt and nut. Tighten the nut finger-tight only at this stage.

73 Where applicable, refit the steering gear heat shield and secure with the three bolts.

74 Refit the alternator upper mounting bolt, locate the coolant hose support bracket in position then refit the mounting nut. Tighten the upper and lower mounting nuts to the specified torque, then refit the coolant hose to the support bracket.

75 Locate the alternator wiring trough back in position and secure with the three bolts. Reconnect the oil pressure switch wiring connector.

76 Reconnect the wiring to the alternator terminals and tighten the retaining nuts securely.

77 Refit the starter motor heat shield and secure with the nut and two bolts.

78 Refit the auxiliary drivebelt as described in Chapter 1B.

79 Refit the exhaust system, the air cleaner assembly, and air intake duct as described in Chapter 4B.

80 Refit the roadwheel then lower the car to the ground. Tighten the roadwheel bolts to the specified torque.

81 On completion, reconnect the battery negative terminal and refit the engine cover.

9 Alternator – testing and overhaul

If the alternator is thought to be suspect, it should be removed from the vehicle and taken to an auto-electrician for testing. Most auto-electricians will be able to supply and fit brushes at a reasonable cost. However, check on the cost of repairs before proceeding as it may prove more economical to obtain a new or exchange alternator.

10 Starting system – testing

Note: *Refer to the precautions given in 'Safety first!' and in Section 1 of this Chapter before starting work.*

1 If the starter motor fails to operate when the ignition key is turned to the appropriate position, the possible causes are as follows:

  a) *The engine immobiliser is faulty.*
  b) *The battery is faulty.*
  c) *The electrical connections between the switch, solenoid, battery and starter motor are somewhere failing to pass the necessary current from the battery through the starter to earth.*
  d) *The solenoid is faulty.*
  e) *The starter motor is mechanically or electrically defective.*

2 To check the battery, switch on the headlights. If they dim after a few seconds, this indicates that the battery is discharged – recharge (see Section 3) or renew the battery. If the headlights glow brightly, operate the starter switch while watching the headlights. If they dim, then this indicates that current is reaching the starter motor, therefore the fault must lie in the starter motor. If the lights continue to glow brightly (and no clicking sound can be heard from the starter motor solenoid), this indicates that there is a fault in the circuit or solenoid – see the following paragraphs. If the starter motor turns slowly when operated, but the battery is in good condition, then this indicates either that the starter motor is faulty, or there is

considerable resistance somewhere in the circuit.

3 If a fault in the circuit is suspected, disconnect the battery leads (including the earth connection to the body), the starter/solenoid wiring and the engine/transmission earth strap. Thoroughly clean the connections, and reconnect the leads and wiring. Use a voltmeter or test light to check that full battery voltage is available at the battery positive lead connection to the solenoid. Smear petroleum jelly around the battery terminals to prevent corrosion – corroded connections are among the most frequent causes of electrical system faults.

4 If the battery and all connections are in good condition, check the circuit by disconnecting the ignition switch supply wire from the solenoid terminal. Connect a voltmeter or test lamp between the wire end and a good earth (such as the battery negative terminal), and check that the wire is live when the ignition switch is turned to the 'start' position. If it is, then the circuit is sound – if not the circuit wiring can be checked as described in Chapter 12.

5 The solenoid contacts can be checked by connecting a voltmeter or test light between the battery positive feed connection on the starter side of the solenoid and earth. When the ignition switch is turned to the 'start' position, there should be a reading or lighted bulb, as applicable. If there is no reading or lighted bulb, the solenoid is faulty and should be renewed.

6 If the circuit and solenoid are proved sound, the fault must lie in the starter motor. In this event, it may be possible to have the starter motor overhauled by a specialist, but check on the cost of spares before proceeding, as it may prove more economical to obtain a new or exchange motor.

11 Starter motor – removal and refitting

Removal

1.8 litre petrol engines

1 Disconnect the battery negative terminal

11.5 Disconnect the wiring connectors from the starter solenoid – 1.8 litre petrol engines

(refer to *Disconnecting the battery* in the Reference Chapter).

2 Firmly apply the handbrake, then jack up the front of the car and support it securely on axle stands (see *Jacking and vehicle support*).

3 Disconnect the oxygen sensor wiring at the cable connector below the intake manifold.

4 Undo the two retaining bolts and remove the support bracket from the underside of the intake manifold, noting the location of the earth cable.

5 Slacken and remove the two retaining nuts and disconnect the wiring from the starter motor solenoid **(see illustration)**. Recover the washers under the nuts.

6 Where applicable, unscrew the retaining nut and disconnect the earth lead from the starter motor upper bolt.

7 Slacken and remove the retaining bolts then manoeuvre the starter motor out from underneath the engine **(see illustration)**.

2.2 litre petrol engines

8 Disconnect the battery negative terminal (refer to *Disconnecting the battery* in the Reference Chapter).

9 Firmly apply the handbrake, then jack up the front of the car and support it securely on axle stands (see *Jacking and vehicle support*).

10 Disconnect the wiring connector at the oil level sensor located on the front face of the sump.

11 Slacken and remove the two retaining nuts, release the cable tie and disconnect the wiring from the starter motor solenoid. Recover the washers under the nuts.

12 Disconnect the crankshaft sensor wiring connector.

13 Slacken and remove the two retaining bolts then manoeuvre the starter motor out from underneath the engine.

1.9 litre diesel engines

14 Disconnect the battery negative terminal (refer to *Disconnecting the battery* in the Reference Chapter).

15 Firmly apply the handbrake, then jack up the front of the car and support it securely on axle stands (see *Jacking and vehicle support*).

16 On Z19DT engines, remove the oil filler cap and unscrew the two bolts securing the plastic cover over the top of the engine. Release the

11.7 Remove the starter motor from underneath the engine – 1.8 litre petrol engines

11.16a Remove the oil filler cap . . .

11.16b . . . unscrew the two bolts (arrowed) . . .

11.16c . . . release the engine breather hose . . .

11.16d . . . and lift off the plastic engine cover – 1.9 litre Z19DT diesel engines

11.18 Undo the nuts (arrowed) and disconnect the starter solenoid wiring connectors – 1.9 litre diesel engines

11.19 Unscrew the nut (arrowed) and disconnect the earth lead from the starter motor stud bolt – 1.9 litre diesel engines

engine breather hose, then lift off the cover and refit the oil filler cap **(see illustrations)**. On Z19DTH engines, remove the plastic cover by pulling it upwards off the mounting studs.

17 Undo the ten bolts and remove the undertray from beneath the engine.

18 Slacken and remove the two retaining nuts and disconnect the wiring from the starter motor solenoid **(see illustration)**. Recover the washers under the nuts.

19 Unscrew the retaining nut and disconnect the earth lead from the starter motor lower stud bolt **(see illustration)**.

20 Open the retaining clips and release the two heater hoses from the coolant pipe support bracket.

21 Undo the two nuts and release the wiring harness from the support bracket above the starter motor **(see illustration)**.

22 Carefully lift the cooling system expansion tank out of its mounting bracket and place the tank to one side.

23 Unscrew the starter motor lower stud bolt and the two upper mounting bolts **(see illustration)**. Collect the wiring harness support bracket then manoeuvre the starter motor upwards and out of position.

2.0 and 2.2 litre diesel engines

24 Disconnect the battery negative terminal (refer to *Disconnecting the battery* in the Reference Chapter).

25 Firmly apply the handbrake, then jack up the front of the car and support it securely on axle stands (see *Jacking and vehicle support*).

26 Undo the ten bolts and remove the undertray from beneath the engine.

27 Remove the complete exhaust system as described in Chapter 4B.

28 Slacken the retaining nut, unscrew the two retaining bolts and remove the starter motor heat shield.

29 Disconnect the oil pressure switch wiring connector and move the cable to one side.

30 Undo the lower retaining bolt and the two upper retaining bolts securing the alternator wiring trough in position **(see illustration)**.

31 Undo the two bolts and remove the

11.21 Undo the nuts and release the wiring harness from the support bracket – 1.9 litre diesel engines

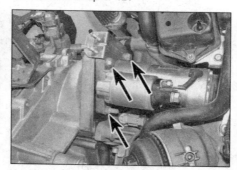

11.23 Unscrew the bolts (arrowed), collect the wiring harness bracket and remove the starter from above – 1.9 litre diesel engines

11.30 Starter motor attachments – 2.0 and 2.2 litre diesel engines

1 *Starter motor retaining bolts*
2 *Wiring trough retaining bolts*
3 *Wiring trough*
4 *Starter bracket and exhaust manifold support bolts*
5 *Starter wiring connections*

exhaust manifold support bracket. Where applicable, unbolt the bracket from the rear of the starter motor.

32 Slacken and remove the two retaining nuts and disconnect the wiring from the starter motor solenoid. Recover the washers under the nuts.

33 Unscrew the retaining nut and disconnect the earth lead from the starter motor lower stud bolt.

34 Unscrew the starter motor upper mounting bolt and lower stud bolt. Carefully push the alternator wiring trough upwards, then manoeuvre the starter motor out from underneath the engine.

Refitting

35 Refitting is a reversal of removal tightening the retaining bolts to the specified torque. Ensure all wiring is correctly routed and its retaining nuts are securely tightened.

12 Starter motor –
testing and overhaul

If the starter motor is thought to be suspect, it should be removed from the vehicle and taken to an auto-electrician for testing. Most auto-electricians will be able to supply and fit brushes at a reasonable cost. However, check on the cost of repairs before proceeding as it may prove more economical to obtain a new or exchange motor.

13 Ignition switch –
removal and refitting

The switch is integral with the steering column lock, and removal and refitting is described in Chapter 10.

14.3 Oil pressure warning light switch (arrowed) – 1.8 litre petrol engines

14 Oil pressure warning light switch –
removal and refitting

Removal

1.8 litre petrol engines

1 The switch is screwed into the rear of the oil pump housing which is located on the right-hand end of the engine, on the end of the crankshaft.

2 Firmly apply the handbrake, then jack up the front of the car and support it securely on axle stands (see *Jacking and vehicle support*).

3 Disconnect the wiring connector then unscrew the switch and recover the sealing washer. Be prepared for oil spillage, and if the switch is to be left removed from the engine for any length of time, plug the switch aperture **(see illustration)**.

2.2 litre petrol engines

4 The switch is screwed into the front of the cylinder block, behind the starter motor **(see illustration)**. To gain access to the switch, it will be necessary to remove the starter motor as described in Section 11.

14.4 Oil pressure warning light switch (arrowed) – 2.2 litre petrol engines

5 Disconnect the wiring connector then unscrew the switch and recover the sealing washer. Be prepared for oil spillage, and if the switch is to be left removed from the engine for any length of time, plug the switch aperture.

Diesel engines

6 The switch is screwed into the oil filter housing (1.9 litre engines), or into the rear of the cylinder block (2.0 and 2.2 litre engines), above the right-hand driveshaft **(see illustrations)**.

7 Firmly apply the handbrake, then jack up the front of the car and support it securely on axle stands (see *Jacking and vehicle support*).

8 Undo the ten bolts and remove the undertray from beneath the engine.

9 Disconnect the wiring connector then unscrew the switch and recover the sealing washer. Be prepared for oil spillage, and if the switch is to be left removed from the engine for any length of time, plug the switch aperture.

Refitting

10 Examine the sealing washer for signs of damage or deterioration and if necessary renew.

11 Refit the switch and washer, tightening

14.6a Oil pressure warning light switch (arrowed) – 1.9 litre diesel engines

H32442

14.6b Oil pressure warning light switch (2) and wiring connector (1) – 2.0 and 2.2 litre diesel engines

15.5 Remove the oil level sensor and renew the seal – 1.8 litre petrol engines

15.9 Where fitted, undo the retaining bolts and remove the oil baffle plate

15.8 Slide off the retaining clip (arrowed) and free the oil level sensor wiring connector from the sump

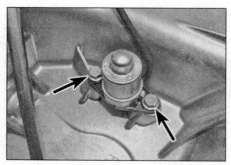

15.10 Undo the two bolts (arrowed) and remove the oil level sensor from the sump

it to the specified torque, and reconnect the wiring connector.
12 On 2.2 litre petrol engine models, refit the starter motor as described in Section 11.
13 On diesel engine models, refit the engine undertray.
14 Lower the vehicle to the ground then check and, if necessary, top-up the engine oil as described in *Weekly checks*.

15 Oil level sensor – removal and refitting

1.8 litre petrol engines

Removal

1 The oil level sensor is located on the front face of the engine sump.

16.1 Oil temperature sensor location on the front face of the sump – 2.0 and 2.2 litre diesel engines

2 Firmly apply the handbrake, then jack up the front of the car and support it securely on axle stands (see *Jacking and vehicle support*).
3 Drain the engine oil into a clean container then refit the drain plug and tighten it to the specified torque (see Chapter 1A).
4 Disconnect the wiring connector from the sensor.
5 Unscrew the retaining bolts then ease the sensor out from the sump and remove it along with its sealing ring/washer. Discard the sealing ring/washer, a new one should be used on refitting **(see illustration)**.

Refitting

6 Refitting is the reverse of removal ensuring the wiring is correctly routed and securely reconnected. On completion refill the engine with oil (see Chapter 1A).

16.4 Unscrew the oil temperature sensor from the sump – 2.0 and 2.2 litre diesel engines

All other models

Removal

7 The oil level sensor is located inside the sump which must first be removed (see the appropriate Part of Chapter 2).
8 With the sump removed, slide off the retaining clip and free the sensor wiring connector from the sump **(see illustration)**.
9 Where fitted, undo the retaining bolts and remove the oil baffle plate from inside the sump **(see illustration)**.
10 Note the correct routing of the wiring then undo the retaining bolts and remove the sensor assembly from the sump **(see illustration)**. Check the wiring connector seal for signs or damage and renew if necessary.

Refitting

11 Prior to refitting remove all traces of locking compound from the sensor retaining bolt and sump threads. Apply a drop of fresh locking compound to the bolt threads and lubricate the wiring connector seal with a smear of engine oil.
12 Fit the sensor, making sure the wiring is correctly routed, and securely tighten its retaining bolts. Ease the wiring connector through the sump, taking care not to damage its seal, and secure it in position with the retaining clip.
13 Ensure the sensor is correctly refitted then, where applicable, refit the oil baffle plate.
14 Refit the sump as described in the appropriate Part of Chapter 2.

16 Oil temperature sensor (diesel engine models) – removal and refitting

Note: *An oil temperature sensor is only fitted to 2.0 and 2.2 litre diesel engines.*

Removal

1 The sensor is screwed into the front face of the sump **(see illustration)**. To gain access, firmly apply the handbrake, then jack up the front of the car and support it securely on axle stands (see *Jacking and vehicle support*).
2 Undo the ten bolts and remove the undertray from beneath the engine.
3 Drain the engine oil as described in Chapter 1B.
4 Disconnect the wiring connector, then unscrew the sensor from the sump **(see illustration)**.

Refitting

5 With a new sealing ring fitted, refit the sensor to the sump and tighten it to the specified torque.
6 Reconnect the sensor wiring connector.
7 Refit the engine undertray and lower the car to the ground.
8 On completion refill the engine with oil as described in Chapter 1B.

17 Pre/post-heating system (diesel engine models) – description and testing

Description

1 Each cylinder of the engine is fitted with a heater plug (commonly called a glow plug) screwed into it. The plugs are electrically-operated before and during start-up when the engine is cold. Electrical feed to the glow plugs is controlled via the pre/post-heating system control unit.
2 A warning light in the instrument panel tells the driver that pre/post-heating is taking place. When the light goes out, the engine is ready to be started. The voltage supply to the glow plugs continues for several seconds after the light goes out. If no attempt is made to start, the timer then cuts off the supply, in order to avoid draining the battery and overheating the glow plugs.
3 The glow plugs also provide a 'post-heating' function, whereby the glow plugs remain switched on after the engine has started. The length of time 'post-heating' takes place is also determined by the control unit, and is dependent on engine temperature.
4 The fuel filter is fitted with a heating element to prevent the fuel 'waxing' in extreme cold temperature conditions and to improve combustion. The heating element is an integral part of the fuel filter housing and is controlled by the pre/post-heating system control unit.

Testing

5 If the system malfunctions, testing is ultimately by substitution of known good units, but some preliminary checks may be made as follows.
6 Connect a voltmeter or 12 volt test lamp between the glow plug supply cable and earth (engine or vehicle metal). Make sure that the live connection is kept clear of the engine and bodywork.
7 Have an assistant switch on the ignition, and check that voltage is applied to the glow plugs. Note the time for which the warning light is lit, and the total time for which voltage is applied before the system cuts out. Switch off the ignition.
8 At an underbonnet temperature of 20°C, typical times noted should be approximately 3 seconds for warning light operation. Warning light time will increase with lower temperatures and decrease with higher temperatures.
9 If there is no supply at all, the control unit or associated wiring is at fault.
10 To locate a defective glow plug, disconnect the wiring connector from each plug.
11 Use a continuity tester, or a 12 volt test lamp connected to the battery positive terminal, to check for continuity between each glow plug terminal and earth. The resistance of a glow plug in good condition is very low (less than 1 ohm), so if the test lamp does not light or the

continuity tester shows a high resistance, the glow plug is certainly defective.
12 If an ammeter is available, the current draw of each glow plug can be checked. After an initial surge of 15 to 20 amps, each plug should draw 12 amps. Any plug which draws much more or less than this is probably defective.
13 As a final check, the glow plugs can be removed and inspected as described in the following Section.

18 Glow plugs (diesel engine models) – removal, inspection and refitting

Caution: If the pre/post-heating system has just been energised, or if the engine has been running, the glow plugs will be very hot.

Removal

1.9 litre engines

1 The glow plugs are located at the rear of the cylinder head above the inlet manifold.
2 On Z19DT engines, remove the oil filler cap and unscrew the two bolts securing the plastic cover over the top of the engine. Release the engine breather hose, then lift off the cover and refit the oil filler cap **(see illustrations 11.16a to 11.16d)**. On Z19DTH engines, remove the plastic cover by pulling it upwards off the mounting studs.
3 On Z19DT engines, undo the two retaining bolts, disconnect the four vacuum hoses and remove the vacuum pipe assembly from the top of the camshaft cover.
4 Disconnect the wiring from the glow plugs by squeezing the connectors with thumb and forefinger, and pulling them from the plugs.
5 Unscrew the glow plugs and remove them from the cylinder head **(see illustration)**.

2.0 and 2.2 litre engines

6 The glow plugs are located at the rear of the cylinder head above the exhaust manifold.
7 Undo the three bolts and lift off the plastic cover over the top of the engine **(see illustration 8.33)**.
8 Undo the two bolts securing the charge air pipe to the camshaft cover **(see illustration)**. Slacken the retaining clip and disconnect the charge air pipe connecting hose from the turbocharger elbow. Move the charge air pipe to one side.
9 Disconnect the wiring from the glow plugs by squeezing the connectors with thumb and forefinger, and pulling them from the plugs.
10 Unscrew the glow plugs and remove them from the cylinder head.

Inspection

11 Inspect each glow plug for physical damage. Burnt or eroded glow plug tips can be caused by a bad injector spray pattern. Have the injectors checked if this type of damage is found.

18.5 Unscrew the glow plugs and remove them from the cylinder head – 1.9 litre Z19DTH diesel engines

12 If the glow plugs are in good physical condition, check them electrically using a 12 volt test lamp or continuity tester as described in the previous Section.
13 The glow plugs can be energised by applying 12 volts to them to verify that they heat up evenly and in the required time. Observe the following precautions.
   a) *Support the glow plug by clamping it carefully in a vice or self-locking pliers. Remember it will become red-hot.*
   b) *Make sure that the power supply or test lead incorporates a fuse or overload trip to protect against damage from a short-circuit.*
   c) *After testing, allow the glow plug to cool for several minutes before attempting to handle it.*
14 A glow plug in good condition will start to glow red at the tip after drawing current for 5 seconds or so. Any plug which takes much longer to start glowing, or which starts glowing in the middle instead of at the tip, is defective.

Refitting

15 Carefully refit the plugs and tighten to the specified torque. Do not overtighten, as this can damage the glow plug element. Push the electrical connectors firmly onto the glow plugs.
16 The remainder of refitting is a reversal of removal, checking the operation of the glow plugs on completion.

18.8 Undo the two bolts (arrowed) securing the charge air pipe to the camshaft cover

19.3 Unclip the control unit and slide it up and off the battery box

19 Pre/post-heating system control unit (diesel engine models) – removal and refitting

Removal

1 The pre/post-heating system control unit is located on the left-hand side of the engine compartment where it is mounted onto the side of the battery box.

2 Disconnect the battery negative terminal (refer to *Disconnecting the battery* in the Reference Chapter).

3 Unclip the control unit and slide it up and off the battery box **(see illustration)**.

4 Disconnect the wiring connector from the base of the control unit and remove the unit from the engine compartment.

Refitting

5 Refitting is a reversal of removal.

Chapter 5 Part B:
Ignition system – petrol engines

Contents

Degrees of difficulty

Easy, suitable for novice with little experience	**Fairly easy,** suitable for beginner with some experience	**Fairly difficult,** suitable for competent DIY mechanic	**Difficult,** suitable for experienced DIY mechanic	**Very difficult,** suitable for expert DIY or professional

Specifications

General
System type	Distributorless ignition system
System application:	
1.8 litre engines	Simtec 71.5
2.2 litre engines:	
Z22SE	GMPT – E16
Z22YH	Simtec 81.1
Location of No 1 cylinder	Timing chain/timing belt end of engine
Firing order	1-3-4-2

Torque wrench setting
	Nm	lbf ft
Ignition module retaining bolts	8	6

1 Ignition system – general information

The ignition system is integrated with the fuel injection system to form a combined engine management system under the control of one electronic control unit (ECU) – see Chapter 4A for further information. The ignition side of the system is of the distributorless type, and consists of the ignition module and the knock sensor.

The ignition module consists of four ignition coils, one per cylinder, in one casing mounted directly above the spark plugs. This module eliminates the need for any HT leads as the coils locate directly onto the relevant spark plug. The ECU uses its inputs from the various sensors to calculate the required ignition advance setting and coil charging time.

The knock sensor is mounted onto the cylinder block and informs the ECU when the engine is 'pinking' under load. The sensor is sensitive to vibration and detects the knocking which occurs when the engine starts to 'pink' (pre-ignite). The knock sensor sends an electrical signal to the ECU which in turn retards the ignition advance setting until the 'pinking' ceases.

The ignition systems fitted to the engines covered by this manual all operate in a similar fashion under the overall control of the engine management ECU. The systems comprise various sensors (whose inputs also provide data to control the fuel injection system), and the ECU, in addition to the ignition module and spark plugs. Further details of the system sensors and the ECU are given in Chapter 4A.

The ECU selects the optimum ignition advance setting based on the information received from the various sensors, and fires the relevant ignition coil accordingly. The degree of advance can thus be constantly varied to suit the prevailing engine operating conditions.

Warning: Due to the high voltages produced by the electronic ignition system, extreme care must be taken when working on the system with the ignition switched on. Persons with surgically-implanted cardiac pacemaker devices should keep well clear of the ignition circuits, components and test equipment.

2 Ignition system – testing

1 If a fault appears in the engine management system, first ensure that all the system wiring connectors are securely connected and free of corrosion. Ensure that the fault is not due to poor maintenance; ie, check that the air cleaner filter element is clean, the spark plugs are in good condition and correctly gapped, the cylinder compression pressures are correct and that the engine breather hoses are clear and undamaged, referring to Chapters 1A, 2A and 2B for further information.

2 If these checks fail to reveal the cause of the problem, the vehicle should be taken to a suitably-equipped Vauxhall/Opel dealer or engine management diagnostic specialist for testing. A diagnostic socket is located at the base of the facia, behind the ashtray, to which a fault code reader or other suitable test equipment can be connected (see illustration). By using the code reader or test equipment, the engine management ECU can be interrogated, and any stored fault codes

2.2 The vehicle diagnostic socket (arrowed) is located at the base of the facia, behind the ashtray

can be retrieved. This will allow the fault to be quickly and simply traced, alleviating the need to test all the system components individually, which is a time-consuming operation that carries a risk of damaging the ECU.

3 The only ignition system checks which can be carried out by the home mechanic are those described in Chapter 1A relating to the spark plugs. If necessary, the system wiring and wiring connectors can be checked as described in Chapter 12, ensuring that the ECU wiring connector(s) have first been disconnected.

3.1 Unclip and lift off the cover over the ignition module – 2.2 litre engines

3 Ignition module – removal and refitting

Removal

1 On 1.8 litre engines, remove the oil filler cap and unscrew the two bolts securing the plastic cover over the top of the engine. Lift off the cover and refit the oil filler cap. On 2.2 litre engines simply unclip the plastic cover and lift it off. Additionally on 2.2 litre engines, lift off the cover over the ignition module **(see illustration)**.
2 The ignition module is mounted at the top of the engine, between the inlet and exhaust camshaft casings. Disconnect the wiring connector at the left-hand end of the module **(see illustration)**.
3 Undo the retaining bolts, and lift the module up and out of position **(see illustration)**. If the module proves reluctant to separate from the spark plugs, insert two long 8 mm bolts into the threaded holes in the top of the module, and pull up on the bolts to free the module from the plugs.

Refitting

4 Locate the module in position, refit the

3.2 Disconnect the ignition module wiring connector

retaining bolts and tighten to the specified torque.
5 Reconnect the wiring connector to the ignition module, making sure it is fitted securely.
6 Refit the engine cover on completion.

4 Ignition timing – checking and adjustment

Due to the nature of the ignition system, the ignition timing is constantly being monitored and adjusted by the engine management ECU.
The only way in which the ignition timing can be checked is by using specialist diagnostic test equipment, connected to the engine management system diagnostic socket. No adjustment of the ignition timing is possible. Should the ignition timing be incorrect, then a fault is likely to be present in the engine management system.

5 Knock sensor – removal and refitting

Refer to the procedures contained in Chapter 4A.

3.3 Undo the retaining bolts (arrowed) and pull the ignition module up and off from the top of the spark plugs

Chapter 6
Clutch

Contents

Degrees of difficulty

Easy, suitable for novice with little experience	**Fairly easy,** suitable for beginner with some experience	**Fairly difficult,** suitable for competent DIY mechanic	**Difficult,** suitable for experienced DIY mechanic	**Very difficult,** suitable for expert DIY or professional

Specifications

Type . . . . Single dry plate with diaphragm spring, hydraulically-operated

Friction disc

Diameter:
  Petrol engine models:
    1.8 litre engines. . . . . 205 mm
    2.2 litre engines. . . . . 228 mm
  Diesel engine models:
    1.9 litre engines. . . . . 239 mm
    2.0 litre engines. . . . . 228 mm
    2.2 litre engines. . . . . 239 mm
New lining thickness:
  Petrol engine models:
    1.8 litre engines. . . . . 7.65 mm
    2.2 litre engines. . . . . 8.4 mm
  Diesel engine models:
    1.9 litre engines. . . . . 7.8 mm
    2.0 and 2.2 litre engines . . . . 8.4 mm

Torque wrench settings

	Nm	lbf ft
ABS hydraulic modulator mounting bracket bolts	20	15
Brake master cylinder retaining nuts*	50	37
Clutch master cylinder retaining nuts*	20	15
Hydraulic pipe to release cylinder	14	10
Pedal mounting bracket nuts*	20	15
Pressure plate retaining bolts:		
M7 bolts	15	11
M8 bolts	28	21
Release cylinder mounting bolts	5	4
Vacuum servo unit stud bolts*	20	15

* Use new nuts/bolts

1 General information

1 The clutch consists of a friction disc, a pressure plate assembly, and the hydraulic release cylinder (which incorporates the release bearing); all of these components are contained in the large cast-aluminium alloy bellhousing, sandwiched between the engine and the transmission.

2 The friction disc is fitted between the engine flywheel and the clutch pressure plate, and is allowed to slide on the transmission input shaft splines.

3 The pressure plate assembly is bolted to the engine flywheel. When the engine is running, drive is transmitted from the crankshaft, via the flywheel, to the friction disc (these components being clamped securely together by the pressure plate assembly) and from the friction disc to the transmission input shaft.

4 To interrupt the drive, the spring pressure must be relaxed. This is achieved using a hydraulic release mechanism which consists of the master cylinder, the release cylinder and the pipe/hose linking the two components. Depressing the pedal pushes on the master cylinder pushrod which hydraulically forces the release cylinder piston against the pressure plate spring fingers. This causes the springs to deform and releases the clamping force on the friction disc.

5 The clutch is self-adjusting and requires no manual adjustment.

6 The clutch pedal support and clutch pedal are one assembly and must be renewed as a complete unit. In the event of a frontal collision, the clutch pedal is released from its bearing in the support bracket to prevent injury to the driver's feet and legs (this also applies to the brake pedal). If an airbag has been deployed, inspect the clutch pedal assembly and if necessary renew the complete unit.

2 Clutch hydraulic system – bleeding

⚠️ *Warning: Hydraulic fluid is poisonous; wash off immediately and thoroughly in the case of skin contact, and seek immediate medical advice if any fluid is swallowed or gets into the eyes. Certain types of hydraulic fluid are flammable, and may ignite when allowed into contact with hot components; when servicing any hydraulic system, it is safest to assume that the fluid is flammable, and to take precautions against the risk of fire as though it is petrol that is being handled. Hydraulic fluid is also an effective paint stripper, and will attack plastics; if any is spilt, it should be washed off immediately, using copious quantities of fresh water. Finally, it is hygroscopic (it*

2.8 Clutch bleed screw (arrowed)

absorbs moisture from the air) – old fluid may be contaminated and unfit for further use. When topping-up or renewing the fluid, always use the recommended type, and ensure that it comes from a freshly-opened sealed container.

General information

1 The correct operation of any hydraulic system is only possible after removing all air from the components and circuit; this is achieved by bleeding the system.

2 The manufacturer's stipulate that the system must be initially bled by the 'back-bleeding' method using Vauxhall/Opel special bleeding equipment. This entails connecting a pressure bleeding unit containing fresh brake fluid, to the release cylinder bleed screw, with a collecting vessel connected to the brake fluid master cylinder reservoir. The pressure bleeding unit is then switched on, the bleed screw is opened and hydraulic fluid is delivered under pressure, backwards, to be expelled from the reservoir into the collecting vessel. Final bleeding is then carried out in the conventional way.

3 In practice, this method would normally only be required if new hydraulic components have been fitted, or if the system has been completely drained of hydraulic fluid. If the system has only been disconnected to allow component removal and refitting procedures to be carried out, such as removal and refitting of the transmission (for example for clutch renewal) or engine removal and refitting, then it is quite likely that normal bleeding will be sufficient.

4 Our advice would therefore be as follows:
 a) *If the hydraulic system has only been partially disconnected, try bleeding by the conventional methods described in paragraphs 10 to 15, or 16 to 19.*
 b) *If the hydraulic system has been completely drained and new components have been fitted, try bleeding by using the pressure bleeding method described in paragraphs 20 to 22.*
 c) *If the above methods fail to produce a firm pedal on completion, it will be necessary to 'back-bleed' the system using Vauxhall/Opel bleeding equipment, or suitable alternative equipment as described in paragraphs 23 to 28.*

5 During the bleeding procedure, add

only clean, unused hydraulic fluid of the recommended type; never re-use fluid that has already been bled from the system. Ensure that sufficient fluid is available before starting work.

6 If there is any possibility of incorrect fluid being already in the system, the hydraulic circuit must be flushed completely with uncontaminated, correct fluid.

7 If hydraulic fluid has been lost from the system, or air has entered because of a leak, ensure that the fault is cured before continuing further.

8 The bleed screw is located in the hose end fitting which is situated on the top of the transmission housing **(see illustration)**. On some models access to the bleed screw is limited and it may be necessary to jack up the front of the vehicle and support it on axle stands so that the screw can be reached from below, or remove the battery and battery box as described in Chapter 5A, so that the screw can be reached from above.

9 Check that all pipes and hoses are secure, unions tight and the bleed screw is closed. Clean any dirt from around the bleed screw.

Bleeding procedure

Conventional method

10 Collect a clean glass jar, a suitable length of plastic or rubber tubing which is a tight fit over the bleed screw, and a ring spanner to fit the screw. The help of an assistant will also be required.

11 Unscrew the master cylinder fluid reservoir cap (the clutch shares the same fluid reservoir as the braking system), and top the master cylinder reservoir up to the upper (MAX) level line. Ensure that the fluid level is maintained at least above the lower level line in the reservoir throughout the procedure.

12 Remove the dust cap from the bleed screw. Fit the spanner and tube to the screw, place the other end of the tube in the jar, and pour in sufficient fluid to cover the end of the tube.

13 Have the assistant fully depress the clutch pedal several times to build-up pressure, then maintain it on the final down stroke.

14 While pedal pressure is maintained, unscrew the bleed screw (approximately one turn) and allow the compressed fluid and air to flow into the jar. The assistant should maintain pedal pressure and should not release it until instructed to do so. When the flow stops, tighten the bleed screw again, have the assistant release the pedal slowly, and recheck the reservoir fluid level.

15 Repeat the steps given in paragraphs 13 and 14 until the fluid emerging from the bleed screw is free from air bubbles. If the master cylinder has been drained and refilled allow approximately five seconds between cycles for the master cylinder passages to refill.

Conventional method using a one-way valve kit

16 As their name implies, these kits consist of a length of tubing with a one-way valve

fitted, to prevent expelled air and fluid being drawn back into the system; some kits include a translucent container, which can be positioned so that the air bubbles can be more easily seen flowing from the end of the tube.

17 The kit is connected to the bleed screw, which is then opened.

18 The user returns to the driver's seat, depresses the clutch pedal with a smooth, steady stroke, and slowly releases it; this is repeated until the expelled fluid is clear of air bubbles.

19 Note that these kits simplify work so much that it is easy to forget the clutch fluid reservoir level; ensure that this is maintained at least above the lower level line at all times.

Pressure-bleeding method

20 These kits are usually operated by the reservoir of pressurised air contained in the spare tyre. However, note that it will probably be necessary to reduce the pressure to a lower level than normal; refer to the instructions supplied with the kit.

21 By connecting a pressurised, fluid-filled container to the clutch fluid reservoir, bleeding can be carried out simply by opening the bleed screw and allowing the fluid to flow out until no more air bubbles can be seen in the expelled fluid.

22 This method has the advantage that the large reservoir of fluid provides an additional safeguard against air being drawn into the system during bleeding.

'Back-bleeding' method

23 The following procedure describes the bleeding method using Vauxhall/Opel equipment. Alternative equipment is available and should be used in accordance with the maker's instructions.

24 Connect the pressure hose (MKM-6174-1) to the bleed screw located in the hose end fitting situated on the top of the transmission housing **(see illustration 2.8)**. Connect the other end of the hose to a suitable pressure bleeding device set to operate at approximately 2.0 bar.

25 Attach the cap (MKM-6174-2) to the master cylinder reservoir, and place the hose in a collecting vessel.

26 Switch on the pressure bleeding equipment, open the bleed screw, and allow fresh hydraulic fluid to flow from the pressure bleeding unit, through the system and out through the top of the reservoir and into the collecting vessel. When fluid, free from air bubbles appears in the reservoir, close the bleed screw and switch off the bleeding equipment.

27 Disconnect the bleeding equipment from the bleed screw and reservoir.

28 Carry out a final conventional bleeding procedure as described in paragraphs 10 to 15, or 16 to 19.

All methods

29 When bleeding is complete, no more

bubbles appear and correct pedal feel is restored, tighten the bleed screw securely (do not overtighten). Remove the tube and spanner, and wash off any spilt fluid. Refit the dust cap to the bleed screw.

30 Check the hydraulic fluid level in the master cylinder reservoir, and top-up if necessary (see *Weekly checks*).

31 Discard any hydraulic fluid that has been bled from the system; it will not be fit for re-use.

32 Check the operation of the clutch pedal. If the clutch is still not operating correctly, air must still be present in the system, and further bleeding is required. Failure to bleed satisfactorily after a reasonable repetition of the bleeding procedure may be due to worn master cylinder/release cylinder seals.

3 Master cylinder – removal and refitting

Note: *New master cylinder retaining nuts will be required for refitting.*

Removal

Right-hand drive models

1 Where fitted, remove the plastic cover over the top of the engine.

2 Release the clutch hydraulic pipe from the support clip(s) on the bulkhead.

3 Unscrew the brake/clutch hydraulic fluid reservoir filler cap, and top-up the reservoir to the MAX mark (see *Weekly checks*). Place a piece of polythene over the filler neck, and secure the polythene with the filler cap. This will minimise brake fluid loss during subsequent operations.

4 Remove all traces of dirt from the outside of the master cylinder and the brake/clutch hydraulic fluid reservoir, then position some cloth beneath the cylinder to catch any spilt fluid.

5 Extract the retaining clip and disconnect the hydraulic pipe from the connector on the end of the master cylinder **(see illustration)**. Plug the pipe end and master cylinder port to minimise fluid loss and prevent the entry of dirt.

6 Release the retaining clip (where fitted) and disconnect the fluid supply hose from the brake/clutch hydraulic fluid reservoir **(see illustration)**.

7 From inside the car, remove the lower facia panel on the driver's side as described in Chapter 11.

8 Where fitted, remove the clutch switch from the pedal mounting bracket.

9 Separate the clutch pedal from the master cylinder piston rod by releasing the retaining clip at the pedal. Vauxhall technicians use a special tool to do this, however, the clip may be released by pressing the retaining tabs together using screwdrivers, while at the same time pulling the clutch pedal rearwards.

Note: *Do not remove the clip from the master*

3.5 Extract the retaining clip (arrowed) and disconnect the hydraulic pipe from the master cylinder connector

cylinder piston rod, just release it from the pedal.

10 On diesel engine models, move the bulkhead insulation to one side for access to the master cylinder retaining nuts. Use a plastic wedge or similar tool to retain the insulation clear of the nuts.

11 Unscrew the two nuts securing the master cylinder to the bulkhead, then return to the engine compartment and remove the master cylinder from the vehicle. If the master cylinder is faulty it must be renewed; overhaul of the unit is not possible.

Left-hand drive models

12 Remove the battery and battery box as described in Chapter 5A.

13 Pull up the locking bar and disconnect the ABS wiring harness multiplug connector from the electronic control unit located on the hydraulic modulator.

14 Undo the two bolts securing the ABS hydraulic modulator mounting bracket to the bulkhead. Taking great care not to strain the hydraulic brake pipes, carefully lift the modulator and mounting bracket upward to disengage the mounting bracket lower guide. Move the assembly to one side as far as the brake pipes will allow and support it in this position.

15 Release the clutch hydraulic pipe from the two support clips beneath the battery box location.

16 Continue with the removal procedure as described in paragraphs 3 to 11.

3.6 Release the retaining clip (arrowed) and disconnect the fluid supply hose from the reservoir

4.2 Clutch release cylinder hydraulic pipe union nut (arrowed)

Refitting

Right-hand drive models

17 Manoeuvre the master cylinder into position whilst ensuring that the piston rod and its retaining clip align correctly with the pedal. Fit two new master cylinder retaining nuts and tighten them to the specified torque.
18 On diesel engine models, locate the bulkhead insulation back into position.
19 Push the master cylinder piston rod retaining clip into the clutch pedal, ensuring that the two lugs on the clip fully engage.
20 Where applicable, refit the clutch switch to the pedal mounting bracket.
21 Refit the lower facia panel on the driver's side as described in Chapter 11.
22 Connect the fluid supply hose to the brake/clutch hydraulic fluid reservoir and, where applicable, secure with the retaining clip.
23 Press the hydraulic pipe back into the connector on the end of the master cylinder and refit the retaining clip. Ensure that the retaining clip engages fully and the pipe is securely retained. Secure the pipe with the support clip(s).
24 Bleed the clutch hydraulic system as described in Section 2, then refit the engine cover (where applicable).

Left-hand drive models

25 Carry out the operations described in paragraphs 17 to 24.
26 Carefully locate the ABS hydraulic modulator and mounting bracket back into

4.5 Extract the retaining clip (arrowed) and remove the hydraulic hose end fitting from the fastening sleeve

4.3 Clutch release cylinder retaining bolts (arrowed)

position and secure with the two bolts, tightened to the specified torque.
27 Connect the ABS wiring harness multiplug connector to the electronic control unit and secure with the locking bar.
28 Refit the battery box and battery described in Chapter 5A.

4 Release cylinder – removal and refitting

Note 1: *Due to the amount of work necessary to remove and refit clutch components, it is usually considered good practice to renew the clutch friction disc, pressure plate assembly and release cylinder as a matched set, even if only one of these is actually worn enough to require renewal. It is also worth considering the renewal of the clutch components on a preventative basis if the engine and/or transmission have been removed for some other reason.*
Note 2: *Refer to the warning concerning the dangers of asbestos dust at the beginning of Section 6.*

Removal

1 Unless the complete engine/transmission unit is to be removed from the car and separated for major overhaul (see the relevant Part of Chapter 2), the clutch release cylinder can be reached by removing the transmission only, as described in Chapter 7A.
2 Wipe clean the outside of the release cylinder then slacken the union nut and disconnect the

4.10 Make sure the lug (arrowed) on the fastening sleeve is located correctly in the transmission housing

hydraulic pipe **(see illustration)**. Wipe up any spilt fluid with a clean cloth.
3 Unscrew the three retaining bolts and slide the release cylinder off from the transmission input shaft **(see illustration)**. Remove the sealing ring which is fitted between the cylinder and transmission housing and discard it; a new one must be used on refitting. Whilst the cylinder is removed, take care not to allow any debris to enter the transmission unit.
4 The release cylinder is a sealed unit and cannot be overhauled. If the cylinder seals are leaking or the release bearing is noisy or rough in operation, then the complete unit must be renewed.
5 To remove the hydraulic pipe, extract the retaining clip and remove the hydraulic hose end fitting from the fastening sleeve on top of the transmission housing **(see illustration)**. Gently squeeze the legs of the retaining clip together and re-insert the clip back into position in the end fitting.
6 Using a small screwdriver, carefully spread the retaining lugs of the fastening sleeve to release the hydraulic pipe connection, and remove the pipe from inside the transmission housing. Check the condition of the sealing ring on the hydraulic pipe and renew if necessary.
7 If required, the fastening sleeve can be removed by squeezing the lower retaining lugs together with pointed-nose pliers, then withdrawing the sleeve upwards and out of the transmission. Note that if the fastening sleeve is removed, a new one must be obtained for refitting.

Refitting

8 Ensure the release cylinder and transmission mating surfaces are clean and dry and fit the new sealing ring to the transmission recess.
9 Lubricate the release cylinder seal with a smear of transmission oil then carefully ease the cylinder along the input shaft and into position.
Note: *Vauxhall/Opel technicians use a special tapered sleeve on the input shaft to prevent damage to the seal. If necessary, wrap suitable tape around the end of the shaft.* Ensure the sealing ring is still correctly seated in its groove then refit the release cylinder retaining bolts and tighten them to the specified torque.
10 If removed, fit the new fastening sleeve, engaging the lug on the sleeve with the cut-out in the housing **(see illustration)**. Ensure that the sleeve can be felt to positively lock in position.
11 Insert the hydraulic pipe into the fastening sleeve until the end fitting can be felt to positively lock in position.
12 Reconnect the hydraulic pipe to the release cylinder, tightening its union nut to the specified torque.
13 Refit the hydraulic hose end fitting to the fastening sleeve ensuring that it is positively retained by its clip.
14 Refit the transmission unit as described in Chapter 7A.
15 Bleed the clutch hydraulic system as described in Section 2.

5 Clutch pedal –
removal and refitting

Note 1: *The clutch pedal mounting bracket, the clutch pedal and the brake pedal are one assembly and must be renewed as a complete unit. In the event of a frontal collision, the clutch pedal is released from its bearing in the mounting bracket to prevent injury to the driver's feet and legs (this also applies to the brake pedal). If an airbag has been deployed, inspect the pedal and mounting bracket assembly and if necessary renew the complete unit.*
Note 2: *New pedal mounting bracket retaining nuts, vacuum servo unit stud bolts and brake master cylinder retaining nuts will be required for refitting.*

Removal

1 Disconnect the battery negative terminal (refer to *Disconnecting the battery* in the Reference Chapter).
2 Remove the steering column as described in Chapter 10.
3 Remove the complete facia assembly and the facia crossmember as described in Chapter 11.
4 Remove the stop-light switch from the pedal mounting bracket as described in Chapter 9.
5 Refer to Chapter 4A or 4B as applicable and remove the air cleaner assembly, the accelerator pedal/position sensor and, where fitted, the clutch switch from the pedal mounting bracket.
6 Working in the engine compartment, unscrew the two nuts securing the brake master cylinder to the vacuum servo unit. Now unscrew the two stud bolts securing the vacuum servo unit to the bulkhead **(see illustration)**.
7 Separate the clutch pedal from the clutch master cylinder piston rod by releasing the retaining clip at the pedal. Vauxhall technicians use a special tool to do this, however, the clip may be released by pressing the retaining tabs together using screwdrivers, while at the same time pulling the clutch pedal rearwards. **Note:** *Do not remove the clip from the master cylinder piston rod, just release it from the pedal.*
8 Unhook the return spring from behind the brake pedal to release all tension in the spring.
9 Carefully prise open and remove the retaining clip, and withdraw the clevis pin securing the brake pedal to the vacuum servo unit pushrod.
10 From inside the car, slacken and remove the three nuts securing the pedal mounting bracket to the bulkhead. Note that two of the three nuts also secure the clutch master cylinder. On diesel engine models, move the bulkhead insulation to one side for access to the nuts, and use a plastic wedge or similar tool to retain the insulation clear.

11 Withdraw the mounting bracket and pedal assembly from the bulkhead, while at the same time guiding the clutch master cylinder piston rod and retaining clip out of the clutch pedal.

Refitting

12 Manoeuvre the mounting bracket and pedal assembly into position, whilst ensuring that the clutch master cylinder piston rod and its retaining clip align correctly with the clutch pedal. Also ensure that the vacuum servo unit pushrod locates around the brake pedal. Fit three new pedal mounting bracket retaining nuts and tighten them to the specified torque.
13 On diesel engine models, locate the bulkhead insulation back into position.
14 Push the clutch master cylinder piston rod retaining clip into the clutch pedal, ensuring that the two lugs on the clip fully engage.
15 Apply a smear of multipurpose grease to the clevis pin then align the vacuum servo unit pushrod with the brake pedal hole and insert the pin. Secure the pin in position with the retaining clip, making sure it is correctly located in the groove.
16 Hook the return spring into position behind the brake pedal.
17 Working in the engine compartment, fit the two new stud bolts securing the vacuum servo unit to the bulkhead and tighten the bolts to the specified torque. Fit the two new brake master cylinder retaining nuts and tighten the nuts to the specified torque.
18 Refer to Chapter 4A or 4B as applicable and refit the air cleaner assembly and the accelerator pedal/position sensor. Where fitted, refit the clutch switch to the pedal mounting bracket.
19 Refit the stop-light switch to the pedal mounting bracket as described in Chapter 9.
20 Refit the facia crossmember and facia assembly as described in Chapter 11.
21 Refit the steering column as described in Chapter 10.
22 Reconnect the battery negative terminal on completion.

6 Clutch assembly –
removal, inspection and refitting

⚠ **Warning: Dust created by clutch wear and deposited on the clutch components may contain asbestos, which is a health hazard. DO NOT blow it out with compressed air, or inhale any of it. DO NOT use petrol or petroleum-based solvents to clean off the dust. Brake system cleaner or methylated spirit should be used to flush the dust into a suitable receptacle. After the clutch components are wiped clean with rags, dispose of the contaminated rags and cleaner in a sealed, marked container.**
Note: *To prevent possible damage to the ends of the pressure plate diaphragm spring fingers, Vauxhall recommend the use of a special jig*

5.6 Vacuum servo unit retaining stud bolts (arrowed)

(KM-6263) to remove the clutch assembly, however, with care it is possible to carry out the work without the jig.

Removal

1 Unless the complete engine/transmission unit is to be removed from the car and separated for major overhaul (see Chapter 2F), the clutch can be reached by removing the transmission as described in Chapter 7A.
2 Before disturbing the clutch, use chalk or a marker pen to mark the relationship of the pressure plate assembly to the flywheel.
3 At this stage, Vauxhall technicians fit the special jig KM-6263 to the rear of the engine and compress the diaphragm spring fingers until the friction disc is released **(see illustrations overleaf)**. The pressure plate mounting bolts are then unscrewed, and the jig spindle backed off.
4 If the jig is not available, progressively unscrew the pressure plate retaining bolts in diagonal sequence by half a turn at a time, until spring pressure is released and the bolts can be unscrewed by hand.
5 Remove the pressure plate assembly and collect the friction disc, noting which way round the disc is fitted. It is recommended that new pressure plate retaining bolts are obtained.

Inspection

Note: *Due to the amount of work necessary to remove and refit clutch components, it is usually considered good practice to renew the clutch friction disc, pressure plate assembly and release bearing as a matched set, even if only one of these is actually worn enough to require renewal. It is also worth considering the renewal of the clutch components on a preventative basis if the engine and/or transmission have been removed for some other reason.*
6 When cleaning clutch components, read first the warning at the beginning of this Section; remove dust using a clean, dry cloth, and working in a well-ventilated atmosphere.
7 Check the friction disc facings for signs of wear, damage or oil contamination. If the friction material is cracked, burnt, scored or damaged, or if it is contaminated with oil or grease (shown by shiny black patches), the friction disc must be renewed.

6.3a Vauxhall special jig KM-6263 for removing the clutch
pressure plate and friction disc

6.3b Thrust piece (1) in contact with the diaphragm spring
fingers (3) of the pressure plate (2)

1, 3 and 6 Bolts securing the jig to the engine
2 and 5 Bolts for adjusting the jig to the centre of the crankshaft

8 If the friction material is still serviceable, check that the centre boss splines are unworn, that the torsion springs are in good condition and securely fastened, and that all the rivets are tight. If any wear or damage is found, the friction disc must be renewed.

9 If the friction material is fouled with oil, this must be due to an oil leak from the crankshaft oil seal, from the sump-to-cylinder block joint, or from the release cylinder assembly (either the main seal or the sealing ring). Renew the crankshaft oil seal or repair the sump joint as described in the appropriate Part of Chapter 2, before installing the new friction disc. The clutch release cylinder is covered in Section 4.

10 Check the pressure plate assembly for obvious signs of wear or damage; shake it to check for loose rivets, or worn or damaged fulcrum rings, and check that the drive straps securing the pressure plate to the cover do not show signs of overheating

(such as a deep yellow or blue discoloration). If the diaphragm spring is worn or damaged, or if its pressure is in any way suspect, the pressure plate assembly should be renewed.

11 Examine the machined bearing surfaces of the pressure plate and of the flywheel; they should be clean, completely flat, and free from scratches or scoring. If either is discoloured from excessive heat, or shows signs of cracks, it should be renewed – although minor damage of this nature can sometimes be polished away using emery paper.

12 Check that the release cylinder bearing rotates smoothly and easily, with no sign of noise or roughness. Also check that the surface itself is smooth and unworn, with no signs of cracks, pitting or scoring. If there is any doubt about its condition, the clutch release cylinder should be renewed (it is not possible to renew the bearing separately).

Refitting

13 On 1.9 and 2.2 litre diesel models the clutch pressure plate is unusual, as there is a pre-adjustment mechanism to compensate for wear in the friction disc (this is termed by Vauxhall/Opel as a self-adjusting clutch (SAC), which is slightly ambiguous as all clutches fitted to these models are essentially self-adjusting). However, this mechanism must be reset before refitting the pressure plate. A new plate may be supplied preset, in which case this procedure can be ignored.

14 A large diameter bolt (M14 at least) long enough to pass through the pressure plate, a matching nut, and several large diameter washers, will be needed for this procedure. Mount the bolt head in the jaws of a sturdy bench vice, with one large washer fitted.

15 Offer the plate over the bolt, friction disc surface facing down, and locate it centrally over the bolt and washer – the washer should bear on the centre hub **(see illustration)**.

16 Fit several further large washers over the bolt, so that they bear on the ends of the spring fingers, then add the nut and tighten by hand to locate the washers **(see illustration)**.

17 The purpose of the procedure is to turn the plate's internal adjuster disc so that the three small coil springs visible on the plate's outer surface are fully compressed. Tighten the nut just fitted until the adjuster disc is free to turn. Using a pair of thin-nosed, or circlip pliers, in one of the three windows in the top surface, open the jaws of the pliers to turn the adjuster disc anti-clockwise, so that the springs are fully compressed **(see illustrations)**.

6.15 Mount a large bolt and washer into a
vice, then fit the pressure plate over it

6.16 Fit large washers and a nut to the bolt
and hand-tighten

6.17a Tighten the nut until the spring adjuster is free to turn . . .

6.17b . . . then open up the jaws of suitable pliers to compress the springs

6.21 The lettering 'transmission side' or 'Getriebeseite' on the friction disc must point towards the transmission

18 Hold the pliers in this position, then unscrew the centre nut. Once the nut is released, the adjuster disc will be gripped in position, and the pliers can be removed. Take the pressure plate from the vice, and it is ready to fit.
19 On reassembly, ensure that the friction surfaces of the flywheel and pressure plate are completely clean, smooth, and free from oil or grease. Use solvent to remove any protective grease from new components.
20 Lightly grease the teeth of the friction disc hub with high melting-point grease. Do not apply too much, otherwise it may eventually contaminate the friction disc linings.

Using the Vauxhall jig

21 Fit the special Vauxhall guide bush to the centre of the crankshaft, and locate the friction disc on it, making sure that the lettering 'transmission side' or 'Getriebeseite' points towards the transmission (see illustration).
22 Locate the pressure plate on the special centring pins on the flywheel, then compress the diaphragm spring fingers with the jig, until the friction disc is in full contact with the flywheel.
23 Insert new pressure plate retaining bolts, and progressively tighten them to the specified torque. If necessary, hold the flywheel stationary while tightening the bolts, using a screwdriver engaged with the teeth of the starter ring gear.
24 Back off the jig spindle so that the

6.27 Fit the pressure plate assembly over the friction disc

diaphragm spring forces the pressure plate against the friction disc and flywheel, then remove the jig and guide bush from the engine.
25 Refit the transmission as described in Chapter 7A.

Without using the Vauxhall jig

26 Locate the friction disc on the flywheel, making sure that the lettering 'transmission side' or 'Getriebeseite' points towards the transmission (see illustration 6.21).
27 Refit the pressure plate assembly, aligning the marks made on dismantling (if the original pressure plate is re-used). Fit new pressure plate bolts, but tighten them only finger-tight so that the friction disc can still be moved (see illustration).
28 The friction disc must now be centralised

6.29 Centralise the friction disc using a clutch aligning tool or similar

so that, when the transmission is refitted, its input shaft will pass through the splines at the centre of the friction disc.
29 Centralisation can be achieved by passing a screwdriver or other long bar through the friction disc and into the hole in the crankshaft. The friction disc can then be moved around until it is centred on the crankshaft hole. Alternatively, a clutch-aligning tool can be used to eliminate the guesswork; these can be obtained from most accessory shops (see illustration).
30 When the friction disc is centralised, tighten the pressure plate bolts evenly and in a diagonal sequence to the specified torque setting.
31 Refit the transmission as described in Chapter 7A.

Chapter 7 Part A:
Manual transmission

Contents

Degrees of difficulty

Easy, suitable for novice with little experience	**Fairly easy,** suitable for beginner with some experience	**Fairly difficult,** suitable for competent DIY mechanic	**Difficult,** suitable for experienced DIY mechanic	**Very difficult,** suitable for expert DIY or professional

Specifications

General

Type:
All except 1.9 litre diesel engine models	Five forward speeds and reverse. Synchromesh on all forward speeds
1.9 litre diesel engine models	Six forward speeds and reverse. Synchromesh on all forward speeds

Manufacturer's designation:
1.8 litre petrol engine models	F17+ WR/CR
2.2 litre petrol engine models	F23 SR
1.9 litre diesel engine models	F40 WR
2.0 litre diesel engine models	F23 WR
2.2 litre diesel engine models	F35 WR

WR = Wide Ratio (wide ratio gear set)
SR = Standard Ratio (standard ratio gear set)
CR = Close Ratio (close ratio gear set)

Lubrication

Lubricant type	See *Lubricants and fluids*
Lubricant capacity	See Chapter 1A or 1B

Final drive ratios

F17+ transmissions	3.94:1

F23 transmissions:
Petrol engine models:	
Saloon and Hatchback	3.95:1
Estate	4.17:1
Diesel engine models	3.74:1
F35 transmissions	3.61:1
F40 transmissions	3.55:1

Gear ratios

F17+ WR transmissions:
1st.	3.73:1
2nd	1.96:1
3rd	1.32:1
4th.	0.95:1
5th.	0.76:1
Reverse.	3.31:1

F17+ CR transmissions:
1st.	3.73:1
2nd	2.14:1
3rd	1.14:1
4th.	1.12:1
5th.	0.89:1
Reverse.	3.31:1

F23 SR transmissions:
1st.	3.58:1
2nd	2.02:1
3rd	1.35:1
4th.	0.98:1
5th.	0.81:1
Reverse.	3.31:1

F23 WR transmissions:
1st.	3.58:1
2nd	1.89:1
3rd	1.19:1
4th.	0.85:1
5th.	0.69:1
Reverse.	3.31:1

F35 WR transmissions:
1st.	3.67:1
2nd	1.88:1
3rd	1.18:1
4th.	0.89:1
5th.	0.66:1
Reverse.	3.43:1

F40 WR transmissions:
1st.	3.92:1
2nd	2.04:1
3rd	1.32:1
4th.	0.95:1
5th.	0.76:1
6th.	0.62:1
Reverse.	3.75:1

Torque wrench settings

	Nm	lbf ft
Differential lower cover plate bolts (F17+ transmissions).	18	13
Engine/transmission mountings.	See the relevant Part of Chapter 2	
Engine-to-transmission bolts	See the relevant Part of Chapter 2	
Gearchange lever assembly mounting bolts	10	7
Oil drain plug:		
F23 transmissions	35	26
F35 transmissions	50	37
F40 transmissions	50	37
Oil filler plug:		
F23 transmissions	35	26
F40 transmissions	50	37
Oil level plug:		
F17+ transmissions:		
Stage 1	4	3
Stage 2	Angle-tighten a further 45°	
Stage 3	Angle-tighten a further 135°	
F23 transmissions	35	26
F35 transmissions	50	37
Reversing light switch	20	15
Roadwheel bolts.	110	81

1 General information

The transmission is contained in a cast-aluminium alloy casing bolted to the engine's left-hand end, and consists of the gearbox and final drive differential – often called a transaxle.

Drive is transmitted from the crankshaft via the clutch to the input shaft, which has a splined extension to accept the clutch friction disc, and rotates in sealed ball-bearings. From the input shaft, drive is transmitted to the output shaft, which rotates in a roller bearing at its right-hand end, and a sealed ball-bearing at its left-hand end. From the output shaft, the drive is transmitted to the differential crown-wheel, which rotates with the differential case and planetary gears, thus driving the sun gears and driveshafts. The rotation of the planetary gears on their shaft allows the inner roadwheel to rotate at a slower speed than the outer roadwheel when the car is cornering.

The input and output shafts are arranged side-by-side, parallel to the crankshaft and driveshafts, so that their gear pinion teeth are in constant mesh. In the neutral position, the output shaft gear pinions rotate freely, so that drive cannot be transmitted to the crownwheel.

Gear selection is via a floor-mounted lever and cable-operated selector linkage mechanism. The selector linkage cause the appropriate selector fork to move its respective synchro-sleeve along the shaft, to lock the gear pinion to the synchro-hub. Since the synchro-hubs are splined to the output shaft, this locks the pinion to the shaft, so that drive can be transmitted. To ensure that gearchanging can be made quickly and quietly, a synchromesh system is fitted to all forward gears, consisting of baulk rings and spring-loaded fingers, as well as the gear pinions and synchro-hubs. The synchromesh cones are formed on the mating faces of the baulk rings and gear pinions.

2 Transmission oil – draining and refilling

1 This operation is much more efficient if the car is first taken on a journey of sufficient length to warm the engine/transmission up to normal operating temperature.
Caution: If the procedure is to be carried out on a hot transmission unit, take care not to burn yourself on the hot exhaust or the transmission/engine unit.
2 Position the vehicle over an inspection pit, on vehicle ramps, or jack it up and support it securely on axle stands (see *Jacking and vehicle support*), but make sure that it is level. On diesel engine models, undo the ten bolts

2.5 Undo the bolts (arrowed) and remove the cover plate – F17+ transmissions

and remove the undertray from beneath the engine.

F17+ transmissions

Note: *A new differential lower cover plate gasket will be required for this operation.*

Draining

3 Since the transmission oil is not renewed as part of the manufacturer's maintenance schedule, no drain plug is fitted to the transmission. If the transmission needs to be drained, the only way of doing so is to remove the differential lower cover plate.
4 Wipe clean the area around the differential cover plate and position a suitable container underneath the cover.
5 Evenly and progressively slacken and remove the retaining bolts then withdraw the cover plate and allow the transmission oil to drain into the container **(see illustration)**. Remove the gasket and discard it; a new one should be used on refitting.
6 Allow the oil to drain completely into the container. If the oil is hot, take precautions against scalding. Remove all traces of dirt and oil from the cover and transmission mating surfaces and wipe clean the inside of the cover plate.
7 Once the oil has finished draining, ensure the mating surfaces are clean and dry then refit the cover plate to the transmission unit, complete with a new gasket. Refit the retaining bolts and evenly and progressively tighten them to the specified torque.

Refilling

8 Wipe clean the area around the level plug.

2.9 Using a funnel to fill the transmission via the reversing light switch aperture – F17+ transmissions

2.8 Transmission oil level plug (arrowed) – F17+ transmissions

The level plug is located behind the driveshaft inner joint on the left-hand side of the transmission **(see illustration)**. Unscrew the plug and clean it.
9 The transmission is refilled via the reversing light switch aperture **(see illustration)**. Wipe clean the area around the reversing light switch, and remove the switch as described in Section 6. Refill the transmission with the specified grade of oil given in *Lubricants and fluids*, until it reaches the bottom of the level plug aperture. Allow any excess oil to drain, then refit and tighten the level plug to the specified torque.
10 Refit the reversing light switch with reference to Section 6, then lower the vehicle to the ground.

F23 transmissions

Draining

11 Wipe clean the area around the drain plug, located below the left-hand driveshaft, and position a suitable container under the plug.
12 Undo the drain plug and allow the oil to drain.
13 Once the oil has finished draining, refit the drain plug with a new sealing washer where applicable, and tighten the plug to the specified torque.

Refilling

14 Wipe clean the area around the level plug located on the rear of the differential housing **(see illustration)**. Unscrew the plug and clean it.
15 The transmission is refilled via the oil filler plug on the top of the casing **(see illustration)**.

2.14 Transmission oil level plug (arrowed) – F23 transmissions

**2.15 Transmission oil filler plug (arrowed) –
F23 transmissions**

**2.24 Transmission oil drain plug (arrowed)
– F40 transmissions**

**2.27 Transmission oil filler plug (arrowed) –
F40 transmissions**

**2.28 Use a graduated container to fill the
transmission with the specified quantity of
oil – F40 transmissions**

Wipe clean the area around the plug and
unscrew it. Refill the transmission with the
specified grade of oil given in *Lubricants and
fluids*, until it reaches the bottom of the level
plug aperture. Allow any excess oil to drain,
then refit and tighten the level plug to the
specified torque.
16 Refit the oil filler plug and tighten it to the
specified torque. Where applicable, refit the
engine undertray, then lower the vehicle to the
ground.

F35 transmissions

Draining

17 Wipe clean the area around the drain plug,
located below the left-hand driveshaft, and
position a suitable container under the plug.
18 Undo the drain plug and allow the oil to
drain.
19 Once the oil has finished draining, refit

the drain plug with a new sealing washer
where applicable, and tighten the plug to the
specified torque.

Refilling

20 Wipe clean the area around the level plug.
The level plug is located behind the driveshaft
inner joint on the left-hand side of the
transmission **(see illustration 2.8)**. Unscrew
the plug and clean it.
21 The transmission is refilled via the
reversing light switch aperture. Wipe clean
the area around the reversing light switch, and
remove the switch as described in Section 6.
Refill the transmission with the specified grade
of oil given in *Lubricants and fluids*, until it
reaches the bottom of the level plug aperture.
Allow any excess oil to drain, then refit and
tighten the level plug to the specified torque.
22 Refit the reversing light switch with
reference to Section 6.

23 Refit the engine undertray, then lower the
vehicle to the ground.

F40 transmissions

Draining

24 Wipe clean the area around the drain plug,
located at the base of the differential housing,
and position a suitable container under the
plug **(see illustration)**.
25 Undo the drain plug and allow the oil to
drain.
26 Once the oil has finished draining, refit
the drain plug with a new sealing washer,
where applicable, and tighten the plug to the
specified torque.

Refilling

27 The transmission is refilled via the oil filler
plug on the top of the casing **(see illustration)**.
To gain access to the plug, remove the battery
and battery box as described in Chapter 5A.
28 Wipe clean the area around the plug and
unscrew it. Refill the transmission with *exactly*
3.2 litres of the specified grade of oil given in
Lubricants and fluids, then refit and tighten
the oil filler plug to the specified torque **(see
illustration)**.
29 Refit the engine undertray, then lower the
vehicle to the ground.
30 Refit the battery box and battery as
described in Chapter 5A.

**3 Gearchange mechanism –
adjustment**

F17+ and F40 transmissions

Note: *A 5 mm drill bit or dowel rod will be
required to carry out this procedure.*
1 From inside the car, unclip the gearchange
lever gaiter retaining frame from the centre
console and lift it off the gearchange lever
(see illustration).
2 Remove the ashtray from the centre console
by opening the lid, depressing the internal tabs
each side and lifting out **(see illustration)**.
3 Release the retaining lugs around the
sides and rear of the gearchange lever gaiter.
Disengage the locating pegs at the front and
fold the gaiter up over the gearchange lever
knob **(see illustrations)**.

**3.1 Unclip and remove the gearchange
lever gaiter retaining frame from the centre
console**

**3.2 Remove the ashtray by depressing the
internal tabs each side and lifting out**

**3.3a Release the retaining lugs around
the sides and rear of the gearchange lever
gaiter . . .**

3.3b . . . then disengage the pegs (arrowed) and fold the gaiter up the lever

3.4a Using a small screwdriver, open the clamping piece on the end of each selector cable . . .

3.4b . . . until the lug (arrowed) rests on the notch

4 Using a small screwdriver, open the clamping piece on the end of each selector cable as far as the notch. Opening them any further may damage the clamping pieces **(see illustrations)**.

5 Pull up the reverse gear detent ring on the gearchange lever to expose the two tabs on the locking block. Depress the two tabs until the locking block releases and moves down the lever **(see illustration)**.

6 Move the gearchange lever to the left and engage the lug at the base of the locking block with the slot on the side of the gearchange lever base **(see illustration)**. The lever is now locked in the adjustment position.

7 In the engine compartment, set the gearchange selector on the transmission to the 'neutral' position. Press the selector down (F17+ transmissions) or pull it up (F40 transmissions) and lock it in the adjustment position by inserting a 5 mm drill bit or dowel rod through the hole in the side of the housing **(see illustration)**. Ensure that the drill bit or dowel rod fully engages with the selector.

8 Working back inside the car, lock both gearshift cable clamping pieces by pushing them down.

9 Remove the drill bit or dowel rod used to lock the gearchange selector on the transmission.

10 Lift the locking block on the gearchange lever out of the slot on the lever base, and slide it fully up the lever until it locks back in its original position.

11 Refit the gearchange lever gaiter and retaining frame to the centre console, then refit the ashtray. Check the gear selector mechanism for correct operation.

F23 transmissions

12 Carry out the operations described in paragraphs 1 to 4 above.

13 In the engine compartment, set the gearchange selector on the transmission to 'neutral' position.

14 Working back inside the car, position the gearchange lever in the 'neutral' position, and lock it there by pushing in the clamp **(see illustration)**.

15 Lock both gearshift cable clamping pieces by pushing them down.

3.5 Pull up the reverse gear detent ring on the gearchange lever to expose the two tabs (arrowed) on the locking block

16 Pull out the clamp locking the gearchange lever, then refit the lever gaiter and retaining frame to the centre console. Refit the ashtray and check the gear selector mechanism for correct operation.

F35 transmissions

Note: *Vauxhall/Opel special tool KM-6325 will be required to carry out this procedure.*

17 Carry out the operations described in paragraphs 1 to 5 above.

18 Move the gearchange lever rearwards to the 4th gear position and engage the lug at the base of the locking block with the slot on the rear of the gearchange lever base.

19 In the engine compartment, set the

3.7 Using a 5 mm drill bit (arrowed) to lock the selector mechanism in the adjustment position – F40 transmission shown

3.6 Engage the lug (arrowed) at the base of the locking block with the slot on the side of the gearchange lever base

selector mechanism on the transmission to the 4th gear position. Insert the special tool (KM-6325) onto the selector mechanism lower lever ensuring that the tool positively locks into position.

20 Working back inside the car, lock both gearshift cable clamping pieces by pushing them down.

21 Remove the special tool from the transmission selector mechanism.

22 Lift the locking block on the gearchange lever out of the slot on the lever base, and slide it fully up the lever until it locks back in its original position.

23 Refit the gearchange lever gaiter and retaining frame to the centre console, then refit the ashtray. Check the gear selector mechanism for correct operation.

3.14 Lock the gearchange lever in 'neutral' by pushing in the clamp with a screwdriver – F23 transmissions

4.2a Extract the retaining clip . . .

4.2b . . . and remove the rear passenger air duct

4.5 Depress the lugs on the sides of the outer cable ends and lift the cables from the gearchange lever base

4.7a Gearchange lever assembly front retaining bolts (arrowed) . . .

4.7b . . . and rear retaining bolts (arrowed)

10 Position the gearchange lever assembly on the floor, insert the securing bolts and tighten to the specified torque.

11 Engage the selector inner cables with the clamping pieces, then refit the outer cables to the gearchange lever base. Do not lock the clamping pieces at this stage.

12 Carry out the gearchange mechanism adjustment procedure, as described in the previous Section.

13 Refit the rear passenger air duct and secure with the retaining clip.

14 Reconnect the wiring connector to the diagnostic socket then refit the mounting bracket and secure with the two bolts.

15 Refit the centre console as described in Chapter 11.

4 Gearchange mechanism – removal and refitting

Gearchange lever

Removal

1 Remove the centre console as described in Chapter 11.

2 Extract the retaining clip and remove the rear passenger air duct **(see illustrations)**.

3 Undo the retaining bolt each side and release the diagnostic socket mounting bracket from the base of the facia. Disconnect the wiring connector and remove the bracket and diagnostic socket.

4 Using a small screwdriver, open the clamping piece on the end of each selector cable as far as the notch. Opening them any

further may damage the clamping pieces **(see illustrations 3.4a and 3.4b)**.

5 Note the fitted locations of the two cables, then depress the lugs on the sides of the outer cable ends and lift the outer cables from the gearchange lever base **(see illustration)**.

6 Move the two selector cables forward to disengage the inner cables from the gearchange lever clamping pieces.

7 Undo the four retaining bolts and lift the gearchange lever assembly from the floor **(see illustrations)**.

8 If required, the cable clamping pieces attached to the gearchange lever can be carefully prised from their position using a forked tool. No further dismantling of the assembly is recommended.

Refitting

9 If previously removed, attached the cable clamping pieces to the base of the lever using a pair of pliers.

Selector cables

Removal

16 Carry out the operations described in paragraphs 1 to 6 above.

17 Working in the engine compartment, note the fitted locations of the cables at their transmission attachments.

18 Using a suitable forked tool, release the inner cable end fittings from the transmission selector levers **(see illustration)**.

19 Pull back the retaining sleeves and detach the outer cables from the mounting bracket on the transmission **(see illustration)**.

20 Release the rubber grommet at the cable entry point on the engine compartment bulkhead, then pull the cables (complete with grommet) out of the bulkhead and into the engine compartment **(see illustration)**.

4.18 Release the inner cable end fittings from the transmission selector levers

4.19 Pull back the retaining sleeves and detach the outer cables from the transmission mounting bracket

4.20 Release the bulkhead rubber grommet (arrowed), then pull the cables into the engine compartment

Refitting

21 Push the selector cables through the bulkhead passage from the engine compartment and locate the rubber grommet back into position in the bulkhead.

22 Refit the outer cables to the mounting bracket on the transmission.

23 Engage the inner cable end fittings with the transmission selector levers, squeezing them together with pliers if necessary.

24 Carry out the operations described in paragraphs 11 to 15 above.

5 Oil seals – renewal

Driveshaft oil seals

1 Firmly apply the handbrake, then jack up the front of the car and support it securely on axle stands (see *Jacking and vehicle support*).

2 Drain the transmission oil as described in Section 2.

3 Remove the driveshaft as described in Chapter 8.

4 Note the correct fitted depth of the seal in its housing then carefully prise it out of position using a large flat-bladed screwdriver **(see illustration)**.

5 Remove all traces of dirt from the area around the oil seal aperture, then apply a smear of grease to the outer lip of the new oil seal. Ensure the seal is correctly positioned, with its sealing lip facing inwards, and tap it squarely into position, using a suitable tubular drift (such as a socket) which bears only on the hard outer edge of the seal **(see illustration)**. Ensure the seal is fitted at the same depth in its housing that the original was.

6 Refit the driveshaft as described in Chapter 8.

7 Refill the transmission with the specified type and amount of oil, as described in Section 2.

Input shaft oil seal

8 The input shaft oil seal is an integral part of the clutch release cylinder; if the seal is leaking the complete release cylinder assembly must be renewed. Before condemning the release cylinder, check that the leak is not coming from the sealing ring which is fitted between the cylinder and the transmission housing; the sealing ring can be renewed once the release cylinder assembly has been removed. Refer to Chapter 6 for removal and refitting details.

6 Reversing light switch – testing, removal and refitting

F17+ transmissions

1 The reversing light circuit is controlled by a plunger-type switch screwed into the top

5.4 Prising out a driveshaft oil seal

of the transmission towards the front of the housing.

Testing

2 If a fault develops in the circuit, first ensure that the circuit fuse has not blown and that the reversing light bulbs are sound.

3 To test the switch, disconnect the wiring connector. Use a multimeter (set to the resistance function) or a battery-and-bulb test circuit to check that there is continuity between the switch terminals only when reverse gear is selected. If this is not the case, and there are no obvious breaks or other damage to the wires, the switch is faulty, and must be renewed.

Removal

4 Disconnect the wiring connector, then unscrew the switch and remove it from the transmission casing along with its sealing washer **(see illustration)**.

Refitting

5 Fit a new sealing washer to the switch, then screw it back into position in the top of the transmission housing and tighten it to the specified torque. Reconnect the wiring connector, then test the operation of the circuit.

F23 transmissions

6 The reversing light circuit is controlled by a plunger-type switch screwed into the rear of the transmission above the left-hand driveshaft.

7 To gain access to the switch, firmly apply

6.4 Unscrew and remove the reversing light switch together with its sealing washer – F17+ transmissions

5.5 Fitting a new driveshaft oil seal using a socket as a tubular drift

the handbrake, then jack up the front of the car and support it securely on axle stands (see *Jacking and vehicle support*). On diesel engine models, undo the ten bolts and remove the undertray from beneath the engine.

Testing

8 Proceed as described in paragraphs 2 and 3 above.

Removal

9 Disconnect the wiring connector, then unscrew the switch and remove it from the transmission casing along with its sealing washer **(see illustration)**.

Refitting

10 Fit a new sealing washer to the switch, then screw it back into position in the rear of the transmission housing and tighten it to the specified torque. Reconnect the wiring connector, then test the operation of the circuit.

11 On completion, refit the engine undertray (where applicable) and lower the vehicle to the ground.

F35 transmissions

12 The reversing light circuit is controlled by a plunger-type switch screwed into the top of the transmission towards the front of the housing.

13 To gain access to the switch, unclip the pre/post-heating system control unit and slide it up and off the side of the battery box.

Testing

14 Proceed as described in paragraphs 2 and 3 above.

6.9 The reversing light switch (arrowed) is positioned above the left-hand driveshaft – F23 transmissions

6.20 The reversing light switch (arrowed) is screwed into the transmission selector lever housing – F40 transmissions

Removal

15 Disconnect the wiring connector, then unscrew the switch and remove it from the transmission casing along with its sealing washer.

Refitting

16 Fit a new sealing washer to the switch, then screw it back into position in the top of the transmission housing and tighten it to the specified torque. Reconnect the wiring connector, then test the operation of the circuit.

17 On completion, refit the pre/post-heating system control unit to the battery box.

F40 transmissions

18 The reversing light circuit is controlled by a plunger-type switch screwed into the selector lever housing on top of the transmission.

Testing

19 Proceed as described in paragraphs 2 and 3 above.

Removal

20 Disconnect the wiring connector, then unscrew the switch and remove it from the selector lever housing along with its sealing washer **(see illustration)**.

Refitting

21 Fit a new sealing washer to the switch, then screw it back into position in the selector lever housing and tighten it to the specified torque. Reconnect the wiring connector, then test the operation of the circuit.

7.7a Using a small screwdriver, prise out the retaining clip . . .

7 Transmission – removal and refitting

Removal

1 Apply the handbrake, then jack up the front of the vehicle and support it on axle stands (see *Jacking and vehicle support*). Allow sufficient working room to remove the transmission from under the left-hand side of the engine compartment. Remove both front roadwheels then, on diesel engine models, undo the ten bolts and remove the undertray from beneath the engine. Also remove the engine top cover where fitted.

2 Remove the battery, battery box, and the starter motor as described in Chapter 5A.

3 Remove the air cleaner housing and intake ducts as described in the relevant Part of Chapter 4.

4 Remove the front bumper as described in Chapter 11.

5 Drain the transmission oil as described in Section 2.

6 Remove the filler cap from the brake/clutch fluid reservoir on the bulkhead, then tighten it onto a piece of polythene. This will reduce the loss of fluid when the clutch hydraulic hose is disconnected. Alternatively, fit a hose clamp to the flexible hose next to the clutch hydraulic connection on the transmission housing.

7 Place some cloth rags beneath the hose, then prise out the retaining clip securing the clutch hydraulic hose to the end fitting on top of the transmission bellhousing. Detach the hose from the end fitting **(see illustrations)**. Gently squeeze the two legs of the retaining clip together and re-insert the retaining clip back into position in the end fitting. Discard the sealing ring from the hose end; a new sealing ring must be used on refitting. Plug/cover both the end fitting and hose end to minimise fluid loss and prevent the entry of dirt into the hydraulic system. **Note:** *Whilst the hose is disconnected, do not depress the clutch pedal.*

8 Note the fitted locations of the gearchange selector cables at their transmission attachments. Using a suitable forked tool,

7.7b . . . and disconnect the clutch hydraulic hose from the end fitting on the transmission bellhousing

release the inner cable end fittings from the transmission selector levers. Pull back the retaining sleeves and release the outer cables from the mounting bracket on the transmission **(see illustrations 4.18 and 4.19)**. Undo the retaining bolts and remove the cable mounting bracket(s) from the transmission.

9 Disconnect the wiring connector from the reversing light switch and free the wiring from the transmission unit and retaining brackets.

10 Disconnect the inner ends of both driveshafts from the differential as described in Chapter 8. There is no need to disconnect the driveshafts from the swivel hub. Support the driveshafts by suspending them with wire or string – do not allow the driveshafts to hang down under their own weight, or the joints may be damaged.

11 Unscrew and remove the upper bolts securing the transmission to the rear of the engine. Where necessary, pull up the coolant hoses and secure them away from the transmission using plastic cable ties.

12 Remove the front subframe assembly as described in Chapter 10, ensuring that the engine unit is securely supported by connecting a hoist to the engine assembly. If available, the type of support bar which locates in the engine compartment side channels is to be preferred.

13 Unbolt and remove the front and rear engine/transmission mounting torque link brackets with reference to the relevant Part of Chapter 2.

14 Place a jack with a block of wood beneath the transmission, and raise the jack to take the weight of the transmission.

15 Unbolt and remove the left-hand engine/transmission mounting bracket from the transmission with reference to the relevant Part of Chapter 2.

16 Lower the engine and transmission by approximately 5 cm making sure that the coolant hoses and wiring harnesses are not stretched.

17 Slacken and remove the remaining bolts securing the transmission to the engine and sump flange. Note the correct fitted positions of each bolt, and the relevant brackets, as they are removed to use as a reference on refitting. Make a final check that all components have been disconnected, and are positioned clear of the transmission so that they will not hinder the removal procedure.

18 With the bolts removed, move the trolley jack and transmission, to free it from its locating dowels. Once the transmission is free, lower the jack and manoeuvre the unit out from under the car. Remove the locating dowels from the transmission or engine if they are loose, and keep them in a safe place.

Refitting

19 The transmission is refitted by a reversal of the removal procedure, bearing in mind the following points.

a) *Ensure the locating dowels are correctly positioned prior to installation.*

b) Tighten all nuts and bolts to the specified torque (where given).

c) Renew the driveshaft oil seals (see Section 5) before refitting the driveshafts.

d) Refit the front subframe assembly as described in Chapter 10.

e) Fit a new sealing ring to the clutch hydraulic hose before clipping the hose into the end fitting. Ensure the hose is securely retained by its clip then bleed the hydraulic system as described in Chapter 6.

f) Refill the transmission with the specified type and quantity of oil, as described in Section 2.

g) On completion, adjust the gearchange mechanism as described in Section 3.

8 Transmission overhaul – general information

1 Overhauling a manual transmission unit is a difficult and involved job for the DIY home mechanic. In addition to dismantling and reassembling many small parts, clearances must be precisely measured and, if necessary, changed by selecting shims and spacers. Internal transmission components are also often difficult to obtain, and in many instances, extremely expensive. Because of this, if the transmission develops a fault or becomes noisy, the best course of action is to have the unit overhauled by a specialist repairer, or to obtain an exchange reconditioned unit.

2 Nevertheless, it is not impossible for the more experienced mechanic to overhaul the transmission, provided the special tools are available, and the job is done in a deliberate step-by-step manner, so that nothing is overlooked.

3 The tools necessary for an overhaul include internal and external circlip pliers, bearing pullers, a slide hammer, a set of pin punches, a dial test indicator, and possibly a hydraulic press. In addition, a large, sturdy workbench and a vice will be required.

4 During dismantling of the transmission, make careful notes of how each component is fitted, to make reassembly easier and more accurate.

5 Before dismantling the transmission, it will help if you have some idea what area is malfunctioning. Certain problems can be closely related to specific areas in the transmission, which can make component examination and renewal easier. Refer to the Fault finding Section of this manual for more information.

9 Transmission oil level check

1 Position the vehicle over an inspection pit, on vehicle ramps, or jack it up and support it securely on axle stands (see Jacking and vehicle support), but make sure that it is level. The oil must be checked before the car is driven, or at least 5 minutes after the engine has been switched off. If the oil is checked immediately after driving the car, some of the oil will remain distributed around the transmission components, resulting in an inaccurate level reading.

F17+ and F35 transmissions

2 On diesel engine models, undo the ten bolts and remove the undertray from beneath the engine.

3 Wipe clean the area around the level plug. The level plug is located behind the driveshaft inner joint on the left-hand side of the transmission (see illustration 2.8). Unscrew the plug and clean it.

4 The oil level should reach the lower edge of the level plug aperture. If topping-up is necessary, wipe clean the area around the reversing light switch, and remove the switch as described in Section 6.

5 Add the specified grade of oil given in Lubricants and fluids, through the reversing light switch aperture, until it reaches the bottom of the level plug aperture. Allow any excess oil to drain, then refit and tighten the level plug to the specified torque.

6 Refit the reversing light switch with reference to Section 6.

7 Where applicable, refit the engine undertray, then lower the vehicle to the ground.

F23 transmissions

8 Wipe clean the area around the level plug located on the rear of the differential housing (see illustration 2.14). Unscrew the plug and clean it.

9 The oil level should reach the lower edge of the level plug aperture. If topping-up is necessary, wipe clean the area around the filler plug on the top of the casing and unscrew the plug (see illustration 2.15).

10 Add the specified grade of oil given in Lubricants and fluids, through the filler plug aperture, until it reaches the bottom of the level plug aperture. Allow any excess oil to drain, then refit and tighten the level plug to the specified torque.

11 Refit the oil filler plug and tighten it to the specified torque. Where applicable, refit the engine undertray, then lower the vehicle to the ground.

F40 transmissions

12 On the F40 type transmission, there is no provision for oil level checking once the transmission has been initially filled. If for any reason it is thought that the oil level may be low, the transmission oil must be completely drained, then refilled with an exact specified quantity of oil as described in Section 2.

Chapter 7 Part B:
Automatic transmission

Contents

Degrees of difficulty

Easy, suitable for novice with little experience	**Fairly easy,** suitable for beginner with some experience	**Fairly difficult,** suitable for competent DIY mechanic	**Difficult,** suitable for experienced DIY mechanic	**Very difficult,** suitable for expert DIY or professional

Specifications

General

Type:

All except 1.9 litre diesel engine models . . . . Electronically-controlled adaptive automatic, five forward speeds and reverse, with sequential manual gear selection capability

1.9 litre diesel engine models . . . . Electronically-controlled adaptive automatic, six forward speeds and reverse, with sequential manual gear selection capability

Manufacturer's designation:
2.2 litre petrol engine models	AF23
1.9 litre diesel engine models	AF40
2.2 litre diesel engine models	AF33

Lubrication
Lubricant type	See *Lubricants and fluids*
Lubricant capacity	See Chapter 1A or 1B

Torque wrench settings

	Nm	lbf ft
Automatic transmission fluid drain/filler plugs:		
AF23 and AF33 transmissions:		
Dipstick retaining bolt	20	15
Drain plug	40	30
Filler plug	30	22
AF40 transmissions:		
Drain plug	50	37
Filler plug	40	30
Level checking plug	8	6
Electronic control unit mounting bolts (AF40 transmissions)	25	18
Engine/transmission mountings	See the relevant Part of Chapter 2	
Engine-to-transmission bolts	See the relevant Part of Chapter 2	
Fluid cooler pipes to transmission	7	5
Input shaft speed sensor bolt	6	4
Output shaft speed sensor bolt	6	4
Roadwheel bolts	110	81
Selector lever assembly mounting bolts	8	6
Selector lever position switch:		
Lever to selector shaft	15	11
Selector shaft main nut	7	5
Switch retaining bolts	25	18
Torque converter-to-driveplate bolts:*		
AF23 and AF33 transmissions	60	44
AF40 Transmissions	30	22

* *Use new bolts*

2.2 Transmission fluid drain plug (1) – AF23 and AF33 transmissions

1 General information

A five- or six-speed, electronically-controlled automatic transmission was optionally available on certain models covered by this manual. The transmission consists of a torque converter, an epicyclic geartrain, and hydraulically-operated clutches and brakes. The unit is controlled by the electronic control unit (ECU) via electrically-operated solenoid valves. In addition to the fully automatic operation, the transmission can also be operated manually with five-speed or six-speed sequential gear selection.

The torque converter provides a fluid coupling between engine and transmission, which acts as an automatic clutch, and also provides a degree of torque multiplication when accelerating. The torque converter incorporates a lock-up function whereby the engine and transmission can be directly coupled by means of a clutch unit inside the torque converter. The lock-up function is controlled by the ECU according to operating conditions.

The epicyclic geartrain provides either of the five, or six forward or one reverse gear ratios, according to which of its component parts are held stationary or allowed to turn. The components of the geartrain are held or released by hydraulically actuated brakes and clutches. A fluid pump within the transmission provides the necessary hydraulic pressure to operate the brakes and clutches.

In automatic mode, the transmission is fully adaptive, whereby the shift points are dependent on driver input, roadspeed, engine speed and vehicle operating conditions. The ECU receives inputs from various engine and drivetrain related sensors, and determines the appropriate shift point for each gear. Additionally, the transmission can be placed into winter mode using the button on the selector lever indicator panel. The transmission will select fourth gear as the vehicle pulls away from a standing start; this helps to maintain traction on very slippery surfaces.

Driver control of the transmission is by a four-position selector lever. The drive D position, allows automatic changing throughout the range of forward gear ratios. An automatic kickdown facility shifts the transmission down a gear if the accelerator pedal is fully depressed. If the selector lever is moved to the left from the D position, the transmission enters manual mode. In manual mode the gear selector lever can be used to shift the transmission up or down each gear sequentially.

Due to the complexity of the automatic transmission, any repair or overhaul work must be left to a Vauxhall/Opel dealer or transmission specialist with the necessary special equipment for fault diagnosis and repair. The contents of the following Sections are therefore confined to supplying general information, and any service information and instructions that can be used by the owner.

2 Transmission fluid – draining and refilling

AF23 and AF33 transmissions
Draining

1 Firmly apply the handbrake, then jack up the front of the car and support it securely on axle stands (see *Jacking and vehicle support*). On diesel engine models, undo the ten bolts and remove the undertray from beneath the engine.
2 Position a container under the drain plug at the rear right-hand side of the transmission, below the driveshaft. Unscrew the plug and remove it along with its sealing washer **(see illustration)**.
3 Allow the fluid to drain completely into the container.
4 When the fluid has finished draining, clean the drain plug threads and those of the transmission casing, fit a new sealing washer and refit the drain plug, tightening it to the specified torque. Refit the engine undertray (where applicable) and lower the vehicle to the ground.

Refilling

5 Where applicable, undo the three bolts and lift off the plastic cover over the top of the engine.
6 Using a suitable forked tool, release the selector cable end fitting from the selector lever position switch on the top of the transmission **(see illustration)**.
7 Move the selector cable to one side and wipe clean the area around the transmission fluid filler plug, located just to the rear of the selector lever position switch. Unscrew and remove the filler plug along with its sealing washer.
8 Refill the transmission using approximately 3.0 litres of the specified type of fluid via the filler plug aperture. Use a funnel with a fine mesh gauze, to avoid spillage, and to ensure that no foreign matter enters the transmission.

H46362

2.6 Transmission fluid dipstick and related components – AF23 and AF33 transmissions

1 Dipstick retaining bolt	4 Selector cable end fitting
2 Dipstick	5 Selector lever position switch
3 Transmission fluid filler plug	6 HOT mark grooves on dipstick

Automatic transmission 7B•3

9 Refit and securely tighten the filler plug, then reconnect the selector cable to the selector lever position switch.

10 Start the engine, and allow it to idle for a few minutes whilst moving the selector lever through its various positions. Take the car on a moderate run to fully distribute the new fluid around the transmission, and to bring the transmission up to normal operating temperature (70° to 80°C). On returning, park the car on level ground and leave the engine idling.

11 Slowly move the selector lever from position P to position D and back to position P.

12 Unscrew the retaining bolt and withdraw the transmission fluid dipstick, located at the front left-hand side of the transmission. Where necessary, unclip the transmission wiring harness and move it to one side for improved access to the dipstick.

13 Wipe the dipstick with a clean cloth and insert it fully into the transmission. Withdraw the dipstick and check the fluid level which must be between the grooves of the HOT mark. Note that 0.3 litres of fluid is required to raise the level from the COLD mark to the HOT mark on the dipstick.

14 If topping-up is necessary, stop the engine, and remove the fluid filler plug as described previously. Add additional fluid, as required, then refit the filler plug, using a new sealing washer. Tighten the filler plug to the specified torque, then reconnect the selector cable to the selector lever position switch.

15 Refit the dipstick and secure with the retaining bolt, tightened to the specified torque. If disturbed, clip the transmission wiring harness back into position.

16 Where applicable, refit the plastic cover over the top of the engine.

AF40 transmissions

Draining

17 Position the vehicle over an inspection pit, on vehicle ramps, or jack it up and support it securely on axle stands (see *Jacking and vehicle support*), but make sure that it is level. Undo the ten bolts and remove the undertray from beneath the engine.

18 Position a container under the combined drain plug/level checking plug at the base of the transmission. Note that the drain plug and level checking plug are incorporated into one unit – the drain plug is the larger of the two plugs, with the level checking plug screwed into the centre of it **(see illustration)**.

19 Unscrew the level checking plug and remove it, along with its sealing washer, from the centre of the drain plug. Now unscrew the drain plug and remove it, along with its sealing washer, from the transmission. Allow the fluid to drain completely into the container.

20 When the fluid has finished draining, clean the drain plug threads and those of the transmission casing, fit a new sealing washer and refit the drain plug, tightening it to the specified torque.

Refilling

21 Wipe clean the area around the transmission fluid filler plug, located on the top of the transmission housing, adjacent to the selector cable **(see illustration)**. Unscrew and remove the filler plug along with its sealing washer.

22 Slowly refill the transmission with the specified type of fluid, via the filler plug aperture until fluid just starts to drip out of the level checking plug aperture. Use a funnel with a fine mesh gauze, to avoid spillage, and

to ensure that no foreign matter enters the transmission.

23 Refit the level checking plug and tighten it securely.

24 Add a further 0.5 litre of fluid via the filler plug aperture.

25 Start the engine and allow it to idle. With the footbrake firmly applied, slowly move the selector lever from position P to position D and back to position P, stopping at each position for at least two seconds. Repeat this procedure twice.

26 With the engine still idling, unscrew the fluid level checking plug once more. Allow the excess fluid to run from the level checking plug aperture until it is only dripping out. Refit the level checking plug with a new sealing washer, and tighten the plug to the specified torque.

27 If no fluid runs from the level checking plug aperture, switch the engine off and repeat paragraphs 24 to 26.

28 Once the fluid level is correct, refit the filler plug with a new sealing washer, and tighten the plug to the specified torque.

29 On completion, refit the engine undertray and lower the vehicle to the ground.

3 Selector cable – adjustment

Note: *If the battery is disconnected with the selector lever in the P (park) position, the lever will be locked in position. To manually release the lever, remove the ashtray from the centre console by opening the lid, depressing the internal tabs each side and lifting out. Using a flat-bladed screwdriver, depress*

2.18 Transmission fluid level checking plug (1) and drain plug (2) – AF40 transmissions

2.21 Transmission fluid filler plug (1) – AF40 transmissions

3.4b . . . until the lug (arrowed) rests on the notch

6 Check the operation of the selector lever and, if necessary, repeat the adjustment procedure. On completion, refit the ashtray to the centre console.

3.5 Move the lever on the selector lever position switch fully forwards so the transmission is in the P position

3.4a Use a small screwdriver to open the clamping piece on the selector cable . . .

the emergency release lever in the ashtray aperture, whilst moving the selector lever to the N (neutral) position.

1 Operate the selector lever throughout its entire range and check that the transmission engages the correct gear indicated on the selector lever position indicator. If adjustment is necessary, continue as follows.

2 Position the selector lever in the P (park) position.

3 Remove the ashtray from the centre console by opening the lid, depressing the internal tabs each side and lifting out.

4 Working in the ashtray aperture, use a small screwdriver to open the clamping piece on the selector cable as far as the notch **(see illustrations)**. Opening any further may damage the clamping piece.

5 Working in the engine compartment, move the lever on the transmission selector lever position switch fully forwards so that the transmission is also positioned in the P position **(see illustration)**. With both the selector lever and transmission correctly positioned, lock the clamping piece on the selector cable by pushing it down until it clicks in position.

4 **Selector cable –**
removal and refitting

Removal

1 Remove the centre console as described in Chapter 11 then position the selector lever in the P (park) position.

2 Undo the retaining bolt and remove the rear passenger air duct **(see illustration)**.

3 Undo the retaining bolt each side and release the diagnostic socket mounting bracket from the base of the facia. Disconnect the wiring connector and remove the bracket and diagnostic socket.

4 Using a small screwdriver, open the clamping piece on the end of the selector cable as far as the notch. Opening any further may damage the clamping piece **(see illustration 3.4b)**.

5 Again using a small screwdriver, lift up the locking clip securing the outer cable to the selector lever housing **(see illustration)**.

6 Move the selector cable forward to disengage the inner cable from the selector lever clamping piece.

7 Working in the engine compartment, use a forked tool or flat-bladed screwdriver, and carefully lever the selector inner cable end fitting off the balljoint on the selector lever position switch. Pull back the retaining sleeve and detach the outer cable from the mounting bracket on the transmission **(see illustration)**.

8 Release the rubber grommet at the cable entry point on the engine compartment bulkhead, then pull the cable (complete with

4.2 Undo the retaining bolt and remove the rear passenger air duct

4.5 Lift up the locking clip securing the outer cable to the selector lever housing

4.7 Selector inner cable end fitting (1) and outer cable retaining sleeve (2)

grommet) out of the bulkhead and into the engine compartment.

Refitting

9 Push the selector cable through the bulkhead passage from the engine compartment and locate the rubber grommet back into position in the bulkhead.
10 Refit the outer cable to the mounting bracket on the transmission.
11 Engage the inner cable end fitting with the balljoint on the selector lever position switch, squeezing them together with pliers if necessary.
12 Move the lever on the selector lever position switch fully forwards so that the transmission is positioned in the P position.
13 From inside the car, position the selector lever in the P position and guide the cable back into its location in the selector lever housing, engaging the inner cable with the clamping piece. Push down the outer cable locking clip and the inner cable clamping piece ensuring they both lock fully into position.
14 Refit the rear passenger air duct and securely tighten the retaining bolt.
15 Reconnect the wiring connector to the diagnostic socket then refit the mounting bracket and secure with the two bolts.
16 Refit the centre console as described in Chapter 11.

5 Selector lever assembly – removal and refitting

Removal

1 Carry out the operations described in Section 4, paragraphs 1 to 6.
2 Disconnect the selector lever assembly wiring connector and release the wiring harness from the retaining clips and ties.
3 Undo the four mounting bolts and lift the selector lever assembly from the floor.

Refitting

4 Working in the engine compartment, check that the transmission is in the P (park) position by moving the lever on the selector lever position switch fully forwards **(see illustration 3.5)**.
5 From inside the car, position the selector lever in the P position, then manoeuvre the selector lever assembly into place, engaging it with the selector cable. Refit the mounting bolts and tighten them to the specified torque.
6 Reconnect the selector lever assembly wiring connector and secure the wiring harness with the retaining clips and ties.
7 Push down the selector outer cable locking clip and the inner cable clamping piece ensuring they both lock fully into position.
8 Refit the rear passenger air duct and securely tighten the retaining bolt.
9 Reconnect the wiring connector to the diagnostic socket then refit the mounting bracket and secure with the two bolts.

H46369

6.2 Rotate the locking sleeve (1) clockwise, and push it down, away from the knob

10 Refit the centre console as described in Chapter 11.

6 Selector lever assembly components – removal and refitting

Selector lever knob

Removal

1 Move the selector lever to the D (drive) position.
2 Rotate the locking sleeve, located directly beneath the lever knob, clockwise, and push it down, away from the knob, using a screwdriver **(see illustration)**.
3 Using a small screwdriver, open the lug at the base of the lever knob, and pull the knob up and off the selector lever **(see illustration)**.
4 Slide the locking sleeve up and off the lever.

Refitting

5 Make sure the selector lever is still in the D position, then refit the locking sleeve and slide it down the lever.
6 Place the knob on the selector lever, press the button on the front of the knob, and push the knob fully into position.
7 Slide the locking sleeve up the lever and turn it anti-clockwise to secure.

Selector lever position indicator

Removal

8 Remove the selector lever knob as described previously.
9 Remove the ashtray from the centre console by opening the lid, depressing the internal tabs each side and lifting out.
10 Carefully unclip and remove the upper trim panel around the edge of the position indicator panel.
11 Release the wiring harness at the front of the selector lever housing from its retaining clips and ties, and disconnect the wiring harness connector **(see illustration)**.
12 Lift the position indicator assembly and

H46370

6.3 Open the lug (arrowed) with a small screwdriver, and pull the knob up and off the selector lever

remove the intermediate mounting frame. Withdraw the unit up and off the selector lever.
13 Release the two clips each side securing the position indicator panel, then remove the panel and slide from the indicator body.

Refitting

14 Insert the slide into the indicator body, then clip the indicator panel into position.
15 Refit the position indicator assembly and intermediate mounting frame to the selector lever housing.
16 Reconnect the wiring harness and secure the harness with the clips and ties.
17 Refit the upper trim panel and ashtray, then refit the selector lever knob as described previously.

Selector lever control unit

Removal

18 Remove the centre console as described in Chapter 11.

H46371

6.11 Selector lever position indicator components

1 Wiring harness
2 Wiring harness connector
3 Intermediate mounting frame
4 Position indicator assembly

7B•6 Automatic transmission

19 Undo the retaining bolt and remove the rear passenger air duct **(see illustration 4.2)**.
20 Undo the retaining bolt each side and release the diagnostic socket mounting bracket from the base of the facia. Disconnect the wiring connector and remove the bracket and diagnostic socket.
21 Carefully unclip the selector emergency release lever from its guides on the side of the selector lever housing.
22 Disconnect the three wiring harness connectors then unclip and remove the control unit from the side of the selector lever housing.

Refitting

23 Refitting is a reversal of removal.

Selector lever lock switch

Removal

24 Carry out the operations described in paragraphs 18 to 21.
25 Disconnect the wiring harness connector then withdraw the switch from its guide on the side of the selector lever housing.

Refitting

26 Refitting is a reversal of removal.

7 Oil seals – renewal

Driveshaft oil seals

1 Firmly apply the handbrake, then jack up the front of the car and support it securely on axle stands (see *Jacking and vehicle support*).
2 Drain the transmission fluid as described in Section 2.
3 Remove the driveshaft as described in Chapter 8.
4 Note the correct fitted depth of the seal in its housing then carefully prise it out of position using a large flat-bladed screwdriver.
5 Remove all traces of dirt from the area around the oil seal aperture, then lubricate the new oil seal with automatic transmission fluid. Ensure the seal is correctly positioned, with its sealing lip facing inwards, and tap it squarely into position, using a suitable tubular drift (such as a socket) which bears only on the hard outer edge of the seal. Ensure the seal is fitted at the same depth in its housing that the original was.
6 Refit the driveshaft as described in Chapter 8.
7 Refill the transmission with fresh fluid as described in Section 2.

Torque converter oil seal

8 Remove the transmission as described in Section 12.
9 Carefully slide the torque converter off of the transmission shaft whilst being prepared for fluid spillage.
10 Note the correct fitted position of the seal in the oil pump housing then carefully lever the

seal out of position taking care not to mark the housing or input shaft.
11 Remove all traces of dirt from the area around the oil seal aperture then press the new seal into position, ensuring its sealing lip is facing inwards.
12 Lubricate the seal with clean transmission fluid then carefully ease the torque converter into position. On the AF40 transmissions, slide the torque converter onto the transmission shaft by turning it until it fully engages with the oil pump.
13 Refit the transmission as described in Section 12.

8 Fluid cooler – general information

The transmission fluid cooler is an integral part of the radiator assembly. Refer to Chapter 3 for removal and refitting details, if the cooler is damaged the complete radiator assembly must be renewed.

9 Selector lever position switch – removal and refitting

AF23 and AF33 transmissions

1 The switch is a dual-function switch, performing the reversing light and starter inhibitor switch functions. The switch operates the reversing lights when reverse gear is selected and prevents the engine being started when the transmission is in gear. If at any time the reversing light operation becomes faulty, or it is noted that the engine can be started with the selector lever in any position other than P (park) or N (neutral), then it is likely that the switch is faulty. If adjustment fails to correct the fault then the complete switch must be renewed as a unit.

Removal

2 Ensure the handbrake is fully applied, then move the gear selector lever to the N (neutral) position.
3 Where applicable, undo the three bolts and lift off the plastic cover over the top of the engine.
4 On diesel engine models, unclip the pre/post-heating system control unit from the side of the battery box.
5 Unscrew the retaining bolt and nut and release the wiring harness support bracket (where fitted) from the selector lever position switch.
6 Using a forked tool or flat-bladed screwdriver, carefully lever the selector inner cable end fitting off the balljoint on the selector lever position switch. Pull back the retaining sleeve and detach the outer cable from the mounting bracket on the transmission **(see illustration 4.7)**.
7 Unscrew the retaining nut and remove the lever from the transmission selector shaft.

8 Disconnect the selector lever position switch wiring connector.
9 Bend back the lockwasher then unscrew and remove the main nut and the lockwasher from the transmission selector shaft.
10 Unscrew and remove the two switch retaining bolts, and manoeuvre the switch assembly upwards and off the transmission selector shaft.

Refitting

11 Prior to refitting, first make sure that the transmission selector shaft is still in the N (neutral) position. If there is any doubt, temporarily engage the selector shaft lever with the transmission selector shaft and move the lever fully forwards (to the P position) then move it two notches backwards.
12 Locate the switch on the transmission selector shaft then refit the two retaining bolts, tightening them by hand only at this stage.
13 Refit the lockwasher and main nut to the selector shaft. Tighten the nut to the specified torque setting and secure it in position by bending up the locking washer against one of its flats.
14 Adjust the switch as described in paragraph 21.
15 Once the switch is correctly adjusted, reconnect the wiring connector, ensuring that the wiring is correctly routed.
16 Refit the selector lever to the shaft and tighten its retaining nut to the specified torque.
17 Refit the selector outer cable to the mounting bracket on the transmission. Engage the selector inner cable end fitting with the balljoint on the selector lever, squeezing them together with pliers if necessary.
18 Where applicable, refit the wiring harness support bracket, the pre/post-heating control unit and the plastic engine cover.
19 If necessary, adjust the selector cable as described in Section 3.

Adjustment

20 Carry out the operations described in paragraphs 2 to 7.
21 With the transmission in neutral, the flats on the selector shaft should be parallel to the marking on the switch assembly **(see illustration opposite)**. Place a straight-edge against the flats on the shaft to check this. If adjustment is necessary, slacken the switch retaining bolts and rotate the switch assembly as necessary before retightening the bolts to the specified torque.
22 Refit the selector lever to the shaft and tighten its retaining nut to the specified torque.
23 Refit the selector outer cable to the mounting bracket on the transmission. Engage the selector inner cable end fitting with the balljoint on the selector lever, squeezing them together with pliers if necessary.
24 Where applicable, refit the wiring harness support bracket, the pre/post-heating control unit and the plastic engine cover.
25 If necessary, adjust the selector cable as described in Section 3.

AF40 transmissions

26 On the AF40 transmissions, the selector lever position switch is an integral part of the transmission electronic control unit and cannot be separated. Removal and refitting procedures for the electronic control unit are contained in Section 11.

10 Transmission input/ output speed sensors – removal and refitting

AF23 and AF33 transmissions

Removal

1 The speed sensors are fitted to the top of the transmission unit. The input shaft speed sensor is the front of the two sensors and is situated beneath the selector cable. The output shaft sensor is the rear of the two.
2 Where applicable, undo the three bolts and lift off the plastic cover over the top of the engine.
3 On diesel engine models, unclip the pre/post-heating system control unit from the side of the battery box.
4 If removing the input shaft speed sensor, use a forked tool or flat-bladed screwdriver, and carefully lever the selector inner cable end fitting off the balljoint on the selector lever position switch. Pull back the retaining sleeve and detach the outer cable from the mounting bracket on the transmission.
5 Wipe clean the area around the relevant sensor, then undo the retaining bolt and withdraw the sensor from the transmission.
6 Disconnect the wiring connector and remove the sensor. Remove the sealing ring from the sensor and discard it, a new one should be used on refitting.

Refitting

7 Fit the new sealing ring to the sensor groove and lubricate it with a smear of transmission fluid.
8 Reconnect the wiring connector, then ease the sensor into position and refit the retaining bolt. Tighten the bolt to the specified torque.
9 If working on the input shaft speed sensor, refit the selector outer cable to the mounting bracket on the transmission. Engage the selector inner cable end fitting with the balljoint on the selector lever, squeezing them together with pliers if necessary.
10 Where applicable, refit the pre/post-heating control unit and the plastic engine cover.

AF40 transmissions

11 On the AF40 transmissions, the input and output shaft speed sensors are located internally within the transmission and are not individually available. If one or both speed sensors are diagnosed as faulty, it will be necessary to obtain a complete new transmission.

9.21 Selector lever position switch adjustment – AF23 and AF33 transmissions

1 Switch retaining bolt
2 Switch retaining bolt
3 Selector shaft
4 Straight-edge parallel with mark on switch assembly (arrows)

11 Electronic control unit – removal and refitting

Note: *If a new ECU is to be fitted, this work must be entrusted to a Vauxhall/Opel dealer or suitably-equipped specialist. It is necessary to reset the transmission electronic control system prior to removal, and to programme the new ECU after installation. This work requires the use of dedicated Vauxhall/Opel diagnostic equipment or a compatible alternative.*

AF23 and AF33 transmissions

Removal

1 The ECU is located at the front, left-hand

11.14 Electronic control unit mounting bolts (arrowed) – AF40 transmissions

side of the engine compartment, inside the battery box.
2 Open the battery box by releasing the lid at the front and pivoting it upwards.
3 Release the ECU wiring harness from its retaining clips, then disconnect the upper wiring harness connector from the ECU.
4 Unclip the ECU mounting bracket from the battery box, then lift the ECU and mounting bracket upwards.
5 Release the ECU wiring harness from its retaining clips, then disconnect the lower wiring harness connector from the ECU. Remove the ECU and mounting bracket from the car.

Refitting

6 Refitting is a reversal of removal.

AF40 transmissions

Removal

7 The combined ECU and selector lever position switch are located on the top of the transmission housing.
8 Ensure the handbrake is fully applied, then move the gear selector lever to the N (neutral) position.
9 Remove the battery and battery box as described in Chapter 5A.
10 Unclip the pre/post-heating system control unit wiring harness from the battery box support.
11 Release the ECU wiring harness from its retaining clips, then disconnect the wiring harness connector from the ECU.
12 Using a forked tool or flat-bladed screwdriver, carefully lever the selector inner cable end fitting off the balljoint on the selector lever position switch. Pull back the retaining sleeve and detach the outer cable from the mounting bracket on the transmission **(see illustration 4.7)**.
13 Unscrew the retaining nut and remove the lever from the transmission selector shaft.
14 Unscrew and remove the three mounting bolts, then carefully lift the ECU upwards and remove it from the transmission **(see illustration)**. Take great care not to damage the wiring connector pins on the underside of the ECU as it is lifted off.

Refitting

15 Prior to refitting, first make sure that the transmission selector shaft is still in the N (neutral) position. If there is any doubt, temporarily engage the selector shaft lever with the transmission selector shaft and move the lever fully forwards (to the P position) then move it two notches backwards.
16 Set the selector lever position switch on the ECU to the N position by turning the switch until the two arrows are aligned.
17 Check that the transmission wiring harness is correctly located, then carefully place the ECU in position. Take great care not to damage the wiring connector pins as the ECU is fitted.
18 Refit the three bolts and tighten to the specified torque.

19 Refit the selector lever to the shaft and tighten its retaining nut to the specified torque.
20 Refit the selector outer cable to the mounting bracket on the transmission. Engage the selector inner cable end fitting with the balljoint on the selector lever, squeezing them together with pliers if necessary.
21 Reconnect the ECU wiring harness connector, then secure the harness in its retaining clips.
22 Clip the pre/post-heating system control unit wiring harness to the battery box support.
23 Refit the battery box and battery as described in Chapter 5A.

12 Automatic transmission – removal and refitting

Note: *New torque converter-to-driveplate bolts will be required for refitting.*

Removal

1 Apply the handbrake, then jack up the front of the vehicle and support it on axle stands (see *Jacking and vehicle support*). Allow sufficient working room to remove the transmission from under the left-hand side of the engine compartment. Remove both front roadwheels then, on diesel engine models, undo the ten bolts and remove the undertray from beneath the engine. Also remove the engine top cover where fitted.
2 Remove the battery, battery box, and the starter motor as described in Chapter 5A.
3 Remove the air cleaner housing and intake ducts as described in the relevant Part of Chapter 4.

4 Remove the front bumper as described in Chapter 11.
5 Drain the transmission fluid as described in Section 2.
6 Using a forked tool or flat-bladed screwdriver, carefully lever the selector inner cable end fitting off the balljoint on the selector lever position switch. Pull back the retaining sleeve and detach the outer cable from the mounting bracket on the transmission.
7 On the AF23 and AF33 transmissions, disconnect the transmission main wiring harness connector, then release the harness from the clips or ties securing it to the engine/transmission unit.
8 On the AF40 transmissions, unclip the pre/post-heating system control unit wiring harness from the battery box support. Release the ECU wiring harness from its retaining clips, then disconnect the wiring harness connector from the ECU.
9 Disconnect the breather hose (where fitted) from the top of the transmission unit.
10 Unscrew the central retaining bolt (or nut) and detach the fluid cooler pipes from the transmission. Suitably cover the pipe ends and plug the transmission orifices to prevent dirt entry.
11 Disconnect the inner ends of both driveshafts from the differential as described in Chapter 8. There is no need to disconnect the driveshafts from the swivel hub. Support the driveshafts by suspending them with wire or string – do not allow the driveshafts to hang down under their own weight, or the joints may be damaged.
12 Unscrew and remove the upper bolts securing the transmission to the rear of the engine. Where necessary, pull up the coolant

hoses and secure them away from the transmission using plastic cable ties.
13 Remove the front subframe assembly as described in Chapter 10, ensuring that the engine unit is securely supported by connecting a hoist to the engine assembly. If available, the type of support bar which locates in the engine compartment side channels is to be preferred.
14 Unbolt and remove the front and rear engine/transmission mounting torque link brackets with reference to the relevant Part of Chapter 2.
15 Using a socket and extension bar, turn the crankshaft pulley until one of the bolts securing the torque converter to the driveplate becomes accessible through the starter motor aperture. Slacken and remove the bolt, then turn the crankshaft pulley as necessary and undo the remaining bolts as they become accessible. On the AF23 and AF33 transmissions there are three securing bolts and on the AF40 transmissions there are six. Discard the bolts, new ones must be used on refitting.
16 Place a jack with a block of wood beneath the transmission, and raise the jack to take the weight of the transmission.
17 Unbolt and remove the left-hand engine/transmission mounting bracket from the transmission with reference to the relevant Part of Chapter 2.
18 Lower the engine and transmission by approximately 5 cm making sure that the coolant hoses and wiring harnesses are not stretched.
19 Slacken and remove the remaining bolts securing the transmission to the engine and sump flange. Note the correct fitted positions of each bolt, and the relevant brackets, as they are removed to use as a reference on refitting. Make a final check that all components have been disconnected, and are positioned clear of the transmission so that they will not hinder the removal procedure.
20 With all the bolts removed, move the trolley jack and transmission, to free it from its locating dowels. Once the transmission is free, lower the jack and manoeuvre the unit out from under the car, taking care to ensure that the torque converter does not fall off. Remove the locating dowels from the transmission or engine if they are loose, and keep them in a safe place. Retain the torque converter while the transmission is removed by bolting a strip of metal across the transmission bellhousing end face.

Refitting

21 The transmission is refitted by a reversal of the removal procedure, bearing in mind the following points.
a) *Prior to refitting, remove all traces of old locking compound from the torque converter threads by running a tap of the correct thread diameter and pitch down the holes. In the absence of a suitable tap, use one of the old bolts with slots cut in its threads.*

J44609

12.21 Check that the torque converter is fully entered

1   *Straight-edge*
2   *Vernier calipers on bolt hole*
3   *Torque converter centre stub*

b) Ensure the engine/transmission locating dowels are correctly positioned and apply a smear of molybdenum disulphide grease to the torque converter locating pin and its centering bush in the crankshaft end.
c) Check that the torque converter is fully entered inside the transmission bellhousing by measuring the distance from the flange to the bolt holes in the torque converter, using a straight-edge and vernier calipers *(see illustration)*. The distance must measure approximately 16.0 mm (AF23 and AF33 transmissions) or 20.0 mm (AF40 transmissions).
d) Once the transmission and engine are correctly joined, refit the securing bolts, tightening them to the specified torque setting.
e) Fit the new torque converter-to-driveplate bolts and tighten them lightly only to start then go around and tighten them to the specified torque setting in a diagonal sequence.
f) Tighten all nuts and bolts to the specified torque (where given).
g) Renew the driveshaft oil seals (see Section 7) and refit the driveshafts to the transmission as described in Chapter 8.
h) Refit the front subframe assembly as described in Chapter 10.
i) On completion, refill the transmission with the specified type and quantity of fluid as described in Section 2 and adjust the selector cable as described in Section 3.

13 Automatic transmission overhaul – general information

1 In the event of a fault occurring with the transmission, it is first necessary to determine whether it is of a mechanical, electrical or hydraulic nature, and to do this, special test equipment is required. It is therefore essential to have the work carried out by a Vauxhall/Opel dealer or suitably equipped specialist if a transmission fault is suspected.
2 Do not remove the transmission from the car for possible repair before professional fault diagnosis has been carried out, since most tests require the transmission to be in the vehicle.

Chapter 8
Driveshafts

Contents

Degrees of difficulty

Easy, suitable for novice with little experience	**Fairly easy,** suitable for beginner with some experience	**Fairly difficult,** suitable for competent DIY mechanic	**Difficult,** suitable for experienced DIY mechanic	**Very difficult,** suitable for expert DIY or professional

Specifications

General
Driveshaft type . . . . Solid steel shafts with inner and outer constant velocity (CV) joints. Right-hand driveshaft incorporating intermediate shaft (except on 1.8 litre petrol engine models)

Lubrication (overhaul only – see text)
Lubricant type/specification. . . . . Use only special grease supplied in sachets with gaiter kits – joints are otherwise pre-packed with grease and sealed

Torque wrench settings

	Nm	lbf ft
Anti-roll bar connecting link retaining nut*	65	48
Driveshaft retaining nut:*		
Stage 1	150	111
Stage 2	Slacken the nut by 45°	
Stage 3	250	185
Intermediate shaft bearing housing to support bracket.	18	13
Lower arm balljoint clamp bolt nut:*		
Stage 1	30	22
Stage 2	Angle-tighten through a further 60°	
Stage 3	Angle-tighten through a further 15°	
Roadwheels	110	81
Track rod end to swivel hub*	35	26

Use new nuts/bolts.

2.3 Where fitted, tap off the driveshaft retaining nut dust cap

1 General information

Drive is transmitted from the differential to the front wheels by means of two, unequal-length driveshafts.

Both driveshafts are splined at their outer ends to accept the wheel hubs, and are threaded so that each hub can be fastened by a large nut. The inner end of each driveshaft is splined to accept the intermediate shaft or differential sun gear and is held in place by an internal circlip.

Constant velocity (CV) joints are fitted to each end of the driveshafts, to ensure the smooth and efficient transmission of drive at all the angles possible as the roadwheels move up-and-down with the suspension, and as they turn from side-to-side under steering.

2.6 Unscrew the retaining nut, then use a balljoint separator tool to remove the track rod end from the swivel hub

2.8a Unscrew the retaining nut (arrowed) . . .

TOOL TiP

A tool to hold the wheel hub stationary whilst the driveshaft retaining nut is slackened can be fabricated from two lengths of steel strip (one long, one short) and a nut an bolt; the nut and bolt forming the pivot of a forked tool.

Both inner and outer constant velocity joints are of the ball-and-cage type.

On all except 1.8 litre petrol engine models the right-hand driveshaft has an intermediate shaft attached to the rear of the cylinder block.

2 Driveshaft – removal and refitting

Note: *A new driveshaft retaining nut, inner joint circlip, lower arm balljoint clamp bolt and nut, anti-roll bar connecting link retaining nut*

2.7 Unscrew the nut securing the connecting link to the anti-roll bar, while holding the link stub with a further spanner

2.8b . . . and withdraw the clamp bolt from the swivel hub

and a new track rod end retaining nut will be needed for refitting. The driveshaft outer joint splines may be a tight fit in the hub and it is possible that a puller/extractor will be required to draw the hub assembly off the driveshaft during removal.

Removal

1 Firmly apply the handbrake, then jack up the front of the car and support it securely on axle stands (see *Jacking and vehicle support*). Remove the relevant front roadwheel.
2 On diesel engine models, undo the ten bolts and remove the undertray from beneath the engine.
3 Where fitted, tap off the driveshaft retaining nut dust cap using a cold chisel or large screwdriver **(see illustration)**.
4 To prevent rotation of the wheel hub as the driveshaft retaining nut is slackened, make up a holding tool and bolt the tool to the wheel hub using two wheel bolts **(see Tool Tip)**.
5 With the holding tool in place, slacken and remove the driveshaft retaining nut using a socket and long bar. Where necessary, support the socket on an axle stand to prevent it slipping off the nut. This nut is very tight; make sure that there is no risk of pulling the car off the axle stands as the nut is slackened.
6 Unscrew the nut securing the track rod end to the steering arm on the swivel hub, then use a balljoint separator tool to remove the track rod end **(see illustration)**.
7 Unscrew and remove the nut securing the connecting link to the anti-roll bar, while holding the link stub on the flats provided with a further spanner **(see illustration)**. Release the link from the anti-roll bar and move it to one side.
8 Unscrew the nut and remove the clamp bolt securing the front suspension lower arm to the swivel hub. Note that the bolt head faces the front of the vehicle **(see illustrations)**.
9 Using a lever, push down on the suspension lower arm to free the balljoint from the swivel hub, then move the swivel hub to one side and release the arm, taking care not to damage the balljoint rubber boot **(see illustration)**. It is advisable to place a protective cover over the rubber boot, such as the plastic cap from an aerosol can, suitably cut to fit.
10 The hub must now be freed from the end

2.9 Push down the lower suspension arm to free the balljoint from the swivel hub

of the driveshaft **(see illustration)**. It may be possible to pull the hub off the driveshaft, but if the end of the driveshaft is tight in the hub, temporarily refit the driveshaft retaining nut to protect the driveshaft threads, then tap the end of the driveshaft with a soft-faced hammer while pulling outwards on the swivel hub. Alternatively, use a suitable puller to press the driveshaft through the hub.

11 With the driveshaft detached from the swivel hub, tie the suspension strut to one side and support the driveshaft on an axle stand.

12 If working on the left-hand driveshaft (or the right-hand driveshaft on 1.8 litre petrol models), place a suitable container beneath the differential, to collect escaping transmission oil/fluid when the driveshaft is withdrawn.

13 Using a stout bar, release the inner end of the driveshaft from the differential or intermediate shaft. Lever between the constant velocity joint and differential housing, or between the constant velocity joint and intermediate shaft bearing housing, to release the driveshaft retaining circlip **(see illustration)**.

14 Withdraw the driveshaft, ensuring that the constant velocity joints are not placed under excessive strain, and remove the driveshaft from beneath the vehicle. Whilst the driveshaft is removed, plug or tape over the differential aperture to prevent dirt entry.

Caution: Do not allow the vehicle to rest on its wheels with one or both driveshafts removed, as damage to the wheel bearings(s) may result. If the vehicle must be moved on its wheels, clamp the wheel bearings using spacers and a long threaded rod to take the place of the driveshaft.

Refitting

15 Before refitting the driveshaft, examine the oil seal in the transmission housing and renew it if necessary as described in the relevant Part of Chapter 7.

16 Remove the circlip from the end of the driveshaft inner joint splines, or from the end of the intermediate shaft (as applicable) and discard it. Fit a new circlip, making sure it is correctly located in the groove.

17 Thoroughly clean the driveshaft splines, intermediate shaft splines (where applicable), and the apertures in the transmission and hub assembly. Apply a thin film of grease to the oil seal lips, and to the driveshaft splines and shoulders. Check that all gaiter clips are securely fastened.

18 Offer up the driveshaft, and engage the inner joint splines with those of the differential sun gear or intermediate shaft, taking care not to damage the oil seal. Push the joint fully into position, then check that the circlip is correctly located and securely holds the joint in position. If necessary, use a soft-faced mallet or drift to drive the driveshaft inner joint fully into position.

19 Align the outer constant velocity joint

2.10 Pull the swivel hub outwards then withdraw the driveshaft from the hub splines

splines with those of the hub, and slide the joint back into position in the hub.

20 Using a lever, push down on the lower suspension arm, then relocate the balljoint and release the arm. Make sure that the balljoint stub is fully entered in the swivel hub.

21 Insert a new lower arm balljoint clamp bolt with its head facing the front of the vehicle, fit a new retaining nut and tighten the nut to the specified torque in the stages given in the Specifications.

22 Refit the track rod end to the steering arm on the swivel hub and tighten the new nut to the specified torque.

23 Locate the connecting link on the anti-roll bar, fit a new retaining nut and tighten the nut to the specified torque.

24 Lubricate the inner face and threads of the new driveshaft retaining nut with clean engine oil, and refit it to the end of the driveshaft. Use the method employed on removal to prevent the hub from rotating, and tighten the driveshaft retaining nut to the specified torque in the stages given in the Specifications. Check that the hub rotates freely.

25 Where fitted, tap a new driveshaft retaining nut dust cap into position.

26 On diesel engine models, refit the engine undertray and secure with the ten retaining bolts.

27 Refit the roadwheel, lower the vehicle to the ground and tighten the roadwheel bolts to the specified torque.

28 Check and if necessary top-up the transmission oil/fluid level, using the information given in the relevant Part of Chapter 7.

3.6 Intermediate shaft bearing housing retaining bolts (arrowed)

2.13 Using a stout bar, release the inner end of the driveshaft from the differential or intermediate shaft

3 Intermediate shaft – removal and refitting

Note 1: *An intermediate shaft is not fitted to 1.8 litre petrol engine models.*

Note 2: *A new driveshaft inner joint circlip, lower arm balljoint clamp bolt and nut, anti-roll bar connecting link retaining nut and a new track rod end retaining nut will be needed for refitting.*

Removal

1 Firmly apply the handbrake, then jack up the front of the car and support it securely on axle stands (see *Jacking and vehicle support*). Remove the right-hand front roadwheel.

2 On diesel engine models, undo the ten bolts and remove the undertray from beneath the engine.

3 Carry out the operations described in paragraphs 6 to 9 of Section 2.

4 Using a stout bar, release the inner end of the driveshaft from the intermediate shaft. Lever between the constant velocity joint and intermediate shaft bearing housing to release the driveshaft retaining circlip. Support driveshaft to one side.

5 Place a suitable container beneath the differential, to collect escaping transmission oil/fluid when the intermediate shaft is withdrawn.

6 Undo the three bolts securing the intermediate shaft bearing housing to the support bracket on the cylinder block **(see illustration)**. Pull the intermediate shaft out of the transmission, slide it through the support bracket and remove the shaft from under the car.

Refitting

7 Before refitting the intermediate shaft, examine the oil seal in the transmission housing and renew it if necessary as described in the relevant Part of Chapter 7.

8 Remove the circlip from the end of the driveshaft inner joint splines, or from the end of the intermediate shaft (as applicable) and discard it. Fit a new circlip, making sure it is correctly located in the groove.

9 Thoroughly clean the driveshaft splines,

4.3 Extract the circlip (arrowed) securing the intermediate shaft in the bearing

intermediate shaft splines, and the aperture in the transmission. Apply a thin film of grease to the oil seal lips, and to the driveshaft and intermediate shaft splines and shoulders.

10 Insert the intermediate shaft into the transmission, engaging the splines with the differential sun gear, taking care not to damage the oil seal.

11 Refit the three bolts securing the intermediate shaft bearing housing to the support bracket on the cylinder block. Tighten the bolts to the specified torque.

12 Locate the driveshaft inner joint on the intermediate shaft splines, then use a soft-metal drift to drive the joint onto the intermediate shaft until it is retained by the circlip.

13 Using a lever, push down on the lower suspension arm, then relocate the balljoint and release the arm. Make sure that the balljoint stub is fully entered in the swivel hub.

5.2 Release the rubber gaiter retaining clips by cutting through them using a hacksaw

5.5 Outer CV joint snap-ring (arrowed)

14 Insert a new lower arm balljoint clamp bolt with its head facing the front of the vehicle, fit a new retaining nut and tighten the nut to the specified torque in the stages given in the Specifications.

15 Refit the track rod end to the steering arm on the swivel hub and tighten the new nut to the specified torque.

16 Locate the connecting link on the anti-roll bar, fit a new retaining nut and tighten the nut to the specified torque.

17 On diesel engine models, refit the engine undertray and secure with the ten retaining bolts.

18 Refit the roadwheel, lower the vehicle to the ground and tighten the roadwheel bolts to the specified torque.

19 Check and if necessary top-up the transmission oil/fluid level, using the information given in the relevant Part of Chapter 7.

4 Intermediate shaft bearing – renewal

Note: *A hydraulic press, together with tubes and mandrels of suitable diameters will be needed for this operation. A new intermediate shaft circlip and, where fitted, a new O-ring will also be required.*

1 Remove the intermediate shaft as described in Section 3.

2 Where fitted, remove the O-ring from the end of the intermediate shaft.

3 Using circlip pliers, or a small screwdriver,

5.3 Cut the gaiter open using a suitable knife and remove it from the driveshaft

5.6a Sharply strike the edge of the outer joint to drive it off the end of the shaft

extract the circlip securing the intermediate shaft in the bearing **(see illustration)**.

4 Support the underside of the bearing housing on the press bed and press the intermediate shaft downwards out of the bearing.

5 With the intermediate shaft removed, press the bearing out of the housing using a suitable mandrel.

6 Locate the new bearing in the housing and press it fully into position using a suitable tube in contact with the bearing outer race.

7 With the bearing supported on its inner race, press the intermediate shaft back into the bearing until it is fully engaged.

8 Secure the intermediate shaft with a new circlip then, where applicable, fit a new O-ring to the end of the shaft.

9 On completion, refit the intermediate shaft as described in Section 3.

5 Driveshaft joint gaiters – renewal

Outer CV joint

1 Remove the driveshaft from the car as described in Section 2, then secure the shaft in a vice equipped with soft jaws.

2 Release the rubber gaiter inner and outer retaining clips by cutting through them using a junior hacksaw **(see illustration)**. Spread the clips and remove them from the gaiter.

3 Slide the rubber gaiter down the shaft to expose the CV joint or, alternatively, cut the gaiter open using a suitable knife and remove it from the driveshaft **(see illustration)**.

4 Using old rags, clean away as much of the old grease as possible from the CV joint. It is advisable to wear disposable rubber gloves during this operation.

5 The outer CV joint will be retained on the driveshaft either by an external snap-ring, or by an internal circlip **(see illustration)**. If an external snap-ring is fitted, use circlip pliers to expand the snap-ring as the CV joint is removed.

6 Using a mallet, sharply strike the edge of the outer joint to drive it off the end of the shaft **(see illustrations)**.

7 Once the joint has been removed, extract

5.6b If an external snap-ring is fitted, use circlip pliers to expand the snap-ring as the joint is removed

5.7 Removing the circlip from the groove in the driveshaft splines

5.12 Components required for driveshaft gaiter renewal

5.13 Slide the new rubber gaiter and retaining clips onto the driveshaft

5.14a Fit a new snap-ring to the constant velocity joint . . .

5.14b . . . or a new circlip to the groove in the driveshaft

5.15 Pack the joint with the grease supplied in the repair kit

the snap-ring from the joint, or remove the circlip from the groove in the driveshaft splines **(see illustration)**. A new snap-ring or circlip must be fitted on reassembly.

8 If still in place, withdraw the rubber gaiter from the driveshaft.

9 With the CV joint removed from the driveshaft, wipe away the remaining grease (do not use any solvent) to allow the joint components to be inspected.

10 Move the inner splined driving member from side-to-side, to expose each ball in turn at the top of its track. Examine the balls for cracks, flat spots, or signs of surface pitting.

11 Inspect the ball tracks on the inner and outer members. If the tracks have widened, the balls will no longer be a tight fit. At the same time, check the ball cage windows for wear or cracking between the windows.

12 If on inspection any of the constant velocity joint components are found to be

worn or damaged, it will be necessary to renew the complete joint assembly. If the joint is in satisfactory condition, obtain a repair kit consisting of a new gaiter and retaining clips, a constant velocity joint snap-ring or circlip, and the correct type and quantity of grease **(see illustration)**.

13 Slide the new rubber gaiter and retaining clips onto the driveshaft **(see illustration)**.

14 Fit a new snap-ring to the constant velocity joint, or a new circlip to the groove in the driveshaft, as applicable **(see illustrations)**.

15 Pack the joint with the grease supplied in the repair kit **(see illustration)**. Work the grease well into the bearing tracks whilst twisting the joint, and fill the rubber gaiter with any excess.

16 Screw on the driveshaft retaining nut two or three turns to protect the threads, then engage the joint with the driveshaft splines. Tap the joint onto the driveshaft until the

snap-ring or circlip engages in its groove **(see illustration)**. Make sure that the joint is securely retained, by pulling on the joint, not the shaft.

17 Ease the gaiter over the joint, and ensure that the gaiter lips are correctly located in the grooves on both the driveshaft and constant velocity joint. Lift the outer sealing lip of the gaiter, to equalise air pressure within the gaiter.

18 Pull the large gaiter retaining clip as tight as possible, and locate the hooks on the clip in their slots. Remove any slack in the gaiter retaining clip by carefully compressing the raised section of the clip. In the absence of the special tool, a pair of side-cutters may be used. Secure the small retaining clip using the same procedure **(see illustrations)**.

19 Check that the constant velocity joint moves freely in all directions, then refit the driveshaft to the car as described in Section 2.

5.16 Tap the joint onto the driveshaft until the snap-ring or circlip engages in its groove

5.18a Secure the large gaiter retaining clip in position by compressing the raised section of the clip

5.18b The small inner retaining clip is secured in the same way

5.21a Remove the circlip from the groove in the inner CV joint splines . . .

5.21b . . . then, where fitted, slide off the rubber dust cover

5.22 Cut off the rubber gaiter retaining clips, then slide the gaiter down the shaft

5.24 Clean away as much of the old grease as possible from the CV joint

5.25a Expand the joint retaining snap-ring using circlip pliers . . .

5.25b . . . then remove the joint by tapping it off the driveshaft with a hammer and punch

Inner CV joint

20 Remove the driveshaft from the car as described in Section 2, then secure the shaft in a vice equipped with soft jaws.

21 Remove the circlip from the groove in the CV joint splines then, where fitted, slide off the rubber dust cover **(see illustrations)**. Note that a new circlip must be fitted on reassembly.

22 Release the rubber gaiter inner and outer retaining clips by cutting through them using a junior hacksaw **(see illustration)**. Spread the clips and remove them from the gaiter.

23 Slide the rubber gaiter down the shaft to expose the CV joint.

24 Using old rags, clean away as much of the old grease as possible from the CV joint **(see illustration)**. It is advisable to wear disposable rubber gloves during this operation.

25 Expand the CV joint retaining snap-ring using circlip pliers, then remove the joint by tapping it off the driveshaft with a hammer and

punch in contact with the joint inner member **(see illustrations)**.

26 Once the joint has been removed, extract the snap-ring, noting that a new snap-ring must be fitted on reassembly.

27 Withdraw the rubber gaiter from the driveshaft.

28 With the CV joint removed from the driveshaft, wipe away the remaining grease (do not use any solvent) and inspect the joint components as described previously in paragraphs 10 and 11.

29 If on inspection any of the constant velocity joint components are found to be worn or damaged, it will be necessary to renew the complete joint assembly. If the joint is in satisfactory condition, obtain a repair kit consisting of a new gaiter and retaining clips, a constant velocity joint snap-ring and circlip, and the correct type and quantity of grease.

30 Slide the new rubber gaiter and retaining clips onto the driveshaft **(see illustration)**.

31 Fit a new snap-ring to the constant velocity joint, then engage the joint with the driveshaft splines. Tap the joint onto the driveshaft until the snap-ring engages in its groove **(see illustration)**. Make sure that the joint is securely retained, by pulling on the joint, not the shaft.

32 Pack the joint with the grease supplied in the repair kit **(see illustration)**. Work the grease well into the bearing tracks whilst twisting the joint, and fill the rubber gaiter with any excess.

33 Ease the gaiter over the joint, and ensure that the gaiter lips are correctly located in the grooves on both the driveshaft and constant velocity joint. Lift the outer sealing lip of the gaiter, to equalise air pressure within the gaiter.

34 Pull the large gaiter retaining clip as tight as possible, and locate the hooks on the clip in their slots. Remove any slack in the gaiter retaining clip by carefully compressing the raised section of the clip. In the absence of

5.30 Slide the new rubber gaiter and retaining clips onto the driveshaft

5.31 Tap the joint onto the driveshaft until the snap-ring engages in its groove

5.32 Pack the joint with the grease supplied in the repair kit

the special tool, a pair of side-cutters may be used. Secure the small retaining clip using the same procedure **(see illustrations)**.

35 Where applicable, slide the rubber dust cover onto the CV joint, then fit a new circlip to the groove in the joint splines.

36 Check that the constant velocity joint moves freely in all directions, then refit the driveshaft to the car as described in Section 2.

6 Driveshaft overhaul – general information

1 If any of the checks described in Chapter 1A or 1B reveal possible wear in any driveshaft joint, carry out the following procedures to identify the source of the problem.

2 Firmly apply the handbrake, then jack up the front of the vehicle and support it securely on axle stands (see *Jacking and vehicle support*).

3 Referring to the information contained in Section 2, make up a tool to hold the wheel hub, and bolt the tool to the hub. Use a torque

5.34a Secure the large gaiter retaining clip in position by compressing the raised section of the clip

wrench to check that the driveshaft retaining nut is securely fastened, then repeat this check on the remaining driveshaft nut.

4 Road test the vehicle, and listen for a metallic clicking from the front as the vehicle is driven slowly in a circle on full-lock. If a clicking noise is heard, this indicates wear in the outer constant velocity joint.

5.34b The small inner retaining clip is secured in the same way

5 If vibration, consistent with roadspeed, is felt through the car when accelerating, there is a possibility of wear in the inner constant velocity joints.

6 To check the joints for wear, remove the driveshafts, then dismantle them as described in Section 5; if any wear or free play is found, the affected joint must be renewed.

Chapter 9
Braking system

Contents

Degrees of difficulty

Easy, suitable for novice with little experience	Fairly easy, suitable for beginner with some experience	Fairly difficult, suitable for competent DIY mechanic	Difficult, suitable for experienced DIY mechanic	Very difficult, suitable for expert DIY or professional

Specifications

Front brakes

Type	Ventilated disc, with single-piston sliding caliper
Disc diameter	285.0 mm
Disc thickness:	
New	25.0 mm
Minimum	22.0 mm
Maximum disc run-out	0.12 mm
Brake pad thickness:	
New (including backing plate)	20.0 mm
Minimum thickness (including backing plate)	9.0 mm
Brake caliper piston diameter	57.0 mm

Rear Brakes

Type	Solid disc, with single-piston sliding caliper
Disc diameter	278.0 mm
Disc thickness:	
New	12.0 mm
Minimum	10.0 mm
Maximum disc run-out	0.03 mm
Brake pad thickness:	
New (including backing plate)	17.0 mm
Minimum thickness (including backing plate)	8.0 mm
Brake caliper piston diameter	38.0 mm

Handbrake

Type	Cabke-operated, acting on rear brake calipers. Self-adjusting

ABS system type

Standard ABS system	EBC 430 EV
ABS with traction control	EBC 430 EV/TC
ABS with electronic stability program	EBC 430 EV/ESP

Torque wrench settings

	Nm	lbf ft
ABS hydraulic modulator mounting bracket bolts	20	15
ABS hydraulic modulator to mounting bracket	10	7
Brake caliper bleed screws	6	4
Brake caliper guide bolts	30	22
Brake caliper mounting bracket bolts:*		
Front caliper	230	170
Rear caliper	130	96
Brake fluid pipe unions.	16	12
Brake hydraulic hose banjo union bolts	40	30
Brake pedal mounting bracket nuts*	20	15
Handbrake lever retaining nuts	10	7
Master cylinder retaining nuts*	50	37
Roadwheel bolts.	110	81
Vacuum pump mounting bolts:		
1.9 litre engines	20	15
2.0 and 2.2 litre engines	8	6
Vacuum servo unit stud bolts*	20	15

* Use new fasteners

1 General information

The braking system is of servo-assisted, dual-circuit hydraulic type split diagonally. The arrangement of the hydraulic system is such that each circuit operates one front and one rear brake from a tandem master cylinder. Under normal circumstances, both circuits operate in unison. However, in the event of hydraulic failure in one circuit, full braking force will still be available at two wheels.

All models are fitted with front and rear disc brakes. The disc brakes are actuated by single-piston sliding type calipers, which ensure that equal pressure is applied to each disc pad.

An Anti-lock Braking System (ABS) is fitted as standard equipment to all vehicles covered in this manual. On higher specification models, the ABS may also incorporate traction control or an electronic stability program. Refer to Section 17 for further information on ABS operation.

The self-adjusting, cable-operated handbrake provides an independent mechanical means of rear brake application.

On diesel engine models, since there is no throttling as such of the inlet manifold, the manifold is not a suitable source of vacuum to operate the vacuum servo unit. The servo unit is therefore connected to a separate vacuum pump bolted to the left-hand end of the cylinder head and driven by the camshaft.

⚠ **Warning: When servicing any part of the system, work carefully and methodically; also observe scrupulous cleanliness when overhauling any part of the hydraulic system. Always renew components (in axle sets, where applicable) if in doubt about their condition, and use only genuine Vauxhall/Opel parts, or at least those of known good quality. Note the warnings given in 'Safety first!' and at relevant points in this Chapter concerning the dangers of asbestos dust and hydraulic fluid.**

2 Hydraulic system – bleeding

⚠ **Warning: Hydraulic fluid is poisonous; wash off immediately and thoroughly in the case of skin contact, and seek immediate medical advice if any fluid is swallowed or gets into the eyes. Certain types of hydraulic fluid are inflammable, and may ignite when allowed into contact with hot components; when servicing any hydraulic system, it is safest to assume that the fluid is inflammable, and to take precautions against the risk of fire as though it is petrol that is being handled. Hydraulic fluid is also an effective paint stripper, and will attack plastics; if any is spilt, it should be washed off immediately, using copious quantities of fresh water. Finally, it is hygroscopic (it absorbs moisture from the air) – old fluid may be contaminated and unfit for further use. When topping-up or renewing the fluid, always use the recommended type, and ensure that it comes from a freshly-opened sealed container.**

General

1 The correct operation of any hydraulic system is only possible after removing all air from the components and circuit; this is achieved by bleeding the system.
2 During the bleeding procedure, add only clean, unused hydraulic fluid of the recommended type; never re-use fluid that has already been bled from the system. Ensure that sufficient fluid is available before starting work.
3 If there is any possibility of incorrect fluid being already in the system, the brake components and circuit must be flushed completely with uncontaminated, correct fluid, and new seals should be fitted to the various components.
4 If hydraulic fluid has been lost from the system, or air has entered because of a leak, ensure that the fault is cured before proceeding further.

5 Park the vehicle over an inspection pit or on car ramps. Alternatively, apply the handbrake then jack up the front and rear of the vehicle and support it on axle stands (see *Jacking and vehicle support*). For improved access with the vehicle jacked up, remove the roadwheels.
6 Check that all pipes and hoses are secure, unions tight and bleed screws closed. Clean any dirt from around the bleed screws.
7 Unscrew the master cylinder reservoir cap, and top the master cylinder reservoir up to the MAX level line; refit the cap loosely, and remember to maintain the fluid level at least above the MIN level line throughout the procedure, otherwise there is a risk of further air entering the system.
8 There is a number of one-man, do-it-yourself brake bleeding kits currently available from motor accessory shops. It is recommended that one of these kits is used whenever possible, as they greatly simplify the bleeding operation, and also reduce the risk of expelled air and fluid being drawn back into the system. If such a kit is not available, the basic (two-man) method must be used, which is described in detail below.
Caution: Vauxhall recommend using a pressure bleeding kit for this operation (see paragraphs 24 to 27).
9 If a kit is to be used, prepare the vehicle as described previously, and follow the kit manufacturer's instructions, as the procedure may vary slightly according to the type being used; generally, they are as outlined below in the relevant sub-section.
10 Whichever method is used, the same sequence should be followed (paragraphs 11 and 12) to ensure the removal of all air from the system.

Bleeding sequence

11 If the system has been only partially disconnected, and suitable precautions were taken to minimise fluid loss, it should only be necessary to bleed that part of the system (ie, the primary or secondary circuit). If the master cylinder or main brake lines have been disconnected, then the complete system must be bled.

12 The manufacturer does not give any sequence for bleeding the brake circuit, however, we recommend the following for right-hand drive models; for left-hand drive models, bleed the opposite sides:

 a) *Left-hand rear brake.*
 b) *Right-hand front brake.*
 c) *Right-hand rear brake.*
 d) *Left-hand front brake.*

Bleeding

Basic (two-man) method

13 Collect together a clean glass jar, a suitable length of plastic or rubber tubing which is a tight fit over the bleed screw, and a ring spanner to fit the screw. The help of an assistant will also be required.

14 Remove the dust cap from the first bleed screw in the sequence **(see illustrations)**. Fit the spanner and tube to the screw, place the other end of the tube in the jar, and pour in sufficient fluid to cover the end of the tube.

15 Ensure that the master cylinder reservoir fluid level is maintained at least above the MIN level line throughout the procedure.

16 Have the assistant fully depress the brake pedal several times to build-up pressure, then maintain it on the final downstroke.

17 While pedal pressure is maintained, unscrew the bleed screw (approximately one turn) and allow the compressed fluid and air to flow into the jar. The assistant should maintain pedal pressure, following it down to the floor if necessary, and should not release it until instructed to do so. When the flow stops, tighten the bleed screw again, have the assistant release the pedal slowly, and recheck the reservoir fluid level.

18 Repeat the steps given in paragraphs 16 and 17 until the fluid emerging from the bleed screw is free from air bubbles. If the master cylinder has been drained and refilled, and air is being bled from the first screw in the sequence, allow approximately five seconds between cycles for the master cylinder passages to refill.

19 When no more air bubbles appear, securely tighten the bleed screw, remove the tube and spanner, and refit the dust cap. Do not overtighten the bleed screw.

20 Repeat the procedure on the remaining screws in the sequence, until all air is removed from the system and the brake pedal feels firm again.

Using a one-way valve kit

21 As the name implies, these kits consist of a length of tubing with a one-way valve fitted, to prevent expelled air and fluid being drawn back into the system; some kits include a translucent container, which can be positioned so that the air bubbles can be more easily seen flowing from the end of the tube.

22 The kit is connected to the bleed screw, which is then opened. The user returns to the driver's seat, depresses the brake pedal with a smooth, steady stroke, and slowly releases it; this is repeated until the expelled fluid is clear of air bubbles.

2.14a Remove the dust caps from the front . . .

23 Note that these kits simplify work so much that it is easy to forget the master cylinder reservoir fluid level; ensure that this is maintained at least above the MIN level line at all times.

Using a pressure-bleeding kit

24 These kits are usually operated by a reservoir of pressurised air contained in the spare tyre. However, note that it will probably be necessary to reduce the pressure to a lower level than normal; refer to the instructions supplied with the kit.

25 By connecting a pressurised, fluid-filled container to the master cylinder reservoir, bleeding can be carried out simply by opening each screw in turn (in the specified sequence), and allowing the fluid to flow out until no more air bubbles can be seen in the expelled fluid.

26 This method has the advantage that the large reservoir of fluid provides an additional safeguard against air being drawn into the system during bleeding.

27 Pressure-bleeding is particularly effective when bleeding 'difficult' systems, or when bleeding the complete system at the time of routine fluid renewal.

All methods

28 When bleeding is complete, and firm pedal feel is restored, wash off any spilt fluid, securely tighten the bleed screws, and refit the dust caps.

29 Check the hydraulic fluid level in the master cylinder reservoir, and top-up if necessary (see *Weekly checks*).

30 Discard any hydraulic fluid that has been

3.2a Pull out the spring clip . . .

2.14b . . . and rear bleed screws

bled from the system; it will not be fit for re-use.

31 Check the feel of the brake pedal. If it feels at all spongy, air must still be present in the system, and further bleeding is required. Failure to bleed satisfactorily after a reasonable repetition of the bleeding procedure may be due to worn master cylinder seals.

---

3 Hydraulic pipes and hoses – renewal

Note: *Before starting work, refer to the note at the beginning of Section 2 concerning the dangers of hydraulic fluid.*

1 If any pipe or hose is to be renewed, minimise fluid loss by first removing the master cylinder reservoir cap and screwing it down onto a piece of polythene. Alternatively, flexible hoses can be sealed, if required, using a proprietary brake hose clamp. Metal brake pipe unions can be plugged (if care is taken not to allow dirt into the system) or capped immediately they are disconnected. Place a wad of rag under any union that is to be disconnected, to catch any spilt fluid.

2 If a flexible hose is to be disconnected, unscrew the brake pipe union nut before removing the spring clip which secures the hose to its mounting bracket. Where applicable, unscrew the banjo union bolt securing the hose to the caliper and recover the copper washers. When removing the front flexible hose, pull out the spring clip and disconnect it from the strut **(see illustrations)**.

3.2b . . . and disconnect the hydraulic hose from the strut bracket

3 To unscrew union nuts, it is preferable to obtain a brake pipe spanner of the correct size; these are available from most motor accessory shops. Failing this, a close-fitting open-ended spanner will be required, though if the nuts are tight or corroded, their flats may be rounded-off if the spanner slips. In such a case, a self-locking wrench is often the only way to unscrew a stubborn union, but it follows that the pipe and the damaged nuts must be renewed on reassembly. Always clean a union and surrounding area before disconnecting it. If disconnecting a component with more than one union, make a careful note of the connections before disturbing any of them.

4 If a brake pipe is to be renewed, it can be obtained, cut to length and with the union nuts and end flares in place, from Vauxhall/Opel dealers. All that is then necessary is to bend it to shape, following the line of the original, before fitting it to the car. Alternatively, most motor accessory shops can make up brake pipes from kits, but this requires very careful measurement of the original, to ensure that the new one is of the correct length. The safest answer is usually to take the original to the shop as a pattern.

5 On refitting, do not overtighten the union nuts.

6 When refitting hoses to the calipers, always use new copper washers and tighten the banjo union bolts to the specified torque. Make sure that the hoses are positioned so that they will not touch surrounding bodywork or the roadwheels.

7 Ensure that the pipes and hoses are correctly routed, with no kinks, and that they are secured in the clips or brackets provided. After fitting, remove the polythene from the reservoir, and bleed the hydraulic system as described in Section 2. Wash off any spilt fluid, and check carefully for fluid leaks.

4 Front brake pads – renewal

⚠️ *Warning: Renew BOTH sets of front brake pads at the same time – NEVER renew the pads on only one wheel, as uneven braking may result. Note that the dust created by wear of the pads may contain asbestos, which is a health hazard. Never blow it out with compressed air, and do not inhale any of it. An approved filtering mask should be worn when working on the brakes. DO NOT use petroleum-based solvents to clean brake parts – use brake cleaner or methylated spirit only.*

Note: *Two different types of front brake caliper may be encountered. The type 1 caliper was fitted up to approximately 2005, with the type 2 caliper being used from that date onward. Identify the caliper type fitted with reference to the accompanying illustrations and proceed as described under the relevant sub-heading, according to type.*

Type 1 caliper

1 Apply the handbrake, then jack up the front of the vehicle and support it on axle stands (see *Jacking and vehicle support*). Remove the front roadwheels.

2 If working on the left-hand caliper, disconnect the wiring connector for the pad wear warning indicator. Release the wiring from the brackets on the inner wheel arch and suspension strut, and from under the rubber cap on the caliper bleed screw.

3 Push in the caliper piston by sliding the caliper body towards the outside of the vehicle by hand.

4 Follow the accompanying photos (**illustrations 4.4a to 4.4s**) for the actual pad renewal procedure, bearing in mind the additional points listed below. Be sure to stay in order and read the caption under each illustration. Note that if the old pads are to be refitted, ensure that they are identified so that they can be returned to their original positions.

5 After removing the caliper from the mounting bracket, tie it to the suspension strut using a cable tie or suitable piece of wire. Do not allow the caliper to hang unsupported on the flexible brake hose.

4.4a Extract the retaining clip and release the hydraulic hose from the suspension strut

4.4b Release the legs of the retaining spring from the caliper mounting bracket . . .

4.4c . . . then remove the spring from the caliper body

4.4d Remove the dust caps from the upper . . .

4.4e . . . and lower guide bolts

4.4f Unscrew the upper and lower guide bolts and remove them from the caliper

4.4g Lift the caliper and inner pad off the mounting bracket

4.4h Remove the inner pad from the caliper piston, noting that it is retained by a spring clip attached to the pad backing plate

4.4i Remove the outer pad from the mounting bracket

4.4j Measure the thickness of the pad friction material and backing plate. If any are worn down to the specified minimum, or fouled with oil or grease, all four pads must be renewed

4.3k Apply a little high melting-point copper brake grease to the pad backing plate contact areas on the mounting bracket

4.4l If new pads are to be fitted, before refitting the caliper, push back the caliper piston whilst opening the bleed screw. This is to prevent any dirt/debris being forced back up the hydraulic circuit in the ABS modulator

4.4m Fit the outer pad to the caliper mounting bracket, ensuring that its friction material is facing the brake disc

4.4n Fit the inner pad to the caliper, ensuring that its clip is correctly located in the caliper piston

4.4o Slide the caliper into position in the mounting bracket and refit the guide bolts

4.4p Tighten the guide bolts to the specified torque . . .

4.4q . . . then refit the dust caps

4.4r Locate the retaining spring into the holes in the caliper, then position the spring legs over the mounting bracket

4.4s Refit the hydraulic hose to the suspension strut and secure with the retaining clip. Reconnect and secure the pad wear warning indicator to complete

6 If the original brake pads are still serviceable, carefully clean them using a clean, fine wire brush or similar, paying particular attention to the sides and back of the metal backing plate. Clean out the grooves in the friction material, and pick out any large embedded particles of dirt or debris. Carefully clean the pad locations in the caliper body/mounting bracket.

7 Prior to fitting the pads, check that the guide bolts are a snug fit in the caliper mounting bracket. Brush the dust and dirt from the caliper and piston, but do not inhale it, as it is injurious to health. Inspect the dust seal around the piston for damage, and the piston for evidence of fluid leaks, corrosion or damage. If attention to any of these components is necessary, refer to Section 7.

8 If new brake pads are to be fitted, the caliper piston must be pushed back into the cylinder to allow for the extra pad thickness. Either use a G-clamp or similar tool, or use suitable pieces of wood as levers. Clamp off the flexible brake hose leading to the caliper then connect a brake bleeding kit to the caliper bleed screw. Open the bleed screw as the piston is retracted, the surplus brake fluid will then be collected in the bleed kit vessel **(see illustration 4.4l)**. Close the bleed screw just before the caliper piston is pushed fully into the caliper. This should ensure no air enters the hydraulic system.

Caution: The ABS unit contains hydraulic components that are very sensitive to impurities in the brake fluid. Even the smallest particles can cause the system to fail through blockage. The pad retraction method described here prevents any debris in the brake fluid expelled from the caliper from being passed back to the ABS hydraulic unit, as well as preventing any chance of damage to the master cylinder seals.

9 With the brake pads installed, depress the brake pedal repeatedly, until normal (non-assisted) pedal pressure is restored, and the pads are pressed into firm contact with the brake disc.

10 Repeat the above procedure on the remaining front brake caliper.

11 Refit the roadwheels, then lower the vehicle to the ground and tighten the roadwheel bolts to the specified torque setting.

12 Check the hydraulic fluid level as described in *Weekly checks*.

Caution: New pads will not give full braking efficiency until they have bedded-in. Be prepared for this, and avoid hard braking as far as possible for the first hundred miles or so after pad renewal.

Type 2 caliper

13 Apply the handbrake, then jack up the front of the vehicle and support it on axle stands (see *Jacking and vehicle support*). Remove the front roadwheels.

14 Push in the caliper piston by sliding the caliper body towards the outside of the vehicle by hand.

15 Follow the accompanying photos **(illustrations 4.15a to 4.15ab)** for the actual pad renewal procedure, bearing in mind the additional points listed previously in paragraphs 5 to 12. Be sure to stay in order and read the caption under each illustration. Note that if the old pads are to be refitted, ensure that they are identified so that they can be returned to their original positions.

4.15a Extract the retaining clip and release the hydraulic hose from the suspension strut

4.15b If working on the left-hand caliper, lift up the bleed screw cap to release the wire for the pad wear warning indicator

4.15c Unclip the wiring guide from the brake hose

4.15d Depress the locking tab and release the wiring connector from the suspension strut

4.15e Slide the locking bar on the wiring connector downward . . .

4.15f . . . then hold the upper part of the connector and twist the lower part in the direction of the arrow

4.15g Disconnect the pad wear warning indicator wire from the connector

4.15h Release the legs of the retaining spring from the caliper body . . .

4.15i . . . then remove the spring from the caliper mounting bracket

4.15j Remove the dust caps from the upper and lower guide bolts

4.15k Unscrew the upper . . .

4.15l . . . and lower guide bolts and remove them from the caliper

4.15m Lift the caliper and inner pad off the mounting bracket

4.15n Remove the inner pad from the caliper piston, noting that it is retained by a spring clip attached to the pad backing plate

4.15o Remove the outer pad from the mounting bracket

4.15p Measure the thickness of the pad friction material and backing plate. If any are worn down to the specified minimum, or fouled with oil or grease, all four pads must be renewed

4.15q It may be necessary to transfer the pad wear warning indicator wire to the new pad, if so extract the retaining clip and the wire from the old pad

4.15r With the retaining clip in place on the end of the wire, push the wire back into position on the new pad

4.15s Apply a little high melting-point copper brake grease to the pad backing plate contact areas on the mounting bracket

4.15t If new pads are to be fitted, before refitting the caliper, push back the caliper piston whilst opening the bleed screw. This is to prevent any dirt/debris being forced back up the hydraulic circuit in the ABS modulator

4.15u Fit the outer pad to the caliper mounting bracket, ensuring that its friction material is facing the brake disc

4.15v Where applicable, feed the pad wear warning indicator wire through the hole in the caliper . . .

4.15w . . . then fit the inner pad to the caliper, ensuring that its clip is correctly located in the caliper piston

4.15x Slide the caliper into position in the mounting bracket and refit the guide bolts

4.15y Tighten the guide bolts to the specified torque, then refit the dust caps . . .

4.15z Locate the retaining spring legs into the holes in the caliper . . .

4.15aa . . . then hold the legs in place and locate the upper part of the spring behind the lugs on the mounting bracket

4.15ab Refit the hydraulic hose to the suspension strut and secure with the retaining clip. Where applicable, reconnect and secure the pad wear warning indicator to complete

5 Rear brake pads – renewal

⚠ **Warning: Renew BOTH sets of rear brake pads at the same time – NEVER renew the pads on only one wheel, as uneven braking may result. Note that the dust created by wear of the pads may contain asbestos, which is a health hazard. Never blow it out with compressed air, and do not inhale any of it.**

An approved filtering mask should be worn when working on the brakes. DO NOT use petroleum-based solvents to clean brake parts – use brake cleaner or methylated spirit only.

1 Chock the front wheels then jack up the rear of the car and securely support it on axle stands (see *Jacking and vehicle support*). Remove the rear roadwheels.

2 Follow the accompanying photos (illustrations 5.2a to 5.2o) for the actual pad renewal procedure, bearing in mind the additional points listed below. Be sure

to stay in order and read the caption under each illustration. Note that if the old pads are to be refitted, ensure that they are identified so that they can be returned to their original positions.

3 If the original brake pads are still serviceable, carefully clean them using a clean, fine wire brush or similar, paying particular attention to the sides and back of the metal backing plate. Clean out the grooves in the friction material, and pick out any large embedded particles of dirt or debris. Carefully clean the pad locations in the caliper body/mounting bracket.

5.2a Release the legs of the retaining spring from the caliper body and remove the spring

5.2b Remove the dust caps from the upper and lower caliper guide bolts . . .

5.2c . . . then unscrew both guide bolts and remove them from the caliper

5.2d Lift the caliper off the mounting bracket and suspend it from a suitable place under the wheel arch using a cable tie or similar

5.2e Remove the outer pad . . .

5.2f . . . and inner pad from the caliper mounting bracket

5.2g Measure the thickness of the pad friction material and backing plate. If any are worn down to the specified minimum, or fouled with oil or grease, all four pads must be renewed

5.2h Turn and press the caliper piston firmly clockwise using suitable pliers . . .

5.2i . . . or alternatively use a caliper retracting tool to retract the piston

5.2j Apply a little high melting-point copper brake grease to the pad backing plate contact areas on the mounting bracket

5.2k Fit the inner pad to the caliper mounting bracket . . .

5.2l . . . followed by the outer pad

5.2m Slide the caliper into position in the mounting bracket and refit the guide bolts

5.2n Tighten the guide bolts to the specified torque, then refit the dust caps

5.2o Locate the retaining spring legs into the holes in the caliper, then hold the legs in place and locate the upper part of the spring behind the lugs on the mounting bracket

4 Prior to fitting the pads, check that the guide bolts are a snug fit in the caliper mounting bracket. Brush the dust and dirt from the caliper and piston, but do not inhale it, as it is injurious to health. Inspect the dust seal around the piston for damage, and the piston for evidence of fluid leaks, corrosion or damage. If attention to any of these components is necessary, refer to Section 8.

5 If new brake pads are to be fitted, it will be necessary to retract the piston fully into the caliper bore by rotating it in a clockwise direction. This can be achieved by using sturdy circlip pliers, noting that as well as being turned, the piston has to be pressed in very firmly. Special tools are readily available to achieve this with less effort. While the caliper is being retracted, clamp off the flexible brake hose leading to the caliper then connect a brake bleeding kit to the caliper bleed screw. Open the bleed screw as the piston is retracted, the surplus brake fluid will then be collected in the bleed kit vessel (see illustrations 5.2h and 5.2i). Close the bleed screw just before the caliper piston is pushed fully into the caliper. This should ensure no air enters the hydraulic system.

Caution: The ABS unit contains hydraulic components that are very sensitive to impurities in the brake fluid. Even the smallest particles can cause the system to fail through blockage. The pad retraction method described here prevents any debris in the brake fluid expelled from the caliper from being passed back to the ABS hydraulic unit, as well as preventing any

6.10a Undo the two bolts (arrowed) . . .

chance of damage to the master cylinder seals.

6 With the brake pads installed, depress the brake pedal repeatedly, until normal (non-assisted) pedal pressure is restored, and the pads are pressed into firm contact with the brake disc.

7 Repeat the above procedure on the remaining rear brake caliper.

8 Refit the roadwheels, then lower the vehicle to the ground and tighten the roadwheel bolts to the specified torque setting.

9 Check the hydraulic fluid level as described in *Weekly checks*.

Caution: New pads will not give full braking efficiency until they have bedded-in. Be prepared for this, and avoid hard braking as far as possible for the first hundred miles or so after pad renewal.

6 Front/rear brake disc – inspection, removal and refitting

Note: *Before starting work, refer to the warning at the beginning of Section 4 or 5 concerning the dangers of asbestos dust. If either disc requires renewal, both should be renewed at the same time together with new pads, to ensure even and consistent braking.*

Inspection

1 Remove the wheel trim, then loosen the roadwheel bolts. If checking a front disc, apply the handbrake, and if checking a rear disc, chock the front wheels and release the

6.10b . . . and remove the caliper mounting bracket from the swivel hub

handbrake, then jack up the relevant end of the vehicle and support on axle stands (see *Jacking and vehicle support*). Remove the roadwheel.

2 Check that the brake disc securing screw is tight, then fit a spacer approximately 10.0 mm thick to one of the roadwheel bolts, and refit and tighten the bolt in the hole opposite the disc securing screw.

3 Rotate the brake disc, and examine it for deep scoring or grooving. Light scoring is normal, but if excessive, the disc should be removed and either renewed or machined (within the specified limits) by an engineering works. The minimum thickness is given in the Specifications at the start of this Chapter.

4 Using a dial gauge, or a flat metal block and feeler blades, check that the disc run-out does not exceed the figure given in the Specifications. Measure the run-out 10.0 mm in from the outer edge of the disc.

5 If the disc run-out is excessive, remove the disc as described later, and check that the disc-to-hub surfaces are perfectly clean. Refit the disc and check the run-out again.

6 If the run-out is still excessive, the disc should be renewed.

7 To remove a disc, proceed as follows.

Front disc

Removal

8 Remove the roadwheel bolt and spacer used when checking the disc.

9 Remove the front brake pads as described in Section 4.

10 Undo the two bolts securing the caliper mounting bracket to the swivel hub and remove the mounting bracket (see illustrations).

11 Remove the securing screw and withdraw the disc from the hub. (see illustrations).

Refitting

12 Refit the disc, making sure that the mating faces of the disc and hub are perfectly clean, and apply a little locking fluid to the threads of the securing screw.

13 Refit the caliper mounting bracket and tighten the bolts to the specified torque.

14 Refit the brake pads as described in Section 4.

6.11a Remove the securing screw . . .

6.11b . . . and withdraw the disc from the hub

6.17 Undo the two bolts and remove the brake caliper mounting bracket from the hub carrier

Rear disc

Removal

15 Where applicable, remove the roadwheel bolt and spacer used when checking the disc.
16 Remove the rear brake pads as described in Section 5.
17 Undo the two bolts securing the caliper mounting bracket to the hub carrier and remove the mounting bracket **(see illustration)**.
18 Remove the securing screw and withdraw the disc from the hub **(see illustrations)**.

Refitting

19 Refit the disc, making sure that the mating faces of the disc and hub are perfectly clean, and apply a little locking fluid to the threads of the securing screw.
20 Refit the caliper mounting bracket and tighten the bolts to the specified torque.
21 Refit the brake pads as described in Section 5.

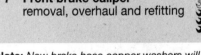

7 Front brake caliper –
removal, overhaul and refitting

Note: *New brake hose copper washers will be required when refitting. Before starting work, refer to the note at the beginning of Section 2 concerning the dangers of hydraulic fluid, and to the warning at the beginning of Section 4 concerning the dangers of asbestos dust.*

Removal

1 Apply the handbrake, then jack up the front of the vehicle and support it on axle stands (see *Jacking and vehicle support*). Remove the roadwheel.
2 Minimise fluid loss by first removing the master cylinder reservoir cap and screwing it down onto a piece of polythene. Alternatively, use a brake hose clamp to clamp the flexible hose leading to the brake caliper.
3 Clean the area around the caliper brake hose union. Unscrew and remove the union bolt, and recover the copper sealing washer from each side of the hose union. Discard the washers; new ones must be used on refitting. Plug the hose end and caliper hole,

6.18a Remove the securing screw (arrowed)

to minimise fluid loss and prevent the ingress of dust and dirt into the hydraulic system.
4 Remove the brake pads as described in Section 4, then remove the caliper from the vehicle.

Overhaul

5 With the caliper on the bench, wipe it clean with a cloth rag.
6 Withdraw the partially-ejected piston from the caliper body, and remove the dust seal. The piston can be withdrawn by hand, or if necessary pushed out by applying compressed air to the brake hose union hole. Only low pressure should be required, such as is generated by a foot pump.
7 Using a small screwdriver, carefully remove the piston seal from the groove in the caliper, taking care not to mark the bore **(see illustration)**.

7.7 Removing the piston seal from the caliper body

6.18b . . . and withdraw the disc from the hub

8 Carefully press the guide bushes out of the caliper body.
9 Thoroughly clean all components, using only methylated spirit or clean hydraulic fluid. Never use mineral-based solvents such as petrol or paraffin, which will attack the rubber components of the hydraulic system. Dry the components using compressed air or a clean, lint-free cloth. If available, use compressed air to blow clear the fluid passages.

⚠️ *Warning: Wear eye protection when using compressed air.*

10 Check all components, and renew any that are worn or damaged. If the piston and/or cylinder bore are scratched excessively, renew the complete caliper body. Similarly check the condition of the guide bushes and bolts; both bushes and bolts should be undamaged and (when cleaned) a reasonably tight sliding fit. If there is any doubt about the condition of any component, renew it.
11 If the caliper is fit for further use, obtain the necessary components from your Vauxhall/Opel dealer. Renew the caliper seals and dust covers as a matter of course; these should never be re-used.
12 On reassembly, ensure that all components are absolutely clean and dry.
13 Dip the piston and the new piston seal in clean hydraulic fluid, and smear clean fluid on the cylinder bore surface.
14 Locate the new seal in the cylinder bore groove, using only the fingers to manipulate it into position.

8.3 Rear caliper brake hose union bolt (arrowed)

8.4a Disengage the handbrake inner cable from the caliper lever . . .

8.4b . . . then pull the outer cable grommet out of the caliper bracket

15 Fit the new dust seal to the piston, then insert the piston into the cylinder bore using a twisting motion to ensure it enters the seal correctly. Locate the dust seal in the body groove, and push the piston fully into the caliper bore.

16 Insert the guide bushes into position in the caliper body.

Refitting

17 Refit the brake pads as described in Section 4, together with the caliper which at this stage will not have the hose attached.

18 Position a new copper sealing washer on each side of the hose union, and connect the brake hose to the caliper. Ensure that the hose is correctly positioned against the caliper body lug, then install the union bolt and tighten it to the specified torque setting.

19 Remove the brake hose clamp or polythene, and bleed the hydraulic system as described in Section 2. Note that, providing the precautions described were taken to minimise brake fluid loss, it should only be necessary to bleed the relevant front brake circuit.

20 Refit the roadwheel, then lower the vehicle to the ground and tighten the roadwheel bolts to the specified torque.

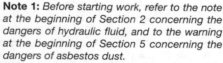

8 Rear brake caliper – removal, overhaul and refitting

Note 1: *Before starting work, refer to the note at the beginning of Section 2 concerning the dangers of hydraulic fluid, and to the warning at the beginning of Section 5 concerning the dangers of asbestos dust.*
Note 2: *Due to the integral handbrake operating mechanism incorporated in the caliper piston, it is not possible to fully dismantle the caliper. Only the guide bushes and dust seal can be individually renewed.*

Removal

1 Chock the front wheels, then jack up the rear of the vehicle and support on axle stands (see *Jacking and vehicle support*). Remove the roadwheel.

2 Minimise fluid loss by first removing the master cylinder reservoir cap and screwing it

down onto a piece of polythene. Alternatively, use a brake hose clamp to clamp the flexible hose leading to the brake caliper.

3 Clean the area around the caliper brake hose union. Unscrew and remove the union bolt, and recover the copper sealing washer from each side of the hose union **(see illustration)**. Discard the washers; new ones must be used on refitting. Plug the hose end and caliper hole, to minimise fluid loss and prevent the ingress of dust and dirt into the hydraulic system.

4 Disengage the handbrake inner cable from the caliper lever, then pull the outer cable grommet out of the caliper bracket **(see illustrations)**.

5 Remove the brake pads as described in Section 5, then remove the caliper from the vehicle.

Overhaul

6 With the caliper on the bench, wipe it clean with a cloth rag.

7 Using a small screwdriver, carefully prise out the dust seal from the caliper, taking care not to damage the piston.

8 Carefully press the guide bushes out of the caliper body.

9 Further dismantling of the caliper is not possible as individual parts are not available separately.

10 Thoroughly clean all components, using only methylated spirit or clean hydraulic fluid. Dry the components using a clean, lint-free cloth.

11 Check the condition of the exposed portion of the caliper piston. If the piston and/or cylinder bore are scratched excessively or corroded, renew the complete caliper body. Similarly check the condition of the guide bushes and bolts; both bushes and bolts should be undamaged and (when cleaned) a reasonably tight sliding fit. If there is any doubt about the condition of any component, renew it.

12 If the caliper is fit for further use, obtain the necessary components from your Vauxhall/Opel dealer. Renew the caliper dust cover as a matter of course; it should never be re-used.

13 Fit the new dust seal to the piston, then locate the dust seal in the caliper body groove.

14 Insert the guide bushes into position in the caliper body.

Refitting

15 Refit the brake pads as described in Section 5, together with the caliper which at this stage will not have the hose attached.

16 Position a new copper sealing washer on each side of the hose union, and connect the brake hose to the caliper. Ensure that the hose is correctly positioned against the caliper body lug, then install the union bolt and tighten it to the specified torque setting.

17 Engage the handbrake outer cable grommet with the caliper bracket, then pull back the operating lever and reconnect the handbrake inner cable.

18 Remove the brake hose clamp or polythene, and bleed the hydraulic system as described in Section 2. Note that, providing the precautions described were taken to minimise brake fluid loss, it should only be necessary to bleed the relevant rear brake circuit.

19 Refit the roadwheel, then lower the vehicle to the ground and tighten the roadwheel bolts to the specified torque.

9 Master cylinder – removal, overhaul and refitting

Note 1: *Before starting work, refer to the warning at the beginning of Section 2 concerning the dangers of hydraulic fluid.*
Note 2: *New master cylinder retaining nuts will be required for refitting.*

Removal

1 Remove the master cylinder reservoir cap, and syphon the hydraulic fluid from the reservoir. **Note:** *Do not syphon the fluid by mouth, as it is poisonous; use a syringe or an old hydrometer.* Alternatively, open any convenient bleed screw in the system, and gently pump the brake pedal to expel the fluid through a plastic tube connected to the screw (see Section 2).

2 On 2.0 and 2.2 litre right-hand drive diesel engine models, remove the air cleaner housing and air intake duct as described in Chapter 4B.

3 On left-hand drive models, lift up the cooling system expansion tank and remove it from the mounting bracket. Place the tank to one side.

4 Disconnect the wiring connector from the brake fluid level sensor at the base of the reservoir **(see illustration)**.

5 On models with manual transmission, release the clip and disconnect the clutch hydraulic pipe from the fluid reservoir **(see illustration)**. Tape over or plug the outlet.

6 Place cloth rags beneath the fluid reservoir then carefully prise it from the top of the master cylinder and withdraw from the engine compartment. If necessary, prise the reservoir seals from the top of the cylinder.

7 Place cloth rags beneath the master cylinder to collect escaping brake fluid. Identify the brake lines for position, then unscrew the union nuts and move the lines to one side. Tape over or plug the line outlets.

8 Unscrew the mounting nuts and withdraw the master cylinder from the vacuum servo unit **(see illustration)**. Recover the seal. Take care not to spill fluid on the vehicle paintwork. Note that new retaining nuts will be required for refitting.

Overhaul

9 At the time of writing, master cylinder overhaul is not possible as no spares are available.

10 The only parts available individually are the fluid reservoir, its mounting seals, the filler cap and the master cylinder mounting seal.

11 If the master cylinder is worn excessively, it must be renewed.

12 To remove the fluid reservoir, undo the retaining bolt and pull the reservoir out of the rubber seals in the master cylinder body. Place absorbent rags under the master cylinder as you do this to catch the escaping hydraulic fluid.

13 Remove the reservoir seals from the master cylinder body and obtain new seals for reassembly.

14 Lubricate the new seals with clean brake hydraulic fluid and push the new seals into position.

15 Refit the reservoir and secure with the retaining bolt.

Refitting

16 Ensure that the mating surfaces are clean and dry then fit the new seal to the rear of the master cylinder.

17 Fit the master cylinder to the servo unit, ensuring that the servo unit pushrod enters the master cylinder piston centrally. Fit the new retaining nuts and tighten them to the specified torque setting.

18 Refit the brake lines and tighten the union nuts securely.

19 On manual transmission models, reconnect the clutch hydraulic pipe and secure with the clip.

20 Reconnect the wiring connector to the brake fluid level sensor.

21 On left-hand drive models, refit the

9.4 Disconnect the wiring connector (arrowed) from the brake fluid level sensor

cooling system expansion tank to its mounting bracket.

22 Where applicable, refit the air cleaner housing and air intake duct as described in Chapter 4B.

23 Remove the reservoir filler cap and polythene, then top-up the reservoir with fresh hydraulic fluid to the MAX mark (see *Weekly checks*).

24 Bleed the hydraulic systems as described in Section 2 and Chapter 6 then refit the filler cap. Thoroughly check the operation of the brakes and clutch before using the vehicle on the road.

10 Brake pedal –
removal and refitting

Note 1: *The brake pedal mounting bracket, the brake pedal and the clutch pedal are one assembly and must be renewed as a complete unit. In the event of a frontal collision, the brake pedal is released from its bearing in the mounting bracket to prevent injury to the driver's feet and legs (this also applies to the clutch pedal). If an airbag has been deployed, inspect the pedal and mounting bracket assembly and if necessary renew the complete unit.*

Note 2: *New pedal mounting bracket retaining nuts, vacuum servo unit stud bolts and brake master cylinder retaining nuts will be required for refitting.*

Removal

1 Disconnect the battery negative terminal (refer to *Disconnecting the battery* in the Reference Chapter).

2 Remove the steering column as described in Chapter 10.

3 Remove the complete facia assembly and the facia crossmember as described in Chapter 11.

4 Remove the stop-light switch from the pedal mounting bracket as described in Section 15.

5 Refer to Chapter 4A or 4B as applicable and remove the air cleaner assembly and the accelerator pedal/position sensor. Where fitted, remove the clutch switch from the pedal mounting bracket.

9.5 Release the clip (arrowed) and disconnect the clutch hydraulic pipe from the fluid reservoir

6 Working in the engine compartment, unscrew the two nuts securing the brake master cylinder to the vacuum servo unit. Now unscrew the two stud bolts securing the vacuum servo unit to the bulkhead **(see illustration 9.8)**.

7 Separate the clutch pedal from the clutch master cylinder piston rod by releasing the retaining clip at the pedal. Vauxhall/Opel technicians use a special tool to do this, however, the clip may be released by pressing the retaining tabs together using screwdrivers, while at the same time pulling the clutch pedal rearwards. **Note:** *Do not remove the clip from the master cylinder piston rod, just release it from the pedal.*

8 Unhook the return spring from behind the brake pedal to release all tension in the spring.

9 Carefully prise open and remove the retaining clip, and withdraw the clevis pin securing the brake pedal to the vacuum servo unit pushrod.

10 From inside the car, slacken and remove the three nuts securing the pedal mounting bracket to the bulkhead. Note that two of the three nuts also secure the clutch master cylinder. On diesel engine models, move the bulkhead insulation to one side for access to the nuts, and use a plastic wedge or similar tool to retain the insulation clear.

11 Withdraw the mounting bracket and pedal assembly from the bulkhead, while at the same time guiding the clutch master cylinder piston rod and retaining clip out of the clutch pedal.

9.8 Master cylinder mounting nuts (A) and vacuum servo unit stud bolts (B)

Refitting

12 Manoeuvre the mounting bracket and pedal assembly into position, whilst ensuring that the clutch master cylinder piston rod and its retaining clip align correctly with the clutch pedal. Also ensure that the vacuum servo unit pushrod locates around the brake pedal. Fit three new pedal mounting bracket retaining nuts and tighten them to the specified torque.

13 On diesel engine models, locate the bulkhead insulation back into position.

14 Push the clutch master cylinder piston rod retaining clip into the clutch pedal, ensuring that the two lugs on the clip fully engage.

15 Apply a smear of multipurpose grease to the clevis pin then align the vacuum servo unit pushrod with the brake pedal hole and insert the pin. Secure the pin in position with the retaining clip, making sure it is correctly located in the groove.

16 Hook the return spring into position behind the brake pedal.

17 Working in the engine compartment, fit the two new stud bolts securing the vacuum servo unit to the bulkhead and tighten the bolts to the specified torque. Fit the two new brake master cylinder retaining nuts and tighten the nuts to the specified torque.

18 Refer to Chapter 4A or 4B as applicable and refit the air cleaner assembly and the accelerator pedal/position sensor. Where fitted, refit the clutch switch to the pedal mounting bracket.

19 Refit the stop-light switch to the pedal mounting bracket as described in Section 15.

20 Refit the facia crossmember and facia assembly as described in Chapter 11.

21 Refit the steering column as described in Chapter 10.

22 Reconnect the battery negative terminal on completion.

---

11 Vacuum servo unit – testing, removal and refitting

Testing

1 To test the operation of the servo unit, with the engine off, depress the footbrake several times to exhaust the vacuum. Now start the engine, keeping the pedal firmly depressed. As the engine starts, there should be a noticeable 'give' in the brake pedal as the vacuum builds-up. Allow the engine to run for at least two minutes, then switch it off. The brake pedal should now feel normal, but further applications should result in the pedal feeling firmer, the pedal stroke decreasing with each application.

2 If the servo does not operate as described, first inspect the servo unit check valve as described in Section 12.

3 If the servo unit still fails to operate satisfactorily, the fault lies within the unit itself. Repairs to the unit are not possible; if faulty, the servo unit must be renewed.

Removal

Right-hand drive models

4 On 1.9 litre diesel engine models, it will first be necessary to remove the engine and transmission assembly as described in Chapter 2F to obtain the necessary clearance for removal of the servo unit.

5 Disconnect the battery negative terminal (refer to *Disconnecting the battery* in the Reference Chapter).

6 Remove the master cylinder as described in Section 9.

7 Remove the facia footwell trim panel on the driver's side as described in Chapter 11.

8 Unhook the return spring from behind the brake pedal to release all tension in the spring.

9 Carefully prise open and remove the retaining clip, and withdraw the clevis pin securing the brake pedal to the vacuum servo unit pushrod.

10 Pull out the vacuum hose from the rubber grommet in the vacuum servo **(see illustration)**.

11 Unscrew the two stud bolts securing the vacuum servo unit to the bulkhead, and remove the servo unit from the engine compartment **(see illustration 9.8)**. Note that new bolts will be required for refitting.

Left-hand drive models

12 Remove the battery and battery box as described in Chapter 5A.

13 Lift up the cooling system expansion tank and remove it from the mounting bracket. Place the tank to one side.

14 Remove the ABS hydraulic modulator together with its mounting bracket as described in Section 18.

15 Remove the master cylinder as described in Section 9.

16 Remove the facia footwell trim panel on the driver's side as described in Chapter 11.

17 Unhook the return spring from behind the brake pedal to release all tension in the spring.

18 Carefully prise open and remove the retaining clip, and withdraw the clevis pin securing the brake pedal to the vacuum servo unit pushrod.

19 Pull out the vacuum hose from the rubber grommet in the vacuum servo **(see illustration 11.10)**.

11.10 Pull out the vacuum hose (arrowed) from the rubber grommet in the vacuum servo

20 Unscrew the two stud bolts securing the vacuum servo unit to the bulkhead, and remove the servo unit from the engine compartment **(see illustration 9.8)**. Note that new bolts will be required for refitting.

Refitting

Right-hand drive models

21 Locate the vacuum servo unit in position on the bulkhead ensuring that the servo unit pushrod locates correctly around the brake pedal. Refit the two new retaining stud bolts and tighten them to the specified torque.

22 Refit the vacuum hose to the servo grommet, ensuring that the hose is correctly seated.

23 Apply a smear of multipurpose grease to the clevis pin then align the servo unit pushrod with the brake pedal hole and insert the pin. Secure the pin in position with the retaining clip, making sure it is correctly located in the groove.

24 Hook the return spring into position behind the brake pedal, then refit the facia footwell trim panel as described in Chapter 11.

25 Refit the brake master cylinder as described in Section 9.

26 On 1.9 litre diesel engine models, refit the engine and transmission assembly as described in Chapter 2F.

27 On completion, reconnect the battery negative terminal.

Left-hand drive models

28 Locate the vacuum servo unit in position on the bulkhead ensuring that the servo unit pushrod locates correctly around the brake pedal. Refit the two new retaining stud bolts and tighten them to the specified torque.

29 Refit the vacuum hose to the servo grommet, ensuring that the hose is correctly seated.

30 Apply a smear of multipurpose grease to the clevis pin then align the servo unit pushrod with the brake pedal hole and insert the pin. Secure the pin in position with the retaining clip, making sure it is correctly located in the groove.

31 Hook the return spring into position behind the brake pedal, then refit the facia footwell trim panel as described in Chapter 11.

32 Refit the brake master cylinder as described in Section 9, but don't bleed the hydraulic circuits at this stage.

33 Refit the ABS hydraulic modulator and mounting bracket as described in Section 18.

34 Refit the cooling system expansion tank to the mounting bracket.

35 Refit the battery box and battery as described in Chapter 5A.

36 Remove the master cylinder reservoir filler cap and polythene, then top-up the reservoir with fresh hydraulic fluid to the MAX mark (see *Weekly checks*).

37 Bleed the hydraulic systems as described in Section 2 and Chapter 6 then refit the filler cap. Thoroughly check the operation of the brakes and clutch before using the vehicle on the road.

12 Vacuum servo unit check valve and hose – removal, testing and refitting

Removal

1 Pull out the vacuum hose from the rubber grommet in the vacuum servo unit **(see illustration 11.10)**.
2 Remove the plastic cover over the top of the engine.
3 Disconnect the hose quick-release fitting from the inlet manifold (petrol engines) or vacuum pump (diesel engines) **(see illustration)**.
4 Unclip the vacuum hose from its supports on the bulkhead and engine, then remove the hose and check valve from the car.

Testing

5 Examine the check valve and hose for signs of damage, and renew if necessary. The valve may be tested by blowing through it in both directions. Air should flow through the valve in one direction only – when blown through from the servo unit end. If air flows in both directions, or not at all, renew the valve and hose as an assembly.
6 Examine the servo unit rubber sealing grommet for signs of damage or deterioration, and renew as necessary.

Refitting

7 Refitting is a reversal of removal ensuring that the quick-release connector audibly locks in position, and that the hose is correctly seated in the servo grommet.
8 On completion, start the engine and check that there are no air leaks.

13 Handbrake lever – removal and refitting

Removal

1 Remove the rear centre console as described in Chapter 11.
2 Ensure that the handbrake lever is released (off).

12.3 Disconnect the vacuum hose quick-release fitting at the vacuum pump on diesel engines

3 Set the handbrake cable self-adjusting mechanism to the fully released position as follows. Push the piston rod and spring rearward with a suitable tool. Hold them in this position and press down the transport fixing to lock the mechanism in the released position **(see illustration)**.
4 Remove the complete exhaust system and centre heat shield as described in Chapter 4A or 4B as applicable.
5 From under the car, use a suitable socket to depress the lugs of the clevis pin retaining collar **(see illustrations)**. Pull the clevis pin upwards and out of the handbrake cable equaliser to release the handbrake lever connecting rod. Note that a new retaining collar will be required for refitting.

13.3 Push the piston rod and spring rearward with a suitable tool, then press down the transport fixing to lock the mechanism

6 From inside the car, disconnect the wiring connector from the handbrake lever warning light switch **(see illustration)**. Release the plastic cable guide from the handbrake lever mounting stud and move the cable to one side.
7 Undo the four retaining nuts and remove the handbrake lever assembly from inside the car **(see illustration)**. Recover the seal between the handbrake lever and vehicle floor.

Refitting

8 Ensure that the seal is correctly seated on the vehicle floor then locate the handbrake lever assembly in position over the mounting studs. Refit the four retaining nuts and tighten to the specified torque.
9 Reconnect the handbrake lever warning light switch wiring connector and clip the plastic guide onto the mounting stud.
10 Fit a new retaining collar to the handbrake lever connecting rod clevis pin. Align the connecting rod with the hole in the equaliser and fit the retaining collar from above. Ensure that the clevis pin is pushed fully home so that the lugs on the retaining collar lock the clevis pin in position.
11 Refit the heat shield and the exhaust system as described in Chapter 4A or 4B, as applicable.
12 Pull the handbrake lever up to release the transport fixing and automatically adjust the handbrake cable.
13 Refit the centre console as described in Chapter 11.

13.5a Push a suitable socket over the clevis pin . . .

13.5b . . . to depress the lugs (arrowed) of the clevis pin retaining collar

13.6 Disconnect the wiring connector (arrowed) from the handbrake lever warning light switch

13.7 Handbrake lever retaining nuts (arrowed)

14.4 Undo the bolt (arrowed) securing the handbrake cable support bracket to the underbody on each side

14.5b . . . from the cable guides (arrowed) . . .

14.5a Release the handbrake cable from the mounting bracket (arrowed) . . .

14.5c . . . and support clips (arrowed)

14 Handbrake cable – removal and refitting

Removal

1 The handbrake cable consists of two parts, a short front connecting rod which connects the lever to the equaliser plate, and the main cable which links the equaliser plate to the left-hand and right-hand rear brakes. The connecting rod is an integral part of the handbrake lever assembly and cannot be separated. The main cable is supplied as one part, together with the equaliser plate.
2 Carry out the operations described in Section 13, paragraphs 1 to 5.
3 Disengage the handbrake inner cable from the rear brake caliper levers, then pull

the outer cable grommets out of the caliper brackets **(see illustrations 8.4a and 8.4b)**.
4 Undo the bolt securing the handbrake cable support bracket to the underbody on each side **(see illustration)**.
5 Release the cable from the remaining support brackets and clips on the underbody and suspension arms, and remove the cable from under the car **(see illustrations)**.

Refitting

6 Locate the cable in position in the underbody support clips and brackets, and tighten the support bracket bolt on each side securely.
7 Engage the handbrake outer cable grommet with the caliper bracket on each side, then pull back the caliper operating levers and reconnect the handbrake inner cable.
8 Carry out the operations described in Section 13, paragraphs 10 to 13.

15 Stop-light switch – removal, refitting and adjustment

Removal

1 The stop-light switch is located on the pedal bracket in the driver's footwell, behind the facia **(see illustration)**.
2 Remove the facia footwell trim panel on the driver's side as described in Chapter 11.
3 Disconnect the wiring plug from the stop-light switch.
4 Push the brake pedal down, pull out the brake switch actuating pin, then unclip the locking sleeve from around the actuating pin **(see illustrations)**.
5 Release the securing clips and pull the switch to disengage it from the pedal mounting bracket.

Refitting and adjustment

6 With the actuating pin pulled out, and the locking sleeve unclipped, refit the switch to the pedal bracket.
7 Secure the switch with the locking sleeve.
8 Release the brake pedal and the pedal will automatically adjust the position of the actuating pin.
9 Reconnect the wiring connector, then refit the facia footwell trim panel as described in Chapter 11.

16 Handbrake warning light switch – removal and refitting

Removal

1 Remove the rear centre console as described in Chapter 11.
2 Disconnect the wiring connector from the warning light switch on the side of the handbrake lever.
3 Unclip the trim on the side of the handbrake lever, then unscrew the mounting bolt and remove the switch from the handbrake lever bracket **(see illustration)**.

Refitting

4 Refitting is a reversal of removal.

15.1 Stop-light switch location (arrowed) on the brake pedal bracket

15.4a Pull out the centre actuating pin arrowed (switch removed for clarity) . . .

15.4b . . . and unclip the locking sleeve

16.3 Handbrake warning light switch mounting bolt (arrowed)

17 Anti-lock Braking and Traction Control systems – general information

ABS is fitted as standard to all models. On higher specification models, the ABS may also incorporate traction control or an electronic stability program as additional safety features.

The ABS system comprises a hydraulic modulator and electronic control unit together with four wheel speed sensors. The hydraulic modulator contains the electronic control unit (ECU), the hydraulic solenoid valves (one set for each brake) and the electrically-driven pump. The purpose of the system is to prevent the wheel(s) locking during heavy braking. This is achieved by automatic release of the brake on the relevant wheel, followed by re-application of the brake.

The solenoid valves are controlled by the ECU, which itself receives signals from the four wheel speed sensors which monitor the speed of rotation of each wheel. By comparing these signals, the ECU can determine the speed at which the vehicle is travelling. It can then use this speed to determine when a wheel is decelerating at an abnormal rate, compared to the speed of the vehicle, and therefore predicts when a wheel is about to lock. During normal operation, the system functions in the same way as a conventional braking system.

If the ECU senses that a wheel is about to lock, it operates the relevant solenoid valve(s) in the hydraulic unit, which then isolates from the master cylinder the relevant brake(s) on the wheel(s) which is/are about to lock, effectively sealing-in the hydraulic pressure.

If the speed of rotation of the wheel continues to decrease at an abnormal rate, the ECU operates the electrically-driven pump which pumps the hydraulic fluid back into the master cylinder, releasing the brake. Once the speed of rotation of the wheel returns to an acceptable rate, the pump stops, and the solenoid valves switch again, allowing the hydraulic master cylinder pressure to return to the caliper, which then re-applies the brake. This cycle can be carried out many times a second.

The action of the solenoid valves and return pump creates pulses in the hydraulic circuit.

When the ABS system is functioning, these pulses can be felt through the brake pedal.

On early models with traction control, the ABS hydraulic modulator incorporates an additional set of solenoid valves which operate the traction control system. The system operates at speeds up to approximately 30 mph using the signals supplied by the wheel speed sensors. If the ECU senses that a driving wheel is about to lose traction, it prevents this by momentarily applying the relevant front brake. The ABS ECU also communicates with the engine management ECU during traction control operation. In severe cases of traction loss the engine management ECU will reduce engine power to assist with traction recovery. On later models, with traction control, the additional solenoids in the modulator are not used, and the traction control function is provided solely by a reduction in engine power.

The electronic stability program (ESP) is a further development of ABS and traction control. Using additional sensors to monitor steering wheel position, vehicle yaw rate, acceleration and deceleration, in conjunction with the ABS sensors, the ECU can intervene under conditions of vehicle instability. Using the signals from the various sensors, the ECU can determine driver intent (steering wheel position, throttle position, vehicle speed and engine speed). From the sensor inputs from the wheel speed sensors, yaw rate sensors and acceleration sensors the ECU can calculate whether the vehicle is responding to driver input, or whether an unstable driving situation is occurring. If instability is detected, the ECU will intervene by applying or releasing the relevant front or rear brake, in conjunction with a power reduction, until vehicle stability returns.

The operation of the ABS, traction control, and stability programs is entirely dependent on electrical signals. To prevent the system responding to any inaccurate signals, a built-in safety circuit monitors all signals received by the ECU. If an inaccurate signal or low battery voltage is detected, the system is automatically shut down, and the relevant warning light on the instrument panel is illuminated, to inform the driver that the system is not operational. Normal braking is still available, however.

If a fault develops in the ABS/traction control/ESP system, the vehicle must be taken to a Vauxhall/Opel dealer for fault diagnosis and repair.

18 Anti-lock Braking and Traction Control system components – removal and refitting

Note 1: *Faults on the ABS system can only be diagnosed using Vauxhall/Opel diagnostic equipment or compatible alternative equipment.*
Note 2: *Before starting work, refer to the note at the beginning of Section 2 concerning the dangers of hydraulic fluid.*

18.3 Pull out the locking bar (arrowed) to disconnect the wiring harness plug from the ECU

Hydraulic modulator and ECU

1 Remove the battery and battery box as described in Chapter 5A.
2 Minimise fluid loss by first removing the master cylinder reservoir cap and screwing it down onto a piece of polythene.
3 Pull out the locking bar and disconnect the wiring harness plug from the ECU **(see illustration)**.
4 Note and record the fitted position of the brake pipes at the modulator, then unscrew the union nuts and release the pipes. As a precaution, place absorbent rags beneath the brake pipe unions when unscrewing them. Suitably plug or cap the disconnected unions to prevent dirt entry and fluid loss.
5 Unscrew the retaining bolts and remove the hydraulic modulator from the mounting bracket.
6 Refitting is the reverse of the removal procedure, noting the following points:
  a) *Tighten the modulator retaining bolts to the specified torque.*
  b) *Refit the brake pipes to their respective locations, and tighten the union nuts to the specified torque.*
  c) *Ensure that the wiring is correctly routed, and that the ECU wiring harness plug is firmly pressed into position and secured with the locking bar.*
  d) *Refit the battery box and battery as described in Chapter 5A.*
  e) *On completion, bleed the complete hydraulic system as described in Section 2. Ensure that the system is bled in the correct order, to prevent air entering the modulator return pump.*

Electronic control unit (ECU)

7 Remove the hydraulic modulator from the car as described previously in this Section.
8 Undo the two retaining bolts and carefully withdraw the ECU upwards and off the hydraulic modulator.
9 Prior to refitting, clean and then carefully inspect, the condition of the gasket sealing surfaces on the ECU and hydraulic modulator. If the surfaces are in any way deformed, damaged, or rough to the extent that a perfect gasket seal cannot be maintained, the

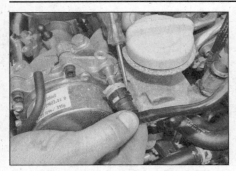

19.2 Disconnect the quick-release fitting and detach the servo unit vacuum hose – 1.9 litre engines

19.3a Undo the three mounting bolts (arrowed) . . .

19 Vacuum pump (diesel engine models) – removal and refitting

19.3b . . . and remove the vacuum pump from the cylinder head/camshaft housing – 1.9 litre engines

19.6 Vacuum hose connections (arrowed) – 2.0 and 2.2 litre engines

complete modulator and ECU assembly must be renewed.
10 Holding the ECU by the outer edges, carefully lower it over the solenoid valves on the modulator, keeping it square and level. Ensure that the wiring connectors correctly engage.
11 Fit the two retaining bolts and tighten securely.
12 On completion, refit the hydraulic

modulator as described previously in this Section.

Wheel speed sensors

13 The front and rear wheel speed sensors are an integral part of the hub bearings and cannot be separated.
14 Refer to Chapter 10 for front and rear hub bearing removal and refitting procedures.

Removal

1.9 litre engines

1 Remove the plastic cover over the top of the engine.
2 Disconnect the quick-release fitting and detach the vacuum servo unit vacuum hose from the pump **(see illustration)**. Disconnect the smaller vacuum hose from the outlet on the side of the pump.
3 Undo the three mounting bolts and remove the pump from the cylinder head/camshaft housing **(see illustrations)**. Recover the gasket.

2.0 and 2.2 litre engines

4 Remove the plastic cover over the top of the engine.
5 Undo the bolt and detach the coolant pipe bracket from the top of the pump.
6 Disconnect the quick-release fitting and detach the vacuum servo unit vacuum hose from the pump **(see illustration)**.
7 Undo the three bolts and detach the wiring harness support bracket from the left-hand end of the cylinder head.
8 Undo the four mounting bolts and withdraw the pump from the cylinder head. Detach the lower vacuum hose as the pump is withdrawn. Recover the O-ring seal.

Refitting

9 Refitting is a reversal of removal, but clean the mating faces of the pump and cylinder head/camshaft housing, and fit a new gasket or O-ring as applicable. Tighten the mounting bolts to the specified torque.

Chapter 10
Suspension and steering

Contents

Degrees of difficulty

Easy, suitable for novice with little experience	**Fairly easy,** suitable for beginner with some experience	**Fairly difficult,** suitable for competent DIY mechanic	**Difficult,** suitable for experienced DIY mechanic	**Very difficult,** suitable for expert DIY or professional

Specifications

Front suspension
Type .... Independent, with MacPherson struts and anti-roll bar

Rear suspension
Type .... Independent multilink with coil springs, gas-filled shock absorbers and anti-roll bar

Steering
Type .... Rack and pinion with electro-hydraulic power steering (EHPS)

Front and rear hub bearings
Bearing play (maximum)................................... 0.1 mm
Bearing radial run-out.................................... 0.04 mm
Bearing lateral run-out .... 0.05 mm

Torque wrench settings

	Nm	lbf ft
Front suspension		
Anti-roll bar link:*		
To strut	65	48
To anti-roll bar.	65	48
Anti-roll bar to subframe*	20	15
Driveshaft retaining nut:*		
Stage 1	150	111
Stage 2	Slacken the nut by 45°	
Stage 3	250	185
Hub bearing assembly to swivel hub:*		
Stage 1	100	74
Stage 2	Angle-tighten a further 60°	
Stage 3	Angle-tighten a further 15°	
Lower arm balljoint clamp bolt nut:*		
Stage 1	30	22
Stage 2	Angle-tighten through a further 60°	
Stage 3	Angle-tighten through a further 15°	
Lower arm front pivot bolt:*		
Stage 1	90	66
Stage 2	Angle-tighten a further 75°	
Stage 3	Angle-tighten a further 15°	
Lower arm rear mounting bush to lower arm:*		
Stage 1	40	30
Stage 2	Angle-tighten a further 40°	
Lower arm rear mounting bush to subframe:*		
Stage 1	90	66
Stage 2	Angle-tighten a further 75°	
Stage 3	Angle-tighten a further 15°	
Subframe:		
Front engine mounting/torque link to subframe*	80	59
Rear engine mounting/torque link to subframe*.	60	44
Front mounting bolts:*		
Stage 1	80	59
Stage 2	Angle-tighten a further 120°	
Stage 3	Angle-tighten a further 15°	
Rear mounting reinforcement plates to underbody:*		
Early models – outer bolts:		
Stage 1	55	41
Stage 2	Angle-tighten a further 45°	
Stage 3	Angle-tighten a further 15°	
Early models – inner bolts:		
Stage 1	90	66
Stage 2	Angle-tighten a further 45°	
Stage 3	Angle-tighten a further 15°	
Later models:		
Stage 1	90	66
Stage 2	Angle-tighten a further 45°	
Stage 3	Angle-tighten a further 15°	
Rear mounting reinforcement plates to subframe:*		
Stage 1	100	74
Stage 2	Angle-tighten a further 90°	
Stage 3	Angle-tighten a further 15°	
Suspension strut piston rod nut*	100	74
Suspension strut to swivel hub:*		
Stage 1	50	37
Stage 2	85	63
Stage 3	Angle-tighten a further 75°	
Stage 4	Angle-tighten a further 15°	
Suspension strut upper mounting bolts:*		
Stage 1	20	15
Stage 2	Angle-tighten a further 45°	
Stage 3	Angle-tighten a further 15°	

Torque wrench settings (continued)

	Nm	lbf ft
Rear suspension		
Anti-roll bar clamp bolts:*		
Stage 1	25	18
Stage 2	Angle-tighten a further 30°	
Stage 3	Angle-tighten a further 15°	
Anti-roll bar link rod to hub carrier:*		
Stage 1	45	33
Stage 2	Angle-tighten a further 60°	
Stage 3	Angle-tighten a further 15°	
Auxiliary control arm to hub carrier:*		
Stage 1	150	111
Stage 2	Angle-tighten a further 45°	
Stage 3	Angle-tighten a further 15°	
Auxiliary control arm to rear axle body:*		
Stage 1	90	66
Stage 2	Angle-tighten a further 60°	
Stage 3	Angle-tighten a further 15°	
Hub bearing assembly to hub carrier:*		
Stage 1	60	44
Stage 2	Angle-tighten a further 60°	
Stage 3	Angle-tighten a further 15°	
Lower control arm to hub carrier and rear axle body:*		
Stage 1	90	66
Stage 2	Angle-tighten a further 60°	
Stage 3	Angle-tighten a further 15°	
Rear axle body mounting bolts:*		
Stage 1	90	66
Stage 2	Slacken bolts	
Stage 3	90	66
Stage 4	Angle-tighten a further 90°	
Stage 5	Angle-tighten a further 15°	
Shock absorber lower mounting bolt*	150	111
Shock absorber upper mounting bolt*	90	66
Trailing arm front mounting bracket bolts:*		
Stage 1	90	66
Stage 2	Slacken bolts	
Stage 3	90	66
Stage 4	Angle-tighten a further 90°	
Stage 5	Angle-tighten a further 15°	
Trailing arm to hub carrier*	150	111
Upper control arm to hub carrier:*		
Stage 1	150	111
Stage 2	Angle-tighten a further 45°	
Stage 3	Angle-tighten a further 15°	
Upper control arm to rear axle body:*		
Stage 1	90	66
Stage 2	Angle-tighten a further 60°	
Stage 3	Angle-tighten a further 15°	
Steering		
EHPS supply unit:		
Fluid supply pipe union	30	22
Mounting bracket to subframe........................	20	15
Mounting bracket to underbody:		
Upper bolts......................................	22	16
Lower bolt (subframe mounting bolt):*		
Stage 1	80	59
Stage 2	Angle-tighten a further 120°	
Stage 3	Angle-tighten a further 15°	
Supply unit to mounting bracket	7	5
Hydraulic fluid pipes to steering gear..................	11	8
Intermediate shaft to steering column*	25	18
Intermediate shaft to steering gear pinion*	25	18
Steering column mounting bolts*........................	25	18

Torque wrench settings (continued)

	Nm	lbf ft
Steering (continued)		
Steering gear to subframe:*		
Stage 1	45	33
Stage 2	Angle-tighten through a further 45°	
Stage 3	Angle-tighten through a further 15°	
Steering wheel bolt	30	22
Track rod inner balljoint to steering rack	90	66
Track rod outer balljoint to swivel hub*	35	26
Roadwheels		
All models	110	81

* Use new nuts/bolts.

1 General information

The independent front suspension is of the MacPherson strut type, incorporating coil springs and integral telescopic shock absorbers. The MacPherson struts are located by transverse lower suspension arms, which utilise rubber inner mounting bushes, and incorporate a balljoint at the outer ends. The front swivel hubs, which carry the hub bearings, brake calipers and disc assemblies, are bolted to the MacPherson struts, and connected to the lower arms via the balljoints. A front anti-roll bar is fitted, which has link rods with balljoints at each end to connect it to the strut.

The rear suspension is of fully independent multilink type, with a central axle body (crossmember), gas-filled shock absorbers, coil springs, trailing arms, upper and lower transverse control arms, auxiliary transverse control arms and an anti-roll bar. The shock absorbers are attached at their upper ends to the vehicle underbody and at their lower ends to the hub carriers. The rear hub carriers are attached to the trailing arms, upper and lower control arms and auxiliary control arms by means of flexible rubber bushes. The anti-roll bar is mounted on the axle body and is connected to the hub carriers by drop links.

The steering system is of the electro-hydraulic power steering (EHPS) type. This system utilises a conventional rack-and-pinion type steering gear mounted on the front subframe, with variable power assistance generated by a hydraulic pump, driven by an electric motor. The degree of power assistance available is governed by the speed of the electric motor which is controlled by the steering system electronic control unit. The ECU receives input signals on steering wheel position (from a steering angle sensor) and roadspeed (from the ABS wheel speed sensors) and calculates the amount of power assistance required. Two versions of the EHPS system are used on the Vectra, according to engine type; a standard EHPS system and a compact EHPS system. The standard EHPS system has the hydraulic pump, electric motor and hydraulic fluid reservoir assembly, remotely sited under the front wheel arch and connected to the rack-and-pinion steering gear by hydraulic supply and return pipes. On the compact EHPS system, the hydraulic pump, electric motor and hydraulic fluid reservoir are mounted above the rack-and-pinion steering gear on the front subframe.

The steering column is linked to the steering gear by an intermediate shaft. The intermediate shaft has a universal joint fitted to its upper end, and is secured to the column by a clamp bolt. The lower end of the intermediate shaft is attached to the steering gear pinion by means of a clamp bolt.

2 Front swivel hub – removal and refitting

Note: A new driveshaft retaining nut, lower arm balljoint clamp bolt and nut, anti-roll bar connecting link retaining nut, brake caliper mounting bracket bolts and a new track rod end retaining nut will be needed for refitting. The driveshaft outer joint splines may be a tight fit in the hub and it is possible that a puller/extractor will be required to draw the hub assembly off the driveshaft during removal.

Caution: The front wheel camber setting is controlled by the bolts securing the hub carrier to the front suspension strut. Before removing the bolts, mark the hub carrier in relation to the strut accurately. On completion, the camber setting must be checked and adjusted by a suitably-equipped garage.

Removal

1 Firmly apply the handbrake, then jack up the front of the car and support it securely on axle stands (see *Jacking and vehicle support*). Remove the relevant front roadwheel.

2 On diesel engine models, undo the ten bolts and remove the undertray from beneath the engine.

3 On early models, remove the ABS wheel speed sensor wiring plug from the suspension strut bracket and disconnect the wiring connector **(see illustration)**.

4 On later models, depress the locking tab and release the wiring connector from the suspension strut. Slide the locking bar on the connector downward, then hold the upper part of the connector and twist the lower part to open the connector. Disconnect the ABS wheel speed sensor wire from the connector and, if working on the left-hand swivel hub, also disconnect the brake pad wear warning indicator wire **(see illustrations)**.

5 Where fitted, tap off the driveshaft retaining nut dust cap using a cold chisel or large screwdriver **(see illustration)**.

6 To prevent rotation of the wheel hub as the driveshaft retaining nut is slackened, make up a holding tool and bolt the tool to the wheel hub using two wheel bolts **(see Tool Tip)**.

7 With the holding tool in place, slacken and remove the driveshaft retaining nut using a socket and long bar. Where necessary, support the socket on an axle stand to prevent it slipping off the nut. This nut is very tight; make sure that there is no risk of pulling the car off the axle stands as the nut is slackened.

8 Extract the retaining clip and release the hydraulic hose from the suspension strut **(see**

2.3 On early models, remove the ABS wheel speed sensor wiring plug (arrowed)

2.4a Depress the locking tab and release the connector from the suspension strut

2.4b Slide the locking bar on the wiring connector downward . . .

2.4c . . . then hold the upper part of the connector and twist the lower part in the direction of the arrow

2.4d Disconnect the wires from the connector

illustration). If working on the left-hand swivel hub on early models, also release the brake pad wear warning indicator wire from the strut bracket.

9 Undo the two bolts securing the brake caliper mounting bracket to the swivel hub. Slide the mounting bracket, complete with brake caliper and pads off the brake disc, and tie it to the coil spring using wire or a cable tie. Note that new caliper mounting bracket bolts will be required for refitting.

10 Undo the securing screw and remove the brake disc from the wheel hub **(see illustrations).**

11 Unscrew the nut securing the track rod end to the steering arm on the swivel hub, then use a balljoint separator tool to remove the track rod end **(see illustration).**

12 Unscrew the nut and remove the clamp bolt securing the front suspension lower arm balljoint to the swivel hub **(see illustrations).**

2.5 Where fitted, tap off the driveshaft retaining nut dust cap

Note that a new clamp bolt and nut will be required for refitting.

13 Using a lever, push down on the suspension lower arm to free the balljoint from the swivel hub, then move the swivel hub to one side and

TOOL TiP

A tool to hold the wheel hub stationary whilst the driveshaft retaining nut is slackened can be fabricated from two lengths of steel strip (one long, one short) and a nut an bolt; the nut and bolt forming the pivot of a forked tool.

2.8 Extract the retaining clip and release the hose from the suspension strut

2.10a Undo the securing screw . . .

2.10b . . . and remove the brake disc from the wheel hub

2.11 Unscrew the retaining nut, then use a balljoint separator tool to remove the track rod end from the swivel hub

2.12a Unscrew the retaining nut (arrowed) . . .

2.12b . . . and withdraw the clamp bolt from the swivel hub

2.13 Push down the lower suspension arm to free the balljoint from the swivel hub

2.14 Pull the swivel hub outwards then withdraw the driveshaft from the hub splines

2.16 Slacken and remove the two nuts and bolts securing the suspension strut to the swivel hub

release the arm, taking care not to damage the balljoint rubber boot **(see illustration)**. It is advisable to place a protective cover over the rubber boot such as the plastic cap from an aerosol can, suitably cut to fit.

14 The hub must now be freed from the end of the driveshaft **(see illustration)**. It may be possible to pull the hub off the driveshaft, but if the end of the driveshaft is tight in the hub, temporarily refit the driveshaft retaining nut to protect the driveshaft threads, then tap the end of the driveshaft with a soft-faced hammer while pulling outwards on the swivel hub. Alternatively, use a suitable puller to press the driveshaft through the hub.

15 Mark the position of the suspension strut on the swivel hub by drawing a circle around the heads of the two retaining bolts. **Note:** *This is important to maintain the camber setting.*

16 Slacken and remove the two nuts and bolts securing the suspension strut to the swivel hub, noting that new nuts and bolts will be required for refitting **(see illustration)**. Disengage the swivel hub from the strut and remove it from the car.

Refitting

17 Ensure that the driveshaft outer constant velocity joint and hub splines are clean, then slide the hub onto the driveshaft splines. Fit the new driveshaft retaining nut, tightening it by hand only at this stage.

18 Engage the swivel hub with the suspension strut, and insert the new bolts from the front of the strut so that their threads are facing to the rear. Fit the new nuts, tightening them by hand only at this stage.

19 Locate the lower arm balljoint in the swivel hub. Insert the clamp bolt from the front of the swivel hub, so that its threads are facing to the rear. Fit the new nut to the clamp bolt, and tighten it to the specified torque and through the specified angles given in the Specifications, using a torque wrench and angle-tightening gauge.

20 With the hub correctly located, align the strut-to-swivel hub bolt heads with the marks made on the strut during removal. Tighten the bolts to the specified torque and through the specified angles given in the Specifications, using a torque wrench and angle-tightening gauge.

21 Engage the track rod balljoint in the swivel hub, then fit the new retaining nut and tighten it to the specified torque setting.

22 Refit the brake disc and tighten its retaining screw securely.

23 Slide the brake pads, caliper and mounting bracket over the disc and into position on the swivel hub. Fit the two new caliper mounting bracket retaining bolts and tighten them to the specified torque (see Chapter 9).

24 Reconnect the ABS wheel speed sensor wiring connector and, where applicable, the break pad wear warning indicator wire. Secure the wiring in the relevant support brackets and clips.

25 Refit the brake hydraulic hose to the suspension strut and secure with the retaining clip.

26 Using the method employed on removal to prevent rotation, tighten the driveshaft retaining nut through the stages given in the Specifications. Where fitted, tap a new driveshaft retaining nut dust cap into position.

27 Refit the roadwheel, then lower the vehicle to the ground and tighten the roadwheel bolts to the specified torque.

---

3 Front hub bearings – checking and renewal

Note: *The front hub bearing and integral ABS wheel speed sensor is a sealed unit and no repairs are possible. If the bearing is worn or the speed sensor is faulty, a new bearing assembly must be obtained.*

3.13 Undo the three bolts (arrowed) securing the bearing assembly to the swivel hub

Checking

1 Firmly apply the handbrake, then jack up the front of the car and support it securely on axle stands (see *Jacking and vehicle support*). Remove the roadwheel.

2 A dial test indicator (DTI) will be required to measure the amount of play in the bearing. Locate the DTI on the suspension strut and zero the probe on the brake disc.

3 Lever the hub in and out and measure the amount of play in the bearing.

4 To measure the bearing lateral and radial run-out, undo the two bolts securing the brake caliper mounting bracket to the swivel hub. Slide the mounting bracket, complete with brake caliper and pads off the brake disc, and tie it to the coil spring using wire or a cable tie. Note that new caliper mounting bracket bolts will be required for refitting.

5 Undo the securing screw and remove the brake disc from the wheel hub.

6 To check the lateral run-out, locate the DTI on the suspension strut and zero the probe on the front face of the hub flange. Rotate the hub and measure the run-out.

7 To check the radial run-out, zero the DTI probe on the upper face of the extended portion at the centre of the hub. Rotate the hub and measure the run-out.

8 If the play or run-out exceeds the specified amounts, renew the hub bearing as described below.

9 If the bearing is satisfactory, refit the brake disc and tighten its retaining screw securely.

10 Slide the brake pads, caliper and mounting bracket over the disc and into position on the swivel hub. Fit the two new caliper mounting bracket retaining bolts and tighten them to the specified torque (see Chapter 9).

11 Refit the roadwheel, then lower the vehicle to the ground and tighten the roadwheel bolts to the specified torque.

Renewal

Note: *New hub bearing retaining bolts will be required for refitting.*

12 Remove the swivel hub as described in Section 2.

13 Undo the three bolts securing the bearing assembly to the swivel hub **(see illustration)**.

14 Remove the bearing and the brake shield from the swivel hub **(see illustrations)**.

15 Thoroughly clean the swivel hub and brake shield, then place the shield in position on the swivel hub.

16 Locate the wheel bearing over the brake shield and into the swivel hub. Position the bearing so that the wheel speed sensor wiring connector is toward the brake caliper side of the swivel hub (ie, towards the front of the vehicle). Align the retaining bolt holes and fit the three new bolts.

17 Tighten the retaining bolts progressively to the specified Stage 1 torque setting using a torque wrench, and then through the specified Stage 2 and Stage 3 angles, using an angle tightening gauge.

18 Refit the swivel hub as described in Section 2.

3.14a Remove the bearing . . .

3.14b . . . and the brake shield from the swivel hub

| 4 | **Front suspension strut –** removal, overhaul and refitting |

Note: *New strut-to-swivel hub bolts and nuts, strut upper mounting bolts and strut link rod nut, will be required for refitting. Ideally, both front suspension struts should be renewed at the same time in order to maintain good steering and suspension characteristics.*

Removal

1 Apply the handbrake, then jack up the front of the vehicle and support it on axle stands (see *Jacking and vehicle support*). Remove the front roadwheel.

2 Extract the retaining clip and release the hydraulic hose from the suspension strut **(see illustration 2.8)**. If working on the left-hand suspension strut on early models, also release the brake pad wear warning indicator wire from the strut bracket.

3 On early models, unscrew the retaining bolt and release the ABS wheel speed sensor wiring plug support plate from the suspension strut bracket **(see illustration)**.

4 On later models, depress the locking tab and release the wiring connector from the suspension strut bracket **(see illustration 2.4a)**.

5 Unscrew the nut and disconnect the anti-roll bar link rod from the strut. Use a spanner on the special flats to hold the

link while the nut is being loosened **(see illustration)**.

6 Mark the position of the suspension strut on the swivel hub by drawing a circle around the heads of the two retaining bolts. **Note:** *This is important to maintain the camber setting.*

7 Slacken and remove the two nuts and bolts securing the suspension strut to the swivel hub, noting that new nuts and bolts will be required for refitting **(see illustration 2.16)**. Disengage the top of the swivel hub from the strut.

8 Support the strut beneath the front wing then, from within the engine compartment, unscrew the three strut upper mounting bolts **(see illustration)**.

9 Lower the strut and withdraw it from under the front wing.

Overhaul

Note 1: *A spring compressor tool will be*

required for this operation. Before overhaul, mark the position of each component in relationship with each other for reassembly.

Note 2: *A new piston rod nut will be required for reassembly.*

10 Using a screwdriver, prise out the plastic cap from the upper mounting **(see illustration)**.

11 With the suspension strut resting on a bench, or clamped in a vice, fit a spring compressor tool, and compress the coil spring to relieve the pressure on the spring seats. Ensure that the compressor tool is securely located on the spring, in accordance with the tool manufacturer's instructions.

12 Mark the position of the spring relevant to the top and bottom mountings, then counterhold the strut piston rod with an Allen key or suitable bit, and unscrew the piston rod nut **(see illustration)**.

4.3 On early models, unscrew the retaining bolt (arrowed) and release the wiring plug support plate from the strut bracket

4.5 Use a spanner on the flats to hold the link while the nut is being loosened

4.8 Unscrew the three suspension strut upper mounting bolts (arrowed)

4.10 Prise out the plastic cap from the strut upper mounting

4.12 Counterhold the strut piston rod with an Allen key or suitable bit, and unscrew the piston rod nut

4.13a Remove the strut upper mounting . . .

4.13b . . . upper spring seat . . .

4.13c . . . rubber gaiter . . .

4.13d . . . buffer . . .

4.13e . . . and spring from the strut

4.18 Locate the spring on the strut making sure that its lower end (A) is against the raised stop (B)

13 Remove the strut upper mounting, upper spring seat, rubber gaiter, buffer and spring from the strut **(see illustrations)**.
14 With the strut assembly now completely dismantled, examine all the components for wear, damage or deformation. Renew any of the components as necessary.
15 Examine the strut for signs of fluid leakage. Check the strut piston for signs of pitting along its entire length, and check the strut body for signs of damage. While holding it in an upright position, test the operation of the strut by moving the piston through a full stroke, and then through short strokes of 50 to 100 mm. In both cases, the resistance felt should be smooth and continuous. If the resistance is jerky or uneven or if there is any visible sign of wear or damage to the strut, renewal is necessary.
16 If any doubt exists as to the condition of the coil spring, carefully remove the spring compressors and check the spring for distortion and signs of cracking. Renew the spring if it is damaged or distorted, or if there is any doubt as to its condition.
17 Inspect all other components for damage or deterioration, and renew any that are suspect.
18 With the spring compressed with the compressor tool, locate the spring on the strut making sure that it is correctly seated with its lower end against the raised stop **(see illustration)**.
19 Refit the buffer, rubber gaiter, upper spring seat and the upper mounting.
20 Refit the new piston rod nut and tighten it to the specified torque while counterholding

the piston rod. Refit the plastic cap to the upper mounting.
21 Slowly slacken the spring compressor tool to relieve the tension in the spring. Check that the ends of the spring locate correctly against the stops on the spring seats. If necessary, turn the spring and the upper seat so that the components locate correctly before the compressor tool is removed. Remove the compressor tool when the spring is fully seated.

Refitting

22 Locate the strut in position under the front wing and refit the three new retaining bolts. Tighten the retaining bolts progressively to the specified Stage 1 torque setting using a torque wrench, and then through the specified Stage 2 and Stage 3 angles, using an angle tightening gauge.
23 Engage the swivel hub with the suspension strut, and insert the new bolts from the front of the strut so that their threads are facing to the rear. Fit the new nuts, tightening them by hand only at this stage.
24 Align the strut-to-swivel hub bolt heads with the marks made on the strut during removal. Tighten the bolts to the specified torque and through the specified angles given in the Specifications, using a torque wrench and angle-tightening gauge.
25 Locate the hydraulic hose in the strut bracket and secure with the retaining clip. Where applicable, also refit the brake pad wear warning indicator wire to the strut bracket.
26 On early models, refit the ABS wheel speed sensor wiring plug support plate to

the suspension strut bracket and tighten the retaining bolt securely.
27 On later models, refit the wiring connector to the suspension strut bracket.
28 Connect the anti-roll bar link rod to the strut and use a spanner on the flats to hold the link while tightening the nut to the specified torque.
29 Refit the roadwheel, then lower the vehicle to the ground and tighten the roadwheel bolts to the specified torque.

5 Front lower arm – removal, overhaul and refitting

Note: *New lower arm pivot bolts, and new lower arm-to-balljoint nut/bolt, will be required.*

Removal

1 Firmly apply the handbrake, then jack up the front of the car and support it securely on axle stands (see *Jacking and vehicle support*). Remove the appropriate front roadwheel.
2 On models with xenon headlights, if working on the left-hand lower arm, undo the bolt securing the range control sensor to the lower arm, and the two bolts securing the sensor to the subframe. Move the sensor to one side.
3 Unscrew the nut and remove the clamp bolt securing the lower arm balljoint to the swivel hub **(see illustrations 2.12a and 2.12b)**. Note that a new bolt and nut will be required for refitting.

4 Using a lever, push down on the lower arm to free the balljoint from the swivel hub, then move the swivel hub to one side and release the arm, taking care not to damage the balljoint rubber boot **(see illustration 2.13)**. It is advisable to place a protective cover over the rubber boot such as the plastic cap from an aerosol can, suitably cut to fit.

5 Unscrew the pivot bolt securing the lower arm front mounting to the subframe. Note that a new bolt will be required for refitting.

6 Undo the two bolts securing the lower arm rear mounting bush to the subframe. Note that new bolts will be required for refitting.

7 Disengage the front mounting from the subframe and remove the lower arm from under the car.

Overhaul

8 Thoroughly clean the lower arm and the area around the arm mountings, removing all traces of dirt and underseal if necessary. Check carefully for cracks, distortion, or any other signs of wear or damage, paying particular attention to the mounting bushes and lower arm balljoint. If the front mounting bush or the balljoint are worn, the lower arm must be renewed as these components are not available separately.

9 To renew the rear mounting bush, undo the retaining bolt and remove the bush from the arm. Fit the new bush together with a new retaining bolt. Tighten the bolt just sufficiently to retain the bush. Final tightening is carried out with the car on its roadwheels.

Refitting

10 Offer up the lower arm, aligning the front end of the arm with its subframe bracket. Insert the new front pivot bolt, and secure the rear mounting with two new retaining bolts. Tighten the rear mounting bush retaining bolts to the specified torque and through the specified angles given in the Specifications. Only tighten the pivot bolts hand tight at this stage.

11 Locate the lower arm balljoint in the swivel hub. Insert the clamp bolt from the front of the swivel hub, so that its threads are facing to the rear. Fit the new nut to the clamp bolt, and tighten it to the specified torque and through the specified angles given in the Specifications, using a torque wrench and angle-tightening gauge.

12 On models with xenon headlights, if working on the left-hand lower arm, refit and tighten the bolt securing the range control sensor to the lower arm, and the two bolts securing the sensor to the subframe.

13 Refit the roadwheel, lower the car to the ground, and tighten the roadwheel bolts to the specified torque setting.

14 Push the car forwards and backwards slightly to settle the suspension and allow the car to adopt its normal ride height. Now tighten the lower arm front pivot bolt to the specified torque and through the specified angles given in the Specifications. If the rear

6.5 Unscrew the bolt (arrowed) securing the steering column intermediate shaft to the steering gear pinion

mounting bush has been renewed, tighten its mounting bolt to the specified torque and through the specified angles also.

---

6 Front subframe – removal and refitting

Note: *Vauxhall/Opel technicians use special jigs to ensure that the front subframe is correctly aligned when refitting. An alternative method of aligning the subframe using a home-made tool is described in the text.*

Removal

1 Jack up the front and rear of the car and support it securely on axle stands (see *Jacking and vehicle support*). Preferably, position the car over an inspection pit, or on a lift. The help of an assistant will be needed for this procedure.

2 On diesel engine models, undo the ten bolts and remove the engine undertray.

3 Set the front wheels in the straight-ahead position, then remove the ignition key and lock the column by turning the steering wheel as required. Remove both front road-wheels.

4 Remove the complete exhaust system as described in Chapter 4A or 4B, as applicable.

5 Working in the engine compartment, unscrew the bolt securing the bottom of the steering column intermediate shaft to the steering gear pinion **(see illustration)**. Use paint or a suitable marker pen to make

6.7 Undo the nut securing the front engine mounting/torque link to the subframe and withdraw the through-bolt (arrowed)

6.6 Undo the through-bolt (arrowed) securing the rear engine mounting/torque link to the subframe

alignment marks between the intermediate shaft and the steering gear pinion, then pull the shaft from the pinion and position to one side.

6 Undo the through-bolt securing the rear engine mounting/torque link to the subframe **(see illustration)**.

7 Similarly, slacken and remove the nut securing the front engine mounting/torque link to the subframe bracket. Withdraw the through-bolt **(see illustration)**.

8 Disconnect the steering track rod balljoints from the swivel hubs by unscrewing the nuts and using a balljoint separator tool **(see illustration 2.11)**.

9 Unscrew the nut and remove the clamp bolt each side securing the lower arm balljoint to the swivel hub **(see illustrations 2.12a and 2.12b)**. Note that new bolts and nuts will be required for refitting.

10 Working on one side at a time, use a lever to push down on the lower arm to free the balljoint from the swivel hub, then move the swivel hub to one side and release the arm, taking care not to damage the balljoint rubber boot **(see illustration 2.13)**. It is advisable to place a protective cover over the rubber boot such as the plastic cap from an aerosol can, suitably cut to fit.

11 Unscrew the nuts and disconnect the anti-roll bar link rods from the anti-roll bar on both sides. Use a further spanner to hold the studs while the nuts are being loosened **(see illustration)**.

12 Undo the retaining screws, release the

6.11 Unscrew the nuts and disconnect the anti-roll bar link rods from the anti-roll bar on both sides

6.12 Undo the retaining screws, release the clips and remove the wheel arch liner from the wheel arch and subframe

clips and remove the wheel arch liner from the wheel arch and subframe on the right-hand side (see illustration).

13 Remove the front bumper as described in Chapter 11.

6.17a Attach a nut and bolt to one end of the steel strip . . .

6.17c . . . to make the subframe aligning tool

6.17e . . . and engage the socket at the other end of the tool with the hole in the underbody

6.14 Disconnect the wiring connectors (arrowed) at the EHPS supply unit – standard EHPS unit shown

14 Disconnect the wiring connectors at the EHPS supply unit. On models with standard EHPS, the supply unit is located under the wheel arch on the right-hand side. On models with compact EHPS, the supply unit

6.17b . . . and attach a 40 mm diameter socket to the other end . . .

6.17d Engage the bolt on the tool with the hole in the subframe . . .

6.20a Undo the bolts (arrowed) each side securing the subframe reinforcement plates to the underbody . . .

is mounted on the subframe, above the rack-and-pinion steering gear (see illustration).

15 On models with standard EHPS, release the wiring harness from the clips on the subframe and hydraulic pipes.

16 On models with xenon headlights, disconnect the wiring connector from the range control sensor, and release the wiring harness from the clips on the subframe.

17 If the Vauxhall/Opel alignment jigs are not being used, it will be necessary to make up an alignment tool to ensure the subframe is correctly positioned when refitting. Obtain a length of steel strip long enough to reach from the 12 mm hole in the side of the subframe, just in front of the lower arm front mounting, to the 40 mm hole in the underbody, outboard and to the rear of the subframe. Mark the position of these two holes as accurately as possible on the steel strip, then drill a 12 mm hole at each marked position. Attach a nut and bolt to one hole, and secure a 40 mm diameter socket, using a nut and bolt, to the other hole. Engage the bolt on the tool with the hole in the subframe and engage the socket at the other end of the tool with the hole in the underbody. Reposition the bolt and socket as necessary until the tool is an accurate fit. It may be necessary to elongate the holes in the strip to achieve perfect alignment. Once the tool fits accurately on one side of the car, try it on the other side; the fit should be the same (see illustrations).

18 Use cable-ties to secure the top of the radiator on each side to prevent the radiator dropping when the subframe is removed.

19 Support the subframe with a cradle across a trolley jack. Alternatively, two trolley jacks and the help of an assistant will be required.

20 Undo the three bolts (early models) or two bolts (later models) each side securing the subframe rear mountings and the reinforcement plates to the underbody (see illustrations). Remove the reinforcement plates.

21 Undo the subframe front mounting bolt on the right-hand side, noting that, on models with standard EHPS, this bolt also secures the EHPS supply unit mounting bracket (see illustration).

22 On 1.9 litre diesel engine models, remove the engine management system ECU as described in Chapter 4B.

6.20b . . . and to the subframe – later models shown

23 On models with standard EHPS, undo the two upper mounting bolts securing the EHPS supply unit mounting bracket to the underbody.

24 Undo the subframe front mounting bolt on the left-hand side **(see illustration)**.

25 Slowly and carefully lower the subframe to the ground. As the subframe is lowered, make sure there are no cables or wiring still attached.

26 Remove the lower suspension arms from the subframe with reference to Section 5, the anti-roll bar with reference to Section 7, the rear engine mounting/torque link with reference to the relevant part of Chapter 2, and the steering gear with reference to Section 22.

Refitting

27 Refitting is a reversal of removal, bearing in mind the following points:

a) *Ensure that the radiator lower mounting pegs engage correctly in the subframe brackets as the subframe is refitted.*

b) *Tighten all nuts and bolts to the specified torque and, where necessary, in the stages given. Note that new nuts/bolts should be used on all disturbed fittings.*

c) *Make sure that the subframe is correctly aligned with the underbody before fully tightening the mounting bolts.*

7 Front anti-roll bar – removal and refitting

Note: *It is recommended that all mounting nuts and bolts are renewed when refitting.*

Removal

1 Remove the front subframe assembly as described in Section 6.

2 Prior to removal of the anti-roll bar, mark the position of each anti-roll bar mounting clamp rubber.

3 Unscrew the retaining nut and disconnect the link rod from the ends of the anti-roll bar, discard the retaining nut; a new one should be used on refitting **(see illustration 6.11)**. Use a spanner on the flats to hold the link while the nut is being loosened.

4 Unscrew the two bolts from each mounting clamp, and remove the clamp **(see**

7.4 Anti-roll bar clamp mounting bolts (arrowed)

6.21 Undo the subframe front mounting bolt on the right-hand side

illustration). As the last clamp is removed, support the anti-roll bar and remove it from the subframe.

5 Inspect the mounting clamp rubbers for signs of damage and deterioration, and renew if necessary **(see illustrations)**.

Refitting

6 Align the mounting rubbers with the marks made on the anti-roll bar prior to refitting.

7 Refit the anti-roll bar to the subframe, and fit the mounting clamps. Ensure that the clamp half is correctly engaged with the anti-roll bar rubbers, then tighten each clamp retaining bolt, by hand only at this stage.

8 With the two clamps loosely installed, check the position of the anti-roll bar to the marks made on removal, then tighten the clamp bolts to the specified torque setting.

9 Refit the link rods to the ends of the anti-roll bar using new retaining nuts, tighten to the specified torque setting.

10 Refit the front subframe assembly as described in Section 6.

11 Refit the roadwheels if not already done, then lower the vehicle to the ground and tighten the roadwheel bolts to the specified torque setting.

8 Rear hub bearings – checking and renewal

Note: *The rear hub bearing and integral ABS wheel speed sensor is a sealed unit and no repairs are possible. If the bearing is worn*

7.5a Remove the clamps from the rubber bushes . . .

6.24 Subframe left-hand side front mounting bolt (arrowed)

or the speed sensor is faulty, a new bearing assembly must be obtained.

Checking

1 Chock the front wheels then jack up the rear of the car and securely support it on axle stands (see *Jacking and vehicle support*). Remove the roadwheel.

2 A dial test indicator (DTI) will be required to measure the amount of play in the bearing. Locate the DTI on the trailing arm and zero the probe on the brake disc.

3 Lever the hub in and out and measure the amount of play in the bearing.

4 To measure the bearing lateral and radial run-out, undo the two bolts securing the brake caliper mounting bracket to the hub carrier. Slide the mounting bracket, complete with brake caliper and pads off the brake disc, and tie it to the shock absorber upper mounting using wire or cable ties. Note that new caliper mounting bracket bolts will be required for refitting.

5 Undo the securing screw and remove the brake disc from the wheel hub.

6 To check the lateral run-out, locate the DTI on the trailing arm and zero the probe on the front face of the hub flange. Rotate the hub and measure the run-out.

7 To check the radial run-out, zero the DTI probe on the upper face of the extended portion at the centre of the hub. Rotate the hub and measure the run-out.

8 If the play or run-out exceeds the specified amounts, renew the hub bearing as described below.

9 If the bearing is satisfactory, refit the brake disc and tighten its retaining screw securely.

7.5b . . . then remove the bushes and inspect for wear

8.15 Disconnect the ABS wheel speed sensor wiring connector (arrowed) from the rear of the bearing assembly

10 Slide the brake pads, caliper and mounting bracket over the disc and into position on the hub carrier. Fit the two new caliper mounting bracket retaining bolts and tighten them to the specified torque (see Chapter 9).

11 Refit the roadwheel, then lower the vehicle to the ground and tighten the roadwheel bolts to the specified torque.

Renewal

Note: *New hub bearing retaining nuts will be required for refitting.*

12 Chock the front wheels then jack up the rear of the car and securely support it on axle stands (see *Jacking and vehicle support*). Remove the roadwheel.

13 Undo the two bolts securing the brake caliper mounting bracket to the hub carrier. Slide the mounting bracket, complete with brake caliper and pads off the brake disc, and tie it to the shock absorber upper mounting using wire

9.2a Disengage the handbrake inner cable from the caliper lever . . .

9.3 Undo the bolt (arrowed) securing the handbrake cable support bracket to the trailing arm front mounting

8.16 Undo the four retaining nuts (arrowed) and remove the bearing unit and brake disc shield from the hub carrier

or cable ties. Note that new caliper mounting bracket bolts will be required for refitting.

14 Undo the securing screw and remove the brake disc from the wheel hub.

15 Disconnect the ABS wheel speed sensor wiring connector from the rear of the bearing assembly **(see illustration)**.

16 Undo the four retaining nuts and remove the bearing unit and brake disc shield from the hub carrier **(see illustration)**.

17 Thoroughly clean the hub carrier, bearing unit and brake shield mating faces, then place the shield in position on the bearing unit.

18 Refit the bearing unit and brake shield to the hub carrier, and screw on four new retaining nuts.

19 Tighten the retaining nuts progressively to the specified Stage 1 torque setting using a torque wrench, and then through the specified Stage 2 and Stage 3 angles, using an angle tightening gauge.

9.2b . . . then pull the outer cable grommet out of the caliper bracket

9.7 Undo the four bolts (arrowed) securing the trailing arm front mounting bracket to the underbody

20 Reconnect the ABS wheel speed sensor wiring connector.

21 Refit the brake disc and tighten its retaining screw securely.

22 Slide the brake pads, caliper and mounting bracket over the disc and into position on the hub carrier. Fit the two new caliper mounting bracket retaining bolts and tighten them to the specified torque (see Chapter 9).

23 Refit the roadwheel, then lower the vehicle to the ground and tighten the roadwheel bolts to the specified torque.

9 Rear hub carrier – removal and refitting

Note 1: *Suitable coil spring compressors will be required for this operation.*
Note 2: *It is recommended that all mounting nuts and bolts are renewed when refitting.*

Removal

1 Chock the front wheels then jack up the rear of the car and securely support it on axle stands (see *Jacking and vehicle support*). Remove the roadwheel.

2 Disengage the handbrake inner cable from the rear brake caliper lever, then pull the outer cable grommet out of the caliper bracket **(see illustrations)**.

3 Release the handbrake cable from the clip on the trailing arm, then undo the bolt securing the handbrake cable support bracket to the trailing arm front mounting **(see illustration)**. Move the handbrake cable to one side.

4 Remove the rear hub bearing as described in Section 8.

5 Remove the rear coil spring as described in Section 10.

6 Unscrew the shock absorber lower mounting bolt and detach the shock absorber from the hub carrier.

7 Unclip the ABS wheel speed sensor wiring harness from the trailing arm, then undo the four bolts securing the trailing arm front mounting bracket to the underbody **(see illustration)**.

8 Undo the bolt and detach the anti-roll bar link rod from the hub carrier **(see illustration)**.

9.8 Undo the bolt (arrowed) and detach the anti-roll bar link rod from the hub carrier

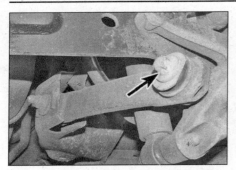

9.10a Undo the bolts securing the auxiliary control arm (arrowed) . . .

9.10b . . . upper control arm (arrowed) . . .

9.10c . . . and lower control arm (arrowed) to the hub carrier

9 Undo the three bolts securing the trailing arm to the hub carrier and remove the trailing arm from the car.

10 Undo the bolts securing the auxiliary control arm, upper control arm and lower control arm to the hub carrier, and remove the hub carrier from the car **(see illustrations)**.

Refitting

11 Refitting is a reversal of removal, bearing in mind the following points:
a) Tighten all nuts and bolts to the specified torque and, where necessary, in the stages given. Note that new nuts/bolts should be used on all disturbed fittings.
b) Refit the rear coil spring as described in Section 10.
c) Refit the rear hub bearing as described in Section 8.
d) Have the rear wheel toe-in setting and camber angle checked and if necessary adjusted at the earliest opportunity.

10 Rear coil spring – removal and refitting

Note 1: Always renew coil springs in pairs and the correct version for model, to maintain good handling.
Note 2: Suitable coil spring compressors will be required for this operation.

Removal

1 Chock the front wheels then jack up the rear of the car and securely support it on axle stands (see Jacking and vehicle support). Remove the roadwheel.

2 Undo the two bolts securing the brake caliper mounting bracket to the hub carrier. Slide the mounting bracket, complete with brake caliper and pads off the brake disc, and tie it to the shock absorber upper mounting using wire or cable ties. Note that new caliper mounting bracket bolts will be required for refitting.

3 Fit a spring compressor tool to the coil spring, and compress the spring to relieve the pressure on the spring seats. Ensure that the compressor tool is securely located on the spring, in accordance with the tool manufacturer's instructions. Remove the

spring together with the upper damper ring and lower spring stop.

Refitting

4 Locate the compressed spring in position ensuring that the upper damper ring and lower spring stop are correctly seated. Release the tension on the spring compressor and remove the compressor from the spring.

5 Slide the brake pads, caliper and mounting bracket over the disc and into position on the hub carrier. Fit the two new caliper mounting bracket retaining bolts and tighten them to the specified torque (see Chapter 9).

6 Refit the roadwheel, then lower the vehicle to the ground and tighten the roadwheel bolts to the specified torque.

11 Rear suspension upper control arm – removal and refitting

Note: It is recommended that all mounting nuts and bolts are renewed when refitting.

Removal

1 Chock the front wheels then jack up the rear of the car and securely support it on axle stands (see Jacking and vehicle support). Remove the roadwheel.

2 Remove the rear coil spring as described in Section 10.

3 Release the clips securing the ABS wheel speed sensor wiring harness to the upper control arm.

11.6 Undo the bolt (arrowed) securing the upper control arm to the rear axle body

4 Place a jack under the hub carrier and just take the weight of the rear suspension assembly.

5 Undo the bolt securing the upper control arm to the hub carrier **(see illustration 9.10b)**.

6 Undo the bolt securing the upper control arm to the rear axle body and remove the control arm from the car **(see illustration)**.

Refitting

7 Refitting is a reversal of removal, bearing in mind the following points:
a) Tighten all nuts and bolts to the specified torque and, where necessary, in the stages given. Note that new nuts/bolts should be used on all disturbed fittings.
b) Refit the rear coil spring as described in Section 10.
c) Have the rear wheel toe-in setting and camber angle checked and if necessary adjusted at the earliest opportunity.

12 Rear suspension lower control arm – removal and refitting

Note: It is recommended that all mounting nuts and bolts are renewed when refitting.

Removal

1 Chock the front wheels then jack up the rear of the car and securely support it on axle stands (see Jacking and vehicle support). Remove the roadwheel.

2 If working on the left-hand lower control arm, suitably support the exhaust system and release the rubber mounting blocks at the rear. Lower the system slightly for access to the control arm.

3 If working on the left-hand lower control arm on models with xenon headlights, undo the retaining bolt and detach the headlight range control linkage from the lower control arm.

4 Remove the rear coil spring as described in Section 10.

5 Undo the bolt securing the lower control arm to the hub carrier **(see illustration 9.10c)**.

6 Accurately mark the position of the camber adjustment eccentric disc on the lower control arm inner mounting **(see illustration)**. Undo the bolt securing the lower control arm to the

12.6 Camber adjustment eccentric disc (arrowed) on the lower control arm inner mounting

rear axle body and remove the control arm from the car.

Refitting

7 Refitting is a reversal of removal, bearing in mind the following points:
 a) *Tighten all nuts and bolts to the specified torque and, where necessary, in the stages given. Note that new nuts/bolts should be used on all disturbed fittings.*
 b) *Align the camber adjustment eccentric disc with the marks made on removal when tightening the control arm inner mounting bolt.*
 c) *Refit the rear coil spring as described in Section 10.*
 d) *Have the rear wheel toe-in setting and camber angle checked and if necessary adjusted at the earliest opportunity.*

13 Rear suspension auxiliary control arm – removal and refitting

Note: *It is recommended that all mounting nuts and bolts are renewed when refitting.*

Removal

1 Chock the front wheels then jack up the rear of the car and securely support it on axle stands (see *Jacking and vehicle support*). Remove the roadwheel.
2 Remove the rear coil spring as described in Section 10.
3 Place a jack under the hub carrier and just take the weight of the rear suspension assembly.
4 Undo the bolt securing the auxiliary control arm to the hub carrier **(see illustration 9.10a)**.
5 Accurately mark the position of the toe-in adjustment eccentric disc on the auxiliary control arm inner mounting **(see illustration)**. Undo the bolt securing the auxiliary control arm to the rear axle body and remove the control arm from the car.

Refitting

6 Refitting is a reversal of removal, bearing in mind the following points:
 a) *Tighten all nuts and bolts to the specified torque and, where necessary, in the*

13.5 Toe-in adjustment eccentric disc (arrowed) on the auxiliary control arm inner mounting

stages given. Note that new nuts/bolts should be used on all disturbed fittings.
 b) *Align the toe-in adjustment eccentric disc with the marks made on removal when tightening the control arm inner mounting bolt.*
 c) *Refit the rear coil spring as described in Section 10.*
 d) *Have the rear wheel toe-in setting and camber angle checked and if necessary adjusted at the earliest opportunity.*

14 Rear suspension trailing arm – removal and refitting

Note: *It is recommended that all mounting nuts and bolts are renewed when refitting.*

Removal

1 Chock the front wheels then jack up the rear of the car and securely support it on axle stands (see *Jacking and vehicle support*). Remove the roadwheel.
2 Release the handbrake cable from the clip on the trailing arm, then undo the bolt securing the handbrake cable support bracket to the trailing arm front mounting **(see illustration 9.3)**. Move the handbrake cable to one side.
3 Unclip the ABS wheel speed sensor wiring harness from the trailing arm.
4 Place a jack under the hub carrier and just take the weight of the rear suspension assembly.
5 Unscrew the shock absorber lower

15.4 Shock absorber upper mounting bolt (arrowed)

mounting bolt and detach the shock absorber from the hub carrier.
6 Undo the four bolts securing the trailing arm front mounting bracket to the underbody **(see illustration 9.7)**.
7 Undo the three bolts securing the trailing arm to the hub carrier and remove the trailing arm from the car.

Refitting

8 Refitting is a reversal of removal, bearing in mind the following points:
 a) *Tighten all nuts and bolts to the specified torque and, where necessary, in the stages given. Note that new nuts/bolts should be used on all disturbed fittings.*
 b) *Have the rear wheel toe-in setting and camber angle checked and if necessary adjusted at the earliest opportunity.*

15 Rear shock absorber – removal, testing and refitting

Note 1: *Always renew shock absorbers in pairs and the correct version for model, to maintain good handling.*
Note 2: *It is recommended that the shock absorber mounting bolts are renewed when refitting.*

Removal

1 Chock the front wheels then jack up the rear of the car and securely support it on axle stands (see *Jacking and vehicle support*). Remove the roadwheel.
2 Place a jack under the hub carrier and just take the weight of the rear suspension assembly.
3 Unscrew the shock absorber lower mounting bolt and detach the shock absorber from the hub carrier.
4 Unscrew the shock absorber upper mounting bolt and remove the shock absorber from the car **(see illustration)**.

Testing

5 Examine the shock absorber for signs of fluid leakage or damage. Test the operation of the strut, while holding it in an upright position, by moving the piston through a full stroke, and then through short strokes of 50 to 100 mm. In both cases, the resistance felt should be smooth and continuous. If the resistance is jerky, or uneven, or if there is any visible sign of wear or damage to the strut, renewal is necessary. Also check the rubber mounting bush(es) for damage and deterioration. If the bushes are damaged or worn, the complete shock absorber will have to be renewed, as the mounting bushes are not available separately. Inspect the shanks of the mounting bolts for signs of wear or damage, and renew as necessary.

Refitting

6 Refitting is a reversal of removal, tightening the new mounting bolts to the specified torque.

16 Rear axle body –
removal and refitting

Note 1: *Vauxhall technicians use special jigs to ensure that the rear axle body is correctly aligned. Without the use of these tools it is important to note and suitably mark the position of the axle body accurately before removal. If necessary, refer to the information contained in Section 6 regarding the fabrication of a home-made aligning tool, and adapt the principle for the rear axle body.*

Note 2: *It is recommended that all mounting nuts and bolts are renewed when refitting.*

Removal

1 Chock the front wheels then jack up the rear of the car and securely support it on axle stands (see *Jacking and vehicle support*). Remove both rear the roadwheels.

2 Remove the complete exhaust system as described in Chapter 4A or 4B as applicable.

3 Disengage the handbrake inner cable from the rear brake caliper levers, then pull the outer cable grommet out of the caliper brackets **(see illustrations 9.2a and 9.2b)**.

4 Undo the two bolts securing the brake caliper mounting bracket to the hub carrier on each side. Slide the mounting bracket, complete with brake caliper and pads off the brake disc, and tie it to the shock absorber upper mounting using wire or cable ties. Note that new caliper mounting bracket bolts will be required for refitting.

5 Release the handbrake cable from the clip on each trailing arm, then undo the bolt securing the handbrake cable support bracket to the trailing arm front mounting on each side **(see illustration 9.3)**. Move the handbrake cables to one side.

6 Trace the ABS wheel speed sensor wiring harness back to the wiring connector on the underbody and disconnect the connector. Release the harness from the underbody clips so that it's free to be removed with the rear axle body.

7 On models with a tyre pressure monitoring system, undo the screws and clips and remove the wheel arch liners on both sides. Trace the wiring harness back to the connectors, and disconnect the wiring connectors on each side. Release the harness from the clips on the underbody.

8 On models with xenon headlights, undo the retaining bolt and detach the headlight range control linkage from the lower control arm on the left-hand side.

9 Remove the rear coil spring on each side as described in Section 10.

10 Unscrew the shock absorber lower mounting bolt and detach the shock absorber from the hub carrier.

11 Undo the four bolts securing the trailing arm front mounting bracket to the underbody **(see illustration 9.7)**.

16.13a Rear axle body front mounting bolt (arrowed) . . .

12 Support the rear axle body with a cradle across a trolley jack. Alternatively, two trolley jacks and the help of an assistant will be required.

13 Undo the four bolts securing the rear axle body to the vehicle underbody **(see illustrations)**.

14 Slowly and carefully lower the rear axle body to the ground. As the assembly is lowered, make sure there are no cables or wiring still attached.

15 With the rear axle body removed from the car, if required, carry out further dismantling to remove the attached components, with reference to the applicable Sections of this Chapter.

Refitting

16 Refitting is a reversal of removal, bearing in mind the following points:
a) *Tighten all nuts and bolts to the specified torque and, where necessary, in the stages given. Note that new nuts/bolts should be used on all disturbed fittings.*
b) *Make sure that the rear axle body is correctly aligned with the vehicle underbody before fully tightening the mounting bolts.*

17 Rear anti-roll bar –
removal and refitting

Note: *It is recommended that all mounting nuts and bolts are renewed when refitting.*

Removal

1 Remove the rear axle body as described in Section 16.

2 Undo the bolt and detach the anti-roll bar link rod from the hub carrier on each side **(see illustration 9.8)**.

3 Prior to removal of the anti-roll bar, mark the position of each anti-roll bar mounting clamp rubber.

4 Unscrew the two bolts from each mounting clamp, and remove the clamp. As the last clamp is removed, support the anti-roll bar and remove it from the rear axle body.

5 Inspect the mounting clamp rubbers for signs of damage and deterioration, and renew if necessary.

16.13b . . . and rear mounting bolt (arrowed)

Refitting

6 Align the mounting rubbers with the marks made on the anti-roll bar prior to removal.

7 Refit the anti-roll bar to the rear axle body, and fit the mounting clamps. Ensure that the clamp half is correctly engaged with the anti-roll bar rubbers, then tighten each clamp retaining bolt, by hand only at this stage.

8 With the two clamps loosely installed, check the position of the anti-roll bar to the marks made on removal, then tighten the clamp bolts to the specified torque setting.

9 Refit the link rods to the hub carriers using new bolts, and tighten the bolts to the specified torque setting.

10 Refit the rear axle body as described in Section 16.

18 Steering wheel –
removal and refitting

 Warning: Make sure that the airbag safety recommendations given in Chapter 12 are followed, to prevent personal injury.

Removal

1 Remove the airbag as described in Chapter 12.

2 Set the front wheels in the straight-ahead position, then lock the column in position after removing the ignition key.

3 Disconnect the wiring harness connector for the steering wheel switches **(see illustration)**.

18.3 Disconnect the wiring harness connector (arrowed) for the steering wheel switches

18.4 Alignment marks (arrowed) between the steering column shaft and steering wheel

18.5 Steering wheel retaining bolt (arrowed)

18.7 Guide the wiring for the airbag through the aperture in the wheel, taking care not to damage the wiring connectors

4 Check that there are alignment marks between the steering column shaft and steering wheel **(see illustration)**. If no marks are visible, centre punch the wheel and column shaft to ensure correct alignment when refitting.

5 Unscrew the steering wheel retaining bolt, but don't remove it completely **(see illustration)**.

6 Grip the steering wheel with both hands and carefully rock it from side-to-side to release it from the splines on the steering column.

7 With the steering wheel loose on the splines, the retaining bolt can now be completely removed. As the steering wheel is being removed, guide the wiring for the airbag through the aperture in the wheel, taking care not to damage the wiring connectors **(see illustration)**.

Refitting

8 Refit the steering wheel, aligning the marks made prior to removal. Route the airbag wiring connectors through the steering wheel aperture. **Note:** *Make sure the steering wheel centre hub locates correctly with the contact unit on the steering column.*

9 Clean the threads on the retaining bolt and the threads in the steering column. Coat the retaining bolt with locking compound, then fit the retaining bolt and tighten to the specified torque.

10 Reconnect the wiring connector for the steering wheel switches.

11 Release the steering lock, and refit the airbag as described in Chapter 12.

19 Ignition switch/ steering column lock – removal and refitting

Removal

1 Disconnect the battery negative terminal (refer to *Disconnecting the battery* in the Reference Chapter).

2 Remove the steering column shrouds as described in Chapter 11.

3 Insert the ignition key into the ignition switch/lock, and turn it to position I.

4 Insert a thin rod into the hole in the lock housing, press the rod to release the detent spring, and pull out the lock cylinder using the key **(see illustration)**.

Refitting

5 Insert the ignition switch/lock into the lock housing, while the key is in position I. Remove the rod from the lock housing.

6 Refit steering column shrouds as described in Chapter 11, then reconnect the battery.

20 Steering column – removal and refitting

Note: *It is recommended that all mounting nuts and bolts are renewed when refitting.*

Removal

1 Remove the steering wheel as described in Section 18.

2 Remove the facia footwell trim panel on the driver's side as described in Chapter 11.

3 Remove the steering column shrouds as described in Chapter 11.

4 Remove the steering column electronics module as described in Chapter 12.

5 If applicable, make sure the steering column adjustment handle is in the locked position.

6 Using paint or similar, make alignment marks between the steering column and intermediate shaft, then slacken and remove the clamp bolt securing the intermediate shaft to the steering column **(see illustration)**. Separate the intermediate shaft from the steering column shaft.

7 Undo the retaining bolt and disconnect the earth cable from the column. Unscrew the plastic retainer and release the wiring harness from the side of the column **(see illustration)**.

8 Where fitted, remove the clutch switch from the pedal bracket assembly.

9 Unscrew the steering column lower fastening clamp bolt, and the two upper mounting bolts **(see illustrations)**. Withdraw the steering column from the facia crossmember, and remove the column from inside the vehicle.

Refitting

10 Refitting is a reversal of removal, bearing in mind the following points:

a) Tighten all nuts and bolts to the

19.4 Insert a thin rod into the lock housing hole, press the rod to release the detent spring, and pull out the lock cylinder

20.6 Slacken and remove the clamp bolt (arrowed) securing the intermediate shaft to the steering column

20.7 Unscrew the plastic retainer (arrowed) and release the wiring harness from the side of the column

specified torque and, where necessary, in the stages given. Note that new nuts/bolts should be used on all disturbed fittings.

b) Ensure that the marks made on the steering column and intermediate shaft are correctly aligned.

c) Refit the steering column electronics module as described in Chapter 12.

d) Refit the steering column shrouds and facia footwell trim panel as described in Chapter 11.

e) Refit the steering wheel as described in Section 18.

20.9a Unscrew the steering column lower fastening clamp bolt (arrowed) . . .

20.9b . . . and the two upper mounting bolts (one side arrowed

21 Power steering system – filling and bleeding

Note: *Checking of the power steering fluid level is not a routine service operation and should only be necessary if the low-fluid level warning light on the instrument panel is illuminated.*

Models with standard EHPS

1 Firmly apply the handbrake, then jack up the front of the car and support it securely on axle stands (see *Jacking and vehicle support*). Remove the right-hand front roadwheel.

2 Undo the retaining screws, release the clips and remove the wheel arch liner from the wheel arch and subframe on the right-hand side **(see illustration 6.12)**.

3 Check that the fluid level is between the upper MAX line and lower MIN line on the side of the EHPS supply unit reservoir **(see illustration)**.

4 If topping-up is necessary, remove the filler cap from the top of the reservoir. Obtain a clean funnel and a long length of flexible pipe to fit the end of the funnel. From within the engine compartment, insert the pipe through the gap between the air cleaner housing and the headlight and insert the pipe into the top of the reservoir **(see illustration)**.

5 Using power steering fluid of the specified type (see *Lubricants and fluids*), fill the reservoir up to the MAX line, by means of the funnel and tube.

6 If the system has been completely drained and is being refilled after a repair operation, carry out the following bleeding procedure. If the system was only being topped-up, remove the funnel and tube and refit the reservoir filler cap. Refit the wheel arch liner and roadwheel, then lower the car to the ground.

7 To bleed the system, make sure the fluid level in the reservoir is up to the MAX mark and check the level constantly during the bleeding procedure.

8 Start the engine, then switch it off again after approximately five seconds. Repeat this procedure two more times, pausing briefly between each stop/start and maintaining the fluid level in the reservoir.

9 Now start the engine again and allow it to idle. Turn the steering to full left lock, then full right lock five times. Switch the engine off.

10 Recheck the fluid level in the reservoir and top-up if necessary. Remove the funnel and tube and refit the reservoir filler cap.

11 Refit the wheel arch liner and roadwheel, then lower the car to the ground.

12 It is possible that some air may still remain in the system after bleeding but this will be expelled when the car is driven on the road.

Models with compact EHPS

13 Reach down behind the engine and unscrew the filler cap from the EHPS supply unit reservoir **(see illustration)**.

14 Wipe clean the dipstick which is integral with the cap. Refit the cap, then remove it

21.3 Fluid level MAX and MIN lines on the side of the standard EHPS supply unit reservoir

21.13 Reach down behind the engine and unscrew the filler cap from the compact EHPS supply unit reservoir

once more and observe the fluid level on the dipstick. The level should be up to the MAX mark **(see illustration)**.

15 If topping-up is necessary, obtain a clean funnel and a long length of flexible pipe to fit the end of the funnel. Insert the pipe down behind the engine and into the top of the reservoir. Using power steering fluid of the specified type (see *Lubricants and fluids*), fill the reservoir by means of the funnel and tube until the level is up to the MAX line on the dipstick.

16 If the system has been completely drained and is being refilled after a repair operation, carry out the bleeding procedure described previously in paragraphs 7 to 10. If the system was only being topped-up, remove the funnel and tube and refit the reservoir filler cap.

21.4 Insert a pipe through the gap between the air cleaner housing and the headlight into the top of the reservoir

21.14 Maximum mark (arrowed) on the fluid level dipstick

22.5 Steering gear mounting bolt retaining nut (arrowed)

22 Steering gear assembly – removal, inspection and refitting

Note: *It is recommended that all mounting nuts and bolts are renewed when refitting.*

Removal

1 Remove the front subframe as described in Section 6.
2 On models with compact EHPS, remove the EHPS supply unit and mounting bracket as described in Section 23.
3 Disconnect the steering angle sensor wiring connector from the steering gear. Note the routing of the wiring harness, then release it from the clips on the hydraulic pipes and steering gear and move the harness to one side.
4 Place a suitable container beneath the hydraulic supply and return pipes on the steering gear and be prepared for escaping hydraulic fluid. Undo the bolt securing the hydraulic supply and return pipe retaining plate to the steering gear. Withdraw the pipes from the steering gear and collect the retaining plate. Collect the escaping fluid in the container. Note that new sealing O-rings will be required for the hydraulic pipes for refitting. Suitably cover or plug the disconnected unions to prevent dirt entry.
5 Undo the nuts from the two steering gear mounting bolts, while counterholding the bolts from under the subframe **(see illustration)**.

Lift off the two washers then remove the bolts. Note that new nuts and bolts will be required for refitting.
6 Twist the anti-roll bar upwards, then lift the steering gear off the subframe.
7 If a new steering gear assembly is to be fitted, then the track rod balljoints will need to be removed from each end of the steering track rod arms (see Section 25).

Inspection

8 Examine the steering gear assembly for signs of wear or damage, and check that the rack moves freely throughout the full length of its travel, with no signs of roughness or excessive free play between the steering gear pinion and rack. If any problems of this nature are noted, renewal of the steering gear will be necessary. The only components which can be renewed separately are the steering gear gaiters, the track rod balljoints and the track rods. Steering gear gaiter, track rod balljoint and track rod renewal procedures are covered in Sections 24, 25 and 26 respectively.

Refitting

9 Refitting is a reverse of the removal procedure, bearing in mind the following points:
a) Renew the sealing O-rings on the hydraulic supply and return pipes.
b) Tighten the steering gear mounting bolt nuts to the specified torque in the stages given. Note that new nuts/bolts should be used.
c) On models with compact EHPS, refit the supply unit and mounting bracket as described in Section 23.
d) Set the steering gear in the straight-ahead position prior to refitting the front subframe.
e) Refit the front subframe as described in Section 6.
f) Where applicable, fit new track rod balljoints as described in Section 25.
g) On completion, fill and bleed the power steering system as described in Section 21.
h) Have the front wheel toe setting checked and if necessary adjusted at the earliest opportunity.

23 Electro-hydraulic power steering (EHPS) supply unit – removal and refitting

Note 1: *The EHPS supply unit comprises the power steering pump, electric pump drive motor and the EHPS electronic control unit. The supply unit is a sealed component and the individual parts cannot be removed separately.*
Note 2: *If a new EHPS supply unit is to be fitted, it will be necessary to programme the new ECU after installation. This work requires the use of dedicated Vauxhall/Opel diagnostic equipment or a compatible alternative.*

Standard EHPS

Removal

1 The EHPS supply unit is located under the front wheel-arch on the right-hand side, behind the wheel arch liner.
2 Firmly apply the handbrake, then jack up the front of the car and support it securely on axle stands (see *Jacking and vehicle support*). Remove the right-hand front roadwheel.
3 On diesel engine models, undo the ten bolts and remove the engine undertray.
4 Undo the retaining screws, release the clips and remove the wheel arch liner from the wheel arch and subframe on the right-hand side **(see illustration 6.12)**.
5 Disconnect the wiring connectors at the EHPS supply unit, then release the wiring harness from the retaining clips on the mounting bracket **(see illustration)**.
6 Place a suitable container beneath the hydraulic supply and return pipes on the side of the EHPS supply unit and be prepared for escaping hydraulic fluid **(see illustration)**.
7 Wipe clean the area around the supply pipe and return hose connections. Undo the supply pipe union and withdraw the pipe from the EHPS supply unit. Collect the escaping fluid in the container.
8 Slacken the hose clip and disconnect the fluid return hose from the supply unit. Suitably cover or plug the disconnected unions to prevent dirt entry.
9 Undo the lower EHPS supply unit mounting

23.5 Disconnect the wiring connectors (arrowed) at the EHPS supply unit

23.6 Hydraulic supply and return pipe connections (arrowed) on the side of the EHPS supply unit

23.9 Undo the lower EHPS supply unit mounting bracket retaining bolt

bracket retaining bolt, noting that this bolt also secures the front subframe (see illustration). Note that a new bolt will be required for refitting.

10 Undo the two upper supply unit mounting bracket retaining bolts and withdraw the supply unit and mounting bracket from under the wheel arch.

11 If required, undo the three nuts and remove the supply unit from the mounting bracket.

Refitting

12 Refitting is a reverse of the removal procedure, bearing in mind the following points:
  a) *Renew the sealing O-ring on the hydraulic supply pipe if there is any sign of deterioration.*
  b) *Tighten all nuts, bolts and unions to the specified torque and, where necessary, in the stages given. Note that a supply unit mounting bracket lower retaining bolt must be used.*
  c) *On completion, fill and bleed the power steering system as described in Section 21.*

Compact EHPS

Removal

13 The EHPS supply unit is mounted on the front subframe, above the steering gear.

14 Firmly apply the handbrake, then jack up the front of the car and support it securely on axle stands (see *Jacking and vehicle support*). On diesel engine models, undo the ten bolts and remove the engine undertray.

15 On 1.9 litre diesel engine models, remove the fuel filter crash box as described in Chapter 4B.

16 If necessary, for improved access below the car, remove the exhaust system as described in Chapter 4A or 4B, as applicable.

17 Disconnect the wiring connectors at the EHPS supply unit.

18 Place a suitable container beneath the hydraulic supply and return pipes on the steering gear and be prepared for escaping hydraulic fluid. Undo the bolt securing the hydraulic supply and return pipe retaining plate to the steering gear. Withdraw the pipes from the steering gear and collect the retaining plate. Collect the escaping fluid in the container. Note that new sealing O-rings will be required for the hydraulic pipes for refitting. Suitably cover or plug the disconnected unions to prevent dirt entry.

19 Undo the three nuts securing the EHPS supply unit to its mounting bracket. Lift the supply unit, complete with hydraulic pipes, and remove it from the car. On 1.9 litre diesel engine models, the unit is removed from above; on all other models, from below.

20 If required the supply unit mounting bracket can be removed from the subframe, after undoing the three retaining bolts.

Refitting

21 Refitting is a reverse of the removal

procedure, bearing in mind the following points:
  a) *Renew the sealing O-rings on the hydraulic supply and return pipes.*
  b) *Tighten all nuts, bolts and unions to the specified torque.*
  c) *On 1.9 litre diesel engine models, refit the fuel filter crash box as described in Chapter 4B.*
  d) *If removed, refit the exhaust system as described in Chapter 4A or 4B as applicable.*
  e) *On completion, fill and bleed the power steering system as described in Section 21.*

24 Steering gear rubber gaiters – renewal

1 Remove the track rod balljoint as described in Section 25.

2 Mark the correct fitted position of the gaiter on the track rod, then release the retaining clips, and slide the gaiter off the steering gear housing and track rod end.

3 Thoroughly clean the track rod and the steering gear housing, clean off any corrosion, burrs or sharp edges which might damage the new gaiter's sealing lips on installation.

4 Carefully slide the new gaiter onto the track rod end, and locate it on the steering gear housing. Align the outer edge of the gaiter with the mark made on the track rod prior to removal, then secure it in position with new retaining clips.

5 Refit the track rod balljoint as described in Section 25.

25 Track rod balljoint – removal and refitting

Note: *A new track rod balljoint-to-swivel hub nut will be required when refitting.*

Removal

1 Firmly apply the handbrake, then jack up the front of the car and support it securely on axle stands (see *Jacking and vehicle support*). Remove the appropriate front roadwheel.

2 If the balljoint is to be re-used, use a scriber, or similar, to mark its relationship to the track rod.

3 Hold the track rod arm, and unscrew the balljoint locknut by a quarter of a turn.

4 Slacken and remove the nut securing the track rod balljoint to the swivel hub, and release the balljoint tapered shank using a universal balljoint separator (see illustration). Discard the nut; a new one must be used of refitting.

5 Counting the exact number of turns necessary to do so, unscrew the balljoint from the track rod arm.

6 Count the number of exposed threads between the end of the track rod and the

25.4 Release the balljoint tapered shank using a universal balljoint separator

locknut, and record this figure. If a new gaiter is to be fitted, unscrew the locknut from the track rod.

7 Carefully clean the balljoint and the track rod threads. Renew the balljoint if there is excessive free play of the balljoint shank, or if the shank is excessively stiff. If the balljoint gaiter is damaged, the complete balljoint assembly must be renewed; it is not possible to obtain the gaiter separately.

Refitting

8 If it was removed, screw the locknut onto the track rod threads, and position it so that the same number of exposed threads are visible as was noted prior to removal.

9 Screw the balljoint on to the track rod by the number of turns noted on removal. This should bring the balljoint locknut to within approximately quarter of a turn from the locknut, with the alignment marks that were noted on removal.

10 Refit the balljoint shank to the swivel hub, then fit a new retaining nut and tighten it to the specified torque setting. If the balljoint stud turns as the nut is being tightened, press down on the track rod balljoint to force the tapered part of the stud into the arm on the swivel hub.

11 Tighten the track rod balljoint securing locknut on the track rod arm while holding the track rod arm stationary with a second spanner on the flats provided.

12 Refit the roadwheel, then lower the vehicle to the ground and tighten the roadwheel bolts to the specified torque setting.

13 Have the front wheel toe setting checked and if necessary adjusted at the earliest opportunity.

26 Track rod – renewal

Note: *When refitting, a new track rod balljoint-to-swivel hub nut and new gaiter retaining clips will be required. Vauxhall/Opel special tool KM-6321, or a suitable equivalent, will be required to unscrew the track rod inner balljoint from the end of the steering rack.*

1 Remove the track rod balljoint as described in Section 25.

2 Release the retaining clips, and slide the steering gear gaiter off the end of the track rod as described in Section 24.

3 If the track rod on the passenger's side is being removed, it will be necessary to release the clip and fold back the gaiter on the driver's side also. A flat is provided on the rack, on the driver's side, to enable the rack to be held stationary while the track rod is unscrewed.

4 Turn the steering on full lock, so that the rack protrudes from the steering gear housing on the relevant side, slide the cover (where fitted) off the inner balljoint.

5 Engage the help of an assistant, if necessary, and prevent the rack from rotating using an open-ended spanner located on the rack flat on the driver's side. Unscrew and remove the track rod inner balljoint from the end of the steering rack using the special tool or suitable equivalent.

6 Remove the track rod assembly, and examine the track rod inner balljoint for signs of slackness or tight spots. Check that the track rod itself is straight and free from damage. If necessary, renew the track rod; it is also recommended that the steering gear gaiter/dust cover is renewed.

7 Screw the balljoint into the end of the steering rack. Tighten the track rod inner balljoint to the specified torque, whilst retaining the steering rack with an open-ended spanner.

8 Install the steering gaiter(s) and track rod balljoint as described in Sections 24 and 25.

27 Wheel alignment and steering angles – general information

Definitions

1 A car's steering and suspension geometry is defined in four basic settings – all angles are expressed in degrees (toe settings are also expressed as a measurement); the steering axis is defined as an imaginary line drawn through the axis of the suspension strut, extended where necessary to contact the ground.

2 Camber is the angle between each roadwheel and a vertical line drawn through its centre and tyre contact patch, when viewed from the front or rear of the car. Positive camber is when the roadwheels are tilted outwards from the vertical at the top; negative camber is when they are tilted inwards. Slight adjustment of the front camber angle is possible, by altering the position of the swivel hub at its attachment to the front suspension strut. The rear camber angle can be adjusted by altering the position of the eccentric disc on the lower control arm inner mounting.

3 Castor is the angle between the steering axis and a vertical line drawn through each roadwheel's centre and tyre contact patch, when viewed from the side of the car. Positive castor is when the steering axis is tilted so that it contacts the ground ahead of the vertical; negative castor is when it contacts the ground behind the vertical. The castor angle is not adjustable.

4 Toe is the difference, viewed from above, between lines drawn through the roadwheel centres and the car's centre-line. 'Toe-in' is when the roadwheels point inwards, towards each other at the front, while 'toe-out' is when they splay outwards from each other at the front.

5 The front wheel toe setting is adjusted by screwing the track rod in or out of its balljoints, to alter the effective length of the track rod assembly. The rear wheel toe setting can be adjusted by altering the position of the eccentric disc on the auxiliary control arm inner mounting.

Checking and adjustment

6 Due to the special measuring equipment necessary to check the wheel alignment and steering angles, and the skill required to use it properly, the checking and adjustment of these settings is best left to a Vauxhall/Opel dealer or similar expert. Note that most tyre-fitting shops now possess sophisticated checking equipment.

Chapter 11
Bodywork and fittings

Contents

Degrees of difficulty

Easy, suitable for novice with little experience	Fairly easy, suitable for beginner with some experience	Fairly difficult, suitable for competent DIY mechanic	Difficult, suitable for experienced DIY mechanic	Very difficult, suitable for expert DIY or professional

Specifications

Torque wrench settings	Nm	lbf ft
Front seat belt anchorage bolts	25	18
Front seat belt inertia reel bolt	20	15
Front seat mounting bolts	25	18
Rear seat belt anchorage bolts	35	26
Rear seat belt inertia reel bolt	35	26
Rear seat belt stalk retaining bolts	35	26
Rear seat belt tensioner mounting bolts	35	26
Seat belt-to-height adjuster mounting bolts	35	26

1 General information

The bodyshell is made of pressed-steel sections, and is available in three- and five-door Saloon, Hatchback and Estate versions. Most components are welded together, but some use is made of structural adhesives; the front wings are bolted on.

The bonnet is made of aluminium, whereas the doors, and some other vulnerable panels, are made of zinc-coated metal. These are further protected by being coated with an anti-chip primer, prior to being sprayed.

Extensive use is made of plastic materials, mainly on the interior, but also in exterior components. The front and rear bumpers are injection-moulded from a synthetic material which is very strong and yet light. Plastic components such as wheel arch liners are fitted to the underside of the vehicle, to improve the body's resistance to corrosion.

2 Maintenance – bodywork and underframe

The general condition of a vehicle's bodywork is the one thing that significantly affects its value. Maintenance is easy, but needs to be regular. Neglect, particularly after minor damage, can lead quickly to further deterioration and costly repair bills. It is important also to keep watch on those parts of the vehicle not immediately visible, for instance the underside, inside all the wheel arches, and the lower part of the engine compartment.

The basic maintenance routine for the bodywork is washing – preferably with a lot of water, from a hose. This will remove all the loose solids which may have stuck to the vehicle. It is important to flush these off in such a way as to prevent grit from scratching the finish. The wheel arches and underframe need washing in the same way, to remove any accumulated mud, which will retain moisture and tend to encourage rust. Paradoxically enough, the best time to clean the underframe and wheel arches is in wet weather, when the mud is thoroughly wet and soft. In very wet weather, the underframe is usually cleaned of large accumulations automatically, and this is a good time for inspection.

Periodically, except on vehicles with a wax-based underbody protective coating, it is a good idea to have the whole of the underframe of the vehicle steam-cleaned, engine compartment included, so that a thorough inspection can be carried out to see what minor repairs and renovations are necessary. Steam-cleaning is available at many garages, and is necessary for the removal of the accumulation of oily grime, which sometimes is allowed to become thick

in certain areas. If steam-cleaning facilities are not available, there are some excellent grease solvents available which can be brush-applied; the dirt can then be simply hosed off. Note that these methods should not be used on vehicles with wax-based underbody protective coating, or the coating will be removed. Such vehicles should be inspected annually, preferably just prior to Winter, when the underbody should be washed down, and any damage to the wax coating repaired. Ideally, a completely fresh coat should be applied. It would also be worth considering the use of such wax-based protection for injection into door panels, sills, box sections, etc, as an additional safeguard against rust damage, where such protection is not provided by the vehicle manufacturer.

After washing paintwork, wipe off with a chamois leather to give an unspotted clear finish. A coat of clear protective wax polish will give added protection against chemical pollutants in the air. If the paintwork sheen has dulled or oxidised, use a cleaner/polisher combination to restore the brilliance of the shine. This requires a little effort, but such dulling is usually caused because regular washing has been neglected. Care needs to be taken with metallic paintwork, as special non-abrasive cleaner/polisher is required to avoid damage to the finish. Always check that the door and ventilator opening drain holes and pipes are completely clear, so that water can be drained out. Brightwork should be treated in the same way as paintwork. Windscreens and windows can be kept clear of the smeary film which often appears, by the use of proprietary glass cleaner. Never use any form of wax or other body or chromium polish on glass.

3 Maintenance of upholstery and carpets – general

Mats and carpets should be brushed or vacuum-cleaned regularly, to keep them free of grit. If they are badly stained, remove them from the vehicle for scrubbing or sponging, and make quite sure they are dry before refitting. Seats and interior trim panels can be kept clean by wiping with a damp cloth. If they do become stained (which can be more apparent on light-coloured upholstery), use a little liquid detergent and a soft nail brush to scour the grime out of the grain of the material. Do not forget to keep the headlining clean in the same way as the upholstery. When using liquid cleaners inside the vehicle, do not over-wet the surfaces being cleaned. Excessive damp could get into the seams and padded interior, causing stains, offensive odours or even rot.

If the inside of the vehicle gets wet accidentally, it is worthwhile taking some trouble to dry it out properly, particularly where carpets are involved. Do not leave oil or electric heaters inside the vehicle for this purpose.

4 Minor body damage – repair

Minor scratches

If the scratch is very superficial, and does not penetrate to the metal of the bodywork, repair is very simple. Lightly rub the area of the scratch with a paintwork renovator, or a very fine cutting paste, to remove loose paint from the scratch, and to clear the surrounding bodywork of wax polish. Rinse the area with clean water.

Apply touch-up paint to the scratch using a fine paint brush; continue to apply fine layers of paint until the surface of the paint in the scratch is level with the surrounding paintwork. Allow the new paint at least two weeks to harden, then blend it into the surrounding paintwork by rubbing the scratch area with a paintwork renovator or a very fine cutting paste. Finally, apply wax polish.

Where the scratch has penetrated right through to the metal of the bodywork, causing the metal to rust, a different repair technique is required. Remove any loose rust from the bottom of the scratch with a penknife, then apply rust-inhibiting paint to prevent the formation of rust in the future. Using a rubber or nylon applicator, fill the scratch with bodystopper paste. If required, this paste can be mixed with cellulose thinners to provide a very thin paste which is ideal for filling narrow scratches. Before the stopper-paste in the scratch hardens, wrap a piece of smooth cotton rag around the top of a finger. Dip the finger in cellulose thinners, and quickly sweep it across the surface of the stopper-paste in the scratch; this will ensure that the surface of the stopper-paste is slightly hollowed. The scratch can now be painted over as described earlier in this Section.

Dents

When deep denting of the vehicle's bodywork has taken place, the first task is to pull the dent out, until the affected bodywork almost attains its original shape. There is little point in trying to restore the original shape completely, as the metal in the damaged area will have stretched on impact, and cannot be reshaped fully to its original contour. It is better to bring the level of the dent up to a point which is about 3 mm below the level of the surrounding bodywork. In cases where the dent is very shallow anyway, it is not worth trying to pull it out at all. If the underside of the dent is accessible, it can be hammered out gently from behind, using a mallet with a wooden or plastic head. Whilst doing this, hold a suitable block of wood firmly against the outside of the panel, to absorb the impact from the hammer blows and thus prevent a large area of the bodywork from being 'belled-out'.

Should the dent be in a section of the

bodywork which has a double skin, or some other factor making it inaccessible from behind, a different technique is called for. Drill several small holes through the metal inside the area – particularly in the deeper section. Then screw long self-tapping screws into the holes, just sufficiently for them to gain a good purchase in the metal. Now the dent can be pulled out by pulling on the protruding heads of the screws with a pair of pliers.

The next stage of the repair is the removal of the paint from the damaged area, and from an inch or so of the surrounding 'sound' bodywork. This is accomplished most easily by using a wire brush or abrasive pad on a power drill, although it can be done just as effectively by hand, using sheets of abrasive paper. To complete the preparation for filling, score the surface of the bare metal with a screwdriver or the tang of a file, or alternatively, drill small holes in the affected area. This will provide a really good 'key' for the filler paste.

To complete the repair, see the Section on filling and respraying.

Rust holes or gashes

Remove all paint from the affected area, and from an inch or so of the surrounding 'sound' bodywork, using an abrasive pad or a wire brush on a power drill. If these are not available, a few sheets of abrasive paper will do the job most effectively. With the paint removed, you will be able to judge the severity of the corrosion, and therefore decide whether to renew the whole panel (if this is possible) or to repair the affected area. New body panels are not as expensive as most people think, and it is often quicker and more satisfactory to fit a new panel than to attempt to repair large areas of corrosion.

Remove all fittings from the affected area, except those which will act as a guide to the original shape of the damaged bodywork (eg headlight shells etc). Then, using tin snips or a hacksaw blade, remove all loose metal and any other metal badly affected by corrosion. Hammer the edges of the hole inwards, in order to create a slight depression for the filler paste.

Wire-brush the affected area to remove the powdery rust from the surface of the remaining metal. Paint the affected area with rust-inhibiting paint, if the back of the rusted area is accessible, treat this also.

Before filling can take place, it will be necessary to block the hole in some way. This can be achieved by the use of aluminium or plastic mesh, or aluminium tape.

Aluminium or plastic mesh, or glass-fibre matting, is probably the best material to use for a large hole. Cut a piece to the approximate size and shape of the hole to be filled, then position it in the hole so that its edges are below the level of the surrounding bodywork. It can be retained in position by several blobs of filler paste around its periphery.

Aluminium tape should be used for small or very narrow holes. Pull a piece off the roll,

trim it to the approximate size and shape required, then pull off the backing paper (if used) and stick the tape over the hole; it can be overlapped if the thickness of one piece is insufficient. Burnish down the edges of the tape with the handle of a screwdriver or similar, to ensure that the tape is securely attached to the metal underneath.

Filling and respraying

Before using this Section, see the Sections on dent, deep scratch, rust holes and gash repairs.

Many types of bodyfiller are available, but generally speaking, those proprietary kits which contain a tin of filler paste and a tube of resin hardener are best for this type of repair. A wide, flexible plastic or nylon applicator will be found invaluable for imparting a smooth and well-contoured finish to the surface of the filler.

Mix up a little filler on a clean piece of card or board – measure the hardener carefully (follow the maker's instructions on the pack), otherwise the filler will set too rapidly or too slowly. Using the applicator, apply the filler paste to the prepared area; draw the applicator across the surface of the filler to achieve the correct contour and to level the surface. As soon as a contour that approximates to the correct one is achieved, stop working the paste – if you carry on too long, the paste will become sticky and begin to 'pick-up' on the applicator. Continue to add thin layers of filler paste at 20-minute intervals, until the level of the filler is just proud of the surrounding bodywork.

Once the filler has hardened, the excess can be removed using a metal plane or file. From then on, progressively-finer grades of abrasive paper should be used, starting with a 40-grade production paper, and finishing with a 400-grade wet-and-dry paper. Always wrap the abrasive paper around a flat rubber, cork, or wooden block – otherwise the surface of the filler will not be completely flat. During the smoothing of the filler surface, the wet-and-dry paper should be periodically rinsed in water. This will ensure that a very smooth finish is imparted to the filler at the final stage.

At this stage, the 'dent' should be surrounded by a ring of bare metal, which in turn should be encircled by the finely 'feathered' edge of the good paintwork. Rinse the repair area with clean water, until all of the dust produced by the rubbing-down operation has gone.

Spray the whole area with a light coat of primer – this will show up any imperfections in the surface of the filler. Repair these imperfections with fresh filler paste or bodystopper, and once more smooth the surface with abrasive paper. Repeat this spray-and-repair procedure until you are satisfied that the surface of the filler, and the feathered edge of the paintwork, are perfect. Clean the repair area with clean water, and allow to dry fully.

The repair area is now ready for final spraying. Paint spraying must be carried out in a warm, dry, windless and dust-free atmosphere. This condition can be created artificially if you have access to a large indoor working area, but if you are forced to work in the open, you will have to pick your day very carefully. If you are working indoors, dousing the floor in the work area with water will help to settle the dust which would otherwise be in the atmosphere. If the repair area is confined to one body panel, mask off the surrounding panels; this will help to minimise the effects of a slight mis-match in paint colours. Bodywork fittings (eg chrome strips, door handles etc) will also need to be masked off. Use genuine masking tape, and several thicknesses of newspaper, for the masking operations.

Before commencing to spray, agitate the aerosol can thoroughly, then spray a test area (an old tin, or similar) until the technique is mastered. Cover the repair area with a thick coat of primer; the thickness should be built up using several thin layers of paint, rather than one thick one. Using 400-grade wet-and-dry paper, rub down the surface of the primer until it is really smooth. While doing this, the work area should be thoroughly doused with water, and the wet-and-dry paper periodically rinsed in water. Allow to dry before spraying on more paint.

Spray on the top coat, again building up the thickness by using several thin layers of paint. Start spraying at one edge of the repair area, and then, using a side-to-side motion, work until the whole repair area and about 2 inches of the surrounding original paintwork is covered. Remove all masking material 10 to 15 minutes after spraying on the final coat of paint.

Allow the new paint at least two weeks to harden, then, using a paintwork renovator, or a very fine cutting paste, blend the edges of the paint into the existing paintwork. Finally, apply wax polish.

Plastic components

With the use of more and more plastic body components by the vehicle manufacturers (eg bumpers. spoilers, and in some cases major body panels), rectification of more serious damage to such items has become a matter of either entrusting repair work to a specialist in this field, or renewing complete components. Repair of such damage by the DIY owner is not really feasible, owing to the cost of the equipment and materials required for effecting such repairs. The basic technique involves making a groove along the line of the crack in the plastic, using a rotary burr in a power drill. The damaged part is then welded back together, using a hot-air gun to heat up and fuse a plastic filler rod into the groove. Any excess plastic is then removed, and the area rubbed down to a smooth finish. It is important that a filler rod of the correct plastic is used, as body components can be made of a variety of different types (eg polycarbonate, ABS, polypropylene).

6.1 Undo the screws (arrowed) securing the wheel arch liner to the front bumper on each side

6.2 Release the four plastic rivets (arrowed) securing the bumper to the front subframe

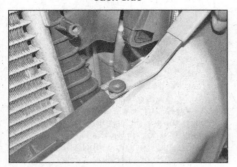

6.3 Extract the upper bumper retaining clip each side

6.5 Pull the bumper out at the sides to disengage the support bracket

Damage of a less serious nature (abrasions, minor cracks etc) can be repaired by the DIY owner using a two-part epoxy filler repair material. Once mixed in equal proportions, this is used in similar fashion to the bodywork filler used on metal panels. The filler is usually cured in twenty to thirty minutes, ready for sanding and painting.

If the owner is renewing a complete component himself, or if he has repaired it with epoxy filler, he will be left with the problem of finding a suitable paint for finishing which is compatible with the type of plastic used. At one time, the use of a universal paint was not possible, owing to the complex range of plastics encountered in body component applications. Standard paints, generally speaking, will not bond to plastic or rubber satisfactorily. However, it is now possible to obtain a plastic body parts finishing kit which consists of a pre-primer treatment, a primer

and coloured top coat. Full instructions are normally supplied with a kit, but basically, the method of use is to first apply the pre-primer to the component concerned, and allow it to dry for up to 30 minutes. Then the primer is applied, and left to dry for about an hour before finally applying the special-coloured top coat. The result is a correctly-coloured component, where the paint will flex with the plastic or rubber, a property that standard paint does not normally possess.

5 Major body damage repair – general

Where serious damage has occurred, or large areas need renewal due to neglect, it means that complete new panels will need welding-in, and this is best left to

professionals. If the damage is due to impact, it will also be necessary to check completely the alignment of the bodyshell, and this can only be carried out accurately by a Vauxhall/Opel dealer, or accident repair specialist, using special jigs. If the body is left misaligned, it is primarily dangerous as the car will not handle properly, and secondly, uneven stresses will be imposed on the steering, suspension and possibly transmission, causing abnormal wear, or complete failure, particularly to such items as the tyres.

6 Front bumper – removal and refitting

Removal

1 Working under the wheel arch, undo the six retaining screws (three on each side) securing the wheel arch liner to the bumper **(see illustration)**.
2 Release the four plastic rivets securing the lower centre of the bumper to the front subframe **(see illustration)**.
3 Using a forked tool, extract the upper retaining clip each side, adjacent to the headlights **(see illustration)**.
4 Where applicable, disconnect any wiring block connector(s) and washer hoses from the rear of the bumper.
5 With the aid of an assistant, pull the bumper out at the sides to disengage the support bracket, then remove it forward and off the car **(see illustration)**.

Refitting

6 Refitting is a reversal of the removal procedure, ensuring that all bumper fasteners are securely tightened.

7 Rear bumper – removal and refitting

Removal

Saloon and Hatchback models

1 Remove the rear light cluster each side and the number plate lights as described in Chapter 12.
2 Working under the wheel arch, undo the six retaining screws (three on each side) securing the wheel arch liner to the bumper **(see illustration)**.
3 Undo the retaining screw above the number plate on each side **(see illustration)**.
4 Open the two locking catches securing the underside of the bumper to the support bracket **(see illustration)**.
5 With the aid of an assistant, pull the bumper out at the sides to disengage the support bracket. Disengage the bumper from the peg and guides on each side and withdraw it from the support bracket **(see illustrations)**.

7.2 Undo the screws (arrowed) securing the wheel arch liner to the rear bumper on each side

7.3 Undo the retaining screw (arrowed) above the number plate on each side

6 Detach the wiring harness clip from the bumper, then remove the bumper from the car **(see illustration)**.

Estate models

7 Remove the rear light cluster each side and the number plate lights as described in Chapter 12.
8 Working under the wheel arch, undo the six retaining screws (three on each side) securing the wheel arch liner to the bumper **(see illustration 7.2)**.
9 Remove the trim panel from the top of the bumper by pulling it sharply rearward **(see illustration)**.
10 Undo the two upper screws on each side of the bumper, and the four screws in the tailgate aperture **(see illustrations)**.
11 Open the two locking catches securing the underside of the bumper to the support bracket **(see illustration 7.4)**.
12 Where fitted, unclip the four parking sensors.
13 With the aid of an assistant, pull the bumper out at the sides to disengage the support bracket, and remove the bumper from the car.

Refitting

14 Refitting is a reversal of the removal procedure, ensuring that all bumper fasteners are securely tightened.

---

8 Bonnet and support strut – removal, refitting and adjustment

Bonnet

Removal

1 Open the bonnet, and have an assistant support it.
2 Using a marker pen or paint, mark around the hinge positions on the bonnet.
3 Using a screwdriver prise out the retaining spring clip and disconnect the support strut from the bonnet.
4 With the aid of the assistant, unscrew the bolts securing the bonnet to the hinges on both sides.
5 Lift off the bonnet taking care not to damage the vehicle paintwork.

Refitting

6 Align the marks made on the bonnet before removal with the hinges, then refit and tighten the bonnet securing bolts.
7 Check the bonnet adjustment as follows.

Adjustment

8 Close the bonnet, and check that there is an equal gap (approximately 4.0 mm) at each side, between the bonnet and the wing panels. Check also that the bonnet sits flush in relation to the surrounding body panels.
9 The bonnet should close smoothly and positively without excessive pressure. If this is not the case, adjustment will be required.

7.4 Open the two locking catches securing the underside of the bumper to the support bracket

7.5b . . . disengage the bumper from the peg (arrowed) . . .

10 To adjust the bonnet alignment, loosen the bonnet-to-hinge mounting bolts, and move the bonnet on the bolts as required (the bolt holes in the hinges are enlarged). If necessary, the scissor-type hinge mounting bolts may

7.6 Detach the wiring harness clip from the bumper

7.10a Undo the two upper screws (arrowed) on each side of the bumper . . .

7.5a Pull the bumper out at the sides to disengage the support bracket . . .

7.5c . . . and guides (arrowed) on each side

be loosened as well. Access to the hinge retaining bolts can be gained after removing the water deflector (see Section 23). To adjust the bonnet front height in relation to the front wings, adjustable rubber bump stops are

7.9 Remove the trim panel from the top of the bumper by pulling it sharply rearward

7.10b . . . and the four screws (arrowed) in the tailgate aperture

9.4a Move the bonnet release handle rearward slightly to free the detent lugs . . .

9.4b . . . then lift the release handle off the mounting bracket

10.3a Disengage the bonnet lock spring leg from the front crossmember . . .

10.3b . . . slide the other end off the release cable and remove the spring from the crossmember

fitted to the front corners of the bonnet. These may be screwed in or out as necessary. After making an adjustment, the bonnet striker must be adjusted so that the lock spring holds the bonnet firmly against the rubber bump stops. Loosen the locknut and screw the striker in or out as necessary.

Support strut

Removal

11 Open the bonnet, and have an assistant support it.
12 Using a screwdriver prise out the retaining spring clips and disconnect the strut from the bonnet and body. Note which way round the strut is fitted.

Refitting

13 Refitting is a reversal of removal.

9 Bonnet release cable – removal and refitting

Removal

1 Remove the facia footwell trim panel and the front footwell side trim panel on the driver's side as described in Section 27.
2 Remove the water deflector as described in Section 23.
3 Remove the bonnet lock spring as described in Section 10.
4 Insert a small screwdriver through the opening at the top of the release handle, and move the handle rearward slightly to free the detent lugs. Lift the release handle off the mounting bracket (see illustrations).
5 Release the cable from the support clips

and brackets in the engine compartment, then withdraw the cable through the rubber grommet and into the passenger compartment. As an aid to refitting, tie a length of string to the cable before removing it and leave the string in position ready for refitting.

Refitting

6 Refitting is a reversal of removal, but tie the string to the end of the cable, and use the string to pull the cable into position. Ensure that the cable is routed as noted before removal, and make sure that the grommet is correctly seated. On completion, refit the water deflector and the interior trim panels as described in Section 23 and 27.

10 Bonnet lock spring – removal and refitting

Removal

1 The bonnet is held in its locked position with a strong spring which engages with the striker on the front edge of the bonnet. The release cable is connected to the end of the spring.
2 The striker may be removed from the bonnet by unscrewing the locknut, however measure its fitted length first as a guide to refitting it.
3 To remove the lock spring, disengage the spring leg from the front crossmember, slide the other end of the spring off the release cable and remove the spring from the crossmember (see illustrations).

Refitting

4 Refitting is a reversal of removal.

11 Door – removal, refitting and adjustment

Removal

1 Open the door and disconnect the wiring connector which is fitted to the front edge of the door (see illustration).
2 Undo the bolt securing the door check strap to the vehicle body (see illustration).

11.1 Disconnect the door wiring connector (arrowed) – front door shown

11.2 Undo the bolt (arrowed) securing the door check strap to the body

11.3 Undo the grub screw (arrowed) from the upper and lower hinge

11.7 Door striker retaining screws (arrowed)

12.2a Prise out the control switch assembly . . .

12.2b . . . and disconnect the wiring connector

3 Undo the grub screw from the upper and lower hinge (**see illustration**).

4 With the aid of an assistant, lift the door upward and off the hinge pins.

Refitting and adjustment

5 Refit the door using the reverse of the removal procedure, then close the door and check that it fits correctly in its aperture, with equal gaps at all points between it and the surrounding bodywork.

6 If adjustment is required, slacken the bolts securing the hinges to the door and reposition the door as required. Securely tighten the bolts after completing the adjustment.

7 The striker alignment should be checked after either the door or the lock has been disturbed. To adjust a striker, slacken its screws, reposition it and securely tighten the screws (**see illustration**).

12 Door inner trim panel – removal and refitting

Front door

Removal

1 Open the door window.

2 If working on the driver's door, carefully prise out the control switch assembly and disconnect the wiring connector (**see illustrations**).

3 Using a plastic wedge or similar tool, carefully prise the door grab handle plastic cover away from the handle at the top. Disengage the lower retaining lug from the door panel and remove the cover (**see illustrations**).

4 Undo the two screws now exposed after removal of the grab handle plastic cover (**see illustration**).

5 Undo the three screws securing the lower edge of the trim panel to the door (**see illustration**).

6 Using a wide-bladed screwdriver or removal tool, carefully prise the bottom and sides of the panel away from door to release the internal clips (**see illustration**). Lift the panel upward to release it from the window aperture.

7 Once the panel is free, reach behind, and using a small screwdriver, lift the front edge of the door lock operating cable retainer. Slide the outer cable to the rear and disengage the inner cable end from the interior handle (**see illustrations**).

8 If working on the passenger's door, disconnect the wiring connector from the window control switch.

12.3a Prise the door grab handle plastic cover away from the handle at the top . . .

12.3b . . . then disengage the lower retaining lug (arrowed)

12.4 Undo the two screws now exposed

12.5 Undo the three screws (arrowed) securing the lower edge of the trim panel to the door

12.6 Prise the bottom and sides of the panel away from door to release the internal clips

12.7a Lift the front edge (arrowed) of the lock operating cable retainer . . .

12.7b . . . slide the outer cable to the rear and disengage the inner cable end from the interior handle

12.11 Prise the triangular panel away from the door to release the retaining clips – Hatchback and Estate models

12.12a Where a manual regulator is fitted, use a cloth rag to release the handle spring clip . . .

12.12b . . . remove the handle from the splined shaft . . .

12.12c . . . and refit the spring clip to the handle

12.15 Undo the two screws (arrowed) securing the lower edge of the trim panel to the door

Refitting

9 Refitting is a reversal of removal. If working on the driver's door, make sure the control switch wiring is pulled through the aperture in the trim panel as the panel is fitted.

Rear door

Removal

10 Open the door window.
11 On Hatchback and Estate models, using a plastic wedge or similar tool, carefully prise the triangular panel away from the door to release the three retaining clips **(see illustration)**.
12 Where a manual window regulator is fitted, locate a cloth rag between the handle and the trim panel and pull it to one side to release the spring clip. Remove the handle from the splined shaft and refit the spring clip to the handle **(see illustrations)**.

12.16 Prise the bottom and sides of the panel away from door to release the internal clips

13 Using a plastic wedge or similar tool, carefully prise the door grab handle plastic cover away from the handle at the top. Disengage the lower retaining lug from the door panel and remove the cover **(see illustration 12.3a and 12.3b)**.
14 Undo the two screws now exposed after removal of the grab handle plastic cover **(see illustration 12.4)**.
15 Undo the two screws securing the lower edge of the trim panel to the door **(see illustration)**.
16 Using a wide-bladed screwdriver or removal tool, carefully prise the bottom and sides of the panel away from door to release the internal clips. Lift the panel upward to release it from the window aperture **(see illustration)**.
17 Once the panel is free, reach behind and, using a small screwdriver, lift the front edge of

13.2a Prise out the blanking cap from the rear edge of the door . . .

the door lock operating cable retainer. Slide the outer cable to the rear and disengage the inner cable end from the interior handle **(see illustrations 12.7a and 12.7b)**.
18 Disconnect the wiring connector from the window control switch and tweeter speaker, where applicable.
19 Disconnect the interior lock button operating rod from the bellcrank, and remove the panel from the door.

Refitting

20 Refitting is a reversal of removal.

---

13 Door handles and lock components – removal and refitting

Door interior handle

1 The door interior handle is an integral part of the door inner trim panel and cannot be individually removed. If there are any problems with the interior handle, a new inner trim panel will be required.

Front door exterior handle

Removal

2 Open the door and carefully prise out the blanking cap from the rear edge of the door to gain access to the handle locking screw **(see illustrations)**.
3 Pull the exterior door handle outwards and hold it in that position. With the exterior door handle held in the open position, turn

13.2b . . . to gain access to the handle locking screw (arrowed)

13.4 Withdraw the fixed part of the handle, containing the lock cylinder, from the door

13.5 Slide the handle to the rear, disengage the front pivot from the frame and remove the handle

13.10a Prise out the blanking cap from the rear edge of the door . . .

13.10b . . . to gain access to the handle locking screw (arrowed)

13.11 With the exterior handle held open, turn the locking screw anti-clockwise until it reaches its stop

the handle locking screw anti-clockwise until it reaches its stop. The exterior door handle should now be fixed in the open position.

4 Withdraw the fixed part of the handle, containing the lock cylinder, from the door **(see illustration)**.

5 Slide the exterior door handle to the rear, disengage the front pivot from the handle frame and remove the handle from the door **(see illustration)**.

Refitting

6 Engage the handle front pivot with the frame and move the handle back into position.

7 Refit the fixed part of the handle with the lock cylinder to the door.

8 Hold the exterior handle and turn the handle locking screw clockwise to retain the handle.

9 Check the operation of the handle then refit the blanking cap to the edge of the door.

Rear door exterior handle

Removal

10 Open the door and carefully prise out the blanking cap from the rear edge of the door to gain access to the handle locking screw **(see illustrations)**.

11 Pull the exterior door handle outwards and hold it in that position. With the exterior door handle held in the open position, turn the handle locking screw anti-clockwise until it reaches its stop **(see illustration)**. The exterior door handle should now be fixed in the open position.

12 Withdraw the fixed part of the handle from the door **(see illustration)**.

13 Slide the exterior door handle to the rear, disengage the front pivot from the handle frame and remove the handle from the door **(see illustration 13.5)**.

Refitting

14 Engage the handle front pivot with the frame and move the handle back into position.

15 Refit the fixed part of the handle to the door.

16 Hold the exterior handle and turn the handle locking screw clockwise to retain the handle.

17 Check the operation of the handle then refit the blanking cap to the edge of the door.

Front door lock cylinder

Removal

18 Remove the exterior handle as described previously in this Section.

13.12 Withdraw the fixed part of the handle from the door

19 Unclip the trim cap and remove the cap from the lock cylinder housing **(see illustration)**.

20 The lock cylinder body is an integral part of the housing and no further dismantling is possible.

Refitting

21 Refitting is a reversal of removal.

Front door exterior handle frame

Note: *A pop-rivet gun and suitable rivets will be required when refitting. The rivet heads should be approximately 4.8 mm in diameter and 11 mm in length.*

Removal

22 Disconnect the battery negative terminal (refer to *Disconnecting the battery* in the Reference Chapter).

23 Remove the exterior handle as described previously in this Section.

13.19 Unclip the trim cap and remove the cap from the lock cylinder housing

13.25a Undo the screws (arrowed) and withdraw the loudspeaker . . .

13.25b . . . disconnect the wiring connector and unclip the wiring from the guide (arrowed)

13.26a Undo the screws (arrowed) and withdraw the door electronics module . . .

13.26b . . . pull out the locking bar and disconnect the wiring connector

13.27 Push out the clips securing the wiring harness to the door

13.28 Carefully peel back the protective plastic sheet and remove the sheet from the door

24 Remove the door inner trim panel as described in Section 12.
25 Undo the three screws securing the loudspeaker to the door. Withdraw the speaker and disconnect the wiring connector.

Unclip the wiring from the guide and remove the speaker **(see illustrations)**.
26 Undo the three screws securing the door electronics module to the door. Pull out the locking bar, disconnect the wiring

connector and remove the module **(see illustrations)**.
27 Reach in through the loudspeaker aperture and push out the clips securing the wiring harness to the door **(see illustration)**.
28 Carefully peel back the protective plastic sheet and remove the sheet from the door **(see illustration)**.
29 Using an 8.5 mm drill bit, drill out the two rivets securing the window rear guide rail to the door, taking great care not to damage the door panel **(see illustrations)**.
30 Disengage the top of the guide rail from the window lifting channel by moving it rearward, and remove the guide rail through the door aperture **(see illustrations)**.
31 Undo the two screws securing the security cover to the exterior handle frame and door lock, and remove the cover through the door aperture **(see illustrations)**.
32 Release the retaining clip and disconnect

13.29a Drill out the upper rivet . . .

13.29b . . . and lower rivet securing the window rear guide rail to the door

13.30a Disengage the top of the guide rail (arrowed) from the window lifting channel . . .

13.30b . . . then remove the guide rail through the door aperture

13.31a Undo the two screws (arrowed) . . .

13.31b ... and remove the security cover through the door aperture

13.32 Release the retaining clip (arrowed) and disconnect the lock operating rod from the lever

13.33a Slacken the exterior handle frame front retaining screw (arrowed) approximately five turns ...

the lock operating rod from the lever on the exterior handle frame (see illustration).

33 Slacken the exterior handle frame front retaining screw approximately five turns. Slide the handle frame forward to release the rear locating lugs, disengage the lock cylinder operating rod and remove the frame through the door aperture (see illustrations).

34 Clean out the remains of the old rivets from inside the door.

Refitting

35 Connect the lock cylinder operating rod, then place the exterior handle frame in position in the door. Tighten the front retaining screw securely.

36 Engage the lock operating rod with the lever on the exterior handle frame and push the retaining clip back into position on the rod.

37 Refit the security cover and secure with the two screws.

38 Engage the top of the window guide rail with the lifting channel and position the guide rail in the door. Secure the guide rail with new pop rivets (see illustration).

39 Refit the protective plastic sheet to the door ensuring it is firmly stuck with no air bubbles. If the sheet was damaged during removal it should be renewed. This entails cutting a new sheet to the correct size and shape using the old sheet as a template. The new sheet can then be attached to the door with fresh adhesive.

40 Refit the wiring harness clips to the door ensuring they are firmly attached.

41 Refit the door electronics module, securely tighten the three retaining screws and reconnect the wiring connector.

42 Reconnect the wiring to the loudspeaker, position the speaker in the door and secure with the three screws.

43 Refit the door inner trim panel as described in Section 12.

44 Refit the exterior handle as described previously in this Section, then reconnect the battery negative terminal.

Rear door exterior handle frame

Removal

45 Disconnect the battery negative terminal

13.33b ... slide the frame forward to release the rear lugs, disengage the lock cylinder operating rod (arrowed)

(refer to *Disconnecting the battery* in the Reference Chapter).

46 Remove the exterior handle as described previously in this Section.

47 Remove the door inner trim panel as described in Section 12.

48 Remove the rear door lock as described later in this Section.

49 Slacken the exterior handle frame front retaining screw approximately five turns. Slide the handle frame forward to release the rear locating lugs and remove the frame through the door aperture (see illustrations 13.33a and 13.33b).

Refitting

50 Place the exterior handle frame in position in the door and tighten the front retaining screw securely.

51 Refit the rear door lock as described later in this Section.

13.55 Undo the three screws (arrowed) securing the lock to the door

13.38 Secure the window guide rail with new pop rivets

52 Refit the door inner trim panel as described in Section 12.

53 Refit the exterior handle as described previously in this Section, then reconnect the battery negative terminal.

Front door lock

Removal

54 Remove the front door exterior handle frame as described earlier in this Section.

55 Undo the three screws securing the lock to the door (see illustration).

56 Withdraw the lock from its location, then lift the locking bar and disconnect the wiring connector (see illustration).

57 Lower the lock assembly down into the door, bringing the interior lock button and rod in through the hole provided. Now remove the lock assembly through the upper door aperture (see illustrations).

13.56 Lift the locking bar and disconnect the wiring connector

13.57a Lower the lock and bring the interior lock button and rod in through the hole provided . . .

13.57b . . . then remove the lock assembly through the upper door aperture

13.58 If required, disconnect the operating cables from the lock linkage and bracket

13.61 Carefully peel back the protective plastic sheet and remove the sheet from the door

13.62a Undo the upper screw (arrowed) . . .

13.62b . . . and lower screw securing the window rear guide rail to the door

58 If required, disconnect the operating cables from the lock linkage and bracket **(see illustration)**.

Refitting

59 Refitting is a reversal of removal.

Rear door lock

Removal – Hatchback models

60 Remove the door inner trim panel as described in Section 12.

61 Carefully peel back the protective plastic sheet and remove the sheet from the door **(see illustration)**.

62 Undo the upper and lower screws securing the window rear guide rail to the door **(see illustrations)**.

63 Pull the rubber window channel out of the guide rail, then remove the guide rail through the door aperture **(see illustrations)**.

64 Undo the screw securing the door lock

operating cable guide to the door, then disconnect the inner cable from the bellcrank **(see illustration)**.

65 Release the retaining clip and disconnect the lock operating rod from the lever on the exterior handle frame **(see illustration 13.32)**.

66 Undo the three screws securing the lock to the door **(see illustration 13.55)**.

67 Withdraw the lock from its location, then lift the locking bar and disconnect the wiring connector **(see illustration 13.56)**. Unclip the wiring harness from the lock body.

68 Remove the lock assembly through the upper door aperture.

69 If required, disconnect the operating cables from the lock linkage and bracket **(see illustration 13.58)**.

Refitting – Hatchback models

70 If removed, reconnect the operating cables to the lock linkage and bracket.

71 Insert the lock assembly into the door and

reconnect the wiring connector. Secure the wiring harness to the lock body.

72 Position the lock assembly in its location, refit the three retaining screws and tighten securely.

73 Engage the lock operating rod with the lever on the exterior handle frame, and push the retaining clip back into position on the rod.

74 Connect the lock operating cable to the bellcrank, then secure the cable guide with the retaining screw.

75 Locate the guide rail in position in the door and refit the rubber window channel to the guide rail. Secure the guide rail with the upper and lower retaining screws.

76 Refit the protective plastic sheet to the door ensuring it is firmly stuck with no air bubbles. If the sheet was damaged during removal it should be renewed. This entails cutting a new sheet to the correct size and

13.63a Pull the rubber window channel out of the guide rail . . .

13.63b . . . then remove the guide rail through the door aperture

13.64 Undo the screw (arrowed) securing the lock operating cable guide to the door

shape using the old sheet as a template. The new sheet can then be attached to the door with fresh adhesive.

77 Refit the door inner trim panel as described in Section 12.

Removal – Saloon and Estate models

78 Remove the door inner trim panel as described in Section 12.

79 Carefully peel back the protective plastic sheet and remove the sheet from the door **(see illustration 13.61)**.

80 Using a plastic wedge or similar tool, tap up the window outer waist seal from the door aperture. Lift the seal up and remove it from the door **(see illustration)**.

81 Remove the door sealing weatherstrip from the top and rear side of the door.

82 Lift the fixed window glass upward and remove it rearwards from the door.

83 Undo the screw securing the window rear guide rail to the door **(see illustration 13.62a)**. Slide the guide rail down to release it from its upper location, then remove it upwards and out from the outside of the door.

84 Undo the screw securing the door lock operating cable guide to the door, then disconnect the inner cable from the bellcrank **(see illustration 13.64)**.

85 Release the retaining clip and disconnect the lock operating rod from the lever on the exterior handle frame **(see illustration 13.32)**.

86 Undo the three screws securing the lock to the door **(see illustration 13.55)**.

87 Withdraw the lock from its location, then lift the locking bar and disconnect the wiring connector **(see illustration 13.56)**. Unclip the wiring harness from the lock body.

88 Remove the lock assembly through the upper door aperture.

89 If required, disconnect the operating cables from the lock linkage and bracket **(see illustration 13.58)**.

Refitting – Saloon and Estate models

90 If removed, reconnect the operating cables to the lock linkage and bracket.

91 Insert the lock assembly into the door and reconnect the wiring connector. Secure the wiring harness to the lock body.

92 Position the lock assembly in its location, refit the three retaining screws and tighten securely.

13.80 Tap up the window outer waist seal from the door aperture, then lift the seal up and remove it from the door

93 Engage the lock operating rod with the lever on the exterior handle frame, and push the retaining clip back into position on the rod.

94 Connect the lock operating cable to the bellcrank, then secure the cable guide with the retaining screw.

95 Locate the window rear guide rail in position in the door and engage its upper mounting location. Secure the guide rail with the retaining screw.

96 Place the fixed window glass in position in the door.

97 Refit the door sealing weatherstrip to the top and rear side of the door.

98 Refit the window outer waist seal to the door aperture, ensuring that the retaining clips securely engage.

99 Refit the protective plastic sheet to the door ensuring it is firmly stuck with no air bubbles. If the sheet was damaged during removal it should be renewed. This entails cutting a new sheet to the correct size and shape using the old sheet as a template. The new sheet can then be attached to the door with fresh adhesive.

100 Refit the door inner trim panel as described in Section 12.

14 Door window regulator and glass – removal and refitting

Front door window regulator

Note: A pop-rivet gun and suitable rivets will

be required when refitting. The rivet heads should be approximately 4.8 mm in diameter and 11 mm in length.

Removal

1 Remove the door inner trim panel as described in Section 12.

2 Open the window so that it is approximately 50 mm downward from the closed position. Using adhesive tape over the top of the door frame, retain the window in this position.

3 Undo the three screws securing the loudspeaker to the door. Withdraw the speaker and disconnect the wiring connector. Unclip the wiring from the guide and remove the speaker **(see illustrations 13.25a and 13.25b)**.

4 Undo the three screws securing the door electronics module to the door. Pull out the locking bar, disconnect the wiring connector and remove the module **(see illustrations 13.26a and 13.26b)**.

5 Reach in through the loudspeaker aperture and push out the clips securing the wiring harness to the door **(see illustration 13.27)**.

6 Carefully peel back the protective plastic sheet and remove the sheet from the door **(see illustration 13.28)**.

7 Using an 8.5 mm drill bit, drill out the two rivets securing the window rear guide rail to the door, taking great care not to damage the door panel **(see illustrations 13.29a and 13.29b)**.

8 Disengage the top of the guide rail from the window lifting channel by moving it rearward, and remove the guide rail through the door aperture **(see illustrations 13.30a and 13.30b)**.

9 Undo the screw securing the regulator front lifting arm to the window lift channel **(see illustration)**.

10 Unclip the wiring harness support panel from the base of the door **(see illustration)**.

11 Pull out the locking bar and disconnect the window regulator wiring connector **(see illustration)**.

12 Using an 8.5 mm drill bit, drill out the six rivets securing the window regulator to the door, taking great care not to damage the door panel **(see illustration)**.

13 Lift the regulator up to disengage the front locating dowel, slide it sideways to disengage the regulator arm from the window guide channel, then remove the regulator through the door aperture **(see illustrations)**.

14.9 Undo the screw (arrowed) securing the regulator front lifting arm to the window lift channel

14.10 Unclip the wiring harness support panel from the base of the door

14.11 Pull out the locking bar and disconnect the window regulator wiring connector

14.12 Drill out the rivets (arrowed) securing the window regulator to the door

14.13a Lift the regulator up to disengage the front locating dowel (arrowed) . . .

14.13b . . . slide it sideways to disengage the regulator arm (arrowed) from the window guide channel . . .

14.13c . . . then remove the regulator through the door aperture

14 Clean out the remains of the old rivets from inside the door.

Refitting

15 Engage the regulator arm with the window guide channel, then locate the regulator dowel in the slot in the door panel. Secure the regulator with new pop rivets.

16 Reconnect the regulator wiring connector, then clip the wiring harness support panel back into position.

17 Refit and tighten the screw securing the regulator front lifting arm to the window lift channel.

18 Engage the top of the window guide rail with the lifting channel and position the guide rail in the door. Secure the guide rail with new pop rivets **(see illustration 13.38)**.

19 Refit the protective plastic sheet to the door ensuring it is firmly stuck with no air bubbles. If the sheet was damaged during removal it should be renewed. This entails

14.27 Position the window so that the window fixing clip is accessible through the small opening (arrowed) in the door

cutting a new sheet to the correct size and shape using the old sheet as a template. The new sheet can then be attached to the door with fresh adhesive.

20 Refit the wiring harness clips to the door ensuring they are firmly attached.

21 Refit the door electronics module, securely tighten the three retaining screws and reconnect the wiring connector.

22 Reconnect the wiring to the loudspeaker, position the speaker in the door and secure with the three screws.

23 Remove the adhesive tape used to retain the window, then refit the door inner trim panel as described in Section 12.

Rear door window regulator

Note: *A pop-rivet gun and suitable rivets will be required when refitting. The rivet heads should be approximately 4.8 mm in diameter and 11 mm in length.*

Removal

24 Remove the door inner trim panel as described in Section 12.

25 Carefully peel back the protective plastic sheet and remove the sheet from the door **(see illustration 13.61)**.

26 Undo the screw securing the door lock operating cable guide to the door, then disconnect the inner cable from the bellcrank **(see illustration 13.64)**.

27 Position the window in the assembly position so that the window fixing clip is accessible through the small opening in the door **(see illustration)**. On models with manually-operated windows, temporarily refit the regulator handle to reposition the window. On models with electric windows, it will be necessary to remove the window control switch from the door trim panel and temporarily reconnect the switch wiring.

28 Obtain a scribe or similar pointed tool with a 4.0 mm shaft diameter. Push the tool through the centre of the two-part window fixing clip to expand the internal locking lugs and separate the clip **(see illustrations)**. Disengage the window from the regulator lifting block and recover the two parts of the fixing clip.

29 Slide the window to the fully closed position. Using adhesive tape over the top of the door frame, retain the window in this position.

30 On models with electric windows, pull out the locking bar and disconnect the window regulator wiring connector.

31 Using an 8.5 mm drill bit, drill out the two rivets (electric windows) or five rivets

14.28a Push the tool through the centre of the two-part window fixing clip . . .

14.28b . . . to expand the internal locking lugs (shown with clip removed) . . .

14.28c . . . and separate the clip

(manual windows) securing the window regulator to the door, taking great care not to damage the door panel **(see illustration)**. On models with electric windows, also undo the retaining bolt located just in front of the regulator motor.

32 Push the regulator into the door, turn it clockwise and manipulate it out through the door aperture **(see illustration)**.

33 Clean out the remains of the old rivets from inside the door.

Refitting

34 Manipulate the regulator back into position in the door, then secure the regulator with new pop rivets **(see illustration)**.

35 On models with electric windows, refit the additional motor retaining bolt and reconnect the wiring connector.

36 Reposition the regulator in the assembly position to provide access for the window fixing clip.

37 Refit the two parts of the fixing clip to the window, remove the tape retaining the window in position and slide the window down and into engagement with the regulator lifting block.

38 Connect the lock operating cable to the bellcrank, then secure the cable guide with the retaining screw.

39 Refit the protective plastic sheet to the door ensuring it is firmly stuck with no air bubbles. If the sheet was damaged during removal it should be renewed. This entails cutting a new sheet to the correct size and shape using the old sheet as a template. The new sheet can then be attached to the door with fresh adhesive.

40 Refit the door inner trim panel as described in Section 12.

Front door window glass

Removal

41 Remove the regulator as previously described in this Section.

42 Using a plastic wedge or similar tool, tap up the window outer waist seal from the door aperture. Lift the seal up and remove it from the door **(see illustration)**.

43 Tilt the window glass down at the front, then carefully lift it upwards and remove it from the outside of the door.

Refitting

44 Refitting is a reversal of removal. Position the window glass so that it is approximately 50 mm downward from the closed position. Using adhesive tape over the top of the door frame, retain the window in this position during the remainder of refitting.

Rear door window glass

Removal – Hatchback models

45 Remove the door inner trim panel as described in Section 12.

46 Carefully peel back the protective plastic sheet and remove the sheet from the door **(see illustration 13.61)**.

47 Using a plastic wedge or similar tool, tap

14.31 Drill out the rivets (arrowed) securing the window regulator to the door

up the window outer waist seal from the door aperture. Lift the seal up and remove it from the door **(see illustration 13.80)**.

48 Undo the upper and lower screws securing the window rear guide rail to the door **(see illustrations 13.62a and 13.62b)**.

49 Pull the rubber window channel out of the guide rail, then remove the guide rail through the door aperture **(see illustrations 13.63a and 13.63b)**.

50 Release the window glass from the regulator as described previously in paragraphs 27 and 28.

51 Move the window and regulator to the fully open position.

52 Pull the rubber window channel out of the triangular panel at the rear of the door, then carefully lift the window glass upwards and remove it from the outside of the door.

Refitting – Hatchback models

53 Position the window regulator in the assembly position as described previously in paragraph 27.

54 Refit the two parts of the fixing clip to the window, place the window in the door and slide it down and into engagement with the regulator lifting block.

55 Refit the rubber window channel to the triangular panel at the rear of the door.

56 Locate the guide rail in position in the door and refit the rubber window channel to the guide rail. Secure the guide rail with the upper and lower retaining screws.

57 Refit the window outer waist seal to the door aperture, ensuring that the retaining clips securely engage.

14.34 Secure the regulator with new pop rivets

58 Refit the protective plastic sheet to the door ensuring it is firmly stuck with no air bubbles. If the sheet was damaged during removal it should be renewed. This entails cutting a new sheet to the correct size and shape using the old sheet as a template. The new sheet can then be attached to the door with fresh adhesive.

59 Refit the door inner trim panel as described in Section 12.

Removal – Saloon and Estate models

60 Remove the door inner trim panel as described in Section 12.

61 Carefully peel back the protective plastic sheet and remove the sheet from the door **(see illustration 13.61)**.

62 Using a plastic wedge or similar tool, tap up the window outer waist seal from the door aperture. Lift the seal up and remove it from the door **(see illustration 13.80)**.

63 Remove the door sealing weatherstrip from the top and rear side of the door.

64 Lift the fixed window glass upward and remove it rearwards from the door.

65 Undo the screw securing the window rear guide rail to the door **(see illustration 13.62b)**. Slide the guide rail down to release it from its upper location, then remove it upwards and out from the outside of the door.

66 Release the window glass from the regulator as described previously in paragraphs 27 and 28.

67 Move the window and regulator to the fully open position.

68 Carefully lift the window glass upwards and remove it from the outside of the door.

14.32 Manipulate the regulator out through the door aperture

14.42 Tap up the front door window outer waist seal and remove it from the door

Refitting – Saloon and Estate models

69 Position the window regulator in the assembly position as described previously in paragraph 27.

70 Refit the two parts of the fixing clip to the window, place the window in the door and slide it down and into engagement with the regulator lifting block.

71 Locate the window rear guide rail in position in the door and engage its upper mounting location. Secure the guide rail with the retaining screw.

72 Place the fixed window glass in position in the door.

73 Refit the door sealing weatherstrip to the top and rear side of the door.

74 Refit the window outer waist seal to the door aperture, ensuring that the retaining clips securely engage.

75 Refit the protective plastic sheet to the door ensuring it is firmly stuck with no air bubbles. If the sheet was damaged during removal it should be renewed. This entails cutting a new sheet to the correct size and shape using the old sheet as a template. The new sheet can then be attached to the door with fresh adhesive.

76 Refit the door inner trim panel as described in Section 12.

15 Rear quarter window glass – removal and refitting

Removal

1 Remove the relevant inner trim panels for access to the rear quarter window glass with reference to Section 27.

2 Unscrew the plastic retaining nuts and remove the window glass from the body. On Estate models there are 10 nuts; on Hatchback models there are 6 nuts.

Refitting

3 Refitting is a reversal of removal, using new plastic retaining nuts.

16 Boot lid and support struts – removal, refitting and adjustment

Boot lid

Removal

1 Open the boot lid, and have an assistant support it.

2 Disconnect the wiring at the connector.

3 Using a pencil or marker pen, mark around the hinges on the boot lid as a guide for refitting.

4 Using a screwdriver prise out the retaining spring clips and disconnect the upper ends of the support struts from the boot lid.

5 Unscrew the mounting bolts then lift the boot lid from the hinges.

6 The hinges can be removed if required by unbolting the hinges from the body.

Refitting and adjustment

7 Refitting is a reversal of removal, but make sure that the hinges are positioned as noted on removal and tighten the mounting bolts securely. With the boot lid closed, check that it is positioned centrally within the body aperture. If adjustment is necessary, loosen the boot lid mounting bolts and/or hinge mounting bolts and reposition the boot lid, then retighten the bolts. Check that the striker enters the lock centrally, and if necessary adjust the striker position by loosening the mounting bolts. Tighten the bolts on completion.

Support struts

Removal

8 Open the boot lid, and have an assistant support it.

9 Using a screwdriver prise out the retaining spring clips and disconnect the struts from the boot lid and body. Note which way round the strut is fitted.

Refitting

10 Refitting is a reversal of removal.

17 Boot lid lock components – removal and refitting

Lock assembly

Removal

1 Open the boot lid and remove the trim panel. Use a forked tool or removal tool to prise out the thirteen retaining clips, and the centre pins of the four plastic rivets.

2 Spread the retaining legs of the lock trim panel and remove the panel from the lock **(see illustrations)**.

3 Disconnect the lock wiring connector **(see illustration)**.

4 Undo the three lock assembly retaining screws **(see illustration)**.

5 Using a small screwdriver, depress the retaining lugs on each side of the lock extension **(see illustration)**.

6 Lift the lock assembly up and withdraw it from the inside **(see illustration)**.

Refitting

7 Refitting is a reversal of removal. Check that when closed the boot lid lock engages the lock striker centrally. If necessary loosen

17.2a Spread the retaining legs of the lock trim panel . . .

17.2b . . . and remove the panel from the lock

17.3 Disconnect the lock wiring connector

17.4 Undo the three lock assembly retaining screws (arrowed)

17.5 Depress the retaining lugs on each side of the lock extension

17.6 Lift the lock assembly up and withdraw it from the inside

17.10a Undo the two retaining screws (arrowed) . . .

17.10b . . . free the lock cylinder from its location and disconnect the wiring connector

the bolts and adjust the position of the striker, then tighten the bolts.

Lock cylinder

Removal

8 Open the boot lid and remove the trim panel as previously described.
9 Remove the lock assembly as previously described.
10 Undo the two retaining screws, free the lock cylinder from its location and disconnect the wiring connector **(see illustrations)**.
11 Where applicable, depress the retaining catch and release the operating cable from the lock cylinder. Disconnect the operating cable inner end fitting from the lock cylinder and remove the cylinder.

Refitting

12 Refitting is a reversal of removal.

---

18 Tailgate and support struts – removal, refitting and adjustment

Tailgate

Removal

1 Open the tailgate, release the wiring harness grommet, then depress the locking catch and disconnect the tailgate wiring connector on each side **(see illustration)**.
2 Have an assistant support the tailgate, then disconnect the tops of the support struts by prising out the spring clips with a small screwdriver. Lower the struts to the body.
3 Drive out the tailgate hinge pins from outside to inside with a suitable drift, while the assistant supports the tailgate **(see illustration)**. Withdraw the tailgate from the body.

Refitting

4 Refitting is a reversal of removal, but apply a little grease to the pivot pins, and check that when closed the tailgate is positioned centrally within the body aperture and flush with the surrounding bodywork. If necessary, adjust the position of the rubber supports so that the tailgate is flush with the surrounding bodywork. After making adjustments, check

that the striker enters the lock centrally and if necessary loosen the striker bolts to reposition it. Tighten the bolts on completion.

Support struts

Removal

5 Open the tailgate and note which way round the struts are fitted. Have an assistant support the tailgate in its open position.
6 Using a small screwdriver, prise the spring clip from the top of the strut and disconnect it from the ball on the tailgate **(see illustrations)**.
7 Similarly prise the spring clip from the bottom of the strut and disconnect it from the ball on the body. Withdraw the strut.

Refitting

8 Refitting is a reversal of removal.

18.1 Disconnect the tailgate wiring connector on each side

18.6a Prise the spring clip from the top of the strut . . .

---

19 Tailgate lock components – removal and refitting

Removal

Hatchback models

1 Open the tailgate and remove the trim caps over the upper side trim panel retaining screws. Undo the screw each side **(see illustrations)**.
2 Unscrew the parcel shelf lifting pins on each side.
3 Carefully prise free the side trim panel on each side to release the three retaining clips **(see illustration)**.
4 Using a forked tool, or removal tool, extract

18.3 Drive out the tailgate hinge pins (arrowed) from outside to inside

18.6b . . . and disconnect it from the ball on the tailgate

19.1a Remove the trim caps over the upper side trim panel retaining screws . . .

19.1b . . . then undo the screw (arrowed) each side

19.3 Prise free the side trim panel on each side to release the three retaining clips

19.4 Extract the four stud retaining clips at the lower edge of the lower trim panel

19.6 Pull the panel away from the tailgate to release the remaining internal clips

19.8 Undo the retaining screw located in the release handle aperture, and remove the release handle

the four stud retaining clips at the lower edge of the lower trim panel **(see illustration)**.

5 Undo the retaining screws in the centre of the panel and pull out the centre pins of the four plastic rivets.

6 Pull the panel away from the tailgate to

release the remaining internal clips and remove the panel from the tailgate **(see illustration)**.

7 With the trim panel removed, proceed as described in Section 17 for the lock assembly and lock cylinder removal and refitting procedures.

Estate models

8 Undo the retaining screw located in the tailgate release handle aperture, and remove the release handle **(see illustration)**.

9 Using a small screwdriver, extract the centre pins and remove the plastic securing rivets **(see illustration)**.

10 Pull the lower trim panel away from the tailgate to release the remaining internal clips and remove the panel from the tailgate **(see illustration)**.

11 With the trim panel removed, proceed as described in Section 17 for the lock assembly and lock cylinder removal and refitting procedures.

Refitting

12 Refitting is a reversal of removal.

19.9 Extract the centre pins and remove the plastic securing rivets

19.10 Pull the lower trim panel away from the tailgate to release the remaining internal clips

20 Exterior mirrors and associated components – removal and refitting

Exterior mirror

Removal

1 Fully open the door window.

2 Remove the door inner trim panel as described in Section 12.

3 Carefully prise off the mirror interior trim panel to release the two retaining clips **(see illustration)**.

4 Disconnect the wiring connector from the mirror **(see illustration)**.

20.3 Prise off the mirror interior trim panel to release the two retaining clips

20.4 Disconnect the wiring connector from the mirror

20.5a Release the tweeter speaker wiring harness retaining clip . . .

20.5b . . . and disconnect the tweeter wiring connector

20.6 Extract the blanking plug from the front edge of the door and undo the mirror lower retaining bolt now exposed

20.7 Undo the two upper retaining bolts (arrowed) and remove the mirror assembly from the door

20.10 Prise the outer edge of the glass outwards to release the internal retaining clips

20.11 Withdraw the mirror glass and disconnect the wiring connectors

5 Release the tweeter speaker wiring harness retaining clip from the interior trim panel, and disconnect the tweeter wiring connector **(see illustrations)**. Remove the trim panel.
6 Extract the blanking plug from the front edge of the door and undo the mirror lower retaining bolt now exposed **(see illustration)**.
7 Undo the two upper retaining bolts and remove the mirror assembly from the door **(see illustration)**.

Refitting

8 Refitting is a reversal of removal.

Mirror glass

Removal

9 Press the inner edge of the glass inwards so that the glass is forced out from the centre.
10 Using a plastic wedge, prise the outer edge of the glass outwards to release the internal retaining clips **(see illustration)**.
11 Withdraw the mirror glass and disconnect the wiring connectors **(see illustration)**.

Refitting

12 Refitting is a reversal of removal. Carefully press the mirror glass into the housing until the centre retainer clips are engaged.

Outer cover

Removal

13 Remove the mirror glass as described previously in this Section.
14 Using a small screwdriver, carefully prise the outer cover away from the mirror body to release the inner locating pin from its hole **(see illustration)**.
15 Compress the four clips securing the cover to the mirror body, starting with the two inner clips, then the two outer clips **(see illustration)**. Withdraw the cover from the mirror body.

20.14 Prise the outer cover away from the mirror body to release the inner locating pin (arrowed) from its hole

20.15 Compress the four clips securing the cover to the mirror body

20.18 Remove the rubber seal from the mirror frame

20.19a Carefully release the base cover from the mirror frame . . .

20.19b . . . and mirror body . . .

20.19c . . . and withdraw the cover

Refitting

16 Refitting is a reversal of removal.

Base cover

Removal

17 Remove the mirror from the car as described previously in this Section.
18 Remove the rubber seal from the mirror frame **(see illustration)**.
19 Using a small screwdriver carefully release the base cover from the mirror frame and mirror body and withdraw the cover **(see illustrations)**.

Refitting

20 Refitting is a reversal of removal.

21 Windscreen and fixed window glass – general information

The windscreen and tailgate glass are cemented in position with a special adhesive and require the use of specialist equipment for their removal and refitting. Renewal of such fixed glass is considered beyond the scope of the home mechanic. Owners are strongly advised to have the work carried out by one of the many specialist windscreen fitting specialists.

22 Sunroof – general information

A manual or electric sunroof was offered as

an optional extra on most models, and is fitted as standard equipment on some models.

Due to the complexity of the sunroof mechanism, considerable expertise is needed to repair, renew or adjust the sunroof components successfully. Removal of the roof first requires the headlining to be removed, which is a complex and tedious operation in itself, and not a task to be undertaken lightly. Therefore, any problems with the sunroof should be referred to a Vauxhall/Opel dealer.

On models with an electric sunroof, if the sunroof motor fails to operate, first check the relevant fuse. If the fault cannot be traced and rectified, the sunroof can be opened and closed manually using an Allen key to turn the motor spindle. To gain access to the motor spindle, carefully prise out the trim cover situated at the rear of the sunroof. Insert the Allen key in the motor spindle,

23.7 Pull up the rubber weatherseal from the flange at the rear of the engine compartment

and turn to move the sunroof to the required position. A suitable Allen key is supplied with the vehicle, and is attached to the inside of the trim cover.

23 Body exterior fittings – removal and refitting

Radiator grille

1 To remove the upper radiator grille, open the bonnet and undo the eight radiator grille retaining screws. Unclip the grille and remove it from the bonnet. Refit the grille to the bonnet and secure with the retaining screws.
2 To remove lower radiator grille, remove the front bumper as described in Section 6. Where fitted, unclip the headlight washer hose, then release the twenty tabs and remove the grille. Refit the grille, clip the washer hose into position (where applicable), then refit the front bumper as described in Section 6.

Wheel arch liners and body under-panels

3 The various plastic covers fitted to the underside of the vehicle are secured in position by a mixture of screws, nuts and retaining clips, and removal will be fairly obvious on inspection. Work methodically around the liner/panel, removing its retaining screws and releasing its retaining clips until it is free to be removed from the underside of the vehicle. Most clips used on the vehicle, with the exception of the fasteners which are used to secure the wheel arch liners, are simply prised out of position. The wheel arch liner clips are released by tapping their centre pins through the clip, and then removing the outer section of the clip; new clips will be required on refitting if the centre pins are not recovered.
4 On diesel engine models an undertray is fitted beneath the engine/transmission assembly. The undertray is secured to the front subframe and underbody with ten bolts.
5 When refitting, renew any retaining clips that may have been broken on removal, and ensure that the panel is securely retained by all the relevant clips, nuts and screws. Vauxhall/Opel also recommend that plastic nuts (where used) are renewed, regardless of their apparent condition, whenever they are disturbed.

Water deflector

6 Remove the windscreen wiper arms as described in Chapter 12.
7 Open the bonnet, and pull up the rubber weatherseal from the flange at the rear of the engine compartment **(see illustration)**.
8 Carefully prise free the water deflector from the base of the windscreen to release the retaining clips, and remove the water deflector from the car **(see illustration)**.
9 Refit the water deflector using a reversal of

23.8 Prise free the water deflector from the base of the windscreen to release the retaining clips

the removal procedure. Refit the wiper arms as described in Chapter 12.

Body trim strips and badges

10 The various body trim strips and badges are held in position with a special adhesive tape. Removal requires the trim/badge to be heated, to soften the adhesive, and then cut away from the surface. Due to the high risk of damage to the vehicle's paintwork during this operation, it is recommended that this task should be entrusted to a Vauxhall/Opel dealer.

24 Seats – removal and refitting

Warning: The front seats are equipped with seat belt tensioners, and side airbags may be built into

the outer sides of the seats. The seat belt tensioners and side airbags may cause injury if triggered accidentally. If the tensioner has been triggered due to a sudden impact or accident, the unit must be renewed, as it cannot be reset. If a seat is to be disposed of, the tensioner must be triggered before the seat is removed from the vehicle. Due to safety considerations, tensioner renewal or seat disposal must be entrusted to a Vauxhall/Opel dealer. Where side airbags are fitted, refer to Chapter 12 for the precautions which should be observed when dealing with an airbag system.

1 Disconnect the battery negative terminal (refer to *Disconnecting the battery* in the Reference Chapter). Wait 2 minutes for the capacitors to discharge, before working on the seat electrics.

Front seat removal

2 Depress the two tabs and remove the front seat headrest.
3 Slide the seat adjustment fully forward.
4 Unclip the cover over the seat belt mounting, then undo the seat belt retaining bolt **(see illustration)**.
5 Pull out the locking bar and disconnect the wiring connector from the underside of the seat, at the rear **(see illustration)**.
6 Slacken and remove the seat retaining bolts from the rear of the guide rails **(see illustration)**.
7 Pull the seat backwards to disengage the guide rail front mounting lugs from the floor. The seat can now be lifted out of the vehicle.

Rear seat removal

Cushion

8 Pull the front of the rear seat cushion upwards to disengage the front mountings. Where applicable, disconnect the wiring for the seat heater.
9 On Saloon and Hatchback models, lift the cushion out of the rear mountings and remove it from the car.
10 On Estate models, push the cushion and move it to the left to disengage the left-hand rear mounting, then move it to the right to disengage the right-hand rear mounting. Remove the cushion from the car.

Backrest

11 Remove the rear seat cushion as described previously in this Section.
12 Pull the upper portion of the backrest side padding forward to disengage the upper mounting, then lift it up to disengage the lower hook **(see illustrations)**. Remove the side padding from the car.
13 Unscrew the retaining nut and remove the centre seat belt buckle.
14 Fold the backrest forward, then using a screwdriver, press the outer hinge pin locking collar in, to free the hinge pin, while at the same time pulling upward to release the backrest **(see illustration)**.
15 Fold the backrest upward, then pull the hinge pin out of the centre support (left-hand side), or pull the backrest off the hinge pin (right-hand side) **(see illustration)**. Remove the backrest from the vehicle.

24.4 Undo the seat belt retaining bolt from the front seat

24.5 Pull out the locking bar and disconnect the wiring connector from the underside of the seat

24.6 Slacken and remove the seat retaining bolts (arrowed) from the rear of the guide rails

24.12a Pull the upper portion of the backrest side padding forward to disengage the upper mounting . . .

24.12b . . . then lift it up to disengage the lower hook

24.14 Press the outer hinge pin locking collar in, while at the same time pulling upward to release the backrest

24.15 Pull the backrest off the hinge pin (arrowed) – right-hand backrest shown

Front seat refitting

16 Refitting is a reverse of the removal procedure, noting the following points:

a) *Remove all traces of old thread-locking compound from the threads of the seat retaining bolts, and clean the threaded holes in the vehicle floor, ideally by running a tap of the correct size and pitch down them.*

b) *Apply a suitable thread-locking compound to the threads of the seat bolts. Refit the bolts, and tighten them to the specified torque setting.*

c) *Reconnect the seat wiring connector making sure it has locked securely, then reconnect the battery negative terminal.*

Rear seat refitting

17 Refitting is a reverse of the removal procedure.

26.3 Undo the front seat belt upper mounting bolt

26.4b ... for access to the front seat belt reel mounting nut (arrowed)

25 Seat belt tensioning mechanism – general information

All models covered in this manual are fitted with a front seat belt pyrotechnic tensioner system. On certain models, this system is also fitted to the rear outer seat belts. The system is designed to instantaneously take up any slack in the seat belt in the case of a sudden frontal impact, therefore reducing the possibility of injury to the front seat occupants. Each front seat is fitted with its own system, the components of which are mounted on the seat frame.

The seat belt tensioner is triggered by a frontal impact causing a deceleration of six times the force of gravity or greater. Lesser impacts, including impacts from behind, will not trigger the system.

When the system is triggered, a pretensioned spring draws back the seat belt via a cable which acts on the seat belt stalk. The cable can move by up to 80.0 mm, which therefore reduces the slack in the seat belt around the shoulders and waist of the occupant by a similar amount.

There is a risk of injury if the system is triggered inadvertently when working on the vehicle, and it is therefore strongly recommended that any work involving the seat belt tensioner system is entrusted to a Vauxhall/Opel dealer. Refer to the warning given at the beginning of Section 24 before contemplating any work on the front seats.

26.4a Prise the cover from the lower outside of the B-pillar ...

26.8a Slide out the wiring connector locking bar ...

26 Seat belt components – removal and refitting

⚠ *Warning: The front seats (and on certain models, the rear outer seats) are fitted with pyrotechnic seat belt tensioners which are triggered by the airbag control system. Before removing a seat belt, disconnect the battery and wait at least 2 minutes to allow the system capacitors to discharge.*

Front belt and reel

Removal

1 Unclip the cover over the seat belt mounting on the front seat, then undo the seat belt retaining bolt **(see illustration 24.4)**.
2 Remove the B-pillar inner trim panel and sill trim panel as described in Section 27.
3 Undo the seat belt upper mounting bolt **(see illustration)**.
4 Prise the cover from the lower outside of the B-pillar for access to the front seat belt reel mounting nut **(see illustrations)**. Using a 13 mm socket, 65 mm deep on the inside, unscrew the nut taking care not to drop it inside the B-pillar. Note that an extension pin is provided to enable the nut to be removed safely.
5 With the nut removed, remove the reel from the inside of the pillar.

Refitting

6 Refitting is a reversal of removal, but tighten the mounting bolts to the specified torque.

Front belt stalk and tensioner

Removal

7 Remove the front seat as described in Section 24.
8 From underneath the seat, slide out the wiring connector locking bar and disconnect the wiring connector **(see illustrations)**. Unclip the wiring harness from the seat.
9 Undo the retaining bolt and withdraw the tensioner from the seat **(see illustration)**.
10 Release the cable retaining clip and remove the tensioner **(see illustration)**.

26.8b ... and disconnect the seat belt tensioner wiring connector

26.9 Undo the retaining bolt (arrowed) and withdraw the tensioner from the seat

26.10 Release the cable retaining clip (arrowed) and remove the tensioner

26.14 Undo the rear seat belt lower mounting bolt (arrowed)

Refitting

11 Refitting is a reverse of the removal procedure, noting the following points:
a) *Remove all traces of old thread-locking compound from the thread of the tensioner retaining bolt, and clean the threaded hole in the seat, ideally by running a tap of the correct size and pitch down it.*
b) *Apply a suitable thread-locking compound to the thread of the tensioner retaining bolt. Refit the bolt, and tighten it to the specified torque setting.*

Rear outer belt and reel

Removal

12 Remove the rear seat cushion as described in Section 24.
13 Remove the luggage compartment upper side trim and sill rear trim panel as described in Section 27.
14 Undo the seat belt lower mounting bolt **(see illustration)**.
15 Undo the seat belt reel mounting bolt and remove the reel and belt from the car **(see illustration)**.

Refitting

16 Refitting is a reversal of removal, but tighten the mounting bolts to the specified torque.

Rear centre belt and reel

17 The inertia reel for the centre rear seat belt is located internally within the rear seat backrest. To gain access, the backrest must be removed and completely dismantled. This is a complex operation and considerable expertise is needed to remove and refit the seat upholstery and internal components without damage. Therefore, any problems with the centre seat belt and reel should be referred to a Vauxhall/Opel dealer.

Rear belt stalk and tensioner

Removal

18 Remove the rear seat cushion as described in Section 24.
19 On models without seat belt tensioners, undo the retaining nut and remove the relevant stalk from the floor **(see illustration)**.

26.15 Undo the rear seat belt reel mounting bolt (arrowed) and remove the reel and belt from the car

20 On models with seat belt tensioners, slide out the wiring connector locking bar and disconnect the wiring connector.
21 Undo the retaining nut and remove the relevant tensioner from the floor. Note that a new retaining nut will be required for refitting.

Refitting

22 Refitting is a reversal of removal, but tighten the mounting bolts to the specified torque.

---

27 Interior trim – removal and refitting

1 The interior trim panels are secured by a combination of clips and screws. Removal and refitting is generally self-explanatory, noting that it may be necessary to remove or loosen

27.2 Pull off the front door weather strip in the vicinity of the A-pillar trim panel

26.19 Undo the retaining nut (arrowed) and remove the relevant stalk from the floor

surrounding panels to allow a particular panel to be removed. The following paragraphs describe the general removal and refitting details of the major panels.

A-pillar trim panel

2 Pull off the front door weather strip in the vicinity of the A-pillar trim panel **(see illustration)**.
3 On models equipped with curtain airbags, pull out the airbag positioning clip from the trim panel **(see illustration)**.
4 Pull the trim panel away from the A-pillar and remove it from the car **(see illustration)**.
5 Refitting is a reversal of removal.

Front footwell side trim panel

6 Open the front door and pull the weatherstrip away from the side trim panel and side sill panel.

27.3 Pull out the airbag positioning clip from the trim panel

27.4 Pull the trim panel away from the A-pillar and remove it from the car

7 Undo the two screws securing the footwell side trim panel to the body **(see illustration)**.
8 Pull the overlapping side sill panel from its location at the front, then disengage and remove the footwell panel **(see illustration)**.
9 Refitting is a reversal of removal.

B-pillar upper trim panel

10 Open the front and rear doors and pull the weatherstrip away from the B-pillar.
11 Unclip the cover over the seat belt mounting on the front seat, then undo the seat belt retaining bolt **(see illustration 24.4)**.
12 Prise out the plastic cover at the top of the panel **(see illustration)**.
13 Prise the trim panel away from the B-pillar at the top **(see illustration)**.
14 Disengage the lower end of the panel from the B-pillar lower trim panel, feed the seat belt through the opening and remove the panel from the car **(see illustration)**.

27.12 Prise out the plastic cover at the top of the B-pillar upper trim panel

27.18 Unclip the B-pillar lower trim panel from the upper panel at the top

27.7 Undo the two screws (arrowed) securing the footwell side trim panel to the body

15 Refitting is a reversal of removal.

B-pillar lower trim panel

16 Open the front and rear doors and pull the weatherstrip away from the B-pillar.
17 Pull the overlapping side sill panel from its location to allow the B-pillar lower trim to be removed.
18 Unclip the B-pillar lower trim panel from the upper panel at the top **(see illustration)**.
19 Unclip the bottom of the panel from the B-pillar and remove the panel from the car.
20 Refitting is a reversal of removal.

Side sill inner trim panel

21 Open the front and rear doors and pull the weatherstrip away from the B-pillar and the lower part of the door apertures.
22 Remove the rear seat cushion as described in Section 24.
23 Pull the upper portion of the seat backrest side padding forward to disengage the upper

27.13 Prise the trim panel away from the B-pillar at the top

27.24 Spread the sides of the side sill inner trim panel outward and release it from the B-pillar lower trim panel

27.8 Pull the overlapping side sill panel from its location, then disengage and remove the footwell panel

mounting, then lift it up to disengage the lower hook **(see illustrations 24.12a and 24.12b)**. Remove the side padding from the car.
24 Spread the sides of the side sill inner trim panel outward and release it from the B-pillar lower trim panel **(see illustration)**.
25 Starting at the front and working rearwards, unclip the panel from the sill and remove the panel from the car.
26 Refitting is a reversal of removal.

Luggage compartment lower side trim panel

Saloon and Hatchback models

27 Fold the rear seat backrests forward.
28 Open the boot lid or tailgate.
29 Remove the luggage compartment floor covering.
30 Pull the tailgate aperture trim panel away to release the internal retaining clips and remove the panel from the car **(see illustration)**.

27.14 Disengage the lower end of the panel from the B-pillar lower trim panel and feed the seat belt through the opening

27.30 Pull the tailgate aperture trim panel away to release the internal retaining clips and remove the panel from the car

27.31 Pull the weatherstrip away from the boot lid/tailgate aperture

31 Pull the weatherstrip away from the boot lid/tailgate aperture (see illustration).
32 Using a forked tool, or removal tool, prise out the retaining clips at the rear of the panel (see illustration).
33 Pull the panel away to release the internal clips, disconnect the wiring for the luggage compartment light (where applicable) and remove the panel.
34 Refitting is a reversal of removal.

Estate models

35 Open the tailgate.
36 Remove the luggage compartment floor covering.
37 Pull the weatherstrip away from the rear door aperture.
38 Remove the tailgate aperture lower centre trim panel, as described later in this Section.
39 Carefully unclip the upper and lower cover strips from the side trim panel (see illustration).

27.40 Unscrew the six panel retaining screws

27.43 Pull the panel away to release the internal clips, and remove the panel from the car

27.32 Prise out the retaining clips at the rear of the panel

40 Unscrew the six panel retaining screws (see illustration).
41 Unclip and remove the covers over the luggage retaining lugs (see illustration).
42 Undo the retaining bolts and remove the luggage retaining lugs (see illustration).
43 Pull the panel away to release the internal clips, and remove the panel from the car (see illustration).
44 Refitting is a reversal of removal.

C-pillar trim panel
Saloon models

45 Pull the weatherstrip away from the rear door aperture.
46 Pull the upper portion of the seat backrest side padding forward to disengage the upper mounting, then lift it up to disengage the lower hook (see illustrations 24.12a and 24.12b). Remove the side padding from the car.
47 Prise off the cover and undo the rear seat belt upper mounting bolt.

27.41 Unclip and remove the covers over the luggage retaining lugs

27.53a Prise off the cover . . .

27.39 Carefully unclip the upper and lower cover strips from the side trim panel

48 On models with curtain airbags, pull out the airbag positioning clip from the trim panel.
49 Pull the panel away to release the internal clips, and remove the panel from the car.
50 Refitting is a reversal of removal, but tighten the seat belt retaining bolt to the specified torque.

C/D-pillar trim panel
Hatchback and Estate models

51 Remove the luggage compartment lower side trim panel as described previously in this Section.
52 Pull the upper portion of the seat backrest side padding forward to disengage the upper mounting, then lift it up to disengage the lower hook (see illustrations 24.12a and 24.12b). Remove the side padding from the car.
53 Prise off the cover and undo the rear seat belt upper mounting bolt (see illustrations).

27.42 Undo the retaining bolts and remove the luggage retaining lugs

27.53b . . . and undo the rear seat belt upper mounting bolt

27.55 Pull out the airbag positioning clip from the trim panel

27.56a Undo the three screws at the front (arrowed) . . .

27.56b . . . and the screw at the rear (arrowed) securing the panel to the body

27.57 Pull the panel away to release the internal clips, and remove the panel from the car

27.60 Pull the panel away to release the internal clips, and remove the panel from the car

27.64a On Estate models, prise up the trim caps . . .

27.64b . . . and undo the panel retaining screws

27.65 Pull the panel away to release the internal clips, and remove the panel from the car

28.3 Remove the centre console storage compartment

54 Pull the weatherstrip away from the rear door aperture.

55 On models equipped with curtain airbags, pull out the airbag positioning clip from the trim panel (see illustration).

56 Undo the three screws at the front and the screw at the rear securing the panel to the body (see illustrations).

57 Pull the panel away to release the internal clips, and remove the panel from the car (see illustration).

58 Refitting is a reversal of removal, but

tighten the seat belt retaining bolt to the specified torque.

Tailgate aperture upper centre trim panel

59 Open the boot lid or tailgate.

60 Pull the panel away to release the internal clips, and remove the panel from the car (see illustration).

61 Refitting is a reversal of removal.

Tailgate aperture lower centre trim panel

62 Open the boot lid or tailgate.

63 Remove the luggage compartment floor covering.

64 On Estate models, prise up the trim caps and undo the panel retaining screws (see illustrations).

65 Pull the panel away to release the internal clips, and remove the panel from the car (see illustration).

66 Refitting is a reversal of removal.

Interior mirror

67 On models fitted with a rain sensor, unclip and remove the sensor trim panel and release the retaining clip(s) and disconnect the wiring connectors from the mirror assembly.

68 Press the retaining clip at the top of the interior mirror mounting bracket, then carefully release the interior mirror in the downwards direction to remove it from the windscreen.

69 Refitting is the reverse of removal.

28 Centre console – removal and refitting

Front console

Removal

1 Disconnect the battery negative terminal (refer to *Disconnecting the battery* in the Reference Chapter).

2 Remove the rear centre console as described later in this Section.

3 Unclip and remove the centre console storage compartment below the heater/ventilation control panel (see illustration).

4 Carefully release the facia decorative strip

28.4a Carefully release the facia decorative strip using a plastic spatula or similar tool . . .

28.4b . . . and remove the strip from the facia

28.5 Prise up and remove the trim panel around the cigarette lighter/accessory socket

using a plastic spatula or similar tool (see illustrations).

5 Carefully prise up and remove the trim panel around the cigarette lighter/accessory socket (see illustration).

6 Remove the ashtray from the centre console by opening the lid, depressing the internal tabs each side and lifting out (see illustration).

7 Disconnect the wiring connector at the rear of the cigarette lighter/accessory socket.

8 Unclip the gearchange/selector lever gaiter retaining frame from the centre console and lift it off the gearchange lever (see illustration).

9 On manual transmission models, release the retaining lugs around the sides and rear of the gearchange lever gaiter. Disengage the locating pegs at the front and fold the gaiter up over the gearchange lever knob (see illustrations).

10 Undo the two upper screws securing the centre console to the facia (see illustration).

28.6 Remove the ashtray by opening the lid, depressing the internal tabs each side and lifting out

28.8 Unclip the gearchange/selector lever gaiter retaining frame from the centre console

11 Undo the retaining screw at the rear left-hand side of the centre console (see illustration).

12 Prise out the two trim caps on each

side of the centre console at the front, and undo the screw and nut each side (see illustrations).

13 Lift the console up and slide it to the rear,

28.9a Release the retaining lugs around the sides and rear of the gearchange lever gaiter . . .

28.9b . . . then disengage the locating pegs at the front and fold the gaiter up over the gearchange lever knob

28.10 Undo the two upper screws (arrowed) securing the centre console to the facia

28.11 Undo the retaining screw (arrowed) at the rear left-hand side of the centre console

28.12a Prise out the two trim caps on each side of the centre console at the front . . .

28.12b . . . and undo the screw and nut each side

28.13 Lift the console up and slide it to the rear, then remove the console from the car

28.16 Prise free the cigarette lighter/ accessory socket panel at the rear of the centre console

28.17 Undo the two screws (arrowed) securing the rear of the centre console to the floor

28.18 Undo the four bolts (arrowed) and remove the armrest and rear vent housing from the console

then remove the console from the car **(see illustration)**.

Refitting

14 Refitting is a reversal of removal.

28.19a Carefully prise free the storage compartment at the front of the centre console . . .

Rear console

Removal

15 Disconnect the battery negative terminal (refer to *Disconnecting the battery* in the Reference Chapter).

28.19b . . . then undo the screw (arrowed) in the storage compartment aperture

16 Carefully prise free the cigarette lighter/ accessory socket panel at the rear of the centre console **(see illustration)**. Disconnect the wiring connector and remove the panel.
17 Undo the two screws, now exposed, securing the rear of the centre console to the floor **(see illustration)**.
18 Undo the four bolts and remove the armrest and rear vent housing from the console **(see illustration)**.
19 Carefully prise free the storage compartment at the front of the centre console, then undo the screw in the storage compartment aperture **(see illustrations)**.
20 Pull the console to the rear to disengage the front locating pegs, lift it over the handbrake lever and remove the console from the car **(see illustration)**.

Refitting

21 Refitting is a reversal of removal.

28.20 Pull the console to the rear to disengage the front locating pegs

29.2 Prise out the glovebox interior light and disconnect the wiring connector

29 Facia panel components – removal and refitting

Glovebox

Removal

1 Carefully release the facia decorative strip using a plastic spatula or similar tool **(see illustrations 28.4a and 28.4b)**.
2 Prise out the glovebox interior light and disconnect the wiring connector **(see illustration)**.
3 Undo the screw each side securing the base of the glovebox to the facia **(see illustrations)**.

29.3a Undo the right-hand screw (arrowed) . . .

29.3b . . . and left-hand screw (arrowed) securing the base of the glovebox to the facia

29.4 Undo the three screws (arrowed) securing the top of the glovebox to the facia

29.7 Prise out the trim cap on the side of the centre console at the front, and undo the retaining nut

29.8 Undo the screw securing the footwell trim panel at the front

4 Open the glovebox and undo the three screws securing the top of the glovebox to the facia **(see illustration).**
5 Withdraw the glovebox from the facia and remove it from the car.

Refitting

6 Refitting is a reversal of removal.

Facia footwell trim panel

Removal

7 Prise out the trim cap on the side of the centre console at the front, and undo the retaining nut **(see illustration).**
8 Undo the screw securing the footwell trim panel at the front **(see illustration).**
9 Ease the front of the centre console outwards to expose the recessed hidden bolt **(see illustration).** Unscrew and remove the bolt.
10 While still holding the front of the centre console outwards, remove the footwell trim panel from the side of the facia **(see illustration).**

Refitting

11 Refitting is a reversal of removal.

Centre air vents

Removal

12 Carefully release the facia decorative strip using a plastic spatula or similar tool **(see illustrations 28.4a and 28.4b).**
13 Undo the four bolts securing the centre vent housing to the facia and withdraw the housing from its location **(see illustrations).** Lift the locking bar(s) and disconnect the wiring connector(s) from the rear of the information display unit, then remove the vent housing from the facia.

Refitting

14 Refitting is a reversal of removal.

Side air vents

Removal

15 To remove the vent from the driver's side of the facia, carefully release the facia decorative strip using a plastic spatula or similar tool **(see illustration).**
16 Undo the two screws securing the base

29.9 Ease the front of the centre console outwards to expose the recessed hidden bolt (arrowed)

29.10 While still holding the front of the centre console outwards, remove the footwell trim panel from the side of the facia

of the vent to the facia. Pull the vent out at the bottom, disengage the two upper retaining lugs, and remove the vent from the facia **(see illustrations).**

17 To remove the vent from the passenger's side of the facia, release the facia decorative strip as described in paragraph 12, then remove the vent as described in paragraph 16.

29.13a Undo the four bolts (arrowed) securing the centre vent housing to the facia (arrowed) . . .

29.13b . . . and withdraw the housing from its location

29.15 Release the facia decorative strip using a plastic spatula or similar

29.16a Undo the two screws (arrowed) securing the base of the vent to the facia . . .

29.16b . . . pull the vent out at the bottom and disengage the two upper retaining lugs (arrowed)

29.19 Undo the screw (arrowed) at the top of the headlight switch aperture

29.20a Undo the two upper screws and three lower screws (arrowed) . . .

29.20b . . . and remove the lower trim panel from under the facia

29.25 Undo the two screws (arrowed) and remove the steering column height adjuster handle

29.26 Prise off the circular trim panel around the ignition switch

Refitting

18 Refitting is a reversal of removal.

Driver's side lower trim panel

Removal

19 Remove the headlight switch as described

29.27a Hook out the trim caps . . .

29.27b . . . and undo the shroud upper retaining screw on each side

in Chapter 12, then undo the screw at the top of the light switch aperture (see illustration).
20 Undo the two upper screws and three lower screws, and remove the lower trim panel from under the facia (see illustrations).

Refitting

21 Refitting is a reversal of removal.

Steering column shrouds

Removal

22 Carefully release the facia decorative strip below the side vent panel using a plastic spatula or similar tool (see illustration 29.15).
23 Remove the driver's side lower trim panel as described previously in this Section.
24 Move the steering column to its lowest position by means of the height adjuster.
25 Undo the two screws and remove the steering column height adjuster handle (see illustration).
26 Carefully prise off the circular trim panel around the ignition switch (see illustration).
27 Using a small screwdriver, hook out the trim caps and undo the shroud upper retaining screw on each side (see illustrations).
28 Undo the shroud lower retaining screw in the column height adjuster handle aperture (see illustration).
29 Carefully prise the upper shroud off the lower shroud.
30 Unhook the shroud inner panel from the facia on both sides, then lift the upper shroud up and off the steering column (see illustration).
31 Undo the screw each side securing the

29.28 Undo the shroud lower retaining screw (arrowed) in the column height adjuster handle aperture

29.30 Unhook the shroud inner panel from the facia (arrowed) on both sides, then lift the upper shroud off the steering column

29.31 Undo the screw (arrowed) each side securing the lower shroud to the switch assembly

29.41 Remove the side cover panels at the left-hand and right-hand ends of the facia

29.42a Undo the bolt (arrowed) securing the radio/cassette/CD player mounting frame to the facia . . .

lower shroud to the switch assembly (see illustration).

32 Disengage the lower shroud from the steering column height adjuster and ignition switch, and remove the shroud from the column.

Refitting

33 Refitting is a reversal of removal.

Complete facia assembly

Note: *This is an involved operation entailing the removal of numerous components and assemblies, and the disconnection of a multitude of wiring connectors. Make notes on the location of all disconnected wiring, or attach labels to the connectors, to avoid confusion when refitting.*

Removal

34 Disconnect the battery negative terminal (refer to *Disconnecting the battery* in the Reference Chapter).

35 Remove the A-pillar trim panels on both sides as described in Section 27.

36 Remove the front centre console as described in Section 28.

37 Remove the following facia panels as described previously in this Section:
 a) *Glovebox.*
 b) *Facia footwell trim panels.*
 c) *Centre and side air vents.*
 d) *Driver's side lower trim panel.*
 e) *Steering column shrouds.*

38 Remove the steering wheel as described in Chapter 10.

39 Remove the steering column electronics

29.42b . . . prise free the upper and lower retaining tabs . . .

module, instrument panel, radio/cassette/CD player and all the facia switches as described in Chapter 12.

40 Remove the heater control assembly as described in Chapter 3.

41 Remove the side cover panels at the left-hand and right-hand ends of the facia (see illustration).

42 Undo the bolt securing the radio/cassette/CD player mounting frame to the facia. Prise free the upper and lower retaining tabs and remove the frame from the facia (see illustrations).

43 Release the locking catches with a small screwdriver, and detach the switch plug strips on the left-hand and right-hand side of the radio/cassette/CD player aperture (see illustrations).

44 Carefully prise out the sun sensor panel from the top of the facia and disconnect

29.42c . . . and remove the frame from the facia

the wiring connector (see illustration). On models fitted with a loudspeaker in the sun sensor aperture, undo the two retaining bolts, remove the speaker and disconnect the wiring connector.

45 Unclip and remove the glovebox cooling duct, then undo the bolt and remove the footwell air duct on the passenger's side.

46 Extract the plastic rivet and remove the footwell air duct on the driver's side (see illustration).

47 Undo the following fasteners securing the facia to the mounting bracket (see illustrations):
 a) *1 bolt at the left-hand and right-hand end.*
 b) *1 bolt each side at the lower left-hand and right-hand corners of the facia.*
 c) *1 lower centre bolt each side.*
 d) *1 nut in the centre vent panel aperture.*

48 With the help of an assistant, carefully

29.43a Release the locking catches with a small screwdriver . . .

29.43b . . . and detach the switch plug strips

29.44 Carefully prise out the sun sensor panel from the top of the facia

29.46 Extract the plastic rivet and remove the footwell air duct on the driver's side

29.47a Undo the bolt (arrowed) at each end of the facia . . .

29.47b . . . the bolt at each lower corner (arrowed) . . .

29.47c . . . the lower centre bolt (arrowed) each side . . .

29.47d . . . and the nut (arrowed) in the centre vent aperture

29.57 Undo the through-bolt (arrowed) securing the crossmember to the A-pillar on each side

29.58a Undo the upper outer bolt (arrowed) . . .

29.58b . . . and lower nut (arrowed) securing the crossmember to the body on each side

lift the facia from its location. Check that all wiring has been disconnected, then remove the facia from the car.

Refitting

49 Refitting is a reversal of removal ensuring that all wiring is correctly reconnected and all mounting securely tightened.

Facia crossmember

Note: *This is an involved operation entailing*

the disconnection of a multitude of wiring connectors. Make notes on the location of all disconnected wiring, or attach labels to the connectors, to avoid confusion when refitting.

Removal

50 Remove the facia as described previously in this Section.
51 Remove the steering column as described in Chapter 10.

52 Remove the passenger's airbag as described in Chapter 12.
53 Undo the retaining bolts and remove the electronics modules from the crossmember on each side.
54 Disconnect all remaining earth cables and wiring connections, making careful notes as to their locations.
55 Undo the upper and lower retaining bolts and remove the crossmember centre brace.
56 Undo the bolts securing the crossmember to the heater/air conditioning system air distribution housing.
57 From outside the car, undo the long throughbolt securing the crossmember to the A-pillar on each side **(see illustration)**.
58 Undo the upper and lower outer bolt and nut securing the crossmember to the body on each side **(see illustrations)**.
59 With the help of an assistant, check that all wiring has been disconnected, then remove the crossmember from the car.

Refitting

60 Refitting is a reversal of removal ensuring that all wiring is correctly reconnected and all mounting securely tightened.

Chapter 12
Body electrical systems

Contents

Degrees of difficulty

Easy, suitable for novice with little experience	**Fairly easy,** suitable for beginner with some experience	**Fairly difficult,** suitable for competent DIY mechanic	**Difficult,** suitable for experienced DIY mechanic	**Very difficult,** suitable for expert DIY or professional

Specifications

System type . . . . 12 volt negative earth

Bulbs   **Wattage**

Direction indicator side repeater 5
Direction indicator 21
Front foglight 55
Headlight 55
Interior lights. 10
Number plate light 10
Rear foglight 21
Reversing light 21
Sidelight 5
Stop/tail-light 21/5

1 General information and precautions

⚠️ **Warning: Before carrying out any work on the electrical system, read through the precautions given in 'Safety first!' at the beginning of this manual, and in Chapter 5A.**

1 The electrical system is of the 12 volt negative earth type. Power for the lights and all electrical accessories is supplied by a lead-acid type battery, which is charged by the engine-driven alternator.

2 This Chapter covers repair and service procedures for the various electrical components not associated with the engine. Information on the battery, alternator and starter motor can be found in Chapter 5A.

3 It should be noted that, prior to working on any component in the electrical system, the battery negative terminal should first be disconnected, to prevent the possibility of electrical short-circuits and/or fires.

Caution: Before proceeding, refer to 'Disconnecting the battery' in the Reference Chapter for further information.

2 Electrical fault finding – general information

Note: *Refer to the precautions given in 'Safety first!' and in Section 1 before starting work. The following tests relate to testing of the main electrical circuits, and should not be used to test delicate electronic circuits (such as the anti-lock braking system or fuel injection system), particularly where an electronic control unit is used.*

General

1 A typical electrical circuit consists of an electrical component, any switches, relays, motors, fuses, fusible links or circuit breakers related to that component, and the wiring and connectors which link the component to both the battery and the vehicle body. To help to pinpoint a problem in an electrical circuit, wiring diagrams are shown at the end of this Chapter.

2 Before attempting to diagnose an electrical fault, first study the appropriate wiring diagram to obtain a complete understanding of the components included in the particular circuit concerned. The possible sources of a fault can be narrowed down by noting if other components related to the circuit are operating properly. If several components or circuits fail at one time, the problem is likely to be related to a shared fuse or earth connection.

3 Electrical problems usually stem from simple causes, such as loose or corroded connections, a faulty earth connection, a blown fuse, a melted fusible link, or a faulty relay (refer to Section 3 for details of testing relays). Inspect the condition of all fuses, wires and connections in a problem circuit before testing the components. Use the wiring diagrams to determine which terminal connections will need to be checked in order to pinpoint the trouble-spot.

4 The basic tools required for electrical fault finding include a circuit tester or voltmeter (a 12 volt bulb with a set of test leads can also be used for certain tests); a self-powered test light (sometimes known as a continuity tester); an ohmmeter (to measure resistance); a battery and set of test leads; and a jumper wire, preferably with a circuit breaker or fuse incorporated, which can be used to bypass suspect wires or electrical components. Before attempting to locate a problem with test instruments, use the wiring diagram to determine where to make the connections.

5 To find the source of an intermittent wiring fault (usually due to a poor or dirty connection, or damaged wiring insulation), a 'wiggle' test can be performed on the wiring. This involves wiggling the wiring by hand to see if the fault occurs as the wiring is moved. It should be possible to narrow down the source of the fault to a particular section of wiring. This method of testing can be used in conjunction with any of the tests described in the following sub-Sections.

6 Apart from problems due to poor connections, two basic types of fault can occur in an electrical circuit – open-circuit, or short-circuit.

7 Open-circuit faults are caused by a break somewhere in the circuit, which prevents current from flowing. An open-circuit fault will prevent a component from working, but will not cause the relevant circuit fuse to blow.

8 Short-circuit faults are caused by a 'short' somewhere in the circuit, which allows the current flowing in the circuit to 'escape' along an alternative route, usually to earth. Short-circuit faults are normally caused by a breakdown in wiring insulation, which allows a feed wire to touch either another wire, or an earthed component such as the bodyshell. A short-circuit fault will normally cause the relevant circuit fuse to blow.

Finding an open-circuit

9 To check for an open-circuit, connect one lead of a circuit tester or voltmeter to either the negative battery terminal or a known good earth.

10 Connect the other lead to a connector in the circuit being tested, preferably nearest to the battery or fuse.

11 Switch on the circuit, bearing in mind that some circuits are live only when the ignition switch is turned to a particular position.

12 If voltage is present (indicated either by the tester bulb lighting or a voltmeter reading, as applicable), this means that the section of the circuit between the relevant connector and the battery is problem-free.

13 Continue to check the remainder of the circuit in the same fashion.

14 When a point is reached at which no voltage is present, the problem must lie between that point and the previous test point with voltage. Most problems can be traced to a broken, corroded or loose connection.

Finding a short-circuit

15 To check for a short-circuit, first disconnect the load(s) from the circuit (loads are the components which draw current from a circuit, such as bulbs, motors, heating elements, etc).

16 Remove the relevant fuse from the circuit, and connect a circuit tester or voltmeter to the fuse connections.

17 Switch on the circuit, bearing in mind that some circuits are live only when the ignition switch is turned to a particular position.

18 If voltage is present (indicated either by the tester bulb lighting or a voltmeter reading, as applicable), this means that there is a short-circuit.

19 If no voltage is present, but the fuse still blows with the load(s) connected, this indicates an internal fault in the load(s).

Finding an earth fault

20 The battery negative terminal is connected to 'earth' – the metal of the engine/transmission unit and the car body – and most systems are wired so that they only receive a positive feed, the current returning via the metal of the car body. This means that the component mounting and the body form part of that circuit. Loose or corroded mountings can therefore cause a range of electrical faults, ranging from total failure of a circuit, to a puzzling partial fault. In particular, lights may shine dimly (especially when another circuit sharing the same earth point is in operation), motors (eg, wiper motors or the radiator cooling fan motor) may run slowly, and the operation of one circuit may have an apparently-unrelated effect on another. Note that on many vehicles, earth straps are used between certain components, such as the engine/transmission and the body, usually where there is no metal-to-metal contact between components, due to flexible rubber mountings, etc.

21 To check whether a component is properly earthed, disconnect the battery, and connect one lead of an ohmmeter to a known good earth point. Connect the other lead to the wire or earth connection being tested. The resistance reading should be zero; if not, check the connection as follows.

22 If an earth connection is thought to be faulty, dismantle the connection, and clean back to bare metal both the bodyshell and the wire terminal or the component earth connection mating surface. Be careful to remove all traces of dirt and corrosion, then use a knife to trim away any paint, so that a clean metal-to-metal joint is made. On reassembly, tighten the joint fasteners securely; if a wire terminal is being refitted, use serrated washers between the terminal

and the bodyshell, to ensure a clean and secure connection. When the connection is remade, prevent the onset of corrosion in the future by applying a coat of petroleum jelly or silicone-based grease. Alternatively, at regular intervals, spray on a proprietary ignition sealer or a water-dispersant lubricant.

3 Fuses and relays – general information

Fuses

1 The main fuses are located behind a cover on the left-hand edge of the facia, with additional fuses and relays located in the fuse/relay box on the left-hand side of the engine compartment, and in the left-hand side of the luggage compartment.
2 To gain access to the facia fuses, pull open and remove the cover (see illustration).
3 To gain access to the engine compartment fuses, open the battery box cover and lift the lid off the fusebox (see illustration).
4 Access to the fuses in the luggage compartment can be gained by opening the stowage compartment cover (see illustration).
5 To remove a fuse, first switch off the circuit concerned (or the ignition), then pull the fuse out of its terminals using the plastic removal tool provided (see illustration). The wire within the fuse is clearly visible; if the fuse is blown, it will be broken or melted.
6 Always renew a fuse with one of an identical rating; never use a fuse with a different rating from the original, nor substitute anything else. Never renew a fuse more than once without tracing the source of the trouble. The fuse rating is stamped on top of the fuse; note that the fuses are also colour-coded for easy recognition.
7 If a new fuse blows immediately, find the cause before renewing it again; a short to earth as a result of faulty insulation is most likely. Where a fuse protects more than one circuit, try to isolate the defect by switching on each circuit in turn (if possible) until the fuse blows again. Always carry a supply of spare fuses of each relevant rating on the vehicle, a spare of each rating should be clipped into the base of the fuse/relay box.

Relays

8 Most of the relays are located in the fuse/relay box in the engine compartment (see illustration 3.3).
9 If a circuit or system controlled by a relay develops a fault and the relay is suspect, operate the system; if the relay is functioning, it should be possible to hear it click as it is energised. If this is the case, the fault lies with the components or wiring of the system. If the relay is not being energised, then either the relay is not receiving a main supply or a switching voltage, or the relay itself is faulty.

3.2 Pull open and remove the cover for access to the fuses in the facia

3.4 Access to the fuses in the luggage compartment can be gained by opening the stowage compartment cover

Testing is by the substitution of a known good unit, but be careful; while some relays are identical in appearance and in operation, others look similar but perform different functions.
10 To renew a relay, first ensure that the ignition switch is off. The relay can then simply be pulled out from the socket and the new relay pressed in.

4 Switches – removal and refitting

Note: *Disconnect the battery negative terminal (refer to 'Disconnecting the battery' in the Reference Chapter) before removing any switch, and reconnect the terminal after refitting.*

Ignition switch/ steering column lock

1 Refer to Chapter 10.

4.4a Press switch the knob in and turn it to the vertical position . . .

3.3 Open the battery box cover and lift off the fusebox lid for access to the engine compartment fuses

3.5 Pull the fuse out of its terminals using the plastic removal tool provided

Steering column switches

2 The direction indicator and windscreen wiper switches are an integral part of the steering column electronics module, and cannot be individually renewed.
3 To remove the steering column electronics module, which also contains the airbag rotary connector, proceed as described in Section 23.

Lighting switch assembly

4 With the light switch knob in the off position, press the knob in and turn it to the vertical position (sidelights 'on'). The switch assembly internal catch is now unlocked and the switch assembly can be withdrawn from the facia (see illustrations). Once the switch is released, turn the switch off.
5 Release the locking catch and disconnect the switch wiring connector.
6 Note that the switch assembly cannot be

4.4b . . . then withdraw the switch assembly from the facia

4.13a Carefully prise out the control switch assembly . . .

4.13b . . . and disconnect the wiring connector

4.21 Undo the retaining screw from the rear of the steering wheel to release the switches

dismantled; if any of its functions are faulty, the complete assembly must be renewed.

7 Reconnect the wiring connector and push the switch back into the facia.

Facia centre switches

8 Using a small screwdriver inserted at the top of the switch, carefully ease the relevant switch from its location.

9 To refit, push the switch back into position in the facia.

Heated rear window/ blower motor switch

10 The heated rear window and blower motor switches are an integral part of the heater control assembly. Removal and refitting procedures are contained in Chapter 3.

Handbrake warning light switch

11 Refer to Chapter 9.

5.2 Unscrew the plastic cover from the rear of the headlight

4.22 Unclip the switch surround from the steering wheel, then disconnect the switch wiring connector

Stop-light switch

12 Refer to Chapter 9.

Electric window/mirror switches

Driver's door

13 Carefully prise out the control switch assembly and disconnect the wiring connector **(see illustrations)**.

14 Refitting is the reverse of removal.

Passenger's door

15 Remove the front/rear door inner trim panel as described in Chapter 11.

16 Carefully release the retaining clips at the rear of the trim panel and remove the switch from the panel.

17 Refitting is the reverse of removal.

Air conditioning system switch

18 The air conditioning system control switch

5.3 Rotate the dipped beam bulbholder anti-clockwise to release the bayonet fitting

is an integral part of the heating/ventilation control unit, and cannot be removed. Should the switch become faulty, the complete control unit assembly must be renewed (see Chapter 3).

19 The air conditioning system control switch is an integral part of the heater control assembly. Removal and refitting procedures are contained in Chapter 3.

Steering wheel switches

20 Remove the driver's airbag as described in Section 23.

21 Turn the steering wheel so that the switch retaining screw opening is accessible, then undo the retaining screw from the rear of the steering wheel **(see illustration)**.

22 Unclip the switch surround from the steering wheel, then disconnect the wiring connector from the switch **(see illustration)**.

35 Refitting is the reverse of removal. On completion, refit the airbag as described in Section 23.

5 Bulbs (exterior lights) – renewal

General

1 Whenever a bulb is renewed, note the following points:

a) *Make sure the switch is in the OFF position, for the bulb you are working on.*

b) *Remember that if the light has just been in use, the bulb may be extremely hot.*

c) *Always check the bulb contacts and holder, ensuring that there is clean metal-to-metal contact between the bulb and its live(s) and earth. Clean off any corrosion or dirt before fitting a new bulb.*

d) *Wherever bayonet-type bulbs are fitted, ensure that the live contact(s) bear firmly against the bulb contact.*

e) *Always ensure that the new bulb is of the correct rating, and that it is completely clean before fitting it; this applies particularly to headlight/foglight bulbs.*

Halogen type headlight unit

Note 1: *If working on the left-hand headlight unit it will be necessary to unclip and remove the filler neck for the windscreen washer reservoir for access to the rear of the headlight unit. If working on the right-hand headlight unit, it will be necessary to unclip the intake duct from the air cleaner housing.*

Note 2: *The outer bulb in the headlight unit is the dipped beam bulb and the inner bulb is the main beam bulb.*

Dipped beam

2 Rotate the plastic cover anti-clockwise and remove it from the rear of the headlight unit **(see illustration)**.

3 Rotate the bulbholder anti-clockwise to release the bayonet fitting, then withdraw the bulbholder from the light unit **(see illustration)**.

5.4 Hold the bulb by its base and withdraw it from the bulbholder

5.7 Depress the catch and remove the plastic cover from the rear of the headlight

5.8 Rotate the main beam bulbholder anti-clockwise to release the bayonet fitting

5.9 Hold the bulb by its base and withdraw it from the bulbholder

5.13a Withdraw the sidelight bulbholder from the rear of the headlight unit

5.13b The bulb is a push-fit in the bulbholder

4 Hold the bulb by its base and withdraw it from the bulbholder **(see illustration)**. When handling the new bulb, use a tissue or clean cloth to avoid touching the glass with the fingers; moisture and grease from the skin can cause blackening and rapid failure of this type of bulb. If the glass is accidentally touched, wipe it clean using methylated spirit.

5 Fit the new bulb to the bulbholder, then refit the bulbholder to the headlight unit. Turn the bulbholder clockwise to lock it in position.

6 Refit the plastic cover to the rear of the headlight unit, then refit any components removed for access.

Main beam

7 Depress the catch and remove the plastic cover from the rear of the headlight unit **(see illustration)**.

8 Rotate the bulbholder anti-clockwise to release the bayonet fitting, then withdraw the bulbholder from the light unit **(see illustration)**.

9 Hold the bulb by its base and withdraw it from the bulbholder **(see illustration)**. When handling the new bulb, use a tissue or clean cloth to avoid touching the glass with the fingers; moisture and grease from the skin can cause blackening and rapid failure of this type of bulb. If the glass is accidentally touched, wipe it clean using methylated spirit.

10 Fit the new bulb to the bulbholder, then refit the bulbholder to the headlight unit. Turn the bulbholder clockwise to lock it in position.

11 Refit the plastic cover to the rear of the headlight unit, then refit any components removed for access.

Front sidelight

12 Depress the catch and remove the plastic cover from the rear of the headlight unit **(see illustration 5.7)**.

13 Withdraw the sidelight bulbholder from the rear of the headlight unit. The bulb is of the capless (push-fit) type, and can be removed by simply pulling it out of the bulbholder **(see illustrations)**.

14 Refitting is the reverse of the removal procedure, ensuring that the bulbholder is fully engaged. On completion, refit any components removed for access.

Front indicator

15 Twist the indicator bulbholder anti-clockwise, and remove it from the rear of the headlight unit **(see illustration)**.

16 The bulb is a bayonet fit in the holder, and can be removed by pressing it and twisting in an anti-clockwise direction **(see illustration)**.

17 Refitting is a reverse of the removal procedure. On completion, refit any components removed for access.

Xenon type headlight unit

⚠ *Warning: Xenon dipped beam headlights operate at very high voltage. Do not touch the associated wiring when the headlights are switched on.*

Note: *The outer bulb in the headlight unit is the dipped beam bulb and the inner bulb is the main beam bulb.*

Dipped beam

18 Remove the headlight unit as described in Section 7.

19 Undo the three screws and lift off the plastic cover at the rear of the headlight unit.

20 Disconnect the xenon starter unit from the bulb by turning it anti-clockwise.

21 Compress the legs of the retaining spring

5.15 Twist the indicator bulbholder anti-clockwise, and remove it from the rear of the headlight unit

5.16 The bulb is a bayonet fit in the bulbholder

5.31 Twist the cover and free it from the foglight unit

5.32 Release the spring clip and withdraw the foglight bulb from the light unit

5.33 Disconnect the wiring connector and remove the bulb

clip and pivot the clip off the bulb. Withdraw the bulb from the rear of the headlight unit.

22 When handling the new bulb, use a tissue or clean cloth to avoid touching the glass with the fingers; moisture and grease from the skin can cause blackening and rapid failure of this type of bulb. If the glass is accidentally touched, wipe it clean using methylated spirit.

23 Install the new bulb, ensuring that its locating tabs are correctly located in the headlight unit cut-outs. Secure the bulb with the retaining spring clip and reconnect the starter unit. Turn the starter unit clockwise to lock it in position

24 Refit the plastic cover to the rear of the unit, then refit the headlight unit as described in Section 7.

Main beam

25 Renewal of the main beam bulb is as described previously in this Section for the halogen type headlight unit.

Front sidelight

26 Renewal of the front sidelight bulb is as described previously in this Section for the halogen type headlight unit.

Front indicator

27 Renewal of the front indicator bulb is as described previously in this Section for the halogen type headlight unit.

Indicator side repeater

28 Push the light unit toward the front door, and release the front edge of the unit from the wing. If necessary, assist removal using a

suitable plastic wedge, taking great care not damage the painted finish of the wing.

29 Withdraw the light unit from the wing, and pull the bulbholder out of the light unit. The bulb is of the capless (push-fit) type, and can be removed by simply pulling it out of the bulbholder.

30 Refitting is a reverse of the removal procedure.

Front foglight

31 Twist the cover and free it from the foglight unit **(see illustration)**.

32 Release the spring clip and withdraw the foglight bulb from the light unit **(see illustration)**.

33 Disconnect the wiring connector and remove the bulb **(see illustration)**.

34 When handling the new bulb, use a tissue or clean cloth to avoid touching the glass with the fingers; moisture and grease from the skin can cause blackening and rapid failure of this type of bulb. If the glass is accidentally touched, wipe it clean using methylated spirit.

35 Connect the wiring connector to the new bulb.

36 Insert the new bulb, making sure it is correctly located, and secure it in position with the spring clip.

37 Refit the cover to the rear of the unit.

Rear light cluster

Saloon and Hatchback models

38 Press the catch and remove the access cover from the stowage compartment.

39 Reach in through the stowage compartment and disconnect the wiring connector from the bulbholder.

40 Depress the sides of the bulbholder in the area of the light unit retaining tabs and withdraw the bulbholder from the light unit **(see illustration)**.

41 The relevant bulb can then be renewed; all bulbs have a bayonet fitting **(see illustration)**. Note that the stop/tail-light bulb has offset locating pins, to prevent it being installed incorrectly.

42 Refitting is the reverse of the removal sequence, ensuring that the bulbholder locates securely into position.

Estate models – rear wing light cluster

43 Press the catch and remove the access cover from the stowage compartment.

44 Reach in through the stowage compartment and use the wheel brace from the tool kit to slacken the three light cluster plastic nuts **(see illustration)**.

45 Hold the light cluster from the outside and unscrew the plastic nuts by hand the rest of the way.

46 Withdraw the light cluster and disconnect the wiring connector **(see illustrations)**.

47 Undo the three retaining screws and separate the bulbholder from the light cluster **(see illustrations)**.

48 The relevant bulb can then be renewed; both bulbs have a bayonet fitting.

49 Refitting is the reverse of the removal sequence.

5.40 Depress the sides of the bulbholder in the area of the light unit retaining tabs (arrowed)

5.41 The relevant bulb can then be renewed

5.44 Slacken and remove the three light cluster plastic nuts (arrowed)

5.46a Withdraw the light cluster . . .

5.46b . . . and disconnect the wiring connector

5.47a Undo the three retaining screws (arrowed) . . .

5.47b . . . and separate the bulbholder from the light cluster

5.50 Undo the retaining screw located in the release handle aperture, and remove the release handle

5.51 Extract the centre pins and remove the plastic securing rivets

Estate models – tailgate light cluster

50 Open the tailgate, undo the retaining screw located in the release handle aperture, and remove the release handle **(see illustration)**.
51 Using a small screwdriver, extract the centre pins and remove the plastic securing rivets **(see illustration)**.
52 Pull the lower trim panel away from the tailgate to release the remaining internal clips and remove the panel from the tailgate **(see illustration)**.
53 Release the bulbholder bayonet fitting, and remove the relevant bulbholder from the light cluster **(see illustration)**.
54 The relevant bulb can then be renewed; all bulbs have a bayonet fitting.
55 Refitting is the reverse of the removal sequence.

Number plate light

56 Using a small flat-bladed screwdriver, carefully prise the light unit out from its location **(see illustration)**.
57 Lift the tab and disconnect the wiring

connector from the bulbholder **(see illustration)**.
58 Twist the bulbholder to remove it from the light unit, and remove the bulb **(see illustrations)**.

5.52 Pull the lower trim panel away from the tailgate to release the remaining internal clips

5.53 Release the bayonet fitting, and remove the relevant bulbholder from the light cluster

5.56 Carefully prise the number plate light unit out from its location

5.57 Lift the tab and disconnect the wiring connector

5.58a Twist the bulbholder to remove it from the light unit . . .

5.58b . . . and remove the push-fit bulb

59 Refitting is a reverse of the removal procedure.

High-level stop-light

60 The high-level stop-light bulbs are of the LED (light emitting diode) type and cannot be individually renewed. Remove the complete light unit as described in Section 7.

6 Bulbs (interior lights) – renewal

General

1 Refer to Section 5, paragraph 1.

Front courtesy light

2 Using a small screwdriver, carefully prise the light unit lens from the overhead console **(see illustration)**.

6.2 Carefully prise the light unit lens from the overhead console

3 Pull the relevant bulb from its socket **(see illustration)**.
4 Install the new bulb, ensuring that it is securely held in position by the contacts, and clip the light unit lens back into position.

Rear courtesy light

5 Using a suitable screwdriver, carefully prise the right-hand side of the light unit out of position, and withdraw the light unit.
6 Release the locking plate and disconnect the wiring connector. Remove the relevant bulb from the light unit.
7 Install the new bulb, ensuring that it is securely held in position by the contacts. Refit the wiring connector and locking plate, then clip the light unit back into position.

Luggage compartment light

8 Using a suitable screwdriver, carefully prise the light unit out of position, and release

6.3 Pull the relevant bulb from its socket

the bulb from the light unit contacts **(see illustrations)**.
9 Install the new bulb, ensuring that it is securely held in position by the contacts, and clip the light unit back into position.

Cigarette lighter/ ashtray illumination

10 Carefully prise up and remove the trim panel around the cigarette lighter **(see illustration)**.
11 Remove the ashtray from the centre console by opening the lid, depressing the internal tabs each side and lifting out **(see illustration)**.
12 Disconnect the wiring connector at the rear of the cigarette lighter socket.
13 Using a small screwdriver, carefully prise the cigarette lighter body out of the illumination ring, then remove the illumination ring from the console.

6.8a Carefully prise the luggage compartment light unit out of position . . .

6.8b . . . and release the bulb from the light unit contacts

6.10 Prise up and remove the trim panel around the cigarette lighter

6.11 Remove the ashtray by opening the lid, depressing the internal tabs each side and lifting out

6.16a Carefully prise the glovebox light unit out of position . . .

6.16b . . . then release the bulb from its contacts

7.2a Undo the two upper retaining bolts (arrowed) . . .

7.2b . . . and the lower retaining bolt (arrowed) . . .

7.2c . . . then withdraw the headlight unit . . .

7.2d . . . and disconnect the wiring connectors

7.3a Rotate the adjustment motor anti-clockwise to free it from the headlight unit . . .

7.3b . . . then unclip the balljoint from the rear of the light reflector

14 Pull the bulbholder out of the illumination ring and renew the bulb.

15 Refitting is a reverse of the removal procedure.

Glovebox light

16 Open the glovebox. Using a small flat-bladed screwdriver, carefully prise the light unit out of position, then release the bulb from its contacts **(see illustrations)**. Install the new bulb, ensuring it is securely held in position by the contacts, and clip the light unit back into position.

Switch illumination

17 All the switches are fitted with illumination bulbs; some are also fitted with a bulb to show when the circuit concerned is operating. These bulbs are an integral part of the switch assembly, and cannot be obtained separately.

> **7 Exterior light units –** removal and refitting

Note: *Disconnect the battery negative terminal (refer to 'Disconnecting the battery' in the Reference Chapter) before removing any light unit, and reconnect the terminal after refitting.*

Headlight

⚠ *Warning: Xenon dipped beam headlights operate at very high voltage. Do not touch the associated wiring when the headlights are switched on.*

1 Remove the front bumper as described in Chapter 11.

2 Undo the three retaining bolts and withdraw the headlight unit from the vehicle. Disconnect the wiring connectors from rear of the headlight unit as it is withdrawn **(see illustrations)**.

3 On models fitted with halogen type headlight units, the headlight beam adjustment motor can be removed and refitted as follows. Unclip the cover then rotate the adjustment motor anti-clockwise to free the motor from the rear of the headlight unit. Unclip the balljoint from the rear of the light reflector and disconnect the wiring connector **(see illustrations)**.

4 On refitting, align the motor balljoint with the light unit socket, and clip it into position. Engage the motor assembly with the light, and twist it clockwise to secure it in position.

5 Refitting is a reverse of the removal procedure. On completion, check the headlight beam alignment using the information given in Section 8.

Front indicator light

6 The front direction indicator lights are integral with the headlight units. Removal and refitting is as described above.

Indicator side repeater light

7 Push the light unit toward the front door, and release the front edge of the unit from the wing. If necessary, assist removal using a suitable plastic wedge, taking great care not damage the painted finish of the wing.

8 Withdraw the light unit from the wing, and disconnect its wiring connector. Tie a piece of

string to the wiring, to prevent it falling back into the wing.

9 On refitting, connect the wiring connector, and clip the light unit back into position.

Front foglight

10 Remove the front bumper as described in Chapter 11.

11 Undo the three foglight retaining bolts and remove the light unit from the bumper **(see illustration)**.

12 Refit the light unit to the bumper, and securely tighten its retaining bolts.

13 Refit the front bumper as described in Chapter 11.

Rear light cluster

Saloon and Hatchback models

14 Press the catch and remove the access cover from the stowage compartment.

7.11 Front foglight retaining bolts (arrowed)

7.16a Undo the three retaining nuts (arrowed) . . .

7.16b . . . and remove the light cluster from the rear wing

7.26 Extract the two blanking caps from the tailgate . . .

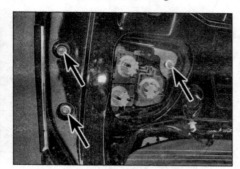

7.27 . . . and undo the light cluster retaining nuts (arrowed)

15 Reach in through the stowage compartment and disconnect the wiring connector from the bulbholder.

16 Undo the three retaining nuts and remove the light cluster from the rear wing (see illustrations).

17 Refitting is a reversal of removal.

Estate models – rear wing light cluster

18 Press the catch and remove the access cover from the stowage compartment.

19 Reach in through the stowage com-

7.33a Remove the trim caps over the upper side trim panel retaining screws . . .

7.33b . . . then undo the screw (arrowed) each side

7.34 Unscrew the parcel shelf lifting pins on each side

7.35 Prise free the side trim panel on each side to release the three retaining clips

partment and use the wheel brace from the tool kit to slacken the three light cluster plastic nuts (see illustration 5.44).

20 Hold the light cluster from the outside and unscrew the plastic nuts by hand the rest of the way.

21 Withdraw the light cluster and disconnect the wiring connector (see illustrations 5.46a and 5.46b)

22 Refitting is a reversal of removal.

Estate models – tailgate light cluster

23 Open the tailgate, undo the retaining screw located in the release handle aperture, and remove the release handle (see illustration 5.50).

24 Using a small screwdriver, extract the centre pins and remove the plastic securing rivets (see illustration 5.51).

25 Pull the lower trim panel away from the tailgate to release the remaining internal clips and remove the panel from the tailgate (see illustration 5.52).

26 Extract the blanking caps from the tailgate for access to the light cluster retaining nuts (see illustration).

27 Undo the three retaining nuts and remove the light unit from the tailgate (see illustration).

28 Refitting is a reversal of removal.

Number plate light

29 Using a small flat-bladed screwdriver, carefully prise the light unit out from its location (see illustration 5.56).

30 Lift the tab and disconnect the wiring connector from the bulbholder (see illustration 5.57).

31 Refitting is a reversal of removal.

High-level stop-light

Saloon models

32 To remove the high-level stop-light, it is necessary to drill holes in the inside of the boot lid panelling, for access to the stop-light retaining bolts. At the time of writing information on the position of these holes was not available. It is recommended that any problems with the high-level stop-light should be referred to a Vauxhall/Opel dealer.

Hatchback models

33 Open the tailgate and remove the trim caps over the upper side trim panel retaining screws. Undo the screw each side (see illustrations).

34 Unscrew the parcel shelf lifting pins on each side (see illustration).

35 Carefully prise free the side trim panel on each side to release the three retaining clips (see illustration).

36 Using a forked tool, or removal tool, extract the four stud retaining clips at the lower edge of the lower trim panel (see illustration).

37 Undo the retaining screws in the centre of the panel and pull out the centre pins of the four plastic rivets.

38 Pull the panel away from the tailgate to

7.36 Extract the four stud retaining clips at the lower edge of the lower trim panel

7.38 Pull the panel away from the tailgate to release the remaining internal clips

7.39a Compress the light unit locking clip (arrowed) with pliers, push in the lugs at the end . . .

release the remaining internal clips and remove the panel from the tailgate **(see illustration)**.

39 Working on one side of the light unit at a time, compress the locking clip with pliers, push in the lugs at the end and release one side of the unit from the tailgate **(see illustrations)**. Repeat this procedure on the other side.

40 Once the light unit is free, withdraw it from the tailgate and disconnect the wiring connector **(see illustration)**.

41 Reconnect the wiring connector then push the light unit into the tailgate until it locks in position.

Estate models

42 Open the tailgate, undo the retaining screw located in the release handle aperture, and remove the release handle **(see illustration 5.50)**.

43 Using a small screwdriver, extract the centre pins and remove the plastic securing rivets **(see illustration 5.51)**.

44 Pull the lower trim panel away from the tailgate to release the remaining internal clips and remove the panel from the tailgate **(see illustration 5.52)**.

45 Pull the upper trim panel away from the tailgate to release the internal retaining clips **(see illustration)**.

46 Disconnect the high-level stop-light wiring connector.

7.39b . . . and release one side of the unit at a time from the tailgate

47 Release the three retaining catches and remove the high-level stop-light from the tailgate upper trim panel **(see illustration)**.

48 Refitting is a reversal of removal.

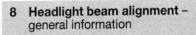

8 Headlight beam alignment – general information

1 Accurate adjustment of the headlight beam is only possible using optical beam-setting equipment, and this work should therefore be carried out by a Vauxhall/Opel dealer or suitably-equipped workshop.

2 For reference, the headlights can be adjusted

7.40 Withdraw the light unit from the tailgate and disconnect the wiring connector

using the adjuster assemblies fitted to the top of each light unit. The inner adjuster, alters the vertical position of the beam. The outer adjuster alters the horizontal aim of the beam.

3 Most models have an electrically-operated headlight beam adjustment system, controlled via a switch in the facia. The recommended settings are as follows.

0 Front seat(s) occupied
1 All seats occupied
2 All seats occupied, and load in luggage compartment
3 Driver's seat occupied and load in the luggage compartment

Note: *When adjusting the headlight aim, ensure that the switch is set to position 0.*

7.45 Pull the upper trim panel away from the tailgate to release the internal retaining clips

7.47 Release the retaining catches (arrowed) and remove the high-level stop-light from the trim panel

9.3a Undo the two lower retaining screws (arrowed) . . .

9.3b . . . then pull the instrument panel away from the facia at the bottom

9.4 Disengage the top of the panel from the facia and disconnect the wiring connector

9 Instrument panel – removal and refitting

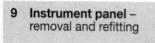

Note: *The instrument panel is a complete sealed assembly, and no dismantling of the instrument panel is possible.*

Removal

1 Disconnect the battery negative terminal (refer to *Disconnecting the battery* in the Reference Chapter).
2 Remove the steering column shrouds as described in Chapter 11, Section 29.
3 Undo the two lower retaining screws, then pull the panel away from the facia at the bottom **(see illustrations)**.
4 Disengage the top of the panel from the facia, disconnect the wiring connector and remove the panel from the car **(see illustration)**.

Refitting

5 Refitting is a reversal of removal.

10 Information display unit – removal and refitting

Removal

1 Disconnect the battery negative terminal (refer to *Disconnecting the battery* in the Reference Chapter).
2 Remove the centre vent housing as described in Chapter 3.
3 Undo the four screws and remove the information display unit from the centre vent housing **(see illustration)**.

Refitting

4 Refitting is a reversal of removal.

11 Cigarette lighter – removal and refitting

Proceed as described in Section 6, paragraphs 10 to 15.

12 Horn – removal and refitting

Removal

1 Firmly apply the handbrake, then jack up the front of the car and support it securely on axle stands (see *Jacking and vehicle support*).
2 Working under the bumper on the left-hand side, undo the retaining nut/bolt and remove the horn, disconnecting its wiring connector as they become accessible **(see illustration)**.

Refitting

3 Refitting is the reverse of removal.

13 Wiper arm – removal and refitting

10.3 Undo the screws (arrowed) and remove the information display unit from the centre vent housing

12.2 Horn retaining nut and wiring connector

Removal

1 Operate the wiper motor, then switch it off so that the wiper arm returns to the at-rest (parked) position.

 HAYNES HiNT *Stick a piece of masking tape along the edge of the wiper blade, to use as an alignment aid on refitting.*

2 Unclip the wiper arm spindle nut cover (windscreen wiper arm), or pivot the cover up (tailgate wiper arm), then slacken and remove the spindle nut and washer **(see illustrations)**.
3 Using a suitable puller, free the wiper arm from the spindle and remove the arm **(see**

13.2a Unclip the windscreen wiper arm spindle nut cover . . .

13.2b . . . then slacken and remove the spindle nut and washer

illustration). **Note:** *If both windscreen wiper arms are to be removed at the same time, mark them for identification. The arms are not interchangeable; the passenger-side wiper arm is longer than the driver's-side arm, and its shaft is also cranked slightly.*

Refitting

4 Ensure that the wiper arm and spindle splines are clean and dry, then refit the arm to the spindle, aligning the wiper blade with the tape fitted on removal. Refit the spindle nut, tightening it securely, and clip the nut cover back in position.

14 Windscreen wiper motor and linkage – removal and refitting

Removal

1 Disconnect the battery negative terminal (refer to *Disconnecting the battery* in the Reference Chapter).
2 Remove the wiper arms as described in the Section 13.
3 Remove the water deflector as described in Chapter 11, Section 23.
4 Undo the retaining bolts and disconnect the wiring connector from the wiper motor (**see illustrations**).
5 Undo the three retaining bolts, and remove the wiper motor and linkage assembly out from the vehicle (**see illustrations**).
6 If necessary, mark the relative positions of the motor shaft and linkage arm, then unscrew the retaining nut from the motor spindle. Free the wiper linkage from the spindle, then remove the three motor retaining bolts, and separate the motor and linkage (**see illustration**).

Refitting

7 Where necessary, assemble the motor and linkage, and securely tighten the motor retaining bolts. Locate the linkage arm on the motor spindle, aligning the marks made prior to removal, and securely tighten its retaining nut.
8 Manoeuvre the motor assembly back into position in the vehicle. Refit the retaining bolts, and tighten them securely.

13.3 Using a suitable puller, free the wiper arm from the spindle

9 Reconnect the wiper motor wiring connector.
10 Refit the water deflector as described in Chapter 11.
11 Install both the wiper arms as described in Section 13, and reconnect the battery negative terminal.

15 Tailgate wiper motor – removal and refitting

Removal

Hatchback models

1 Open the tailgate and remove the trim caps over the upper side trim panel retaining screws. Undo the screw each side (**see illustrations 7.33a and 7.33b**).

14.4a Undo the retaining bolts (two shown, arrowed) . . .

2 Unscrew the parcel shelf lifting pins on each side (**see illustration 7.34**).
3 Carefully prise free the side trim panel on each side to release the three retaining clips (**see illustration 7.35**).
4 Using a forked tool, or removal tool, extract the four stud retaining clips at the lower edge of the lower trim panel (**see illustration 7.36**).
5 Undo the retaining screws in the centre of the panel and pull out the centre pins of the four plastic rivets.
6 Pull the panel away from the tailgate to release the remaining internal clips and remove the panel from the tailgate (**see illustration 7.38**).

Estate models

7 Open the tailgate, undo the retaining screw located in the release handle aperture, and remove the release handle (**see illustration 5.50**).
8 Using a small screwdriver, extract the centre pins and remove the plastic securing rivets (**see illustration 5.51**).
9 Pull the lower trim panel away from the tailgate to release the remaining internal clips and remove the panel from the tailgate (**see illustration 5.52**).

All models

10 Remove the wiper arm as described in Section 13.
11 Disconnect the wiring connector, then slacken and remove the wiper motor mounting bolts and remove the wiper motor (**see illustrations**).

14.4b . . . and disconnect the wiring connector from the wiper motor

14.5a Undo the three retaining bolts (arrowed) . . .

14.5b . . . and remove the wiper motor and linkage assembly

14.6 Wiper motor retaining bolts (arrowed)

15.11a Disconnect the wiring connector . . .

Refitting

12 Refitting is the reverse of removal, ensuring the wiper motor retaining bolts are securely tightened.

16 Windscreen/tailgate washer system components – removal and refitting

Washer system reservoir

1 Remove the front bumper as described in Chapter 11.
2 If necessary, partially detach the wheel arch liner.
3 From within the engine compartment, unclip and remove the filler neck for the windscreen washer reservoir.
4 Disconnect the wiring connectors at the

16.5a Washer reservoir upper retaining nuts (arrowed) . . .

16.11 Depress the retaining clip, then carefully prise the washer nozzle from the water deflector panel

15.11b . . . then slacken and remove the tailgate wiper motor mounting bolts (arrowed)

washer pump(s) and washer fluid level sensor, as applicable.
5 Undo the two upper nuts, and one lower nut and remove the reservoir from under the car **(see illustrations)**.
6 Refitting is the reverse of removal, ensuring that the washer hose(s) are securely connected.

Washer pump

7 Remove the washer reservoir as described above.
8 Tip out the contents of the reservoir, then carefully ease the pump out from the reservoir and recover its sealing grommet.
9 Refitting is the reverse of removal, using a new sealing grommet if the original one shows signs of damage or deterioration.

Windscreen washer jets

10 Remove the water deflector as described in Chapter 11, Section 23.

16.5b . . . and lower retaining nut (arrowed)

16.14 Carefully prise the washer jet out of the radio aerial base

11 Depress the retaining clip, then carefully prise the nozzle from the water deflector panel **(see illustration)**.
12 Disconnect the nozzle from its fluid hose, and remove it from the vehicle.
13 On refitting, securely connect the nozzle to the hose, and clip it into position in the water deflector panel. Refit the water deflector panel, then check the operation of the jet. If necessary, adjust the nozzle using a pin, aiming the spray to a point slightly above the centre of the swept area.

Tailgate washer jet

14 Carefully prise the washer jet out of the radio aerial base and disconnect it from its supply pipe **(see illustration)**. Whilst the jet is removed, tie a piece of string to the supply pipe, to ensure that it does not fall back into the tailgate.
15 When refitting, ensure that the jet is clipped securely in position. Check the operation of the jet. If necessary, adjust the nozzle using a pin, aiming the spray to a point slightly above the centre of the swept area.

17 Radio/cassette/CD player – removal and refitting

Note: *The following removal and refitting procedure is for the range of radio/cassette/ CD units which Vauxhall/Opel fit as standard equipment. Removal and refitting procedures of non-standard units may differ slightly.*

Removal

1 All the radio/cassette/CD players fitted by Vauxhall have DIN standard fixings. Two special tools, obtainable from most car accessory shops, are required for removal. Alternatively, suitable tools can be fabricated from 3 mm diameter wire, such as welding rod.
2 Disconnect the battery negative terminal (refer to *Disconnecting the battery* in the Reference Chapter).
3 Insert the tools into the holes on the front of the unit, and push them until they snap into place. The radio/cassette/CD player can then be slid out of the facia **(see illustration)**.

17.3 Using welding rod to compress the clips (arrowed) on the radio/cassette/CD player

4 Disconnect the wiring and aerial connections at the rear of the unit, and remove the unit from the car.

Refitting

5 To refit the radio/cassette player/CD, reconnect the wiring and simply push the unit into the facia until the retaining lugs snap into place. On completion, reconnect the battery and enter the radio security code, where applicable.

18 Speakers – removal and refitting

Front small (tweeter) speaker

1 Remove the front door inner trim panel as described in Chapter 11, Section 12.
2 Carefully prise off the door mirror interior trim panel to release the two retaining clips (see illustration).
3 Disconnect the wiring connector from the mirror (see illustration).
4 Release the speaker wiring harness retaining clip from the interior trim panel, and disconnect the wiring connector (see illustrations). Remove the trim panel.
5 Remove the rubber pad from the panel base, then undo the three screws and remove the speaker from the panel (see illustration).
6 Refitting is the reverse of removal.

Rear small (tweeter) speaker

7 Remove the rear door inner trim panel as described in Chapter 11, Section 12.

8 Unclip the control switch panel from the door trim panel.
9 Unclip the speaker from the switch panel.
10 Refitting is the reverse of removal.

Large (bass) speaker

11 Remove the door inner trim panel as described in Chapter 11.
12 Undo the retaining screws, then free the speaker from the door (see illustration). Disconnect the wiring connectors and remove the speaker.
13 Refitting is the reverse of removal.

19 Radio aerial – general information

1 Where required, the aerial mast can be unscrewed from the base unit.
2 Removal of the base unit entails removal of the headlining, which is a complicated operation, considered to be outside the scope of this manual. Therefore, any problems relating to the aerial base unit or wiring should be entrusted to a Vauxhall/Opel dealer.

20 Anti-theft alarm system – general information

Note: This information is applicable only to the anti-theft alarm system fitted by Vauxhall/Opel as standard equipment.

1 Most models in the range are fitted with an anti-theft alarm system as standard equipment. The alarm is automatically armed and disarmed when the deadlocks are operated using the driver's door lock or remote control key. The alarm has switches on all the doors (including the tailgate), the bonnet, the radio/cassette/CD player and the ignition and starter circuits. If the tailgate, bonnet or any of the doors are opened whilst the alarm is set, the alarm horn will sound and the hazard warning lights will flash. The alarm also has an immobiliser function which makes the ignition and starter circuits inoperable whilst the alarm is triggered.
2 The alarm system performs a self-test every time it is switched on; this test takes approximately 10 seconds. During the self-test, the LED (light emitting diode) in the hazard warning light switch will come on. If the LED flashes, then either the tailgate, bonnet or one of the doors is open, or there is a fault in the circuit. After the initial 10 second period, the LED will flash to indicate that the alarm is switched on. On unlocking the driver's door lock, the LED will illuminate for approximately 1 second, then go out, indicating that the alarm has been switched off.
3 With the alarm set, if the tailgate is unlocked, the tailgate switch sensing will automatically be switched off, but the door and bonnet switches will still be active. Once the tailgate is shut and locked again, the tailgate switch sensing will be switched back on after approximately 10 seconds.
4 Should the alarm system develop a fault, the vehicle should be taken to a Vauxhall/Opel dealer for examination.

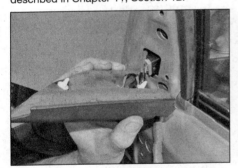

18.2 Carefully prise off the door mirror interior trim panel

18.3 Disconnect the wiring connector from the mirror

18.4a Release the wiring harness retaining clip from the interior trim panel . . .

18.4b . . . and disconnect the tweeter wiring connector

18.5 Undo the three screws (arrowed) and remove the speaker from the panel

18.12 Door loudspeaker retaining screws (arrowed)

23.2a Depress the airbag internal spring retainers . . .

21 Heated seat components – general information

On models with heated seats, a heater mat is fitted to both the seat back and seat cushion. Renewal of either heater mat involves peeling back the upholstery, removing the old mat, sticking the new mat in position and then refitting the upholstery. Note that upholstery removal and refitting requires considerable skill and experience if it is to be carried out successfully, and is therefore best entrusted to your Vauxhall/Opel dealer. In practice, it will be very difficult for the home mechanic to carry out the job without ruining the upholstery.

22 Airbag system – general information and precautions

General information

A driver's airbag is fitted as standard equipment on all models. The airbag is fitted in the steering wheel centre pad. Additionally, a passenger's airbag located in the facia, side airbags located in the front seats, and curtain airbags located in the headlining are optionally available.

The system is armed only when the ignition is switched on, however, a reserve power source maintains a power supply to the system in the event of a break in the main electrical

23.2b . . . and at the same time pull the airbag unit away from the steering wheel

supply. The steering wheel and facia airbags are activated by a 'g' sensor (deceleration sensor), and controlled by an electronic control unit located under the centre console. The side airbags and curtain airbags are activated by severe side impact and operate independently of the main system. A separate electrical supply, control unit and sensor is provided for the side/curtain airbags on each side of the car.

The airbags are inflated by a gas generator, which forces the bag out from its location in the steering wheel, facia, seat back frame, or headlining.

Precautions

⚠ *Warning: The following precautions must be observed when working on vehicles equipped with an airbag system, to prevent the possibility of personal injury.*

General precautions

The following precautions must be observed when carrying out work on a vehicle equipped with an airbag:

a) *Do not disconnect the battery with the engine running.*
b) *Before carrying out any work in the vicinity of the airbag, removal of any of the airbag components, or any welding work on the vehicle, de-activate the system as described in the following sub-Section.*
c) *Do not attempt to test any of the airbag system circuits using test meters or any other test equipment.*
d) *If the airbag warning light comes on, or any fault in the system is suspected, consult a Vauxhall/Opel dealer without delay.* **Do not** *attempt to carry out fault diagnosis, or any dismantling of the components.*

Precautions when handling an airbag

a) *Transport the airbag by itself, bag upward.*
b) *Do not put your arms around the airbag.*
c) *Carry the airbag close to the body, bag outward.*
d) *Do not drop the airbag or expose it to impacts.*
e) *Do not attempt to dismantle the airbag unit.*
f) *Do not connect any form of electrical equipment to any part of the airbag circuit.*

Precautions when storing an airbag

a) *Store the unit in a cupboard with the airbag upward.*
b) *Do not expose the airbag to temperatures above 80°C.*
c) *Do not expose the airbag to flames.*
d) *Do not attempt to dispose of the airbag – consult a Vauxhall/Opel dealer.*
e) *Never refit an airbag which is known to be faulty or damaged.*

De-activation of airbag system

The system must be de-activated

before carrying out any work on the airbag components or surrounding area:

a) *Switch on the ignition and check the operation of the airbag warning light on the instrument panel. The light should illuminate when the ignition is switched on, then extinguish.*
b) *Switch off the ignition.*
c) *Remove the ignition key.*
d) *Switch off all electrical equipment.*
e) *Disconnect the battery negative terminal (refer to 'Disconnecting the battery' in the Reference Chapter).*
f) *Insulate the battery negative terminal and the end of the battery negative lead to prevent any possibility of contact.*
g) *Wait for at least two minutes before carrying out any further work. Wait at least ten minutes if the airbag warning light did not operate correctly.*

Activation of airbag system

To activate the system on completion of any work, proceed as follows:

a) *Ensure that there are no occupants in the vehicle, and that there are no loose objects around the vicinity of the steering wheel. Close the vehicle doors and windows.*
b) *Ensure that the ignition is switched off then reconnect the battery negative terminal.*
c) *Open the driver's door and switch on the ignition, without reaching in front of the steering wheel. Check that the airbag warning light illuminates briefly then extinguishes.*
d) *Switch off the ignition.*
e) *If the airbag warning light does not operate as described in paragraph c), consult a Vauxhall/Opel dealer before driving the vehicle.*

23 Airbag system components – removal and refitting

⚠ *Warning: Refer to the precautions given in Section 22 before attempting to carry out work on any of the airbag components.*

1 De-activate the airbag system as described in the previous Section, then proceed as described under the relevant heading.

Driver's airbag

2 Insert a screwdriver into the holes on both sides of the rear of the steering wheel, to depress the internal spring retainers, and at the same time pull the airbag unit away from the steering wheel to release it **(see illustrations)**.
3 Release the locking clips, then disconnect the wiring connectors at the rear of the airbag unit **(see illustration)**. Remove the airbag unit. Note that the airbag must not be knocked or dropped, and should be stored the correct way up, with its padded surface uppermost.

23.3 Release the locking clips, then disconnect the wiring connectors

23.6 Passenger's airbag wiring connectors . . .

23.7 . . . and retaining bolts (arrowed)

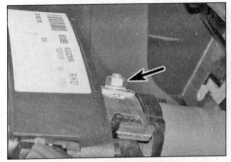

23.18a Slacken the upper clamp nut (arrowed) . . .

23.18b . . . and the lower clamp bolt (arrowed)

23.19 Disconnect the wiring connector and remove the module

4 Refitting is a reversal of the removal procedure.

Passenger's airbag

5 Remove the glovebox as described in Chapter 11, Section 29.

6 Disconnect the airbag wiring connector(s) from the side of the unit (see illustration).

7 Undo the two bolts securing the airbag to the facia crossmember and withdraw the airbag out through the glovebox aperture (see illustration). Note that the airbag must not be knocked or dropped, and should be stored the correct way up (as mounted in the vehicle).

8 Refitting is a reversal of the removal procedure, tightening the retaining bolts securely.

Side airbags

9 The side airbags are located internally within the front seat back and no attempt should be made to remove them. Any suspected

problems with the side airbag system should be referred to a Vauxhall/Opel dealer.

Curtain airbags

10 The curtain airbags are located behind the headlining above the doors on each side and no attempt should be made to remove them. Any suspected problems with curtain airbag system should be referred to a Vauxhall/Opel dealer.

Airbag control unit

11 The airbag control unit is located beneath the centre console and no attempt should be made to remove it. Any suspected problems with the control unit should be referred to a Vauxhall/Opel dealer.

Airbag rotary connector

12 The airbag rotary connector is an integral part of the steering column electronics

module. Removal and refitting procedures for the module are as follows:

13 Disconnect the battery negative terminal (refer to *Disconnecting the battery* in the Reference Chapter) and wait for 2 minutes.

14 Set the roadwheels in the straight-ahead position and ensure they remain in that position during the removal and refitting procedures.

15 Remove the steering wheel as described in Chapter 10.

16 Remove the steering column shrouds as described in Chapter 11, Section 29.

17 Mark the position of the electronics module in relation to the steering column.

18 Slacken the upper clamp nut, and the lower clamp bolt, and withdraw the module from the steering column (see illustrations).

19 Disconnect the wiring connector and remove the module (see illustration).

20 Refitting is a reversal of the removal procedure.

VAUXHALL VECTRA wiring diagrams

Diagram 1

Key to symbols

Bulb	⊗
Flashing bulb	⊗
Switch contact	—o o—
Fuse/fusible link and current rating	F5 30A
Wire splice, soldered joint or unspecified connection	
Connecting wires	
Variable resistor	
Resistor	

Item no.	2
Single speed pump/motor	Ⓜ
Gauge/meter	⊘
Earth point and location	E4
Diode	▶⊢
Light emitting diode (LED)	
Heating element	
Solenoid actuator	

Wire colour (blue with white tracer) — Bu/Wh

Dashed outline denotes part of a larger item, containing in this case an electronic or solid state device. e.g. connector no. XC30, pin 2.

XC30/2

Engine fusebox 2

Fuse	Rating	Circuit protected
F1	20A	Engine management, automatic transmission
F2	25A	Starter
F3	15A	Horn
F4	10A	Air conditioning, climate control
F5	15A	Wash/wipe system
F6	-	
F7	15A	Central control unit, ESP
F8	10A	Headlights, heated washer
F9	7.5A	Power steering
F10	10A	Adaptive lighting
F11	30A	Windscreen wiper
F12	30A	Windscreen wiper
F13	7.5A	Central control unit, ESP
F14	30A	Headlight wash system
F15	10A	Engine control unit
F16	7.5A	ABS
F17	-	
F18	-	
F19	10A	Adaptive lighting,
F19	5A	Headlight levelling
F19	15A	Xenon headlights
F20	5A	Headlight levelling
F21	-	
F22	30A	Wash/wipe
F23	20A	Auxiliary heating
F24	30A	Battery voltage, terminal 30
F25	30A	Battery voltage, terminal 30
F26	-	
F27	-	
F28	60A	Tailgate module control unit
F29	40A	ABS
F30	60A	Tailgate module control unit
F31	60A	Vehicle interior module control unit
F32	40A	ABS
F33	60A	Vehicle interior module control unit
F34	60A	Tailgate module control unit
F35	30A	Engine cooling fan
F36	20A	Engine cooling fan
F37	-	Adaptive lighting (slot for changing lighting for abroad)
F38	-	

Passenger fusebox 12

Fuse	Rating	Circuit protected
F1	20A	Infotainment system, DVD
F2	7.5A	Heater blower, heating, air conditioning
F3	20A	Sunroof
F4	-	
F5	7.5A	Door control units
F6	7.5A	Brake light
F7	30A	Body control unit
F8	30A	LH front door control unit
F9	7.5A	Central control unit
F10	7.5A	Steering column control unit
F11	7.5A	Diagnostic connector
F12	15A	Battery control unit
F13	-	
F14	-	
F15	30A	RH front door control unit
F16	-	
F17	15A	Instrument, info display
F18	7.5A	Ignition terminal 15, air conditioning
F19	-	
F20	7.5A	Yaw sensor (ESP)
F21	7.5A	Telematics
F22	30A	Cigar lighter, DVD
F23	40A	Heater blower, air conditioning, climate control
F24	-	
F25	7.5A	Heating, air conditioning
F26	7.5A	Instruments, info display
F27	-	

Rear fusebox 11

Fuse	Rating	Circuit protected
F1	-	-
F2	-	-
F3	40A	Electric seat adjustment
F4	40A	Heated rear window
F5	40A	Electric seat adjustment
F6	30A	RH rear electric window
F7	30A	LH rear electric window
F8	15A	RH rear seat heater
F9	15A	Horn, alarm
F10	20A	Fuel pump
F11	25A	Battery voltage
F12	15A	LH rear seat heater
F13	20A	Towing equipment
F14	15A	Rear wiper
F15	15A	LH front seat heater
F16	15A	RH front seat heater
F17	15A	Accessory socket
F18	30A	Tailgate lock
F19	10A	Terminal 30
F20	7.5A	Central locking
F21	5A	Alarm
F22	30A	Electrically operated tailgate
F23	7.5A	Alarm
F24	25A	Battery voltage
F25	10A	Electronic chassis
F26	25A	Terminal 15 (ignition lock)
F27	5A	Seat occupancy recognition, tyre pressure monitor, rain sensor, air conditioning
F28	7.5A	Parking distance sensor
F29	-	

Earth locations

E1	Engine compartment strut tower RH side
E2	RH 'A' pillar
E3	Instrument panel cross member front passenger side
E4	LH engine compartment
E5	Instrument panel cross member front passenger side
E6	LH front frame side member
E7	Rear panel RH side
E8	Transmission tunnel
E9	LH 'A' pillar
E10	Engine starter/alternator
E11	RH 'C' pillar
E12	Rear panel LH side
E13	On engine
E14	Steering column bracket
E15	On tailgate
E16	Engine compartment strut tower LH side
E17	Rear panel RH side

H33648

Wire colours

Bg	Beige	**LBu**	Light blue
Bk	Black	**LGn**	Light green
Bn	Brown	**Og**	Orange
DBu	Dark blue	**Bn**	Brown
DGn	Dark green	**Pu**	Purple
Ye	Yellow	**Pk**	Pink
Gn	Green	**Rd**	Red
Gy	Grey	**Wh**	White
Vt	Violet	**Bu**	Blue

Key to items

1   Battery
2   Engine fusebox
   a = under bonnet control unit
   k1 = starter relay
   k3 = terminal 15 relay
   k4 = horn relay
3   Starter motor
4   Alternator

5   LH horn
6   RH horn
7   Horn switch
8   Steering column control unit
9   Engine cooling fan & control unit

Diagram 2

H33649

Starting & charging

Horn

Single engine cooling fan

Dual engine cooling fan

Wire colours

Bg	Beige	**LBu**	Light blue
Bk	Black	**LGn**	Light green
Bn	Brown	**Og**	Orange
DBu	Dark blue	**Bn**	Brown
DGn	Dark green	**Pu**	Purple
Ye	Yellow	**Pk**	Pink
Gn	Green	**Rd**	Red
Gy	Grey	**Wh**	White
Vt	Violet	**Bu**	Blue

Key to items

1 Battery
2 Engine fusebox
   a = under bonnet control unit
   k3 = terminal 15 relay
8 Steering column control unit
11 Rear fusebox
   a = rear electronic control unit
12 Passenger fusebox
13 Stop light switch
14 Reversing light switch
15 LH rear light unit (saloon/hatch)
   a = reversing light
   b = stop light
   c = tail light

16 RH rear light unit (saloon/hatch)
   a = reversing light
   b = stop light
   c = tail light
17 LH inner rear light unit (estate)
   a = reversing light
   b = tail light
18 RH inner rear light unit (estate)
   a = reversing light
   b = tail light
19 High level brake light
20 LH outer rear light unit (estate)
   a = stop light

21 RH outer rear light unit (estate)
   a = stop light
22 Number plate light
23 LH front light unit
   a = side light
24 RH front light unit
   a = side light
25 Light switch
   a = side/headlight switch
26 Body control unit

Diagram 3

H33650

Stop & reversing lights

Side, tail & number plate lights

Diagram 4

Wire colours

Bg	Beige	LBu	Light blue
Bk	Black	LGn	Light green
Bn	Brown	Og	Orange
DBu	Dark blue	Bn	Brown
DGn	Dark green	Pu	Purple
Ye	Yellow	Pk	Pink
Gn	Green	Rd	Red
Gy	Grey	Wh	White
Vt	Violet	Bu	Blue

Key to items

1 Battery
2 Engine fusebox
  a = under bonnet control unit
11 Rear fusebox
  a = rear electronic control unit
15 LH rear light unit (saloon/hatch)
  e = direction indicator
16 RH rear light unit (saloon/hatch)
  d = foglight
  e = direction indicator
18 RH inner rear light unit (estate)
  c = foglight
20 LH outer rear light unit (estate)
  b = direction indicator

21 RH outer rear light unit (estate)
  b = direction indicator
23 LH front light unit
  b = main beam
  c = dip beam
  d = ignition module
  e = controller
  f = direction indicator
24 RH front light unit
  (as above)
25 Light switch
  a = side/headlight switch
  b = front foglight switch
  c = rear foglight switch

26 Body control unit
30 LH front fog light
31 RH front fog light
32 LH front indicator side repeater
33 RH front indicator side repeater
34 Hazard warning light switch
35 Trailer warning buzzer
36 Trailer hitch position switch
37 Trailer socket

H33651

Headlights

Direction indicators & hazard warning lights

Fog lights

Trailer socket

Wire colours

Bg	Beige	**LBu**	Light blue
Bk	Black	**LGn**	Light green
Bn	Brown	**Og**	Orange
DBu	Dark blue	**Bn**	Brown
DGn	Dark green	**Pu**	Purple
Ye	Yellow	**Pk**	Pink
Gn	Green	**Rd**	Red
Gy	Grey	**Wh**	White
Vt	Violet	**Bu**	Blue

Key to items

1   Battery
2   Engine fusebox
    a = under bonnet control unit
    k3 = terminal 15 relay
8   Steering column control unit
23 LH front light unit
    g = headlight levelling
24 RH front light unit
    g = headlight levelling
25 Light switch
    a = side/headlight switch
    d = headlight levelling

26 Body control unit
43 Headlight levelling control unit
44 Front level sensor
45 Rear level sensor
46 Front interior light
47 Rear interior light
48 Glovebox light
49 Luggage compartment light
50 Ashtray light
51 LH front door light
52 RH front door light
53 LH rear door light

54 RH rear door light
55 LH front door control unit
56 RH front door control unit
57 LH vanity mirror illumination
58 RH vanity mirror illumination

Diagram 5

H33652

**Headlight levelling –
without xenon lighting**

**Headlight levelling –
with xenon lighting**

Interior lighting

See diagram 9
Central locking

Wire colours

Bg	Beige	LBu	Light blue
Bk	Black	LGn	Light green
Bn	Brown	Og	Orange
DBu	Dark blue	Bn	Brown
DGn	Dark green	Pu	Purple
Ye	Yellow	Pk	Pink
Gn	Green	Rd	Red
Gy	Grey	Wh	White
Vt	Violet	Bu	Blue

Key to items

1 Battery
2 Engine fusebox
  a = under bonnet control unit
  k3 = terminal 15 relay
  k5 = front wiper slow/fast
  k6 = front wiper on/off
  k7 = headlight washer relay
  k9 = washer relay
8 Steering column control unit
11 Rear fusebox
  a = rear electronic control unit
  k1 = terminal 15 relay
  k2 = rear wiper relay

12 Passenger fusebox
  k3 = terminal 15 relay
26 Body control unit
60 Cigar lighter
61 Accessory socket
65 LH washer jet heater
66 RH washer jet heater
67 Front wiper motor
68 Rear wiper motor
69 Rain sensor
70 Screen washer pump
71 Headlight washer pump

Diagram 6

H33653

Cigar lighter & accessory socket

Heated washer jets

Wash/wipe & headlight washer

Wire colours

Bg	Beige	**LBu**	Light blue
Bk	Black	**LGn**	Light green
Bn	Brown	**Og**	Orange
DBu	Dark blue	**Bn**	Brown
DGn	Dark green	**Pu**	Purple
Ye	Yellow	**Pk**	Pink
Gn	Green	**Rd**	Red
Gy	Grey	**Wh**	White
Vt	Violet	**Bu**	Blue

Key to items

1 Battery
2 Engine fusebox
8 Steering column control unit
11 Rear fusebox
  a = rear electronic control unit
  k7 = heated rear window relay
12 Passenger fusebox
  k3 = terminal 15 relay
  k4 = blower relay
  k5 = blower relay
26 Body control unit

75 Heated rear window
76 Heater assembly
  a = control unit
  b = heater blower motor
  c = heater blower resistors
  d = recirculation flap motor
  e = air distriubution falp motor
  f = air mixer flap motor
77 Sunroof assembly
78 Sunroof switch

Diagram 7

H33654

Wire colours

Bg	Beige	**LBu**	Light blue
Bk	Black	**LGn**	Light green
Bn	Brown	**Og**	Orange
DBu	Dark blue	**Bn**	Brown
DGn	Dark green	**Pu**	Purple
Ye	Yellow	**Pk**	Pink
Gn	Green	**Rd**	Red
Gy	Grey	**Wh**	White
Vt	Violet	**Bu**	Blue

Key to items

1 Battery
2 Engine fusebox
8 Steering column control unit
12 Passenger fusebox
  k3 = terminal 15 relay
26 Body control unit
55 LH front door control unit
56 RH front door control unit

80 Instrument cluster
  a = illumination
  b = engine management warning light
  c = warning lights/gauges/display
81 Low washer fluid switch
82 LH front brake pad wear sensor
83 Low ccolant level switch
84 Handbrake switch

85 Low brake fluid level switch
86 LH mirror assembly
87 RH mirror assembly
88 RH front door switch unit
  a = mirror select switch
  b = mirror position switch

Diagram 8

H33655

Wire colours

Bg	Beige	**LBu**	Light blue
Bk	Black	**LGn**	Light green
Bn	Brown	**Og**	Orange
DBu	Dark blue	**Bn**	Brown
DGn	Dark green	**Pu**	Purple
Ye	Yellow	**Pk**	Pink
Gn	Green	**Rd**	Red
Gy	Grey	**Wh**	White
Vt	Violet	**Bu**	Blue

Key to items

1	Battery
2	Engine fusebox
11	Rear fusebox
	a = rear electronic control unit
	k8 = central locking relay (fuel filler flap)
12	Passenger fusebox
26	Body control unit
55	LH front door control unit
56	RH front door control unit
88	RH front door switch unit
	c = locking open/close
	d = tailgate release
	e = child security
	f = child security illumination
	g = switch illumination
90	LH front door switch unit
	c = locking open/close
	d = tailgate release
91	LH front door lock
92	LH rear door lock
93	RH front door lock
94	RH rear door lock
95	Tailgate unlock switch
96	Tailgate lock
97	Fuel filler flap motor

Diagram 9

H33656

Central locking

Wire colours

Bg	Beige	**LBu**	Light blue
Bk	Black	**LGn**	Light green
Bn	Brown	**Og**	Orange
DBu	Dark blue	**Bn**	Brown
DGn	Dark green	**Pu**	Purple
Ye	Yellow	**Pk**	Pink
Gn	Green	**Rd**	Red
Gy	Grey	**Wh**	White
Vt	Violet	**Bu**	Blue

Key to items

1 Battery
2 Engine fusebox
11 Rear fusebox
  a = rear electronic control unit
12 Passenger fusebox
26 Body control unit
55 LH front door control unit
56 RH front door control unit
88 RH front door switch unit
  h = LH front window switch
  i = RH front window switch
  j = window selector

90 LH front door switch unit
  h = LH front window switch
100 LH front window motor
101 LH rear window motor
102 RH front window motor
103 RH rear window motor
104 LH rear window switch
105 RH rear window switch

Diagram 10

H33657

Electric windows

Dimensions and weights

Note: *All figures are approximate and may vary according to model. Refer to manufacturer's data for exact figures.*

Dimensions

Overall length:
    Saloon and Hatchback. . . . . 4596 mm
    Estate . . . . 4822 mm
Overall width (including door mirrors) . . . . 2036 mm
Overall height (unladen):
    Saloon and Hatchback. . . . . 1460 mm
    Estate 1500
Wheelbase:
    Saloon and Hatchback. . . . . 2700 mm
    Estate . . . . 2830 mm
Turning circle diameter (wall to wall) . . . . 11.50 metres
Front track . . . . 1536 mm
Rear track. . . . . 1525 mm

Weights

Kerb weight:
    1.8 litre petrol engine models:
        Saloon. . . . . 1375 to 1395 kg
        Hatchback . . . . 1390 to 1410 kg
        Estate . . . . 1470 to 1490 kg
    2.2 litre petrol engine models:
        Saloon. . . . . 1435 to 1485 kg
        Hatchback . . . . 1450 to 1500 kg
        Estate . . . . 1530 to 1580 kg
    1.9 litre diesel models:
        Saloon. . . . . 1503 to 1548 kg
        Hatchback . . . . 1503 to 1580 kg
        Estate . . . . 1605 to 1633 kg
    2.0 litre diesel models:
        Saloon. . . . . 1490 to 1510 kg
        Hatchback . . . . 1505 to 1525 kg
        Estate . . . . 1580 to 1600 kg
    2.2 litre diesel models:
        Saloon. . . . . 1505 to 1550 kg
        Hatchback . . . . 1503 to 1548 kg
        Estate . . . . 1600 to 1633 kg
Gross vehicle weight . . . . Refer to information contained on the vehicle identification plate
Maximum roof load (including weight of rack):
    Saloon and Hatchback. . . . . 75 kg
    Estate . . . . 100 kg

Conversion factors

Length (distance)

Inches (in)	x 25.4	=	Millimetres (mm)	x 0.0394 =	Inches (in)
Feet (ft)	x 0.305	=	Metres (m)	x 3.281 =	Feet (ft)
Miles	x 1.609	=	Kilometres (km)	x 0.621 =	Miles

Volume (capacity)

Cubic inches (cu in; in³)	x 16.387	=	Cubic centimetres (cc; cm³)	x 0.061 =	Cubic inches (cu in; in³)
Imperial pints (Imp pt)	x 0.568	=	Litres (l)	x 1.76 =	Imperial pints (Imp pt)
Imperial quarts (Imp qt)	x 1.137	=	Litres (l)	x 0.88 =	Imperial quarts (Imp qt)
Imperial quarts (Imp qt)	x 1.201	=	US quarts (US qt)	x 0.833 =	Imperial quarts (Imp qt)
US quarts (US qt)	x 0.946	=	Litres (l)	x 1.057 =	US quarts (US qt)
Imperial gallons (Imp gal)	x 4.546	=	Litres (l)	x 0.22 =	Imperial gallons (Imp gal)
Imperial gallons (Imp gal)	x 1.201	=	US gallons (US gal)	x 0.833 =	Imperial gallons (Imp gal)
US gallons (US gal)	x 3.785	=	Litres (l)	x 0.264 =	US gallons (US gal)

Mass (weight)

Ounces (oz)	x 28.35	=	Grams (g)	x 0.035 =	Ounces (oz)
Pounds (lb)	x 0.454	=	Kilograms (kg)	x 2.205 =	Pounds (lb)

Force

Ounces-force (ozf; oz)	x 0.278	=	Newtons (N)	x 3.6 =	Ounces-force (ozf; oz)
Pounds-force (lbf; lb)	x 4.448	=	Newtons (N)	x 0.225 =	Pounds-force (lbf; lb)
Newtons (N)	x 0.1	=	Kilograms-force (kgf; kg)	x 9.81 =	Newtons (N)

Pressure

Pounds-force per square inch (psi; lbf/in²; lb/in²)	x 0.070	=	Kilograms-force per square centimetre (kgf/cm²; kg/cm²)	x 14.223 =	Pounds-force per square inch (psi; lbf/in²; lb/in²)
Pounds-force per square inch (psi; lbf/in²; lb/in²)	x 0.068	=	Atmospheres (atm)	x 14.696 =	Pounds-force per square inch (psi; lbf/in²; lb/in²)
Pounds-force per square inch (psi; lbf/in²; lb/in²)	x 0.069	=	Bars	x 14.5 =	Pounds-force per square inch (psi; lbf/in²; lb/in²)
Pounds-force per square inch (psi; lbf/in²; lb/in²)	x 6.895	=	Kilopascals (kPa)	x 0.145 =	Pounds-force per square inch (psi; lbf/in²; lb/in²)
Kilopascals (kPa)	x 0.01	=	Kilograms-force per square centimetre (kgf/cm²; kg/cm²)	x 98.1 =	Kilopascals (kPa)
Millibar (mbar)	x 100	=	Pascals (Pa)	x 0.01 =	Millibar (mbar)
Millibar (mbar)	x 0.0145	=	Pounds-force per square inch (psi; lbf/in²; lb/in²)	x 68.947 =	Millibar (mbar)
Millibar (mbar)	x 0.75	=	Millimetres of mercury (mmHg)	x 1.333 =	Millibar (mbar)
Millibar (mbar)	x 0.401	=	Inches of water (inH₂O)	x 2.491 =	Millibar (mbar)
Millimetres of mercury (mmHg)	x 0.535	=	Inches of water (inH₂O)	x 1.868 =	Millimetres of mercury (mmHg)
Inches of water (inH₂O)	x 0.036	=	Pounds-force per square inch (psi; lbf/in²; lb/in²)	x 27.68 =	Inches of water (inH₂O)

Torque (moment of force)

Pounds-force inches (lbf in; lb in)	x 1.152	=	Kilograms-force centimetre (kgf cm; kg cm)	x 0.868 =	Pounds-force inches (lbf in; lb in)
Pounds-force inches (lbf in; lb in)	x 0.113	=	Newton metres (Nm)	x 8.85 =	Pounds-force inches (lbf in; lb in)
Pounds-force inches (lbf in; lb in)	x 0.083	=	Pounds-force feet (lbf ft; lb ft)	x 12 =	Pounds-force inches (lbf in; lb in)
Pounds-force feet (lbf ft; lb ft)	x 0.138	=	Kilograms-force metres (kgf m; kg m)	x 7.233 =	Pounds-force feet (lbf ft; lb ft)
Pounds-force feet (lbf ft; lb ft)	x 1.356	=	Newton metres (Nm)	x 0.738 =	Pounds-force feet (lbf ft; lb ft)
Newton metres (Nm)	x 0.102	=	Kilograms-force metres (kgf m; kg m)	x 9.804 =	Newton metres (Nm)

Power

Horsepower (hp)	x 745.7	=	Watts (W)	x 0.0013 =	Horsepower (hp)

Velocity (speed)

Miles per hour (miles/hr; mph)	x 1.609	=	Kilometres per hour (km/hr; kph)	x 0.621 =	Miles per hour (miles/hr; mph)

Fuel consumption*

Miles per gallon, Imperial (mpg)	x 0.354	=	Kilometres per litre (km/l)	x 2.825 =	Miles per gallon, Imperial (mpg)
Miles per gallon, US (mpg)	x 0.425	=	Kilometres per litre (km/l)	x 2.352 =	Miles per gallon, US (mpg)

Temperature

Degrees Fahrenheit = (°C x 1.8) + 32   Degrees Celsius (Degrees Centigrade; °C) = (°F - 32) x 0.56

It is common practice to convert from miles per gallon (mpg) to litres/100 kilometres (l/100km), where mpg x l/100 km = 282

Spare parts are available from many sources, including maker's appointed garages, accessory shops, and motor factors. To be sure of obtaining the correct parts, it will sometimes be necessary to quote the vehicle identification number. If possible, it can also be useful to take the old parts along for positive identification. Items such as starter motors and alternators may be available under a service exchange scheme – any parts returned should be clean.

Our advice regarding spare parts is as follows.

Officially appointed garages

This is the best source of parts which are peculiar to your car, and which are not otherwise generally available (eg, badges, interior trim, certain body panels, etc). It is also the only place at which you should buy parts if the vehicle is still under warranty.

Accessory shops

These are very good places to buy materials and components needed for the maintenance of your car (oil, air and fuel filters, light bulbs, drivebelts, greases, brake pads, touch-up paint, etc). Components of this nature sold by a reputable shop are of the same standard as those used by the car manufacturer.

Besides components, these shops also sell tools and general accessories, usually have convenient opening hours, charge lower prices, and can often be found close to home. Some accessory shops have parts counters where components needed for almost any repair job can be purchased or ordered.

Motor factors

Good factors will stock all the more important components which wear out comparatively quickly, and can sometimes supply individual components needed for the overhaul of a larger assembly (eg, brake seals and hydraulic parts, bearing shells, pistons, valves). They may also handle work such as cylinder block reboring, crankshaft regrinding, etc.

Tyre and exhaust specialists

These outlets may be independent, or members of a local or national chain. They frequently offer competitive prices when compared with a main dealer or local garage, but it will pay to obtain several quotes before making a decision. When researching prices, also ask what 'extras' may be added – for instance fitting a new valve and balancing the wheel are both commonly charged on top of the price of a new tyre.

Other sources

Beware of parts or materials obtained from market stalls, car boot sales or similar outlets. Such items are not invariably sub-standard, but there is little chance of compensation if they do prove unsatisfactory. In the case of safety-critical components such as brake pads, there is the risk not only of financial loss, but also of an accident causing injury or death.

Second-hand components or assemblies obtained from a car breaker can be a good buy in some circumstances, but his sort of purchase is best made by the experienced DIY mechanic.

Vehicle identification

Modifications are a continuing and unpublished process in vehicle manufacture, quite apart from major model changes. Spare parts manuals and lists are compiled upon a numerical basis, the individual vehicle numbers being essential to correct identification of the component required.

When ordering spare parts, always give as much information as possible. Quote the car model, year of manufacture and vehicle identification and/or engine numbers as appropriate.

The *vehicle identification plate* is attached to the front right-hand side door pillar **(see illustration)** and includes the Vehicle Identification Number (VIN), vehicle weight information and paint and trim colour codes.

The *Vehicle Identification Number (VIN)* is given on the vehicle identification plate and is also stamped into the body floor panel between the right-hand front seat and the door sill panel **(see illustration)**; lift the flap in the carpet to see it.

Vauxhall/Opel use a 'Car pass' scheme for vehicle identification. This is a card which is issued to the customer when the car is first purchased. It contains important information, eg, VIN number, key number and radio code. It also includes a special code for diagnostic equipment, therefore it must be kept in a secure place and not in the vehicle.

The engine number is stamped on a horizontal flat located on the front of the cylinder block, at the transmission end. The first part of the engine number gives the engine code – eg Z18XE.

Engine codes are as follows

1.8 litre (1796 cc) DOHC 16-valve petrol engine.............Z18XE and Z18XEL

2.2 litre (2198 cc) DOHC 16-valve petrol engine.............Z22SE and Z22YH

1.9 litre (1910 cc) SOHC 8-valve diesel engine.............Z19DT

1.9 litre (1910 cc) DOHC 16-valve diesel engine.............Z19DTH

2.0 litre (1994 cc) SOHC 16-valve diesel engine.............Y20DTH

2.2 litre (2171 cc) SOHC 16-valve diesel engine.............Y22DTR

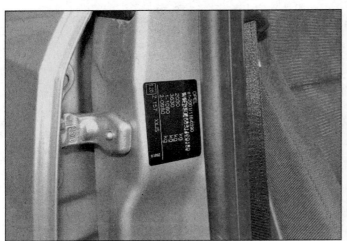

Vehicle Identification Number (VIN) plate attached to the front right-hand side door pillar

The VIN number is stamped into the body floor next to the right-hand front seat

Whenever servicing, repair or overhaul work is carried out on the car or its components, observe the following procedures and instructions. This will assist in carrying out the operation efficiently and to a professional standard of workmanship.

Joint mating faces and gaskets

When separating components at their mating faces, never insert screwdrivers or similar implements into the joint between the faces in order to prise them apart. This can cause severe damage which results in oil leaks, coolant leaks, etc upon reassembly. Separation is usually achieved by tapping along the joint with a soft-faced hammer in order to break the seal. However, note that this method may not be suitable where dowels are used for component location.

Where a gasket is used between the mating faces of two components, a new one must be fitted on reassembly; fit it dry unless otherwise stated in the repair procedure. Make sure that the mating faces are clean and dry, with all traces of old gasket removed. When cleaning a joint face, use a tool which is unlikely to score or damage the face, and remove any burrs or nicks with an oilstone or fine file.

Make sure that tapped holes are cleaned with a pipe cleaner, and keep them free of jointing compound, if this is being used, unless specifically instructed otherwise.

Ensure that all orifices, channels or pipes are clear, and blow through them, preferably using compressed air.

Oil seals

Oil seals can be removed by levering them out with a wide flat-bladed screwdriver or similar implement. Alternatively, a number of self-tapping screws may be screwed into the seal, and these used as a purchase for pliers or some similar device in order to pull the seal free.

Whenever an oil seal is removed from its working location, either individually or as part of an assembly, it should be renewed.

The very fine sealing lip of the seal is easily damaged, and will not seal if the surface it contacts is not completely clean and free from scratches, nicks or grooves. If the original sealing surface of the component cannot be restored, and the manufacturer has not made provision for slight relocation of the seal relative to the sealing surface, the component should be renewed.

Protect the lips of the seal from any surface which may damage them in the course of fitting. Use tape or a conical sleeve where possible. Lubricate the seal lips with oil before fitting and, on dual-lipped seals, fill the space between the lips with grease.

Unless otherwise stated, oil seals must be fitted with their sealing lips toward the lubricant to be sealed.

Use a tubular drift or block of wood of the appropriate size to install the seal and, if the seal housing is shouldered, drive the seal down to the shoulder. If the seal housing is unshouldered, the seal should be fitted with its face flush with the housing top face (unless otherwise instructed).

Screw threads and fastenings

Seized nuts, bolts and screws are quite a common occurrence where corrosion has set in, and the use of penetrating oil or releasing fluid will often overcome this problem if the offending item is soaked for a while before attempting to release it. The use of an impact driver may also provide a means of releasing such stubborn fastening devices, when used in conjunction with the appropriate screwdriver bit or socket. If none of these methods works, it may be necessary to resort to the careful application of heat, or the use of a hacksaw or nut splitter device.

Studs are usually removed by locking two nuts together on the threaded part, and then using a spanner on the lower nut to unscrew the stud. Studs or bolts which have broken off below the surface of the component in which they are mounted can sometimes be removed using a stud extractor. Always ensure that a blind tapped hole is completely free from oil, grease, water or other fluid before installing the bolt or stud. Failure to do this could cause the housing to crack due to the hydraulic action of the bolt or stud as it is screwed in.

When tightening a castellated nut to accept a split pin, tighten the nut to the specified torque, where applicable, and then tighten further to the next split pin hole. Never slacken the nut to align the split pin hole, unless stated in the repair procedure.

When checking or retightening a nut or bolt to a specified torque setting, slacken the nut or bolt by a quarter of a turn, and then retighten to the specified setting. However, this should not be attempted where angular tightening has been used.

For some screw fastenings, notably cylinder head bolts or nuts, torque wrench settings are no longer specified for the latter stages of tightening, "angle-tightening" being called up instead. Typically, a fairly low torque wrench setting will be applied to the bolts/nuts in the correct sequence, followed by one or more stages of tightening through specified angles.

Locknuts, locktabs and washers

Any fastening which will rotate against a component or housing during tightening should always have a washer between it and the relevant component or housing.

Spring or split washers should always be renewed when they are used to lock a critical component such as a big-end bearing retaining bolt or nut. Locktabs which are folded over to retain a nut or bolt should always be renewed.

Self-locking nuts can be re-used in non-critical areas, providing resistance can be felt when the locking portion passes over the bolt or stud thread. However, it should be noted that self-locking stiffnuts tend to lose their effectiveness after long periods of use, and should then be renewed as a matter of course.

Split pins must always be replaced with new ones of the correct size for the hole.

When thread-locking compound is found on the threads of a fastener which is to be re-used, it should be cleaned off with a wire brush and solvent, and fresh compound applied on reassembly.

Special tools

Some repair procedures in this manual entail the use of special tools such as a press, two or three-legged pullers, spring compressors, etc. Wherever possible, suitable readily-available alternatives to the manufacturer's special tools are described, and are shown in use. In some instances, where no alternative is possible, it has been necessary to resort to the use of a manufacturer's tool, and this has been done for reasons of safety as well as the efficient completion of the repair operation. Unless you are highly-skilled and have a thorough understanding of the procedures described, never attempt to bypass the use of any special tool when the procedure described specifies its use. Not only is there a very great risk of personal injury, but expensive damage could be caused to the components involved.

Environmental considerations

When disposing of used engine oil, brake fluid, antifreeze, etc, give due consideration to any detrimental environmental effects. Do not, for instance, pour any of the above liquids down drains into the general sewage system, or onto the ground to soak away. Many local council refuse tips provide a facility for waste oil disposal, as do some garages. If none of these facilities are available, consult your local Environmental Health Department, or the National Rivers Authority, for further advice.

With the universal tightening-up of legislation regarding the emission of environmentally-harmful substances from motor vehicles, most vehicles have tamperproof devices fitted to the main adjustment points of the fuel system. These devices are primarily designed to prevent unqualified persons from adjusting the fuel/air mixture, with the chance of a consequent increase in toxic emissions. If such devices are found during servicing or overhaul, they should, wherever possible, be renewed or refitted in accordance with the manufacturer's requirements or current legislation.

OIL CARE
FOLLOW THE CODE

OIL BANK LINE
0800 66 33 66
www.oilbankline.org.uk

Note: It is antisocial and illegal to dump oil down the drain. To find the location of your local oil recycling bank, call this number free.

The jack supplied with the vehicle tool kit should only be used for changing roadwheels – see *Wheel changing* at the front of this manual. Ensure the jack head is correctly engaged before attempting to raise the vehicle. When carrying out any other kind of work, raise the vehicle using a hydraulic jack, and always supplement the jack with axle stands positioned under the vehicle jacking points.

When jacking up the vehicle with a trolley jack, position the jack head under one of the relevant jacking points. Use a block of wood between the jack or axle stand and the sill – the block of wood should have a groove cut into it , in which the welded flange of the sill will locate. **Do not** jack the vehicle under the sump or any of the steering or suspension components. Supplement the jack using axle stands **(see illustrations)**.

⚠️ *Warning: Never work under, around, or near a raised vehicle, unless it is adequately supported in at least two places.*

Front jacking point for hydraulic jack or axle stands

Rear jacking point for hydraulic jack or axle stands

Axle stands should be placed under, or adjacent to the jacking point (arrowed)

Disconnecting the battery

Numerous systems fitted to the vehicle require battery power to be available at all times, either to ensure their continued operation (such as the clock) or to maintain control unit memories which would be erased if the battery were to be disconnected. Whenever the battery is to be disconnected therefore, first note the following, to ensure that there are no unforeseen consequences of this action:

a) *First, on any vehicle with central locking, it is a wise precaution to remove the key from the ignition, and to keep it with you, so that it does not get locked in, if the central locking should engage accidentally when the battery is reconnected.*

b) *Depending on model and specification, the Vauxhall anti-theft alarm system may be of the type which is automatically activated when the vehicle battery is disconnected and/or reconnected. To prevent the alarm sounding on models so equipped, switch the ignition on, then off, and disconnect the battery within15 seconds. If the alarm is activated when the battery is reconnected, switch the ignition on then off to deactivate the alarm.*

c) *If a security-coded audio unit is fitted, and the unit and/or the battery is disconnected, the unit will not function again on reconnection until the correct*

security code is entered. Details of this procedure, which varies according to the unit fitted, are given in the vehicle audio system operating instructions. Ensure you have the correct code before you disconnect the battery. If you do not have the code or details of the correct procedure, but can supply proof of ownership and a legitimate reason for wanting this information, a Vauxhall dealer may be able to help.

d) *The engine management electronic control unit is of the 'self-learning' type, meaning that as it operates, it also monitors and stores the settings which give optimum engine performance under all operating conditions. When the battery is disconnected, these settings are lost and the ECU reverts to the base settings programmed into its memory at the factory. On restarting, this may lead to the engine running/idling roughly for a short while, until the ECU has re-learned the optimum settings. This process is best accomplished by taking the vehicle on a road test (for approximately 15 minutes), covering all engine speeds and loads, concentrating mainly in the 2500 to 3500 rpm region.*

e) *On models equipped with automatic transmission, the transmission selector lever assembly incorporates an*

electrically-operated selector lever lock mechanism that prevents the lever being moved out of the P position unless the ignition is switched on and the brake pedal is depressed. If the selector lever is in the P position and the battery is disconnected, it will not be possible to move the selector lever out of position P by the normal means. Although it is possible to manually override the system (see Chapter 7B), it is sensible to move the selector lever to the N position before disconnecting the battery.

f) *On models with electric windows, it will be necessary to reprogramme the motors to restore the one-touch function of the buttons, after reconnection of the battery. To do this, fully close both front windows. With the windows closed, depress the up button of the driver's side window for approximately 5 seconds, then release it and depress the passenger side window up button for approximately 5 seconds.*

g) *On models with an electric sliding sunroof, it will be necessary to fully open and fully close the sunroof after battery reconnection, to recalibrate the sensors.*

h) *On all models, when reconnecting the battery after disconnection, switch on the ignition and wait 10 seconds to allow the electronic vehicle systems to stabilise and re-initialise.*

Introduction

A selection of good tools is a fundamental requirement for anyone contemplating the maintenance and repair of a motor vehicle. For the owner who does not possess any, their purchase will prove a considerable expense, offsetting some of the savings made by doing-it-yourself. However, provided that the tools purchased meet the relevant national safety standards and are of good quality, they will last for many years and prove an extremely worthwhile investment.

To help the average owner to decide which tools are needed to carry out the various tasks detailed in this manual, we have compiled three lists of tools under the following headings: *Maintenance and minor repair*, *Repair and overhaul*, and *Special*. Newcomers to practical mechanics should start off with the *Maintenance and minor repair* tool kit, and confine themselves to the simpler jobs around the vehicle. Then, as confidence and experience grow, more difficult tasks can be undertaken, with extra tools being purchased as, and when, they are needed. In this way, a *Maintenance and minor repair* tool kit can be built up into a *Repair and overhaul* tool kit over a considerable period of time, without any major cash outlays. The experienced do-it-yourselfer will have a tool kit good enough for most repair and overhaul procedures, and will add tools from the *Special* category when it is felt that the expense is justified by the amount of use to which these tools will be put.

Maintenance and minor repair tool kit

The tools given in this list should be considered as a minimum requirement if routine maintenance, servicing and minor repair operations are to be undertaken. We recommend the purchase of combination spanners (ring one end, open-ended the other); although more expensive than open-ended ones, they do give the advantages of both types of spanner.

- ☐ *Combination spanners:*
  Metric - 8 to 19 mm inclusive
- ☐ *Adjustable spanner - 35 mm jaw (approx.)*
- ☐ *Spark plug spanner (with rubber insert) - petrol models*
- ☐ *Spark plug gap adjustment tool - petrol models*
- ☐ *Set of feeler gauges*
- ☐ *Brake bleed nipple spanner*
- ☐ *Screwdrivers:*
  Flat blade - 100 mm long x 6 mm dia
  Cross blade - 100 mm long x 6 mm dia
  Torx - various sizes (not all vehicles)
- ☐ *Combination pliers*
- ☐ *Hacksaw (junior)*
- ☐ *Tyre pump*
- ☐ *Tyre pressure gauge*
- ☐ *Oil can*
- ☐ *Oil filter removal tool*
- ☐ *Fine emery cloth*
- ☐ *Wire brush (small)*
- ☐ *Funnel (medium size)*
- ☐ *Sump drain plug key (not all vehicles)*

Repair and overhaul tool kit

These tools are virtually essential for anyone undertaking any major repairs to a motor vehicle, and are additional to those given in the *Maintenance and minor repair* list. Included in this list is a comprehensive set of sockets. Although these are expensive, they will be found invaluable as they are so versatile - particularly if various drives are included in the set. We recommend the half-inch square-drive type, as this can be used with most proprietary torque wrenches.

The tools in this list will sometimes need to be supplemented by tools from the *Special* list:

- ☐ *Sockets (or box spanners) to cover range in previous list (including Torx sockets)*
- ☐ *Reversible ratchet drive (for use with sockets)*
- ☐ *Extension piece, 250 mm (for use with sockets)*
- ☐ *Universal joint (for use with sockets)*
- ☐ *Flexible handle or sliding T "breaker bar" (for use with sockets)*
- ☐ *Torque wrench (for use with sockets)*
- ☐ *Self-locking grips*
- ☐ *Ball pein hammer*
- ☐ *Soft-faced mallet (plastic or rubber)*
- ☐ *Screwdrivers:*
  Flat blade - long & sturdy, short (chubby), and narrow (electrician's) types
  Cross blade – long & sturdy, and short (chubby) types
- ☐ *Pliers:*
  Long-nosed
  Side cutters (electrician's)
  Circlip (internal and external)
- ☐ *Cold chisel - 25 mm*
- ☐ *Scriber*
- ☐ *Scraper*
- ☐ *Centre-punch*
- ☐ *Pin punch*
- ☐ *Hacksaw*
- ☐ *Brake hose clamp*
- ☐ *Brake/clutch bleeding kit*
- ☐ *Selection of twist drills*
- ☐ *Steel rule/straight-edge*
- ☐ *Allen keys (inc. splined/Torx type)*
- ☐ *Selection of files*
- ☐ *Wire brush*
- ☐ *Axle stands*
- ☐ *Jack (strong trolley or hydraulic type)*
- ☐ *Light with extension lead*
- ☐ *Universal electrical multi-meter*

Sockets and reversible ratchet drive

Brake bleeding kit

Torx key, socket and bit

Hose clamp

Angular-tightening gauge

Special tools

The tools in this list are those which are not used regularly, are expensive to buy, or which need to be used in accordance with their manufacturers' instructions. Unless relatively difficult mechanical jobs are undertaken frequently, it will not be economic to buy many of these tools. Where this is the case, you could consider clubbing together with friends (or joining a motorists' club) to make a joint purchase, or borrowing the tools against a deposit from a local garage or tool hire specialist. It is worth noting that many of the larger DIY superstores now carry a large range of special tools for hire at modest rates.

The following list contains only those tools and instruments freely available to the public, and not those special tools produced by the vehicle manufacturer specifically for its dealer network. You will find occasional references to these manufacturers' special tools in the text of this manual. Generally, an alternative method of doing the job without the vehicle manufacturers' special tool is given. However, sometimes there is no alternative to using them. Where this is the case and the relevant tool cannot be bought or borrowed, you will have to entrust the work to a dealer.

- ☐ Angular-tightening gauge
- ☐ Valve spring compressor
- ☐ Valve grinding tool
- ☐ Piston ring compressor
- ☐ Piston ring removal/installation tool
- ☐ Cylinder bore hone
- ☐ Balljoint separator
- ☐ Coil spring compressors (where applicable)
- ☐ Two/three-legged hub and bearing puller
- ☐ Impact screwdriver
- ☐ Micrometer and/or vernier calipers
- ☐ Dial gauge
- ☐ Stroboscopic timing light
- ☐ Dwell angle meter/tachometer
- ☐ Fault code reader
- ☐ Cylinder compression gauge
- ☐ Hand-operated vacuum pump and gauge
- ☐ Clutch plate alignment set
- ☐ Brake shoe steady spring cup removal tool
- ☐ Bush and bearing removal/installation set
- ☐ Stud extractors
- ☐ Tap and die set
- ☐ Lifting tackle
- ☐ Trolley jack

Buying tools

Reputable motor accessory shops and superstores often offer excellent quality tools at discount prices, so it pays to shop around.

Remember, you don't have to buy the most expensive items on the shelf, but it is always advisable to steer clear of the very cheap tools. Beware of 'bargains' offered on market stalls or at car boot sales. There are plenty of good tools around at reasonable prices, but always aim to purchase items which meet the relevant national safety standards. If in doubt, ask the proprietor or manager of the shop for advice before making a purchase.

Care and maintenance of tools

Having purchased a reasonable tool kit, it is necessary to keep the tools in a clean and serviceable condition. After use, always wipe off any dirt, grease and metal particles using a clean, dry cloth, before putting the tools away. Never leave them lying around after they have been used. A simple tool rack on the garage or workshop wall for items such as screwdrivers and pliers is a good idea. Store all normal spanners and sockets in a metal box. Any measuring instruments, gauges, meters, etc, must be carefully stored where they cannot be damaged or become rusty.

Take a little care when tools are used. Hammer heads inevitably become marked, and screwdrivers lose the keen edge on their blades from time to time. A little timely attention with emery cloth or a file will soon restore items like this to a good finish.

Working facilities

Not to be forgotten when discussing tools is the workshop itself. If anything more than routine maintenance is to be carried out, a suitable working area becomes essential.

It is appreciated that many an owner-mechanic is forced by circumstances to remove an engine or similar item without the benefit of a garage or workshop. Having done this, any repairs should always be done under the cover of a roof.

Wherever possible, any dismantling should be done on a clean, flat workbench or table at a suitable working height.

Any workbench needs a vice; one with a jaw opening of 100 mm is suitable for most jobs. As mentioned previously, some clean dry storage space is also required for tools, as well as for any lubricants, cleaning fluids, touch-up paints etc, which become necessary.

Another item which may be required, and which has a much more general usage, is an electric drill with a chuck capacity of at least 8 mm. This, together with a good range of twist drills, is virtually essential for fitting accessories.

Last, but not least, always keep a supply of old newspapers and clean, lint-free rags available, and try to keep any working area as clean as possible.

Micrometers

Dial test indicator ("dial gauge")

Strap wrench

Compression tester

Fault code reader

This is a guide to getting your vehicle through the MOT test. Obviously it will not be possible to examine the vehicle to the same standard as the professional MOT tester. However, working through the following checks will enable you to identify any problem areas before submitting the vehicle for the test.

Where a testable component is in borderline condition, the tester has discretion in deciding whether to pass or fail it. The basis of such discretion is whether the tester would be happy for a close relative or friend to use the vehicle with the component in that condition. If the vehicle presented is clean and evidently well cared for, the tester may be more inclined to pass a borderline component than if the vehicle is scruffy and apparently neglected.

It has only been possible to summarise the test requirements here, based on the regulations in force at the time of printing. Test standards are becoming increasingly stringent, although there are some exemptions for older vehicles.

An assistant will be needed to help carry out some of these checks.

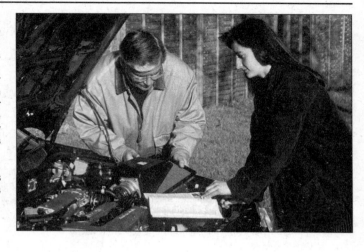

The checks have been sub-divided into four categories, as follows:

1 Checks carried out **FROM THE DRIVER'S SEAT**

2 Checks carried out **WITH THE VEHICLE ON THE GROUND**

3 Checks carried out **WITH THE VEHICLE RAISED AND THE WHEELS FREE TO TURN**

4 Checks carried out on **YOUR VEHICLE'S EXHAUST EMISSION SYSTEM**

---

1 Checks carried out **FROM THE DRIVER'S SEAT**

Handbrake

☐ Test the operation of the handbrake. Excessive travel (too many clicks) indicates incorrect brake or cable adjustment.

☐ Check that the handbrake cannot be released by tapping the lever sideways. Check the security of the lever mountings.

Footbrake

☐ Depress the brake pedal and check that it does not creep down to the floor, indicating a master cylinder fault. Release the pedal, wait a few seconds, then depress it again. If the pedal travels nearly to the floor before firm resistance is felt, brake adjustment or repair is necessary. If the pedal feels spongy, there is air in the hydraulic system which must be removed by bleeding.

☐ Check that the brake pedal is secure and in good condition. Check also for signs of fluid leaks on the pedal, floor or carpets, which would indicate failed seals in the brake master cylinder.

☐ Check the servo unit (when applicable) by operating the brake pedal several times, then keeping the pedal depressed and starting the engine. As the engine starts, the pedal will move down slightly. If not, the vacuum hose or the servo itself may be faulty.

Steering wheel and column

☐ Examine the steering wheel for fractures or looseness of the hub, spokes or rim.

☐ Move the steering wheel from side to side and then up and down. Check that the steering wheel is not loose on the column, indicating wear or a loose retaining nut. Continue moving the steering wheel as before, but also turn it slightly from left to right.

☐ Check that the steering wheel is not loose on the column, and that there is no abnormal

movement of the steering wheel, indicating wear in the column support bearings or couplings.

Windscreen, mirrors and sunvisor

☐ The windscreen must be free of cracks or other significant damage within the driver's field of view. (Small stone chips are acceptable.) Rear view mirrors must be secure, intact, and capable of being adjusted.

290mm

☐ The driver's sunvisor must be capable of being stored in the "up" position.

Seat belts and seats

Note: *The following checks are applicable to all seat belts, front and rear.*

☐ Examine the webbing of all the belts (including rear belts if fitted) for cuts, serious fraying or deterioration. Fasten and unfasten each belt to check the buckles. If applicable, check the retracting mechanism. Check the security of all seat belt mountings accessible from inside the vehicle.

☐ Seat belts with pre-tensioners, once activated, have a "flag" or similar showing on the seat belt stalk. This, in itself, is not a reason for test failure.

☐ The front seats themselves must be securely attached and the backrests must lock in the upright position.

Doors

☐ Both front doors must be able to be opened and closed from outside and inside, and must latch securely when closed.

2 Checks carried out WITH THE VEHICLE ON THE GROUND

Vehicle identification

☐ Number plates must be in good condition, secure and legible, with letters and numbers correctly spaced – spacing at (A) should be at least twice that at (B).

☐ The VIN plate and/or homologation plate must be legible.

Electrical equipment

☐ Switch on the ignition and check the operation of the horn.

☐ Check the windscreen washers and wipers, examining the wiper blades; renew damaged or perished blades. Also check the operation of the stop-lights.

☐ Check the operation of the sidelights and number plate lights. The lenses and reflectors must be secure, clean and undamaged.

☐ Check the operation and alignment of the headlights. The headlight reflectors must not be tarnished and the lenses must be undamaged.

☐ Switch on the ignition and check the operation of the direction indicators (including the instrument panel tell-tale) and the hazard warning lights. Operation of the sidelights and stop-lights must not affect the indicators - if it does, the cause is usually a bad earth at the rear light cluster.

☐ Check the operation of the rear foglight(s), including the warning light on the instrument panel or in the switch.

☐ The ABS warning light must illuminate in accordance with the manufacturers' design. For most vehicles, the ABS warning light should illuminate when the ignition is switched on, and (if the system is operating properly) extinguish after a few seconds. Refer to the owner's handbook.

Footbrake

☐ Examine the master cylinder, brake pipes and servo unit for leaks, loose mountings, corrosion or other damage.

☐ The fluid reservoir must be secure and the fluid level must be between the upper (**A**) and lower (**B**) markings.

☐ Inspect both front brake flexible hoses for cracks or deterioration of the rubber. Turn the steering from lock to lock, and ensure that the hoses do not contact the wheel, tyre, or any part of the steering or suspension mechanism. With the brake pedal firmly depressed, check the hoses for bulges or leaks under pressure.

Steering and suspension

☐ Have your assistant turn the steering wheel from side to side slightly, up to the point where the steering gear just begins to transmit this movement to the roadwheels. Check for excessive free play between the steering wheel and the steering gear, indicating wear or insecurity of the steering column joints, the column-to-steering gear coupling, or the steering gear itself.

☐ Have your assistant turn the steering wheel more vigorously in each direction, so that the roadwheels just begin to turn. As this is done, examine all the steering joints, linkages, fittings and attachments. Renew any component that shows signs of wear or damage. On vehicles with power steering, check the security and condition of the steering pump, drivebelt and hoses.

☐ Check that the vehicle is standing level, and at approximately the correct ride height.

Shock absorbers

☐ Depress each corner of the vehicle in turn, then release it. The vehicle should rise and then settle in its normal position. If the vehicle continues to rise and fall, the shock absorber is defective. A shock absorber which has seized will also cause the vehicle to fail.

Exhaust system

☐ Start the engine. With your assistant holding a rag over the tailpipe, check the entire system for leaks. Repair or renew leaking sections.

3 Checks carried out **WITH THE VEHICLE RAISED AND THE WHEELS FREE TO TURN**

Jack up the front and rear of the vehicle, and securely support it on axle stands. Position the stands clear of the suspension assemblies. Ensure that the wheels are clear of the ground and that the steering can be turned from lock to lock.

Steering mechanism

☐ Have your assistant turn the steering from lock to lock. Check that the steering turns smoothly, and that no part of the steering mechanism, including a wheel or tyre, fouls any brake hose or pipe or any part of the body structure.

☐ Examine the steering rack rubber gaiters for damage or insecurity of the retaining clips. If power steering is fitted, check for signs of damage or leakage of the fluid hoses, pipes or connections. Also check for excessive stiffness or binding of the steering, a missing split pin or locking device, or severe corrosion of the body structure within 30 cm of any steering component attachment point.

Front and rear suspension and wheel bearings

☐ Starting at the front right-hand side, grasp the roadwheel at the 3 o'clock and 9 o'clock positions and rock gently but firmly. Check for free play or insecurity at the wheel bearings, suspension balljoints, or suspension mountings, pivots and attachments.

☐ Now grasp the wheel at the 12 o'clock and 6 o'clock positions and repeat the previous inspection. Spin the wheel, and check for roughness or tightness of the front wheel bearing.

☐ If excess free play is suspected at a component pivot point, this can be confirmed by using a large screwdriver or similar tool and levering between the mounting and the component attachment. This will confirm whether the wear is in the pivot bush, its retaining bolt, or in the mounting itself (the bolt holes can often become elongated).

☐ Carry out all the above checks at the other front wheel, and then at both rear wheels.

Springs and shock absorbers

☐ Examine the suspension struts (when applicable) for serious fluid leakage, corrosion, or damage to the casing. Also check the security of the mounting points.

☐ If coil springs are fitted, check that the spring ends locate in their seats, and that the spring is not corroded, cracked or broken.

☐ If leaf springs are fitted, check that all leaves are intact, that the axle is securely attached to each spring, and that there is no deterioration of the spring eye mountings, bushes, and shackles.

☐ The same general checks apply to vehicles fitted with other suspension types, such as torsion bars, hydraulic displacer units, etc. Ensure that all mountings and attachments are secure, that there are no signs of excessive wear, corrosion or damage, and (on hydraulic types) that there are no fluid leaks or damaged pipes.

☐ Inspect the shock absorbers for signs of serious fluid leakage. Check for wear of the mounting bushes or attachments, or damage to the body of the unit.

Driveshafts (fwd vehicles only)

☐ Rotate each front wheel in turn and inspect the constant velocity joint gaiters for splits or damage. Also check that each driveshaft is straight and undamaged.

Braking system

☐ If possible without dismantling, check brake pad wear and disc condition. Ensure that the friction lining material has not worn excessively, (A) and that the discs are not fractured, pitted, scored or badly worn (B).

☐ Examine all the rigid brake pipes underneath the vehicle, and the flexible hose(s) at the rear. Look for corrosion, chafing or insecurity of the pipes, and for signs of bulging under pressure, chafing, splits or deterioration of the flexible hoses.

☐ Look for signs of fluid leaks at the brake calipers or on the brake backplates. Repair or renew leaking components.

☐ Slowly spin each wheel, while your assistant depresses and releases the footbrake. Ensure that each brake is operating and does not bind when the pedal is released.

☐ Examine the handbrake mechanism, checking for frayed or broken cables, excessive corrosion, or wear or insecurity of the linkage. Check that the mechanism works on each relevant wheel, and releases fully, without binding.

☐ It is not possible to test brake efficiency without special equipment, but a road test can be carried out later to check that the vehicle pulls up in a straight line.

Fuel and exhaust systems

☐ Inspect the fuel tank (including the filler cap), fuel pipes, hoses and unions. All components must be secure and free from leaks.

☐ Examine the exhaust system over its entire length, checking for any damaged, broken or missing mountings, security of the retaining clamps and rust or corrosion.

Wheels and tyres

☐ Examine the sidewalls and tread area of each tyre in turn. Check for cuts, tears, lumps, bulges, separation of the tread, and exposure of the ply or cord due to wear or damage. Check that the tyre bead is correctly seated on the wheel rim, that the valve is sound and properly seated, and that the wheel is not distorted or damaged.

☐ Check that the tyres are of the correct size for the vehicle, that they are of the same size

and type on each axle, and that the pressures are correct.

☐ Check the tyre tread depth. The legal minimum at the time of writing is 1.6 mm over at least three-quarters of the tread width. Abnormal tread wear may indicate incorrect front wheel alignment.

Body corrosion

☐ Check the condition of the entire vehicle structure for signs of corrosion in load-bearing areas. (These include chassis box sections, side sills, cross-members, pillars, and all suspension, steering, braking system and seat belt mountings and anchorages.) Any corrosion which has seriously reduced the thickness of a load-bearing area is likely to cause the vehicle to fail. In this case professional repairs are likely to be needed.

☐ Damage or corrosion which causes sharp or otherwise dangerous edges to be exposed will also cause the vehicle to fail.

4 Checks carried out on YOUR VEHICLE'S EXHAUST EMISSION SYSTEM

Petrol models

☐ The engine should be warmed up, and running well (ignition system in good order, air filter element clean, etc).

☐ Before testing, run the engine at around 2500 rpm for 20 seconds. Let the engine drop to idle, and watch for smoke from the exhaust. If the idle speed is too high, or if dense blue or black smoke emerges for more than 5 seconds, the vehicle will fail. Typically, blue smoke signifies oil burning (engine wear); black smoke means unburnt fuel (dirty air cleaner element, or other fuel system fault).

☐ An exhaust gas analyser for measuring carbon monoxide (CO) and hydrocarbons (HC) is now needed. If one cannot be hired or borrowed, have a local garage perform the check.

CO emissions (mixture)

☐ The MOT tester has access to the CO limits for all vehicles. The CO level is measured at idle speed, and at 'fast idle' (2500 to 3000 rpm). The following limits are given as a general guide:

At idle speed – Less than 0.5% CO
At 'fast idle' – Less than 0.3% CO
Lambda reading – 0.97 to 1.03

☐ If the CO level is too high, this may point to poor maintenance, a fuel injection system problem, faulty lambda (oxygen) sensor or catalytic converter. Try an injector cleaning treatment, and check the vehicle's ECU for fault codes.

HC emissions

☐ The MOT tester has access to HC limits for all vehicles. The HC level is measured at 'fast idle' (2500 to 3000 rpm). The following limits are given as a general guide:

At 'fast idle' – Less then 200 ppm

☐ Excessive HC emissions are typically caused by oil being burnt (worn engine), or by a blocked crankcase ventilation system ('breather'). If the engine oil is old and thin, an oil change may help. If the engine is running badly, check the vehicle's ECU for fault codes.

Diesel models

☐ The only emission test for diesel engines is measuring exhaust smoke density, using a calibrated smoke meter. The test involves accelerating the engine at least 3 times to its maximum unloaded speed.

Note: *On engines with a timing belt, it is VITAL that the belt is in good condition before the test is carried out.*

☐ With the engine warmed up, it is first purged by running at around 2500 rpm for 20 seconds. A governor check is then carried out, by slowly accelerating the engine to its maximum speed. After this, the smoke meter is connected, and the engine is accelerated quickly to maximum speed three times. If the smoke density is less than the limits given below, the vehicle will pass:

Non-turbo vehicles: 2.5m-1
Turbocharged vehicles: 3.0m-1

☐ If excess smoke is produced, try fitting a new air cleaner element, or using an injector cleaning treatment. If the engine is running badly, where applicable, check the vehicle's ECU for fault codes. Also check the vehicle's EGR system, where applicable. At high mileages, the injectors may require professional attention.

Engine

- [ ] Engine fails to rotate when attempting to start
- [ ] Engine rotates, but will not start
- [ ] Engine difficult to start when cold
- [ ] Engine difficult to start when hot
- [ ] Starter motor noisy or excessively-rough in engagement
- [ ] Engine starts, but stops immediately
- [ ] Engine idles erratically
- [ ] Engine misfires at idle speed
- [ ] Engine misfires throughout the driving speed range
- [ ] Engine hesitates on acceleration
- [ ] Engine stalls
- [ ] Engine lacks power
- [ ] Engine backfires
- [ ] Oil pressure warning light illuminated with engine running
- [ ] Engine runs-on after switching off
- [ ] Engine noises

Cooling system

- [ ] Overheating
- [ ] Overcooling
- [ ] External coolant leakage
- [ ] Internal coolant leakage
- [ ] Corrosion

Fuel and exhaust systems

- [ ] Excessive fuel consumption
- [ ] Fuel leakage and/or fuel odour
- [ ] Excessive noise or fumes from exhaust system

Clutch

- [ ] Pedal travels to floor – no pressure or very little resistance
- [ ] Clutch fails to disengage (unable to select gears)
- [ ] Clutch slips (engine speed increases, with no increase in vehicle speed)
- [ ] Judder as clutch is engaged
- [ ] Noise when depressing or releasing clutch pedal

Manual transmission

- [ ] Noisy in neutral with engine running
- [ ] Noisy in one particular gear
- [ ] Difficulty engaging gears
- [ ] Jumps out of gear
- [ ] Vibration
- [ ] Lubricant leaks

Automatic transmission

- [ ] Fluid leakage
- [ ] Transmission fluid brown, or has burned smell
- [ ] General gear selection problems
- [ ] Transmission will not downshift (kickdown) with accelerator pedal fully depressed
- [ ] Engine will not start in any gear, or starts in gears other than Park or Neutral
- [ ] Transmission slips, shifts roughly, is noisy, or has no drive in forward or reverse gears

Driveshafts

- [ ] Vibration when accelerating or decelerating
- [ ] Clicking or knocking noise on turns (at slow speed on full-lock)

Braking system

- [ ] Vehicle pulls to one side under braking
- [ ] Noise (grinding or high-pitched squeal) when brakes applied
- [ ] Excessive brake pedal travel
- [ ] Brake pedal feels spongy when depressed
- [ ] Excessive brake pedal effort required to stop vehicle
- [ ] Judder felt through brake pedal or steering wheel when braking
- [ ] Brakes binding
- [ ] Rear wheels locking under normal braking

Suspension and steering

- [ ] Vehicle pulls to one side
- [ ] Wheel wobble and vibration
- [ ] Excessive pitching and/or rolling around corners, or during braking
- [ ] Wandering or general instability
- [ ] Excessively-stiff steering
- [ ] Excessive play in steering
- [ ] Lack of power assistance
- [ ] Tyre wear excessive

Electrical system

- [ ] Battery will not hold a charge for more than a few days
- [ ] Ignition/no-charge warning light remains illuminated with engine running
- [ ] Ignition/no-charge warning light fails to come on
- [ ] Lights inoperative
- [ ] Instrument readings inaccurate or erratic
- [ ] Horn inoperative, or unsatisfactory in operation
- [ ] Windscreen wipers inoperative, or unsatisfactory in operation
- [ ] Windscreen washers inoperative, or unsatisfactory in operation
- [ ] Electric windows inoperative, or unsatisfactory in operation
- [ ] Central locking system inoperative, or unsatisfactory in operation

Introduction

The vehicle owner who does his or her own maintenance according to the recommended service schedules should not have to use this section of the manual very often. Modern component reliability is such that, provided those items subject to wear or deterioration are inspected or renewed at the specified intervals, sudden failure is comparatively rare. Faults do not usually just happen as a result of sudden failure, but develop over a period of time. Major mechanical failures in particular are usually preceded by characteristic symptoms over hundreds or even thousands of miles. Those components which do occasionally fail without warning are often small and easily carried in the vehicle.

With any fault-finding, the first step is to decide where to begin investigations. Sometimes this is obvious, but on other occasions, a little detective work will be necessary. The owner who makes half a dozen haphazard adjustments or replacements may be successful in curing a fault (or its symptoms), but will be none the wiser if the fault recurs, and ultimately may have spent more time and money than was necessary. A calm and logical approach will be found to be more satisfactory in the long run. Always take into account any warning signs or abnormalities that may have been noticed in the period preceding the fault – power loss, high or low gauge readings, unusual smells,

etc – and remember that failure of components such as fuses or spark plugs may only be pointers to some underlying fault.

The pages which follow provide an easy-reference guide to the more common problems which may occur during the operation of the vehicle. These problems and their possible causes are grouped under headings denoting various components or systems, such as Engine, Cooling system, etc. The general Chapter which deals with the problem is also shown in brackets; refer to the relevant part of that Chapter for system-specific information. Whatever the fault, certain basic principles apply. These are as follows:

Verify the fault. This is simply a matter of

being sure that you know what the symptoms are before starting work. This is particularly important if you are investigating a fault for someone else, who may not have described it very accurately.

Don't overlook the obvious. For example, if the vehicle won't start, is there fuel in the tank? (Don't take anyone else's word on this particular point, and don't trust the fuel gauge either!) If an electrical fault is indicated, look for loose or broken wires before digging out the test gear.

Cure the disease, not the symptom. Substituting a flat battery with a fully-charged one will get you off the hard shoulder, but if the underlying cause is not attended to, the new battery will go the same way. Similarly, changing oil-fouled spark plugs for a new set will get you moving again, but remember that the reason for the fouling (if it wasn't simply an incorrect grade of plug) will have to be established and corrected.

Don't take anything for granted. Particularly, don't forget that a 'new' component may itself be defective (especially if it's been rattling around in the boot for months), and don't leave components out of a fault diagnosis sequence just because they are new or recently-fitted. When you do finally diagnose a difficult fault, you'll probably realise that all the evidence was there from the start.

Consider what work, if any, has recently been carried out. Many faults arise through careless or hurried work. For instance, if any work has been performed under the bonnet, could some of the wiring have been dislodged or incorrectly routed, or a hose trapped? Have all the fasteners been properly tightened? Were new, genuine parts and new gaskets used? There is often a certain amount of detective work to be done in this case, as an apparently-unrelated task can have far-reaching consequences.

Diesel fault diagnosis

The majority of starting problems on small diesel engines are electrical in origin. The mechanic who is familiar with petrol engines but less so with diesel may be inclined to view the diesel's injectors and pump in the same light as the spark plugs and distributor, but this is generally a mistake.

When investigating complaints of difficult starting for someone else, make sure that the correct starting procedure is understood and is being followed. Some drivers are unaware of the significance of the preheating warning light – many modern engines are sufficiently forgiving for this not to matter in mild weather, but with the onset of winter, problems begin.

As a rule of thumb, if the engine is difficult to start but runs well when it has finally got going, the problem is electrical (battery, starter motor or preheating system). If poor performance is combined with difficult starting, the problem is likely to be in the fuel system. The low-pressure (supply) side of the fuel system should be checked before suspecting the injectors and high-pressure pump. The most common fuel supply problem is air getting into the system, and any pipe from the fuel tank forwards must be scrutinised if air leakage is suspected. Normally the pump is the last item to suspect, since unless it has been tampered with, there is no reason for it to be at fault.

Engine

Engine fails to rotate when attempting to start

- [ ] Battery terminal connections loose or corroded (see *Weekly checks*)
- [ ] Battery discharged or faulty (Chapter 5A)
- [ ] Broken, loose or disconnected wiring in the starting circuit (Chapter 5A)
- [ ] Defective starter solenoid or ignition switch (Chapter 5A or 12)
- [ ] Defective starter motor (Chapter 5A)
- [ ] Starter pinion or flywheel ring gear teeth loose or broken (Chapter 2A, 2B, 2C, 2D or 2E or 5A)
- [ ] Engine earth strap broken or disconnected (Chapter 5A)
- [ ] Engine suffering 'hydraulic lock' (eg from water drawn into the engine after traversing flooded roads, or from a serious internal coolant leak) – consult a main dealer for advice
- [ ] Automatic transmission not in position P or N (Chapter 7B)

Engine rotates, but will not start

- [ ] Fuel tank empty
- [ ] Battery discharged (engine rotates slowly) (Chapter 5A)
- [ ] Battery terminal connections loose or corroded (see *Weekly checks*)
- [ ] Ignition components damp or damaged – petrol models (Chapter 1A or 5B)
- [ ] Immobiliser fault, or 'uncoded' ignition key being used (Chapter 12 or Roadside repairs)
- [ ] Broken, loose or disconnected wiring in the ignition circuit – petrol models (Chapter 1A or 5B)
- [ ] Worn, faulty or incorrectly-gapped spark plugs – petrol models (Chapter 1A)
- [ ] Preheating system faulty – diesel models (Chapter 5A)
- [ ] Fuel injection/engine management system fault (Chapter 4A, 4B or 4C)
- [ ] Air in fuel system – diesel models (Chapter 4B)
- [ ] Major mechanical failure (eg timing /beltchain snapped) (Chapter 2A, 2B, 2C, 2D or 2E)

Engine difficult to start when cold

- [ ] Battery discharged (Chapter 5A)
- [ ] Battery terminal connections loose or corroded (see *Weekly checks*)

- [ ] Worn, faulty or incorrectly-gapped spark plugs – petrol models (Chapter 1A)
- [ ] Other ignition system fault – petrol models (Chapter 1A or 5B)
- [ ] Preheating system faulty – diesel models (Chapter 5A)
- [ ] Fuel injection/engine management system fault (Chapter 4A, 4B or 4C)
- [ ] Wrong grade of engine oil used (*Weekly checks*, Chapter 1A or 1B)
- [ ] Low cylinder compression (Chapter 2A, 2B, 2C, 2D or 2E)

Engine difficult to start when hot

- [ ] Air filter element dirty or clogged (Chapter 1A or 1B)
- [ ] Fuel injection/engine management system fault (Chapter 4A, 4B or 4C)
- [ ] Low cylinder compression (Chapter 2A, 2B, 2C, 2D or 2E)

Starter motor noisy or excessively-rough in engagement

- [ ] Starter pinion or flywheel ring gear teeth loose or broken (Chapter 2A, 2B, 2C, 2D or 2E or 5A)
- [ ] Starter motor mounting bolts loose or missing (Chapter 5A)
- [ ] Starter motor internal components worn or damaged (Chapter 5A)

Engine starts, but stops immediately

- [ ] Loose or faulty electrical connections in the ignition circuit – petrol models (Chapter 1A or 5B)
- [ ] Vacuum leak at the throttle body or inlet manifold – petrol models (Chapter 4A)
- [ ] Blocked injectors/fuel injection system fault (Chapter 4A or 4B)

Engine idles erratically

- [ ] Air filter element clogged (Chapter 1A or 1B)
- [ ] Vacuum leak at the throttle body, inlet manifold or associated hoses – petrol models (Chapter 4A)
- [ ] Worn, faulty or incorrectly-gapped spark plugs – petrol models (Chapter 1A)
- [ ] Uneven or low cylinder compression (Chapter 2A, 2B, 2C, 2D or 2E)
- [ ] Camshaft lobes worn (Chapter 2A, 2B, 2C, 2D or 2E)
- [ ] Blocked injectors/fuel injection system fault (Chapter 4A or 4B)

Engine (continued)

Engine misfires at idle speed

- [ ] Worn, faulty or incorrectly-gapped spark plugs – petrol models (Chapter 1A)
- [ ] Vacuum leak at the throttle body, inlet manifold or associated hoses – petrol models (Chapter 4A)
- [ ] Blocked injectors/fuel injection system fault (Chapter 4A, 4B or 4C)
- [ ] Faulty injector(s) – diesel models (Chapter 4B)
- [ ] Uneven or low cylinder compression (Chapter 2A, 2B, 2C, 2D or 2E)
- [ ] Disconnected, leaking, or perished crankcase ventilation hoses (Chapter 4C)

Engine misfires throughout the driving speed range

- [ ] Fuel filter choked (Chapter 1A or 1B)
- [ ] Fuel pump faulty, or delivery pressure low – petrol models (Chapter 4A)
- [ ] Fuel tank vent blocked, or fuel pipes restricted (Chapter 4A, 4B or 4C)
- [ ] Vacuum leak at the throttle body, inlet manifold or associated hoses – petrol models (Chapter 4A)
- [ ] Worn, faulty or incorrectly-gapped spark plugs – petrol models (Chapter 1A)
- [ ] Faulty injector(s) – diesel models (Chapter 4B)
- [ ] Faulty ignition module – petrol models (Chapter 5B)
- [ ] Uneven or low cylinder compression (Chapter 2A, 2B, 2C, 2D or 2E)
- [ ] Blocked injector/fuel injection system fault (Chapter 4A or 4B)
- [ ] Blocked catalytic converter (Chapter 4A or 4B)
- [ ] Engine overheating (Chapter 3)

Engine hesitates on acceleration

- [ ] Worn, faulty or incorrectly-gapped spark plugs – petrol models (Chapter 1A)
- [ ] Vacuum leak at the throttle body, inlet manifold or associated hoses – petrol models (Chapter 4A)
- [ ] Blocked injectors/fuel injection system fault (Chapter 4A or 4B)
- [ ] Faulty injector(s) – diesel models (Chapter 4B)

Engine stalls

- [ ] Vacuum leak at the throttle body, inlet manifold or associated hoses – petrol models (Chapter 4A)
- [ ] Fuel filter choked (Chapter 1A or 1B)
- [ ] Fuel pump faulty, or delivery pressure low – petrol models (Chapter 4A)
- [ ] Fuel tank vent blocked, or fuel pipes restricted (Chapter 4A, 4B or 4C)
- [ ] Blocked injectors/fuel injection system fault (Chapter 4A or 4B)
- [ ] Faulty injector(s) – diesel models (Chapter 4B)

Engine lacks power

- [ ] Air filter element blocked (Chapter 1A or 1B)
- [ ] Fuel filter choked (Chapter 1A or 1B)
- [ ] Fuel pipes blocked or restricted (Chapter 4A, 4B or 4C)
- [ ] Worn, faulty or incorrectly-gapped spark plugs – petrol models (Chapter 1A)
- [ ] Engine overheating (Chapter 3)
- [ ] Accelerator pedal position sensor faulty (Chapter 4A or 4B)
- [ ] Vacuum leak at the throttle body, inlet manifold or associated hoses – petrol models (Chapter 4A)
- [ ] Blocked injectors/fuel injection system fault (Chapter 4A or 4B)
- [ ] Faulty injector(s) – diesel models (Chapter 4B)
- [ ] Fuel pump faulty, or delivery pressure low – petrol models (Chapter 4A)
- [ ] Uneven or low cylinder compression (Chapter 2A, 2B, 2C, 2D or 2E)
- [ ] Blocked catalytic converter (Chapter 4A or 4B)
- [ ] Brakes binding (Chapter 1A, 1B or 9)
- [ ] Clutch slipping (Chapter 6)

Engine backfires

- [ ] Vacuum leak at the throttle body, inlet manifold or associated hoses – petrol models (Chapter 4A)
- [ ] Blocked injectors/fuel injection system fault (Chapter 4A or 4B)
- [ ] Blocked catalytic converter (Chapter 4A or 4B)
- [ ] Faulty ignition module – petrol models (Chapter 5B)

Oil pressure warning light illuminated with engine running

- [ ] Low oil level, or incorrect oil grade (see *Weekly checks*)
- [ ] Faulty oil pressure sensor, or wiring damaged (Chapter 2A, 2B, 2C, 2D or 2E)
- [ ] Worn engine bearings and/or oil pump (Chapter 2A, 2B, 2C, 2D, 2E or 2F)
- [ ] High engine operating temperature (Chapter 3)
- [ ] Oil pump pressure relief valve defective (Chapter 2A, 2B, 2C, 2D or 2E)
- [ ] Oil pump pick-up strainer clogged (Chapter 2A, 2B, 2C, 2D or 2E)

Engine runs-on after switching off

- [ ] Excessive carbon build-up in engine (Chapter 2A, 2B, 2C, 2D, 2E or 2F)
- [ ] High engine operating temperature (Chapter 3)
- [ ] Fuel injection/engine management system fault (Chapter 4A, 4B or 4C)

Engine noises

Pre-ignition (pinking) or knocking during acceleration or under load

- [ ] Ignition system/engine management system fault – petrol models (Chapter 1A, 4A or 5B)
- [ ] Incorrect grade of spark plug – petrol models (Chapter 1A)
- [ ] Incorrect grade of fuel (Chapter 4A or 4B)
- [ ] Knock sensor faulty – petrol models (Chapter 4A or 5B)
- [ ] Vacuum leak at the throttle body, inlet manifold or associated hoses – petrol models (Chapter 4A)
- [ ] Excessive carbon build-up in engine (Chapter 2A, 2B, 2C, 2D, 2E or 2F)
- [ ] Fuel injection/engine management system fault (Chapter 4A, 4B or 4C)
- [ ] Faulty injector(s) – diesel models (Chapter 4C)

Whistling or wheezing noises

- [ ] Leaking inlet manifold or throttle body gasket – petrol models (Chapter 4A)
- [ ] Leaking exhaust manifold gasket or pipe-to-manifold joint (Chapter 4A or 4B)
- [ ] Leaking vacuum hose (Chapter 4A, 4B, 4C or 9)
- [ ] Blowing cylinder head gasket (Chapter 2A, 2B, 2C, 2D or 2E)
- [ ] Partially blocked or leaking crankcase ventilation system (Chapter 4C)

Tapping or rattling noises

- [ ] Worn valve gear or camshaft (Chapter 2A, 2B, 2C, 2D or 2E)
- [ ] Ancillary component fault (coolant pump, alternator, etc) (Chapter 3, 5A, etc)

Knocking or thumping noises

- [ ] Worn big-end bearings (regular heavy knocking, perhaps less under load) (Chapter 2F)
- [ ] Worn main bearings (rumbling and knocking, perhaps worsening under load) (Chapter 2F)
- [ ] Piston slap – most noticeable when cold, caused by piston/bore wear (Chapter 2F)
- [ ] Ancillary component fault (coolant pump, alternator, etc) (Chapter 3, 5A, etc)
- [ ] Engine mountings worn or defective (Chapter 2A, 2B, 2C, 2D or 2E)
- [ ] Front suspension or steering components worn (Chapter 10)

Cooling system

Overheating

- ☐ Insufficient coolant in system (see *Weekly checks*)
- ☐ Thermostat faulty (Chapter 3)
- ☐ Radiator core blocked, or grille restricted (Chapter 3)
- ☐ Cooling fan or cooling module faulty (Chapter 3)
- ☐ Inaccurate coolant temperature sensor (Chapter 3)
- ☐ Airlock in cooling system (Chapter 1A, 1B or 3)
- ☐ Expansion tank pressure cap faulty (Chapter 3)
- ☐ Engine management system fault (Chapter 4A, 4B or 4C)

Overcooling

- ☐ Thermostat faulty (Chapter 3)
- ☐ Inaccurate coolant temperature sensor (Chapter 3)
- ☐ Cooling fan faulty (Chapter 3)
- ☐ Engine management system fault (Chapter 4A, 4B or 4C)

External coolant leakage

- ☐ Deteriorated or damaged hoses or hose clips (Chapter 1A or 1B)
- ☐ Radiator core or heater matrix leaking (Chapter 3)
- ☐ Expansion tank pressure cap faulty (Chapter 1A or 1B)
- ☐ Coolant pump internal seal leaking (Chapter 3)
- ☐ Coolant pump gasket leaking (Chapter 3)
- ☐ Boiling due to overheating (Chapter 3)
- ☐ Cylinder block core plug leaking (Chapter 2E)

Internal coolant leakage

- ☐ Leaking cylinder head gasket (Chapter 2A, 2B, 2C, 2D or 2E)
- ☐ Cracked cylinder head or cylinder block (Chapter 2A, 2B, 2C, 2D or 2E)

Corrosion

- ☐ Infrequent draining and flushing (Chapter 1A or 1B)
- ☐ Incorrect coolant mixture or inappropriate coolant type (see *Weekly checks*)

Fuel and exhaust systems

Excessive fuel consumption

- ☐ Air filter element dirty or clogged (Chapter 1A or 1B)
- ☐ Fuel injection system fault (Chapter 4A or 4B)
- ☐ Engine management system fault (Chapter 4A, 4B or 4C)
- ☐ Crankcase ventilation system blocked (Chapter 4C)
- ☐ Tyres under-inflated (see *Weekly checks*)
- ☐ Brakes binding (Chapter 1A, 1B or 9)
- ☐ Fuel leak, causing apparent high consumption (Chapter 1A, 1B, 4A, 4B or 4C)

Fuel leakage and/or fuel odour

- ☐ Damaged or corroded fuel tank, pipes or connections (Chapter 4A or 4B)
- ☐ Evaporative emissions system fault – petrol models (Chapter 4C)

Excessive noise or fumes from exhaust system

- ☐ Leaking exhaust system or manifold joints (Chapter 1A, 1B, 4A or 4B)
- ☐ Leaking, corroded or damaged silencers or pipe (Chapter 1A, 1B, 4A or 4B)
- ☐ Broken mountings causing body or suspension contact (Chapter 1A, 1B, 4A or 4B)

Clutch

Pedal travels to floor – no pressure or very little resistance

- ☐ Air in hydraulic system/faulty master or slave cylinder (Chapter 6)
- ☐ Faulty hydraulic release system (Chapter 6)
- ☐ Clutch pedal return spring detached or broken (Chapter 6)
- ☐ Faulty clutch release cylinder (Chapter 6)
- ☐ Broken diaphragm spring in clutch pressure plate (Chapter 6)

Clutch fails to disengage (unable to select gears)

- ☐ Air in hydraulic system/faulty master or slave cylinder (Chapter 6)
- ☐ Faulty hydraulic release system (Chapter 6)
- ☐ Clutch disc sticking on transmission input shaft splines (Chapter 6)
- ☐ Clutch disc sticking to flywheel or pressure plate (Chapter 6)
- ☐ Faulty pressure plate assembly (Chapter 6)
- ☐ Clutch release mechanism worn or incorrectly assembled (Chapter 6)

Clutch slips (engine speed increases, with no increase in vehicle speed)

- ☐ Faulty hydraulic release system (Chapter 6)
- ☐ Clutch disc linings excessively worn (Chapter 6)
- ☐ Clutch disc linings contaminated with oil or grease (Chapter 6)
- ☐ Faulty pressure plate or weak diaphragm spring (Chapter 6)

Judder as clutch is engaged

- ☐ Clutch disc linings contaminated with oil or grease (Chapter 6)
- ☐ Clutch disc linings excessively worn (Chapter 6)
- ☐ Faulty or distorted pressure plate or diaphragm spring (Chapter 6).
- ☐ Worn or loose engine or transmission mountings (Chapter 2A, 2B, 2C, 2D or 2E)
- ☐ Clutch disc hub or transmission input shaft splines worn (Chapter 6)

Noise when depressing or releasing clutch pedal

- ☐ Faulty clutch release cylinder (Chapter 6)
- ☐ Worn or dry clutch pedal bushes (Chapter 6)
- ☐ Faulty pressure plate assembly (Chapter 6)
- ☐ Pressure plate diaphragm spring broken (Chapter 6)
- ☐ Broken clutch disc cushioning springs (Chapter 6)

Manual transmission

Noisy in neutral with engine running

☐ Lack of oil (Chapter 7A)
☐ Input shaft bearings worn (noise apparent with clutch pedal released, but not when depressed) (Chapter 7A)*
☐ Clutch release cylinder faulty (noise apparent with clutch pedal depressed, possibly less when released) (Chapter 6)

Noisy in one particular gear

☐ Worn, damaged or chipped gear teeth (Chapter 7A)*

Difficulty engaging gears

☐ Clutch fault (Chapter 6)
☐ Worn, damaged, or poorly-adjusted gearchange (Chapter 7A)
☐ Lack of oil (Chapter 7A or 7C)
☐ Worn synchroniser units (Chapter 7A)*

Jumps out of gear

☐ Worn, damaged, or poorly-adjusted gearchange (Chapter 7A)
☐ Worn synchroniser units (Chapter 7A)*
☐ Worn selector forks (Chapter 7A)*

Vibration

☐ Lack of oil (Chapter 7A or 7C)
☐ Worn bearings (Chapter 7A)*

Lubricant leaks

☐ Leaking driveshaft or selector shaft oil seal (Chapter 7A)
☐ Leaking housing joint (Chapter 7A)*
☐ Leaking input shaft oil seal (Chapter 7A)*

* Although the corrective action necessary to remedy the symptoms described is beyond the scope of the home mechanic, the above information should be helpful in isolating the cause of the condition, so that the owner can communicate clearly with a professional mechanic.

Automatic transmission

Note: *Due to the complexity of the automatic transmission, it is difficult for the home mechanic to properly diagnose and service this unit. For problems other than the following, the vehicle should be taken to a dealer service department or automatic transmission specialist. Do not be too hasty in removing the transmission if a fault is suspected, as most of the testing is carried out with the unit still fitted. Remember that, besides the sensors specific to the transmission, many of the engine management system sensors described in Chapter 4 are essential to the correct operation of the transmission.*

Fluid leakage

☐ Automatic transmission fluid is usually dark red in colour. Fluid leaks should not be confused with engine oil, which can easily be blown onto the transmission by airflow.
☐ To determine the source of a leak, first remove all built-up dirt and grime from the transmission housing and surrounding areas using a degreasing agent, or by steam-cleaning. Drive the vehicle at low speed, so airflow will not blow the leak far from its source. Raise and support the vehicle, and determine where the leak is coming from. The following are common areas of leakage:
a) *Fluid pan*
b) *Dipstick tube (Chapter 7B)*
c) *Transmission-to-fluid cooler unions (Chapter 7B)*

Transmission fluid brown, or has burned smell

☐ Transmission fluid level low (Chapter 7B)

General gear selection problems

☐ Chapter 7B deals with checking the selector cable on automatic transmissions. The following are common problems which may be caused by a faulty cable or sensor:

a) *Engine starting in gears other than Park or Neutral.*
b) *Indicator panel indicating a gear other than the one actually being used.*
c) *Vehicle moves when in Park or Neutral.*
d) *Poor gear shift quality or erratic gear changes.*

Transmission will not downshift (kickdown) with accelerator pedal fully depressed

☐ Low transmission fluid level (Chapter 7B)
☐ Engine management system fault (Chapter 4A or 4B)
☐ Faulty transmission sensor or wiring (Chapter 7B)
☐ Incorrect selector cable adjustment (Chapter 7B)

Engine will not start in any gear, or starts in gears other than Park or Neutral

☐ Faulty transmission sensor or wiring (Chapter 7B)
☐ Engine management system fault (Chapter 4A or 4B)
☐ Incorrect selector cable adjustment (Chapter 7B)

Transmission slips, shifts roughly, is noisy, or has no drive in forward or reverse gears

☐ Transmission fluid level low (Chapter 7B)
☐ Faulty transmission sensor or wiring (Chapter 7B)
☐ Engine management system fault (Chapter 4A or 4B)

Note: *There are many probable causes for the above problems, but diagnosing and correcting them is considered beyond the scope of this manual. Having checked the fluid level and all the wiring as far as possible, a dealer or transmission specialist should be consulted if the problem persists.*

Driveshafts

Vibration when accelerating or decelerating

☐ Worn inner constant velocity joint (Chapter 8)
☐ Bent or distorted driveshaft (Chapter 8)
☐ Worn intermediate bearing (Chapter 8)

Clicking or knocking noise on turns (at slow speed on full-lock)

☐ Worn outer constant velocity joint (Chapter 8)
☐ Lack of constant velocity joint lubricant, possibly due to damaged gaiter (Chapter 8)

Braking system

Note: *Before assuming that a brake problem exists, make sure that the tyres are in good condition and correctly inflated, that the front wheel alignment is correct, and that the vehicle is not loaded with weight in an unequal manner. Apart from checking the condition of all pipe and hose connections, any faults occurring on the anti-lock braking system should be referred to a Vauxhall/Opel dealer for diagnosis.*

Vehicle pulls to one side under braking

☐ Worn, defective, damaged or contaminated brake pads on one side (Chapter 1A, 1B or 9)
☐ Seized or partially-seized brake caliper piston (Chapter 1A, 1B or 9)
☐ A mixture of brake pad lining materials fitted between sides (Chapter 1A, 1B or 9)
☐ Brake caliper mounting bolts loose (Chapter 9)
☐ Worn or damaged steering or suspension components (Chapter 1A, 1B or 10)

Noise (grinding or high-pitched squeal) when brakes applied

☐ Brake pad friction lining material worn down to metal backing (Chapter 1A, 1B or 9)
☐ Excessive corrosion of brake disc (may be apparent after the vehicle has been standing for some time (Chapter 1A, 1B or 9)
☐ Foreign object (stone chipping, etc) trapped between brake disc and shield (Chapter 1A, 1B or 9)

Excessive brake pedal travel

☐ Faulty master cylinder (Chapter 9)
☐ Air in hydraulic system (Chapter 1A, 1B, 6 or 9)
☐ Faulty vacuum servo unit (Chapter 9)

Brake pedal feels spongy when depressed

☐ Air in hydraulic system (Chapter 1A, 1B, 6 or 9)
☐ Deteriorated flexible rubber brake hoses (Chapter 1A, 1B or 9)

☐ Master cylinder mounting nuts loose (Chapter 9)
☐ Faulty master cylinder (Chapter 9)

Excessive brake pedal effort required to stop vehicle

☐ Faulty vacuum servo unit (Chapter 9)
☐ Faulty vacuum pump – diesel models (Chapter 9)
☐ Disconnected, damaged or insecure brake servo vacuum hose (Chapter 9)
☐ Primary or secondary hydraulic circuit failure (Chapter 9)
☐ Seized brake caliper piston (Chapter 9)
☐ Brake pads incorrectly fitted (Chapter 9)
☐ Incorrect grade of brake pads fitted (Chapter 9)
☐ Brake pad linings contaminated (Chapter 1A, 1B or 9)

Judder felt through brake pedal or steering wheel when braking

Note: *Under heavy braking on models equipped with ABS, vibration may be felt through the brake pedal. This is a normal feature of ABS operation, and does not constitute a fault*
☐ Excessive run-out or distortion of discs (Chapter 1A, 1B or 9)
☐ Brake pad linings worn (Chapter 1A, 1B or 9)
☐ Brake caliper mounting bolts loose (Chapter 9)
☐ Wear in suspension or steering components or mountings (Chapter 1A, 1B or 10)
☐ Front wheels out of balance (see *Weekly checks*)

Brakes binding

☐ Seized brake caliper piston (Chapter 9)
☐ Faulty master cylinder (Chapter 9)

Rear wheels locking under normal braking

☐ Rear brake pad linings contaminated or damaged (Chapter 1 or 9)
☐ Rear brake discs warped (Chapter 1 or 9)

Suspension and steering

Note: *Before diagnosing suspension or steering faults, be sure that the trouble is not due to incorrect tyre pressures, mixtures of tyre types, or binding brakes.*

Vehicle pulls to one side

☐ Defective tyre (see *Weekly checks*)
☐ Excessive wear in suspension or steering components (Chapter 1A, 1B or 10)
☐ Incorrect front wheel alignment (Chapter 10)
☐ Accident damage to steering or suspension components (Chapter 1A or 1B)

Wheel wobble and vibration

☐ Front wheels out of balance (vibration felt mainly through the steering wheel) (see *Weekly checks*)
☐ Rear wheels out of balance (vibration felt throughout the vehicle) (see *Weekly checks*)
☐ Roadwheels damaged or distorted (see *Weekly checks*)
☐ Faulty or damaged tyre (see *Weekly checks*)
☐ Worn steering or suspension joints, bushes or components (Chapter 1A, 1B or 10)
☐ Wheel bolts loose (Chapter 1A or 1B)

Excessive pitching and/or rolling around corners, or during braking

☐ Defective shock absorbers (Chapter 1A, 1B or 10)
☐ Broken or weak spring and/or suspension component (Chapter 1A, 1B or 10)
☐ Worn or damaged anti-roll bar or mountings (Chapter 1A, 1B or 10)

Wandering or general instability

☐ Incorrect front wheel alignment (Chapter 10)
☐ Worn steering or suspension joints, bushes or components (Chapter 1A, 1B or 10)
☐ Roadwheels out of balance (see *Weekly checks*)
☐ Faulty or damaged tyre (see *Weekly checks*)
☐ Wheel bolts loose (Chapter 1A or 1B)
☐ Defective shock absorbers (Chapter 1A, 1B or 10)
☐ Power steering system fault (Chapter 10)

Excessively-stiff steering

☐ Seized steering linkage balljoint or suspension balljoint (Chapter 1A, 1B or 10)
☐ Incorrect front wheel alignment (Chapter 10)
☐ Steering rack damaged (Chapter 10)
☐ Power steering system fault (Chapter 10)

Suspension and steering (continued)

Excessive play in steering

- ☐ Worn steering column/intermediate shaft joints (Chapter 10)
- ☐ Worn track rod balljoints (Chapter 1A, 1B or 10)
- ☐ Worn steering rack (Chapter 10)
- ☐ Worn steering or suspension joints, bushes or components (Chapter 1A, 1B or 10)

Lack of power assistance

- ☐ Power steering system fault (Chapter 10)
- ☐ Faulty steering rack (Chapter 10)

Tyre wear excessive

Tyres worn on inside or outside edges

- ☐ Tyres under-inflated (wear on both edges) (see *Weekly checks*)
- ☐ Incorrect camber or castor angles (wear on one edge only) (Chapter 10)

- ☐ Worn steering or suspension joints, bushes or components (Chapter 1A, 1B or 10)
- ☐ Excessively-hard cornering or braking
- ☐ Accident damage

Tyre treads exhibit feathered edges

- ☐ Incorrect toe-setting (Chapter 10)

Tyres worn in centre of tread

- ☐ Tyres over-inflated (see *Weekly checks*)

Tyres worn on inside and outside edges

- ☐ Tyres under-inflated (see *Weekly checks*)

Tyres worn unevenly

- ☐ Tyres/wheels out of balance (see *Weekly checks*)
- ☐ Excessive wheel or tyre run-out
- ☐ Worn shock absorbers (Chapter 1A, 1B or 10)
- ☐ Faulty tyre (see *Weekly checks*)

Electrical system

Note: *For problems associated with the starting system, refer to the faults listed under 'Engine' earlier in this Section.*

Battery will not hold a charge for more than a few days

- ☐ Battery defective internally (Chapter 5A)
- ☐ Battery terminal connections loose or corroded (see *Weekly checks*)
- ☐ Auxiliary drivebelt worn or faulty automatic adjuster (Chapter 1A or 1B)
- ☐ Alternator not charging at correct output (Chapter 5A)
- ☐ Alternator or voltage regulator faulty (Chapter 5A)
- ☐ Short-circuit causing continual battery drain (Chapter 5A or 12)

Ignition/no-charge warning light remains illuminated with engine running

- ☐ Auxiliary drivebelt broken, worn, or or faulty automatic adjuster (Chapter 1A or 1B)
- ☐ Internal fault in alternator or voltage regulator (Chapter 5A)
- ☐ Broken, disconnected, or loose wiring in charging circuit (Chapter 5A or 12)

Ignition/no-charge warning light fails to come on

- ☐ Warning light bulb blown (Chapter 12)
- ☐ Broken, disconnected, or loose wiring in warning light circuit (Chapter 5A or 12)
- ☐ Alternator faulty (Chapter 5A)

Lights inoperative

- ☐ Bulb blown (Chapter 12)
- ☐ Corrosion of bulb or bulbholder contacts (Chapter 12)

- ☐ Blown fuse (Chapter 12)
- ☐ Faulty relay (Chapter 12)
- ☐ Broken, loose, or disconnected wiring (Chapter 12)
- ☐ Faulty switch (Chapter 12)

Instrument readings inaccurate or erratic

Fuel or temperature gauges give no reading

- ☐ Faulty gauge sender unit (Chapter 3 or 4)
- ☐ Wiring open-circuit (Chapter 12)
- ☐ Faulty gauge (Chapter 12)

Fuel or temperature gauges give continuous maximum reading

- ☐ Faulty gauge sender unit (Chapter 3 or 4)
- ☐ Wiring short-circuit (Chapter 12)
- ☐ Faulty gauge (Chapter 12)

Horn inoperative, or unsatisfactory in operation

Horn operates all the time

- ☐ Horn push either earthed or stuck down (Chapter 12)
- ☐ Horn cable-to-horn push earthed (Chapter 12)

Horn fails to operate

- ☐ Blown fuse (Chapter 12)
- ☐ Cable or connections loose, broken or disconnected (Chapter 12)
- ☐ Faulty horn (Chapter 12)

Horn emits intermittent or unsatisfactory sound

- ☐ Cable connections loose (Chapter 12)
- ☐ Horn mountings loose (Chapter 12)
- ☐ Faulty horn (Chapter 12)

Electrical system (continued)

Windscreen wipers inoperative, or unsatisfactory in operation

Wipers fail to operate, or operate very slowly

☐ Wiper blades stuck to screen, or linkage seized or binding (Chapter 12)
☐ Blown fuse (Chapter 12)
☐ Battery discharged (Chapter 5A)
☐ Cable or connections loose, broken or disconnected (Chapter 12)
☐ Faulty relay (Chapter 12)
☐ Faulty wiper motor (Chapter 12)

Wiper blades sweep over too large or too small an area of the glass

☐ Wiper blades incorrectly fitted, or wrong size used (see *Weekly checks*)
☐ Wiper arms incorrectly positioned on spindles (Chapter 12)
☐ Excessive wear of wiper linkage (Chapter 12)
☐ Wiper motor or linkage mountings loose or insecure (Chapter 12)

Wiper blades fail to clean the glass effectively

☐ Wiper blade rubbers dirty, worn or perished (see *Weekly checks*)
☐ Wiper blades incorrectly fitted, or wrong size used (see *Weekly checks*)
☐ Wiper arm tension springs broken, or arm pivots seized (Chapter 12)
☐ Insufficient windscreen washer additive to adequately remove road film (see *Weekly checks*)

Windscreen washers inoperative, or unsatisfactory in operation

One or more washer jets inoperative

☐ Blocked washer jet
☐ Disconnected, kinked or restricted fluid hose (Chapter 12)
☐ Insufficient fluid in washer reservoir (see *Weekly checks*)

Washer pump fails to operate

☐ Broken or disconnected wiring or connections (Chapter 12)
☐ Blown fuse (Chapter 12)
☐ Faulty washer switch (Chapter 12)
☐ Faulty washer pump (Chapter 12)

Washer pump runs for some time before fluid is emitted from jets

☐ Faulty one-way valve in fluid supply hose (Chapter 12)

Electric windows inoperative, or unsatisfactory in operation

Window glass will only move in one direction

☐ Faulty switch (Chapter 12)

Window glass slow to move

☐ Battery discharged (Chapter 5A)
☐ Regulator seized or damaged, or in need of lubrication (Chapter 11)
☐ Door internal components or trim fouling regulator (Chapter 11)
☐ Faulty motor (Chapter 11)

Window glass fails to move

☐ Blown fuse (Chapter 12)
☐ Faulty relay (Chapter 12)
☐ Broken or disconnected wiring or connections (Chapter 12)
☐ Faulty motor (Chapter 11)

Central locking system inoperative, or unsatisfactory in operation

Complete system failure

☐ Remote handset battery discharged, where applicable (Chapter 1A or 1B)
☐ Blown fuse (Chapter 12)
☐ Faulty relay (Chapter 12)
☐ Broken or disconnected wiring or connections (Chapter 12)
☐ Faulty motor (Chapter 11)

Latch locks but will not unlock, or unlocks but will not lock

☐ Remote handset battery discharged, where applicable (Chapter 1A or 1B)
☐ Faulty master switch (Chapter 12)
☐ Broken or disconnected latch operating rods or levers (Chapter 11)
☐ Faulty relay (Chapter 12)
☐ Faulty motor (Chapter 11)

One solenoid/motor fails to operate

☐ Broken or disconnected wiring or connections (Chapter 12)
☐ Faulty operating assembly (Chapter 11)
☐ Broken, binding or disconnected latch operating rods or levers (Chapter 11)
☐ Fault in door latch (Chapter 11)

Note: *References throughout this index are in the form* "**Chapter number**" • "**Page number**". *So, for example, 2C•15 refers to page 15 of Chapter 2C.*

Note: *References throughout this index are in the form* "**Chapter number**" • "**Page number**". *So, for example, 2C•15 refers to page 15 of Chapter 2C.*

Note: *References throughout this index are in the form* **"Chapter number"** *•* **"Page number"**. *So, for example, 2C•15 refers to page 15 of Chapter 2C.*

Note: *References throughout this index are in the form* **"Chapter number"** • **"Page number"**. *So, for example, 2C•15 refers to page 15 of Chapter 2C.*

Haynes Manuals – The Complete **UK Car** List

Title	Book No.
ALFA ROMEO Alfasud/Sprint (74 - 88) up to F *	0292
Alfa Romeo Alfetta (73 - 87) up to E *	0531
AUDI 80, 90 & Coupe Petrol (79 - Nov 88) up to F	0605
Audi 80, 90 & Coupe Petrol (Oct 86 - 90) D to H	1491
Audi 100 & 200 Petrol (Oct 82 - 90) up to H	0907
Audi 100 & A6 Petrol & Diesel (May 91 - May 97) H to P	3504
Audi A3 Petrol & Diesel (96 - May 03) P to 03	4253
Audi A4 Petrol & Diesel (95 - Feb 00) M to V	3575
Audi A4 Petrol & Diesel (Mar 00 - Aug 04) W to 04	4609
AUSTIN A35 & A40 (56 - 67) up to F *	0118
Austin/MG/Rover Maestro 1.3 & 1.6 Petrol (83 - 95) up to M	0922
Austin/MG Metro (80 - May 90) up to G	0718
Austin/Rover Montego 1.3 & 1.6 Petrol (84 - 94) A to L	1066
Austin/MG/Rover Montego 2.0 Petrol (84 - 95) A to M	1067
Mini (59 - 69) up to H *	0527
Mini (69 - 01) up to X	0646
Austin/Rover 2.0 litre Diesel Engine (86 - 93) C to L	1857
Austin Healey 100/6 & 3000 (56 - 68) up to G *	0049
BEDFORD CF Petrol (69 - 87) up to E	0163
Bedford/Vauxhall Rascal & Suzuki Supercarry (86 - Oct 94) C to M	3015
BMW 316, 320 & 320i (4-cyl) (75 - Feb 83) up to Y *	0276
BMW 320, 320i, 323i & 325i (6-cyl) (Oct 77 - Sept 87) up to E	0815
BMW 3- & 5-Series Petrol (81 - 91) up to J	1948
BMW 3-Series Petrol (Apr 91 - 99) H to V	3210
BMW 3-Series Petrol (Sept 98 - 03) S to 53	4067
BMW 520i & 525e (Oct 81 - June 88) up to E	1560
BMW 525, 528 & 528i (73 - Sept 81) up to X *	0632
BMW 5-Series 6-cyl Petrol (April 96 - Aug 03) N to 03	4151
BMW 1500, 1502, 1600, 1602, 2000 & 2002 (59 - 77) up to S *	0240
CHRYSLER PT Cruiser Petrol (00 - 03) W to 53	4058
CITROËN 2CV, Ami & Dyane (67 - 90) up to H	0196
Citroën AX Petrol & Diesel (87 - 97) D to P	3014
Citroën Berlingo & Peugeot Partner Petrol & Diesel (96 - 05) P to 55	4281
Citroën BX Petrol (83 - 94) A to L	0908
Citroën C15 Van Petrol & Diesel (89 - Oct 98) F to S	3509
Citroën C3 Petrol & Diesel (02 - 05) 51 to 05	4197
Citroën CX Petrol (75 - 88) up to F	0528
Citroën Saxo Petrol & Diesel (96 - 04) N to 54	3506
Citroën Visa Petrol (79 - 88) up to F	0620
Citroën Xantia Petrol & Diesel (93 - 01) K to Y	3082
Citroën XM Petrol & Diesel (89 - 00) G to X	3451
Citroën Xsara Petrol & Diesel (97 - Sept 00) R to W	3751
Citroën Xsara Picasso Petrol & Diesel (00 - 02) W to 52	3944
Citroën ZX Diesel (91 - 98) J to S	1922
Citroën ZX Petrol (91 - 98) H to S	1881
Citroën 1.7 & 1.9 litre Diesel Engine (84 - 96) A to N	1379
FIAT 126 (73 - 87) up to E *	0305
Fiat 500 (57 - 73) up to M *	0090
Fiat Bravo & Brava Petrol (95 - 00) N to W	3572
Fiat Cinquecento (93 - 98) K to R	3501
Fiat Panda (81 - 95) up to M	0793
Fiat Punto Petrol & Diesel (94 - Oct 99) L to V	3251
Fiat Punto Petrol (Oct 99 - July 03) V to 03	4066
Fiat Regata Petrol (84 - 88) A to F	1167
Fiat Tipo Petrol (88 - 91) E to J	1625
Fiat Uno Petrol (83 - 95) up to M	0923

Title	Book No.
Fiat X1/9 (74 - 89) up to G *	0273
FORD Anglia (59 - 68) up to G *	0001
Ford Capri II (& III) 1.6 & 2.0 (74 - 87) up to E *	0283
Ford Capri II (& III) 2.8 & 3.0 V6 (74 - 87) up to E	1309
Ford Cortina Mk III 1300 & 1600 (70 - 76) up to P *	0070
Ford Escort Mk I 1100 & 1300 (68 - 74) up to N *	0171
Ford Escort Mk I Mexico, RS 1600 & RS 2000 (70 - 74) up to N *	0139
Ford Escort Mk II Mexico, RS 1800 & RS 2000 (75 - 80) up to W *	0735
Ford Escort (75 - Aug 80) up to V *	0280
Ford Escort Petrol (Sept 80 - Sept 90) up to H	0686
Ford Escort & Orion Petrol (Sept 90 - 00) H to X	1737
Ford Escort & Orion Diesel (Sept 90 - 00) H to X	4081
Ford Fiesta (76 - Aug 83) up to Y	0334
Ford Fiesta Petrol (Aug 83 - Feb 89) A to F	1030
Ford Fiesta Petrol (Feb 89 - Oct 95) F to N	1595
Ford Fiesta Petrol & Diesel (Oct 95 - Mar 02) N to 02	3397
Ford Fiesta Petrol & Diesel (Apr 02 - 05) 02 to 54	4170
Ford Focus Petrol & Diesel (98 - 01) S to Y	3759
Ford Focus Petrol & Diesel (Oct 01 - 04) 51 to 54	4167
Ford Galaxy Petrol & Diesel (95 - Aug 00) M to W	3984
Ford Granada Petrol (Sept 77 - Feb 85) up to B *	0481
Ford Granada & Scorpio Petrol (Mar 85 - 94) B to M	1245
Ford Ka (96 - 02) P to 52	3570
Ford Mondeo Petrol (93 - Sept 00) K to X	1923
Ford Mondeo Petrol & Diesel (Oct 00 - Jul 03) X to 03	3990
Ford Mondeo Petrol & Diesel (July 03 - 07) 03 to 56	4619
Ford Mondeo Diesel (93 - 96) L to N	3465
Ford Orion Petrol (83 - Sept 90) up to H	1009
Ford Sierra 4-cyl Petrol (82 - 93) up to K	0903
Ford Sierra V6 Petrol (82 - 91) up to J	0904
Ford Transit Petrol (Mk 2) (78 - Jan 86) up to C	0719
Ford Transit Petrol (Mk 3) (Feb 86 - 89) C to G	1468
Ford Transit Diesel (Feb 86 - 99) C to T	3019
Ford 1.6 & 1.8 litre Diesel Engine (84 - 96) A to N	1172
Ford 2.1, 2.3 & 2.5 litre Diesel Engine (77 - 90) up to H	1606
FREIGHT ROVER Sherpa Petrol (74 - 87) up to E	0463
HILLMAN Avenger (70 - 82) up to Y	0037
Hillman Imp (63 - 76) up to R *	0022
HONDA Civic (Feb 84 - Oct 87) A to E	1226
Honda Civic (Nov 91 - 96) J to N	3199
Honda Civic Petrol (Mar 95 - 00) M to X	4050
HYUNDAI Pony (85 - 94) C to M	3398
JAGUAR E Type (61 - 72) up to L *	0140
Jaguar MkI & II, 240 & 340 (55 - 69) up to H *	0098
Jaguar XJ6, XJ & Sovereign; Daimler Sovereign (68 - Oct 86) up to D	0242
Jaguar XJ6 & Sovereign (Oct 86 - Sept 94) D to M	3261
Jaguar XJ12, XJS & Sovereign; Daimler Double Six (72 - 88) up to F	0478
Jeep Cherokee Petrol (93 - 96) K to N	1943
LADA 1200, 1300, 1500 & 1600 (74 - 91) up to J	0413
Lada Samara (87 - 91) D to J	1610
LAND ROVER 90, 110 & Defender Diesel (83 - 07) up to 56	3017
Land Rover Discovery Petrol & Diesel (89 - 98) G to S	3016
Land Rover Discovery Diesel (Nov 98 - Jul 04) S to 04	4606
Land Rover Freelander Petrol & Diesel (97 - Sept 03) R to 53	3929
Land Rover Freelander Petrol & Diesel (Oct 03 - 06) 53 to 56	4623
Land Rover Series IIA & III Diesel (58 - 85) up to C	0529

Title	Book No.
Land Rover Series II, IIA & III 4-cyl Petrol (58 - 85) up to C	0314
MAZDA 323 (Mar 81 - Oct 89) up to G	1608
Mazda 323 (Oct 89 - 98) G to R	3455
Mazda 626 (May 83 - Sept 87) up to E	0929
Mazda B1600, B1800 & B2000 Pick-up Petrol (72 - 88) up to F	0267
Mazda RX-7 (79 - 85) up to C *	0460
MERCEDES-BENZ 190, 190E & 190D Petrol & Diesel (83 - 93) A to L	3450
Mercedes-Benz 200D, 240D, 240TD, 300D & 300TD 123 Series Diesel (Oct 76 - 85) up to C	1114
Mercedes-Benz 250 & 280 (68 - 72) up to L *	0346
Mercedes-Benz 250 & 280 123 Series Petrol (Oct 76 - 84) up to B *	0677
Mercedes-Benz 124 Series Petrol & Diesel (85 - Aug 93) C to K	3253
Mercedes-Benz C-Class Petrol & Diesel (93 - Aug 00) L to W	3511
MGA (55 - 62) *	0475
MGB (62 - 80) up to W	0111
MG Midget & Austin-Healey Sprite (58 - 80) up to W *	0265
MINI Petrol (July 01 - 05) Y to 05	4273
MITSUBISHI Shogun & L200 Pick-Ups Petrol (83 - 94) up to M	1944
MORRIS Ital 1.3 (80 - 84) up to B	0705
Morris Minor 1000 (56 - 71) up to K	0024
NISSAN Almera Petrol (95 - Feb 00) N to V	4053
Nissan Bluebird (May 84 - Mar 86) A to C	1223
Nissan Bluebird Petrol (Mar 86 - 90) C to H	1473
Nissan Cherry (Sept 82 - 86) up to D	1031
Nissan Micra (83 - Jan 93) up to K	0931
Nissan Micra (93 - 02) K to 52	3254
Nissan Primera Petrol (90 - Aug 99) H to V	1851
Nissan Stanza (82 - 86) up to D	0824
Nissan Sunny Petrol (May 82 - Oct 86) up to D	0895
Nissan Sunny Petrol (Oct 86 - Mar 91) D to H	1378
Nissan Sunny Petrol (Apr 91 - 95) H to N	3219
OPEL Ascona & Manta (B Series) (Sept 75 - 88) up to F *	0316
Opel Ascona Petrol (81 - 88)	3215
Opel Astra Petrol (Oct 91 - Feb 98)	3156
Opel Corsa Petrol (83 - Mar 93)	3160
Opel Corsa Petrol (Mar 93 - 97)	3159
Opel Kadett Petrol (Nov 79 - Oct 84) up to B	0634
Opel Kadett Petrol (Oct 84 - Oct 91)	3196
Opel Omega & Senator Petrol (Nov 86 - 94)	3157
Opel Rekord Petrol (Feb 78 - Oct 86) up to D	0543
Opel Vectra Petrol (Oct 88 - Oct 95)	3158
PEUGEOT 106 Petrol & Diesel (91 - 04) J to 53	1882
Peugeot 205 Petrol (83 - 97) A to P	0932
Peugeot 206 Petrol & Diesel (98 - 01) S to X	3757
Peugeot 206 Petrol & Diesel (02 - 06) 51 to 06	4613
Peugeot 306 Petrol & Diesel (93 - 02) K to 02	3073
Peugeot 307 Petrol & Diesel (01 - 04) Y to 54	4147
Peugeot 309 Petrol (86 - 93) C to K	1266
Peugeot 405 Petrol (88 - 97) E to P	1559
Peugeot 405 Diesel (88 - 97) E to P	3198
Peugeot 406 Petrol & Diesel (96 - Mar 99) N to T	3394
Peugeot 406 Petrol & Diesel (Mar 99 - 02) T to 52	3982
Peugeot 505 Petrol (79 - 89) up to G	0762
Peugeot 1.7/1.8 & 1.9 litre Diesel Engine (82 - 96) up to N	0950
Peugeot 2.0, 2.1, 2.3 & 2.5 litre Diesel Engines (74 - 90) up to H	1607

* Classic reprint

Title	Book No.
PORSCHE 911 (65 - 85) up to C	0264
Porsche 924 & 924 Turbo (76 - 85) up to C	0397
PROTON (89 - 97) F to P	3255
RANGE ROVER V8 Petrol (70 - Oct 92) up to K	0606
RELIANT Robin & Kitten (73 - 83) up to A *	0436
RENAULT 4 (61 - 86) up to D *	0072
Renault 5 Petrol (Feb 85 - 96) B to N	1219
Renault 9 & 11 Petrol (82 - 89) up to F	0822
Renault 18 Petrol (79 - 86) up to D	0598
Renault 19 Petrol (89 - 96) F to N	1646
Renault 19 Diesel (89 - 96) F to N	1946
Renault 21 Petrol (86 - 94) C to M	1397
Renault 25 Petrol & Diesel (84 - 92) B to K	1228
Renault Clio Petrol (91 - May 98) H to R	1853
Renault Clio Diesel (91 - June 96) H to N	3031
Renault Clio Petrol & Diesel (May 98 - May 01) R to Y	3906
Renault Clio Petrol & Diesel (June 01 - 04) Y to 54	4168
Renault Espace Petrol & Diesel (85 - 96) C to N	3197
Renault Laguna Petrol & Diesel (94 - 00) L to W	3252
Renault Laguna Petrol & Diesel (Feb 01 - Feb 05) X to 54	4283
Renault Mégane & Scénic Petrol & Diesel (96 - 99) N to T	3395
Renault Mégane & Scénic Petrol & Diesel (Apr 99 - 02) T to 52	3916
Renault Megane Petrol & Diesel (Oct 02 - 05) 52 to 55	4284
Renault Scenic Petrol & Diesel (Sept 03 - 06) 53 to 06	4297
ROVER 213 & 216 (84 - 89) A to G	1116
Rover 214 & 414 Petrol (89 - 96) G to N	1689
Rover 216 & 416 Petrol (89 - 96) G to N	1830
Rover 211, 214, 216, 218 & 220 Petrol & Diesel (Dec 95 - 99) N to V	3399
Rover 25 & MG ZR Petrol & Diesel (Oct 99 - 04) V to 54	4145
Rover 414, 416 & 420 Petrol & Diesel (May 95 - 98) M to R	3453
Rover 45/MG ZS Petrol & Diesel (99 - 05) V to 55	4384
Rover 618, 620 & 623 Petrol (93 - 97) K to P	3257
Rover 75/MG ZT Petrol & Diesel (99 - 06) S to 06	4292
Rover 820, 825 & 827 Petrol (86 - 95) D to N	1380
Rover 3500 (76 - 87) up to E *	0365
Rover Metro, 111 & 114 Petrol (May 90 - 98) G to S	1711
SAAB 95 & 96 (66 - 76) up to R *	0198
Saab 90, 99 & 900 (79 - Oct 93) up to L	0765
Saab 900 (Oct 93 - 98) L to R	3512
Saab 9000 (4-cyl) (85 - 98) C to S	1686
Saab 9-3 Petrol & Diesel (98 - Aug 02) R to 02	4614
Saab 9-5 4-cyl Petrol (97 - 04) R to 54	4156
SEAT Ibiza & Cordoba Petrol & Diesel (Oct 93 - Oct 99) L to V	3571
Seat Ibiza & Malaga Petrol (85 - 92) B to K	1609
SKODA Estelle (77 - 89) up to G	0604
Skoda Fabia Petrol & Diesel (00 - 06) W to 06	4376
Skoda Favorit (89 - 96) F to N	1801
Skoda Felicia Petrol & Diesel (95 - 01) M to X	3505
Skoda Octavia Petrol & Diesel (98 - Apr 04) R to 04	4285
SUBARU 1600 & 1800 (Nov 79 - 90) up to H *	0995
SUNBEAM Alpine, Rapier & H120 (67 - 74) up to N *	0051
SUZUKI Supercarry & Bedford/Vauxhall Rascal (86 - Oct 94) C to M	3015
Suzuki SJ Series, Samurai & Vitara (4-cyl) Petrol (82 - 97) up to P	1942
TALBOT Alpine, Solara, Minx & Rapier (75 - 86) up to D	0337

Title	Book No.
Talbot Horizon Petrol (78 - 86) up to D	0473
Talbot Samba (82 - 86) up to D	0823
TOYOTA Avensis Petrol (98 - Jan 03) R to 52	4264
Toyota Carina E Petrol (May 92 - 97) J to P	3256
Toyota Corolla (80 - 85) up to C	0683
Toyota Corolla (Sept 83 - Sept 87) A to E	1024
Toyota Corolla (Sept 87 - Aug 92) E to K	1683
Toyota Corolla Petrol (Aug 92 - 97) K to P	3259
Toyota Corolla Petrol (July 97 - Feb 02) P to 51	4286
Toyota Hi-Ace & Hi-Lux Petrol (69 - Oct 83) up to A	0304
Toyota Yaris Petrol (99 - 05) T to 05	4265
TRIUMPH GT6 & Vitesse (62 - 74) up to N *	0112
Triumph Herald (59 - 71) up to K *	0010
Triumph Spitfire (62 - 81) up to X	0113
Triumph Stag (70 - 78) up to T *	0441
Triumph TR2, TR3, TR3A, TR4 & TR4A (52 - 67) up to F *	0028
Triumph TR5 & 6 (67 - 75) up to P *	0031
Triumph TR7 (75 - 82) up to Y *	0322
VAUXHALL Astra Petrol (80 - Oct 84) up to B	0635
Vauxhall Astra & Belmont Petrol (Oct 84 - Oct 91) B to J	1136
Vauxhall Astra Petrol (Oct 91 - Feb 98) J to R	1832
Vauxhall/Opel Astra & Zafira Petrol (Feb 98 - Apr 04) R to 04	3758
Vauxhall/Opel Astra & Zafira Diesel (Feb 98 - Apr 04) R to 04	3797
Vauxhall/Opel Calibra (90 - 98) G to S	3502
Vauxhall Carlton Petrol (Oct 78 - Oct 86) up to D	0480
Vauxhall Carlton & Senator Petrol (Nov 86 - 94) D to L	1469
Vauxhall Cavalier Petrol (81 - Oct 88) up to F	0812
Vauxhall Cavalier Petrol (Oct 88 - 95) F to N	1570
Vauxhall Chevette (75 - 84) up to B	0285
Vauxhall/Opel Corsa Diesel (Mar 93 - Oct 00) K to X	4087
Vauxhall Corsa Petrol (Mar 93 - 97) K to R	1985
Vauxhall/Opel Corsa Petrol (Apr 97 - Oct 00) P to X	3921
Vauxhall/Opel Corsa Petrol & Diesel (Oct 00 - Sept 03) X to 53	4079
Vauxhall/Opel Corsa Petrol & Diesel (Oct 03 - Aug 06) 53 to 06	4617
Vauxhall/Opel Frontera Petrol & Diesel (91 - Sept 98) J to S	3454
Vauxhall Nova Petrol (83 - 93) up to K	0909
Vauxhall/Opel Omega Petrol (94 - 99) L to T	3510
Vauxhall/Opel Vectra Petrol & Diesel (95 - Feb 99) N to S	3396
Vauxhall/Opel Vectra Petrol & Diesel (Mar 99 - May 02) T to 02	3930
Vauxhall/Opel Vectra Petrol & Diesel (June 02 - 06) 02 to 56	4618
Vauxhall/Opel 1.5, 1.6 & 1.7 litre Diesel Engine (82 - 96) up to N	1222
VW 411 & 412 (68 - 75) up to P *	0091
VW Beetle 1200 (54 - 77) up to S	0036
VW Beetle 1300 & 1500 (65 - 75) up to P	0039
VW 1302 & 1302S (70 - 72) up to L *	0110
VW Beetle 1303, 1303S & GT (72 - 75) up to P	0159
VW Beetle Petrol & Diesel (Apr 99 - 01) T to 51	3798
VW Golf & Jetta Mk 1 Petrol 1.1 & 1.3 (74 - 84) up to A	0716
VW Golf, Jetta & Scirocco Mk 1 Petrol 1.5, 1.6 & 1.8 (74 - 84) up to A	0726
VW Golf & Jetta Mk 1 Diesel (78 - 84) up to A	0451
VW Golf & Jetta Mk 2 Petrol (Mar 84 - Feb 92) A to J	1081
VW Golf & Vento Petrol & Diesel (Feb 92 - Mar 98) J to R	3097

Title	Book No.
VW Golf & Bora Petrol & Diesel (April 98 - 00) R to X	3727
VW Golf & Bora 4-cyl Petrol & Diesel (01 - 03) X to 53	4169
VW Golf & Bora Petrol & Diesel (04 - 07) 53 to 07	4610
VW LT Petrol Vans & Light Trucks (76 - 87) up to E	0637
VW Passat & Santana Petrol (Sept 81 - May 88) up to E	0814
VW Passat 4-cyl Petrol & Diesel (May 88 - 96) E to P	3498
VW Passat 4-cyl Petrol & Diesel (Dec 96 - Nov 00) P to X	3917
VW Passat Petrol & Diesel (Dec 00 - May 05) X to 05	4279
VW Polo & Derby (76 - Jan 82) up to X	0335
VW Polo (82 - Oct 90) up to H	0813
VW Polo Petrol (Nov 90 - Aug 94) H to L	3245
VW Polo Hatchback Petrol & Diesel (94 - 99) M to S	3500
VW Polo Hatchback Petrol (00 - Jan 02) V to 51	4150
VW Polo Petrol & Diesel (02 - May 05) 51 to 05	4608
VW Scirocco (82 - 90) up to H *	1224
VW Transporter 1600 (68 - 79) up to V	0082
VW Transporter 1700, 1800 & 2000 (72 - 79) up to V *	0226
VW Transporter (air-cooled) Petrol (79 - 82) up to Y *	0638
VW Transporter (water-cooled) Petrol (82 - 90) up to H	3452
VW Type 3 (63 - 73) up to M *	0084
VOLVO 120 & 130 Series (& P1800) (61 - 73) up to M *	0203
Volvo 142, 144 & 145 (66 - 74) up to N *	0129
Volvo 240 Series Petrol (74 - 93) up to K	0270
Volvo 262, 264 & 260/265 (75 - 85) up to C *	0400
Volvo 340, 343, 345 & 360 (76 - 91) up to J	0715
Volvo 440, 460 & 480 Petrol (87 - 97) D to P	1691
Volvo 740 & 760 Petrol (82 - 91) up to J	1258
Volvo 850 Petrol (92 - 96) J to P	3260
Volvo 940 Petrol (90 - 96) H to N	3249
Volvo S40 & V40 Petrol (96 - Mar 04) N to 04	3569
Volvo S70, V70 & C70 Petrol (96 - 99) P to V	3573
Volvo V70 / S80 Petrol & Diesel (98 - 05) S to 55	4263

AUTOMOTIVE TECHBOOKS

Title	Book No.
Automotive Electrical and Electronic Systems Manual	3049
Automotive Gearbox Overhaul Manual	3473
Automotive Service Summaries Manual	3475
Automotive Timing Belts Manual – Austin/Rover	3549
Automotive Timing Belts Manual – Ford	3474
Automotive Timing Belts Manual – Peugeot/Citroën	3568
Automotive Timing Belts Manual – Vauxhall/Opel	3577

DIY MANUAL SERIES

Title	Book No.
The Haynes Air Conditioning Manual	4192
The Haynes Manual on Bodywork	4198
The Haynes Manual on Brakes	4178
The Haynes Manual on Carburettors	4177
The Haynes Car Electrical Systems Manual	4251
The Haynes Manual on Diesel Engines	4174
The Haynes Manual on Engine Management	4199
The Haynes Manual on Fault Codes	4175
The Haynes Manual on Practical Electrical Systems	4267
The Haynes Manual on Small Engines	4250
The Haynes Manual on Welding	4176

* Classic reprint

CL22.4/07

Preserving Our Motoring Heritage

< *The Model J Duesenberg Derham Tourster. Only eight of these magnificent cars were ever built – this is the only example to be found outside the United States of America*

Almost every car you've ever loved, loathed or desired is gathered under one roof at the Haynes Motor Museum. Over 300 immaculately presented cars and motorbikes represent every aspect of our motoring heritage, from elegant reminders of bygone days, such as the superb Model J Duesenberg to curiosities like the bug-eyed BMW Isetta. There are also many old friends and flames. Perhaps you remember the 1959 Ford Popular that you did your courting in? The magnificent 'Red Collection' is a spectacle of classic sports cars including AC, Alfa Romeo, Austin Healey, Ferrari, Lamborghini, Maserati, MG, Riley, Porsche and Triumph.

A Perfect Day Out

Each and every vehicle at the Haynes Motor Museum has played its part in the history and culture of Motoring. Today, they make a wonderful spectacle and a great day out for all the family. Bring the kids, bring Mum and Dad, but above all bring your camera to capture those golden memories for ever. You will also find an impressive array of motoring memorabilia, a comfortable 70 seat video cinema and one of the most extensive transport book shops in Britain. The Pit Stop Cafe serves everything from a cup of tea to wholesome, home-made meals or, if you prefer, you can enjoy the large picnic area nestled in the beautiful rural surroundings of Somerset.

John Haynes O.B.E., Founder and Chairman of the museum at the wheel of a Haynes Light 12.

< *Graham Hill's Lola Cosworth Formula 1 car next to a 1934 Riley Sports.*

The Museum is situated on the A359 Yeovil to Frome road at Sparkford, just off the A303 in Somerset. It is about 40 miles south of Bristol, and 25 minutes drive from the M5 intersection at Taunton.
Open 9.30am - 5.30pm (10.00am - 4.00pm Winter) 7 days a week, *except Christmas Day, Boxing Day and New Years Day*
Special rates available for schools, coach parties and outings Charitable Trust No. 292048